THE MODERN THEORY OF CORPORATE FINANCE

Hanan Eytan

McGraw-Hill Series in Finance

CONSULTING EDITOR

Charles A. D'Ambrosio, *University of Washington*

Archer and Kerr: Readings and Cases in Corporate Finance
Brealey and Myers: Principles of Corporate Finance
Doherty: Corporate Risk Management: A Financial Exposition
Edmister: Financial Institutions: Markets and Management
Francis: Investments: Analysis and Management
Francis: Management of Investments
Fuller and Farrell: Modern Investments and Security Analysis
Garbade: Securities Markets
Lang: Strategy for Personal Finance
Levi: International Finance: Financial Management and the International Economy
Maness: Introduction to Corporate Finance
Martin, Petty, and Klock: Personal Financial Management
Schall and Haley: Introduction to Financial Management
Sharpe: Portfolio Theory and Capital Markets
Smith: The Modern Theory of Corporate Finance
Stevenson: Fundamentals of Finance

McGraw-Hill Finance Guide Series

CONSULTING EDITOR

Charles A. D'Ambrosio, *University of Washington*

Bowlin, Martin, and Scott: Guide to Financial Analysis
Farrell: Guide to Portfolio Management
Smith: Guide to Working Capital Management

THE MODERN THEORY OF CORPORATE FINANCE

SECOND EDITION

EDITED BY

Clifford W. Smith, Jr.

Clarey Professor of Finance
William E. Simon Graduate School of Business Administration
University of Rochester

With the assistance of
North-Holland Publishing Company

McGRAW-HILL PUBLISHING COMPANY

New York   St. Louis   San Francisco   Auckland   Bogotá   Caracas
Hamburg   Lisbon   London   Madrid   Mexico   Milan
Montreal   New Delhi   Oklahoma City   Paris   San Juan
São Paulo   Singapore   Sydney   Tokyo   Toronto

THE MODERN THEORY OF CORPORATE FINANCE

2 3 4 5 6 7 8 9 0 DOC DOC 8 9 4 3 2 1 0 9

ISBN 0-07-059109-1

See Acknowledgments on pages ix-xi. Copyrights included on this page by reference.

This book was set in Times Roman by Jay's Publishers Services, Inc.
The editors were Suzanne BeDell and Linda Richmond;
the production supervisor was Diane Renda.
The cover was designed by Karen Quigley.
R. R. Donnelley & Sons Company was printer and binder.

Library of Congress Cataloging - in- Publication Data

The Modern Theory of Corporate Finance / edited by Clifford W. Smith, Jr.: with
the assistance of North-Holland Publishing Company- -2nd ed.
    p.   cm. - (McGraw Hill series in finance)
    Includes bibliographies.
ISBN 0-07-059109-1
1. Corporations - -Finance   I. Smith, Clifford W.   II. North-Holland Publishing Company.
III. Series.
HG4026.5.M62 1989
658.15 - - dc20   89-8167

CONTENTS

v

ACKNOWLEDGMENTS

The editor wishes to thank the following authors for permission to reprint their articles:

Randolph P. Beatty, The Wharton School, University of Pennsylvania

Fischer Black, Goldman, Sachs & Co., New York

James A. Brickley, William E. Simon Graduate School of Business Administration, University of Rochester

Larry Y. Dann, College of Business Administration, University of Oregon

Harry DeAngelo, Graduate School of Business Administration, University of Michigan, Ann Arbor

Frank H. Easterbrook, The Law School, University of Chicago

Eugene F. Fama, Graduate School of Business, University of Chicago

Christopher James, College of Business Administration, University of Oregon

Gregg A. Jarrell, William E. Simon Graduate School of Business Administration, University of Rochester

Michael C. Jensen, Graduate School of Business Administration, Harvard University

Ramon E. Johnson, Graduate School of Business, University of Utah

Avner Kalay, Graduate School of Business, University of Utah

Ronald C. Lease, A. B. Freeman School of Business, Tulane University

Nicholas S. Majluf, Engineering and Systems Department, Pontificia-Catholic University of Chile

Ronald W. Masulis, Edwin L. Cox School of Business, Southern Methodist University

John J. McConnell, Krannert School of Management, Purdue University

William H. Meckling, William E. Simon Graduate School of Business Administration, University of Rochester

Stewart C. Myers, Sloan School of Management, Massachusetts Institute of Technology

Jeffry M. Netter, Economics Department, University of Georgia, Athens

Krishna Ramaswamy, The Wharton School, University of Pennsylvania
Jay R. Ritter, Graduate School of Business Administration, University of Michigan, Ann Arbor
Richard S. Ruback, Graduate School of Business Administration, Harvard University
James S. Schallheim, Graduate School of Business, University of Utah
Suresh M. Sundaresan, Graduate School of Business, Columbia University
René M. Stulz, College of Business, Ohio State University
Joseph D. Vu, College of Business Administration, University of Illinois, Chicago
Lee M. Wakeman, Capital Markets Group, Chemical Bank, New York
Jerold B. Warner, William E. Simon Graduate School of Business Administration, University of Rochester

The editor wishes to acknowledge the sources of the articles in this volume as follows:

American Economic Association:

Frank H. Easterbrook, "Two Agency-Cost Explanations of Dividends," *American Economic Review,* vol. 74, no. 4, September 1984, pp. 650–659.

Eugene F. Fama, "The Effect of a Firm's Investment and Financing Decisions on the Welfare of Its Security Holders," *American Economic Review,* vol. 68, no. 3, June 1978, pp. 272–284.

Gregg A. Jarrell, James A. Brickley and Jeffry M. Netter, "The Market for Corporate Control: The Empirical Evidence Since 1980," *Journal of Economic Perspectives,* vol. 2, no. 1, Winter 1988, pp. 49–68.

Michael C. Jensen, "Agency Costs of Free Cash Flow, Corporate Finance, and Takeovers," *American Economic Review,* vol. 76, no. 2, May 1986, pp. 323–329.

American Finance Association:

Clifford W. Smith, Jr., and Lee M. Wakeman, "Determinants of Corporate Leasing Policy," *Journal of Finance,* vol. 40, no. 3, July 1985, pp. 895–908.

Jerold B. Warner, "Bankruptcy Costs: Some Evidence," *Journal of Finance,* vol. 32, no. 2, May 1977, pp. 337–348.

Chase Manhattan Bank:

L. Macdonald Wakeman, "The Real Function of Bond Rating Agencies," *Chase Financial Quarterly,* vol. 1, no. 1, Fall 1981, pp. 18–26.

Institutional Investor:

Fischer Black, "The Dividend Puzzle," *Journal of Portfolio Management,* vol. 2, Winter 1976, pp. 5–8. Copyright © by Institutional Investor, Inc.

North-Holland Publishing Company:

Randolph P. Beatty and Jay R. Ritter, "Investment Banking, Reputation, and the Underpricing of Initial Public Offerings," *Journal of Financial Economics,* vol. 15, nos. 1/2, January/February 1986, pp. 213–232.

James A. Brickley, "Shareholder Wealth, Information Signaling and the Specially Designated Dividend: An Empirical Study," *Journal of Financial Economics,* vol. 12, no. 2, August 1983, pp. 187–209.

Larry Y. Dann, "Common Stock Repurchases: An Analysis of Returns to Bondholders and Stockholders," *Journal of Financial Economics,* vol. 9, no. 2, June 1981, pp. 113–138.

Harry DeAngelo and Ronald W. Masulis, "Optimal Capital Structure Under Corporate and Personal Taxation," *Journal of Financial Economics,* vol. 8, no. 1, March 1980, pp. 3–29.

Christopher James, "Some Evidence on the Uniqueness of Bank Loans," *Journal of Financial Economics,* vol. 19, no. 2, December 1987, pp. 217–235.

Michael C. Jensen and William H. Meckling, "Theory of the Firm: Managerial Behavior, Agency Costs, and Ownership Structure," *Journal of Financial Economics,* vol. 3, no. 4, October 1976, pp. 305–360.

Michael C. Jensen and Richard S. Ruback, "The Market for Corporate Control: The Scientific Evidence," *Journal of Financial Economics,* vol. 11, nos. 1–4, April 1983, pp. 5–50.

Avner Kalay, "Stockholder-Bondholder Conflict and Dividend Constraints," *Journal of Financial Economics,* vol. 10, no. 2, July 1982, pp. 211–233.

Ronald W. Masulis, "The Effects of Capital Structure Change on Security Prices: A Study of Exchange Offers," *Journal of Financial Economics,* vol. 8, no. 2, June 1980, pp. 139–177.

Stewart C. Myers, "Determinants of Corporate Borrowing," *Journal of Financial Economics,* vol. 5, no. 2, November 1977, pp. 147–175.

Stewart C. Myers and Nicholas S. Majluf "Corporate Financing and Investment Decisions When Firms Have Information that Investors Do Not Have," *Journal of Financial Economics,* vol. 13, no. 2, June 1984, pp. 187–221.

Krishna Ramaswamy and Suresh M. Sundaresan, "The Valuation of Floating-Rate Instruments: Theory and Evidence," *Journal of Financial Economics,* vol. 17, no. 2, December 1986, pp. 251–272.

James S. Schallheim, Ramon E. Johnson, Ronald C. Lease, and John J. McConnell, "The Determinants of Yields on Financial Leasing Contracts," *Journal of Financial Economics,* vol. 19, no. 1, September 1987, pp. 45–67.

Clifford W. Smith, Jr., "Applications of Option Pricing Analysis," in James L. Bicksler, ed., *Handbook of Financial Economics,* North-Holland Publishing Company, Amsterdam, 1979, pp. 79–121.

Clifford W. Smith, Jr., "Investment Banking and the Capital Acquisition Process," *Journal of Financial Economics,* vol. 15, nos. 1/2, January/February 1986, pp. 3–29.

Clifford W. Smith, Jr., and Jerold B. Warner, "On Financial Contracting: An Analysis of Bond Covenants," *Journal of Financial Economics,* vol. 7, no. 2, June 1979, pp. 117–161.

René M. Stulz, "Managerial Control of Voting Rights: Financing Policies and the Market for Corporate Control," *Journal of Financial Economics,* vol. 20, nos. 1/2, January/March 1988, pp. 25–54.

Joseph D. Vu, "An Empirical Investigation of Calls of Non-Convertible Bonds," *Journal of Financial Economics,* vol. 16, no. 2, June 1986, pp. 235–265.

I would like to thank Michael C. Jensen, my coauthor on the first edition of this introduction and my coeditor on the first edition of this book, for his input and assistance. Unfortunately, too many commitments and too many miles precluded our collaboration on this edition.

McGraw-Hill and the editor also wish to thank the following reviewers for their many helpful comments and suggestions: Ronald Lease, Tulane University; Ronald Masulis, Southern Methodist University; Edward Rice, University of Chicago; and Ehud Ronn, University of Chicago.

Clifford W. Smith, Jr.

THE MODERN
THEORY OF
CORPORATE
FINANCE

ONE

INTRODUCTION

The Theory of Corporate Finance:
A Historical Overview

Clifford W. Smith, Jr.*

1 INTRODUCTION

My purpose is to provide a brief review of the development of the modern theory of corporate finance as a general background for the articles included in this book. The finance literature through the early 1950s consisted in large part of ad hoc theories and institutional detail, but little systematic analysis. For example, Dewing (1919; 1953), the major corporate finance textbook for generations, describes the birth of a corporation and follows it through various policy decisions to its death (bankruptcy). Corporate financial theory prior to the 1950s was riddled with logical inconsistencies and was almost totally prescriptive, that is, normatively oriented. The major concerns of the field were optimal investment, financing, and dividend policies, but little consideration was given to the effects of individual incentives, or to the nature of equilibrium in financial markets.

The theory of financial markets in the 1950s was in the same undeveloped state as the theory of corporate finance. Portfolio theory was in its infancy, and the pricing and other implications of equilibrium in financial markets were largely ignored. The leading book on security analysis, Graham/Dodd (1951), describes how to "pick winners" by analyzing the firm's assets, earnings, dividends, and so on. Questions such as how those winners are formed into portfolios, or how such analysis could consistently succeed given the widespread competition among investors for undervalued securities were not usually addressed.

In the 1950s, fundamental changes in finance began to occur. The analytical methods and techniques traditional to economics began to be applied to problems in finance, and the resulting transformation has been significant. This evolution was accompanied by a change in the focus of the literature from normative questions such as "What should investment, financing, or dividend policies be?" to positive theories addressing questions such as "What are the effects of alternate investment, financing, or dividend policies on the value of the firm?" This shift in research emphasis was necessary to provide the scientific basis for the formation and analysis of corporate policy decisions.

The logical structure of decision making implies that better answers to normative questions are likely to occur when decision makers have a richer set of positive theories that provide a better understanding of the consequences of their choices. This impor-

*Clarey Professor of Finance, William E. Simon Graduate School of Business Administration, University of Rochester.

tant relation between normative and positive theories often goes unrecognized. Purposeful decisions cannot be made without the explicit or implicit use of positive theories. Managers cannot decide what action to take and expect to meet their objective if they have no idea about how alternative actions affect the desired outcome—and that is what is meant by a positive theory.[1] For example, to choose among alternative financial structures, a manager wants to know how the choices affect expected net cash flows, the level of risk, and therefore the effect on firm value. Using incorrect positive theories leads to decisions that have unexpected and undesirable outcomes.

2   FUNDAMENTAL BUILDING BLOCKS

The years since 1950 have witnessed the formulation of the major building blocks of the modern theory of financial economics:

Efficient Markets Theory—analysis of the behavior of price changes through time in speculative markets.

Portfolio Theory—analysis of optimal security selection procedures for an investor's portfolio of securities.

Capital Asset Pricing Theory—analysis of the determinants of asset prices under conditions of uncertainty.

Option Pricing Theory—analysis of the determinants of the prices of contingent claims such as call options and corporate bonds.

Agency Theory—analysis of the control of incentive conflicts in contractual relations.

The development of a body of theory addressing these questions has evolved over time in roughly this order. Here, I briefly summarize them with emphasis on aspects central to corporate financial policy.

2.1   Efficient Markets Theory

The efficient markets hypothesis holds that a market is efficient if it is impossible to make economic profits by trading on available information. Cowles (1933) documents the inability of 45 professional agencies to forecast stock price changes. Other early work in the field by statisticians such as Working (1934), Kendall (1953), and Osborne (1959, 1962) document that stock and commodity prices behave like a random walk; that is, stock price changes behave as if they were independent random drawings. This means that technical trading rules based on information in the past price series cannot be expected to produce above-normal returns.

Samuelson (1965) and Mandelbrot (1966) provide the modern theoretical rationale behind the efficient markets hypothesis that unexpected price changes in a speculative market must behave as independent random drawings if the market is competitive and

---

[1]Jensen (1983) provides an extended discussion of these and other methodological issues.

economic trading profits are zero.[2] They argue that unexpected price changes reflect new information. Since new information by definition is information that cannot be deduced from previous information, new information must be independent over time. Therefore, unexpected security price changes must be independent through time if expected economic profits are to be zero. In the economics literature, this hypothesis has been independently developed by Muth (1961). Termed the rational expectations hypothesis, it has had a dramatic impact on macroeconomic analysis.

The efficient markets hypothesis is perhaps the most extensively tested hypothesis in all the social sciences. An important factor leading to the substantial body of empirical evidence on this hypothesis is the data made available by the establishment of the Center for Research in Security Prices (CRSP) sponsored by Merrill Lynch at the University of Chicago. The center created accurate computer files of closing prices, dividends, and capital changes for all stocks on the New York and American stock exchanges and the National Association of Security Dealers Automated Quotation (NASDAQ) System. Consistent with the efficient markets hypothesis, detailed empirical studies of stock prices indicate that it is difficult to earn above-normal profits by trading on publicly available data because it is already incorporated in security prices. Fama (1976) reviews much of the evidence. However, the evidence is not completely one-sided; see, for example, Jensen (1978), who provides a review of some anomalies.

If capital markets are efficient, then the market value of the firm reflects the present value of the firm's expected future net cash flows, including expected cash flows from future investment opportunities. Thus the efficient markets hypothesis has several important implications for corporate finance. First, there is no ambiguity about the firm's objective function—managers should maximize the current market value of the firm.[3] Hence management does not have to choose between maximizing the firm's current value or its future value, and there is no reason for management to have a time horizon that is too short. Second, there is no benefit to manipulating earnings per share. Management decisions that increase earnings but do not affect cash flows represent wasted effort. Third, if new securities are issued at market prices which reflect an unbiased assessment of future payoffs, then concern about dilution or the sharing of positive net present value projects with new securityholders is eliminated. Fourth, security returns are meaningful measures of firm performance. This allows scholars to use security returns to estimate the effects of various corporate policies and events on the market value of the corporation. Beginning with the Fama/Fisher/Jensen/Roll (1969) analysis of the effect of stock splits on the value of the firm's shares, empirical research examining abnormal stock price changes has produced a rich array of evidence to augment positive theories in corporate finance. In Section 6, I mention a few of the recent contributions from studies of stock price reactions to announcements of financing decisions, payout policy decisions, and corporate control transactions.

---

[2]Probably the first to characterize pricing in security markets as efficient was Bachelier (1900). Although he anticipated the efficient markets hypothesis and developed models describing the pricing of options and the distribution of price changes, his work went largely unnoticed for more than 50 years.

[3]For securityholders to prefer value maximization also requires that their consumption opportunities are altered by the firm's investment and financing decisions only through wealth changes.

2.2   Portfolio Theory

Prior to Markowitz (1952), little attention was given to portfolio selection. Security analysis focused on picking undervalued securities; a portfolio was generally taken to be just an accumulation of these securities. Markowitz points out that if risk is an undesirable attribute for investors, merely accumulating predicted "winners" is a poor portfolio selection procedure because it ignores the effect of portfolio diversification on risk. He analyzes the normative portfolio question of picking portfolios that maximize the expected utility of investors under conditions where investors choose among portfolios on the basis of expected portfolio return and portfolio risk measured by the variance of portfolio return. He defines the efficient set of portfolios as those that provide both maximum expected return for a given variance and minimum variance for a given expected return. His mean-variance analysis provides (1) formal content to the meaning of diversification, (2) a measure of the contribution of the covariance among security returns to the riskiness of a portfolio, and (3) rules for the construction of an efficient portfolio. Portfolio theory implies that the firm should evaluate projects in the same way that investors evaluate securities. For example, firms do not receive a lower cost of capital from corporate diversification. (Of course, diversification could affect value by affecting expected bankruptcy costs and thus net cash flows.)

2.3   Capital Asset Pricing Theory

Treynor (1961), Sharpe (1964), and Lintner (1965) apply the normative analysis of Markowitz to create a positive theory of the determination of asset prices. Given investor demands for securities implied by the Markowitz mean-variance portfolio selection model and assuming fixed supplies of assets, they solve for equilibrium security prices in a single-period world with no taxes.

Although total risk is measured by the variance of portfolio returns, the above-mentioned authors demonstrate that in equilibrium an individual security is priced to reflect its contribution to total risk (or "systematic" risk), which is measured by the covariance of its return with the return on the market portfolio of all assets. The simplest form of the capital asset pricing model yields the following expression for the equilibrium expected returns, $E(R_j)$, on asset j:

$$E(R_j) = R_F + [E(R_M) - R_F] \beta_j$$

where R_F is the riskless rate of interest; $E(R_M)$ is the expected return on the market portfolio of all assets; and $\beta_j = \text{cov}(R_j, R_M)/\sigma^2(R_M)$, the covariance between the return on asset j and the market return divided by the variance of the market return, is the measure of systematic risk of asset j. Thus, asset pricing theory defines the opportunity cost of capital for the firm's capital budgeting decisions. Much research has been devoted to extensions and empirical tests of the model. Jensen (1972) provides a survey of much of the literature, Roll (1977) offers criticisms of tests of the capital asset pricing model, and Schwert (1983) provides a survey of size-related deviations of average returns from those predicted by the capital asset pricing model.[4]

---

[4]Alternate valuation models such as the arbitrage pricing model suggested by Ross (1976) or the consumption-based asset pricing model suggested by Breeden (1979) may eventually lead to a better

2.4   Option Pricing Theory

The capital asset pricing model provides a positive theory for the determination of expected returns and thus links an asset's price today with that asset's expected future payoffs. However many important corporate policy problems require the valuation of assets which, like call options, have payoffs that are contingent on the future value of another asset. Black/Scholes (1973) provide a key to this problem in their solution to the call option valuation problem. An American call option gives the holder the right to buy a stock at a specified exercise price at any time prior to a specified expiration date. They note that a risk-free position can be maintained by continuously adjusting a hedge portfolio containing an option and its underlying stock. To avoid opportunities for riskless arbitrage profits, the return to the hedge must equal the market risk-free rate. This condition yields an expression for the current call price as a function of the current stock price.

Black/Scholes note that if the firm's cash flow distribution is fixed, the option pricing analysis can be used to value other contingent claims such as the equity of a levered firm. In this view, the equity of a levered firm is a call option on the total value of the firm's assets with an exercise price equal to the face value of the debt and an expiration date equal to the maturity date of the debt. The Black/Scholes analysis shows that the value of the firm's equity is an increasing function of the value of the firm's assets, the time to maturity of the firm's debt, the variance of the return on the firm's assets, the risk-free rate, and a decreasing function of the face value of the firm's debt. For a review of this literature, see **Smith (1979)**[5], and see **Ramaswamy/Sundaresan (1986)** for its application to value floating rate claims.

2.5   Agency Theory

Narrowly defined, an agency relationship is a contract in which one or more persons [the principal(s)] engage another person (the agent) to perform some service on their behalf which involves delegating some decision making authority. Spence/Zeckhauser (1971) and Ross (1973) provide early formal analyses of the problems associated with structuring the compensation of the agent to align his incentives with the interests of the principal. **Jensen/Meckling (1976)** argue that agency problems emanating from conflicts of interest are general to virtually all cooperative activity among self-interested individuals whether or not it occurs in the hierarchical fashion suggested by the principal agent analogy.

Jensen/Meckling define agency costs as the sum of the costs of structuring contracts (formal and informal): monitoring expenditures by the principal, bonding expenditures by the agent, and the residual loss. The residual loss is the opportunity cost associated with the change in real activities that occurs because it does not pay to enforce all contracts perfectly. They argue that the parties to the contracts make rational forecasts of the activities to be accomplished and structure contracts to facilitate those

---

understanding of the structure of security prices and overcome limitations of the capital asset pricing model. Note, however, that each of these models implies that expected returns are related to the contribution of a security to a particular measure of total risk.

[5] Articles reprinted in this volume are highlighted in boldface.

activities. At the time the contracts are negotiated, the actions motivated by the incentives established through the contracts are anticipated and reflected in the contracts' prices and terms. Hence, the agency costs of any relationship are born by the parties to the contracting relationship. This means that some individual(s) can always benefit by devising more effective ways of reducing them. Jensen/Meckling use the agency framework to analyze the resolution of conflicts of interest between stockholders, managers, and bondholders of the firm.

The development of a theory of the optimal contract structure in a firm involves construction of a general theory of organizations. Jensen (1983) outlines the role of agency theory in such an effort. Fama (1980) and Fama/Jensen (1983a,b) analyze the nature of residual claims and the separation of management and riskbearing in the corporation and in other organization forms. They provide a theory based on trade-offs of the risksharing and other advantages of the corporate form with its agency costs to explain the survival of the corporate form in large-scale, complex nonfinancial activities. They also explain the survival of proprietorships, partnerships, mutuals, and nonprofits in other activities. Since the primary distinguishing characteristic among these organizational forms is the nature of their residual or equity claims, this work addresses the question: What type of equity claim should an organization issue? This question is a natural predecessor to the question of the optimal quantity of debt relative to equity—the capital structure issue—that has long been discussed in finance. For a review of this literature, see Jensen/Smith (1985).

3 CAPITAL BUDGETING DECISIONS

Dean (1951) recommends that the firm make investment decisions by looking to the capital markets for the firm's cost of capital, accepting each project with an internal rate of return that exceeds this market-determined cost of capital. (The internal rate of return is the discount rate at which the present value of the net cash flows equals zero.) Subsequently, Lorie/Savage (1955) and Hirshleifer (1958) draw on the earlier analysis of Fisher (1907, 1930) and Lutz/Lutz (1951) to analyze deficiencies in the internal rate of return decision criterion (for example, it can yield decisions that are not unique and it does not account correctly for a nonflat term structure of interest rates). They offer the net present value criterion for investment decisions as a solution. The net present value rule directs the manager to discount project cash flows at the market-based cost of capital and to accept all projects with positive discounted values. Analysis of the firm's investment decisions has been well understood for so long that now the best discussions are in textbooks [e.g., Brealey/Myers (1988)].

The net present value criterion can be implemented in a relatively straightforward manner when the capital market contains traded claims on identical projects, for example, scale-expanding projects. In this case new claims can be priced by observing the prices of existing claims for identical projects. However, for new projects, a theory is required to identify the characteristics of the project that are important in determining the cost of capital. Asset pricing theory identifies those characteristics and the manner in which they determine the project's cost of capital and thus provides a theory for valuing cash flows in capital budgeting under uncertainty.

Some real investment projects have embedded options—some technologies are more flexible than others; for example, a heating plant is constructed to change from oil to gas as a source of fuel by turning a switch. To appropriately value these real investment options (in this example, the value of switching from one fuel source to another), the option pricing model must be employed. See Majd/Pindyck (1987) and Mason/Merton (1985).

4   CAPITAL STRUCTURE POLICY

4.1   The Irrelevance Proposition

In 1958, Modigliani/Miller laid an important foundation for a positive theory of financial structure by developing the implications of market equilibrium for optimal debt policy. They demonstrated that given the firm's investment policy and with no taxes or contracting costs, the firm's choice of financing policy does not affect the current market value of the firm.[6] Their capital structure irrelevance proposition shows that the firm's choice of financing policy cannot affect the value of the firm as long as it does not affect the probability distribution of the total cash flows to the firm. The Modigliani/Miller irrelevance proposition is a special case of the more general proposition developed by Coase (1960) that in the absence of contracting costs and wealth effects, the assignment of property rights leaves the use of real resources unaffected. For a review of the capital structure irrelevance literature, see **Fama (1978).**

4.2   Toward an Optimal Financing Policy

While Modigliani/Miller (1958) permanently changed the role of economic analysis in discussions of capital structure, their work provides no explanations for the corporate financing policies observed in practice. However, the Modigliani/Miller irrelevance proposition does tell us that if the choice of corporate financing policy does affect the current market value of the firm, it must do so in one of only three ways: the choice of financing policy must change either the tax liabilities of the firm or the firm's claimholders, change contracting/agency costs, or change the firm's incentives with respect to its choice of future investment policy.

Taxes   The early analysis addressing the normative question "How should the optimal debt/equity ratio be set?" followed the Modigliani/Miller admonition to avoid confusing investment and financing policies. By explicitly holding investment policy fixed, the analysis focuses on other factors that influence net cash flows. Modigliani/Miller (1963) argue that since the corporate profits tax allows the deduction of interest payments in calculating taxable income, the more debt in the capital structure, the lower the corporate tax liability, the higher after-tax cash flows, and the greater the market value of the firm.

Building on the analysis of Farrar/Selwyn (1967) and Black (1973), Miller (1977) argues that the tax advantage of debt is exaggerated by considering the corporate profits tax in isolation from personal income taxes. He argues that the corporate tax ad-

---

[6]This basic argument was anticipated by Williams (1938, pp. 72–75).

vantage of debt is offset by personal tax rates on investors' debt income that are higher than tax rates on investors' equity income. In addition, Brennan/Schwartz (1978) also argue that the corporate tax advantage of debt is lower because the interest tax shield is lost if the firm goes through bankruptcy and liquidation. Furthermore, **DeAngelo/Masulis (1980)** argue that substitute tax shields, such as investment tax credits, also reduce the corporate tax advantage of debt.

Bankruptcy Costs   Kraus/Litzenberger (1973) produce a theory of the optimal capital structure by formalizing the argument that the corporate tax shield is offset by increased expected bankruptcy costs. Increases in leverage increase the probability of bankruptcy and thus increase expected bankruptcy costs. The optimal capital structure is defined by the point at which additional leverage generates an increase in the value of expected bankruptcy costs that just offsets the tax subsidy to the incremental debt.

Baxter (1967) argues that bankruptcy costs can take two forms, direct and indirect. **Warner (1977)** examines the magnitude of the direct bankruptcy costs for a sample of railroad firms. He finds that the expected present value of the out-of-pocket expenses associated with bankruptcy is small relative to the market value of the firm. His analysis avoids many of the problems of previous studies, which largely consisted of examinations of personal and small business bankruptcies.

In addition to direct bankruptcy costs, Baxter (1967) argues that there are important indirect costs of bankruptcy. Indirect bankruptcy costs are specific contracting costs which arise because the firm's investment policy and other resource allocation decisions (such as corporate compensation and marketing policies) are not fixed.[7] Indirect costs include lost sales, lost profits, costs associated with restrictions on the firm's borrowing, and higher compensation that managers demand because of higher probability of unemployment. Some of these costs arise because the bankruptcy trustee is an agent of the court and thus has limited incentives to make value-maximizing investment or financing decisions. Good estimates of these costs do not yet exist, but in general, they are unlikely to be trivial.

Agency Costs   Conflicts of interest exist among common stockholders, bondholders, and managers because corporate decisions that increase the welfare of one of these groups often reduce the welfare of the others. **Jensen/Meckling (1976)** use the agency framework to provide a positive analysis of the effects of conflicts of interest among stockholders, managers, and bondholders on the investment and financing decisions of the firm. They argue that viewing the financial structure problem as one of determining the optimal quantities of debt versus equity is too narrow. More generally the problem involves determining the optimal ownership structure of the firm including the relative quantities of debt and equity held by managers and outsiders as well as the details of the debt (short-term, long-term; public, private; convertible; callable; and the associated covenants) and equity (common stock with unrestricted or restricted alienability, the allocation of voting rights, preferred stock, warrants, etc.) At its most

---

[7]These indirect bankruptcy costs are thus a special case of what within agency theory would be labeled the residual loss.

general level the capital structure problem involves the joint determination of the entire set of contracts among stockholders, bondholders, and managers as well as other agents in the nexus of contracts, including customers, employees, lessors, insurers, and so on.

Myers (1977) examines a specific aspect of the agency costs of debt, the underinvestment problem. His analysis demonstrates that with fixed claims in the firm's capital structure, stockholders can have incentives to reject positive net present value projects. **Smith/Warner (1979)** provide a detailed analysis of the monitoring and bonding technology for control of the conflict of interest between bondholders and stockholders, demonstrating how observed bond contracts should vary in response to these agency problems. Smith/Watts (1982) examine the control of the conflict between stockholders and managers. They analyze the structure of management compensation contracts focusing on the trade-offs between salaries, stock options, restricted stock, bonus plans, and other frequently observed compensation provisions. Mayers/Smith (1982) analyze corporate insurance purchases and argue that insurance contracts produce an efficient allocation of riskbearing and provide for efficient administration of claims against the corporation.[8]

4.3 Corporate Leasing Policy

Leasing is a contractual arrangement in which a firm acquires the services of an asset for a specified time period and therefore is an alternative to purchasing the asset. **Smith/Wakeman (1985)** analyze the corporate leasing decision. As in the original Modigliani/Miller capital structure analysis, when the cash flow distribution is unaffected, leasing policy has no effect on the value of the firm. However, like debt, leasing can affect the firm's cash flows in a number of ways. Given the investment decision, leasing provides an alternative to purchasing that can affect the incidence of taxes and thus after-tax corporate cash flows. When tax rates differ between lessor and lessee, leasing provides opportunities to reduce total tax payments by shifting tax shields to individuals or companies who value them most highly. Leasing can lower contracting costs when the useful life of the asset is significantly longer than the period over which a particular company expects to use the asset; for example, Hertz and Holiday Inn specialize in providing short-term leasing of durable assets. Leasing can also be employed to engage in certain forms of price discrimination; for example, charging copier lessees a rate based on the number of copies (metering) charges high-intensity users higher prices. Finally, agency costs are reduced when organization-specific assets (assets that are more highly valued within the organization than in their best alternative use) are owned rather than leased [see also Klein/Crawford/Alchian (1978)]. **Schallheim/Johnson/Lease/McConnell (1987)** examine the determination of lease rates for a sample of lease contracts. They demonstrate that observed lease rates reflect explicit compensation for the risk and tax consequences of the contract.

---

[8]There has been significant research relating the corporate choice of accounting procedures to political pressures and the firm's management compensation and financial policies. For a review of this literature, see Watts/Zimmerman (1986).

5   DIVIDEND POLICY

5.1   The Irrelevance Proposition

Miller/Modigliani (1961) extended their capital structure analysis to dividend policy. They argue that as long as the probability distribution of the firm's cash flows is fixed and there are no tax effects, the firm's choice of dividend policy leaves the current market value of the firm unaffected. In their analysis, increased dividends are financed by the sale of new stock. Because the total value of the firm remains constant, the sale of new stock reduces the per share price of the existing shares by an amount equal to the increased dividend per share paid from the proceeds of the sale. This means that for the existing shareholders, there is a one-for-one trade-off between higher expected dividends and lower expected capital gains. Thus, with the probability distribution fixed, dividend policy is irrelevant.

5.2   Toward an Optimal Dividend Policy

Questions regarding (1) why firms pay dividends and (2) the effects of alternative dividend policies when firm cash flow distributions are allowed to vary with dividend policy have been the source of much debate and empirical examination. **Black (1976)** provides a concise summary of the unresolved issues.

Agency Costs and Dividend Policy   Because dividend payments not financed by new equity sales reduce the asset base securing corporate bonds, bond values can be increased by providing appropriate protection from expropriation through unrestricted dividend payments. **Smith/Warner (1979)** and **Kalay (1982)** analyze the restrictions on dividends specified in corporate bond contracts. They show that through the cash flow identity, dividend and investment policies are interdependent; specifying a lower maximum on dividends in the debt covenant imposes a higher minimum on the fraction of earnings retained in the firm. Increased earnings retention, however, imposes overinvestment costs on a firm that expects few profitable projects over the life of its bond. Thus, the theory predicts that an unregulated firm which forecasts recurring profitable future investment projects will set a low maximum on dividends, and therefore a high minimum on retentions. This will reduce both their requirements for externally raised equity capital and the associated equity flotation costs as well as the present value of agency costs.

Rozeff (1982) and **Easterbrook (1984)** note that a policy of paying dividends increases the frequency with which the corporation's managers go to capital markets to obtain new equity. This policy subjects the firm more frequently to the intensive capital market monitoring and discipline that occur at the time new funds are raised and lowers agency costs. They also argue that dividend payments to stockholders allow the firm to raise its debt-equity ratio without requiring the firm to increase its assets by issuing debt. Their arguments predict that firms with high growth rates and high demand for new capital will have less reason to pay high dividends because they are going to the capital markets frequently anyway. Consistent with this prediction, such firms generally have low dividends.

In contrast, utilities have historically had high demands for new capital and high dividend payout rates. **Smith (1986)** argues that utility stockholders are likely to fare less well in the rate regulation process if the dividend rate is lowered to reduce the frequency and costs of floating new equity in the capital markets. In many political jurisdictions, the process effectively makes the required rates of return a function of dividend payments. Moreover, by paying high dividends the regulated firm more frequently subjects both itself and its regulatory body to the discipline of the marketplace. Stockholders are less likely to suffer expropriation through low rates set in the adversarial regulatory setting when the regulatory body is more frequently policed by the capital markets. Giving suppliers of debt and equity capital an opportunity to signal their dissatisfaction with confiscatorily low rates through low prices, or perhaps through denial of funds required to maintain service, accomplishes this. Thus, high dividends are a way of bonding to stockholders that they will receive a normal rate of return on the capital invested in the corporation.

Kalay (1982) has examined corporate dividend covenants and finds that firms do not pay all dividends allowed under the contract. If firms are behaving optimally, this implies there are benefits from maintaining a reservoir that gives the firm the right to pay dividends. These benefits could come from avoiding forced investment at low returns when no profitable projects are available.

Dividend Yields and Expected Returns   In determining an optimal dividend policy, one question is "How do capital markets value cash dividends versus capital gains?" The Miller/Modigliani dividend proposition demonstrates that if, for the marginal supplier, there is not a differential cost of producing dividends or capital gains, then a dollar of dividends and a dollar of capital gains are valued equally. Thus, the "bird-in-hand" argument that dividend policy matters because investors value current dividends more highly than uncertain future capital gains is false. Valuation will be determined by the marginal cost of producing dividends and capital gains; without differential costs of production, preferences will be reflected only in relative quantities of dividends and capital gains, not in the value of firms.

Brennan (1970) suggests that higher effective tax rates on dividends relative to capital gains will result in higher expected pre-tax returns on high-dividend stocks of equivalent risk. Miller/Scholes (1978) argue that the tax disadvantage of dividends is reduced by investors' ability to offset dividend income by interest deductions on borrowings combined with investment of the proceeds from the borrowing in tax-sheltered means of accumulation such as life insurance contracts and retirement accounts. Whether this tax reduction mechanism is used by enough investors to affect prices is unknown at this time.[9]

The results of cross-sectional examinations of the effect of dividend yields on expected returns are unsettled. Litzenberger/Ramaswamy (1979, 1982) conclude that higher dividends are associated with higher expected returns; Black/Scholes (1974)

---

[9] Furthermore, there is an apparent contradiction between the Miller/Scholes analysis of dividends and Miller's (1977) tax-based model of financial structure. The mechanisms which Miller/Scholes apply to avoid taxes on dividends can also be applied to avoid personal taxes on interest income. This apparently eliminates the effective differential tax rates on equity and debt that is the basis of Miller's model. The issue is unresolved as yet. See Hamada/Scholes (1985) for a discussion of these issues.

and Miller/Scholes (1981) conclude that higher dividends have no effect on expected returns; and Long (1978) concludes that higher dividends are associated with lower expected returns. Litzenberger/Ramaswamy argue that their examination of the effect of dividend yield on expected returns employs more prior information about corporate dividend policy and thus produces more efficient estimates. Miller/Scholes argue that the Litzenberger/Ramaswamy procedure introduces bias in estimation, overstating the magnitude of the estimated dividend effect. Long examines the Citizens Utilities Corporation, a unique company with two classes of stock which differ only in terms of their dividends and tax treatment—one class receives cash dividends and the other receives stock dividends. The special circumstances of this company provide powerful controls for potentially confounding differences in investment and financing policies in the usual tests of dividend policy effects. He finds that the class receiving cash dividends is priced at a premium over the class receiving stock dividends.

6   EVIDENCE FROM ANNOUNCEMENTS OF CORPORATE TRANSACTIONS

6.1   Security Sale, Exchange Offer, and Payout Announcements

Optimal Capital Structure   Although a number of researchers argue that the market's reaction to announcements of financing decisions can be employed to test optimal capital structure theories, that evidence appears ill-suited to examine those hypotheses because these events do not hold investment policy fixed. If we assume that stock price changes reflect firms' attempts to move toward an optimal capital structure, then stock price reactions to security announcements should, on average, be positive. Yet the evidence from the announcements of new security sales summarized in **Smith (1986)** indicates that the market's reaction is negative or at best neutral. Thus, gains from moving toward an optimal capital structure are not the dominating factor in the price response to new security offers.

Information Disparity Between Management and Potential Investors   The documented reductions in firm value associated with security sales present financial economists with a puzzle. One explanation is that security sales are optimal responses to changes for the worse in a company's prospects. Investors used to stock offerings under such conditions will discount the stock prices of companies announcing security offerings. The evidence from announcements of security sales is consistent with a disparity of information between management and the market, and the incentives this offers management in timing the issue of new securities. New security offerings appear to affect investors' outlook about a company through two primary channels: (1) the implied change in expected net operating cash flow and (2) the leverage change.

Investors are ultimately interested in a company's capacity to generate cash flow. If unanticipated security issues are associated with reductions in future cash flows from operations, then investors would systematically interpret announcements of security sales as bad news. Miller/Rock (1985) argue that announcements of stock repurchases, increases in investment expenditures, and higher dividend payments signal increases in investment operating cash flow and, thus, are good news for investors. Conversely, security offerings, reductions in investment expenditures, and reductions in dividend payments all imply reductions in expected operating cash flow.

The evidence on market responses to announcements of new securities sales, stock repurchases, dividend changes, and changes in capital spending is broadly consistent with this hypothesis. Announcements of security repurchases [see Masulis (1980a), **Dann (1981),** Vermaelen (1981) and **Vu (1986)**], dividend increases [see Charest (1978), Asquith/Mullins (1983), and **Brickley (1983)**], and increases in capital spending [see McConnell/Muscarella (1985)] are associated with increases in stock prices. The market generally responds negatively to announcements of security sales, dividend reductions, and decreases in new investment. Thus, this evidence is consistent with the market making inferences about changes in operating cash flow from announcements that do not explicitly associate sources with uses of funds.

Myers/Majluf (1984) also assume that a potential purchaser of securities has less information about the prospects of the firm than management, and that management is more likely to issue securities when the market price of the firm's traded securities is higher than management's assessment of their value. Sophisticated investors revise their estimate of the value of the firm if management announces a new security issue; furthermore, the larger the potential disparity in information, the greater the revision in expectations and the larger the negative price reaction to the announcement of a new issue.

Because debt and preferred stock are more senior claims, their values are less sensitive to changes in company value than is the value of common stock. Thus, this information disparity problem is most acute in the case of equity offerings. Similarly, convertible debt and preferred stock values are also generally more sensitive to changes in firm value than nonconvertible debt and preferred because of their equity component, but less sensitive than common stock; hence the information disparity should be more problematic for convertible than for nonconvertible securities. Finally, because the rate regulation process reduces the differential information between manager and outsiders, price reaction of utilities' announcements is smaller than that of industrials.

This second, leverage-related channel through which the information disparity problem operates can be distinguished from the implied cash flow change explanation by examining evidence from events that *explicitly* associate sources and uses of funds: exchange offers, conversion-forcing calls of convertible securities, and security sales in which the proceeds are explicitly intended for debt retirement. Research on announcements of these transactions documents the following: (1) The market responds positively to leverage-increasing transactions and negatively to leverage-decreasing transactions; (2) the larger the change in leverage, the greater the price reaction. [See **Masulis (1980b),** McConnell/Schlarbaum (1981), Mikkelson (1981), and Dietrich (1984).]

In Table 1 the implied cash flow change and leverage change hypotheses are combined to provide additional insight into the information disparity explanation. The events in the upper left portion of the table are predicted to have negative abnormal stock price reactions, events in the lower right are predicted to have positive reactions, and events along the diagonal from the lower left to the upper right are predicted to have insignificant reactions.

TABLE 1
PREDICTED SIGN OF ABNORMAL RETURNS ASSOCIATED WITH VARIOUS CORPORATE CAPITAL MARKET TRANSACTIONS

	Implied cash flow change		
Leverage change	**Negative**	**Zero**	**Positive**
Negative	Common sale Dividend decrease	Common sale to retire debt Convertible bond sale to retire debt Common/preferred exchange offer Preferred/bond exchange offer Common/bond exchange offer Call of convertible bonds Call of convertible preferred	Calls of nonconvertible bonds
Zero	Convertible-preferred sale Convertible-bond sale Investment decrease	Bond/bond exchange offer Bond sale to retire debt	Investment increase
Positive	Preferred sale Debt sale	Common repurchase financed with debt Bond/common exchange offer Preferred/common exchange offer Bond/preferred exchange offer Income bond/preferred exchange offer	Common repurchase Dividend increase Dividend initiations Specially designated dividends

predicted negative abnormal returns

predicted insignificant abnormal returns

predicted positive abnormal returns

Free Cash Flow   **Jensen (1986a,** 1986b) argues that the agency conflict between shareholders and managers over the payout of free cash flow can also explain the stock price reactions to these corporate transactions. He defines free cash flow as cash flow in excess of that required to fund all positive net present value projects; it must be paid to shareholders if the firm is to maximize value. For firms with positive free cash flow, this theory predicts that stock prices will increase with unexpected increases in payouts to corporate claimholders and decrease with unexpected increases in demand for funds via new issues. In addition, the theory predicts stock prices will increase with increasing tightness of the constraints binding the payout of future cash flow to claimholders and decrease with reductions in the tightness of these constraints. These predictions do not apply, however, to those firms with more profitable projects than free cash flow to fund them.

These predictions can also be summarized in terms of Table 1. Simply replace negative, no change, and positive implied cash flow change with reduced, no change, and increased current cash flows to claimholders; and negative, no change, and positive leverage change with reduced, no change, and increased bonding of future cash flows to claimholders. This is because the information disparity hypothesis assumes that the market has a reasonable estimate of investment policy and from an announcement of a higher dividend, for example, learns about internally generated cashflows; in contrast, the free cash flow hypothesis assumes that the market has a reasonably accurate estimate of internally generated cash and from a dividend increase learns about a lower likelihood of wasteful investments. Since both are good news, under each hypothesis, the market responds favorably. The free cash flow hypothesis suggests the returns to firms with no free cash flow will behave differently from those which do. And since extant studies do not distinguish firms with free cash flow, the correspondence between the hypothesis and the evidence might seem surprising. However, the information disparity hypothesis and the free cash flow hypothesis are not mutually exclusive.

6.2   The Structure of the Security Offer

The information disparity hypothesis has implications for structuring a security sale. If potential investors are concerned that the issuing firm has more precise information about the value of the securities than they do, this creates a derived demand for bonding. This implies that where the potential information disparity is greater, the derived demand for bonding is greater. **Smith (1986)** argues that an underwritten offer is better bonded than a rights offer, that a negotiated offer is better bonded than a competitive bid offer, that an offer traditionally registered with the SEC is better bonded than a shelf-registered offer, and that a firm commitment is better bonded than a best-efforts offer. Thus, shelf registration and competitive bids are most frequently observed in debt offers by utilities where the information disparity problems are lowest and the derived demand for bonding is least.[10]

---

[10]Other institutions provide valuable bonding functions: external auditors [Watts (1977)]; bond rating agencies [**Wakeman (1981)**]; insurers [Mayers/Smith (1982)]; outside members of the board of directors [Fama (1980)].

Rock (1986) notes that in initial public equity offers (IPOs) there is substantial underpricing [see Ibbotson (1975) and Ritter (1984)]. He argues that this is because of the information disparity among potential investors. If investment bankers set the offer price equal to the expected after-market price, those issues that were ex post overpriced would be undersubscribed, while ex post underpriced issues would be oversubscribed. A relatively uninformed investor who placed orders for both issues would receive all requested shares in the ex post overpriced issue but be rationed in the ex post underpriced issue. Thus, this investor's realized return would be subnormal. To attract relatively uninformed investors, the offer price must be set below the expected after-market price. **Beatty/Ritter (1986)** test Rock's model on a sample of IPOs. They find that investment bankers who underprice either too much or too little tend to fail.

Thus far, we have focused on public security sales. **James (1987)** examines announcements of new bank credit agreements. He finds a positive abnormal stock price reaction, not zero as with announcements of other debt sales. He suggests that this is because banks have a comparative advantage in monitoring certain corporate activities. Wruck (1989) finds a positive abnormal stock price reaction to announcements of private placements of equity. She interprets this as evidence that a private sale can be negotiated to avoid some problems with public sales: (1) Proprietary information can be disclosed to the security purchaser but not to the firm's competitors; (2) the blockholder frequently takes a board seat and may have a comparative advantage in monitoring certain corporate activities; (3) given the information disparity between the external shareholders and the purchaser of the private placement, the announcement that this individual invests in the block is good news.

6.3 Ownership and Organizational Restructuring

Smith (1986) notes that transactions which increase ownership concentration, such as private equity sales, tender offers [see **Jensen/Ruback (1983)** and **Jarrell/Brickley/ Netter (1988)**], and large block acquisitions [see Holderness/Sheehan (1985) and Mikkelson/Ruback (1988)], are associated with positive abnormal stock price reactions while transactions which reduce ownership concentration, such as secondary distributions [see Mikkelson/Partch (1985)] and targeted share repurchases [see Dann/ DeAngelo (1983) and Bradley/Wakeman (1983)], are associated with negative stock price reactions.

Schipper/Smith (1986) find that announcements of equity carve-outs are associated with a positive stock price reaction. In an equity carve-out, the firm sells a minority interest in a previously wholly owned subsidiary. Thus, in addition to raising capital through selling equity, the firm is voluntarily restructuring.

The evidence on organizational restructuring summarized in **Jensen/Ruback (1983)** and **Jarrell/Brickley/Netter (1988)** suggests that announcements of mergers, spinoffs, sell-offs, joint ventures, going private, voluntary liquidations, and proxy fights are all associated with positive abnormal stock price reactions. They view these transactions as specific transactions in what Manne (1965) calls the market for corporate control. **Jensen/Ruback (1983)** argue that this market is the arena in which alternative management teams compete for the rights to manage corporate resources, with stockholders playing a relatively passive role accepting or rejecting competing takeover offers.

This analysis has provided impetus to authors to integrate mechanisms of the market for corporate control with issues traditionally examined in corporate finance. For example, **Stulz (1988)** and Harris/Raviv (1988) examine the relation between the firm's debt equity ratio and managerial voting right control. They note that manager and nonmanager shareholder interests can diverge if there are benefits from control. Thus the fraction of the equity controlled by management and the fraction of the assets financed by debt affect the attractiveness of a firm as a takeover target. **Jensen (1986a)** notes that debt reduces the agency cost of free cash flow by reducing the cash flow available for spending at the discretion of managers. By issuing debt, managers bond their promise to distribute future cash flows. Hence debt created in a hostile takeover (or in a takeover defense) can control the free cash flow problem. Thus, mergers and tender offers involving firms with large cash flows but low growth prospects (and especially firms that must shrink their operations) can be understood in terms of controlling free cash flow problems. These considerations from the market for corporate control help explain firms' financing and payout policies.

7 CONCLUSIONS

The finance profession has progressed from a largely ad hoc, normatively oriented field with little scientific basis for decision making to one of the richest and most exciting fields in economics. Financial economics has emerged from its stage of policy irrelevance propositions in the 1960s to a stage where the theory and evidence offer much useful guidance to the practicing financial manager. The theory and evidence are sufficiently rich that sensible analyses of many problems, such as the valuation of contingent claims, the choice of bond covenants, and a wide range of contracting problems, are emerging. Our science has not as yet, however, provided a satisfactory framework for resolving many problems facing the corporate financial officer. Some of the more important questions are how to decide on (1) the level and form of corporate payouts to stockholders; (2) the marketing of the firm's securities (i.e., public versus private issues, rights versus underwritten issues); (3) the structure of claims in the firm's capital structure (i.e., long-term versus short-term debt, fixed rate versus floating rate debt, common versus preferred stock). I expect that the frontiers of knowledge in corporate finance will continue to expand. That expansion promises to be rapid over the next decade, and the results of this research promise to be of great value in resolving many problems facing corporate financial managers.

REFERENCES

Asquith, Paul, and David Mullins (1983): "The Impact of Initiating Dividend Payments on Shareholder Wealth," *Journal of Business*, vol. 56, pp. 77–96.

Bachelier, Louis (1900): *Theorie de la Speculation*, Gauthier-Villars: Paris, reprinted in Cootner, Paul, ed. (1964): *The Random Character of Stock Market Prices*, Massachusetts Institute of Technology, Cambridge, Mass., pp. 17–78.

Baxter, Nevins (1967): "Leverage, Risk of Ruin, and the Cost of Capital," *Journal of Finance*, vol. 22, pp. 395–404.

Beatty, Randolph P., and Jay R. Ritter (1986): "Investment Banking, Reputation, and the Underpricing of Initial Public Offerings," *Journal of Financial Economics*, vol. 15, pp. 213–232; **reprinted in this volume.**

Black, Fischer (1973): "Taxes and Capital Market Equilibrium Under Uncertainty," unpublished manuscript.

Black, Fischer (1976): "The Dividend Puzzle," *Journal of Portfolio Management*, vol. 2, pp. 5–8; **reprinted in this volume.**

Black, Fischer, and Myron Scholes (1973): "The Pricing of Options and Corporate Liabilities," *Journal of Political Economy*, vol. 81, pp. 637–659.

Black, Fischer, and Myron Scholes (1974): "The Effects of Dividend Yield and Dividend Policy on Common Stock Prices and Returns," *Journal of Financial Economics*, vol. 1, pp. 1–22.

Bradley, Michael, and L. M. Wakeman (1983): "The Wealth Effects of Targeted Share Repurchases," *Journal of Financial Economics*, vol. 11, pp. 301–328.

Brealey, Richard, and Stewart Myers (1988): *Principles of Corporate Finance*, 3d ed., McGraw-Hill, New York.

Breeden, Douglas (1979): "An Intertemporal Asset Pricing Model with Stochastic Consumption and Investment Opportunities," *Journal of Financial Economics*, vol. 7, pp. 265–296.

Brennan, Michael (1970): "Taxes, Market Valuation, and Corporate Financial Policy," *National Tax Journal*, vol. 23, pp. 417–427.

Brennan, Michael, and Eduardo Schwartz (1978): "Corporate Income Taxes, Valuation, and the Problem of Optimal Capital Structure," *Journal of Business*, vol. 51, pp. 103–114.

Brickley, James (1983): "Shareholder Wealth, Information Signaling and the Specially Designated Dividend: An Empirical Study," *Journal of Financial Economics*, vol. 12, pp. 187–209; **reprinted in this volume.**

Charest, Guy (1978): "Dividend Information, Stock Returns, and Market Efficiency—II," *Journal of Financial Economics*, vol. 6, pp. 297–330.

Coase, Ronald (1960): "The Problem of Social Cost," *Journal of Law and Economics*, vol. 3, pp. 1–44.

Cowles, Alfred, 3rd (1933): "Can Stock Market Forecasters Forecast?" *Econometrica*, vol. 1, pp. 309–324.

Dann, Larry (1981): "Common Stock Repurchases: An Analysis of Returns to Bondholders and Stockholders," *Journal of Financial Economics*, vol. 9, pp. 113–138; **reprinted in this volume.**

Dann, Larry, and Harry DeAngelo (1983): "Standstill Agreements, Privately Negotiated Stock Repurchases and the Market for Corporate Control," *Journal of Financial Economics*, vol. 11, pp. 275–300.

Dean, Joel (1951): *Capital Budgeting*, Columbia University Press, New York.

DeAngelo, Harry, and Ronald Masulis (1980): "Optimal Capital Structure Under Corporate and Personal Taxation," *Journal of Financial Economics*, vol. 8, pp. 3–29; **reprinted in this volume.**

Dewing, Arthur (1919; 1953): *The Financial Policy of Corporations*, Ronald Press, New York.

Dietrich, J. Richard (1984): "Effects of Early Bond Refundings: An Empirical Investigation of Security Returns," *Journal of Accounting and Economics*, vol. 6, pp. 67–96.

Easterbrook, Frank H. (1984): "Two Agency-Cost Explanations of Dividends," *American Economic Review*, vol. 74, pp. 650–659; **reprinted in this volume.**

Fama, Eugene F. (1976): *Foundations of Finance*, Basic Books, New York.

Fama, Eugene F. (1978): "The Effects of a Firm's Investment and Financing Decisions," *American Economic Review*, vol. 68, pp. 272–284; **reprinted in this volume.**

Fama, Eugene F. (1980): "Agency Problems and the Theory of the Firm," *Journal of Political Economy*, vol. 88, pp. 288–307.

Fama, Eugene F., Lawrence Fisher, Michael C. Jensen, and Richard Roll (1969): "The Adjustment of Stock Prices to New Information," *International Economic Review,* vol. 10, pp. 1–21.

Fama, Eugene F., and Michael C. Jensen (1983a): "Agency Problems and Residual Claims," *Journal of Law and Economics,* vol. 26, pp. 327–349.

Fama, Eugene F., and Michael C. Jensen (1983b): "Separation of Ownership and Control," *Journal of Law and Economics,* vol. 26, pp. 301–325.

Farrar, Donald, and Lee Selwyn (1967): "Taxes, Corporate Financial Policy and Return to Investors," *National Tax Journal,* vol. 20, pp. 144–154.

Fisher, Irving (1907): *The Rate of Interest,* MacMillan Company, New York.

Fisher, Irving (1930): *The Theory of Interest,* MacMillan Company, New York.

Graham, Benjamin, and David Dodd (1951): *Security Analysis,* McGraw-Hill, New York.

Hamada, Robert S., and Myron S. Scholes (1984): "Taxes and Corporate Financial Management," *Recent Advances in Corporate Finance,* edited by E. Altman and M. Subrahmanyam, Irwin, Homewood, Ill., pp. 187–226.

Harris, Milton, and Artur Raviv (1988): "Corporate Control Contests and Capital Structure," *Journal of Financial Economics,* vol. 20, pp. 55–86.

Hirshleifer, Jack (1958): "On the Theory of Optimal Investment Decision," *Journal of Political Economy,* vol. 66, pp. 329–352.

Holderness, Clifford G., and Dennis P. Sheehan (1985): "Raiders or Saviors? The Evidence on Six Controversial Investors," *Journal of Financial Economics,* vol. 14, pp. 555–579.

Ibbotson, Roger (1975): "Price Performance of Common Stock New Issues," *Journal of Financial Economics,* vol. 2, pp. 235–272.

James, Christopher (1987): "Some Evidence on the Uniqueness of Bank Loans," *Journal of Financial Economics,* vol. 19, pp. 217–235; **reprinted in this volume.**

Jarrell, Gregg A., James A. Brickley, and Jeffry M. Netter (1988): "The Market for Corporate Control: The Empirical Evidence Since 1980," *Journal of Economic Perspectives,* vol. 2, pp. 49–68; **reprinted in this volume.**

Jensen, Michael C. (1972): "Capital Markets: Theory and Evidence," *Bell Journal of Economics and Management Science,* vol. 3, pp. 357–398.

Jensen, Michael C. (1978): "Some Anomalous Evidence Regarding Market Efficiency," *Journal of Financial Economics,* vol. 6, pp. 95–101.

Jensen, Michael C. (1983): "Organization Theory and Methodology," *Accounting Review,* vol. 58, no. 2, pp. 319–339.

Jensen, Michael C. (1986a): "Agency Costs of Free Cash Flow, Corporate Finance, and Takeovers," *American Economic Review,* vol. 76, May, pp. 323–329; **reprinted in this volume.**

Jensen, Michael C. (1986b): "The Takeover Controversy: Analysis and Evidence," *Midland Corporate Finance Journal,* vol. 4, no. 2, pp. 6–32.

Jensen, Michael C., and William H. Meckling (1976): "Theory of the Firm: Managerial Behavior, Agency Costs, and Ownership Structure," *Journal of Financial Economics,* vol. 3, no. 4, pp. 305–360; **reprinted in this volume.**

Jensen, Michael C., and Richard Ruback (1983): "The Market for Corporate Control: The Scientific Evidence," *Journal of Financial Economics,* vol. 11, pp. 5–50; **reprinted in this volume.**

Jensen, Michael C., and Clifford W. Smith, Jr. (1985): "Stockholder, Manager, and Creditor Interests: Applications of Agency Theory," *Recent Advances in Corporate Finance,* edited by E. Altman and M. Subrahmanyam, Irwin, Homewood, Ill., pp. 93–131.

Kalay, Avner (1982): "Stockholder-Bondholder Conflict and Dividend Constraints," *Journal of Financial Economics,* vol. 10, pp. 211–233; **reprinted in this volume.**

Kendall, Maurice (1953): "The Analysis of Economic Time Series. Part I: Prices," *Journal of the Royal Statistical Society,* vol. 96, pp. 11–25.

Klein, Benjamin, Robert Crawford, and Armen A. Alchian (1978): "Vertical Integration, Appropriable Rents and the Competitive Contracting Process," *Journal of Law and Economics,* vol. 21, no. 2, pp. 297–326.

Kraus, Alan, and Robert Litzenberger (1973): "A State Preference Model of Optimal Financial Leverage," *Journal of Finance,* vol. 28, pp. 911–922.

Lintner, John (1965): "The Valuation of Risk Assets and the Selection of Risky Investments in Stock Portfolios and Capital Budgets," *Review of Economics and Statistics,* vol. 47, pp. 13–37.

Litzenberger, Robert, and Krishna Ramaswamy (1979): "The Effect of Personal Taxes and Dividends on Capital Asset Prices: Theory and Empirical Evidence," *Journal of Financial Economics,* vol. 7, pp. 163–195.

Litzenberger, Robert, and Krishna Ramaswamy (1982): "The Effects of Dividends on Common Stock Prices: Tax Effects or Information Effects," *Journal of Finance,* vol. 37, pp. 429–443.

Long, John (1978): "The Market Valuation of Cash Dividends: A Case to Consider," *Journal of Financial Economics,* vol. 6, pp. 235–264.

Lorie, James, and Leonard Savage (1955): "Three Problems in Rationing Capital," *Journal of Business,* vol. 28, pp. 229–239.

Lutz, Friedrich, and Vera Lutz (1951): *The Theory of Investment of the Firm,* Princeton University Press, Princeton, N.J.

Majd, Saman, and Robert S. Pindyck (1987): "Time to Build, Option Value, and Investment Decisions," *Journal of Financial Economics,* vol. 18, pp. 7–27.

Mandelbrot, Benoit (1966): "Forecasts of Future Prices, Unbiased Markets, and Martingale Models," *Journal of Business,* vol. 39, pp. 242–255.

Manne, Henry (1965): "Mergers and the Market for Corporate Control," *Journal of Political Economy,* vol. 74, pp. 110–120.

Markowitz, Harry (1952): "Portfolio Selection," *Journal of Finance,* vol. 7, pp. 77–91.

Mason, Scott P., and Robert C. Merton (1985): "The Role of Contingent Claims Analysis in Corporate Finance," *Recent Advances in Corporate Finance,* edited by E. Altman and M. Subrahmanyam, Irwin, Homewood, Ill., pp. 7–54.

Masulis, Ronald M. (1980a): "Stock Repurchase by Tender Offer: An Analysis of the Causes of Common Stock Price Changes," *Journal of Finance,* vol. 35, pp. 305–319.

Masulis, Ronald (1980b): "The Effect of Capital Structure Change on Security Prices: A Study of Exchange Offers," *Journal of Financial Economics,* vol. 8, pp. 139–177; **reprinted in this volume.**

Mayers, David, and Clifford Smith (1982): "On the Corporate Demand for Insurance," *Journal of Business,* vol. 55, no. 2, pp. 281–296.

McConnell, John J., and Chris J. Muscarella (1985): "Corporate Capital Expenditure Decisions and the Market Value of the Firm," *Journal of Financial Economics,* vol. 14, pp. 399–422.

McConnell, John, and Gary Schlarbaum (1981): "Evidence on the Impact of Exchange Offers on Security Prices: The Case of Income Bonds," *Journal of Business,* vol. 54, pp. 65–85.

Mikkelson, Wayne (1981): "Convertible Calls and Security Returns," *Journal of Financial Economics,* vol. 9, pp. 237–264.

Mikkelson, Wayne H., and M. Megan Partch (1985): "Stock Price Effects and Costs of Secondary Distributions," *Journal of Financial Economics,* vol. 14, pp. 165–194.

Mikkelson, Wayne H., and Richard S. Ruback (1988): "Targeted Repurchases and Common Stock Returns," unpublished manuscript, Harvard University.

Miller, Merton (1977): "Debt and Taxes," *Journal of Finance,* vol. 32, no. 2, pp. 261–276.

Miller, Merton, and Franco Modigliani (1961): "Dividend Policy, Growth, and the Valuation of Shares," *Journal of Business,* vol. 34, pp. 411–433.

Miller, Merton, and Kevin Rock (1985): "Dividend Policy Under Asymmetric Information," *Journal of Finance,* vol. 40, no. 4, pp. 1031–1051.

Miller, Merton, and Myron Scholes (1978): "Dividends and Taxes," *Journal of Financial Economics,* vol. 6, pp. 333–364.

Miller, Merton, and Myron Scholes (1981): "Dividends and Taxes: Some Empirical Evidence," *Journal of Political Economy,* vol. 90, pp. 1118–1141.

Modigliani, Franco, and Merton Miller (1958): "The Cost of Capital, Corporation Finance and the Theory of Investment," *American Economic Review,* vol. 48, pp. 261–297.

Modigliani, Franco, and Merton Miller (1963): "Corporate Income Taxes and the Cost of Capital: A Correction," *American Economic Review,* vol. 53, pp. 433–443.

Muth, John (1961): "Rational Expectations and the Theory of Price Movements," *Econometrica,* vol. 29, pp. 315–335.

Myers, Stewart (1977): "Determinants of Corporate Borrowing," *Journal of Financial Economics,* vol. 5, no. 2, pp. 147–175; **reprinted in this volume.**

Myers, Stewart C., and Nicholas S. Majluf (1984): "Corporate Financing and Investment Decisions When Firms Have Information that Investors Do Not Have," *Journal of Financial Economics,* vol. 13, pp. 187–221; **reprinted in this volume.**

Osborne, M. F. M. (1959): "Brownian Motion in the Stock Market," *Operations Research,* vol. 7, pp. 145–173.

Osborne, M. F. M. (1962): "Periodic Structure in the Brownian Motion of Stock Prices," *Operations Research,* vol. 10, pp. 345–379.

Ramaswamy, Krishna, and Suresh M. Sundaresan (1986): "The Valuation of Floating-Rate Instruments: Theory and Evidence," *Journal of Financial Economics,* vol. 17, pp. 251–272; **reprinted in this volume.**

Ritter, Jay R. (1984): "The 'Hot Issue' Market of 1980," *Journal of Business,* vol. 57, pp. 215–240.

Rock, Kevin (1986): "Why New Issues Are Underpriced," *Journal of Financial Economics,* vol. 15, pp. 187–212.

Roll, Richard (1977): "A Critique of the Asset Pricing Theory's Tests; Part I: On Past and Potential Testability of the Theory," *Journal of Financial Economics,* vol. 4, pp. 129–176.

Ross, Stephen (1973): "The Economic Theory of Agency: The Principal's Problem," *American Economic Review,* vol. 63, pp. 134–139.

Ross, Stephen (1976): "The Arbitrage Theory of Capital Asset Pricing," *Journal of Economic Theory,* vol. 13, pp. 341–360.

Rozeff, Michael S. (1982): "Growth, Beta and Agency Costs as Determinants of Dividend Payout Ratios," *Journal of Financial Research,* vol. 5, pp. 249–259.

Samuelson, Paul (1965): "Proof That Properly Anticipated Prices Fluctuate Randomly," *Industrial Management Review,* vol. 6, pp. 41–49.

Schallheim, James S., Ramon E. Johnson, Ronald C. Lease, and John J. McConnell (1987): "The Determinants of Yields on Financial Leasing Contracts," *Journal of Financial Economics,* vol. 19, pp. 45–67; **reprinted in this volume.**

Schipper, Katherine, and Abbie Smith (1986): "A Comparison of Equity Carve-Outs and Seasoned Equity Offerings: Share Price Effects and Corporate Restructuring," *Journal of Financial Economics,* vol. 15, pp. 153–186.

Schwert, G. William (1983): "Size and Stock Returns and Other Empirical Regularities," *Journal of Financial Economics,* vol. 12, pp. 3–12.

Sharpe, William (1964): "Capital Asset Prices: A Theory of Market Equilibrium under Conditions of Risk," *Journal of Finance,* vol. 19, pp. 425–442.

Smith, Clifford (1979): "Applications of Option Pricing Analysis," *Handbook of Financial Economics,* J. L. Bicksler, ed., North Holland, Amsterdam, pp. 80–121; **reprinted in this volume.**

Smith, Clifford (1986): "Investment Banking and the Capital Acquisition Process," *Journal of Financial Economics,* vol. 15, pp. 3–29; **reprinted in this volume.**

Smith, Clifford, and Lee Wakeman (1985): "Determinants of Corporate Leasing Policy," *Journal of Finance,* vol. 40, no. 3, pp. 895–908; **reprinted in this volume.**

Smith, Clifford, and Jerold Warner (1979): "On Financial Contracting: An Analysis of Bond Covenants," *Journal of Financial Economics,* vol. 7, pp. 117–161; **reprinted in this volume.**

Smith, Clifford, and Ross Watts (1982): "Incentive and Tax Effects of U.S. Executive Compensation Plans," *Australian Journal of Management,* vol. 7, pp. 139–157.

Spence, Michael, and Richard Zeckhauser (1971): "Insurance, Information, and Individual Action," *American Economic Review,* vol. 61, pp. 119–132.

Stulz, René M. (1988): "Managerial Control of Voting Rights: Financing Policies and the Market for Corporate Control," *Journal of Financial Economics,* vol. 20, pp. 25–54; **reprinted in this volume.**

Treynor, J. L. (1961): "Toward a Theory of Market Value of Risky Assets," unpublished manuscript.

Vermaelen, Theo (1981): "Common Stock Repurchases and Market Signalling," *Journal of Financial Economics,* vol. 9, pp. 139–183.

Vu, Joseph D. (1986): "An Empirical Investigation of Calls of Non-Convertible Bonds," *Journal of Financial Economics,* vol. 16, pp. 235–265; **reprinted in this volume.**

Wakeman, Lee M. (1981): "The Real Function of Bond Rating Agencies," *Chase Financial Quarterly,* vol. 1, pp. 18–26; **reprinted in this volume.**

Warner, Jerold (1977): "Bankruptcy Costs: Some Evidence," *Journal of Finance,* vol. 32, pp. 337–348; **reprinted in this volume.**

Watts, Ross L. (1977): "Corporate Financial Statements: A Product of the Market and Political Processes," *Australian Journal of Management,* vol. 2, pp. 53–75.

Watts, Ross L., and Jerold L. Zimmerman (1986): *Positive Accounting Theory,* Prentice-Hall, Inc., Englewood Cliffs, N.J.

Williams, John (1938): *The Theory of Investment Value,* Harvard University Press, Cambridge, Mass.

Working, Holbrook (1934): "A Random Difference Series for Use in the Analysis of Time Series," *Journal of the American Statistical Association,* vol. 29, pp. 11–24.

Wruck, Karen (1989): "Equity Ownership Concentration and Firm Value: Evidence from Private Equity Financings," *Journal of Financial Economics,* forthcoming.

TWO

FOUNDATIONS OF CORPORATE FINANCE

The Effects of a Firm's Investment and Financing Decisions on the Welfare of Its Security Holders

Eugene F. Fama*

In their classic article, Franco Modigliani and Merton H. Miller showed that in a perfect capital market, and given some other peripheral assumptions, the financing decisions of a firm are of no consequence. Substantial controversy followed, centered in large part on which of the peripheral assumptions are important to the validity of the theorem. For example, Joseph Stiglitz (1969, 1974) argues that in addition to a perfect market, the critical assumption is that bonds issued by individuals and firms are free of default risk. However, in chapter 4 of our book, Miller and I show that the theorem holds when debt is risky as long as stockholders and bondholders protect themselves from one another with what Fama and Miller (hereafter noted F-M) call "me-first rules."

This paper shows that me-first rules are also unnecessary. Propositions about the irrelevance of the financing decisions of firms can be built either on the assumption that investors and firms have equal access to the capital market or on the assumption that no firm issues securities for which there are not perfect substitutes from other firms. With either approach one can show that if the capital market is perfect, then (a) a firm's financing decisions have no effect on its market value, and (b) its financing decisions are of no consequence to its security holders.

The paper begins with a review of existing capital structure theorems, focusing on the work of Stiglitz and F-M. The discussion of old results has two purposes. The literature in this area has tended to become increasingly mathematical. One of the goals here is to show that the capital structure propositions in fact rest on simple economic arguments. Examining previous results also helps put the new results to be presented into perspective.

Finally, F-M and Stiglitz (1972) note that when firms can issue risky debt, the market value rule for the investment decisions of firms is ambiguous. With risky debt, maximizing stockholder wealth, bondholder wealth, or the combined wealth of bondholders and stockholders can imply three different investment decisions. Stiglitz argues that firms are likely to maximize stockholder wealth, even though this might be less economically efficient than maximizing combined stockholder and bondholder wealth. Miller and I leave the issue unresolved. I

*Graduate School of Business, University of Chicago. This research is supported by the National Science Foundation. I am grateful for the comments of R. Ball, M. Blume, G. Borts, H. DeAngelo, N. Gonedes, R. Hamada, M. Jensen, S. Ross, M. Scholes, G. W. Schwert, and R. Weil. If I have any clear thoughts on the subject matter of this paper, they are due in large part to discussions with Merton H. Miller.

argue here that maximizing combined stockholder and bondholder wealth is the only market value rule consistent with a stable equilibrium, and that in its capacity as price setter the market can provide incentives for firms to choose this rule.

1   ARBITRAGE PROOFS OF THE MARKET VALUE PROPOSITION

Much of the early literature is concerned with the proposition that the market value of a firm is unaffected by its financing decisions, and most of the early proofs use arbitrage arguments. The general idea is that if the financing decisions of a firm affect its market value, there are arbitrage opportunities that can be used to produce costless instantaneous increases in wealth. Since the existence of such opportunities is inconsistent with equilibrium in a perfect capital market, one can conclude that the market value of a firm is unaffected by its financing decisions. Examples of this approach are the original "risk class" model of Modigliani and Miller and the "states of the world" model of Jack Hirshleifer (1965, 1966).

In all of the arbitrage proofs of the market value proposition, there are five common assumptions:

Assumption 1: Perfect Capital Market. There are no transactions costs to investors and firms when they issue or trade securities; bankruptcy likewise involves no costs; there are no taxes; and there are no costs in keeping a firm's management to the decision rules set by its security holders. The perfect capital market assumption is maintained throughout the paper. Thus, I shall not discuss the interesting problems that arise from the differential treatment of corporate dividend and interest payments in computing corporate taxes, or the problems that arise from the differential treatment of dividends and capital gains in computing personal taxes. Nor shall I discuss any effects of bankruptcy costs or managerial agency costs on the nature of optimal investment and financing decisions by firms.

Assumption 2: Equal Access. Individuals and firms have equal access to the capital markets. This means that the types of securities that can be issued by firms can be issued by investors on personal account. For example, suppose an investor owns the same proportion of each of a firm's securities, so that he has a direct share in the firm's activities. Equal access implies that, using the firm's securities as exclusive collateral, the investor can issue the same sort of securities as the firm. If firms can issue securities that contain limited liability provisions, such provisions can also be included in securities issued by investors against their holdings in firms. Moreover, the prices of securities are determined by the characteristics of their payoff streams and not by whether they are issued by investors or firms. Equal access could logically be included as a characteristic of a perfect capital market, but it plays such an important role in capital structure propositions that it is stated separately.

Assumption 3: Complete Agreement or Homogeneous Expectations. Any information available is costlessly available to all market agents (investors and firms), and all agents correctly assess the implications of the information for the future prospects of firms and securities. For most of what we do, it would be sufficient to assume that all market agents can correctly determine when securities issued by different investors and firms are perfect substitutes, but it seems at best a short step from this to complete agreement. A perfect capital market could be taken to imply complete agreement, but it is common in the literature to state the two as separate assumptions.

Assumption 4: Only Wealth Counts. Aside from effects on security holder wealth, the financing decisions of a firm do not affect the characteristics of the portfolio opportunities available to investors. Thus the effects of a firm's financing decisions on the welfare of its security holders can be equated with effects on security holder wealth. This assumption is only precise in the context of models that say which characteristics of portfolio opportunities are of concern to investors. We need not be so specific. For our purposes it is sufficient to assume that the capital market satisfies whatever conditions are necessary to ensure the desired correspondence between wealth and welfare. Moreover, we shall see that one of the contributions of more recent treatments of capital structure propositions is to show that this assumption is unnecessary.

Assumption 5: Given Investment Strategies. To focus on the effects of a firm's financing decisions on the welfare of its security holders, all proofs of capital structure propositions take the investment strategies of firms as given. Although decisions to be made in the future are unknown, the rules that firms use to make current and future investment decisions are given. In addition, investment decisions are made independently of how the decisions are financed. In the last section of the paper, we consider the nature of optimal investment strategies for firms.

Stiglitz (1974, Theorem 2) gives the most general arbitrage proof that Assumptions 1–5 imply that the market value of a firm is unaffected by its financing decisions. Suppose there is an optimal capital structure for the firm, but the firm does not choose this capital structure. Any investor can provide the optimal capital structure to the market by buying equal proportions of the firm's securities and then issuing the optimal proportions on personal account. If the market value of the firm were less than the value implied by an optimal capital structure, by providing the optimal capital structure to the market, the investor could earn an arbitrage profit. Since every investor has an incentive to exploit such opportunities and since exploitation is costless, their existence is inconsistent with a market equilibrium. In equilibrium, the market value of a firm is always the value implied by an optimal capital structure, irrespective of the capital structure chosen by the firm. Thus, at least with respect to its effects on the firm's market value, any choice of capital structure by the firm is as good as any other.

II MARKET VALUE AND SECURITY HOLDER INDIFFERENCE

In the fourth chapter of our book, Miller and I show that the absence of a relationship between a firm's market value and its financing decisions does not in itself imply that the financing decisions are of no consequence to the firm's security holders. When the firm can issue risky debt, it may be able to use its financing decisions to shift wealth from its bondholders to its stockholders or vice versa.

To illustrate, assume a discrete time world in which the firm can issue two general types of securities, bonds and common stock. Given a perfect capital market and a market where the financing decisions of a firm do not affect the important characteristics of the portfolio opportunities available to investors, there is nothing the firm can do with its financing decisions at time t that will help or hurt investors who buy the firm's securities at time t. Thus it suffices to examine the effects of the firm's financing decisions at t on the wealths of investors who have held its securities from $t - 1$.

Let $S_{t-1}(t)$ and $B_{t-1}(t)$ be the market values at time t of the firm's common stock and bonds outstanding from $t - 1$. The combined value of these old stocks and bonds at t is the market value of the firm $V(t)$, less the value of new bonds issued at t, $b(t)$, less the market value of new common stock $s(t)$:

$$(1) \quad S_{t-1}(t) + B_{t-1}(t) = V(t) - b(t) - s(t)$$

The firm also makes dividend and interest payments at t, and we assume these are made only on securities outstanding from $t - 1$. Total dividend payments $D(t)$ and interest payments $R(t)$ are defined by

$$(2) \quad D(t) + R(t) = X(t) - I(t) + b(t) + s(t)$$

where $X(t)$ is net cash income at t (cash revenues minus cash costs), and $I(t)$ is the cash outlay for investment. Adding (1) and (2), the total wealth at time t associated with common stock and bonds outstanding from $t - 1$ is

$$(3) \quad [D(t) + S_{t-1}(t)] + [R(t) + B_{t-1}(t)] = X(t) - I(t) + V(t)$$

Since all capital structure propositions take the firm's investment strategy as given, $I(t)$ does not depend on financing decisions at t. The net cash earnings $X(t)$ are the result of past investment decisions and so are independent of financing decisions at t. Assumptions 1–5 ensure that the value of the firm $V(t)$ is unaffected by its financing decisions. Since $X(t)$, $I(t)$, and $V(t)$ are all independent of financing decisions at t, we can conclude from (3) that the combined wealth of old bondholders and stockholders at time t is independent of the firm's financing decisions at t.

However, there might be financing decisions that the firm can make at time t that change the nature of the claims represented by the bonds outstanding from $t - 1$ and so shift wealth from bondholders to stockholders or vice versa. For example, suppose the firm's old bonds are free of default risk if no new debt is issued, but the firm can issue new debt that has the effect of imposing default risk on the old bonds. The new debt thus brings about a change in the characteristics of the old debt which we would expect to lead to a lower value of $B_{t-1}(t)$. Since the combined wealth of the old bonds and stocks is independent of the financing decision, issuing the new debt has the effect of shifting wealth from the old bondholders to the old stockholders. Alternatively, suppose the old debt is already subject to default risk, and at time t the firm retires some of it but not the entire amount. In the event of bankruptcy at a future date, each of the remaining bonds recovers more than if some of the old bonds are not retired at t. When a firm announces such a financing decision at t, we would expect the value $B_{t-1}(t)$ of all the old bonds to be higher than when no retirement takes place. Thus given constant total wealth, the financing decision implies a shift of wealth from the old stockholders to the old bondholders. In short, the fact that the market value of a firm is independent of its financing decisions does not necessarily imply that the financing decisions are a matter of indifference to the firm's security holders.

Given the world of Assumptions 1–5, the indifference proposition will hold if we restrict the types of securities that can be issued by firms so as to guarantee that the characteristics of the payoffs on the firm's old bonds are unaffected by its financing decisions at t. One way to accomplish this is to assume that all debt is free of default risk, which is the approach taken by Stiglitz (1969, 1974). In chapter 4 of our book, however, Miller and I show that the desired result is obtained when investors protect themselves with me-first rules. For example, bondholders insist that any new debt issued is junior to existing debt—in the event of bankruptcy, older bonds are paid off before newer bonds. The stockholders in their turn insist that the firm does not use its financing decisions to improve the positions of any bondholders. For example, if the firm wants to retire debt before its maturity, junior issues must be retired before senior issues, and any issues retired must be retired in full. We formalize these statements with a new assumption.

Assumption 6. A firm's stockholders and bondholders protect themselves from one another with costlessly enforced me-first rules which ensure that the characteristics of the payoffs on the firm's outstanding bonds are unaffected by changes in its capital structure

In sum, Assumptions 1–5 are sufficient to conclude that the market value of a firm is unaffected by its financing decisions. Risk-free debt or the me-first rules of Assumption 6 then lead to the somewhat stronger conclusion that the financing decisions of the firm are a matter of indifference to all of its security holders.

III   THE IRRELEVANCE OF A FIRM'S DIVIDEND DECISIONS

A firm's dividend decision at any time t is part of its financing decision. The preceding analysis implies that when a firm's securities are protected by me-first rules, the firm's dividend decision at t determines how the wealth of its shareholders is split between $D(t)$ and $S_{t-1}(t)$, but the sum of the two components of shareholder wealth is unaffected by the dividend decision. In short, dividend decisions are a matter of indifference to the firm's security holders whenever financing decisions are a matter of indifference.

However, dividend decisions can be a matter of indifference even when other aspects of the firm's financing decisions are of some consequence. Consider a world where the market value of a firm $V(t)$ is unaffected by its financing decisions, but the firm has risky debt outstanding which is not protected by me-first rules. By issuing more or less new bonds $b(t)$ at time t, the firm can affect the value of its old bonds $B_{t-1}(t)$, which in turn affects the split of wealth between its old bonds and its old stock. Any such effects on the wealths of old bonds and stocks are, however, due entirely to the choice of $b(t)$. Since the firm can issue more or less new stock $s(t)$ at time t, we can see from equation (2) that the choice of $b(t)$ need not affect the decision about the dividend $D(t)$. We can see from equations (1) to (3) that given any decision about $b(t)$ and its implication for $B_{t-1}(t)$, the dividend decision again just affects the split of shareholder wealth between dividends and capital value.

Keep in mind that we are taking the investment strategy of the firm as given. For example, if a firm that has risky bonds outstanding unexpectedly increases its dividend by selling off assets, there is a shift in wealth from bondholders to stockholders. However, the shift should be attributed to the investment decision, the sale of assets, rather than to the dividend decision since the same shift of wealth takes place, but in the form of a capital gain instead of a dividend, if the firm announces that the proceeds from the sale of assets will be used to repurchase shares.

IV   DROPPING THE "ONLY WEALTH COUNTS" ASSUMPTION

Beginning with Modigliani and Miller, proofs of capital structure propositions generally include the Assumption 4 that aside from effects on security holder wealth, the financing decisions of firms do not affect the characterstics of the portfolio opportunities available to investors. Thus, the effects of financing decisions on security holder welfare can be evaluated in terms of their effects on security holder wealth. An exception to this approach is Stiglitz (1969, 1974) who shows that assumptions that lead to capital structure propositions also imply a world where the portfolio opportunities facing investors are unaffected by the financing decisions of firms. Formally:

THEOREM 1: *Suppose the capital market is perfect in the sense of Assumption 1, the equal access and complete agreement provisions, Assumptions 2 and 3, hold, the investment strategies of firms are given in the sense of Assumption 5, and debt is either free of default risk or investors insist on the me-first rules of Assumption 6. Then the characteristics of a general equilibrium, that is, the market values of firms, the positions that investors take in firms, and the costs of these positions, are unaffected by the financing decisions of firms. Thus, the financing decisions of firms are of no consequence to investors.*

The intuition of the argument of Stiglitz' theorem is that when investors and firms have equal access to the capital market, the positions in firms that can be created and traded among investors are determined by the investment strategies of firms, and the possibilities are the same for any set of financing decisions by firms. Thus, the financing decisions of firms have no effect on the set of general equilibria that can be achieved in the capital market.

Moreover, once a general equilibrium has been achieved, implying an optimal set of holdings in firms by investors, there is no reason why changes in the financing decisions of firms should move the market to a different general equilibrium. When firms perturb a general equilibrium by changing their financing decisions, their actions neither expand nor contract the types of positions in firms that can be created by investors. It follows that an optimal response to the changes in the financing decisions of firms occurs when the general equilibrium remains unchanged. Specifically, the market responds by leaving the values of firms and their previously existing bonds unchanged. Investors respond by exactly reversing the changes in the financing decisions of firms on personal account so that the positions of investors in firms are unaffected by the changes in the financing decisions of firms.

The formal proof of Theorem 1 requires that changes in the financing decisions of firms can be reversed by investors on personal account. For this, the equal access Assumption 2 is required, but it is also assumed either that bonds are free of default risk [the assumption that Stiglitz (1974) uses in his proof of Theorem 1] or that investors insist on and costlessly enforce appropriate me-first rules (the extension of Stiglitz's analysis suggested by F-M). In the presence of risky bonds and in the absence of me-first rules, the firm can use changes in its financing decisions to, in effect, expropriate the positions of bondholders to the benefit of stockholders, or vice versa. And the expropriations cannot always be neutralized by investors on personal account.

For example, suppose the firm increases the dividend paid to stockholders at time t by issuing new bonds that have the same priority as the firm's old bonds in the event of bankruptcy. Even if the shareholders use the increase in dividends to repurchase the new bonds issued by the firm, things are not as they were. The new bonds are still outstanding, so that in the event of bankruptcy each of the old bonds gets less than if no new bonds are issued. By issuing new bonds that have equal priority with the old bonds, the firm has expropriated part of the holdings of the old bondholders to the benefit of its stockholders. Other examples, some involving expropriations of stockholder positions to the benefit of bondholders, are easily constructed.

V CAPITAL STRUCTURE PROPOSITIONS WITHOUT ME-FIRST RULES

The assumptions that debt is free of default risk or security holders protect themselves with me-first rules are, however, arbitrary restrictions on the types of securities that can be issued. Some firms or investors may want to issue unprotected bonds, and, appropriately priced, other investors may be willing to hold them. It is now argued that such restrictions on investment opportunities are unnecessary, and this is the first new result of the paper.

THEOREM 2: *Suppose the capital market is perfect in the sense of Assumption 1, the equal access and complete agreement provisions, Assumptions 2 and 3, hold, and the investment strategies of firms are given in the sense of Assumption 5. Then the characteristics of a general equilibrium, that is, the market values of firms and the costs of these positions, are unaffected by the financing decisions of firms. Thus, the financing decisions of firms are of no consequence to investors.*

To establish the theorem we return to time 0, the time when the first firms are organized and before they have issued any securities. The firms choose their investment strategies and then they go into the capital market for the resources to finance these investment strategies. At this point it is clear that given a perfect capital market and given equal access to the market by individuals and firms, the financing decisions of firms have no effect on the nature of a general equilibrium. The positions in firms that investors create and hold, the prices of these positions, and thus the market values of firms are independent of the financing decisions of firms.

If unprotected securities are issued at time 0, then when time 1 comes along firms may be able to use their financing decisions to affect the positions of their security holders. When they hold the securities of a firm that are not protected by me-first rules, investors would of course prefer that the firm not engage in financing decisions at time 1 that have the effect of expropriating their positions; or, they would rather that the firm expropriate to their benefit the positions of other investors. But all of this is irrelevant, once we reconsider how it happened that at time 0 some investors put themselves into positions that could be expropriated at time 1. In an equal access market, the financing decisions of firms affect neither the variety of securities that could be traded at time 0 nor the instruments that are chosen by investors. If the positions that investors want to hold in firms are not offered by the firms, investors can buy up the securities of firms and create their desired positions in trades among themselves. Thus, the positions, protected and unprotected, that investors take in firms at time 0 are the same irrespective of the financing decisions of firms at time 0. If at time 1 some investors profit from or are hurt by unprotected positions taken at time 0, all of this happens to exactly the same extent for any set of financing decisions by firms at time 0.

Likewise, at time 1 firms cannot use their financing decisions to affect the positions in firms that investors choose to carry forward to time 2. Given an equal access market, investors can refinance any firm, buying equal proportions of all its securities, and then issuing preferred proportions on personal account. Thus the types and quantities of claims against firms that investors carry forward from time 1 to time 2 are independent of the financing decisions of firms at time 1. If expropriations take place at time 2 as a result of positions taken at time 1, the same investors are helped or hurt by these expropriations and to exactly the same extent when the unprotected securities are issued at time 1 by firms as when they are issued by investors in trades among themselves.

The arguments are general. When investors and firms have equal access to the capital market, at any point in time the positions that investors take in firms, the prices of these postions and thus the market values of firms are unaffected by the financing decisions of firms. Since the financial history of any investor—what happens to him in the market through time—is unaffected by the financing decisions of firms, the financing decisions of firms are of no consequence to investors.

In all versions of the capital structure propositions discussed so far, equal access to the capital market by investors and firms is assumed. However, the assumption is stronger when debt is neither free of default risk nor protected by me-first rules. One is likewise leaning harder on the complete aggreement assumption. Investors must be able to specify the details of potentially expropriative contracts in the same way as firms. If investors issue unprotected bonds against their holdings in firms, they subsequently expropriate (for example, issue more unprotected bonds) in the same circumstances as would the firms. This requires either that the conditions or states of the world in which expropriations will take place at any time t are stated explicitly in loan contracts or that investors make accurate assessments of the probabilities and extent of expropriations in different future states of the world. Probabilistically speaking, neither issuers nor purchasers of loan contracts are ever "fooled" by anything that happens during the life of a contract, and the price of a contract always properly reflects the possibilities for future expropriations.

I now show that the capital structure propositions can be established without the equal access assumption. The cost, however, is a new assumption which precludes a firm from issuing any securities monopolistically. In effect, we set up conditions that lead to a capital market which is perfectly competitive with respect to the financing decisions of a firm.

VI CAPITAL STRUCTURE PROPOSITIONS WITHOUT EQUAL ACCESS

In Theorem 2, as in Theorem 1, the portfolio opportunities facing investors turn out to be independent of the financing decisions of firms. However, firms can still be monopolists in their investment decisions. A firm may have access to investment opportunities that allow it to create securities with payoff streams whose characteristics cannot be replicated by other firms. Nevertheless, when there is equal access to financial markets, investors can issue the same claims against their holdings in firms that the firms themselves can issue. As a consequence, once firms have chosen their investment strategies, there is nothing further they can do through their financing decisions to affect the opportunity set facing investors.

If this result is to hold when the equal access assumption is dropped, we must restructure the world in such a way that the actions that investors (with equal access) take to free the investment opportunity set from any effects of financing decisions by firms, can be taken instead by firms. To accomplish this, firms are no longer allowed to issue securities for which there are not perfect substitutes issued by other firms. This implies that firms can no longer have monopolistic access to investment opportunities. Firms must also be given the motiviation to act in the manner that leads to the validity of the capital structure propositions. In contrast, in an equal access world, once firms choose their investment strategies, what then happens when they get themselves to the capital market is beyond their control.

The specific new assumptions are:

Assumption 7: No firm produces any security monopolistically. There are always perfect substitutes issued by other firms. Moreover, if a firm shifts its capital structure, substituting some types of securities for others, its actions can be exactly offset by other firms who carry out the reverse shift, with the result that aggregate quantities of each type of security are unchanged.

Assumption 8: The goal of a firm in its financing decisions is to maximize its total market value at whatever prices for securities it sees in the market. Since firms are shown to be perfectly competitive in the capital market, the assumption is unobjectionable.

The arguments in the proof of the theorem that follows are similar to those used by the author and Arthur Laffer in discussing sufficient conditions for perfect competition in product markets in a world of perfect certainty. Also relevant are papers by the author (1972) and Fischer Black and Myron Scholes.

THEOREM 3: *Suppose the capital market is perfect in the sense of Assumption 1, the complete agreement assumption, Assumption 3, holds, the investment strategies of firms are given in the sense of Assumption 5, and Assumptions 7 and 8 also hold. Then given a general equilibrium in the capital market at any time* t: (a) *The market value of a firm is unaffected by changes in its financing decisions;* (b) *the financing decisions of a firm are of no consequence to investors; that is, the firm's financing decisions do not affect what happens to any investor through time; and* (c) *the capital market is perfectly competitive in the sense that aggregate supplies and prices of different types of securities are unaffected by changes in the financing decisions of a firm.*

Consider first the case where debt is free of default risk or investors protect themselves from one another with the me-first rules of Assumption 6. Suppose the capital markets achieves a general equilibrium at time t and then, for whatever reason, some firm perturbs the equilibrium by changing its capital structure.

In the original equilibrium, firms, including the firm that subsequently shifts, chose securities so as to maximize their market values at the original equilibrium values of security prices. This means that at the original prices, the new securities that the shifting firm issues had exactly the same market value as the securities it no longer issues. It also means that the market can achieve a "new" general equilibrium if other firms instantly respond to the disturbance of the initial equilibrium by exactly offsetting the change in the shifting firm's capital structure, and if the prices of securities remain at their old equilibrium values. When this happens, the market value of any firm is the same as it was in the old general equilibrium, and firms have no further incentives to change their capital structures. In addition, since debt is assumed to be either free of default risk or securities are protected by me-first rules, the wealths of individual investors are the same in the new general equilibrium as in the old. Since the aggregate supplies and prices of different securities are unchanged, each investor can choose a portfolio identical to the one chosen in the initial general equilibrium; just the names of the firms issuing particular types of securities may be different. In short, with me-first rules and the perfectly competitive capital market produced by the offsetting financing decisions of other firms, investors are completely immunized from any affects of shifts in the financing decisions of any firm.

The same analysis applies in the absence of me-first rules, once we understand the restrictions implied by the perfect substitutes Assumption 7. In particular, the fact that different firms issue securities at time $t - 1$ that are perfect substitutes does not imply that these firms make the same financing decisions at time t. However, if unprotected securities issued by different firms at $t - 1$ are perfect substitutes, any expropriations that take place at time t must be the same for all of these firms. It follows that if a firm issues unprotected securities at any time $t - 1$, the expropriations that take place in any given state of the world at time t must be the same for all financing decisions that the firm might make in that state at t.

Suppose now that time t comes along, the state of the world is known, firms make their financing decisions, and a general equilibrium set of securities prices and values of firms is determined. Some firm then perturbs the general equilibrium by shifting its capital structure. Given what was said above, even though the firm may have unprotected securities in its capital structure, the shift cannot cause expropriations of security holder positions beyond those associated with the firm's original financing decisions at t. Thus, just as in the case where debt is risk free or securities are protected by me-first rules, the market can reattain a general equilibrium if other firms exactly offset the change in the shifting firm's capital structure, leaving aggregate supplies and prices of different securities unchanged. Since no new expropriations take place, the wealths of investors are also unchanged, and each investor can choose a portfolio identical to the one chosen in the initial general equilibrium.

In the initial general equilibrium that follows the occurrence of a state of the world at time t, the positions of a firm's security holders are, of course, affected by any expropriative financing decisions. But in the world of the complete agreement Assumption 3, investors properly assessed the possibilities for future expropriations when they decided to hold the firm's securities at time $t - 1$, and these possibilities were properly reflected in the prices of the securities at $t - 1$. If the firm hadn't issued these potentially expropriative securities, its security holders would have purchased perfect substitutes from other firms. Thus the financing decisions of any firm are of no consequence to any investor in the sense that what happens to any investor through time happens irrespective of the financing decisions of any particular firm.

VII   SOME PERSPECTIVE ON CAPITAL STRUCTURE PROPOSITIONS

Given a perfect capital market, and given the investment strategies of firms, there are two approaches that lead to the conclusions that the market value of a firm is unaffected by its financing decisions, and a firm's financing decisions are of no consequence to its security holders. One approach is based on the assumption that investors and firms have equal access to the capital market. The other assumes that no firm offers securities to the market for which there are not perfect substitutes from other firms. The fundamental argument in both approaches is that, given the investment strategies of firms, there are mechanisms that insulate the opportunity set facing investors from any effects of the financing decisions of firms. With the equal access assumption, the offsetting actions that produce this result can come from investors or firms, while in the perfect substitutes approach, changes in the financing decisions of a firm are offset by other firms.

The types of capital structure propositions obtained with the two approaches are somewhat different. With equal access one gets statements about the effects of the financing decisions of all firms. When investors and firms have equal access to the capital market, then given the investment strategies of firms, the positions in firms that can be traded among investors are independent of the financing decisions of firms. As a consequence, the characteristics of a general equilibrium in the capital market are unaffected by the financing decisions of firms. In contrast, with the perfect substitutes approach, only firms issue securities so one can't conclude that the characteristics of a general equilibrium are independent of the financing decisions of all firms. One is limited to partial equilibrium statements about the irrelevance of the financing decisions of any individual firm.

The analysis here goes beyond earlier treatments in several respects. First, although earlier approaches generally use both assumptions in one form or another, it is evident from the work of Stiglitz (1969, 1974) that in an equal access market, the validity of the capital structure propositions does not also require the perfect substitutes assumption. However, Stiglitz argues that it is necessary to assume debt is risk free if the financing decisions of firms are to be a matter of indifference to security holders. The analysis here shows that in an equal access market, even the me-first rules of F-M are unnecessary restrictions on the types of securities that can be issued. In essence, in an equal access market investors can and will chose the same positions, protected and unprotected, irrespective of the financing decisions of firms. Thus, the fact that firms might issue unprotected securities does not invalidate the proposition that the financing decisions of firms are a matter of indifference to investors.

In a recent paper, Frank Milne argues that with the perfect substitutes assumption, the proposition that the market value of a firm is independent of its financing decisions does not also require the equal access assumption. However, Milne's framework is less general than that examined here. First, he allows unrestricted short selling of all securities, an assumption close to equal access. To emphasize the power of the perfect substitutes assumption, in the analysis presented here securities are only issued by firms. Second, Milne assumes that the capital market is perfectly competitive, whereas we show how the actions of firms lead to a world where the total supplies and prices of securities of different types are unaffected by the financing decisions of any individual firm. Showing how the existence of perfect substitutes leads to such a strong form of perfect competition seems a substantial enrichment of the analysis. Finally, Milne works in a one-period context and investors do not come into the period already holding the securities of firms. In this world, the analytical difficulties that arise from potential expropriations of security holder positions never have to be faced. In contrast, I analyze the capital structure propositions in a multiperiod framework where firms are allowed to issue unprotected securities. It is shown that with the strong form of perfect competition in the capital market that arises from the perfect substitutes assumption, the financial history of any investor, that is, the protected and unprotected portfolio positions that he takes through time, are unaffected by the financing decisions of any individual firm.

Many have quarreled with the realism of the equal access assumption. (See, for example, the comments of David Durand on the Modigliani and Miller paper.) One can certainly also quarrel with the perfect substitutes assumption. It would seem that if for any securities issued by a firm there are perfect substitutes issued by other firms, then either there exist risk classes of firms in the sense of Modigliani and Miller (that is, there are classes of firms wherein the net cash flows of different firms are perfectly correlated) or the markets for contingent claims discussed by Hirshleifer cover all possible future states of the world. The existence of such risk classes or of complete markets for contingent claims is questionable.

In economics, however, formal propositions never provide pictures of the world that are realistic in all their details. The role of such propositions is to pinpoint the factors that can lead to certain kinds of results. In this view, the analysis of capital structure propositions suggests two factors that push the capital market toward equilibria where the market values of firms are independent of their financing decisions, and where the financing decisions of firms are of no consequence to their security holders. The first factor covers any possibilities investors have to issue claims against the securities of firms that they hold. The second is the natural incentive of firms to provide the types of securities desired by investors, and the ability of firms to provide securities that are close substitutes for those of other firms. In pure form, and in combination with a perfect capital market where contracts are costlessly written and enforced, either of these factors leads to irrelevance of capital structure propositions. In less pure form, but perhaps acting together, they are factors that help to push the market in the direction of the capital structure propositions.

VIII   THE MARKET VALUE RULE FOR INVESTMENT DECISIONS

The previous sections discuss the financing decisions of firms, given their investment strategies. I turn now to problems that arise in determining an optimal investment strategy when the capital market is perfect and when a firm can affect the portfolio opportunities facing its security holders only through the effects its investment decisions have on the wealths of its security holders. All other characteristics of portfolio opportunities are assumed to be unaffected by the investment and financing decisions of the firm.

Given that the investment decisions of a firm only affect the wealths of its security holders, the objectives of the security holders are clear. More wealth is better than less. In chapter 4 of our book, however, Miller and I point out that the "maximize securityholder wealth" rule can be ambiguous when the firm has risky debt. The firm might be able to use its investment decisions to make its previously issued bonds more or less risky and so to shift wealth from bondholders to stockholders or vice versa. One can easily construct examples where the rules "maximize stockholder wealth," "maximize bondholder wealth," and "maximize combined stockholder-bondholder wealth" all lead to different investment decisions.

A   The Pressure of Possible Takeovers

We can apply the argument of Ronald Coase to show that of the three market value rules, only the rule maximize combined stockholder-bondholder wealth is consistent with a stable capital market equilibrium. Note first that when the capital market is perfect and when the characteristics of portfolio opportunities are independent of the actions of any individual firm, there is nothing the firm can do with its investment decision at t to help or hurt investors who buy its securities at t. Thus it suffices to examine the effects of the firm's investment decision at t on investors who have held its securities from $t - 1$.

From equation (3), the combined wealth at time t of the firm's bonds and stocks outstanding from $t - 1$ is $X(t) + V(t) - I(t)$. Since net cash earnings $X(t)$ are assumed to result from past decisions, they are unaffected by the investment decision at t. Thus maximum combined stockholder-bondholder wealth implies maximizing $V(t) - I(t)$, the excess of the market value of the firm at t over the investment outlays needed to generate that market value.

Suppose the firm is controlled by its stockholders, and they choose the rule maximize stockholder wealth. It will pay for the firm's bondholders to buy out the stockholders, paying them the value their shares would have under the rule maximize stockholder wealth. If the bondholders then maximize $V(t) - I(t)$, we can see from (3) that their wealth is larger than if they had allowed the shareholders to proceed with the investment rule maximize stockholder wealth. The same arguments apply, but with the roles of the stockholders and bondholders reversed, when the firm is initially controlled by its bondholders who wish to follow the rule maximize bondholder wealth. Alternatively, if the firm announces an investment rule other than "maximize $V(t) - I(t)$," it pays for outsiders to buy up the firm's securities and then to switch to the rule maximize $V(t) - I(t)$. The outsiders can even afford to pay a premium for the firm as long as it is no greater than the difference between the maximum value of $V(t) - I(t)$ and the value of $V(t) - I(t)$ under the investment policy chosen by the firm.

B   The Pressures Applied by the Market in Its Capacity as Price Setter

Potential takeovers are not the only pressure pushing the firm toward the investment rule maximize $V(t) - I(t)$. In its role as price setter, the market has an additional way to motivate the firm to maximize the total wealth of its security holders.

Consider the firm's bondholders. When the firm issues bonds, the price of a given promised stream of payments depends on the investment strategy that the market perceives the firm to follow. If the firm in fact follows this strategy, the investment strategy is of no consequence to the bondholders. If they had the choice again, with the same uncertainties about the future, they would choose to hold the firm's bonds or perfect substitutes for them. In a capital market where the investment and financing decisions of a firm do not affect the portfolio opportunities facing investors, such perfect substitutes exist or they can be created from the securities of other firms. Since the market for shares is likewise a market of perfect substitutes, given that a firm sticks to the investment strategy that investors perceive it to follow, the choice of strategy is of no consequence to those who purchase its shares when it is an ongoing firm. In this situation, the choice of an investment strategy by the firm affects only the firm's original shareholders or organizers, those who own the rights to its investment opportunities before any securities are issued.

Let us return, then, to the point, call it time 0, when the firm is organized. The firm wishes to choose the investment strategy that maximizes the wealth of its organizers. The wealth of the organizers is $V(0) - I(0)$, the difference between the value of the firm and the investment outlays necessary at time 0 to generate that value. Thus the optimal investment decision at time 0 is to maximize $V(0) - I(0)$.

The value of the firm $V(0)$ depends also on the investment strategy the market thinks the firm will follow at time 1. Since the wealth at time 1 of securities outstanding from time 0 is $X(1) + V(1) - I(1)$, the value of the firm at time 0 is just the market value at time 0 of the distribution of $X(1) + V(1) - I(1)$. The earnings $X(1)$ observed at time 1 are a consequence of the investment decision taken at time 0. In every possible state of the world at time 1, the policy "maximize $V(1) - I(1)$" obviously produces as large a value of $V(1) - I(1)$ as any other investment strategy. It follows that if the firm's statements about investment policy are accepted by the market, the announcement at time 0 that the firm will maximize $V(1) - I(1)$ at time 1 maximizes the contribution of the investment decision at time 1 to $V(0)$ and thus to $V(0) - I(0)$.

Since the market value of the firm at time 1 is just the market value of the distribution of $X(2) + V(2) - I(2)$, $V(1)$ and thus $V(1) - I(1)$ depend in turn on the investment strategy that will be followed at time 2. Arguments analogous to those above imply that the announcement, at time 0, that the firm will maximize $V(1) - I(1)$ at time 1 implies the announcement, at time 0, that it will maximize $V(2) - I(2)$ at time 2. In short, to maximize $V(0) - I(0)$, the wealth of its organizers at time 0, the firm must convince the market that its investment strategy in each future period will likewise be maximize $V(t) - I(t)$. If the firm sticks to this strategy, this means that at any time t it chooses the investment decisions that maximize the combined wealth of bonds and stocks outstanding from $t - 1$.

Using the analysis of "agency costs" provided by Michael Jensen and William Meckling one can argue that the essence of the potential problems surrounding conflicting stockholder-bondholder interests is that once time 0 passes it will be difficult for the stockholders to resist the temptation to try to carry out an unexpected shift from the rule maximize $V(t) - I(t)$ to the rule maximize stockholder wealth. But the market has the means to motiviate firms to stay in line. To maximize $V(0) - I(0)$, the wealth of its organizers, the firm must convince the market that it will always follow the investment strategy maximize $V(t) - I(t)$. The market realizes that the firm might later try to shift to another strategy and it will take this into account in setting $V(0)$. To get the market to set $V(0)$ at the value appropriate to the strategy maximize $V(t) - I(t)$, the firm will have to find some way to guarantee that it will stay with this strategy.

The important point is that the onus of providing this guarantee falls on the firm. In pricing a firm's securities, a well-functioning market will, on average, appropriately charge the firm in advance for future departures from currently declared decision rules. The firm can only avoid these discounts in the prices of its securities to the extent that it can provide concrete assurances of its forthrightness. Thus, firms have clear-cut incentives to evolve mechanisms to assure the market that statements of policy can be taken at face value, and they have incentives to provide these assurances at lowest possible cost. In a multiperiod world, this might not be so difficult since firms continually have opportunities to behave in ways that reinforce their credibility.

Remember also that if the firm does not follow the strategy maximize $V(t) - I(t)$, it pays for outsiders to acquire the firm and then switch to this strategy. The outsiders are then in the position of the firm's organizers. That is, the firm will not be priced at the value implied by the strategy maximize $V(t) - I(t)$ unless the market is convinced that the firm will adhere to this strategy in future periods. If other forms of assurance prove difficult or costly, one possibility is to finance the firm entirely with equity, or more generally, never to issue risky debt. Then the rules maximize stockholder wealth and maximize $V(t) - I(t)$ coincide.

REFERENCES

F. Black and M. Scholes, "The Effect of Dividend Yield and Dividend Policy on Common Stock Prices and Returns," *J. Finan. Econ.*, May 1974, *1*, 1–22.

R. H. Coase, "The Problem of Social Cost," *J. Law. Econ.*, Oct. 1960, *3*, 1–44.

D. Durand, "The Cost of Capital in an Imperfect Market: A Reply to Modigliani and Miller," *Amer. Econ. Rev.*, June 1959, *49*, 639–55.

Eugene F. Fama, "Perfect Competition and Optimal Production Decisions under Uncertainty," *Bell J. Econ.*, Autumn 1972, *3*, 509–30.

_____ and A. B. Laffer, "The Number of Firms and Competition," *Amer. Econ. Rev.*, Sept. 1972, *62*, 670–74.

_____ and Merton H. Miller, *The Theory of Finance*, New York 1972.

J. Hirshleifer, "Investment Decisions under Uncertainty: Choice Theoretic Approaches," *Quart. J. Econ.*, Nov. 1965, *79*, 509–36.

_____, "Investment Decisions under Uncertainty: Applications of the State Preference Approach," *Quart. J. Econ.*, May 1966, *80*, 237–77.

M. C. Jensen and W. H. Meckling, "Theory of the Firm: Managerial Behavior, Agency Costs and Ownership Structure," *J. Finan. Econ.*, Oct. 1976, *3*, 305–60.

F. Milne, "Choice over Asset Economics: Default Risk and Corporate Leverage," *J. Finan. Econ.*, June 1975, *2*, 165–85.

F. Modigliani and M. H. Miller, "The Cost of Capital, Corporation Finance, and the Theory of Investment," *Amer. Econ. Rev.*, June 1958, *47*, 261–97.

J. C. Stiglitz, "A Re-Examination of the Modigliani-Miller Theorem" *Amer. Econ. Rev.*, Dec. 1969, *59*, 784–93.

_____, "Some Aspects of the Pure Theory of Corporate Finance: Bankruptcies and Takeovers," *Bell J. Econ.*, Autumn 1972, *3*, 458–82.

_____, "On the Irrelevance of Corporate Financial Policy," *Amer. Econ. Rev.*, Dec. 1974, *64*, 851–66.

OPTIMAL CAPITAL STRUCTURE UNDER CORPORATE AND PERSONAL TAXATION*

Harry DeANGELO

University of Washington, Seattle, WA 98195, USA

Ronald W. MASULIS

University of California, Los Angeles, CA 90024, USA

Securities and Exchange Commission, Washington, DC 20549, USA

Received September 1978, final version received December 1979

In this paper, a model of corporate leverage choice is formulated in which corporate and differential personal taxes exist and supply side adjustments by firms enter into the determination of equilibrium relative prices of debt and equity. The presence of corporate tax shield substitutes for debt such as accounting depreciation, depletion allowances, and investment tax credits is shown to imply a market equilibrium in which each firm has a unique interior optimum leverage decision (with or without leverage-related costs). The optimal leverage model yields a number of interesting predictions regarding cross-sectional and time-series properties of firms' capital structures. Extant evidence bearing on these predictions is examined.

1. Introduction

In his recent 'Debt and Taxes', Merton Miller (1977) argues that in a world of differential personal taxes, (i) the marginal personal tax disadvantage of debt combined with (ii) supply side adjustments by firms will override the corporate tax advantage of debt and drive market prices to an equilibrium implying leverage irrelevancy to any given firm. Miller's pathbreaking contribution raises the following interesting questions:

> Do (i) and (ii) continue to imply leverage irrelevancy under more realistic assumptions about the corporate tax code or in the presence of

*We would like to express our appreciation to Linda DeAngelo, Michael Jensen, David Mayers, two referees, Gailen Hite and Robert Litzenberger, and an anonymous referee, for their helpful comments on an earlier draft. The authors are responsible for any remaining errors. This paper was prepared prior to Professor Masulis' employment by the Commission. *The Securities and Exchange Commission, as a matter of policy, disclaims responsibility for any private publication or statement by any of its employees. The views expressed herein are those of the author and do not necessarily reflect the views of the Commission or of the author's colleagues upon the staff of the Commission.*

Journal of Financial Economics 8 (1980) 3-29. © North-Holland Publishing Company bankruptcy, agency, or other leverage-related costs? Alternatively, will these conditions imply a unique interior optimum leverage decision for each firm?

Can Miller's model be generalized to yield testable hypotheses regarding the determinants of firm and industry level leverage structures?

In this paper, we extend Miller's analysis to address these questions. We show that Miller's irrelevancy theorem is extremely sensitive to realistic and simple modifications in the corporate tax code. Specifically, the existence of non-debt corporate tax shields such as depreciation deductions or investment tax credits is sufficient to overturn the leverage irrelevancy theorem. In our model, these realistic tax code features imply a unique interior optimum leverage decision for each firm in market equilibrium after all supply side adjustments are taken into account. Importantly, the existence of a unique interior optimum does not require the introduction of bankruptcy, agency, or other leverage-related costs. On the other hand, with any of these leverage costs present, each firm will also have a unique interior optimum capital structure regardless of whether non-debt shields are available. Moreover, market prices will capitalize personal and corporate taxes in such a way as to make bankruptcy costs a significant consideration in a tax benefit– leverage cost tradeoff. This last point is of critical interest because it mitigates Miller's 'horse and rabbit stew' criticism of tax benefit–leverage cost models of optimal capital structure.

Our model also yields a number of testable hypotheses regarding the cross-sectional and time-series properties of firms' capital structures. Most interestingly, our model predicts that firms will select a level of debt which is negatively related to the (relatively easily measured) level of available tax shield substitutes for debt such as depreciation deductions or investment tax credits. We conclude the paper with a brief survey of existing empirical evidence which is relevant to the theories developed in earlier sections.

2. Elements of the model

We employ a two-date state-preference model in which firms make leverage decisions and individuals make portfolio decisions at $t = 0$ before the true state of nature prevailing at $t = 1$ is known. At $t = 0$, value-maximizing firms package their state-contingent $t = 1$ earnings into debt and equity vectors of state-contingent before personal tax dollars for sale to individuals. The corporate tax code treats debt charges as deductible in calculating the corporate tax bill. Firms also have deductible non-cash charges (e.g. accounting depreciation and depletion allowances) as well as tax credits. The personal tax code is heterogeneous in that applicable personal tax rates differ both across debt and equity income across investors. For a given investor, the personal tax code treats equity income more favorably than debt income. At $t=0$, utility maximizing investors select portfolios of firms' debt and equity securities which are optimal for their risk-preferences and personal tax status.

2.1. Aggregate demand for debt and equity under differential personal taxation

For simplicity, we assume the following heterogeneous personal tax code.[1] For each investor i, let τ_{PD}^i and τ_{PE}^i represent constant marginal personal tax rates on debt and equity income. The personal tax code is equity biased as the tax rate on debt income exceeds that on equity income: $\tau_{PD}^i > \tau_{PE}^i \geq 0$ for all investors. Equivalently stated, debt and equity are differentially taxed so that the state-contingent after-personal tax cash flow per unit of state s equity income exceeds that per unit of state s debt income: $(1 - \tau_{PE}^i) > (1 - \tau_{PD}^i)$ for all i.

Let $P_D(s)$ and $P_E(s)$ denote the current (time $t=0$) market prices per unit (per $t=1$ dollar) of before personal tax debt and equity income to be delivered in state s.[2] Define $(1 - \tau_{PD}^i)/P_D(s)$ and $(1 - \tau_{PE}^i)/P_E(s)$ as individual i's after-personal tax yields on state s debt and equity. Under our proportional tax code, utility maximization requires investor i to adjust his holdings of state s debt and equity claims to maximize his portfolio's after-personal tax yield. As a consequence, investor i will choose to hold state s debt over equity if $(1 - \tau_{PD}^i)/P_D(s) > (1 - \tau_{PE}^i)/P_E(s)$. Similarly, investor i will choose to hold state s equity over debt if $(1 - \tau_{PD}^i)/P_D(s) < (1 - \tau_{PE}^i)/P_E(s)$. And investor i will be indifferent to holding either state s debt or equity if after-personal tax yields are equal.

Let τ_c denote the cross-sectionally constant corporate tax rate. For simplicity, we assume that investors are differentially taxed so that at least

[1]Many other (simple and complex) personal tax codes imply demand curves as in figs. 1 and 2 and thus would also suffice for our conclusions. See DeAngelo–Masulis (1980) for a discussion of these alternative personal tax codes and associated clientele effects.

[2]In the standard (i.e., no differential personal tax) model, the single price law of markets requires $P_D(s)=P_E(s)$ for market equilibrium because all state s claims (regardless of whether they are labelled debt, equity, etc.) are perfect substitutes to all investors. In this standard case, $P_D(s) \neq P_E(s)$ is inconsistent with equilibrium because no one will be willing to hold the higher priced asset or, if unlimited shorting is possible, a pure arbitrage wealth pump will be available. However, with differential personal taxes, debt and equity are no longer perfect substitutes to all investors: the debt or equity labelling implies different tax treatment for different investors. This assumes, of course, that personal tax arbitrage schemes cannot be devised to remove the differential treatment. Thus, $P_D(s) \neq P_E(s)$ is perfectly consistent with (and will generally obtain in) market equilibrium. Our usage of the state-preference pricing rule with differential personal taxation is analytically identical to the usage in Litzenberger–Van Horne (1977) and DeAngelo–Masulis (1980).

one investor is in each of the following mutually exclusive and exhaustive personal tax brackets.[3]

Bracket B.1:

$$(1 - \tau^i_{PD}) > (1 - \tau^i_{PE})(1 - \tau_c),$$

Bracket B.2:

$$(1 - \tau^i_{PD}) = (1 - \tau^i_{PE})(1 - \tau_c),$$

Bracket B.3:

$$(1 - \tau^i_{PD}) < (1 - \tau^i_{PE})(1 - \tau_c).$$

The effect of differential personal taxes on the aggregate demand for debt is most easily understood for the special case in which all individuals in the economy are risk-neutral and believe that each state s will occur with probability $\pi(s)$. Let $\bar{P}_E$ and $\bar{P}_D$ be the current market prices of before-personal tax expected equity and debt cash flow. In this case, the markets for state-contingent equity claims must set prices to equate all before personal tax *expected* yields so that $\pi(s)/P_E(s) = 1/\bar{P}_E$ for all s.[4] Similarly, before personal tax expected yields on all debt claims must be equated so that $\pi(s)/P_D(s) = 1/\bar{P}_D$ for all s. Thus, with homogeneous beliefs and risk neutrality, we can examine individuals' debt–equity demand decisions and firms' debt–equity supply decisions by examining only two markets: one for before personal tax *expected* cash flow to equity (with current unit price $\bar{P}_E$) and one for before personal tax *expected* cash flow to debt (with current unit price $\bar{P}_D$).

Market prices $\bar{P}_D$ and $\bar{P}_E$ will establish marginal investors denoted by μ, with tax rates τ^μ_{PD} and τ^μ_{PE}, for whom after-personal tax expected yields on debt and equity are equated:

$$\frac{(1 - \tau^\mu_{PD})\pi(s)}{P_D(s)} = \frac{(1 - \tau^\mu_{PD})}{\bar{P}_D} = \frac{(1 - \tau^\mu_{PE})}{\bar{P}_E} = \frac{(1 - \tau^\mu_{PE})\pi(s)}{P_E(s)} \quad \text{for all } s.$$

By definition, these marginal investors are indifferent between taking their next dollar of income in the form of debt or equity. As noted in figs. 1 and 2,

---

[3]The easiest way to interpret this simple proportional tax code is to consider Miller's special case in which equity income is not taxed: $\tau^i_{PE} = 0$ for all i. Bracket B.1 investors have relatively low personal tax rates on debt income, B.2 investors have intermediate tax rates, and B.3 investors have relatively high tax rates — B.1: $\tau^i_{PD} < \tau_c$, B.2: $\tau^i_{PD} = \tau_c$, B.3: $\tau^i_{PD} > \tau_c$.

[4]Among all state-contingent equity securities, every risk-neutral investor whose tax bracket dictates an equity purchase will plunge in the equity claim with the highest *expected* yield. Since all claims must be held in equilibrium, they must be priced to have the same expected yield. As noted in footnote 2, $1/\bar{P}_E \neq 1/\bar{P}_D$ is perfectly consistent with equilibrium.

for prices $\bar{P}_D \geqq \bar{P}_E$, zero units of expected before personal tax debt cash flow are demanded because the after tax expected yield on equity exceeds that on debt for all investors. For these prices, no marginal investors exist. For relative prices $\bar{P}_E > \bar{P}_D > \bar{P}_E(1-\tau_c)$, positive quantities of expected debt cash flow will be demanded by investors in bracket B.1 and associated marginal tax rates satisfy $(1-\tau_{PD}^\mu) > (1-\tau_{PE}^\mu)(1-\tau_c)$. As $\bar{P}_D$ is lowered relative to $\bar{P}_E$, larger quantities of before personal tax expected debt cash flow are demanded in the aggregate and implied marginal personal tax rates change correspondingly. At prices $\bar{P}_D = \bar{P}_E(1-\tau_c)$, investors in bracket B.1 demand only debt and the marginal investors who are indifferent between expected equity and expected debt income are in bracket B.2 with tax rates $(1-\tau_{PD}^\mu)$ $=(1-\tau_{PE}^\mu)(1-\tau_c)$. And $\bar{P}_D < \bar{P}_E(1-\tau_c)$ implies that investors in brackets B.1 and B.2 demand only debt and marginal investors are in bracket B.3 with $(1-\tau_{PD}^\mu) < (1-\tau_{PE}^\mu)(1-\tau_c)$. Introduction of the aggregate debt curve in figs. 1 and 2 endogenously determines the market-clearing relative prices and the tax bracket of marginal investors.

2.2. Firm valuation under differential personal taxation

In this section, we examine firms' leverage choice problems and lay the groundwork for later sections' derivations of aggregate supply curves.

To understand how leverage affects firm value, we must first characterize the effects of leverage on before-personal tax cash flows to debt and equity.[5] For a given firm, define the following (state-contingent where noted) variables:

$X(s) \equiv$ state s earnings before interest and taxes;
  $B \equiv$ face value of debt which is assumed fully deductible in calculating the corporate tax bill (capital structure decision variable);
  $\Delta \equiv$ corporate tax deductions resulting from non-cash charges such as accounting depreciation;
  $\Gamma \equiv$ dollar value of tax credits;
  $\tau_c \equiv$ statutory marginal corporate tax rate;
  $\theta \equiv$ statutory maximum fraction of gross tax liability which can be shielded by tax credits.[6]

For notational simplicity, let earnings $X(s)$ be monotone increasing in s over the set of possible states $[0, \bar{s}]$ with $0 \leq X(0) \leq X(\bar{s}) < \infty$. Segment $[0, \bar{s}]$

---

[5]To emphasize that the interaction of corporate and personal tax code provisions alone implies a unique interior optimum leverage decision in our model, we do not consider default costs until section 5.

[6]For the investment tax credit, Congress has specified $\theta = 0.5$ (with some exceptions for public utilities, airlines, and railroads) but recently raised θ to 0.9.

into sub-intervals so that the state-contingent before personal tax, but after corporate tax cash flows to debt and equity, $D(s)$ and $E(s)$, are given by:[7]

$D(s)$	$E(s)$	State outcome
$X(s)$	0	for $s \in [0, s^1)$
B	$X(s) - B$	for $s \in [s^1, s^2]$
B	$X(s) - B - \tau_c(X(s) - \Delta - B) + \theta\tau_c(X(s) - \Delta - B)$	for $s \in [s^2, s^3]$
B	$X(s) - B - \tau_c(X(s) - \Delta - B) + \Gamma$	for $s \in [s^3, \bar{s}]$

[handwritten annotations: "No taxable income", "corp. tax shield lost"]

Here, s^1 denotes the state in which earnings just cover debt charges. For earnings realizations in the state interval $s \in [0, s^1)$, the firm is in default, all of the firm's earnings are paid to debtholders, the corporate tax bill is zero, and all corporate tax deductions in excess of earnings are unutilized as are all tax credits.

For $s \in [s^1, \bar{s}]$, no default occurs, the residual component of the firm's earnings is paid to equityholders, and the corporate tax bill can be zero or positive. The extent to which corporate taxes are paid over $[s^1, \bar{s}]$ is state-contingent and depends on earnings $X(s)$, the face value of debt B, and tax shield substitutes for debt (Δ and Γ). Accordingly, s^2 denotes the state in which the corporate tax bill is just driven to zero. It follows that, for $s \in [s^1, s^2]$, the corporate tax bill is zero because corporate tax deductions exceed earnings with a consequent loss of excess deductions and all tax credits. Similarly, s^3 denotes the state in which all deductions and credits are just fully utilized. For $s \in (s^2, s^3)$, the corporate tax bill is positive and deductions are fully utilized but credits are only partially utilized due to the statutory ceiling limiting usable credits to a fraction, θ, of the gross tax liability ($= \tau_c(X(s) - B - \Delta)$). For $s \in [s^3, \bar{s}]$, the corporate tax bill is positive and all deductions and credits are fully utilized. Most importantly for our model, notice that for $s \in [s^1, s^3)$, corporate tax shields are lost to the firm even though no default occurs.

The current market value of the firm is $V = D + E$ where D and E are the current market valuations (at prices $\{P_D(s), P_E(s)\}$) of the vectors of state-

[7]This footnote provides technical definitions of s^1, s^2, and s^3. Intuitive interpretations are provided in the text. Technically, s^1 is defined as the unique state satisfying $X(s^1) = B$, assuming $X(0) \leq B \leq X(\bar{s})$. Notice that setting promised debt charges $B > X(\bar{s}) \equiv$ maximum possible earnings is not possible. If $0 \leq B \leq X(0)$, then $s^1 = 0$. Thus, for $s \in [0, s')$, earnings fall short of promises to debt so that default occurs. Similarly, s^2 is the unique state satisfying $X(s^2) = (B + \Delta)$, assuming $X(0) \leq B + \Delta \leq X(\bar{s})$. If $0 \leq B + \Delta \leq X(0)$, then $s^2 = 0$. If $B + \Delta \geq X(\bar{s})$, then $s^2 = \bar{s}$. Thus, for $s \in [s^1, s^2]$, earnings exceed promises to debt ($X(s) \geq B$) so that no default occurs but allowed deductions exceed earnings ($X(s) \leq (B + \Delta)$) so the corporate tax bill is zero. Finally, s^3 is the unique state satisfying $\theta\tau_c(X(s^3) - (B + \Delta)) = \Gamma$, assuming $X(0) \leq B + \Delta + \Gamma/\theta\tau_c \leq X(\bar{s})$. If $0 \leq B + \Delta + \Gamma/\theta\tau_c \leq X(0)$, then $s^3 = 0$. If $B + \Delta + \Gamma/\theta\tau_c \geq X(\bar{s})$, then $s^3 = \bar{s}$. For $s \in (s^2, s^3)$, the corporate tax bill is positive since earnings exceed deductions but tax credits are partially unutilized since θ times the gross tax liability $\tau_c(X(s) - (B + \Delta)) < \Gamma \equiv$ potentially usable credits. For $s \in [s^3, \bar{s}]$, the tax bill is positive and all deductions and credits are utilized.

contingent *before*-personal tax cash flows to debt $\{D(s)\}$ and to equity $\{E(s)\}$:

$$D = \int_0^{\bar{s}} D(s)P_D(s)\,ds = \int_{s^1}^{\bar{s}} BP_D(s)\,ds + \int_0^{s^1} X(s)P_D(s)\,ds,$$

$$E = \int_0^{\bar{s}} E(s)P_E(s)\,ds = \int_{s^3}^{\bar{s}} \{X(s) - B - \tau_c(X(s) - \Delta - B) + \Gamma\}P_E(s)\,ds,$$

$$+ \int_{s^2}^{s^3} \{X(s) - B - (1-\theta)\tau_c(X(s) - \Delta - B)\}P_E(s)\,ds$$

$$+ \int_{s^1}^{s^2} \{X(s) - B\}P_E(s)\,ds.$$

The firm's optimal leverage decision maximizes the current market value of the firm $V = D + E$.[8] To see how alternative leverage decisions affect firm value, calculate the marginal value of debt financing $\partial V/\partial B$ (noting that terms involving the limits of integration vanish),

$$\partial V/\partial B = \int_{s^3}^{\bar{s}} \{P_D(s) - P_E(s)(1 - \tau_c)\}\,ds$$

$$+ \int_{s^2}^{s^3} \{P_D(s) - P_E(s)(1 - \tau_c(1-\theta))\}\,ds$$

$$+ \int_{s^1}^{s^2} \{P_D(s) - P_E(s)\}\,ds. \tag{1}$$

Inspecting (1), we see immediately that the presence of corporate tax shield substitutes for debt ($\Delta, \Gamma > 0$) implies that the leverage decision is necessarily relevant to the firm. The leverage decision is irrelevant if and only if $\partial V/\partial B = 0$ for all feasible decisions B. But with $\Delta > 0$ and/or $\Gamma > 0$, it is impossible for $\partial V/\partial B$ to vanish identically for all B so that at least some leverage decisions are strictly preferred to others.

---

[8]Schneller (forthcoming) asserts that, in a world of differential personal taxation, owners will generally disagree on optimal firm decisions and therefore value maximization is not the proper corporate goal. Contrary to Schneller's claim, the logic of the Fisher Separation Theorem [see DeAngelo (1980)] continues to apply under differential personal taxation. To see why, note first that in the competitive economy formalized above, a given firm cannot affect the economy's risk-sharing capabilities. Both debt and equity markets are complete so that investors' diversification and personal tax attribute demands are fully satisfied. Moreover, market prices $\{P_D(s), P_E(s)\}$ are perceived as independent of the decisions of a given firm. It follows that a given firm's financing and investment decisions impact on pre-exchange owners' consumption opportunities only through their effect on personal wealth. In the absence of technological externalities, the maximization of firm value simultaneously maximizes the wealth and therefore the consumption opportunities and utility of every pre-exchange owner.

To better understand the marginal value of debt expression (1), again consider the special case in which all investors are risk-neutral with homogeneous beliefs. As shown in section 2.1, risk-neutral valuation implies $P_D(s) = \bar{P}_D \pi(s)$ and $P_E(s) = \bar{P}_E \pi(s)$ for all s where $\bar{P}_D$ and $\bar{P}_E$ are the market prices of before-personal tax *expected* cash flow to debt and equity. The marginal value of debt then reduces to the easily interpreted expression

$$\partial V/\partial B = \{\bar{P}_D - \bar{P}_E(1 - \tau_c)\} \int_{s^3}^{\bar{s}} \pi(s)\,ds$$

$$+ \{\bar{P}_D - \bar{P}_E(1 - \tau_c(1 - \theta))\} \int_{s^2}^{s^3} \pi(s)\,ds$$

$$+ \{\bar{P}_D - \bar{P}_E\} \int_{s^1}^{s^2} \pi(s)\,ds. \tag{2}$$

In (2), $\partial V/\partial B$ is the present value of the expected marginal after-corporate (but before personal) tax cash flow resulting from a substitution of one more promised dollar of debt for equity. This marginal present value can be decomposed into three components which depend on the extent to which the corporate tax deduction from the marginal unit of debt is utilized. The first component, $\bar{P}_D - \bar{P}_E(1 - \tau_c)$, is the present value of the debt for equity substitution given full utilization of the corporate tax deduction associated with the marginal unit of debt. The first integral in (2) is the probability of full utilization of the marginal debt deduction. The second component, $\bar{P}_D - \bar{P}_E(1 - \tau_c(1 - \theta))$, represents a lower present value due to partial loss of the corporate tax shield caused by the statutory θ-ceiling on usable tax credits. The second integral is the probability of partial loss of the marginal corporate tax shield due to the θ-ceiling. Similarly, the third component, $\bar{P}_D - \bar{P}_E$, is the present value of the debt for equity substitution given total loss of marginal corporate tax shield because available deductions already shelter all earnings. The third integral is the probability of total loss of the corporate tax deduction on the marginal unit of debt. Eq. (2) does not include a default probability term because additional promised payments to debt have no cash flow (or corporate tax) impact in default states; over the default range, all earnings are already paid to debtholders and no further debt for equity cash flow substitution can occur.

3. Miller's leverage irrelevancy theorem

To highlight the difference between Miller's model and ours, we first characterize market equilibrium for a world analytically similar to Miller's and derive his leverage irrelevancy result. Given no corporate tax shield substitutes for debt,[9] partial or total loss of the marginal corporate tax shield benefits of debt never occur. Technically, with $\Delta = \Gamma = 0$, we have $s^1 = s^2 = s^3$ and $\partial V/\partial B$ reduces to the first term in (2),

$$\partial V/\partial B = \{\bar{P}_D - \bar{P}_E(1 - \tau_c)\} \int_{s^1}^{\bar{s}} \pi(s)\,ds. \tag{3}$$

From (3), we can derive the aggregate debt supply curve. If relative prices satisfy $\bar{P}_D < \bar{P}_E(1 - \tau_c)$, then $\partial V/\partial B < 0$ for all feasible leverage decisions and the firm selects an all equity capital structure. If $\bar{P}_D > \bar{P}_E(1 - \tau_c)$, then $\partial V/\partial B > 0$ for all B and an all debt capital structure is uniquely optimal. If $\bar{P}_D = \bar{P}_E(1 - \tau_c)$, the firm is indifferent among all feasible debt–equity packages of earnings (i.e., riskless and risky debt) so that the supply curve is perfectly elastic over the entire feasible leverage range. Since the above analysis applies to all firms, the aggregate debt supply curve (the sum of all firms' supply curves) is also perfectly elastic at relative prices $\bar{P}_D = \bar{P}_E(1 - \tau_c)$ as shown in fig. 1.

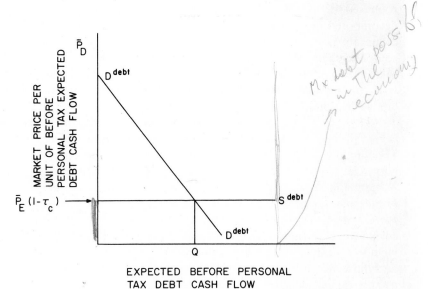

Fig. 1. Market equilibrium in a 'debt and taxes' world; D^{debt} = aggregate demand curve, S^{debt} = aggregate supply curve, Q = equilibrium aggregate quantity of debt, $\bar{P}_D = \bar{P}_E(1 - \tau_c)$ = equilibrium debt price.

_____

[9]We continue to assume that bankruptcy costs are absent. This assumption is critical for Miller's irrelevancy result (see section 5). Also, see DeAngelo–Masulis (1980) for a more complete discussion of the conditions which lead to the irrelevancy theorem.

Given the heterogeneous personal tax code of section 2.1, the downward-sloping aggregate debt demand curve must intersect the aggregate supply curve in the perfectly elastic range at relative prices $\bar{P}_D = \bar{P}_E(1 - \tau_c)$. Thus, the leverage decision is irrelevant to the individual firm facing market equilibrium prices.

On the demand side, in market equilibrium, the marginal investors must be in bracket B.2. As explained in section 2.1, marginal investors are those for whom after-personal tax expected yields on debt and equity are equated at current prices: $(1 - \tau_{PD}^\mu)/\bar{P}_D = (1 - \tau_{PE}^\mu)/\bar{P}_E$. At market equilibrium prices $\bar{P}_D = \bar{P}_E(1 - \tau_c)$, marginal investors are in bracket B.2 with tax rates satisfying $(1 - \tau_{PD}^\mu) = (1 - \tau_{PE}^\mu)(1 - \tau_c)$.

The duality between equilibrium relative market prices and equilibrium relative marginal personal tax rates yields an intuitive interpretation of market equilibrium. Formally, substitute the marginal investors' tax rate condition $\bar{P}_E = \bar{P}_D(1 - \tau_{PE}^\mu)/(1 - \tau_{PD}^\mu)$ into the marginal value of debt expression (3),[10]

$$\partial V/\partial B = \frac{\bar{P}_D}{1 - \tau_{PD}^\mu}\left[\{(1 - \tau_{PD}^\mu) - (1 - \tau_{PE}^\mu)(1 - \tau_c)\}\int_{s^1}^{\bar{s}} \pi(s)\,ds\right]. \tag{4}$$

In equilibrium, the bracketed term is zero as noted above. Intuitively, the market endogenously determines the relative marginal personal tax rates on debt and equity so that the personal tax advantage of equity exactly offsets the corporate tax advantage of debt over the entire feasible leverage range. In Miller's special case in which equity income is not taxed ($\tau_{PE}^\mu = \tau_{PE}^i = 0$ for all i), we have $\tau_c = \tau_{PD}^\mu$ which says that the marginal corporate tax advantage exactly equals the personal tax disadvantage of debt.

4. Tax shield substitutes for debt and interior optimum leverage

With positive corporate tax shield substitutes for debt ($\Delta, \Gamma > 0$), Miller's firm level leverage irrelevancy conclusion no longer holds. Instead, relative

---

[10]Miller's (1977, p. 267) gains from leverage expression can be derived from (4) quite easily. For riskless debt, the probability of default is zero ($s^1 = 0$) and the integral in (4) equals one. Also, for riskless debt, the present market value of debt $D = \bar{P}_D B$. Combining these two facts, (4) may be rewritten as Miller's expression,

$$\partial V/\partial D = [1 - ((1 - \tau_{PE}^\mu)(1 - \tau_c))/(1 - \tau_{PD}^\mu)].$$

It is worth noting that if firms are constrained to issue only riskless debt, then $\bar{P}_D = \bar{P}_E(1 - \tau_c)$ need not hold in equilibrium so that leverage can be relevant to individual firms. See DeAngelo–Masulis (1980) for an explanation of how constraints on firms' supply adjustment capabilities can overturn the leverage irrelevancy result. It is also worth noting that cross-sectional variation in corporate tax rates [as in Black (1971)] implies leverage relevancy to individual firms and corporate capital structure clienteles (firms with relatively high corporate tax rates will be highly levered, etc.).

market prices will adjust until in market equilibrium, each firm has a unique interior optimum leverage decision. This unique interior optimum exists because there is a *constant* expected marginal *personal* tax disadvantage to debt while positive tax shield substitutes imply that the expected marginal *corporate* tax benefit *declines* as leverage is added to the capital structure.[11] At the unique optimum, the expected marginal corporate tax benefit just equals the expected marginal personal tax disadvantage of debt.

We begin, as with Miller's irrelevancy theorem by deriving the aggregate supply curve for before-personal tax expected debt cash flow. With corporate tax shield substitutes for debt, each firm's debt supply curve and therefore the aggregate debt supply curve will have a brief perfectly elastic section and then be smoothly upward sloping as shown in fig. 2. The perfectly elastic

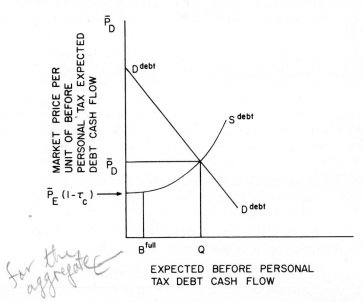

Fig. 2. Market equilibrium with tax shield substitutes for debt; D^{debt} = aggregate demand curve, S^{debt} = aggregate supply curve, Q = equilibrium aggregate quantity of debt, $\bar{P}_D > \bar{P}_E(1-\tau_c)$ is the equilibrium debt price, B^{full} = aggregate quantity of debt supplied when all firms are at the maximum debt level allowing full utilization of all corporate tax shields.

[11]Strictly speaking, the marginal personal tax disadvantage is constant, independent of B, only for risk-free debt. The unique interior optimum still obtains with risky debt, but now the intuitive explanation is that the expected marginal corporate tax benefit of debt declines more rapidly than the expected marginal personal tax disadvantage declines. See footnotes 13 and 17. Our earlier working paper established an unique interior optimum leverage without the assumption of risk neutrality, homogeneous beliefs, and conventional debt contracts.

section occurs at relative prices $\bar{P}_D = \bar{P}_E(1-\tau_c)$ and extends only over those low levels of leverage which allow all corporate tax shields (Δ, Γ, and B) to be fully utilized in every state of nature. Beyond this full utilization level, the supply curve is upward sloping because firms are willing to supply more debt to the market only if they are compensated [with higher unit debt prices $\bar{P}_D > \bar{P}_E(1-\tau_c)$] for the increased probability of partial/total loss of the corporate tax shield associated with additional debt. For any given set of relative prices on this upward sloping section of the supply curve, each firm has a unique interior optimum leverage decision. And under weak assumptions about the personal tax code, the aggregate demand curve intersects the aggregate supply curve in the upward sloping section at relative prices $\bar{P}_E > \bar{P}_D > \bar{P}_E(1-\tau_c)$ which dictates the unique interior optimum for each firm.

To derive the supply curve formally, notice first that $\Delta, \Gamma > 0$ imply $s^3 > s^2 > s^1 \geq 0$ so that the marginal value of debt is once again given by the general expression (2). If relative prices satisfy $\bar{P}_D < \bar{P}_E(1-\tau_c)$, then as in Miller's world, $\partial V/\partial B < 0$ everywhere and no firm will supply any debt. At relative prices $\bar{P}_D = \bar{P}_E(1-\tau_c)$, there is a brief perfectly elastic section of the supply curve which extends only to the point where the selected debt level just results in full utilization of all corporate tax shields (Δ, Γ, and the selected B) in every state of nature. Full utilization of the tax credit Γ in every state requires that leverage B be set low enough that θ times the resulting gross tax liability is always greater than or equal to Γ,

$$\theta\tau_c(X(s)-\Delta-B) \geq \theta\tau_c(X(0)-\Delta-B) \geq \Gamma \quad \text{for all} \quad s.$$

Since $X(0)$ is the lowest possible earnings, the maximum promised debt level or maximum leverage, B^{full}, which is consistent with full utilization of all corporate tax shields in every state is[12]

$$B^{\text{full}} \equiv X(0) - \Delta - \Gamma/\theta\tau_c < X(0).$$

Technically, for leverage B in the range $0 \leq B \leq B^{\text{full}}$, $s^1 = s^2 = s^3 = 0$, because default risk is zero and all corporate tax shields (Δ, Γ, and B) are fully utilized in every state of nature. Over this range (2) reduces to

$$\partial V/\partial B = \bar{P}_D - \bar{P}_E(1-\tau_c) \quad \text{for} \quad 0 \leq B \leq B^{\text{full}} < X(0).$$

[12]We assume $X(0) - \Delta - \Gamma/\theta\tau_c > 0$ for at least some firms. If the reverse inequality holds, firms cannot issue any debt without risking loss of corporate tax shield. In this case the aggregate debt supply curve would be upward sloping everywhere [there would not be a perfectly elastic section at $\bar{P}_D = \bar{P}_E(1-\tau_c)$].

Thus, when relative prices satisfy $\bar{P}_D = \bar{P}_E(1-\tau_c)$, the firm is indifferent among all leverage decisions which allow full utilization of all corporate tax sheild and its supply curve is perfectly elastic over the debt range $0 \leq B \leq B^{full}$. Correspondingly, at $\bar{P}_D = \bar{P}_E(1-\tau_c)$, the aggregate supply curve is perfectly elastic until the quantity at which all firms have reached their full utilization debt levels.

For higher debt levels B in the range $B^{full} < B \leq X(0)$, debt is still riskless but some corporate tax shield is lost in low earnings states. Over this leverage range, $s^1 = 0$ but $s^3 > s^2 \geq 0$ so that, at relative prices $\bar{P}_D = \bar{P}_E(1-\tau_c)$, the first term in (2) vanishes and the sum of the second and third terms is strictly negative. In other words, $\partial V/\partial B < 0$ and no debt will be supplied beyond B^{full} at relative prices $\bar{P}_D = \bar{P}_E(1-\tau_c)$.

Therefore, to induce a supply of debt greater than B^{full}, a higher unit price $\bar{P}_D > \bar{P}_E(1-\tau_c)$ must be paid. This higher debt price is required to compensate for the loss of corporate tax shield which will occur on marginal units of debt in states of the world $[s^1, s^3]$. For any given set of prices $\bar{P}_E > \bar{P}_D > \bar{P}_E(1-\tau_c)$, each firm has a unique interior optimum leverage decision B^* which solves the first-order condition $\partial V/\partial B = 0$.[13] As $\bar{P}_D$ is raised above $\bar{P}_E(1-\tau_c)$ over the range $\bar{P}_E > \bar{P}_D > \bar{P}_E(1-\tau_c)$, each firm's optimum capital structure involves more and more debt so that the aggregate supply curve is indeed smoothly upward sloping over this price range.[14]

Under reasonable conditions, market equilibrium will occur along the upward sloping portion of the debt supply curve. The perfectly elastic section of the supply curve is relatively short because, at $\bar{P}_D = \bar{P}_E(1-\tau_c)$, firms are willing to supply only the 'safest' of riskless debt: they will issue debt only up

[13]With $\bar{P}_E > \bar{P}_D > \bar{P}_E(1-\tau_c)$, it is straightforward to show that the right-hand derivative $(\partial V/\partial B)[B=0] > 0$ and the left-hand derivative $(\partial V/\partial B)[B=X(\bar{s})] < 0$ so that interior leverage decisions strictly dominate corner solutions. A unique interior optimum exists if V is convex in B, $(\partial^2 V/\partial B^2 < 0)$. Differentiating (2) yields

$$\partial^2 V/\partial B^2 = -\theta\tau_c\bar{P}_E(\partial s^3/\partial B)\pi(s^3) - (1-\theta)\tau_c\bar{P}_E(\partial s^2/\partial B)\pi(s^2) - (\bar{P}_D - \bar{P}_E)(\partial s^1/\partial B)\pi(s^1),$$

where s^1, s^2, and s^3 are defined in footnote 7. The first two terms are strictly negative. For riskless debt, $\partial s^1/\partial B = 0$ so that the third term vanishes and $\partial^2 V/\partial B^2 < 0$ necessarily follows. For risky debt, $\partial s^1/\partial B > 0$ so that the third term is positive. In this case, we assume the first two terms dominate the third [which they will, e.g., if $\pi(s^3) = \pi(s^2) = \pi(s^1)$ and $\partial s^1/\partial B = \partial s^2/\partial B = \partial s^3/\partial B$].

Our argument for a unique interior optimum does not require that firms earnings be risky. Under certainty (one state at $t=1$ with earnings X), the firm's unique interior optimum leverage sets $B = X - \Delta - \Gamma/\theta\tau_c$ so that all corporate credits and deductions are fully utilized when $\bar{P}_D - \bar{P}_E(1-\tau_c) > 0$ and $\bar{P}_D - \bar{P}_E(1-\tau_c(1-\theta)) < 0$.

[14]Footnote 13 established the unique interior leverage optimum B^* which solves $(\partial V/\partial B)[B^*] = 0$ at a given set of relative prices $\bar{P}_E > \bar{P}_D > \bar{P}_E(1-\tau_c)$. We wish to show that as $\bar{P}_D$ is raised (relative to fixed $\bar{P}_E$) over this range, larger quantities of debt will be supplied. Define $ECFD \equiv$ expected before-personal tax debt cash flow supplied as debt. Technically, the supply curve is upward sloping if

$$\partial(ECFD)/\partial\bar{P}_D = (\partial(ECFD)/\partial B)(\partial B^*/\partial\bar{P}_D) > 0.$$

to the point where there is not only zero probability of default but also zero probability of losing any corporate tax shield. More precisely, firms are willing to issue debt only over the relatively brief range $0 \leq B \leq B^{\text{full}}$. This requires not only riskless debt but also the stronger condition that earnings never fall so low as to cause any part of available corporate tax shields to be lost in any state of nature.

Recalling the aggregate demand discussion of section 2.1, we know that investors in bracket B.1 will demand positive quantities of corporate debt at relative prices $\bar{P}_{\text{D}} = \bar{P}_{\text{E}}(1 - \tau_c)$. The greater the number of investors (and the amount of current wealth) in B.1, the larger the quantity of debt demanded at these prices. We assume that investors in B.1 are sufficiently important in the market to demand a larger aggregate quantity of debt than B^{full} at $\bar{P}_{\text{D}} = \bar{P}_{\text{E}}(1 - \tau_c)$.[15] In this case, aggregate quantity supplied will fall short of demand and relative prices must adjust to provide $\bar{P}_{\text{D}} > \bar{P}_{\text{E}}(1 - \tau_c)$ to equilibrate supply and demand. In market equilibrium, these relative prices imply that each firm will have a unique interior optimum leverage decision and marginal investors will be in bracket B.1 with tax rates satisfying $(1 - \tau_{\text{PD}}^{\mu}) > (1 - \tau_{\text{PE}}^{\mu})(1 - \tau_c)$.

We can provide an intuitive interpretation of the trade-off which determines the firm's unique interior optimum leverage decision by invoking the duality relationship between relative market prices and relative marginal personal tax rates. Since the analytical expressions are complicated in the general case, we will examine Miller's special case in which equity income is not taxed ($\tau_{\text{PE}}^{\mu} = \tau_{\text{PE}}^{i} = 0$ for all i). In this case, equilibrium prices $\bar{P}_{\text{D}} > \bar{P}_{\text{E}}(1 - \tau_c)$ imply $\tau_{\text{PD}}^{\mu} < \tau_c$ for the marginal investors. Also for simplicity of interpretation, we assume that the firm's interior optimum leverage B^* occurs at a level implying risk-free debt ($B^{\text{full}} < B^* \leq X(0)$ so that $s^1 = 0$).

But this follows immediately because

$$\partial(ECFD)/\partial B = \int_{s^1}^{\bar{s}} \pi(s)\,ds > 0,$$

$$\partial B^*/\partial \bar{P}_{\text{D}} = (\partial^2 V/\partial \bar{P}_{\text{D}} \partial B)/(-\partial^2 V/\partial B^2) = \left(\int_{s^1}^{\bar{s}} \pi(s)\,ds\right)\bigg/\left(-\partial^2 V/\partial B^2\right) > 0.$$

Here, $\partial B^*/\partial \bar{P}_{\text{D}}$ is derived by setting (2) equal to zero and totally differentiating while allowing variation in B^* and $\bar{P}_{\text{D}}$.

[15]If investors in B.1 are relatively unimportant in the market, then in the aggregate, quantity supplied = quantity demanded over the perfectly elastic range of the supply curve. Each firm will be indifferent to leverage satisfying $0 \leq B \leq B^{\text{full}}$ and these capital structures will strictly dominate leverage satisfying $B > B^{\text{full}}$. This is an intuitively unappealing picture of equilibrium as it implies (i) no firm ever defaults on debt and (ii) no firm ever loses any corporate tax shield. [Equilibrium at $\bar{P}_{\text{D}} > \bar{P}_{\text{E}}(1 - \tau_c)$ does not require (i) and (ii).] It seems reasonable that B.1 investors will be important in the market. For example, in Miller's special case in which equity income is not taxed, B.1 investors have $\tau_{\text{PD}}^{i} < \tau_c$. In the U.S., $\tau_c = 0.48$ and a large number of investors have marginal tax rates on ordinary income < 0.48.

Substituting the simplified marginal personal tax rate condition $\bar{P}_E = \bar{P}_D / (1 - \tau_{PD}^\mu)$ into (2) and gathering terms yields the leverage optimality condition

$$\frac{\partial V}{\partial B}[B^*] = \frac{\bar{P}_D}{(1 - \tau_{PD}^\mu)}\left[\tau_c\left\{\int_{s^3}^{\bar{s}}\pi(s)\,ds + (1 - \theta)\int_{s^2}^{s^3}\pi(s)\,ds\right\} - \tau_{PD}^\mu\right] = 0,$$

(5)

At B^*, the term in square brackets equals zero which says that the expected marginal corporate tax benefit is equated to the expected marginal personal tax disadvantage of debt at the optimum. The second term in square brackets, $-\tau_{PD}^\mu$, is the expected marginal *personal* tax disadvantage of debt since, for riskless debt, increasing B by one unit increases the personal tax liability by τ_{PD}^μ in every state of nature. The first term in brackets is the expected marginal *corporate* tax saving from debt which reflects the fact that the corporate shield on the marginal unit of risk-free debt is fully lost in states $[0, s^2)$, partially lost in states $[s^2, s^3)$, and fully realized in states $[s^3, \bar{s}]$.

Examining (5) more closely, we see that the presence of corporate tax shield substitutes for debt affects the extent to which the corporate tax shield from the marginal unit of debt is lost to the firm. This loss of corporate tax shield results from properties of the tax code which rule out negative taxes or subsidies and thereby set a ceiling on the total use of tax shields (Δ, Γ, and B) which are potentially available to the firm.[16] These ceilings ensure that the expected marginal *corporate* tax saving from additional debt declines as debt is added to the capital structure.[17] But for each additional dollar of debt substituted for equity the same higher marginal *personal* tax on debt, rather than on equity income, must be paid. Thus, for relatively low levels of leverage (less than B^*), the marginal value of debt is positive because there is a relatively high probability that

---

[16]The loss of corporate tax shield which is relevant for our model is not triggered by default and, in fact, has nothing to do with risk per se: our arguments go through even under certainty as noted in footnote 13. Brennan–Schwartz (1978) and Kim (1978) consider the default-related loss of corporate tax shield in the context of corporate tax–bankruptcy cost models (without differential personal taxes). See Miller (1977), Chen–Kim (1979), and DeAngelo–Masulis (1980) for a discussion of this phenomenon with differential personal taxes. DeAngelo–Masulis demonstrate that the default-related loss of corporate tax shield has no effect on Miller's irrelevancy theorem. (Also, see section 3 of this paper in which Miller's theorem was shown to hold even though corporate debt tax shelter is lost in default.)

[17]Notice that the expected marginal corporate tax benefit from debt is strictly less than the statutory corporate tax rate τ_c. To see that the expected marginal corporate tax benefit declines with higher leverage, differentiate the first term within the brackets in expression (5) with respect to B and note that

$$\tau_c\{-\theta\pi(s^3)(\partial s^3/\partial B) - (1 - \theta)\pi(s^2)(\partial s^2/\partial B)\} < 0.$$

Notice that this equation is a positive scalar multiple of the second-order condition presented in footnote 13 because, for risk-free debt, $\partial s^1/\partial B = 0$.

additional debt can be fully utilized to reduce the firm's tax liabilities and this corporate tax reduction outweighs the higher personal taxes paid on additional debt. For relatively high levels of leverage (greater than B^*), the marginal value of debt is negative because the tax shield substitutes imply a relatively high probability that the potential corporate shield from additional debt will be partially or totally lost, while an additional personal tax liability for holding debt is incurred. At the unique interior optimum B^*, the expected marginal corporate tax saving just balances the marginal personal tax disadvantage of additional debt.

By using a one-period model, we have implicitly assumed away tax loss carrybacks and carryforwards (CB–CF) which could be introduced in a multi-period formulation. From our one-period model, we can infer the likely effects CB–CF provisions would have on our predictions. CB–CF provisions should reduce the impact of tax shield substitutes on the leverage decision. More specifically, CB provisions reduce the probability that a corporate tax shield will be lost by allowing current tax losses to be applied immediately against several previous years' unsheltered taxable income. Current tax losses can be large relative to previously unsheltered income so that CB provisions will not always result in full utilization of the current period's potential corporate tax shield.[18] Similarly, CF provisions reduce the probability that corporate tax shield will be lost by allowing excess shields to be applied against future taxable income for several years. However, this just shifts the problem forward since future leverage decisions will be affected by the existence of now greater future tax shield substitutes for debt. Furthermore, the CF deferral inherently involves a time-value loss of corporate tax shield. In sum, CB–CF provisions would reduce, but not eliminate, the expected value of the corporate tax shield loss on the marginal unit of debt.

Thus, with CB–CF provisions, we expect that the expected marginal corporate tax savings of debt will still decline as leverage is added to the capital structure (but not as rapidly as in our one-period formulation). As a result, the debt supply curve will still be upward sloping beyond the debt level allowing full utilization of tax shield. The supply curve will be more elastic than in our formulation (but not infinitely elastic) since firms will require smaller price compensation to increase their debt supply because CB–CF provisions reduce the expected loss of corporate tax shield. Given a sufficiently large number of investors in bracket B.1, equilibrium should still obtain in the upward sloping region of the debt supply curve and each firm will have a unique interior optimum leverage decision (but with quantitatively higher leverage than our one-period formulation predicts). Most importantly, we expect that a multi-period formulation encompassing

[18]Moreover, utilizing tax loss carrybacks implies a previous loss of corporate tax shield because taxes were already paid in earlier periods. Although a rebate is obtained in the current period, it does not include interest the government earned on the earlier tax payment.

CB–CF provisions would leave our qualitative predictions unchanged (see section 6).[19]

5. Bankruptcy costs and horse-and-rabbit stew

In section 4, each firm's unique interior optimum leverage decision resulted solely from the interactions of the personal and corporate tax treatment of income. Default-related costs were completely absent in that discussion.[20] With positive default costs (and with or without tax shield substitutes for debt), each firm will still have a unique interior optimum leverage decision in market equilibrium. Moreover, Miller's (1977, pp. 262–264) horse-and-rabbit stew criticism of traditional corporate tax-default cost models is not applicable in this case.[21] Miller faults the traditional models for requiring unrealistically large expected marginal bankruptcy costs to offset the expected marginal corporate tax savings of debt at observed debt–equity ratios. In our model, regardless of whether default costs are large or small, the market's relative prices of debt and equity will adjust so that the net (corporate and marginal personal) tax advantage of debt is of the same order of magnitude as expected marginal default costs. The relative prices must equilibrate in this way to induce firms to supply the proper quantities of debt and equity to satisfy the demands of investors.

More concretely, assume that all tax shield substitutes are absent ($\Delta = \Gamma = 0$) and let $C[B, X(s)]$ denote state-contingent default costs where $C[B, X(s)] \equiv 0$ for no-default states $s \in [s^1, \bar{s}]$ and $C[B, X(s)] > 0$, $\partial C/\partial B > 0$ for $s \in [0, s^1)$. Then the marginal value of debt is easily shown to be

$$\partial V/\partial B = \{\bar{P}_D - \bar{P}_E(1 - \tau_c)\} \int_{s^1}^{\bar{s}} \pi(s)\,ds - \bar{P}_D \int_0^{s^1} \frac{\partial C}{\partial B} \pi(s)\,ds$$

$$= \frac{\bar{P}_D}{(1 - \tau_{PD}^\mu)} \{(1 - \tau_{PD}^\mu) - (1 - \tau_{PE}^\mu)(1 - \tau_c)\} \int_{s^1}^{\bar{s}} \pi(s)\,ds$$

$$\quad - \bar{P}_D \int_0^{s^1} \frac{\partial C}{\partial B} \pi(s)\,ds.$$

[19]We could also modify our model to introduce markets for transferring corporate tax shields. Markets for leasing and acquisitions provide two obvious avenues for transferring non-debt tax shields from one firm to another. Since firms have incentives to avoid excess corporate tax shields, they will be motivated to alter their level of leverage and/or their level of non-debt tax shields. Assuming that markets do not allow costless transfer of tax losses, we would still expect a negative relationship between debt and non-debt tax shield (holding earnings constant).

[20]More generally, agency costs or other leverage-related costs were also ignored [see Jensen–Meckling (1976), Galai–Masulis (1976), and Myers (1977)]. Formally introducing these costs into our framework would have the same effect as introducing default costs: in equilibrium, each firm would have an interior optimum leverage decision and the endogenously determined net tax benefit of debt would be of the same order of magnitude as marginal agency or leverage-related costs.

[21]Some indication that Miller was moving toward this conclusion can be found in 'Debt and Taxes' on p. 271.

In market equilibrium, relative prices will again satisfy $\bar{P}_E > \bar{P}_D > \bar{P}_E(1-\tau_c)$. In this case, the higher debt price $\bar{P}_D > \bar{P}_E(1-\tau_c)$ is required in market equilibrium as compensation for the expected marginal costs of default. Equivalently stated, in market equilibrium there will be a net corporate — marginal personal tax advantage to debt financing $\{(1-\tau_{PD}^\mu) > 1(1-\tau_{PE}^\mu)(1-\tau_c)\}$ which will compensate firms for the expected marginal default costs and thereby induce them to supply risk debt. In market equilibrium, each firm will have a unique interior optimum leverage decision which equates the present value of the expected marginal net tax advantage of debt to the present value of expected marginal default costs.

Thus, even if expected marginal default costs are small relative to the *corporate* tax advantage of debt [such as the 5% average ex-post cost found by Warner (1977) for court costs and lawyers' fees associated with the bankruptcy proceedings of eleven railroads] they can still be significant relative to the net corporate–marginal personal tax advantage of debt: $\{(1-\tau_{PD}^\mu)-(1-\tau_{PE}^\mu)(1-\tau_c)\} > 0$. Moreover, the market-determined marginal personal tax rates will adjust to increases in the supply of debt so as to decrease the expected net tax advantage of debt to firms. In equilibrium, expected default costs equal the expected net tax advantage of debt. In other words, expected marginal default costs are of significant magnitude in our model because the expected net (corporate and marginal personal) tax benefit of debt is *endogenously determined* by the interaction of supply and demand to be of the same order of magnitude as marginal expected default costs.[22]

6. Testable hypotheses

We have demonstrated that each firm has a unique interior optimum capital structure in market equilibrium in a world characterized by (i) the equity-biased personal tax code of section 2.1 and (ii) corporate tax shield substitutes for debt and/or positive default costs.

From this expanded model, we can derive the following cross-sectional and time-series predictions:[23]

---

[22]When both bankruptcy costs and corporate tax shield losses induced by tax shield substitutes are present, we cannot say that bankruptcy costs alone are significant measured relative to net tax savings. We can only say that bankruptcy costs and tax losses taken together are significant.

[23]H.1 and H.2 were derived earlier in the text. Here we sketch the derivation of H.3 (similar calculations lead to H.4 and H.5). Let B^* denote the firm's unique interior optimum leverage decision for which $\partial V/\partial B = 0$. Totally differentiating this first-order condition, letting α denote a dummy parameter (Δ, Γ, τ_c, marginal default-costs), and rearranging terms yields $\partial B^*/\partial \alpha = (\partial^2 V/\partial B\partial\alpha)/(-\partial^2 V/\partial B^2)$. Assuming the second-order condition $\partial^2 V/\partial B^2 < 0$ is satisfied, it follows that $\text{sign}(\partial B^*/\partial\alpha) = \text{sign}(\partial^2 V/\partial\alpha\partial B)$. To derive H.3, note that differentiating the general

H.1: The leverage decision is relevant to the individual firm in the sense that a pure change in debt (holding investment constant) will have a valuation impact.

H.2: In equilibrium, relative market prices will imply a net (corporate and personal) tax advantage to corporate debt financing — i.e., the implied marginal personal tax rates will satisfy $(1-\tau^{\mu}_{PD})>(1-\tau^{\mu}_{PE})(1-\tau_{c})$ or, equivalently, $\tau^{\mu}_{PD}<\tau_{c}+\tau^{\mu}_{PE}(1-\tau_{c})$.

H.3: *Ceteris paribus*, decreases in allowable investment related tax shields (e.g., depreciation deductions or investment tax credits) due to changes in the corporate tax code or due to changes in inflation which reduce the real value of tax shields will increase the amount of debt that firms employ. In cross-sectional analysis, firms with lower investment related tax shields (holding before-tax earnings constant) will employ greater debt in their capital structures.

H.4: *Ceteris paribus*, decreases in firms' marginal bankruptcy costs will increase the use of debt financing. Cross-sectionally, firms subject to greater marginal bankruptcy costs will employ less debt.

H.5: *Ceteris paribus*, as the corporate tax rate is raised, firms will substitute debt for equity financing. Cross-sectionally, firms subject to lower corporate tax rates will employ less debt in their capital structures (holding earnings constant).

Hypotheses H.1 and H.2 are statements about the capital market pricing implications of our tax shield substitutes model. Both are in direct conflict with the predictions of Miller's 'Debt and Taxes' model. Obviously, H.1 predicts that a leverage change will affect the market value of the firm while Miller's model predicts the absence of any valuation impact. H.2 predicts

---

(i.e., not necessarily risk-neutral) valuation expression (1) yields

$$V_{B\Delta}= -\theta\tau_{c}P_{E}(s^{3})(\partial s^{3}/\partial\Delta)-\tau_{c}(1-\theta)P_{E}(s^{2})(\partial s^{2}/\partial\Delta)<0 \quad \text{implies} \quad \partial B^{*}/\partial\Delta<0,$$

$$V_{B\Gamma}= -\theta\tau_{c}P_{E}(s^{3})(\partial s^{3}/\partial\Gamma)<0 \qquad\qquad\qquad\quad \text{implies} \quad \partial B^{*}/\partial\Gamma<0.$$

Notice that H.3 was derived from our general valuation expression (1) while assuming that a unique interior optimum leverage exists. Notice also that we hold investment fixed while allowing debt to vary in response to a parameter shift. While this assumption is consistent with previous analyses of the capital structure decision [e.g., see Scott (1976)], one should nevertheless recognize that potential interactions of investment and financing decisions can technically overturn H.3–H.5 when investment is not held fixed. However, H.3–H.5 can be derived technically when allowing investment to change if we impose sign and/or magnitude assumptions on interaction effects. We have also assumed that market prices are fixed which means that our time series (but not our cross-sectional) predictions must be viewed as partial equilibrium results. Finally, notice that our formulation assumes away progressivity in the corporate tax code. Taking this progressivity into account should, *ceteris paribus*, make leverage more attractive to larger firms.

that relative market prices for debt and equity will imply a net (corporate and personal) tax advantage to debt — i.e., the after-personal tax cash flow to marginal debtholders from investing one more dollar as debt, $(1 - \tau_{PD}^\mu)$, exceeds the after-personal tax cash flow sacrificed by marginal equity holders' $(1 - \tau_{PE}^\mu)(1 - \tau_c)$, due to the debt-for-equity substitution. In contrast, Miller's model predicts that the endogenously determined net tax effect is zero — i.e., $(1 - \tau_{PD}^\mu) = (1 - \tau_{PE}^\mu)(1 - \tau_c)$.

The intuition supporting H.3 is quite appealing. Debt is desirable to firms because it provides a tax shield for corporate income. Depreciation deductions, investment tax credits, and many other features of the corporate tax code provide firms with substitutes for the corporate tax shield attributes of debt. H.3 quite reasonably predicts that the use of leverage will be negatively related to the magnitude of available investment related corporate tax shield substitutes for debt. To our knowledge, H.3 has not been previously derived. However, H.4 and H.5 have been derived by Scott (1976) in a corporate tax–bankruptcy cost model.

7. Empirical evidence

This section reviews existing evidence regarding the empirical relevance of investment tax shields and hypotheses H.1–H.5. While this evidence provides preliminary support of our model, we recognize that a more careful empirical analysis is clearly in order.

In our model, we assumed that investment-related tax shields are economically significant relative to debt tax shields. Two pieces of evidence support this assumption. First, direct measurement by the I.R.S. suggests that both shields are of the same order of magnitude, although debt deductions are larger ($64.3 billion to $49.5 billion for U.S. corporations in 1975). Second, over the period 1964–1973, 27% of all U.S. corporations filing tax returns in a given year paid no taxes at all.[24] Given the relatively low bankruptcy rate for this period,[25] the evidence suggests that investment-

---

[24]The 27% figure was derived from *Statistics of Income* by calculating the ratio of the number of corporations filing income tax returns with net 'taxable' income to the total number of corporations filing returns. The yearly ratio was very stable: it never deviated more than 2% from the ten-year average of 27%. However, over time there is likely to be significant positive serial correlation of firms paying or not paying taxes.

These estimates may not be representative of large firms. However, Vanik (1978) offers some estimates of taxes paid in recent years for some 168 of the largest corporations in the U.S. In 1975 approximately 20% of these firms paid no federal income tax while in 1976 this fell to 10% of these firms. This evidence suggests that even the largest firms experience excess tax shields. The total corporate tax liabilities avoided by investment tax shields is estimated by Muskie (1976).

[25]The average annual failure (bankruptcy) rate of commercial and industrial firms for the period 1965–1974 is 43 per 10,000 concerns based on annual figures of Dun and Bradstreet (1977). Of these failures, approximately 2.5% had liabilities of $1 million or greater.

related tax shields were important in reducing corporate tax bills to zero (and perhaps resulted in excess tax shields) — i.e., not all the low tax bills were a result of financial distress.

7.1. Evidence on the leverage irrelevancy theorem

The fundamental hypothesis of our expanded model, H.1, predicts that firm market value is a function of its capital structure. Early evidence in support of H.1 can be found in Miller–Modigliani's (1966) study of 63 electric utility firms in which they found a significant positive relationship between market values of the firm and the debt tax shield (shown in their table 4). While supportive of H.1, this evidence may justifiably be criticized because of limitations in the statistical methodology as well as the inherent difficulties involved in controlling for cross-sectional differences in firms' underlying asset values and biases associated with studying a regulated industry.

In a more recent study which avoided these difficulties, Masulis (1980) developed a model to estimate the average effect across firms of a change in the debt tax shield on the market value of a given firm. To do this he studied 117 intrafirm exchange offers and recapitalizations which approximated pure capital structure changes, most of which involved a change in the firm's debt tax shield. The basic approach was to utilize the ex post capital structure change to explain the magnitude of the common stock rate of return on the announcement date of the exchange offer. Modelling the hypothesis that a change in the firm's debt tax shield causes a change in the same direction in firm value, Masulis obtained an estimated *average* change in firm value between 10% to 20% of the change in debt market value. Masulis obtained similar estimates under the assumption that only positive changes in debt affected firm value. Together, the Miller–Modigliani and Masulis studies represent direct evidence of the empirical importance of the leverage decision to firm value.

7.2. Industry cross-sectional predictions

Hypotheses H.3 and H.4 predict that differential investment tax shields and/or differential marginal costs of leverage should induce differential optimal leverage ratios for firms. While little empirical evidence of differential leverage-related costs is available, there is considerable evidence of significant variations in investment tax shields across industries as documented in Vanik (1978), Muskie (1976), Siegfried (1974), and Rosenberg (1969). Given these differences across industries, our model predicts that (1) firm leverage (debt–asset ratio) should also differ across industries with differing non-debt tax shields relative to EBIT (earnings before interest and taxes) while exhibiting much greater homogeneity within these individual industry classifications, and (2) as the ratio of non-debt tax shield to EBIT rises, leverage should fall.

Taking a sample of firms from selected industry groups Scott–Martin (1975) and Scott (1972) studied the leverage ratios of twelve major industries and Schwartz–Aronson (1967) studied the leverage ratios of four major industrial groups. They found statistically significant differences in firms' leverage ratios (defined as shareholder equity divided by firm book value) across industries while within industries firm leverage ratios were relatively homogeneous and stable over time. These results were based on a one-way analysis of variance, and are consistent with the predictions of our model. Unfortunately, these studies analyzed only a small number of industries (the industries analyzed in the first two studies being almost identical), which severely limits our ability to deduce evidence supporting or refuting prediction (2) of this section.

One piece of casual evidence in support of H.3 is that Drugs, Mining and Oil Industries had the lowest leverage ratio in the Scott–Martin study and these industries all benefit from special tax code features which increase their investment-related tax shields considerably, e.g., expensing of R&D costs, mineral and oil depletion allowances.

7.3. Aggregate time-series predictions due to changes in the corporate tax code and rate of inflation

Our model predicts changes over time in firms' capital structures due to changes in the cost of leverage (bankruptcy and reorganization or other agency cost of debt) (H.4), changes in the corporate tax rate (H.5), or changes in the firm's investment tax shield (H.3). Over the last fifty years, there have been a number of significant changes in the federal income tax code including major increases in the corporate tax rate as well as increases in the size of corporate investment tax deductions and credits [see Fromm (1971) and Oakland (1972)]. There have also been changes in the personal tax code. Given these non-simultaneous changes in tax rates and investment tax shields, we would expect to see significant *aggregate* changes in firms' leverage decisions over time.

Since a large number of corporate tax deductions are based on historical costs, such as depreciation, depletion allowances, and cost of goods sold, *ceteris paribus*, increases in inflation which increase nominal revenues, will decrease the real value of investment tax shields inducing firms to replace this tax shield loss by increasing their use of debt.[26] Given the significant

---

[26]However, there could be additional effects due to inflation-induced changes in the relative marginal personal tax rates on debt and equity. See Aaron (1976).

increases in the rate of inflation over the period 1965–1974, our model predicts related increases in the level of firm leverage.[27]

The empirical evidence of aggregate firm leverage behavior uncovered in Corcoran (1977) and Zwick (1977) clearly shows that in the period 1948–1975 the behavior of firm leverage has been far from stable. Corcoran observes that the average debt to firm value ratio in market value terms for non-financial corporations 'rose from 22% in 1965 to 42% in 1974, a movement which paralleled the acceleration in the domestic inflation rate'. A similar pattern was found by Zwick using a different measure of leverage (face value of debt to firm book value). The inflation impact was compounded by a corporate tax surcharge over the period 1968–mid 1970, the termination of the investment tax credit between April 1969 and the end of 1970, and a reduction in depletion allowances as of 1969. Together these two studies support the predictions of H.3 and H.5.

In a more comprehensive study, Holland–Myers (1977) measured the year by year aggregate debt and equity market values for all non-financial corporations in the U.S. for the years 1929–1975. The resulting ratios of market values of debt to firm assets was, as expected, highly variable with significant increases in leverage (1) in the 1940–1942 period when corporate taxes were substantially increased and (2) again in the 1967–1975 period of high inflation (early in this period corporate tax rates were also increased). This evidence is consistent with hypotheses H.3 and H.5.[28]

7.4. Equilibrium marginal tax rates

Hypothesis H.2 of our expanded model predicts the market determined marginal tax rate relationship

$$\tau_{PD}^{\mu} < \tau_c + \tau_{PE}^{\mu}(1 - \tau_c).$$

[27]See Nichols (1968), Bradford (1974), and Lintner (1975) for a theoretical discussion. Hong (1977) presents evidence that inflation adversely and differentially affects firms' profitability by causing depreciation and cost of inventory withdrawal expenses to be understated. This evidence is corroborated by the studies of Fama–Schwert (1977), Jaffe–Mandelker (1976), Bodie (1976), and Nelson (1976) which also find a significant negative relationship between common stock rates of return and the rate of inflation.

[28]One piece of apparently non-supportive evidence is Miller's (1963) study for the Commission on Money and Credit. Miller measured the ratio of face value of long-term debt to book value of assets for five-year intervals over the period 1926–1956 for both all non-financial corporations and all manufacturing corporations. He found that this ratio was highly stable for all non-financial corporations but increased significantly for manufacturing corporations. However, by ignoring short-term debt, he admitted that he had downward biased the change in the leverage ratio over the sample period. Moreover, since corporations are likely to make initial adjustments in leverage by altering their short-term debt, Miller's methodology is likely to be dampening the instability in the time series of his measured leverage ratios.

If we assume as Miller does that $\tau_{PE}^{\mu}=0$, then the above condition simplifies to $\tau_{c}>\tau_{PD}^{\mu}$. Notice that $\tau_{PE}^{\mu}=0$ implies that corporate stocks and non-taxable municipal bonds are perfect substitutes in terms of after-personal tax cash flow, so that in equilibrium the before-personal tax yields must be equal (ignoring differences in risk). Given this relationship, one can estimate the marginal personal tax rate on debt by comparing the ratio of the municipal bond yield to the corporate bond yield for bonds of equivalent maturity and risk,[29] since the before-personal tax yield on municipals must be sufficiently below that of the corporate bonds so that there is a marginal investor who is indifferent to holding the two assets. Hence

$$1/P_{M}=(1/P_{D})(1-\tau_{PD}^{\mu})$$

or

$$\tau_{PD}^{\mu}=1-(1/P_{M})/(1/P_{D})$$

where $1/P_{M}=$ yield on non-taxable municipal bonds and $1/P_{D}=$ yield on taxable corporate bonds.[30]

Following this approach, Sharpe (1978) compared the yields on municipal bonds with yields on long-term Aa public utility bonds. For the years 1950–1975 the average ratio of yields was approximately 0.70 which implies a 30% marginal personal tax rate on debt. Given a corporate tax rate of 48%, this finding supports our expanded model's predicted relationship between the equilibrium marginal tax rates and is inconsistent with Miller's prediction.

Moreover, Sharpe's evidence is also inconsistent with the leverage irrelevancy theorem when equity is taxed at the personal level. In this case equilibrium requires $P_{D}=P_{E}(1-\tau_{c})$ and $P_{E}\leqq P_{M}$ because municipal bonds offer a personal tax advantage over equity. Equivalently, equilibrium requires $(1-\tau_{c})\geqq(1/P_{M})/(1/P_{D})$ which is inconsistent with Sharpe's empirical estimates.

8. Summary

In this paper, we generalized Miller's differential personal tax model to include an often overlooked but major feature of the U.S. tax code: the existence of corporate tax shield substitutes for debt such as accounting

---

[29]This is assuming bonds are selling at par so there are no capital gains or losses realized. The methodology is given in Sharpe (1978, pp. 142–143).

[30]The yield on a bond in a one-period model is usually defined as $r_{D}=(1/P_{D})-1$. Here we are interpreting $1/P_{D}$ as the yield which is strictly appropriate in the case of a consol bond (or perpetuity) in a multi-period context. This is consistent with Sharpe's estimation of bond yields from multiperiod cash flows of long term bonds. This is justified because we have formulated our one-period model to approximate the results of a multi-period model where the capital structure decision is permanent.

depreciation deductions and investment tax credits. Introduction of these realistic corporate tax code features leads to a market equilibrium in which each firm has a unique interior optimum leverage decision due solely to the interaction of personal and corporate tax treatment of debt and equity. Our model also allows for positive default costs. In particular, the presence of tax shield substitutes for debt and/or default costs implies a unique interior optimum leverage decision in market equilibrium. Moreover, Miller's horse-and-rabbit stew criticism of corporate tax saving–default cost models is inapplicable to our model because the net corporate–marginal personal tax saving is endogenously determined to be of the same order of magnitude as expected marginal default costs. Our model yields a number of testable hypotheses regarding both the cross-sectional and time-series properties of firms' leverage decisions as well as the marginal personal tax rates implicit in relative market prices. We argued that existing evidence provides indirect support for these hypotheses. However, we believe that a more thorough empirical analysis is clearly in order.

References

Aaron, H., 1976, Inflation and the income tax, American Economic Review 66, 193–199.

Baxter, N., 1967, Leverage, risk of ruin and the cost of capital, Journal of Finance 22, 395–403.

Black, F., 1971, Taxes and capital market equilibrium, Working paper no. 21A, mimeo. (Associates in Finance, Belmont, MA).

Black, F. and M. Scholes, 1974, The effects of dividend yield and dividend policy on common stock prices and returns, Journal of Financial Economics 1, 1–22.

Bodie, Z., 1976, Common stocks as a hedge against inflation, Journal of Finance 31, 459–470.

Bradford, W., 1974, Inflation and the value of the firm: Monetary and depreciation effects, Southern Economic Journal 41, 414–427.

Brennan, M. and E. Schwartz, 1978, Corporate income taxes, valuation, and the problem of optimal capital structure, Journal of Business 51, 103–114.

Chen, A. and H. Kim, 1979, Theories of corporate debt policy: A synthesis, Journal of Finance 34, 371–384.

Corcoran, P., 1977, Inflation, taxes, and corporate investment incentives, Federal Reserve Bank of New York Quarterly Review 2, 1–9.

DeAngelo, H., 1979, Competition and unanimity. Working paper (University of Washington, Seattle, WA).

DeAngelo, H. and R. Masulis, 1980, Leverage and dividend irrelevancy under corporate and personal taxation, Journal of Finance, forthcoming.

Dun & Bradstreet, 1977, The business failure record 1976 (New York).

Fama, E. and M. Miller, 1972, The theory of finance (Holt, Rinehart and Winston, New York).

Fama, E. and G.W. Schwert, 1977, Asset returns and inflation, Journal of Financial Economics, 115–146.

Fromm, G., 1971, Tax incentives and capital spending, Studies of Government Finance (The Brookings Institution, Washington, DC).

Galai, D. and R. Masulis, 1976, The option pricing model and the risk factor of stock, Journal of Financial Economics 3, 115–146.

Holland, D. and S. Myers, 1977, Trends in corporate profitability and capital cost, Working paper (MIT, Cambridge, MA).

Hong, H., 1977, Inflation and the market value of the firm: Theory and tests, Journal of Finance 32, 1031–1048.

Jaffe, J. and G. Mandelkar, 1976, The 'Fisher effect' for risky assets: An empirical investigation Journal of Finance 31, 447–458.

Jensen, M. and W. Meckling, 1976, Theory of the firm: Managerial behavior agency costs and ownership structure, Journal of Financial Economics 3, 305–360.

Kim, H., 1978, A mean-variance theory of optimal capital structure and corporate debt capacity, Journal of Finance 33, 45–64.

Kim, H., W. Lewellen and J. McConnell, 1978, Financial leverage clienteles: Theory and evidence, Journal of Financial Economics 7, 83–109.

Kraus, A. and R. Litzenberger, 1973, A state preference model of optimal financial leverage, Journal of Finance 28, 911–921.

Lintner, J., 1975, Inflation and security return, Presidential address, Journal of Finance 30, 259–280.

Masulis, R., 1978, The effects of capital structure change on security prices, Unpublished Ph.D. dissertation (University of Chicago, Chicago, IL).

Miller, M., 1963, The corporation income tax and corporate financial policies, in: Stabilization policies, Commission on Money and Credit (Prentice-Hall, Englewood Cliffs, NJ).

Miller, M., 1977, Debt and taxes, Journal of Finance 32, 261–275.

Miller, M. and F. Modigliani, 1961, Dividend policy, growth and the valuation of shares, Journal of Business 34, 411–433.

Miller, M. and F. Modigliani, 1966, Some estimates of the cost of capital to the electric utility industry, 1954–57, American Economic Review 56, 333–391.

Modigliani, F. and M. Miller, 1958, The cost of capital, corporation finance and the theory of investment, American Economic Review 48, 261–297.

Modigliani, F. and M. Miller, 1963, Corporation income taxes and the cost of capital: A correction, American Economic Review 53, 433–443.

Muskie, E., 1976, Tax expenditures: Compendium of background material on industrial provisions, Committee on the Budget, U.S. Senate 94th Congress, 2nd session.

Myers, S., 1977, Determinants of corporate borrowing, Journal of Financial Economics 4, 147–176.

Nelson, C., 1976, Inflation and rates of return on common stocks, Journal of Finance 31, 471–483.

Nichols, D., 1968, A note on inflation and common stock values, Journal of Finance 23, 655–657.

Oakland, W., 1973, Corporate earnings and tax shifting in U.S. manufacturing, 1930–1968, Review of Economics and Statistics 54, 235–244.

Robichek, A. and S. Myers, 1966, Problems in the theory of optimal capital structure, Journal of Financial and Quantitative Analysis 1, 1–35.

Rosenberg, L., 1969, Taxation of income from capital by industry group, in: Harberger and Bailey, eds., Taxation of income from capital (Brookings Institution, Washington, DC).

Schneller, M., 1980, Taxes and the optimal capital structure of the firm, Journal of Finance 35, 119–127.

Schwartz, E. and J. Aronson, 1967, Some surrogate evidence in support of the concept of optimal financial structure, Journal of Finance 22, 10–19.

Scott, D., 1973, Evidence on the importance of financial structure, Financial Management, 45–50.

Scott, D. and D. Martin, 1975, Industry influence on financial structure, Financial Management, Spring, 67–73.

Scott, J., 1976, A theory of optimal capital structure, Bell Journal of Economics and Management Science 7, 33–54.

Sharpe, W., 1978, Investments (Prentice-Hall, Englewood Cliffs, NJ).

Siegfried, J., 1974, Effective average U.S. corporation income tax rates, National Tax Journal 27, 245–259.

U.S. Treasury, Internal Revenue Department, Statistics of income, 1964–1973 (U.S. Government Printing Office, Washington, DC).

Vanik, Hon. Charles, 1978, Annual corporate tax study, Tax year 1976, Congressional Record, 95th Congress, 2nd Session, E168-E176.

Warner, J., 1977, Bankruptcy costs: Some evidence, Journal of Finance 32, 337–347.

Zwick, B., 1977, The market for corporate bonds, Federal Reserve Bank of New York Quarterly Review 2, 27–36.

BANKRUPTCY COSTS: SOME EVIDENCE

Jerold B. Warner*

Introduction and Summary

Assumptions about the magnitude of bankruptcy costs will have a considerable bearing on the issue of how much debt it is optimal for the firm to have in its capital structure. For example, in the original Modigliani-Miller model (1958), which abstracted from both corporate taxes and the possibility of bankruptcy, no debt/equity ratio could be regarded as optimal. Given perfect markets and rational investor behavior, they showed that the value of the firm would be invariant to its capital structure. Stiglitz (1969) has shown that the invariance result holds even when there is a positive probability of bankruptcy, but only as long as there are no transactions costs associated with bankruptcy.[1]

Relaxing the assumption that bankruptcy is costless and introducing a corporate tax in which interest payments can be deducted from net income reopens the possibility of optimal debt/equity ratios. Kraus and Litzenberger (1973) have developed a formal model dealing with this case, and on a more general level a central theme in textbook discussion of capital structure policy has become the presumed trade-off between tax savings and bankruptcy costs.[2]

This paper considers some issues surrounding the role of bankruptcy costs in models of capital structure. Evidence on the direct costs of corporate bankruptcy is presented for a number of railroad firms which were in bankruptcy proceedings under Section 77 of the Bankruptcy Act between 1933 and 1955. Elsewhere,[3] I have examined the risk and return characteristics of defaulted debt claims of firms in the railroad industry; the railroad firms whose bankruptcy costs are discussed here are a subsample of the firms whose bond returns were the subject of those studies.

The ratio of direct bankruptcy costs to the market value of the firm appears to fall as the value of the firm increases. As measured here, the cost of bankruptcy is on average about one percent of the market value of the firm prior to bankruptcy. That result seems in striking contrast to the figure of 20 percent reported in a study

* University of Rochester. The author wishes to thank M. Gruber, R. Hamada, F. Jen, M. Jensen, E. H. Kim, E. Kitch, M. Scholes, J. Siegel, C. Smith, B. Stone, H. Stoll, and J. Williams for their comments on previous drafts. I am indebted to N. Gonedes and especially M. Miller for their encouragement and for their criticisms of previous versions of the paper.

1. The work of Arrow (1964), Debreu (1959), and especially Hirshleifer (1965) makes it possible to establish the 'irrelevance' proposition within the context of a 'states of the world' model. For a recent treatment, see Fama and Miller (1972) and Milne (1975).

2. See, for example, Van Horne, (1974), p. 267.

3. Warner (1976, 1977).

by Baxter (1967), although it should be kept in mind that Baxter's data referred to personal bankruptcies and to dollar amounts of individuals' assets which are much smaller than those of the railroad sample. While studies by Stanley and Girth (1971) and Van Horne (1976) also report figures similar to Baxter's, they too deal with entities of much smaller dollar size than the railroad firms. Given the evidence on a "scale" effect, it is important to realize that the findings presented here are by no means inconsistent with previous studies.

In interpreting the results, it must be emphasized that not all bankruptcy costs are measurable, direct costs. Some of the omitted indirect costs may be substantial. Furthermore, it is by no means clear that these findings can be generalized to other industries. The most that can safely be concluded at this point is that the direct costs of bankruptcy, such as legal fees, appear to be lower for large firms than the conventional wisdom suggests.

The Costs of Bankruptcy

The costs of bankruptcy discussed in the literature are of two kinds, direct and indirect. Direct costs include lawyers' and accountants' fees, other professional fees, and the value of the managerial time spent in administering the bankruptcy. Indirect costs include lost sales, lost profits, and possibly the inability of the firm to obtain credit or to issue securities except under especially onerous terms.

It is important to distinguish between these two classes of costs. For direct costs of bankruptcy to arise, it is sufficient that there be transactions costs associated with negotiating disputes between claimholders.[4] But whether indirect costs arise depends upon the market setting. Suppose, for example, that the real operating characteristics of Ford and General Motors are identical, and that the cars they produce are perfect substitutes. If Ford is bankrupt but General Motors is not, the two firms will still face the same production/investment possibilities. If it is optimal (i.e. value maximizing) for General Motors to manufacture a particular product, it will also be optimal for Ford to do so, even if the latter is bankrupt. If it is optimal for General Motors to stay in the industry, it will also be optimal for Ford to do so. Bankruptcy would seem to be irrelevant under these conditions, and the bankrupt and nonbankrupt firm might each operate in the same way, engaging in identical activities to maximize the wealth of their claimholders.

Circumstances can easily be imagined, however, under which the bankrupt firm cannot be treated as if it were "equivalent" but not bankrupt. Baxter (1967) and Jensen and Meckling (1976) point out, for example, that a firm's sales and profits

---

4. If there are costs associated with drawing up all-inclusive contracts, an optimal financing decision may involve issuing debt contracts which are actually ambiguous with respect to the rights of claimholders. Although additional costs are incurred conditional upon bankruptcy, it may be less costly to hire economic agents to negotiate claims in the bankruptcy than to hire them to design contracts to avoid bankruptcy in the first place.

Gould (1973) discusses the conditions under which it will be optimal for the parties to a dispute to settle out of court. If there is agreement on the probable outcome of the bankruptcy proceeding and if side payments are permitted, then there would be no incentive for individual claimholders or the firm to take a dispute to court. When we do observe such cases in the courts, they are likely to be the result of disagreements as to the likely outcome. The cost of such disagreements is presumably taken into account when the firm makes it financing decision.

may decline, and its market value fall, when potential buyers of the product perceive default to be likely. This might be the case because potential users of the product possess imperfect information and use their perception of the firm's financial condition to evaluate its operating characteristics. If so, the fact of bankruptcy is relevant in the sense that it conveys information about the longevity of the firm, and its ability to provide replacement parts or render other types of ongoing support services for the product it sells.

Of perhaps more direct relevance are the indirect bankruptcy costs arising from the bankruptcy process itself. The bankruptcy trustee, as an agent of the court, has the authority to operate the firm. It is not clear that this agency relationship gives the trustee any incentive to run the firm efficiently and make decisions which are in fact value-maximizing. Unlike management, the trustee is responsible to the court and not directly to the firm's claimholders. He might not necessarily act in the claimholder's interests. To the extent that a trustee makes non-optimal decisions which would not have been made in his absence, the firm incurs an opportunity loss which can properly be regarded as a cost of bankruptcy.

EVIDENCE ON DIRECT BANKRUPTCY COSTS FOR RAILROADS

Because the indirect costs of bankruptcy are mainly "lost opportunities," they are inevitably difficult, if not impossible to measure.[5] For the direct costs, however, some quantitative information is available, and the major concern in the remainder of this paper is an examination and evaluation of this evidence.

One salient feature of the bankruptcy process is the extensive use of economic agents by each group of claimholders. Claimholders hire such agents in an effort to maximize the value of their respective claims when the court makes it decision on the terms of the reorganization. The agents include lawyers, accountants, various professional consultants, and "expert" witnesses. The bankruptcy trustee and his counsel are compensated by the firm, hence by the claimholders.

The direct costs of a bankruptcy proceeding includes compensation which must be paid to the various parties just mentioned. By law, each party who performs services related to the bankruptcy must apply to and receive approval of the court before he can be paid. In a typical case, application will be made by the trustee, his counsel, and the counsel for each class of claimholder. Cases with as many as 100 or 200 separate parties applying for fees are not unknown. Fees applied for and awarded are a matter of public record.

It would be exceedingly difficult to document these fees on a case-by-case basis by examining District Court records which are scattered throughout the country. Nor are the data on these costs generally collected in a manner which permits examination of the fees for a large number of companies. However, the Interstate

---

5. Another possible indirect cost of bankruptcy is the higher compensation that the managers of a highly-levered firm will receive because of the higher probability of unemployment they may face. Evidence from the railroad industry does not support the "higher turnover" argument. The study by Warner (1976) reports that in the five-year period following initiation of bankruptcy proceedings, the chief executive officers of the bankrupt firms he examined were replaced with a frequency of 8 percent per year. This compared to a figure of 9 percent per year for the non-bankrupt railroads of his control sample for a similar time period.

Commerce Commission has in the past collected bankruptcy cost data for a limited number of railroad firms.

The data analyzed in this paper are the bankruptcy costs which the ICC reported for 11 bankrupt railroads. The cost data include payments to all parties for legal fees, professional services, trustees' fees, and filing fees. They do not include payments to the managers or employees to reflect the value of the time which they spent in administering the bankruptcy.[6]

Table 1 indicates the firms in the 11 railroad sample, the number of years each was in bankruptcy, and the bankruptcy costs for each firm as reported by the ICC. On average, the bankruptcies took about 13 years to settle. The most lengthy case, that of the Missouri Pacific Railroad, was in the courts from 1933 to 1955. The average direct cost of the bankruptcies was $1.88 million.

TABLE 1

FIRMS IN THE SAMPLE

Name	Number of Years in bankruptcy	Bankruptcy cost, millions of dollars
Chicago and Northwestern	11	2.14
Chicago, Indianapolis, and Louisville	14	0.82
Chicago, Milwaukee, St. Paul and Pacific	11	2.89
Chicago, Rock Island and Pacific	16	2.00
Denver and Rio Grande Western	13	1.37
Erie Railroad	4	2.22
Minneapolis, St. Paul & Slt. Ste Marie	7	0.95
Missouri Pacific	23	2.54
New York, New Haven and Hartford	13	2.15
St. Louis San Francisco Railway	15	2.34
Western Pacific Railroad	10	1.24
High	23	2.89
Low	4	0.82
Mean	12.5	1.88
Median	13	2.00

One problem in measuring bankruptcy costs is to relate these costs to the size of the firm. It is not appropriate simply to look at the bankruptcy cost as a fraction of the market value of the firm at the time of bankruptcy. What should be measured is the fraction of the market value of the firm which potential bankruptcy costs represented at the time the firm originally made its financing decision.[7] This provides the relevant measure of the costs which the firm perceived at the time it

6. Note that Baxter also examined data on the legal costs, but the data in his study were for personal bankruptcy cases. He found that the legal fees in large personal bankruptcy cases totalled about 20 percent of the individuals' assets. While he had no data on corporate bankruptcy costs, Baxter concluded that "for corporate cases the...costs may average a somewhat smaller percentage...but are far from insignificant."

7. Strictly speaking, the future costs should be discounted to reflect their present value. For purposes of this analysis, the discount rate is implicitly assumed to be zero. For a discussion of the problems in dealing with expected bankruptcy costs, see Warner (1974).

decided on the tradeoff to make between bankruptcy costs and the tax advantage to debt. Given that firms may not be able to costlessly or instantaneously adjust their capital structures (due to regulatory constraints, floatation costs, and the like), it is necessary to look at the market value of the firm prior to bankruptcy, and before bankruptcy has become highly likely. Since it is not clear when this happens, it is appropriate to look at the market value of the firm at a number of points before bankruptcy. As long as bankruptcy is likely to be associated with a fall in the total value of the firm, failure to use such a procedure would result in measures of bankruptcy costs which are consistently biased upward when related to firm size.

Define month "0" as the month in which the firm filed a bankruptcy petition. The total market value of each debt and equity issue of each firm has been calculated as of the last day of that month and for several other selected months in the 84 months preceding the bankruptcy filing. Table 2 shows the number of securities whose market values were calculated for each firm. All of the traded securities of each of the railroads were used.

TABLE 2

SECURITIES USED IN COMPUTING MARKET VALUES OF FIRMS IN THE SAMPLE

Name	Total number of issues	Debentures	Common & Preferred
Chicago and Northwestern	14	12	2
Chicago, Indianapolis & Louisville	9	7	2
Chicago, Milwaukee, St. Paul and Pacific	15	13	2
Chicago, Rock Island and Pacific	12	9	3
Denver and Rio Grande Western	5	4	1
Erie Railroad	10	7	3
Minneapolis, St. Paul and Slt. Ste Marie	8	6	2
Missouri Pacific	15	13	2
New York, New Haven and Hartford	12	10	2
St. Louis San Francisco Railway	11	9	2
Western Pacific	4	2	2
High	15	13	
Low	4	2	
Mean	10.5	8.4	
Median	11	9	

Data on the outstanding amounts of each security were compiled from Moody's *Transportation Manual*. The source for price quotations was the *Bank and Quotation Record*. Transaction or bid prices were used in the calculations. As shown in Table 2, the calculations were made for an average of 8 securities per railroad.

Table 3 uses the computed market values of the firms' debt and equity issues and shows the debt/equity ratio for each firm for various months prior to and including the month of bankruptcy. The debt/equity ratio for, say, month "−12" is the ratio of the total market value of the firms' traded debt to the total value of its traded equity on the last trading day of the 12th month before the month in which a bankruptcy petition was filed. The data indicated that the mean debt/equity ratio for firms in the sample rises sharply, starting at 3.8 in month "−84" and eventually increasing to 24.3 in the month of bankruptcy. This is consistent with

TABLE 3

DEBT/EQUITY RATIOS OF FIRMS IN THE SAMPLE

Name	Month				
	0	−12	−36	−60	−84
Chicago and Northwestern	33.9	8.7	21.2	1.9	1.3
Chicago, Indianapolis, and Louisville	16.9	20.8	2.4	2.0	1.9
Chicago, Milwaukee, St. Paul & Pacific	14.4	27.7	15.0	3.0	2.6
Chicago, Rock Island and Pacific	23.9	20.9	1.7	1.4	2.0
Denver and Rio Grande Western	50.3	29.9	43.8	14.9	9.6
Erie Railroad	4.4	3.9	5.2	5.1	1.9
Minneapolis, St. Paul and Slt. Ste Marie	51.0	31.5	50.8	47.8	15.3
Missouri Pacific	33.9	11.7	1.3	1.5	1.6
New York, New Haven and Hartford	3.7	3.5	2.4	0.7	0.9
St. Louis San Francisco Railway	31.7	38.8	3.3	4.7	3.9
Western Pacific	3.7	2.8	3.6	3.6	1.0
High	50.3	38.8	50.8	47.8	15.3
Low	3.7	2.8	1.3	0.7	0.9
Mean	24.3	18.2	13.7	7.8	3.8
Median	23.9	20.8	3.6	3.0	2.0

TABLE 4

MARKET VALUES OF FIRMS, MILLIONS OF DOLLARS

Name	Month					% change in value over observation period
	0	−12	−36	−60	−84	
Chicago and Northwestern	80.4	155.4	88.6	377.2	370.6	−78.3
Chicago, Indianapolis and Louisville	12.5	8.7	43.5	50.9	49.7	−74.8
Chicago, Milwaukee, St. Paul & Pacific	75.2	140.5	78.5	357.7	737.5	−89.8
Chicago, Rock Island and Pacific	114.7	103.0	450.0	464.0	350.7	−67.3
Denver and Rio Grande Western	15.4	24.7	26.9	86.0	93.7	−83.6
Erie Railroad	57.2	205.9	171.4	90.3	216.3	−73.5
Minneapolis, St. Paul & SSM.	10.4	32.5	25.9	29.3	91.2	−88.6
Missouri Pacific	76.9	148.1	392.3	293.4	197.6	−61.0
New York, New Haven and Hartford	54.3	97.1	140.8	202.0	309.6	−82.5
St. Louis San Francisco Railway	39.2	23.9	277.4	378.5	264.2	−85.2
Western Pacific	14.	19.1	21.0	54.4	83.2	−83.2
High	114.7	205.9	450.0	378.5	737.5	−89.8
Low	10.4	8.7	21.0	29.3	49.7	−61.0
Mean	50.0	87.1	156.0	216.7	251.3	−78.9

expectations for firms declaring bankruptcy, namely a greater percentage fall in the market value of the firms' equity than of their debt.

Table 4 shows the total market value of each firm, assumed to be represented by the total market value of its traded securities. 84 months prior to bankruptcy, the average firm in the sample has a market value of $250 million. In the month of bankruptcy, the average firm has a market value of about $50 million. The value of every firm declines over the observation period. The mean percentage change in the market value of the firm between month "−84" and "0" is −78.9.

Table 5 displays the ICC reported bankruptcy costs as a percentage of the total market value of the firm. Using the market value of the firm in the 84th month prior to bankruptcy, bankruptcy costs are on average 1 percent of the value of the firm. If instead the market value of the firm 36 months prior to bankruptcy is used, bankruptcy costs average 2.5 percent of the total market value of the firm. Of the total *change* in the market value of the firm between months "−84" and "0", bankruptcy costs represent 1.3 percent.

It should be noted that the percentages given in Table 5 are subject to several possible biases. One problem which has been ignored is that of non-traded securities. Many short-term liabilities are privately placed, and their market value is unknown. Assuming that the value of such securities is positive, exclusion of these securities from the market value computations biases the percentage figures upward. On the other hand, as discussed earlier, certain bankruptcy costs have not been taken into account. The fact that some components of the costs are not included tends to bias the results downward.

TABLE 5

I.C.C. Reported Bankruptcy Cost as a Percentage of Market Value

Name	Month					Cost as % of change in value
	0	−12	−36	−60	−84	
Chicago and Northwestern	2.7	1.4	2.4	0.6	0.6	0.7
Chicago, Indianapolis & Louisville	6.6	9.4	1.9	1.6	1.6	2.2
Chicago, Milwaukee, St. Paul & Pacific	3.8	2.1	3.7	0.8	0.4	0.4
Chicago, Rock Island and Pacific	1.7	1.9	0.4	0.4	0.6	0.8
Denver and Rio Grande Western	8.9	5.5	5.1	1.6	1.5	1.7
Erie Railroad	3.9	1.1	1.3	2.5	1.0	1.4
Minneapolis, St. Paul & SSM.	9.1	2.9	3.7	3.2	1.0	1.2
Missouri Pacific	3.3	1.7	0.6	0.8	1.3	2.1
New York, New Haven and Hartford	3.9	2.2	1.5	1.1	0.6	0.8
St. Louis San Francisco Railway	6.0	9.8	0.8	0.6	0.9	1.0
Western Pacific	8.8	6.5	5.9	2.3	1.5	1.8
High	9.1	9.8	5.9	3.2	1.6	2.1
Low	1.7	1.1	0.4	0.4	0.6	0.4
Mean	5.3	4.0	2.5	1.4	1.0	1.3

BANKRUPTCY COSTS IN RELATION TO THE MARKET VALUE OF THE FIRM

Figure 1 is a plot of the ICC reported cost of bankruptcy, and the corresponding month "0" value of each firm. Bankruptcy costs tended to be higher, in absolute terms, for the high market-value railroads than for the low market-value railroads. For example, the two railroads in the sample with the smallest market values, the Minneapolis, St. Paul and Sault Ste Marie and the Chicago, Indianapolis and Louisville, each had market values of about $10 million and bankruptcy costs of under $1 million. The two largest railroads, the Chicago and Northwestern and the Chicago, Rock Island and Pacific, each had market values of about $100 million, and bankruptcy costs of about $2 million.

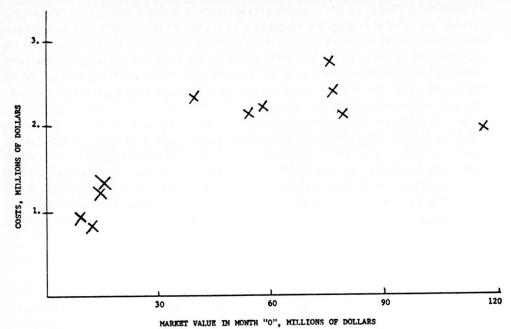

FIGURE 1.   Bankruptcy costs and market value of firms

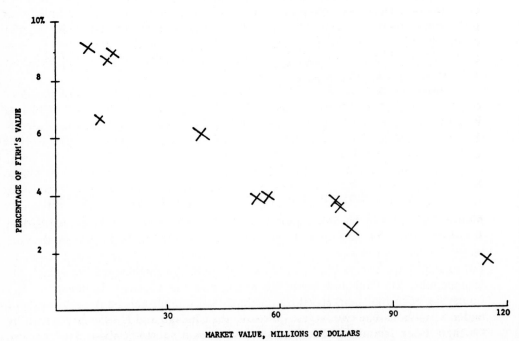

FIGURE 2.   Percentage bankruptcy costs and market value of firms

While the higher market-value railroads generally did incur higher bankruptcy costs, the costs do not appear to be directly proportional to market value. Figure 2 shows the cost of bankruptcy, expressed as a percentage of the month "0" value, for each of the 11 firms. The percentage appears to decline for railroads with relatively high market values. The two smallest railroads, in terms of market values, had bankruptcy costs which were 9.1 and 6.6 percent of their values, while the two largest railroads had bankruptcy costs which represented 2.7 and 1.7 percent of their respective values.[8]

This evidence suggests that there are substantial fixed costs associated with the railroad bankruptcy process, and hence economies of scale with respect to bankruptcy costs. Moreover, when the relationship between the value of the firm and the length of time spent in bankruptcy proceedings was investigated, it was found that the two were uncorrelated. Thus it does not appear that high-market value firms incurred bankruptcy costs simply because they tended to be in bankruptcy proceedings for a longer period of time than low market value firms.

THE EXPECTED COSTS OF BANKRUPTCY

From the standpoint of a firm choosing its capital structure, it is the *expected* cost of bankruptcy that is the relevant measure of bankruptcy costs. These expected costs of bankruptcy cannot be inferred directly from the data presented, since the *ex ante* probability of going bankrupt is not known. However, what these results would imply about expected bankruptcy costs can be shown under different assumptions about the likelihood of bankruptcy.

Suppose, for example, that a given railroad picks a level of debt such that bankruptcy would occur on average once every 20 years (i.e. the probability of going bankrupt is 5 percent in any given year). Assume that when bankruptcy occurs, the firm would pay a lump sum penalty equal to 3 percent of its now current market value. If anything, these numbers tend to overstate the frequency and apparent direct cost of bankruptcy.

Given this background, the firm's expected cost of bankruptcy is equal to fifteen one-hundreths of one percent of its now current market value. If the cost of bankruptcy is doubled to 6 percent and the probability of bankruptcy increased to 10 percent, the expected costs would still be only six-tenths of one percent of the current value of the firm.

These numbers are small indeed. This is not to say that they are small enough to be neglected completely in discussions of capital structure policy. But it would not seem unreasonable to conclude that for firms of the size under consideration, the expected direct costs of bankruptcy are unambiguously lower than the tax savings on debt to be expected at present tax rates in standard valuation models.[9]

8. The squared value of the correlation coefficient between percentage bankruptcy costs and market value is .88. At the .01 level of significance, the hypothesis that the two are uncorrelated must be rejected.

9. See Miller and Modigliani (1963). The analysis here assumes that the relative price of going bankrupt has not changed since the sample bankruptcies took place. This assumption may not be realistic if the price of legal services has increased in relative terms, or if the complexity of the legal system and of the bankruptcy process has increased. The analysis here also ignores the question of

APPLICABILITY TO OTHER INDUSTRIES

The extent to which the results are applicable to firms other than those in the railroad industry is uncertain, since the magnitude of the costs and of the "scale effect" may be industry-specific. One reason that the figures could differ for nonrailroad firms is that the Interstate Commerce Commission plays an active role only in railroad bankruptcies. Some of the railroads' bankruptcy costs may in effect be subsidized. The subsidy exists to the extent that the ICC performs functions which in its absence would have been performed by the railroads or their claimholders. The resources expended by the ICC are not reflected in the cost figures.

From one standpoint, this is unimportant. As long as the bankruptcy costs which the firm itself must bear are known, the fact that the government absorbs certain other costs does not influence the firm's financing decision. The only bankruptcy cost which the firm perceives is the cost which is incident upon the firm and its claimholders. However, if these data are to be used to infer that bankruptcy costs in other industries are similar, and exhibit a similar scale effect, additional assumptions must be made. It must be assumed that the size of the subsidy relative to total bankruptcy costs does not differ across industries, and that total bankruptcy costs are the same for railroad and nonrailroad firms, assuming equivalent size.

There is no obvious factual basis for making such assumptions. While non-railroad firms receive no subsidy from the ICC, they do receive a similar type of subsidy from the Securities and Exchange Commission. It is not clear whether this subsidy differs from the one which the ICC offers, or whether railroad bankruptcies are any more (or less) expensive than bankruptcies for similar-sized nonrailroad firms. Moreover, the differences between railroads and other firms may well be even more important in the case of indirect costs. Restrictions on entry by competitors, owing to ICC regulation, could serve to keep opportunity losses lower for bankrupt railroads than might otherwise be the case. For these reasons, the findings must be regarded as merely suggestive of bankruptcy costs in other industries.

REFERENCES

Kenneth Arrow. "The Role of Securities in the Optimal Allocation of Risk-Bearing," *Review of Economic Studies*, 31 (April, 1964), 91–96.
Bank and Quotation Record. 1926–1955, William B. Dana Company, New York.
Nevins D. Baxter. "Leverage, Risk of Ruin, and the Cost of Capital," *Journal of Finance*, 22 (September, 1967): 395–404.
Gerard Debreu. *The Theory of Value*, New York: John Wiley & Sons, Inc., 1959.
Eugene Fama and Merton Miller. *The Theory of Finance*, New York: Holt, Rinehart and Winston, 1972.
John Gould. "The Economics of Legal Conflicts," *Journal of Legal Studies*, 2 (June, 1973), 279–300.
Jack Hirshleifer. "Investment Decisions Under Uncertainty: Choice Theoretic Approaches," *Quarterly Journal of Economics*, 79 (November, 1965), 509–536.
Michael C. Jensen and William H. Meckling. "Theory of the Firm: Managerial Behavior, Agency Costs, and Capital Structure," *Journal of Financial Economics*, 3 (October, 1976).

whether or not *at the margin* (and not just on average) the direct bankruptcy costs offset the tax advantage.

Alan Kraus and Robert Litzenberger. "A State Preference Model of Optimal Financial Leverage," *Journal of Finance*, 28 (September, 1973), 911–922.

Frank Milne. "Choice Over Asset Economies: Default Risk and Corporate Leverage," *Journal of Financial Economics*, 2 (June, 1975), 165–185.

Merton Miller and Franco Modigliani. "The Cost of Capital, Corporation Finance, and the Theory of Investment," *American Economic Review*, 48 (June, 1958), 261–297.

—— and ——. "Corporate Income Taxes and the Cost of Capital: A Correction," *American Economic Review*, 53 (June, 1963), 433–443.

Moody's Railroad Manual. 1925–1970, Moody's Investors Service, New York.

James Scott. "A Theory of Optimal Capital Structure," *Bell Journal of Economics and Management Science*, 7 (Spring, 1976), 33–54.

David T. Stanley and Marjorie Girth. *Bankruptcy: Problem, Process, Reform*, Washington, D.C.: The Brookings Institution, 1971.

Joseph Stiglitz. "A Reexamination of the Modigliani-Miller Theorem," *American Economic Review*, 59 (September, 1969), 784–793.

United States Congress, House. *Hearings, Committee on Interstate Commerce*, H.R. 2298, 80th Congress, 1947.

United States Government. *Bankruptcy Laws of the United States*, Washington, D.C.: U.S. Government Printing Office, 1972.

James Van Horne. *Fundamentals of Financial Management*, Englewood Cliffs, New Jersey: Prentice-Hall, 1974.

——. "Corporate Bankruptcy and Liquidity Costs," Research Paper No. 205, Stanford Graduate School of Business, 1976.

Jerold B. Warner. "Corporate Bankruptcy," unpublished manuscript, University of Chicago, 1974.

——. "Bankruptcy Absolute Priority, and the Pricing of Risky Debt Claims," *Journal of Financial Economics*, forthcoming.

——. "Bankruptcy Costs, Absolute Priority, and the Pricing of Risky Debt Claims," unpublished Ph.D. thesis, University of Chicago, 1976.

THEORY OF THE FIRM: MANAGERIAL BEHAVIOR, AGENCY COSTS AND OWNERSHIP STRUCTURE

Michael C. JENSEN and William H. MECKLING*

University of Rochester, Rochester, NY 14627, U.S.A.

Received January 1976, revised version received July 1976

This paper integrates elements from the theory of agency, the theory of property rights and the theory of finance to develop a theory of the ownership structure of the firm. We define the concept of agency costs, show its relationship to the 'separation and control' issue, investigate the nature of the agency costs generated by the existence of debt and outside equity, demonstrate who bears these costs and why, and investigate the Pareto optimality of their existence. We also provide a new definition of the firm, and show how our analysis of the factors influencing the creation and issuance of debt and equity claims is a special case of the supply side of the completeness of markets problem.

> The directors of such [joint-stock] companies, however, being the managers rather of other people's money than of their own, it cannot well be expected, that they should watch over it with the same anxious vigilance with which the partners in a private copartnery frequently watch over their own. Like the stewards of a rich man, they are apt to consider attention to small matters as not for their master's honour, and very easily give themselves a dispensation from having it. Negligence and profusion, therefore, must always prevail, more or less, in the management of the affairs of such a company.
>
> Adam Smith, *The Wealth of Nations*, 1776, Cannan Edition
> (Modern Library, New York, 1937) p. 700.

1. Introduction and summary

1.1. Motivation of the paper

In this paper we draw on recent progress in the theory of (1) property rights, (2) agency, and (3) finance to develop a theory of ownership structure[1] for the

---

*Associate Professor and Dean, respectively, Graduate School of Management, University of Rochester. An earlier version of this paper was presented at the Conference on Analysis and Ideology, Interlaken, Switzerland, June 1974, sponsored by the Center for Research in Government Policy and Business at the University of Rochester, Graduate School of Management. We are indebted to F. Black, E. Fama, R. Ibbotson, W. Klein, M. Rozeff, R. Weil, O. Williamson, an anonymous referee, and to our colleagues and members of the Finance Workshop at the University of Rochester for their comments and criticisms, in particular G. Benston, M. Canes, D. Henderson, K. Leffler, J. Long, C. Smith, R. Thompson, R. Watts and J. Zimmerman.

[1]We do not use the term 'capital structure' because that term usually denotes the relative quantities of bonds, equity, warrants, trade credit, etc., which represent the liabilities of a firm. Our theory implies there is another important dimension to this problem – namely the relative amounts of ownership claims held by insiders (management) and outsiders (investors with no direct role in the management of the firm).

Journal of Financial Economics 3 (1976) 305–360. © North-Holland Publishing Company

firm. In addition to tying together elements of the theory of each of these three areas, our analysis casts new light on and has implications for a variety of issues in the professional and popular literature such as the definition of the firm, the "separation of ownership and control", the "social responsibility" of business, the definition of a "corporate objective function", the determination of an optimal capital structure, the specification of the content of credit agreements, the theory of organizations, and the supply side of the completeness of markets problem.

Our theory helps explain:

(1) why an entrepreneur or manager in a firm which has a mixed financial structure (containing both debt and outside equity claims) will choose a set of activities for the firm such that the total value of the firm is *less* than it would be if he were the sole owner and why this result is independent of whether the firm operates in monopolistic or competitive product or factor markets;

(2) why his failure to maximize the value of the firm is perfectly consistent with efficiency;

(3) why the sale of common stock is a viable source of capital even though managers do not literally maximize the value of the firm;

(4) why debt was relied upon as a source of capital before debt financing offered any tax advantage relative to equity;

(5) why preferred stock would be issued;

(6) why accounting reports would be provided voluntarily to creditors and stockholders, and why independent auditors would be engaged by management to testify to the accuracy and correctness of such reports;

(7) why lenders often place restrictions on the activities of firms to whom they lend, and why firms would themselves be led to suggest the imposition of such restrictions;

(8) why some industries are characterized by owner-operated firms whose sole outside source of capital is borrowing;

(9) why highly regulated industries such as public utilities or banks will have higher debt equity ratios for equivalent levels of risk than the average non-regulated firm;

(10) why security analysis can be socially productive even if it does not increase portfolio returns to investors.

1.2. Theory of the firm: An empty box?

While the literature of economics is replete with references to the "theory of the firm", the material generally subsumed under that heading is not a theory of the firm but actually a theory of markets in which firms are important actors. The firm is a "black box" operated so as to meet the relevant marginal conditions with respect to inputs and outputs, thereby maximizing profits, or more accurately, present value. Except for a few recent and tentative steps, however, we have no theory which explains how the conflicting objectives of the individual participants are brought into equilibrium so as to yield this result. The limitations of this black box view of the firm have been cited by Adam Smith and Alfred Marshall, among others. More recently, popular and professional debates over the "social responsibility" of corporations, the separation of ownership and control, and the rash of reviews of the literature on the "theory of the firm" have evidenced continuing concern with these issues.[2]

A number of major attempts have been made during recent years to construct a theory of the firm by substituting other models for profit or value maximization; each attempt motivated by a conviction that the latter is inadequate to explain managerial behavior in large corporations.[3] Some of these reformulation attempts have rejected the fundamental principle of maximizing behavior as well as rejecting the more specific profit maximizing model. We retain the notion of maximizing behavior on the part of all individuals in the analysis to follow.[4]

1.3. Property rights

An independent stream of research with important implications for the theory of the firm has been stimulated by the pioneering work of Coase, and extended by Alchian, Demsetz and others.[5] A comprehensive survey of this literature is given by Furubotn and Pejovich (1972). While the focus of this research has been "property rights",[6] the subject matter encompassed is far broader than that term suggests. What is important for the problems addressed here is that specification of individual rights determines how costs and rewards will be

[2] Reviews of this literature are given by Peterson (1965), Alchian (1965, 1968), Machlup (1967), Shubik (1970), Cyert and Hedrick (1972), Branch (1973), Preston (1975).

[3] See Williamson (1964, 1970, 1975), Marris (1964), Baumol (1959), Penrose (1958), and Cyert and March (1963). Thorough reviews of these and other contributions are given by Machlup (1961) and Alchian (1965).
Simon (1955) developed a model of human choice incorporating information (search) and computational costs which also has important implications for the behavior of managers. Unfortunately, Simon's work has often been misinterpreted as a denial of maximizing behavior, and misused, especially in the marketing and behavioral science literature. His later use of the term 'satisficing' [Simon (1959)] has undoubtedly contributed to this confusion because it suggests rejection of maximizing behavior rather than maximization subject to costs of information and of decision making.

[4] See Meckling (1976) for a discussion of the fundamental importance of the assumption of resourceful, evaluative, maximizing behavior on the part of individuals in the development of theory. Klein (1976) takes an approach similar to the one we embark on in this paper in his review of the theory of the firm and the law.

[5] See Coase (1937, 1959, 1960), Alchian (1965, 1968), Alchian and Kessel (1962), Demsetz (1967), Alchian and Demsetz (1972), Monsen and Downs (1965), Silver and Auster (1969), and McManus (1975).

[6] Property rights are of course human rights, i.e., rights which are possessed by human beings. The introduction of the wholly false distinction between property rights and human rights in many policy discussions is surely one of the all time great semantic flimflams.

allocated among the participants in any organization. Since the specification of rights is generally effected through contracting (implicit as well as explicit), individual behavior in organizations, including the behavior of managers, will depend upon the nature of these contracts. We focus in this paper on the behavioral implications of the property rights specified in the contracts between the owners and managers of the firm.

1.4. Agency costs

Many problems associated with the inadequcy of the current theory of the firm can also be viewed as special cases of the theory of agency relationships in which there is a growing literature.[7] This literature has developed independently of the property rights literature even though the problems with which it is concerned are similar; the approaches are in fact highly complementary to each other.

We define an agency relationship as a contract under which one or more persons (the principal(s)) engage another person (the agent) to perform some service on their behalf which involves delegating some decision making authority to the agent. If both parties to the relationship are utility maximizers there is good reason to believe that the agent will not always act in the best interests of the principal. The *principal* can limit divergences from his interest by establishing appropriate incentives for the agent and by incurring monitoring costs designed to limit the aberrant activities of the agent. In addition in some situations it will pay the *agent* to expend resources (bonding costs) to guarantee that he will not take certain actions which would harm the principal or to ensure that the principal will be compensated if he does take such actions. However, it is generally impossible for the principal or the agent at zero cost to ensure that the agent will make optimal decisions from the principal's viewpoint. In most agency relationships the principal and the agent will incur positive monitoring and bonding costs (non-pecuniary as well as pecuniary), and in addition there will be some divergence between the agent's decisions[8] and those decisions which would maximize the welfare of the principal. The dollar equivalent of the reduction in welfare experienced by the principal due to this divergence is also a cost of the agency relationship, and we refer to this latter cost as the "residual loss". We define *agency costs* as the sum of:

(1) the monitoring expenditures by the principal,[9]
(2) the bonding expenditures by the agent,
(3) the residual loss.

[7]Cf. Berhold (1971), Ross (1973, 1974a), Wilson (1968, 1969), and Heckerman (1975).
[8]Given the optimal monitoring and bonding activities by the principal and agent.
[9]As it is used in this paper the term monitoring includes more than just measuring or observing the behavior of the agent. It includes efforts on the part of the principal to 'control' the behavior of the agent through budget restrictions, compensation policies, operating rules etc.

Note also that agency costs arise in any situation involving cooperative effort (such as the co-authoring of this paper) by two or more people even though there is no clear cut principal–agent relationship. Viewed in this light it is clear that our definition of agency costs and their importance to the theory of the firm bears a close relationship to the problem of shirking and monitoring of team production which Alchian and Demsetz (1972) raise in their paper on the theory of the firm.

Since the relationship between the stockholders and manager of a corporation fit the definition of a pure agency relationship it should be no surprise to discover that the issues associated with the "separation of ownership and control" in the modern diffuse ownership corporation are intimately associated with the general problem of agency. We show below that an explanation of why and how the agency costs generated by the corporate form are born leads to a theory of the ownership (or capital) structure of the firm.

Before moving on, however, it is worthwhile to point out the generality of the agency problem. The problem of inducing an "agent" to behave as if he were maximizing the "principal's" welfare is quite general. It exists in all organizations and in all cooperative efforts – at every level of management in firms,[10] in universities, in mutual companies, in cooperatives, in governmental authorities and bureaus, in unions, and in relationships normally classified as agency relationships such as are common in the performing arts and the market for real estate. The development of theories to explain the form which agency costs take in each of these situations (where the contractual relations differ significantly), and how and why they are born will lead to a rich theory of organizations which is now lacking in economics and the social sciences generally. We confine our attention in this paper to only a small part of this general problem – the analysis of agency costs generated by the contractual arrangements between the owners and top management of the corporation.

Our approach to the agency problem here differs fundamentally from most of the existing literature. That literature focuses almost exclusively on the normative aspects of the agency relationship; that is how to structure the contractual relation (including compensation incentives) between the principal and agent to provide appropriate incentives for the agent to make choices which will maximize

---

[10]As we show below the existence of positive monitoring and bonding costs will result in the manager of a corporation possessing control over some resources which he can allocate (within certain constraints) to satisfy his own preferences. However, to the extent that he must obtain the cooperation of others in order to carry out his tasks (such as divisional vice presidents) and to the extent that he cannot control their behavior perfectly and costlessly they will be able to appropriate some of these resources for their own ends. In short, there are agency costs generated at every level of the organization. Unfortunately, the analysis of these more general organizational issues is even more difficult than that of the 'ownership and control' issue because the nature of the contractual obligations and rights of the parties are much more varied and generally not as well specified in explicit contractual arrangements. Nevertheless, they exist and we believe that extensions of our analysis in these directions show promise of producing insights into a viable theory of organization.

the principal's welfare given that uncertainty and imperfect monitoring exist. We focus almost entirely on the positive aspects of the theory. That is, we assume individuals solve these normative problems and given that only stocks and bonds can be issued as claims, we investigate the incentives faced by each of the parties and the elements entering into the determination of the equilibrium contractual form characterizing the relationship between the manager (i.e., agent) of the firm and the outside equity and debt holders (i.e., principals).

1.5. Some general comments on the definition of the firm

Ronald Coase (1937) in his seminal paper on "The Nature of the Firm" pointed out that economics had no positive theory to determine the bounds of the firm. He characterized the bounds of the firm as that range of exchanges over which the market system was suppressed and resource allocation was accomplished instead by authority and direction. He focused on the cost of using markets to effect contracts and exchanges and argued that activities would be included within the firm whenever the costs of using markets were greater than the costs of using direct authority. Alchian and Demsetz (1972) object to the notion that activities within the firm are governed by authority, and correctly emphasize the role of contracts as a vehicle for voluntary exchange. They emphasize the role of monitoring in situations in which there is joint input or team production.[11] We sympathize with the importance they attach to monitoring, but we believe the emphasis which Alchian–Demsetz place on joint input production is too narrow and therefore misleading. Contractual relations are the essence of the firm, not only with employees but with suppliers, customers, creditors, etc. The problem of agency costs and monitoring exists for all of these contracts, independent of whether there is joint production in their sense; i.e., joint production can explain only a small fraction of the behavior of individuals associated with a firm. A detailed examination of these issues is left to another paper.

It is important to recognize that most organizations are simply *legal fictions*[12] *which serve as a nexus for a set of contracting relationships among individuals.* This includes firms, non-profit institutions such as universities, hospitals and foundations, mutual organizations such as mutual savings banks and insurance companies and co-operatives, some private clubs, and even governmental bodies such as cities, states and the Federal government, government enterprises such as TVA, the Post Office, transit systems, etc.

---

[11]They define the classical capitalist firm as a contractual organization of inputs in which there is '(a) joint input production, (b) several input owners, (c) one party who is common to all the contracts of the joint inputs, (d) who has rights to renegotiate any input's contract independently of contracts with other input owners, (e) who holds the residual claim, and (f) who has the right to sell his contractual residual status.'

[12]By legal fiction we mean the artificial construct under the law which allows certain organizations to be treated as individuals.

The private corporation or firm is simply one form of *legal fiction which serves as a nexus for contracting relationships and which is also characterized by the existence of divisible residual claims on the assets and cash flows of the organization which can generally be sold without permission of the other contracting individuals.* While this definition of the firm has little substantive content, emphasizing the essential contractual nature of firms and other organizations focuses attention on a crucial set of questions – why particular sets of contractual relations arise for various types of organizations, what the consequences of these contractual relations are, and how they are affected by changes exogenous to the organization. Viewed this way, it makes little or no sense to try to distinguish those things which are "inside" the firm (or any other organization) from those things that are "outside" of it. There is in a very real sense only a multitude of complex relationships (i.e., contracts) between the legal fiction (the firm) and the owners of labor, material and capital inputs and the consumers of output.[13]

Viewing the firm as the nexus of a set of contracting relationships among individuals also serves to make it clear that the personalization of the firm implied by asking questions such as "what should be the objective function of the firm", or "does the firm have a social responsibility" is seriously misleading. *The firm is not an individual.* It is a legal fiction which serves as a focus for a complex process in which the conflicting objectives of individuals (some of whom may "represent" other oganizations) are brought into equilibrium within a framework of contractual relations. In this sense the "behavior" of the firm is like the behavior of a market; i.e., the outcome of a complex equilibrium process. We seldom fall into the trap of characterizing the wheat or stock market as an individual, but we often make this error by thinking about organizations as if they were persons with motivations and intentions.[14]

---

[13]For example, we ordinarily think of a product as leaving the firm at the time it is sold, but implicitly or explicitly such sales generally carry with them continuing contracts between the firm and the buyer. If the product does not perform as expected the buyer often can and does have a right to satisfaction. Explicit evidence that such implicit contracts do exist is the practice we occasionally observe of specific provision that 'all sales are final.'

[14]This view of the firm points up the important role which the legal system and the law play in social organizations, especially, the organization of economic activity. Statutory laws sets bounds on the kinds of contracts into which individuals and organizations may enter without risking criminal prosecution. The police powers of the state are available and used to enforce performance of contracts or to enforce the collection of damages for non-performance. The courts adjudicate conflicts between contracting parties and establish precedents which form the body of common law. All of these government activities affect both the kinds of contracts executed and the extent to which contracting is relied upon. This in turn determines the usefulness, productivity, profitability and viability of various forms of organization. Moreover, new laws as well as court decisions often can and do change the rights of contracting parties ex post, and they can and do serve as a vehicle for redistribution of wealth. An analysis of some of the implications of these facts is contained in Jensen and Meckling (1976) and we shall not pursue them here.

1.6. An overview of the paper

We develop the theory in stages. Sections 2 and 4 provide analyses of the agency costs of equity and debt respectively. These form the major foundation of the theory. Section 3 poses some unanswered questions regarding the existence of the corporate form of organization and examines the role of limited liability. Section 5 provides a synthesis of the basic concepts derived in sections 2–4 into a theory of the corporate ownership structure which takes account of the trade-offs available to the entrepreneur–manager between inside and outside equity and debt. Some qualifications and extensions of the analysis are discussed in section 6, and section 7 contains a brief summary and conclusions.

2. The agency costs of outside equity

2.1. Overview

In this section we analyze the effect of outside equity on agency costs by comparing the behavior of a manager when he owns 100 percent of the residual claims on a firm to his behavior when he sells off a portion of those claims to outsiders. If a wholly owned firm is managed by the owner, he will make operating decisions which maximize his utility. These decisions will involve not only the benefits he derives from pecuniary returns but also the utility generated by various non-pecuniary aspects of his entrepreneurial activities such as the physical appointments of the office, the attractiveness of the secretarial staff, the level of employee discipline, the kind and amount of charitable contributions, personal relations ("love", "respect", etc.) with employees, a larger than optimal computer to play with, purchase of production inputs from friends, etc. The optimum mix (in the absence of taxes) of the various pecuniary and non-pecuniary benefits is achieved when the marginal utility derived from an additional dollar of expenditure (measured net of any productive effects) is equal for each non-pecuniary item and equal to the marginal utility derived from an additional dollar of after tax purchasing power (wealth).

If the owner–manager sells equity claims on the corporation which are identical to his (i.e., share proportionately in the profits of the firm and have limited liability) agency costs will be generated by the divergence between his interest and those of the outside shareholders, since he will then bear only a fraction of the costs of any non-pecuniary benefits he takes out in maximizing his own utility. If the manager owns only 95 percent of the stock, he will expend resources to the point where the marginal utility derived from a dollar's expenditure of the firm's resources on such items equals the marginal utility of an additional 95 cents in general purchasing power (i.e., *his* share of the wealth reduction) and not one dollar. Such activities, on his part, can be limited (but probably not eliminated) by the expenditure of resources on monitoring activities by the outside stockholders. But as we show below, the owner will bear the entire wealth effects of these expected costs so long as the equity market anticipates these effects. Prospective minority shareholders will realize that the owner–manager's interests will diverge somewhat from theirs, hence the price which they will pay for shares will reflect the monitoring costs and the effect of the divergence between the manager's interest and theirs. Nevertheless, ignoring for the moment the possibility of borrowing against his wealth, the owner will find it desirable to bear these costs as long as the welfare increment he experiences from converting his claims on the firm into general purchasing power[15] is large enough to offset them.

As the owner–manager's fraction of the equity falls, his fractional claim on the outcomes falls and this will tend to encourage him to appropriate larger amounts of the corporate resources in the form of perquisites. This also makes it desirable for the minority shareholders to expend more resources in monitoring his behavior. Thus, the wealth costs to the owner of obtaining additional cash in the equity markets rise as his fractional ownership falls.

We shall continue to characterize the agency conflict between the owner–manager and outside shareholders as deriving from the manager's tendency to appropriate perquisites out of the firm's resources for his own consumption. However, we do not mean to leave the impression that this is the only or even the most important source of conflict. Indeed, it is likely that the most important conflict arises from the fact that as the manager's ownership claim falls, his incentive to devote significant effort to creative activities such as searching out new profitable ventures falls. He may in fact avoid such ventures simply because it requires too much trouble or effort on his part to manage or to learn about new technologies. Avoidance of these personal costs and the anxieties that go with them also represent a source of on the job utility to him and it can result in the value of the firm being substantially lower than it otherwise could be.

2.2. A simple formal analysis of the sources of agency costs of equity and who bears them

In order to develop some structure for the analysis to follow we make two sets of assumptions. The first set (permanent assumptions) are those which shall carry through almost all of the analysis in sections 2–5. The effects of relaxing some of these are discussed in section 6. The second set (temporary assumptions) are made only for expositional purposes and are relaxed as soon as the basic points have been clarified.

---

[15]For use in consumption, for the diversification of his wealth, or more importantly, for the financing of 'profitable' projects which he could not otherwise finance out of his personal wealth. We deal with these issues below after having developed some of the elementary analytical tools necessary to their solution.

Permanent assumptions

(P.1) All taxes are zero.
(P.2) No trade credit is available.
(P.3) All outside equity shares are non-voting.
(P.4) No complex financial claims such as convertible bonds or preferred stock or warrants can be issued.
(P.5) No outside owner gains utility from ownership in a firm in any way other than through its effect on his wealth or cash flows.
(P.6) All dynamic aspects of the multiperiod nature of the problem are ignored by assuming there is only one production–financing decision to be made by the entrepreneur.
(P.7) The entrepreneur–manager's money wages are held constant throughout the analysis.
(P.8) There exists a single manager (the peak coordinator) with ownership interest in the firm.

Temporary assumptions

(T.1) The size of the firm is fixed.
(T.2) No monitoring or bonding activities are possible.
(T.3) No debt financing through bonds, preferred stock, or personal borrowing (secured or unsecured) is possible.
(T.4) All elements of the owner–manager's decision problem involving portfolio considerations induced by the presence of uncertainty and the existence of diversifiable risk are ignored.

Define:

X $= \{x_1, x_2, \ldots, x_n\}$ = vector of quantities of all factors and activities within the firm from which the manager derives non-pecuniary benefits;[16] the x_i are defined such that his marginal utility is positive for each of them;

$C(X)$ = total dollar cost of providing any given amount of these items;

$P(X)$ = total dollar value to the firm of the productive benefits of X;

$B(X) = P(X) - C(X)$ = net dollar benefit to the firm of X ignoring any effects of X on the equilibrium wage of the manager.

Ignoring the effects of X on the manager's utility and therefore on his equilibrium wage rate, the optimum levels of the factors and activities X are defined by X^* such that

$$\frac{\partial B(X^*)}{\partial X^*} = \frac{\partial P(X^*)}{\partial X^*} - \frac{\partial C(X^*)}{\partial X^*} = 0.$$

[16]Such as office space, air conditioning, thickness of the carpets, friendliness of employee relations, etc.

Thus for any vector $X \geqq X^*$ (i.e., where at least one element of X is greater than its corresponding element of X^*), $F \equiv B(X^*) - B(X) > 0$ measures the dollar cost to the firm (net of any productive effects) of providing the increment $X - X^*$ of the factors and activities which generate utility to the manager. We assume henceforth that for any given level of cost to the firm, F, the vector of factors and activities on which F is spent are those, $\hat{X}$, which yield the manager maximum utility. Thus $F \equiv B(X^*) - B(\hat{X})$.

We have thus far ignored in our discussion the fact that these expenditures on X occur through time and therefore there are tradeoffs to be made across time as well as between alternative elements of X. Furthermore, we have ignored the fact that the future expenditures are likely to involve uncertainty (i.e., they are subject to probability distributions) and therefore some allowance must be made for their riskiness. We resolve both of these issues by defining C, P, B, and F to be the *current market values* of the sequence of probability distributions on the period by period cash flows involved.[17]

Given the definition of F as the current market value of the stream of manager's expenditures on non-pecuniary benefits we represent the constraint which a single owner–manager faces in deciding how much non-pecuniary income he will extract from the firm by the line $\bar{V}F$ in fig. 1. This is analogous to a budget constraint. The market value of the firm is measured along the vertical axis and the market value of the manager's stream of expenditures on non-pecuniary benefits, F, are measured along the horizontal axis. $0\bar{V}$ is the value of the firm when the amount of non-pecuniary income consumed is zero. By definition $\bar{V}$ is the maximum market value of the cash flows generated by the firm for a given money wage for the manager when the manager's consumption of non-pecuniary benefits are zero. At this point all the factors and activities within the firm which generate utility for the manager are at the level X^* defined above. There is a different budget constraint $\bar{V}F$ for each possible scale of the firm (i.e., level of investment, I) and for alternative levels of money wage, W, for the manager. For the moment we pick an arbitrary level of investment (which we assume has already been made) and hold the scale of the firm constant at this level. We also assume that the manager's money wage is fixed at the level W^* which represents the current market value of his wage contract[18] in the optimal compensation package which consists of both wages, W^*, and non-pecuniary benefits, F^*. Since one dollar of current value of non-pecuniary benefits withdrawn from the firm by the manager reduces the market value of the firm by \$1, by definition, the slope of $\bar{V}F$ is -1.

---

[17]And again we assume that for any given market value of these costs, F, to the firm the allocation across time and across alternative probability distributions is such that the manager's current expected utility is at a maximum.

[18]At this stage when we are considering a 100% owner-managed firm the notion of a 'wage contract' with himself has no content. However, the 100% owner-managed case is only an expositional device used in passing to illustrate a number of points in the analysis, and we ask the reader to bear with us briefly while we lay out the structure for the more interesting partial ownership case where such a contract does have substance.

The owner–manager's tastes for wealth and non-pecuniary benefits is represented in fig. 1 by a system of indifference curves, U_1, U_2, etc.[19] The indifference curves will be convex as drawn as long as the owner–manager's marginal rate of

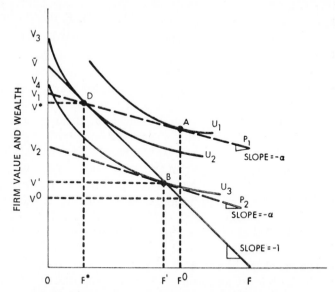

MARKET VALUE OF THE STREAM OF MANAGER'S EXPENDITURES ON NON-PECUNIARY BENEFITS

Fig. 1. The value of the firm (V) and the level of non-pecuniary benefits consumed (F) when the fraction of outside equity is $(1-\alpha)V$, and U_j ($j = 1, 2, 3$) represents owner's indifference curves between wealth and non-pecuniary benefits.

substitution between non-pecuniary benefits and wealth diminishes with increasing levels of the benefits. For the 100 percent owner–manager, this presumes that there are not perfect substitutes for these benefits available on the outside, i.e., to some extent they are job specific. For the fractional owner–manager this presumes the benefits cannot be turned into general purchasing power at a constant price.[20]

[19]The manager's utility function is actually defined over wealth and the future time sequence of vectors of quantities of non-pecuniary benefits, X_t. Although the setting of his problem is somewhat different, Fama (1970b, 1972) analyzes the conditions under which these preferences can be represented as a derived utility function defined as a function of the money value of the expenditures (in our notation F) on these goods conditional on the prices of goods. Such a utility function incorporates the optimization going on in the background which define $\hat{X}$ discussed above for a given F. In the more general case where we allow a time series of consumption, $\hat{X}_t$, the optimization is being carried out across both time and the components of X_t for fixed F.

[20]This excludes, for instance, (a) the case where the manager is allowed to expend corporate resources on anything he pleases in which case F would be a perfect substitute for wealth, or (b) the case where he can 'steal' cash (or other marketable assets) with constant returns to scale – if he could the indifference curves would be straight lines with slope determined by the fence commission.

When the owner has 100 percent of the equity, the value of the firm will be V^* where indifference curve U_2 is tangent to VF, and the level of non-pecuniary benefits consumed is F^*. If the owner sells the entire equity but remains as manager, and if the equity buyer can, at zero cost, force the old owner (as manager) to take the same level of non-pecuniary benefits as he did as owner, then V^* is the price the new owner will be willing to pay for the entire equity.[21]

In general, however, we would not expect the new owner to be able to enforce identical behavior on the old owner at zero costs. If the old owner sells a fraction of the firm to an outsider, he, as manager, will no longer bear the full cost of any non-pecuniary benefits he consumes. Suppose the owner sells a share of the firm, $1-\alpha$, $(0 < \alpha < 1)$ and retains for himself a share, α. If the prospective buyer believes that the owner–manager will consume the same level of non-pecuniary benefits as he did as full owner, the buyer will be willing to pay $(1-\alpha)V^*$ for a fraction $(1-\alpha)$ of the equity. Given that an outsider now holds a claim to $(1-\alpha)$ of the equity, however, the *cost* to the owner–manager of consuming \$1 of non-pecuniary benefits in the firm will no longer be \$1. Instead, it will be $\alpha \times \$1$. If the prospective buyer actually paid $(1-\alpha)V^*$ for his share of the equity, and if thereafter the manager could choose whatever level of non-pecuniary benefits he liked, his budget constraint would be V_1P_1 in fig. 1 and has a slope equal to $-\alpha$. Including the payment the owner receives from the buyer as part of the owner's post-sale wealth, his budget constraint, V_1P_1, must pass through D, since he can if he wishes have the same wealth and level of non-pecuniary consumption he consumed as full owner.

But if the owner–manager is free to choose the level of perquisites, F, subject only to the loss in wealth he incurs as a part owner, his welfare will be maximized by increasing his consumption of non-pecuniary benefits. He will move to point A where V_1P_1 is tangent to U_1 representing a higher level of utility. The value of the firm falls from V^*, to V^0, i.e., by the amount of the cost to the firm of the increased non-pecuniary expenditures, and the owner–manager's consumption of non-pecuniary benefits rises from F^* to F^0.

[21]Point D defines the fringe benefits in the optimal pay package since the value to the manager of the fringe benefits F^* is greater than the cost of providing them as is evidenced by the fact that U_2 is steeper to the left of D than the budget constraint with slope equal to -1.

That D is indeed the optimal pay package can easily be seen in this situation since if the conditions of the sale to a new owner specified that the manager would receive no fringe benefits after the sale he would require a payment equal to V_3 to compensate him for the sacrifice of his claims to V^* and fringe benefits amounting to F^* (the latter with total value to him of $V_3 - V^*$). But if $F = 0$, the value of the firm is only $\bar{V}$. Therefore, if monitoring costs were zero the sale would take place at V^* with provision for a pay package which included fringe benefits of F^* for the manager.

This discussion seems to indicate there are two values for the 'firm', V_3 and V^*. This is not the case if we realize that V^* is the value of the right to be the residual claimant on the cash flows of the firm and $V_3 - V^*$ is the value of the managerial rights, i.e., the right to make the operating decisions which include access to F^*. There is at least one other right which has value which plays no formal role in the analysis as yet – the value of the control right. By control right we mean the right to hire and fire the manager and we leave this issue to a future paper.

If the equity market is characterized by rational expectations the buyers will be aware that the owner will increase his non-pecuniary consumption when his ownership share is reduced. If the owner's response function is known or if the equity market makes unbiased estimates of the owner's response to the changed incentives, the buyer will not pay $(1-\alpha)V^*$ for $(1-\alpha)$ of the equity.

Theorem. For a claim on the firm of $(1-\alpha)$ the outsider will pay only $(1-\alpha)$ times the value he expects the firm to have given the induced change in the behavior of the owner–manager.

Proof. For simplicity we ignore any element of **uncertainty** introduced by the lack of perfect knowledge of the owner–manager's response function. Such uncertainty will not affect the final solution if the equity market is large as long as the estimates are rational (i.e., unbiased) and the errors are independent across firms. The latter condition assures that this risk is diversifiable and therefore equilibrium prices will equal the expected values.

Let W represent the owner's total wealth after he has sold a claim equal to $1-\alpha$ of the equity to an outsider. W has two components. One is the payment, S_o, made by the outsider for $1-\alpha$ of the equity; the rest, S_i, is the value of the owner's (i.e., insider's) share of the firm, so that W, the owner's wealth, is given by

$$W = S_o + S_i = S_o + \alpha V(F, \alpha),$$

where $V(F, \alpha)$ represents the value of the firm given that the manager's fractional ownership share is α and that he consumes perquisites with current market value of F. Let $V_2 P_2$, with a slope of $-\alpha$ represent the tradeoff the owner–manager faces between non-pecuniary benefits and his wealth after the sale. Given that the owner has decided to sell a claim $1-\alpha$ of the firm, his welfare will be maximized when $V_2 P_2$ is tangent to some indifference curve such as U_3 in fig. 1. A price for a claim of $(1-\alpha)$ on the firm that is satisfactory to both the buyer and the seller will require that this tangency occur along $\overline{V}F$, i.e., that the value of the firm must be V'. To show this, assume that such is not the case – that the tangency occurs to the left of the point B on the line $\overline{V}F$. Then, since the slope of $V_2 P_2$ is negative, the value of the firm will be larger than V'. The owner–manager's choice of this lower level of consumption of non-pecuniary benefits will imply a higher value both to the firm as a whole and to the fraction of the firm $(1-\alpha)$ which the outsider has acquired; that is, $(1-\alpha)V' > S_o$. From the owner's viewpoint, he has sold $1-\alpha$ of the firm for less than he could have, given the (assumed) lower level of non-pecuniary benefits he enjoys. On the other hand, if the tangency point B is to the right of the line $\overline{V}F$, the owner–manager's higher consumption of non-pecuniary benefits means the value of the firm is less than V', and hence $(1-\alpha)V(F, \alpha) < S_o = (1-\alpha)V'$. The outside owner then has paid more for his share of the equity than it is worth. S_o will be a mutually satisfactory price if and only if $(1-\alpha)V' = S_o$. But this means that the owner's post-sale wealth is equal to the (reduced) value of the firm V', since

$$W = S_o + \alpha V' = (1-\alpha)V' + \alpha V' = V'.$$

Q.E.D.

The requirement that V' and F' fall on $\overline{V}F$ is thus equivalent to requiring that the value of the claim acquired by the outside buyer be equal to the amount he pays for it and conversely for the owner. *This means that the decline in the total value of the firm ($V^* - V'$) is entirely imposed on the owner–manager.* His total wealth after the sale of $(1-\alpha)$ of the equity is V' and the decline in his wealth is $V^* - V'$.

The distance $V^* - V'$ is the reduction in the market value of the firm engendered by the agency relationship and is a measure of the "residual loss" defined earlier. In this simple example the residual loss represents the total agency costs engendered by the sale of outside equity because monitoring and bonding activities have not been allowed. The welfare loss the owner incurs is less than the residual loss by the value to him of the increase in non-pecuniary benefits ($F' - F^*$). In fig. 1 the difference between the intercepts on the Y axis of the two indifference curves U_2 and U_3 is a measure of the owner–manager's welfare loss due to the incurrence of agency costs,[22] and he would sell such a claim only if the increment in welfare he achieves by using the cash amounting to $(1-\alpha)V'$ for other things was worth more to him than this amount of wealth.

2.3. Determination of the optimal scale of the firm

The case of all equity financing. Consider the problem faced by an entrepreneur with initial pecuniary wealth, W, and monopoly access to a project requiring investment outlay, I, subject to diminishing returns to scale in I. Fig. 2 portrays the solution to the optimal scale of the firm taking into account the agency costs associated with the existence of outside equity. The axes are as defined in fig. 1 except we now plot on the vertical axis the total wealth of the owner, i.e., his initial wealth, W, plus $V(I) - I$, the net increment in wealth he obtains from exploitation of his investment opportunities. The market value of the firm, $V = V(I, F)$, is now a function of the level of investment, I, and the current market value of the manager's expenditures of the firm's resources on non-pecuniary benefits, F. Let $\overline{V}(I)$ represent the value of the firm as a function of the level of investment when the manager's expenditures on non-pecuniary benefits, F, are zero. The schedule with intercept labeled $W + [\overline{V}(I^*) - I^*)]$ and

---

[22]The distance $V^* - V'$ is a measure of what we will define as the gross agency costs. The distance $V_3 - V_4$ is a measure of what we call net agency costs, and it is this measure of agency costs which will be minimized by the manager in the general case where we allow investment to change.

slope equal to -1 in fig. 2 represents the locus of combinations of post-investment wealth and dollar cost to the firm of non-pecuniary benefits which are available to the manager when investment is carried to the value maximizing

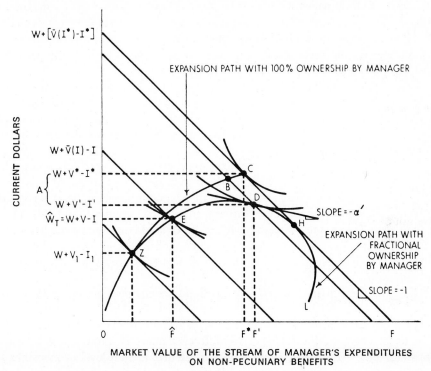

Fig. 2. Determination of the optimal scale of the firm in the case where no monitoring takes place. Point C denotes optimum investment, I^*, and non-pecuniary benefits, F^*, when investment is 100% financed by entrepreneur. Point D denotes optimum investment, I', and non-pecuniary benefits, F, when outside equity financing is used to help finance the investment and the entrepreneur owns a fraction α' of the firm. The distance A measures the gross agency costs.

point, I^*. At this point $\Delta \overline{V}(I) - \Delta I = 0$. If the manager's wealth were large enough to cover the investment required to reach this scale of operation, I^*, he would consume F^* in non-pecuniary benefits and have pecuniary wealth with value $W + V^* - I^*$. However, if outside financing is required to cover the investment he will not reach this point if monitoring costs are non-zero.[23]

The expansion path $OZBC$ represents the equilibrium combinations of wealth and non-pecuniary benefits, F, which the manager could obtain if he had enough

[23]I^* is the value maximizing and Pareto Optimum investment level which results from the traditional analysis of the corporate investment decision if the firm operates in perfectly competitive capital and product markets and the agency cost problems discussed here are ignored. See Debreu (1959, ch. 7), Jensen and Long (1972), Long (1972), Merton and Subrahmanyam (1974), Hirshleifer (1958, 1970), and Fama and Miller (1972).

personal wealth to finance all levels of investment up to I^*. It is the locus of points such as Z and C which represent the equilibrium position for the 100 percent owner–manager at each possible level of investment, I. As I increases we move up the expansion path to the point C where $V(I) - I$ is at a maximum. Additional investment beyond this point reduces the net value of the firm, and as it does the equilibrium path of the manager's wealth and non-pecuniary benefits retraces (in the reverse direction) the curve $OZBC$. We draw the path as a smooth concave function only as a matter of convenience.

If the manager obtained outside financing and if there were zero costs to the agency relationship (perhaps because monitoring costs were zero) the expansion path would also be represented by $OZBC$. Therefore, this path represents what we might call the "idealized" solutions, i.e., those which would occur in the absence of agency costs.

Assume the manager has sufficient personal wealth to completely finance the firm only up to investment level I_1 which puts him at point Z. At this point $W = I_1$. To increase the size of the firm beyond this point he must obtain outside financing to cover the additional investment required, and this means reducing his fractional ownership. When he does this he incurs agency costs, and the lower is his ownership fraction the larger are the agency costs he incurs. However, if the investments requiring outside financing are sufficiently profitable his welfare will continue to increase.

The expansion path $ZEDHL$ in fig. 2 portrays one possible path of the equilibrium levels of the owner's non-pecuniary benefits and wealth at each possible level of investment higher than I_1. This path is the locus of points such as E or D where (1) the manager's indifference curve is tangent to a line with slope equal to $-\alpha$ (his fractional claim on the firm at that level of investment), and (2) the tangency occurs on the "budget constraint" with slope $= -1$ for the firm value and non-pecuniary benefit tradeoff at the same level of investment.[24] As we move along $ZEDHL$ his fractional claim on the firm continues

[24]Each equilibrium point such as that at E is characterized by $(\hat{a}, \hat{F}, \hat{W}_T)$ where $\hat{W}_T$ is the entrepreneur's post-investment financing wealth. Such an equilibrium must satisfy each of the following four conditions:

(1) $\qquad \hat{W}_T + F = \bar{V}(I) + W - I = \bar{V}(I) - K,$

where $K \equiv I - W$ is the amount of outside financing required to make the investment I. If this condition is not satisfied there is an uncompensated wealth transfer (in one direction or the other) between the entrepreneur and outside equity buyers.

(2) $\qquad U_F(\hat{W}_T, \hat{F})/U_{W_T}(\hat{W}_T, \hat{F}) = \hat{a},$

where U is the entrepreneur's utility function on wealth and perquisites, U_F and U_{W_T} are marginal utilities and $\hat{a}$ is the manager's share of the firm.

(3) $\qquad (1 - \hat{a})V(I) = (1 - \hat{a})[\bar{V}(I) - \hat{F}] \geqq K,$

which says the funds received from outsiders are at least equal to K, the minimum required outside financing.

(4) Among all points $(\hat{a}, \hat{F}, \hat{W}_T)$ satisfying conditions (1)–(3), (α, F, W_T) gives the manager highest utility. This implies that $(\hat{a}, \hat{F}, \hat{W}_T)$ satisfy condition (3) as an equality.

to fall as he raises larger amounts of outside capital. This expansion path represents his complete opportunity set for combinations of wealth and non-pecuniary benefits given the existence of the costs of the agency relationship with the outside equity holders. Point D, where this opportunity set is tangent to an indifference curve, represents the solution which maximizes his welfare. At this point, the level of investment is I', his fractional ownership share in the firm is α', his wealth is $W + V' - I'$, and he consumes a stream of non-pecuniary benefits with current market value of F'. The gross agency costs (denoted by A) are equal to $(V^* - I^*) - (V' - I')$. Given that no monitoring is possible, I' is the socially optimal level of investment as well as the privately optimal level.

We can characterize the optimal level of investment as that point, I' which satisfies the following condition for small changes:

$$\Delta V - \Delta I + \alpha' \Delta F = 0. \tag{1}$$

$\Delta V - \Delta I$ is the change in the net market value of the firm, and $\alpha' \Delta F$ is the dollar value to the manager of the incremental fringe benefits he consumes (which cost the firm ΔF dollars).[25] Furthermore, recognizing that $V = \overline{V} - F$, where $\overline{V}$ is the value of the firm at any level of investment when $F = 0$, we can substitute into the optimum condition to get

$$(\Delta \overline{V} - \Delta I) - (1 - \alpha') \Delta F = 0 \tag{3}$$

as an alternative expression for determining the optimum level of investment.

The idealized or zero agency cost solution, I^*, is given by the condition $(\Delta \overline{V} - \Delta I) = 0$, and since ΔF is positive the actual welfare maximizing level of investment I' will be less than I^*, because $(\Delta \overline{V} - \Delta I)$ must be positive at I' if (3) is to be satisfied. Since $-\alpha'$ is the slope of the indifference curve at the optimum and therefore represents the manager's demand price for incremental non-pecuniary benefits, ΔF, we know that $\alpha' \Delta F$ is the dollar value to him of an increment of fringe benefits costing the firm ΔF dollars. The term $(1 - \alpha') \Delta F$ thus measures the dollar "loss" to the firm (and himself) of an additional ΔF dollars spent on non-pecuniary benefits. The term $\Delta \overline{V} - \Delta I$ is the gross increment in the value of the firm ignoring any changes in the consumption of non-pecuniary benefits. Thus, the manager stops increasing the size of the firm when the gross

---

[25]*Proof.* Note that the slope of the expansion path (or locus of equilibrium points) at any point is $(\Delta V - \Delta I)/\Delta F$ and at the optimum level of investment this must be equal to the slope of the manager's indifference curve between wealth and market value of fringe benefits, F. Furthermore, in the absence of monitoring, the slope of the indifference curve, $\Delta W/\Delta F$, at the equilibrium point, D, must be equal to $-\alpha'$. Thus,

$$(\Delta V - \Delta I)/\Delta F = -\alpha' \tag{2}$$

is the condition for the optimal scale of investment and this implies condition (1) holds for small changes at the optimum level of investment, I'.

increment in value is just offset by the incremental "loss" involved in the consumption of additional fringe benefits due to his declining fractional interest in the firm.[26]

2.4. The role of monitoring and bonding activities in reducing agency costs

In the above analysis we have ignored the potential for controlling the behavior of the owner–manager through monitoring and other control activities. In practice, it is usually possible by expending resources to alter the opportunity the owner–manager has for capturing non-pecuniary benefits. These methods include auditing, formal control systems, budget restrictions, and the establishment of incentive compensation systems which serve to more closely identify the manager's interests with those of the outside equity holders, etc. Fig. 3 portrays the effects of monitoring and other control activities in the simple situation portrayed in fig. 1. Figs. 1 and 3 are identical except for the curve BCE in fig. 3 which depicts a "budget constraint" derived when monitoring possibilities are taken into account. Without monitoring, and with outside equity of $(1-\alpha)$, the value of the firm will be V' and non-pecuniary expenditures F'. By incurring monitoring costs, M, the equity holders can restrict the manager's consumption of perquisites to amounts less than F'. Let $F(M, \alpha)$ denote the maximum perquisites the manager can consume for alternative levels of monitoring expenditures, M, given his ownership share α. We assume that increases in monitoring reduce F, and reduce it at a decreasing rate, i.e., $\partial F/\partial M < 0$ and $\partial^2 F/\partial M^2 > 0$.

Since the current value of expected future monitoring expenditures by the outside equity holders reduce the value of any given claim on the firm to them dollar for dollar, the outside equity holders will take this into account in determining the maximum price they will pay for any given fraction of the firm's

---

[26]Since the manager's indifference curves are negatively sloped we know that the optimum scale of the firm, point D, will occur in the region where the expansion path has negative slope, i.e., the market value of the firm will be declining and the *gross* agency costs, A, will be increasing and thus, the manager will not minimize them in making the investment decision (even though he will minimize them for any *given* level of investment). However, we define the *net* agency cost as the dollar equivalent of the welfare loss the manager experiences because of the agency relationship evaluated at $F = 0$ (the vertical distance between the intercepts on the Y axis of the two indifference curves on which points C and D lie). The optimum solution, I', does satisfy the condition that net agency costs are minimized. But this simply amounts to a restatement of the assumption that the manager maximizes his welfare.

Finally, it is possible for the solution point D to be a corner solution and in this case the value of the firm will not be declining. Such a corner solution can occur, for instance, if the manager's marginal rate of substitution between F and wealth falls to zero fast enough as we move up the expansion path, or if the investment projects are 'sufficiently' profitable. In these cases the expansion path will have a corner which lies on the maximum value budget constraint with intercept $\bar{V}(I^*)-I^*$, and the level of investment will be equal to the idealized optimum, I^*. However, the market value of the residual claims will be less than V^* because the manager's consumption of perquisites will be larger than F^*, the zero agency cost level.

equity. Therefore, given positive monitoring activity the value of the firm is given by $V = \bar{V} - F(M, \alpha) - M$ and the locus of these points for various levels of M and for a given level of α lie on the line BCE in fig. 3. The vertical difference between the $\bar{V}F$ and BCE curves is M, the current market value of the future monitoring expenditures.

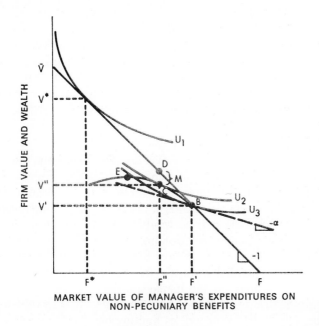

Fig. 3. The value of the firm (V) and level of non-pecuniary benefits (F) when outside equity is $(1-\alpha)$, U_1, U_2, U_3 represent owner's indifference curves between wealth and non-pecuniary benefits, and monitoring (or bonding) activities impose opportunity set BCE as the tradeoff constraint facing the owner.

If it is possible for the outside equity holders to make these monitoring expenditures and thereby to impose the reductions in the owner–manager's consumption of F, he will voluntarily enter into a contract with the outside equity holders which gives them the rights to restrict his consumption of non-pecuniary items to F''. He finds this desirable because it will cause the value of the firm to rise to V''. Given the contract, the optimal monitoring expenditure on the part of the outsiders, M, is the amount $D-C$. The entire increase in the value of the firm that accrues will be reflected in the owner's wealth, but his welfare will be increased by less than this because he forgoes some non-pecuniary benefits he previously enjoyed.

If the equity market is competitive and makes unbiased estimates of the effects of the monitoring expenditures on F and V, potential buyers will be indifferent between the following two contracts:

(i) Purchase of a share $(1-\alpha)$ of the firm at a total price of $(1-\alpha)V'$ and no rights to monitor or control the manager's consumption of perquisites.

(ii) Purchase of a share $(1-\alpha)$ of the firm at a total price of $(1-\alpha)V''$ and the right to expend resources up to an amount equal to $D-C$ which will limit the owner–manager's consumption of perquisites to F;.

Given contract (ii) the outside shareholders would find it desirable to monitor to the full rights of their contract because it will pay them to do so. However, if the equity market is competitive the total benefits (net of the monitoring costs) will be capitalized into the price of the claims. Thus, not surprisingly, the owner–manager reaps all the benefits of the opportunity to write and sell the monitoring contract.[27]

An analysis of bonding expenditures. We can also see from the analysis of fig. 3 that it makes no difference who actually makes the monitoring expenditures – the owner bears the full amount of these costs as a wealth reduction in all cases. Suppose that the owner–manager could expend resources to guarantee to the outside equity holders that he would limit his activities which cost the firm F. We call these expenditures "bonding costs", and they would take such forms as contractual guarantees to have the financial accounts audited by a public account, explicit bonding against malfeasance on the part of the manager, and contractual limitations on the manager's decision making power (which impose costs on the firm because they limit his ability to take full advantage of some profitable opportunities as well as limiting his ability to harm the stockholders while making himself better off).

If the incurrence of the bonding costs were entirely under the control of the manager and if they yielded the same opportunity set BCE for him in fig. 3, he would incur them in amount $D-C$. This would limit his consumption of

---

[27]The careful reader will note that point C will be the equilibrium point only if the contract between the manager and outside equity holders specifies with no ambiguity that they have the right to monitor to limit his consumption of perquisites to an amount no less than F''. If any ambiguity regarding these rights exists in this contract then another source of agency costs arises which is symmetrical to our original problem. If they could do so the outside equity holders would monitor to the point where the net value of *their* holdings, $(1-\alpha)V-M$, was maximized, and this would occur when $(\partial V/\partial M)(1-\alpha)-1 = 0$ which would be at some point between points C and E in fig. 3. Point E denotes the point where the value of the firm net of the monitoring costs is at a maximum, i.e. where $\partial V/\partial M-1 = 0$. But the manager would be worse off than in the zero monitoring solution if the point where $(1-\alpha)V-M$ was at a maximum were to the left of the intersection between BCE and the indifference curve U_3 passing through point B (which denotes the zero monitoring level of welfare). Thus if the manager could not eliminate enough of the ambiguity in the contract to push the equilibrium to the right of the intersection of the curve BCE with indifference curve U_3 he would not engage in any contract which allowed monitoring.

perquisites to F'' from F', and the solution is exactly the same as if the outside equity holders had performed the monitoring. The manager finds it in his interest to incur these costs as long as the net increments in his wealth which they generate (by reducing the agency costs and therefore increasing the value of the firm) are more valuable than the perquisites given up. This optimum occurs at point C in both cases under our assumption that the bonding expenditures yield the same opportunity set as the monitoring expenditures. In general, of course, it will pay the owner–manager to engage in bonding activities and to write contracts which allow monitoring as long as the marginal benefits of each are greater than their marginal cost.

Optimal scale of the firm in the presence of monitoring and bonding activities. If we allow the outside owners to engage in (costly) monitoring activities to limit the manager's expenditures on non-pecuniary benefits and allow the manager to engage in bonding activities to guarantee to the outside owners that he will limit his consumption of F we get an expansion path such as that illustrated in fig. 4 on which Z and G lie. We have assumed in drawing fig. 4 that the cost functions involved in monitoring and bonding are such that some positive levels of the activities are desirable, i.e., yield benefits greater than their cost. If this is not true the expansion path generated by the expenditure of resources on these activities would lie below ZD and no such activity would take place at any level of investment. Points Z, C, and D and the two expansion paths they lie on are identical to those portrayed in fig. 2. Points Z and C lie on the 100 percent ownership expansion path, and points Z and D lie on the fractional owner-ship, zero monitoring and bonding activity expansion path.

The path on which points Z and G lie is the one given by the locus of equilibrium points for alternative levels of investment characterized by the point labeled C in fig. 3 which denotes the optimal level of monitoring and bonding activity and resulting values of the firm and non-pecuniary benefits to the manager given a fixed level of investment. If any monitoring or bonding is cost effective the expansion path on which Z and G lie must be above the non-monitoring expansion path over some range. Furthermore, if it lies anywhere to the right of the indifference curve passing through point D (the zero monitoring–bonding solution) the final solution to the problem will involve positive amounts of monitoring and/or bonding activities. Based on the discussion above we know that as long as the contracts between the manager and outsiders are unambiguous regarding the rights of the respective parties the final solution will be at that point where the new expansion path is just tangent to the highest indifference curve. At this point the optimal level of monitoring and bonding expenditures are M'' and b''; the manager's post-investment-financing wealth is given by $W + V'' - I'' - M'' - b''$ and his non-pecuniary benefits are F''. The total gross agency costs, A, are given by $A(M'', b'', \alpha'', I'') = (V^* - I^*) - (V'' - I'' - M'' - b'')$.

2.5. Pareto optimality and agency costs in manager-operated firms

In general we expect to observe both bonding and external monitoring activities, and the incentives are such that the levels of these activities will satisfy the conditions of efficiency. They will not, however, result in the firm being run in a manner so as to maximize its value. The difference between V^*, the efficient solution under zero monitoring and bonding costs (and therefore zero agency

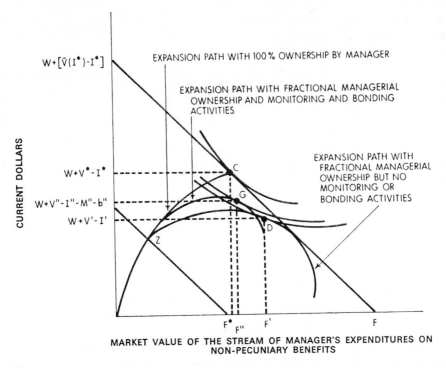

Fig. 4. Determination of optimal scale of the firm allowing for monitoring and bonding activities. Optimal monitoring costs are M'' and bonding costs are b'' and the equilibrium scale of firm, manager's wealth and consumption of non-pecuniary benefits are at point G.

costs), and V'', the value of the firm given positive monitoring costs, are the total gross agency costs defined earlier in the introduction. These are the costs of the "separation of ownership and control" which Adam Smith focused on in the passage quoted at the beginning of this paper and which Berle and Means (1932) popularized 157 years later. The solutions outlined above to our highly simplified problem imply that agency costs will be positive as long as monitoring costs are positive – which they certainly are.

The reduced value of the firm caused by the manager's consumption of perquisites outlined above is "non-optimal" or inefficient only in comparison to a world in which we could obtain compliance of the agent to the principal's wishes at zero cost or in comparison to a *hypothetical* world in which the agency costs were lower. But these costs (monitoring and bonding costs and 'residual loss) are an unavoidable result of the agency relationship. Furthermore, since they are borne entirely by the decision maker (in this case the original owner) responsible for creating the relationship he has the incentives to see that they are minimized (because he captures the benefits from their reduction). Furthermore, these agency costs will be incurred only if the benefits to the owner–manager from their creation are great enough to outweigh them. In our current example these benefits arise from the availability of profitable investments requiring capital investment in excess of the original owner's personal wealth.

In conclusion, finding that agency costs are non-zero (i.e., that there are costs associated with the separation of ownership and control in the corporation) and concluding therefrom that the agency relationship is non-optimal, wasteful or inefficient is equivalent in every sense to comparing a world in which iron ore is a scarce commodity (and therefore costly) to a world in which it is freely available at zero resource cost, and concluding that the first world is "non-optimal" – a perfect example of the fallacy criticized by Coase (1964) and what Demsetz (1969) characterizes as the "Nirvana" form of analysis.[28]

2.6. Factors affecting the size of the divergence from ideal maximization

The magnitude of the agency costs discussed above will vary from firm to firm. It will depend on the tastes of managers, the ease with which they can exercise their own preferences as opposed to value maximization in decision making, and the costs of monitoring and bonding activities.[29] The agency costs will also depend upon the cost of measuring the manager's (agent's) performance and evaluating it, the cost of devising and applying an index for compensating the manager which correlates with the owner's (principal's) welfare, and the cost of devising and enforcing specific behavioral rules or policies. Where the manager has less than a controlling interest in the firm, it will also depend upon the market for managers. Competition from other potential managers limits the costs of obtaining managerial services (including the extent to which a given manager can diverge from the idealized solution which would obtain if all monitoring and bonding costs were zero). The size of the divergence (the agency costs) will be directly related to the cost of replacing the manager. If his responsibilities require

[28]If we could establish the existence of a feasible set of alternative institutional arrangements which would yield net benefits from the reduction of these costs we could legitimately conclude the agency relationship engendered by the corporation was not Pareto optimal. However, we would then be left with the problem of explaining why these alternative institutional arrangements have not replaced the corporate form of organization.

[29]The monitoring and bonding costs will differ from firm to firm depending on such things as the inherent complexity and geographical dispersion of operations, the attractiveness of perquisites available in the firm (consider the mint), etc.

very little knowledge specialized to the firm, if it is easy to evaluate his performance, and if replacement search costs are modest, the divergence from the ideal
will be relatively small and vice versa.

The divergence will also be constrained by the market for the firm itself, i.e.,
by capital markets. Owners always have the option of selling their firm, either
as a unit or piecemeal. Owners of manager-operated firms can and do sample the
capital market from time to time. If they discover that the value of the future
earnings stream to others is higher than the value of the firm to them given that
it is to be manager-operated, they can exercise their right to sell. It is conceivable
that other owners could be more efficient at monitoring or even that a single
individual with appropriate managerial talents and with sufficiently large
personal wealth would elect to buy the firm. In this latter case the purchase by
such a single individual would completely eliminate the agency costs. If there were
a number of such potential owner–manager purchasers (all with talents and
tastes identical to the current manager) the owners would receive in the sale
price of the firm the full value of the residual claimant rights including the capital
value of the eliminated agency costs plus the value of the managerial rights.

Monopoly, competition and managerial behavior. It is frequently argued
that the existence of competition in product (and factor) markets will constrain
the behavior of managers to idealized value maximization, i.e., that monopoly
in product (or monopsony in factor) markets will permit larger divergences from
value maximization.[30] Our analysis does not support this hypothesis. The owners
of a firm with monopoly power have the same incentives to limit divergences of
the manager from value maximization (i.e., the ability to increase their wealth)
as do the owners of competitive firms. Furthermore, competition in the market
for managers will generally make it unnecessary for the owners to share rents
with the manager. The owners of a monopoly firm need only pay the supply price
for a manager.

Since the owner of a monopoly has the same wealth incentives to minimize
managerial costs as would the owner of a competitive firm, both will undertake
that level of monitoring which equates the marginal cost of monitoring to the

---

[30]'Where competitors are numerous and entry is easy, persistent departures from profit
maximizing behavior inexorably leads to extinction. Economic natural selection holds the
stage. In these circumstances, the behavior of the individual units that constitute the supply
side of the product market is essentially routine and uninteresting and economists can confi-
dently predict industry behavior without being explicitly concerned with the behavior of these
individual units.

When the conditions of competition are relaxed, however, the opportunity set of the firm is
expanded. In this case, the behavior of the firm as a distinct operating unit is of separate
interest. Both for purposes of interpreting particular behavior within the firm as well as for
predicting responses of the industry aggregate, it may be necessary to identify the factors that
influence the firm's choices within this expanded opportunity set and embed these in a formal
model.' [Williamson (1964, p. 2)]

marginal wealth increment from reduced consumption of perquisites by the manager. Thus, the existence of monopoly will not increase agency costs.

Furthermore the existence of competition in product and factor markets will not eliminate the agency costs due to managerial control problems as has often been asserted [cf. Friedman (1970)]. If my competitors all incur agency costs equal to or greater than mine I will not be eliminated from the market by their competition.

The existence and size of the agency costs depends on the nature of the monitoring costs, the tastes of managers for non-pecuniary benefits and the supply of potential managers who are capable of financing the entire venture out of their personal wealth. If monitoring costs are zero, agency costs will be zero or if there are enough 100 percent owner–managers available to own and run all the firms in an industry (competitive or not) then agency costs in that industry will also be zero.[31]

3. Some unanswered questions regarding the existence of the corporate form

3.1. The question

The analysis to this point has left us with a basic puzzle: Why, given the existence of positive costs of the agency relationship, do we find the usual corporate form of organization with widely diffuse ownership so widely prevalent? If one takes seriously much of the literature regarding the "discretionary" power held by managers of large corporations, it is difficult to understand the historical fact of enormous growth in equity in such organizations, not only in the United States, but throughout the world. Paraphrasing Alchian (1968): How does it happen that millions of individuals are willing to turn over a significant fraction of their wealth to organizations run by managers who have so little interest in their welfare? What is even more remarkable, why are they willing to make these commitments purely as residual claimants, i.e., on the anticipation that managers will operate the firm so that there will be earnings which accrue to the stockholders?

There is certainly no lack of alternative ways that individuals might invest, including entirely different forms of organizations. Even if consideration is limited to corporate organizations, there are clearly alternative ways capital might be raised, i.e., through fixed claims of various sorts, bonds, notes, mortgages, etc. Moreover, the corporate income tax seems to favor the use of fixed claims since interest is treated as a tax deductible expense. Those who assert that managers do not behave in the interest or stockholders have generally not addressed a very important question: Why, if non-manager-owned shares have

---

[31]Assuming there are no special tax benefits to ownership nor utility of ownership other than that derived from the direct wealth effects of ownership such as might be true for professional sports teams, race horse stables, firms which carry the family name, etc.

such a serious deficiency, have they not long since been driven out by fixed claims?[32]

3.2. Some alternative explanations of the ownership structure of the firm

The role of limited liability. Manne (1967) and Alchian and Demsetz (1972) argue that one of the attractive features of the corporate form vis-a-vis individual proprietorships or partnerships is the limited liability feature of equity claims in corporations. Without this provision each and every investor purchasing one or more shares of a corporation would be potentially liable to the full extent of his personal wealth for the debts of the corporation. Few individuals would find this a desirable risk to accept and the major benefits to be obtained from risk reduction through diversification would be to a large extent unobtainable. This argument, however, is incomplete since limited liability does not eliminate the basic risk, it merely shifts it. The argument must rest ultimately on transactions costs. If all stockholders of GM were liable for GM's debts, the maximum liability for an individual shareholder would be greater than it would be if his shares had limited liability. However, given that many other stockholder's also existed and that each was liable for the unpaid claims in proportion to his ownership it is highly unlikely that the maximum payment each would have to make would be large in the event of GM's bankruptcy since the total wealth of those stock-holders would also be large. However, the existence of unlimited liability would impose incentives for each shareholder to keep track of both the liabilities of GM and the wealth of the other GM owners. It is easily conceivable that the costs of so doing would, in the aggregate, be much higher than simply paying a premium in the form of higher interest rates to the creditors of GM in return for their acceptance of a contract which grants limited liability to the share-holders. The creditors would then bear the risk of any non-payment of debts in the event of GM's bankruptcy.

It is also not generally recognized that limited liability is merely a necessary condition for explaining the magnitude of the reliance on equities, not a sufficient condition. Ordinary debt also carries limited liability.[33] If limited liability is all that is required, why don't we observe large corporations, individually owned, with a tiny fraction of the capital supplied by the entrepreneur,

---

[32]Marris (1964, pp. 7–9) is the exception, although he argues that there exists some 'maximum leverage point' beyond which the chances of 'insolvency' are in some undefined sense too high.

[33]By limited liability we mean the same conditions that apply to common stock. Subordinated debt or preferred stock could be constructed which carried with it liability provisions; i.e., if the corporation's assets were insufficient at some point to pay off all prior claims (such as trade credit, accrued wages, senior debt, etc.) and if the personal resources of the 'equity' holders were also insufficient to cover these claims the holders of this 'debt' would be subject to assessments beyond the face value of their claim (assessments which might be limited or unlimited in amount).

and the rest simply borrowed[34] At first this question seems silly to many people (as does the question regarding why firms would ever issue debt or preferred stock under conditions where there are no tax benefits obtained from the treatment of interest or preferred dividend payments[35]). We have found that oftentimes this question is misinterpreted to be one regarding why firms obtain capital. The issue is not why they obtain capital, but why they obtain it through the particular forms we have observed for such long periods of time. The fact is that no well articulated answer to this question currently exists in the literature of either finance or economics.

The "irrelevance" of capital structure. In their pathbreaking article on the cost of capital, Modigliani and Miller (1958) demonstrated that in the absence of bankruptcy costs and tax subsidies on the payment of interest the value of the firm is independent of the financial structure. They later (1963) demonstrated that the existence of tax subsidies on interest payments would cause the value of the firm to rise with the amount of debt financing by the amount of the capitalized value of the tax subsidy. But this line of argument implies that the firm should be financed almost entirely with debt. Realizing the inconsistence with observed behavior Modigliani and Miller (1963, p. 442) comment:

> "it may be useful to remind readers once again that the existence of a tax advantage for debt financing . . . does not necessarily mean that corporations should at all times seek to use the maximum amount of debt in their capital structures. . . . there are as we pointed out, limitations imposed by lenders . . . as well as many other dimensions (and kinds of costs) in real-world problems of financial strategy which are not fully comprehended within the framework of static equilibrium models, either our own or those of the traditional variety. These additional considerations, which are typically grouped under the rubric of 'the need for preserving flexibility',

---

[34]Alchian–Demsetz (1972, p. 709) argue that one can explain the existence of both bonds and stock in the ownership structure of firms as the result of differing expectations regarding the outcomes to the firm. They argue that bonds are created and sold to 'pessimists' and stocks with a residual claim with no upper bound are sold to 'optimists'.

As long as capital markets are perfect with no taxes or transactions costs and individual investors can issue claims on distributions of outcomes on the same terms as firms, such actions on the part of firms cannot affect their values. The reason is simple. Suppose such 'pessimists' did exist and yet the firm issues only equity claims. The demand for those equity claims would reflect the fact that the individual purchaser could on his own account issue 'bonds' with a limited and prior claim on the distribution of outcomes on the equity which is exactly the same as that which the firm could issue. Similarly, investors could easily unlever any position by simply buying a proportional claim on both the bonds and stocks of a levered firm. Therefore, a levered firm could not sell at a different price than an unlevered firm solely because of the existence of such differential expectations. See Fama and Miller (1972, ch. 4) for an excellent exposition of these issues.

[35]Corporations did use both prior to the institution of the corporate income tax in the U.S. and preferred dividends have, with minor exceptions, never been tax deductible.

will normally imply the maintenance by the corporation of a substantial reserve of untapped borrowing power."

Modigliani and Miller are essentially left without a theory of the determination of the optimal capital structure, and Fama and Miller (1972, p. 173) commenting on the same issue reiterate this conclusion:

"And we must admit that at this point there is little in the way of convincing research, either theoretical or empirical, that explains the amounts of debt that firms do decide to have in their capital structure."

The Modigliani–Miller theorem is based on the assumption that the probability distribution of the cash flows to the firm is independent of the capital structure. It is now recognized that the existence of positive costs associated with bankruptcy and the presence of tax subsidies on corporate interest payments will invalidate this irrelevance theorem precisely because the probability distribution of future cash flows changes as the probability of the incurrence of the bankruptcy costs changes, i.e., as the ratio of debt to equity rises. We believe the existence of agency costs provide stronger reasons for arguing that the probability distribution of future cash flows is *not* independent of the capital or ownership structure.

While the introduction of bankruptcy costs in the presence of tax subsidies leads to a theory which defines an optimal capital structure,[36] we argue that this theory is seriously incomplete since it implies that no debt should ever be used in the absence of tax subsidies if bankruptcy costs are positive. Since we know debt was commonly used prior to the existence of the current tax subsidies on interest payments this theory does not capture what must be some important determinants of the corporate capital structure.

In addition, neither bankruptcy costs nor the existence of tax subsidies can explain the use of preferred stock or warrnts which have no tax advantages, and there is no theory which tells us anything about what determines the fraction of equity claims held by insiders as opposed to outsiders which our analysis in section 2 indicates is so important. We return to these issues later after analyzing in detail the factors affecting the agency costs associated with debt.

4. The agency costs of debt

In general if the agency costs engendered by the existence of outside owners are positive it will pay the absentee owner (i.e., shareholders) to sell out to an owner–manager who can avoid these costs.[37] This could be accomplished in principle by having the manager become the sole equity holder by repurchasing

---

[36]See Kraus and Litzenberger (1972) and Lloyd-Davies (1975).

[37]And if there is competitive bidding for the firm from potential owner–managers the absentee owner will capture the capitalized value of these agency costs.

all of the outside equity claims with funds obtained through the issuance of limited liability debt claims and the use of his own personal wealth. This single-owner corporation would not suffer the agency costs associated with outside equity. Therefore there must be some compelling reasons why we find the diffuse-owner corporate firm financed by equity claims so prevalent as an organizational form.

An ingenious entrepreneur eager to expand, has open to him the opportunity to design a whole hierarchy of fixed claims on assets and earnings, with premiums paid for different levels of risk.[38] Why don't we observe large corporations individually owned with a tiny fraction of the capital supplied by the entre-preneur in return for 100 percent of the equity and the rest simply borrowed? We believe there are a number of reasons: (1) the incentive effects associated with highly leveraged firms, (2) the monitoring costs these incentive effects engender, and (3) bankruptcy costs. Furthermore, all of these costs are simply particular aspects of the agency costs associated with the existence of debt claims on the firm.

4.1. The incentive effects associated with debt

We don't find many large firms financed almost entirely with debt type claims (i.e., non-residual claims) because of the effect such a financial structure would have on the owner–manager's behavior. Potential creditors will not loan $100,000,000 to a firm in which the entrepreneur has an investment of $10,000. With that financial structure the owner–manager will have a strong incentive to engage in activities (investments) which promise very high payoffs if successful even if they have a very low probability of success. If they turn out well, he captures most of the gains, if they turn out badly, the creditors bear most of the costs.[39]

To illustrate the incentive effects associated with the existence of debt and to provide a framework within which we can discuss the effects of monitoring and bonding costs, wealth transfers, and the incidence of agency costs, we again consider a simple situation. Assume we have a manager-owned firm with no debt

[38]The spectrum of claims which firms can issue is far more diverse than is suggested by our two-way classification – fixed vs. residual. There are convertible bonds, equipment trust certificates, debentures, revenue bonds, warrants, etc. Different bond issues can contain different subordination provisions with respect to assets and interest. They can be callable or non-callable. Preferred stocks can be 'preferred' in a variety of dimensions and contain a variety of subordination stipulations. In the abstract, we can imagine firms issuing claims contingent on a literally infinite variety of states of the world such as those considered in the literature on the time–state-preference models of Arrow (1964), Debreu (1959) and Hirshleifer (1970).

[39]An apt analogy is the way one would play poker on money borrowed at a fixed interest rate, with one's own liability limited to some very small stake. Fama and Miller (1972, pp. 179–180) also discuss and provide a numerical example of an investment decision which illustrates very nicley the potential inconsistency between the interests of bondholders and stockholders.

outstanding in a world in which there are no taxes. The firm has the opportunity to take one of two mutually exclusive equal cost investment opportunities, each of which yields a random payoff, $\tilde{X}_j$, T periods in the future ($j = 1, 2$). Production and monitoring activities take place continuously between time 0 and time T, and markets in which the claims on the firm can be traded are open continuously over this period. After time T the firm has no productive activities so the payoff $\tilde{X}_j$ includes the distribution of all remaining assets. For simplicity, we assume that the two distributions are log-normally distributed and have the same expected total payoff, $E(\tilde{X})$, where $\tilde{X}$ is defined as the logarithm of the final payoff. The distributions differ only by their variances with $\sigma_1^2 < \sigma_2^2$. The systematic or covariance risk of each of the distributions, β_j, in the Sharpe (1964) – Lintner (1965) capital asset pricing model, is assumed to be identical. Assuming that asset prices are determined according to the capital asset pricing model, the preceding assumptions imply that the total market value of each of these distributions is identical, and we represent this value by V.

If the owner–manager has the right to decide which investment program to take, and if after he decides this he has the opportunity to sell part or all of his claims on the outcomes in the form of either debt or equity, he will be indifferent between the two investments.[40]

However, if the owner has the opportunity to *first* issue debt, then to decide which of the investments to take, and then to sell all or part of his remaining equity claim on the market, he will not be indifferent between the two investments. The reason is that by promising to take the low variance project, selling bonds and then taking the high variance project he can transfer wealth from the (naive) bondholders to himself as equity holder.

Let X^* be the amount of the "fixed" claim in the form of a non-coupon bearing bond sold to the bondholders such that the total payoff to them, R_j ($j = 1, 2$, denotes the distribution the manager chooses), is

$$
\begin{aligned}
R_j &= X^*, \quad \text{if} \quad \tilde{X}_j \geq X^*, \\
&= X_j, \quad \text{if} \quad \tilde{X}_j \leq X^*.
\end{aligned}
$$

Let B_1 be the current market value of bondholder claims if investment 1 is taken, and let B_2 be the current market value of bondholders claims if investment 2 is taken. Since in this example the total value of the firm, V, is independent of the investment choice and also of the financing decision we can use the Black–Scholes (1973) option pricing model to determine the values of the debt, B_j, and equity, S_j, under each of the choices.[41]

---

[40]The portfolio diversification issues facing the owner–manager are brought into the analysis in section 5 below.

[41]See Smith (1976) for a review of this option pricing literature and its applications and Galai and Masulis (1976) who apply the option pricing model to mergers, and corporate investment decisions.

Black–Scholes derive the solution for the value of a European call option (one which can be exercised only at the maturity date) and argue that the resulting option pricing equation can be used to determine the value of the equity claim on a levered firm. That is the stockholders in such a firm can be viewed as holding a European call option on the total value of the firm with exercise price equal to X^* (the face value of the debt), exercisable at the maturity date of the debt issue. More simply, the stockholders have the right to buy the firm back from the bondholders for a price of X^* at time T. Merton (1973, 1974) shows that as the variance of the outcome distribution rises the value of the stock (i.e., call option) rises, and since our two distributions differ only in their variances, $\sigma_2^2 < \sigma_1^2$, the equity value S_1 is less than S_2. This implies $B_1 > B_2$, since $B_1 = V - S_1$ and $B_2 = V - S_2$.

Now if the owner–manager could sell bonds with face value X^* under the conditions that the potential bondholders believed this to be a claim on distribution 1, he would receive a price of B_1. After selling the bonds, his equity interest in distribution 1 would have value S_1. But we know S_2 is greater than S_1 and thus the manager can make himself better off by changing the investment to take the higher variance distribution 2, thereby redistributing wealth from the bondholders to himself. All this assumes of course that the bondholders could not prevent him from changing the investment program. *If the bondholders cannot do so, and if they perceive that the manager has the opportunity to take distribution 2 they will pay the manager only B_2 for the claim X^*, realizing that his maximizing behavior will lead him to choose distribution 2.* In this event there is no redistribution of wealth between bondholders and stockholders (and in general with rational expectations there never will be) and no welfare loss. It is easy to construct a case, however, in which these incentive effects do generate real costs.

Let cash flow distribution 2 in the previous example have an expected value, $E(X_2)$, which is lower than that of distribution 1. Then we know that $V_1 > V_2$, and if ΔV, which is given by

$$\Delta V = V_1 - V_2 = (S_1 - S_2) + (B_1 - B_2),$$

is sufficiently small relative to the reduction in the value of the bonds the value of the stock will increase.[42] Rearranging the expression for ΔV we see that the

[42]While we used the option pricing model above to motivate the discussion and provide some intuitive understanding of the incentives facing the equity holders, the option pricing solutions of Black and Scholes (1973) do not apply when incentive effects cause V to be a function of the debt/equity ratio as it is in general and in this example. Long (1974) points out this difficulty with respect to the usefulness of the model in the context of tax subsidies on interest and bankruptcy cost. The results of Merton (1974) and Galai and Masulis (1976) must be interpreted with care since the solutions are strictly incorrect in the context of tax subsidies and/or agency costs.

difference between the equity values for the two investments is given by

$$S_2 - S_1 = (B_1 - B_2) - (V_1 - V_2),$$

and the first term on the RHS, $B_1 - B_2$, is the amount of wealth "transferred" from the bondholders and $V_1 - V_2$ is the reduction in overall firm value. Since we know $B_1 > B_2$, $S_2 - S_1$ can be positive even though the reduction in the value of the firm, $V_1 - V_2$, is positive.[43] Again, the bondholders will not actually lose as long as they accurately perceive the motivation of the equity owning manager and his opportunity to take project 2. They will presume he will take investment 2, and hence will pay no more than B_2 for the bonds when they are issued.

In this simple example the reduced value of the firm, $V_1 - V_2$, is the agency cost engendered by the issuance of debt[44] and it is borne by the owner–manager. If he could finance the project out of his personal wealth, he would clearly choose project 1 since its investment outlay was assumed equal to that of project 2 and its market value, V_1, was greater. This wealth loss, $V_1 - V_2$, is the "residual loss" portion of what we have defined as agency costs and it is generated by the cooperation required to raise the funds to make the investment. Another important part of the agency costs are monitoring and bonding costs and we now consider their role.

4.2. The role of monitoring and bonding costs

In principle it would be possible for the bondholders, by the inclusion of various covenants in the indenture provisions, to limit the managerial behavior

[43]The numerical example of Fama and Miller (1972, pp. 179–180) is a close representation of this case in a two-period state model. However, they go on to make the following statement on p. 180:

> 'From a practical viewpoint, however, situations of potential conflict between bond-holders and shareholders in the application of the market value rule are probably unimportant. In general, investment opportunities that increase a firm's market value by more than their cost both increase the value of the firm's shares and strengthen the firm's future ability to meet its current bond commitments.'

This first issue regarding the importance of the conflict of interest between bondholders and stockholders is an empirical one, and the last statement is incomplete – in some circumstances the equity holders could benefit from projects whose net effect was to reduce the total value of the firm as they and we have illustrated. The issue cannot be brushed aside so easily.

[44]Myers (1975) points out another serious incentive effect on managerial decisions of the existence of debt which does not occur in our simple single decision world. He shows that if the firm has the option to take future investment opportunities the existence of debt which matures after the options must be taken will cause the firm (using an equity value maximizing investment rule) to refuse to take some otherwise profitable projects because they would benefit only the bondholders and not the equity holders. This will (in the absence of tax subsidies to debt) cause the value of the firm to fall. Thus (although he doesn't use the term) these incentive effects also contribute to the agency costs of debt in a manner perfectly consistent with the examples discussed in the text.

which results in reductions in the value of the bonds. Provisions which impose constraints on management's decisions regarding such things as dividends, future debt issues,[45] and maintenance of working capital are not uncommon in bond issues.[46] To completely protect the bondholders from the incentive effects, these provisions would have to be incredibly detailed and cover most operating aspects of the enterprise including limitations on the riskiness of the projects undertaken. The costs involved in writing such provisions, the costs of enforcing them and the reduced profitability of the firm (induced because the covenants occasionally limit management's ability to take optimal actions on certain issues) would likely be non-trivial. In fact, since management is a continuous decision making process it will be almost impossible to completely specify such conditions without having the bondholders actually perform the management function. All costs associated with such covenants are what we mean by monitoring costs.

The bondholders will have incentives to engage in the writing of such covenants and in monitoring the actions of the manager to the point where the "nominal" marginal cost to them of such activities is just equal to the marginal benefits they perceive from engaging in them. We use the word nominal here because debtholders will not in fact bear these costs. As long as they recognize their existence, they will take them into account in deciding the price they will pay for any given debt claim,[47] and therefore the seller of the claim (the owner) will bear the costs just as in the equity case discussed in section 2.

In addition the manager has incentives to take into account the costs imposed on the firm by covenants in the debt agreement which directly affect the future cash flows of the firm since they reduce the market value of his claims. Because both the external and internal monitoring costs are imposed on the owner–manager it is in his interest to see that the monitoring is performed in the lowest cost way. Suppose, for example, that the bondholders (or outside equity holders) would find it worthwhile to produce detailed financial statements such as those contained in the usual published accounting reports as a means of monitoring the manager. If the manager himself can produce such information at lower costs than they (perhaps because he is already collecting much of the data they desire for his own internal decision making purposes), it would pay him to agree in advance to incur the cost of providing such reports and to have their

[45]Black–Scholes (1973) discuss ways in which dividend and future financing policy can redistribute wealth between classes of claimants on the firm.

[46]Black, Miller and Posner (1974) discuss many of these issues with particular reference to the government regulation of bank holding companies.

[47]In other words, these costs will be taken into account in determing the yield to maturity on the issue. For an examination of the effects of such enforcement costs on the nominal interest rates in the consumer small loan market, see Benston (1977).

accuracy testified to by an independent outside auditor. This is an example of what we refer to as bonding costs.[48,49]

4.3. Bankruptcy and reorganization costs

We argue in section 5 that as the debt in the capital structure increases beyond some point the marginal agency costs of debt begin to dominate the marginal

[48]To illustrate the fact that it will sometimes pay the manager to incur 'bonding' costs to guarantee the bondholders that he will not deviate from his promised behavior let us suppose that for an expenditure of b of the firm's resources he can guarantee that project 1 will be chosen. If he spends these resources and takes project 1 the value of the firm will be $V_1 - b$ and clearly as long as $(V_1 - b) > V_2$, or alternatively $(V_1 - V_2) > b$ he will be better off, since his wealth will be equal to the value of the firm minus the required investment, I (which we assumed for simplicity to be identical for the two projects).

On the other hand, to prove that the owner–manager prefers the lowest cost solution to the conflict let us assume he can write a covenant into the bond issue which will allow the bondholders to prevent him from taking project 2, if they incur monitoring costs of m, where $m < b$. If he does this his wealth will be higher by the amount $b - m$. To see this note that if the bond market is competitive and makes unbiased estimates, potential bondholders will be indifferent between:

  (i) a claim X^* with no covenant (and no guarantees from management) at a price of B_2,
 (ii) a claim X^* with no covenant (and guarantees from management, through bonding expenditures by the firm of b, that project 1 will be taken) at a price of B_1, and
(iii) a claim X^* with a covenant and the opportunity to spend m on monitoring (to guarantee project 1 will be taken) at a price of $B_1 - m$.

The bondholders will realize that (i) represents in fact a claim on project 2 and that (ii) and (iii) represent a claim on project 1 and are thus indifferent between the three options at the specified prices. The owner–manager, however, will not be indifferent between incurring the bonding costs, b, directly, or including the covenant in the bond identure and letting the bondholders spend m to guarantee that he take project 1. His wealth in the two cases will be given by the value of his equity plus the proceeds of the bond issue less the required investment, and if $m < b < V_1 - V_2$, then his post-investment-financing wealth, W, for the three options will be such that $W_t < W_{tt} < W_{ttt}$. Therefore, since it would increase his wealth, he would voluntarily include the covenant in the bond issue and let the bondholders monitor.

[49]We mention, without going into the problem in detail, that similar to the case in which the outside equity holders are allowed to monitor the manager–owner, the agency relationship between the bondholders and stockholders has a symmetry if the rights of the bondholders to limit actions of the manager are not perfectly spelled out. Suppose the bondholders, by spending sufficiently large amounts of resources, could force management to take actions which would transfer wealth from the equity holder to the bondholders (by taking sufficiently less risky projects). One can easily construct situations where such actions could make the bondholders better off, hurt the equity holders and actually lower the total value of the firm. Given the nature of the debt contract the original owner-manager might maximize his wealth in such a situation by selling off the equity and keeping the bonds as his 'owner's' interest. If the nature of the bond contract is given, this may well be an inefficient solution since the total agency costs (i.e., the sum of monitoring and value loss) could easily be higher than the alternative solution. However, if the owner–manager could strictly limit the rights of the bondholders (perhaps by inclusion of a provision which expressly reserves all rights not specifically granted to the bondholder for the equity holder), he would find it in his interest to establish the efficient contractual arrangement since by minimizing the agency costs he would be maximizing his wealth. These issues involve the fundamental nature of contracts and for now we simply assume that the 'bondholders' rights are strictly limited and unambiguous and all rights not specifically granted them are reserved for the 'stockholders'; a situation descriptive of actual institutional arrangements. This allows us to avoid the incentive effects associated with 'bondholders' potentially exploiting 'stockholders'.

agency costs of outside equity and the result of this is the generally observed phenomenon of the simultaneous use of both debt snd outside equity. Before considering these issues, however, we consider here the third major component of the agency costs of debt which helps to explain why debt doesn't completely dominate capital structures – the existence of bankruptcy and reorganization costs.

It is important to emphasize that bankruptcy and liquidation are very different events. The legal definition of bankruptcy is difficult to specify precisely. In general, it occurs when the firm cannot meet a current payment on a debt obligation,[50] or one or more of the other indenture provisions providing for bankruptcy is violated by the firm. In this event the stockholders have lost all claims on the firm,[51] and the remaining loss, the difference between the face value of the fixed claims and the market value of the firm, is borne by the debtholders. Liquidation of the firm's assets will occur only if the market value of the future cash flows generated by the firm is less than the opportunity cost of the assets, i.e., the sum of the values which could be realized if the assets were sold piecemeal.

If there were no costs associated with the event called bankruptcy the total market value of the firm would not be affected by increasing the probability of its incurrence. However, it is costly, if not impossible, to write contracts representing claims on a firm which clearly delineate the rights of holders for all possible contingencies. Thus even if there were no adverse incentive effects in expanding fixed claims relative to equity in a firm, the use of such fixed claims would be constrained by the costs inherent in defining and enforcing those claims. Firms incur obligations daily to suppliers, to employees, to different classes of investors, etc. So long as the firm is prospering, the adjudication of claims is seldom a problem. When the firm has difficulty meeting some of its obligations, however, the issue of the priority of those claims can pose serious problems. This is most obvious in the extreme case where the firm is forced into bankruptcy. If bankruptcy were costless, the reorganization would be accompanied by an adjustment of the claims of various parties and the business, could, if that proved to be in the interest of the claimants, simply go on (although perhaps under new management).[52]

[50]If the firm were allowed to sell assets to meet a current debt obligation, bankruptcy would occur when the total market value of the future cash flows expected to be generated by the firm is less than the value of a current payment on a debt obligation. Many bond indentures do not, however, allow for the sale of assets to meet debt obligations.

[51]We have been told that while this is true in principle, the actual behavior of the courts appears to frequently involve the provision of some settlement to the common stockholders even when the assets of the company are not sufficient to cover the claims of the creditors.

[52]If under bankruptcy the bondholders have the right to fire the management, the management will have some incentives to avoid taking actions which increase the probability of this event (even if it is in the best interest of the equity holders) if they (the management) are earning rents or if they have human capital specialized to this firm or if they face large adjustment costs in finding new employment. A detailed examination of this issue involves the value of the control rights (the rights to hire and fire the manager) and we leave it to a subsequent paper.

In practice, bankruptcy is not costless, but generally involves an adjudication process which itself consumes a fraction of the remaining value of the assets of the firm. Thus the cost of bankruptcy will be of concern to potential buyers of fixed claims in the firm since their existence will reduce the payoffs to them in the event of bankruptcy. These are examples of the agency costs of cooperative efforts among individuals (although in this case perhaps "non-cooperative" would be a better term). The price buyers will be willing to pay for fixed claims will thus be inversely related to the probability of the incurrence of these costs i.e., to the probability of bankruptcy. Using a variant of the argument employed above for monitoring costs, it can be shown that the total value of the firm will fall, and the owner–manager equity holder will bear the entire wealth effect of the bankruptcy costs as long as potential bondholders make unbiased estimates of their magnitude at the time they initially purchase bonds.[53]

Empirical studies of the magnitude of bankruptcy costs are almost non-existent. Warner (1975) in a study of 11 railroad bankruptcies between 1930 and 1955 estimates the average costs of bankruptcy[54] as a fraction of the value of the firm three years prior to bankruptcy to be 2.5% (with a range of 0.4% to 5.9%). The average dollar costs were $1.88 million. Both of these measures seem remarkably small and are consistent with our belief that bankruptcy costs themselves are unlikely to be the major determinant of corporate capital structures. It is also interesting to note that the annual amount of defaulted funds has fallen significantly since 1940. [See Atkinson (1967).] One possible explanation for this phenomena is that firms are using mergers to avoid the costs of bankruptcy. This hypothesis seems even more reasonable, if, as is frequently the case, reorganization costs represent only a fraction of the costs associated with bankruptcy.

In general the revenues or the operating costs of the firm are not independent of the probability of bankruptcy and thus the capital structure of the firm. As the probability of bankruptcy increases, both the operating costs and the revenues of the firm are adversely affected, and some of these costs can be avoided by merger. For example, a firm with a high probability of bankruptcy will also find that it must pay higher salaries to induce executives to accept the higher risk of unemployment. Furthermore, in certain kinds of durable goods industries the demand function for the firm's product will not be independent of the probability of bankruptcy. The computer industry is a good example. There, the buyer's welfare is dependent to a significant extent on the ability to maintain the equipment, and on continuous hardware and software development. Furthermore, the owner of a large computer often receives benefits from the software

---

[53]Kraus and Litzenberger (1972) and Lloyd-Davies (1975) demonstrate that the total value of the firm will be reduced by these costs.

[54]These include only payments to all parties for legal fees, professional services, trustees' fees and filing fees. They do not include the costs of management time or changes in cash flows due to shifts in the firm's demand or cost functions discussed below.

developments of other users. Thus if the manufacturer leaves the business or loses his software support and development experts because of financial difficulties, the value of the equipment to his users will decline. The buyers of such services have a continuing interest in the manufacturer's viability not unlike that of a bondholder, except that their benefits come in the form of continuing services at lower cost rather than principle and interest payments. Service facilities and spare parts fur automobiles and machinery are other examples.

In summary then the agency costs associated with debt[55] consist of:

(1) the opportunity wealth loss caused by the impact of debt on the investment decisions of the firm,
(2) the monitoring and bonding expenditures by the bondholders and the owner–manager (i.e., the firm),
(3) the bankruptcy and reorganization costs.

4.4. Why are the agency costs of debt incurred?

We have argued that the owner–manager bears the entire wealth effects of the agency costs of debt and he captures the gains from reducing them. Thus, the agency costs associated with debt discussed above will tend, in the absence of other mitigating factors, to discourage the use of corporate debt. What are the factors that encourage its use?

One factor is the tax subsidy on interest payments. (This will not explain preferred stock where dividends are not tax deductible.)[56] Modigliani and Miller (1963) originally demonstrated that the use of riskless perpetual debt will increase the total value of the firm (ignoring the agency costs) by an amount equal to τB, where τ is the marginal and average corporate tax rate and B is the market value of the debt. Fama and Miller (1972, ch. 4) demonstrate that for the case of risky debt the value of the firm will increase by the market value of the (uncertain) tax subsidy on the interest payments. Again, these gains will accrue entirely to

[55]Which, incidentally, exist only when the debt has some probability of default.

[56]Our theory is capable of explaining why in the absence of the tax subsidy on interest payments, we would expect to find firms using both debt and preferred stocks – a problem which has long puzzled at least one of the authors. If preferred stock has all the characteristics of debt except for the fact that its holders cannot put the firm into bankruptcy in the event of nonpayment of the preferred dividends, then the agency costs associated with the issuance of preferred stock will be lower than those associated with debt by the present value of the bankruptcy costs.

However, these lower agency costs of preferred stock exist only over some range if as the amount of such stock rises the incentive effects caused by their existence impose value reductions which are larger than that caused by debt (including the bankruptcy costs of debt). There are two reasons for this. First, the equity holder's claims can be eliminated by the debtholders in the event of bankruptcy, and second, the debtholders have the right to fire the management in the event of bankruptcy. Both of these will tend to become more important as an advantage to the issuance of debt as we compare situations with large amounts of preferred stock to equivalent situations with large amounts of debt because they will tend to reduce the incentive effects of large amounts of preferred stock.

the equity and will provide an incentive to utilize debt to the point where the marginal wealth benefits of the tax subsidy are just equal to the marginal wealth effects of the agency costs discussed above.

However, even in the absence of these tax benefits, debt would be utilized if the ability to exploit potentially profitable investment opportunities is limited by the resources of the owner. If the owner of a project cannot raise capital he will suffer an opportunity loss represented by the increment in value offered to him by the additional investment opportunities. Thus even though he will bear the agency costs from selling debt, he will find it desirable to incur them to obtain additional capital as long as the marginal wealth increments from the new investments projects are greater than the marginal agency costs of debt, and these agency costs are in turn less than those caused by the sale of additional equity discussed in section 2. Furthermore, this solution is optimal from the social viewpoint. However, in the absence of tax subsidies on debt these projects must be unique to this firm[57] or they would be taken by other competitive entrepreneurs (perhaps new ones) who possessed the requisite personal wealth to fully finance the projects[58] and therefore able to avoid the existence of debt or outside equity.

5. A theory of the corporate ownership structure

In the previous sections we discussed the nature of agency costs associated with outside claims on the firm – both debt and equity. Our purpose here is to integrate these concepts into the beginnings of a theory of the corporate ownership structure. We use the term "ownership structure" rather than "capital structure" to highlight the fact that the crucial variables to be determined are not just the relative amounts of debt and equity but also the fraction of the equity held by the manager. Thus, for a given size firm we want a theory to determine three variables:[59]

[57]One other conditions also has to hold to justify the incurrence of the costs associated with the use of debt or outside equity in our firm. If there are other individuals in the economy who have sufficiently large amounts of personal capital to finance the entire firm, our capital constrained owner can realize the full capital value of his current and prospective projects and avoid the agency costs by simply selling the firm (i.e. the, right to take these projects) to one of these individuals. He will then avoid the wealth losses associated with the agency costs caused by the sale of debt or outside equity. If no such individuals exist, it will pay him (and society) to obtain the additional capital in the debt market. This implies, incidentally, that it is somewhat misleading to speak of the owner–manager as the individual who bears the agency costs. One could argue that it is the project which bears the costs since, if it is not sufficiently profitable to cover all the costs (including the agency costs), it will not be taken. We continue to speak of the owner–manager bearing these costs to emphasize the more correct and important point that he has the incentive to reduce them because, if he does, his wealth will be increased.

[58]We continue to ignore for the moment the additional complicating factor involved with the portfolio decisions of the owner, and the implied acceptance of potentially diversifiable risk by such 100% owners in this example.

[59]We continue to ignore such instruments as convertible bonds and warrants.

S_i :   inside equity (held by the manager),
S_o :   outside equity (held by anyone outside of the firm),
B :   debt (held by anyone outside of the firm).

The total market value of the equity is $S = S_i + S_o$, and the total market value of the firm is $V = S + B$. In addition, we also wish to have a theory which determines the optimal size of the firm, i.e., its level of investment.

5.1. Determination of the optimal ratio of outside equity to debt

Consider first the determination of the optimal ratio of outside equity to debt, S_o/B. To do this let us hold the size of the firm constant. V, the actual value of the firm for a given size, will depend on the agency costs incurred, hence we use as our index of size V^*, the value of the firm at a given scale when agency costs are zero. For the moment we also hold the amount of outside financing $(B + S_o)$, constant. Given that a specified amount of financing $(B + S_o)$ is to be obtained externally our problem is to determine the optimal fraction $E^* \equiv S_o^*/(B + S_o)$ to be financed with equity.

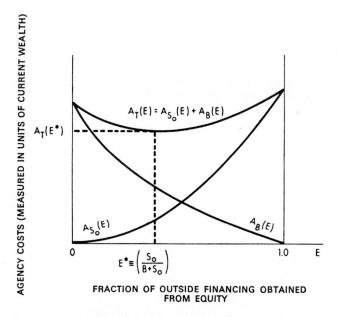

Fig. 5. Total agency costs, $A_T(E)$, as a function of the ratio of outside equity, to total outside financing, $E \equiv S_o/(B + S_o)$, for a given firm size V^* and given total amounts of outside financing $(B + S_o)$. $A_{So}(E) \equiv$ agency costs associated with outside equity, $A_B(E) \equiv$ agency costs associated with debt, B. $A_T(E^*) =$ minimum total agency costs at optimal fraction of outside financing E^*.

We argued above that: (1) as long as capital markets are efficient (i.e., characterized by rational expectations) the prices of assets such as debt and outside equity will reflect unbiased estimates of the monitoring costs and redistributions which the agency relationship will engender, and (2) the selling owner–manager will bear these agency costs. Thus from the owner–manager's standpoint the optimal proportion of outside funds to be obtained from equity (versus debt) *for a given level of internal equity* is that E which results in minimum total agency costs.

Fig. 5 presents a breakdown of the agency costs into two separate components: Define $A_{S_o}(E)$ as the total agency costs (a function of E) associated with the 'exploitation' of the outside equity holders by the owner–manager, and $A_B(E)$ as the total agency costs associated with the presence of debt in the ownership structure. $A_T(E) = A_{S_o}(E) + A_B(E)$ is the total agency cost.

Consider the function $A_{S_o}(E)$. When $E \equiv S_o/(B + S_o)$ is zero, i.e., when there is no outside equity, the manager's incentives to exploit the outside equity is at a minimum (zero) since the changes in the value of the *total* equity are equal to the changes in *his* equity.[60] As E increases to 100 percent his incentives to exploit the outside equity holders increase and hence the agency costs $A_{S_o}(E)$ increase.

The agency costs associated with the existence of debt, $A_B(E)$ are composed mainly of the value reductions in the firm and monitoring costs caused by the manager's incentive to reallocate wealth from the bondholders to himself by increasing the value of his equity claim. They are at a maximum where all outside funds are obtained from debt, i.e., where $S_o = E = 0$. As the amount of debt declines to zero these costs also go to zero because as E goes to 1, his incentive to reallocate wealth from the bondholders to himself falls. These incentives fall for two reasons: (1) the total amount of debt falls, and therefore it is more difficult to reallocate any given amount away from the debtholders, and (2) his share of any reallocation which is accomplished is falling since S_o is rising and therefore $S_i/(S_o + S_i)$, his share of the total equity, is falling.

The curve $A_T(E)$ represents the sum of the agency costs from various combinations of outside equity and debt financing, and as long as $A_{S_o}(E)$ and $A_B(E)$ are

[60]Note, however, that even when outsiders own none of the equity the stockholder–manager still has some incentives to engage in activities which yield him non-pecuniary benefits but reduce the value of the firm by more than he personally values the benefits if there is any risky debt outstanding. Any such actions he takes which reduce the value of the firm, V, tend to reduce the value of the bonds as well as the value of the equity. Although the option pricing model does not in general apply exactly to the problem of valuing the debt and equity of the firm, it can be useful in obtaining some qualitative insights into matters such as this. In the option pricing model $\partial S/\partial V$ indicates the rate at which the stock value changes per dollar change in the value of the firm (and similarly for $\partial B/\partial V$). Both of these terms are less than unity [cf. Black and Scholes (1973)]. Therefore, any action of the manager which reduces the value of the firm, V, tends to reduce the value of both the stock and the bonds, and the larger is the total debt/equity ratio the smaller is the impact of any given change in V on the value of the equity, and therefore, the lower is the cost to him of consuming non-pecuniary benefits.

as we have drawn them the minimum total agency cost for given size firm and outside financing will occur at some point such as $A_T(E^*)$ with a mixture of both debt and equity.[61]

A caveat. Before proceeding further we point out that the issue regarding the exact shapes of the functions drawn in fig. 5 and several others discussed below is essentially an open question at this time. In the end the shape of these functions is a question of fact and can only be settled by empirical evidence. We outline some a priori arguments which we believe lead to some plausible hypotheses about the behavior of the system, but confess that we are far from understanding the many conceptual subtleties of the problem. We are fairly confident of our arguments regarding the signs of the first derivatives of the functions, but the second derivatives are also important to the final solution and much more work (both theoretical and empirical) is required before we can have much confidence regarding these parameters. We anticipate the work of others as well as our own to cast more light on these issues. Moreover, we suspect the results of such efforts will generate revisions to the details of what follows. We believe it is worthwhile to delineate the overall framework in order to demonstrate, if only in a simplified fashion, how the major pieces of the puzzle fit together into a cohesive structure.

5.2. Effects of the scale of outside financing

In order to investigate the effects of increasing the amount of outside financing, $B+S_o$, and therefore reducing the amount of equity held by the manager, S_i, we continue to hold the scale of the firm, V^*, constant. Fig. 6 presents a plot of the agency cost functions, $A_{S_o}(E)$, $A_B(E)$ and $A_T(E) = A_{S_o}(E)+A_B(E)$, for two different levels of outside financing. Define an index of the amount of outside financing to be

$$K = (B+S_o)/V^*,$$

and consider two different possible levels of outside financing K_o and K_1 for a given scale of the firm such that $K_o < K_1$.

As the amount of outside equity increases, the owner's fractional claim on the firm, α, falls. He will be induced thereby to take additional non-pecuniary benefits out of the firm because his share of the cost falls. This also increases the marginal benefits from monitoring activities and therefore will tend to increase the optimal level of monitoring. Both of these factors will cause the locus of agency costs $A_{S_o}(E; K)$ to shift upward as the fraction of outside financing, K,

---

[61]This occurs, of course, not at the intersection of $A_{S_o}(E)$ and $A_B(E)$, but at the point where the absolute value of the slopes of the functions are equal, i.e., where $A'_{S_o}(E)+A'_B(E) = 0$.

increases. This is depicted in fig. 6 by the two curves representing the agency costs of equity, one for the low level of outside financing, $A_{S_o}(E; K_o)$, the other for the high level of outside financing, $A_{S_o}(E; K_1)$. The locus of the latter lies above the former everywhere except at the origin where both are 0.

The agency cost of debt will similarly rise as the amount of outside financing increases. This means that the locus of $A_B(E; K_1)$ for high outside financing, K_1,

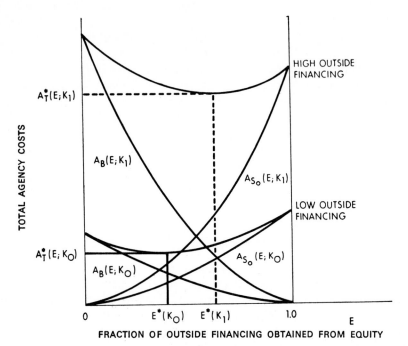

Fig. 6. Agency cost functions and optimal outside equity as a fraction of total outside financing, $E^*(K)$, for two different levels of outside financing, K, for a given size firm, V^*: $K_1 > K_o$.

will lie above the locus of $A_B(E; K_o)$ for low outside financing, K_o because the total amount of resources which can be reallocated from bondholders increases as the total amount of debt increases. However, since these costs are zero when the debt is zero for both K_o and K_1 the intercepts of the $A_B(E; K)$ curves coincide at the right axis.

The net effect of the increased use of outside financing given the cost functions assumed in fig. 6 is to: (1) increase the total agency costs from $A_T(E^*; K_o)$ to $A_T(E^*; K_1)$, and (2) to increase the optimal fraction of outside funds obtained from the sale of outside equity. We draw these functions for illustration only and are unwilling to speculate at this time on the exact form of $E^*(K)$ which gives the general effects of increasing outside financing on the relative quantities of debt and equity.

The locus of points, $A_T(E^*; K)$ where agency costs are minimized (not drawn in fig. 6), determines $E^*(K)$, the optimal proportions of equity and debt to be used in obtaining outside funds as the fraction of outside funds, K, ranges from 0 to 100 percent. The solid line in fig. 7 is a plot of the minimum total agency costs

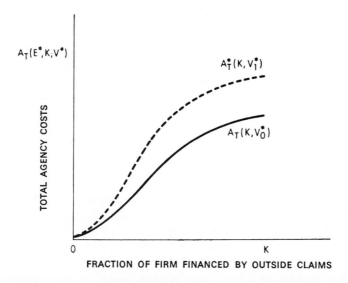

Fig. 7. Total agency costs as a function of the fraction of the firm financed by outside claims for two firm sizes, $V_1^* > V_0^*$.

as a function of the amount of outside financing for a firm with scale V_0^*. The dotted line shows the total agency costs for a larger firm with scale $V_1^* > V_0^*$. That is, we hypothesize that the larger the firm becomes the larger are the total agency costs because it is likely that the monitoring function is inherently more difficult and expensive in a larger organization.

5.3. Risk and the demand for outside financing

The model we have used to explain the existence of minority shareholders and debt in the capital structure of corporations implies that the owner–manager, if he resorts to any outside funding, will have his entire wealth invested in the firm. The reason is that he can thereby avoid the agency costs which additional outside funding impose. This suggests he would not resort to outside funding until he had invested 100 percent of his personal wealth in the firm – an implication which is not consistent with what we generally observe. Most owner–managers hold personal wealth in a variety of forms, and some have only a relatively small fraction of their wealth invested in the corporation they manage.[62] Diversification on the part of owner–managers can be explained by risk aversion and optimal portfolio selection.

If the returns from assets are not perfectly correlated an individual can reduce the riskiness of the returns on his portfolio by dividing his wealth among many different assets, i.e., by diversifying.[63] Thus a manager who invests all of his wealth in a single firm (his own) will generally bear a welfare loss (if he is risk averse) because he is bearing more risk than necessary. He will, of course, be willing to pay something to avoid this risk, and the costs he must bear to accomplish this diversification will be the agency costs outlined above. He will suffer a wealth loss as he reduces his fractional ownership because prospective shareholders and bondholders will take into account the agency costs. Nevertheless, the manager's desire to avoid risk will contribute to his becoming a minority stockholder.

5.4. Determination of the optimal amount of outside financing, K*

Assume for the moment that the owner of a project (i.e., the owner of a prospective firm) has enough wealth to finance the entire project himself. The optimal scale of the corporation is then determined by the condition that, $\Delta V - \Delta I = 0$. In general if the returns to the firm are uncertain the owner–manager can increase his welfare by selling off part of the firm either as debt or equity and reinvesting the proceeds in other assets. If he does this with the optimal combination of debt and equity (as in fig. 6) the total wealth reduction he will incur is given by the agency cost function, $A_T(E^*, K; V^*)$ in fig. 7. The functions $A_T(E^*, K; V^*)$ will be S shaped (as drawn) if total agency costs for a given scale of firm increase at an increasing rate at low levels of outside financing, and at a decreasing rate for high levels of outside financing as monitoring imposes more and more constraints on the manager's actions.

Fig. 8 shows marginal agency costs as a function of K, the fraction of the firm financed with outside funds assuming the total agency cost function is as plotted in fig. 7, and assuming the scale of the firm is fixed. The demand by the owner–manager for outside financing is shown by the remaining curve in fig. 8. This curve represents the marginal value of the increased diversification which the manager

---

[62]On the average, however, top managers seem to have substantial holdings in absolute dollars. A recent survey by Wytmar (*Wall Street Journal*, August 13, 1974, p. 1) reported that the median value of 826 chief executive officers' stock holdings in their companies at year end 1973 was $557,000 and $1.3 million at year end 1972.

[63]These diversification effects can be substantial. Evans and Archer (1968) show that on the average for New York Stock Exchange securities approximately 55% of the total risk (as measured by standard deviation of portfolio returns) can be eliminated by following a naive strategy of dividing one's assets equally among 40 randomly selected securities.

can obtain by reducing his ownership claims and optimally constructing a diversified portfolio. It is measured by the amount he would pay to be allowed to reduce his ownership claims by a dollar in order to increase his diversification. If the liquidation of some of his holdings also influences the owner–manager's consumption set, the demand function plotted in fig. 8 also incorporates the marginal value of these effects. The intersection of these two schedules determines

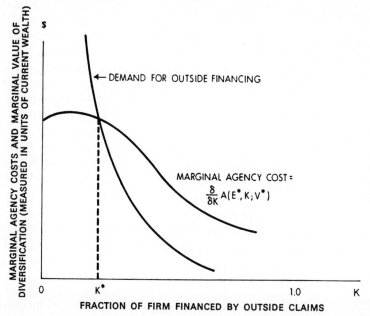

Fig. 8. Determination of the optimal amount of outside financing, K^*, for a given scale of firm

the optimal fraction of the firm to be held by outsiders and this in turn determines the total agency costs borne by the owner. This solution is Pareto optimal; there is no way to reduce the agency costs without making someone worse off.

5.5. Determination of the optimal scale of the firm

While the details of the solution of the optimal scale of the firm are complicated when we allow for the issuance of debt, equity and monitoring and bonding, the general structure of the solution is analogous to the case where monitoring and bonding are allowed for the outside equity example (see fig. 4).

If it is optimal to issue any debt, the expansion path taking full account of such opportunities must lie above the curve ZG in fig. 4. If this new expansion path lies anywhere to the right of the indifference curve passing through point G debt will be used in the optimal financing package. Furthermore, the optimal scale of the firm will be determined by the point at which this new expansion path touches the highest indifference curve. In this situation the resulting level of the owner–manager's welfare must therefore be higher.

6. Qualifications and extensions of the analysis

6.1. Multiperiod aspects of the agency problem

We have assumed throughout our analysis that we are dealing only with a single investment-financing decision by the entrepreneur and have ignored the issues associated with the incentives affecting future financing–investment decisions which might arise after the initial set of contracts are consumated between the entrepreneur–manager, outside stockholders and bondholders. These are important issues which are left for future analysis.[64] Their solution will undoubtedly introduce some changes in the conclusions of the single decision analysis. It seems clear for instance that the expectation of future sales of outside equity and debt will change the costs and benefits facing the manager in making decisions which benefit himself at the (short-run) expense of the current bondholders and stockholders. If he develops a reputation for such dealings he can expect this to unfavourably influence the terms at which he can obtain future capital from outside sources. This will tend to increase the benefits associated with "sainthood" and will tend to reduce the size of the agency costs. Given the finite life of any individual, however, such an effect cannot reduce these costs to zero, because at some point these future costs will begin to weigh more heavily on his successors and therefore the relative benefits to him of acting in his own best interests will rise.[65] Furthermore, it will generally be impossible for him to fully guarantee the outside interests that his successor will continue to follow his policies.

6.2. The control problem and outside owner's agency costs

The careful reader will notice that nowhere in the analysis thus far have we taken into account many of the details of the relationship between the part owner–manager and the outside stockholders and bondholders. In particular we have assumed that all outside equity is nonvoting. If such equity does have voting rights then the manager will be concerned about the effects on his long-run welfare of reducing his fractional ownership below the point where he loses

---

[64]The recent work of Myers (1975) which views future investment opportunities as options and investigates the incentive effects of the existence of debt in such a world where a sequence of investment decisions is made is another important step in the investigation of the multi-period aspects of the agency problem and the theory of the firm.

[65]Becker and Stigler (1972) analyze a special case of this problem involving the use of non-vested pension rights to help correct for this end game play in the law enforcement area.

effective control of the corporation. That is, below the point where it becomes possible for the outside equity holders to fire him. A complete analysis of this issue will require a careful specification of the contractual rights involved on both sides, the role of the board of directors, and the coordination (agency) costs borne by the stockholders in implementing policy changes. This latter point involves consideration of the distribution of the outside ownership claims. Simply put, forces exist to determine an equilibrium distribution of outside ownership. If the costs of reducing the dispersion of ownership are lower than the benefits to be obtained from reducing the agency costs, it will pay some individual or group of individuals to buy shares in the market to reduce the dispersion of ownership. We occasionally witness these conflicts for control which involve outright market purchases, tender offers and proxy fights. Further analysis of these issues is left to the future.

6.3. A note on the existence of inside debt and some conjectures on the use of convertible financial instruments

We have been asked[66] why debt held by the manager (i.e., "inside debt") plays no role in our analysis. We have as yet been unable to incorporate this dimension formally into our analysis in a satisfactory way. The question is a good one and suggests some potentially important extensions of the analysis. For instance, it suggests an inexpensive way for the owner–manager with both equity and debt outstanding to eliminate a large part (perhaps all) of the agency costs of debt. If he binds himself contractually to hold a fraction of the total debt equal to his fractional ownership of the total equity he would have no incentive whatsoever to reallocate wealth from the debt holders to the stockholders. Consider the case where

$$B_i/S_i = B_o/S_o, \tag{4}$$

where S_i and S_o are as defined earlier, B_i is the dollar value of the inside debt held by the owner–manager, and B_o is the debt held by outsiders. In this case if the manager changes the investment policy of the firm to reallocate wealth between the debt and equity holders, the net effect on the total value of his holdings in the firm will be zero. Therefore, his incentives to perform such reallocations are zero.[67]

Why then don't we observe practices or formal contracts which accomplish

[66] By our colleague David Henderson.

[67] This also suggests that *some* outside debt holders can protect themselves from 'exploitation' by the manager by purchasing a fraction of the total equity equal to their fractional ownership of the debt. All debt holders, of course, cannot do this unless the manager does so also. In addition, such an investment rule restricts the portfolio choices of investors and therefore would impose costs if followed rigidly. Thus the agency costs will not be eliminated this way either.

this elimination or reduction of the agency costs of debt? Maybe we do for smaller privately held firms (we haven't attempted to obtain this data), but for large diffuse owner corporations the practice does not seem to be common. One reason for this we believe is that in some respects the claim that the manager holds on the firm in the form of his wage contract has some of the characteristics of debt.[68] If true, this implies that even with zero holdings of formal debt claims he still has positive holdings of a quasi-debt claim and this may accomplish the satisfaction of condition (4). The problem here is that any formal analysis of this issue requires a much deeper understanding of the relationship between formal debt holdings and the wage contract; i.e., how much debt is it equivalent to?

   This line of thought also suggests some other interesting issues. Suppose the implicit debt characteristics of the manager's wage contract result in a situation equivalent to

$$B_i/S_i > B_o/S_o.$$

Then he would have incentives to change the operating characteristics of the firm (i.e., reduce the variance of the outcome distribution) to transfer wealth from the stockholders to the debt holders which is the reverse of the situation we examined in section 4. Furthermore, this seems to capture some of the concern often expressed regarding the fact that managers of large publicly held corporations seem to behave in a risk averse way to the detriment of the equity holders. One solution to this would be to establish incentive compensation systems for the manager or to give him stock options which in effect give him a claim on the upper tail of the outcome distribution. This also seems to be a commonly observed phenomenon.

   This analysis also suggests some additional issues regarding the costs and benefits associated with the use of more complicated financial claims such as warrants, convertible bonds and convertible preferred stock which we have not formally analyzed as yet. Warrants, convertible bonds and convertible preferred stock have some of the characteristics of non-voting shares although they can be converted into voting shares under some terms. Alchian–Demsetz (1972) provide an interesting analysis regarding the use of non-voting shares. They argue that some shareholders with strong beliefs in the talents and judgements of the manager will want to be protected against the possibility that some other shareholders will take over and limit the actions of the manager (or fire him). Given that the securities exchanges prohibit the use of non-voting shares by listed firms the use of option type securities might be a substitute for these claims.

   In addition warrants represents a claim on the upper tail of the distribution of

---

[68]Consider the situation in which the bondholders have the right in the event of bankruptcy to terminate his employment and therefore to terminate the future returns to any specific human capital or rents he may be receiving.

outcomes, and convertible securities can be thought of as securities with non-detachable warrants. It seems that the incentive effects of warrants would tend to offset to some extent the incentive effects of the existence of risky debt because the owner–manager would be sharing part of the proceeds associated with a shift in the distribution of returns with the warrant holders. Thus, we conjecture that potential bondholders will find it attractive to have warrants attached to the risky debt of firms in which it is relatively easy to shift the distribution of outcomes to expand the upper tail of the distribution to transfer wealth from bond-holders. It would also then be attractive to the owner–manager because of the reduction in the agency costs which he would bear. This argument also implies that it would make little difference if the warrants were detachable (and therefore saleable separately from the bonds) since their mere existence would reduce the incentives of the manager (or stockholders) to increase the riskiness of the firm (and therefore increase the probability of bankruptcy). Furthermore, the addition of a conversion privilege to fixed claims such as debt or preferred stock would also tend to reduce the incentive effects of the existence of such fixed claims and therefore lower the agency costs associated with them. The theory predicts that these phenomena should be more frequently observed in cases where the incentive effects of such fixed claims are high than when they are low.

6.4. Monitoring and the social product of security analysts

One of the areas in which further analysis is likely to lead to high payoffs is that of monitoring. We currently have little which could be glorified by the title of a "Theory of Monitoring" and yet this is a crucial building block of the analysis. We would expect monitoring activities to become specialized to those institutions and individuals who possess comparative advantages in these activities. One of the groups who seem to play a large role in these activities is composed of the security analysts employed by institutional investors, brokers and investment advisory services as well as the analysis performed by individual investors in the normal course of investment decision making.

A large body of evidence exists which indicates that security prices incorporate in an unbiased manner all publicly available information and much of what might be called "private information".[69] There is also a large body of evidence which indicates that the security analysis activities of mutual funds and other institutional investors are not reflected in portfolio returns, i.e., they do not increase risk adjusted portfolio returns over a naive random selection buy and hold strategy.[70] Therefore some have been tempted to conclude that the resources expended on such research activities to find under- or over-valued securities is a social loss. Jensen (1974) argues that this conclusion cannot be

---

[69]See Fama (1970) for a survey of this 'efficient markets' literature.
[70]See Jensen (1969) for an example of this evidence and references.

unambiguously drawn because there is a large consumption element in the demand for these services.

Furthermore, the analysis of this paper would seem to indicate that to the extent that security analysis activities reduce the agency costs associated with the separation of ownership and control they are indeed socially productive. Moreover, if this is true we expect the major benefits of the security analysis activity to be reflected in the higher capitalized value of the ownership claims to corporations and *not* in the period to period portfolio returns of the analyst. Equilibrium in the security analysis industry requires that the private returns to analysis (i.e., portfolio returns) must be just equal to the private costs of such activity,[71] and this will not reflect the social product of this activity which will consist of larger output and higher *levels* of the capital value of ownership claims. Therefore, the argument implies that if there is a non-optimal amount of security analysis being performed it is too much[72] not too little (since the shareholders would be willing to pay directly to have the "optimal" monitoring performed), and we don't seem to observe such payments.

6.5. Specialization in the use of debt and equity

Our previous analysis of agency costs suggests at least one other testable hypothesis: i.e., that in those industries where the incentive effects of outside equity or debt are widely different, we would expect to see specialization in the use of the low agency cost financing arrangement. In industries where it is relatively easy for managers to lower the mean value of the outcomes of the enterprise by outright theft, special treatment of favored customers, ease of consumption of leisure on the job, etc. (for example, the bar and restaurant industry) we would expect to see the ownership structure of firms characterized by relatively little outside equity (i.e., 100 percent ownership of the equity by the manager) with almost all outside capital obtained through the use of debt.

The theory predicts the opposite would be true where the incentive effects of debt are large relative to the incentive effects of equity. Firms like conglomerates, in which it would be easy to shift outcome distributions adversely for bondholders (by changing the acquisition or divestiture policy) should be characterized by relatively lower utilization of debt. Conversely in industries where the freedom of management to take riskier projects is severely constrained (for example, regulated industries such as public utilities) we should find more intensive use of debt financing.

The analysis suggests that in addition to the fairly well understood role of uncertainty in the determination of the quality of collateral there is at least one other element of great importance – the ability of the owner of the collateral to

---

[71]Ignoring any pure consumption elements in the demand for security analysis.

[72]Again ignoring the value of the pure consumption elements in the demand for security analysis.

change the distribution of outcomes by shifting either the mean outcome or the variance of the outcomes. A study of bank lending policies should reveal these to be important aspects of the contractual practices observed there.

6.6. Application of the analysis to the large diffuse ownership corporation

While we believe the structure outlined in the proceeding pages is applicable to a wide range of corporations it is still in an incomplete state One of the most serious limitation of the analysis is that as it stands we have not worked out in this paper its application to the very large modern corporation whose managers own little or no equity. We believe our approach can be applied to this case but space limitations precludes discussion of these issues here. They remain to be worked out in detail and will be included in a future paper.

6.7. The supply side of the incomplete markets question

The analysis of this paper is also relevant to the incomplete market issue considered by Arrow (1964), Diamond (1967), Hakansson (1974a, b), Rubinstein (1974), Ross (1974) and others. The problems addressed in this literature derive from the fact that whenever the available set of financial claims on outcomes in a market fails to span the underlying state space [see Arrow (1964) and Debreu (1959)] the resulting allocation is Pareto inefficient. A disturbing element in this literature surrounds the fact that the inefficiency conclusion is generally drawn without explicit attention in the analysis to the costs of creating new claims or of maintaining the expanded set of markets called for to bring about the welfare improvement.

The demonstration of a possible welfare improvement from the expansion of the set of claims by the introduction of new basic contingent claims or options can be thought of as an analysis of the demand conditions for new markets. Viewed from this perspective, what is missing in the literature on this problem is the formulation of a positive analysis of the supply of markets (or the supply of contingent claims). That is, what is it in the maximizing behavior of individuals in the economy that causes them to create and sell contingent claims of various sorts?

The analysis in this paper can be viewed as a small first step in the direction of formulating an analysis of the supply of markets issue which is founded in the self-interested maximizing behavior of individuals. We have shown why it is in the interest of a wealth maximizing entrepreneur to create and sell claims such as debt and equity. Furthermore, as we have indicated above, it appears that extensions of these arguments will lead to a theory of the supply of warrants, convertible bonds and convertible preferred stock. We are not suggesting that the specific analysis offered above is likely to be sufficient to lead to a theory of the supply of the wide range of contracts (both existing and merely potential) in the world at large. However, we do believe that framing the question of the completeness of markets in terms of the joining of both the demand and supply conditions will be very fruitful instead of implicitly assuming that new claims spring forth from some (costless) well head of creativity unaided or unsupported by human effort.

7. Conclusions

The publicly held business corporation is an awesome social invention. Millions of individuals voluntarily entrust billions of dollars, francs, pesos, etc., of personal wealth to the care of managers on the basis of a complex set of contracting relationships which delineate the rights of the parties involved. The growth in the use of the corporate form as well as the growth in market value of established corporations suggests that at least, up to the present, creditors and investors have by and large not been disappointed with the results, despite the agency costs inherent in the corporate form.

Agency costs are as real as any other costs. The level of agency costs depends among other things on statutory and common law and human ingenuity in devising contracts. Both the law and the sophistication of contracts relevant to the modern corporation are the products of a historical process in which there were strong incentives for individuals to minimize agency costs. Moreover, there were alternative organizational forms available, and opportunities to invent new ones. Whatever its shortcomings, the corporation has thus far survived the market test against potential alternatives.

References

Alchian, A.A., 1965, The basis of some recent advances in the theory of management of the firm, Journal of Industrial Economics, Nov., 30–44.

Alchian, A.A., 1968, Corporate management and property rights, in: Economic policy and the regulation of securities (American Enterprise Institute, Washington, DC).

Alchian, A.A., 1974, Some implications of recognition of property right transactions costs, unpublished paper presented at the First Interlaken Conference on Analysis and Ideology, June.

Alchian, A.A. and W.R. Allen, 1969, Exchange and production: Theory in use (Wadsworth, Belmont, CA).

Alchian, A.A. and H. Demsetz, 1972, Production, information costs, and economic organization, American Economic Review LXII, no. 5, 777–795.

Alchian, A.A. and R.A. Kessel, 1962, Competition, monopoly and the pursuit of pecuniary gain, in: Aspects of labor economics (National Bureau of Economic Research, Princeton, NJ).

Arrow, K.J., 1963/4, Control in large organizations, Management Science 10, 397–408.

Arrow, K.J., 1964, The role of securities in the optimal allocation of risk bearing, Review of Economic studies 31, no. 86, 91–96.

Atkinson, T.R., 1967, Trends in corporate bond quality, in: Studies in corporate bond finance 4 (National Bureau of Economic Research, New York).

Baumol, W.J., 1959, Business behavior, value and growth (Macmillan, New York).

Becker, G., 1957, The economics of discrimination (University of Chicago Press, Chicago, IL).

Becker, G.S. and G.J. Stigler, 1972, Law enforcement, corruption and compensation of enforcers, unpublished paper presented at the Conference on Capitalism and Freedom, Oct.

Benston, G., 1977, The impact of maturity regulation on high interest rate lenders and borrowers, Journal of Financial Economics 4, no. 1.

Berhold, M., 1971, A theory of linear profit sharing incentives, Quarterly Journal of Economics LXXXV, Aug., 460–482.

Berle, A.A., Jr. and G.C. Means, 1932, The modern corporation and private property (Macmillan, New York).

Black, F. and M. Scholes, 1973, The pricing of options and corporate liabilities, Journal of Political Economy 81, no. 3, 637–654.

Black, F., M.H. Miller and R.A. Posner, 1974, An approach to the regulation of bank holding companies, unpublished manuscript (University of Chicago, Chicago, IL).

Branch, B., 1973, Corporate objectives and market performance, Financial Management, Summer, 24–29.

Coase, R.H., 1937, The nature of the firm, Economica, New Series, IV, 386–405. Reprinted in: Readings in price theory (Irwin, Homewood, IL) 331–351.

Coase, R.H., 1959, The Federal Communications Commission, Journal of Law and Economics II, Oct., 1–40.

Coase, R.H., 1960, The problem of social cost, Journal of Law and Economics III, Oct., 1–44.

Coase, R.H., 1964, Discussion, American Economic Review LIV, no. 3, 194–197.

Cyert, R.M. and C.L. Hedrick, 1972, Theory of the firm: Past, present and future; An interpretation, Journal of Economic Literature X, June, 398–412.

Cyert, R.M. and J.G. March, 1963, A behavioral theory of the firm (Prentice Hall, Englewood Cliffs, NJ).

De Alessi, L., 1973, Private property and dispersion of ownership in large corporations, Journal of Finance, Sept., 839–851.

Debreu, G., 1959, Theory of value (Wiley, New York).

Demsetz, H., 1967, Toward a theory of property rights, American Economic Review LVII, May, 347–359.

Demsetz, H., 1969, Information and efficiency: Another viewpoint, Journal of Law and Economics XII, April, 1–22.

Diamond, P.A., 1967, The role of a stock market in a general equilibrium model with technological uncertainty, American Economic Review LVII, Sept., 759–776.

Evans, J.L. and S.H. Archer, 1968, Diversification and the reduction of dispersion: An empirical analysis, Journal of Finance, Dec.

Fama, E.F., 1970a, Efficient capital markets: A review of theory and empirical work, Journal of Finance XXV, no. 2.

Fama, E.F., 1970b, Multiperiod consumption–investment decisions, American Economic Review LX, March.

Fama, E.F., 1972, Ordinal and measurable utility, in: M.C. Jensen, ed., Studies in the theory of capital markets (Praeger, New York).

Fama, E.F. and M. Miller, 1972, The theory of finance (Holt, Rinehart and Winston, New York).

Friedman, M., 1970, The social responsibility of business is to increase its profits, New York Times Magazine, 13 Sept, 32ff.

Furubotn, E.G. and S. Pejovich, 1972, Property rights and economic theory: A survey of recent literature, Journal of Economic Literature X, Dec., 1137–1162.

Galai, D. and R.W. Masulis, 1976, The option pricing model and the risk factor of stock, Journal of Financial Economics 3, no. 1/2, 53–82.

Hakansson, N.H., 1974a, The superfund: Efficient paths toward a complete financial market, unpublished manuscript.

Hakansson, N.H., 1974b, Ordering markets and the capital structures of firms with illustrations, Institute of Business and Economic Research Working Paper no. 24 (University of California, Berkeley, CA).

Heckerman, D.G., 1975, Motivating managers to make investment decisions, Journal of Financial Economics 2, no. 3, 273–292.

Hirshleifer, J., 1958, On the theory of optimal investment decisions, Journal of Political Economy, Aug., 329–352.

Hirshleifer, J., 1970, Investment, interest, and capital (Prentice-Hall, Englewood Cliffs, NJ).

Jensen, M.C., 1969, Risk, the pricing of capital assets, and the evaluation of investment portfolios, Journal of Business 42, no. 2, 167–247.

Jensen, M.C., 1974, Tests of capital market theory and implications of the evidence. Graduate School of Management Working Paper Series no.7414 (University of Rochester, Rochester, NY).

Jensen, M.C. and J.B. Long, 1972, Corporate investment under uncertainty and Pareto optimality in the capital markets, Bell Journal of Economics, Spring, 151–174.

Jensen, M.C. and W.H. Meckling, 1976, Can the corporation survive? Center for Research in Government Policy and Business Working Paper no. PPS 76–4 (University of Rochester, Rochester, NY).

Klein, W.A., 1976, Legal and economic perspectives on the firm, unpublished manuscript (University of California, Los Angeles, CA).

Kraus, A. and R. Litzenberger, 1973, A state preference model of optimal financial leverage, Journal of Finance, Sept.

Larner, R.J., 1970, Management control and the large corporation (Dunellen, New York).

Lintner, J., 1965, Security prices, risk, and maximal gains from diversification, Journal of Finance XX, Dec., 587–616.

Lloyd-Davies, P., 1975, Risk and optimal leverage, unpublished manuscript (University of Rochester, Rochester, NY).

Long, J.B., 1972, Wealth, welfare, and the price of risk, Journal of Finance, May, 419–433.

Long, J.B., Jr., 1974, Discussion, Journal of Finance XXXIX, no. 12, 485–488.

Machlup, F., 1967, Theories of the firm: Marginalist, behavioral, managerial, American Economic Review, March, 1–33.

Manne, H.G., 1962, The 'higher criticism' of the modern corporation, Columbia Law Review 62, March, 399–432.

Manne, H.G., 1965, Mergers and the market for corporate control, Journal of Political Economy, April, 110–120.

Manne, H.G., 1967, Our two corporate systems: Law and economics, Virginia Law Review 53, March, 259–284.

Manne, H.G., 1972, The social responsibility of regulated utilities, Wisconsin Law Review V, no. 4, 995–1009.

Marris, R., 1964, The economic theory of managerial capitalism (Free Press of Glencoe, Glencoe, IL).

Mason, E.S., 1959, The corporation in modern society (Harvard University Press, Cambridge, MA).

McManus, J.C., 1975, The costs of alternative economic organizations, Canadian Journal of Economics VIII, Aug., 334–350.

Meckling, W.H., 1976, Values and the choice of the model of the individual in the social sciences, Schweizerische Zeitschrift für Volkswirtschaft und Statistik, Dec.

Merton, R.C., 1973, The theory of rational option pricing, Bell Journal of Economics and Management Science 4, no. 1, 141–183.

Merton, R.C., 1974, On the pricing of corporate debt: The risk structure of interest rates, Journal of Finance XXIX, no. 2, 449–470.

Merton, R.C. and M.G. Subrahmanyam, 1974, The optimality of a competitive stock market, Bell Journal of Economics and Management Science, Spring, 145–170.

Miller, M.H. and F. Modigliani, 1966, Some estimates of the cost of capital to the electric utility industry, 1954–57, American Economic Review, June, 333–391.

Modigliani, F. and M.H. Miller, 1958, The costs of capital, corporation finance, and the theory of investment, American Economic Review 48, June, 261–297.

Modigliani, F. and M.H. Miller, 1963, Corporate income taxes and the cost of capital: A correction, American Economic Review June, 433–443.

Monsen, R.J. and A. Downs, 1965, A theory of large managerial firms, Journal of Political Economy, June, 221–236.

Myers, S.C., 1975, A note on the determinants of corporate debt capacity, unpublished manuscript (London Graduate School of Business Studies, London).

Penrose, E., 1958, The theory of the growth of the firm (Wiley, New York).

Preston, L.E., 1975, Corporation and society: The search for a paradigm, Journal of Economic Literature XIII, June, 434–453.

Ross, S.A., 1973, The economic theory of agency: The principals problems, American Economic Review LXII, May, 134–139.

Ross, S.A., 1974a, The economic theory of agency and the principle of similarity, in: M.D. Balch et al., eds., Essays on economic behavior under uncertainty (North-Holland, Amsterdam).

Ross, S.A., 1974b, Options and efficiency, Rodney L. White Center for Financial Research Working Paper no. 3–74 (University of Pennsylvania, Philadelphia, PA).

Rubinstein, M., 1974, A discrete-time synthesis of financial theory, Parts I and II, Institute of Business and Economic Research Working Papers nos. 20 and 21 (University of California, Berkeley, CA).

Scitovsky, T., 1943, A note on profit maximisation and its implications, Review of Economic Studies XI, 57–60.

Sharpe, W.F., 1964, Capital asset prices : A theory of market equilibrium under conditions of risk, Journal of Finance XIX, Sept., 425–442.

Shubik, M., 1970, A curmudgeon's guide to microeconomics, Journal of Economic Literature VIII, June, 405–434.

Silver, M. and R. Auster, 1969, Entrepreneurship, profit and limits on firm size, Journal of Business 42, July, 277–281.

Simon, H.A., 1955, A behavioral model of rational choice, Quarterly Journal of Economics 69, 99–118.

Simon, H.A., 1959, Theories of decision making in economics and behavioral science, American Economic Review, June, 253–283.

Smith, A., 1937, The wealth of nations, Cannan edition (Modern Library, New York).

Smith, C., 1976, Option pricing: A review, Journal of Financial Economics 3, nos. 1/2, 3–52.

Warner, J.B., 1975, Bankruptcy costs, absolute priority, and the pricing of risky debt claims, unpublished manuscript (University of Chicago, Chicago, IL).

Williamson, O.E., 1964, The economics of discretionary behavior: Managerial objectives in a theory of the firm (Prentice-Hall, Englewood Cliffs, NJ).

Williamson, O.E., 1970, Corporate control and business behavior (Prentice-Hall, Englewood Cliffs, NJ).

Williamson, O.E., 1975, Markets and hierarchies: Analysis and antitrust implications (The Free Press, New York).

Wilson, R., 1968, On the theory of syndicates, Econometrica 36, Jan., 119–132.

Wilson, R., 1969, La decision: Agregation et dynamique des orders de preference, Extrait (Editions du Centre National de la Recherche Scientifique, Paris) 288–307.

DETERMINANTS OF CORPORATE BORROWING*

Stewart C. MYERS

Sloan School, M.I.T., Cambridge, MA 02139, U.S.A.

Received October 1976, revised version received July 1977

Many corporate assets, particularly growth opportunities, can be viewed as call options. The value of such 'real options' depends on discretionary future investment by the firm. Issuing risky debt reduces the present market value of a firm holding real options by inducing a sub-optimal investment strategy or by forcing the firm and its creditors to bear the costs of avoiding the suboptimal strategy. The paper predicts that corporate borrowing is inversely related to the proportion of market value accounted for by real options. It also rationalizes other aspects of corporate borrowing behavior, for example the practice of matching maturities of assets and debt liabilities.

1. Introduction

There is an important gap in modern finance theory on the issue of corporate debt policy. The theory should be able to explain why tax savings generated by debt do not lead firms to borrow as much as possible, and it should explain the phrase 'as much as possible'. It should explain why some firms borrow more than others, why some borrow with short-, and others with long-maturity instruments, and so on.

A variety of ideas has been advanced to fill this gap. Modigliani and Miller (MM) have suggested (1963, p. 111) that firms maintain 'reserve borrowing capacity' – although the need for such flexibility is not clear in the frictionless capital markets MM rely on – and that the incremental tax advantage of borrowing declines as more debt is issued and interest tax shields become less certain. They and others have also noted that personal taxes – specifically the difference between tax rates on capital gains and rates on regular income – reduce the theoretical tax advantage of corporate borrowing,[1] and Miller (1977) has presented a model in which the advantage entirely disappears. These

---

*An earlier version of this paper [Myers (1975)] was presented at seminars at the London Graduate School of Business Studies, Duke University and the Faculté Universitaire Catholique du Mons, Belgium. I wish to thank the London Graduate School of Business Studies for research support and Richard Brealey, Fischer Black, Frederick Grauer, Jeffery Halis, Michael Jensen and Robert Merton for helpful comments.

[1]See Farrar and Selwyn (1967) and Stiglitz (1972).

Journal of Financial Economics 5 (1977) 147–175. © North-Holland Publishing Company

arguments rationalize firms' reluctance to borrow 'as much as possible', but they give little specific guidance beyond that.

There are other lines of argument. Firms' debt policies may reflect imperfect or incomplete capital markets.[2] The literature on credit rationing by banks and other lenders may help explain the limits to corporate borrowing.[3] Perhaps managers avoid high debt ratios in an attempt to protect their jobs and stabilize their personal wealth.[4] Perhaps firms' financing decisions are actually signalling devices, conveying information to investors about the firm's business risk and profitability.[5]

Bankruptcy costs (the transaction costs of liquidation or reorganization) probably discourage borrowing, although recent research by Warner (1977) questions whether these costs are large enough to be significant. Perhaps, as Robicheck and Myers (1966) argue, costs of financial distress are incurred when the firm comes under the threat of bankruptcy, even if bankruptcy is ultimately avoided.[6]

There is doubtless some truth in each of these ideas, but they do not add up to a rigorous, complete and sensible explanation of corporate debt policy. This paper presents a new approach which does not rely on any of the ideas mentioned above. It explains why it is rational for firms to limit borrowing, even when there is a genuine tax advantage to corporate borrowing and capital markets are strictly perfect, efficient, and complete. It shows that a form of capital rationing by lenders can exist in such conditions. It specifies an asset characteristic that encourages relatively heavy borrowing; this characteristic is not 'low risk' in any of the usual senses of that phrase. Finally, it explains a number of previously puzzling phenomena. For example, it clarifies why practical people set target debt ratios in terms of book rather than market values, and why firms tend to 'match maturities' of assets and debt obligations.

The theory rests on a relatively simple argument. It starts with the observation that most firms are valued as going concerns, and that this value reflects an expectation of continued future investment by the firm. However, the investment is discretionary. The amount invested depends on the net present values of opportunities as they arise in the future. In unfavorable future states of nature the firm will invest nothing.

Thus part of the value of a firm is accounted for by the present value of *options* to make further investments on possibly favorable terms. This value

---

[2]Durand's early critique of the MM propositions (1959) rests on market imperfections. The effects of incomplete markets on the firm's capital structure choice were emphasized later by Robichek and Myers (1966) and Stiglitz (1974), among others.

[3]See, for example, Jaffee (1971) and Jaffee and Russell (1976).

[4]Donaldson (1963).

[5]See Ross (1977) and Leland and Pyle (1976).

[6]But Robichek and Myers did not understand *why* a high probability of bankruptcy should in itself make it difficult to raise additional financing, or why it should lead to suboptimal investment decisions. I say this on the best authority.

depends on the rule for deciding whether the options are to be exercised. The paper shows that a firm with risky debt outstanding, and which acts in its stockholders' interest, will follow a different decision rule than one which can issue risk-free debt or which issues no debt at all.[7] The firm financed with risky debt will, in some states of nature, pass up valuable investment opportunities – opportunities which could make a positive net contribution to the market value of the firm.

Issuing risky debt reduces the present market value of the firm by inducing a future strategy that is suboptimal in the sense just described. The loss in market value is absorbed by the firm's current stockholders. Thus, in the absence of taxes, the optimal strategy is to issue no risky debt. If there is a tax advantage to corporate borrowing, the optimal strategy involves a tradeoff between the tax advantages of debt and the costs of the suboptimal future investment strategy. If Miller (1977) is right, and taxes are irrelevant to the firm's debt–equity choice, then we must seek some other reason for explaining why firms use debt. As this paper does not attempt to be a complete theory of corporate debt policy, those other reasons are not pursued here.[8]

In many ways this paper is like Jensen and Meckling's (1976) analysis of agency costs and optimal capital structure. The suboptimal investment policy is an agency cost induced by risky debt. However, this particular cost was not stressed by Jensen and Meckling. Their theory of optimal capital structure is based on different phenomena. On the other hand, this paper resembles theirs in that the analysis finally rests on costs that have traditionally been viewed as market imperfections, in particular costs of negotiation, monitoring and enforcement of contracts.[9]

The paper's formal argument is presented for a simple case in section 2. The assumptions underlying the formal argument are discussed in detail in section 3. Section 4 gives a general statement of the theory and considers how optimal debt policy changes as firms merge, or as different assets are combined in a single firm. Section 5 sketches empirical implications.

2. The basic idea

2.1. Statement of the problem

At first glance, some of the oddest practical rules of thumb for judging debt

---

[7]Of course this point is not in itself new. For example, Fama and Miller (1971, pp. 179–81), and Fama (1976) have noted that conflicts of interest between bondholders and stockholders can affect the firm's operating and investment decisions. However, they argue that such conflicts are easily and cheaply resolved. I disagree, at least with respect to the specific case discussed here. Galai and Masulis (1976) have also recognized that the firm's investment policy depends on capital structure. However, this is a relatively minor part of their paper.

[8]But see Jensen and Meckling (1976).

[9]After I wrote this paper, Michael Brennan showed me preliminary work, done in 1973, which approached the borrowing decision along much the same lines taken here. Unfortunately Brennan's work was never developed and published.

policy are those which depend on ratios of debt to the book value of equity or to total book capitalization. Anyone familiar with modern finance theory considers ratios based on market values much more pertinent. Yet there is an element of sense in the practical procedures. It is not that book values are more accurate than stock market values, but simply that they refer to assets *already in place*. A significant part of many firms' market values is accounted for by assets not yet in place, i.e., by the present value of future growth opportunities. In this section I will show that the amount of debt 'supported by' growth opportunities will be less, other things equal, than is supported by assets already in place. I start with this case because it provides the clearest and most dramatic illustration of the ideas advanced in this paper.

I will assume that there are no corporate taxes and no bankruptcy costs. The firm's managers act in the shareholders' interest. Capital markets are perfect and complete, so that investors can construct portfolios with any conceivable pattern of returns across future states of nature.[10] Let V be the current equilibrium market value of the firm, and V_D and V_E the current equilibrium market values of debt and equity, respectively.

As was previously noted, V can be broken down into the present value of assets already in place and the present value of future growth opportunities,

$$V = V_A + V_G, \tag{1}$$

where V_A is the market value of assets already in place,[11] and V_G is the present value of future investment opportunities.

The usual interpretation is that a positive value of V_G reflects future investments which are expected to yield a rate of return in excess of the opportunity cost of capital. However, since the firm may choose *not* to pursue future investment opportunities, V_G is best regarded as the present value of the firm's *options* to make future investments. The distinction being drawn here is between assets whose ultimate value depends on further, discretionary investment by the firm, and assets whose ultimate value does not depend on such investment.

We start with a firm with no assets in place ($V_A = 0$) and only one future investment opportunity. The firm is initially all-equity financed. It must decide whether to invest I one period hence, at $t = 1$. If it invests, the firm obtains an asset worth $V(s)$ at $t = 1$, where s is the state of nature then obtaining. If it does not invest then the investment opportunity expires and has no value to the firm or to anyone else.

---

[10] I adopt this framework to show that the theory developed below does not depend on some subtle imperfection or gap in *financial* markets. But neither does it depend on full perfection and completeness – these are sufficient, but not necessary conditions. See section 4.

[11] What about future opportunities the firm is contractually obligated to accept? If the obligation really is ironclad, then they should be included in V_A. However, usually the firm can default on such obligations. Given limited liability, the contract can be ironclad only if there is an escrow account or some other security to back up the investment outlay.

Thus the firm's initial (market value) balance sheet is as follows:

Balance sheet at $t = 0$

Value of growth opportunity	V_G	0	Value of debt
		V_E	Value of equity
Value of firm	V	V	

In the next period the firm must decide whether to invest – that is, whether to exercise its option. *If* it decides to invest, additional shares must be issued to raise the required investment I. In that event the value of the firm will be $V(s)$.

Balance sheet at $t = 1$

Value of newly acquired asset	$V(s)$	0	Value of debt
		V_E	Value of equity
Value of firm	$V(s)$	$V(s)$	

If the investment is not made, no additional shares are issued, the option expires, and the firm is worthless. (That is not a necessary assumption: it is sufficient that the value of the option declines if exercise is delayed.)

Obviously, the investment will be made only if $V(s) \geq I$. The decision is shown in fig. 1.[12] For states displayed to the right of s_a ($s \geq s_a$), the investment is made. This is noted by setting the decision variable $x(s) = 1$. For states $s < s_a$, $x(s) = 0$. Thus s_a is the 'breakeven' state.

Given complete markets, the value of the firm at $t = 0$ is

$$V = \int_0^\infty q(s)x(s)[V(s) - I]\mathrm{d}s, \tag{2}$$

where $q(s)$ is the current equilibrium price of a dollar delivered at period $t = 1$ if and only if state s occurs. Under all-equity financing $x(s) = 0$ for $s < s_a$, and $x(s) = 1$ for $s \geq s_a$, so

$$V = \int_{s_a}^\infty q(s)[V(s) - I]\mathrm{d}s. \tag{3}$$

---

[12]For convenience, the states are plotted in order of increasing $V(s)$. This entails no loss in generality. Also, $V(s)$ is not necessarily a linear function of s, although I have drawn it that way.

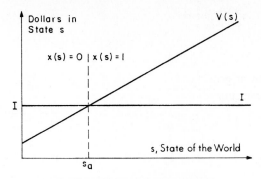

Fig. 1. The firm's investment decision under all-equity financing as a function of the state of the world, s, at the decision point.

2.2. The link between borrowing and the market value of the firm

Since the firm will be worth nothing in states $s < s_a$, it can issue no safe debt. However, it can issue risky debt with the promised payment P. It it does so, its initial balance sheet is

Balance sheet at $t = 0$

Value of growth opportunity	V_G	V_D	Value of debt
		V_E	Value of equity
Value of firm	V	V	

Note that the proceeds of the debt issue are used to reduce the required initial equity investment. They are not held as cash or used to purchase other assets. If they were our mental experiment would be spoiled, for the debt would be partly 'supported by' the cash or other assets, not solely by the investment opportunity.

Assume first that the debt matures before the investment decision is made, but after the true state of nature is revealed. Then if $V(s) - I \geq P$, it will clearly be in the stockholders' interest to pay the debtors off. If $V(s) - I < P$, however, the bondholders will take over, and will exercise the firm's option to invest if $V(s) \geq I$. Thus the equilibrium market value of the debt at $t = 0$ is

$$V_D = \int_{s_a}^{\infty} q(s)[\min(V(s) - I, P)]\,ds. \tag{4}$$

In this case shareholders can borrow the entire value of the firm if they wish.

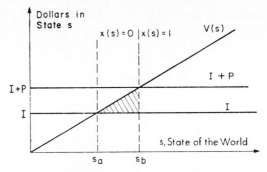

Fig. 2.   The firm's investment decision with prior debt financing as a function of the state of the world, s, at the decision point.

If P is made large enough to exceed $V(s)-I$ in all states, then $V_D = V$ as given by eq. (3). The amount borrowed is a matter of indifference to stockholders – Modigliani and Miller's Proposition I is well known to hold under present assumptions.[13]

The interesting case occurs when the debt matures *after* the firm's investment option expires. Then outstanding debt will change the firm's investment decision in some states.

If the firm raises the amount I and exercises its investment option, its balance sheet will be:

Balance sheet at $t = 1$, given $x(s) = 1$

Value of newly acquired asset	$V(s)$	$\min[V(s), P]$	Value of debt
		$\max[0, V(s)-P]$	Value of equity
Value of firm	$V(s)$	$V(s)$	

But from the shareholders' viewpoint, the option is worth exercising only if $V(s)$ exceeds the sum of I, the required outlay, and P, the promised payment to the firm's creditors. If $V(s) < I+P$ and the investment is made, shareholders' outlay I will exceed the market value of their shares. The new situation is shown in fig. 2. Here $x(s) = 0$ for $s < s_b$ and $x(s) = 1$ for $s \geq s_b$; s_b is the 'breakeven' state in which $V(s) = I+P$.

The firm's value at $t = 0$ is now given by

$$V = \int_{s_b}^{\infty} q(s)[V(s)-I]\,ds, \tag{5}$$

[13]Hirshleifer (1968, pp. 264–268).

where s_b depends on P, the promised payment to creditors. So long as $s_b > s_a$, there is a loss of value in some states of nature. The loss is shown by the shaded triangle in fig. 2. A higher P implies a larger triangle and a lower V. In fact, if P is set high enough, $V(s)$ will be less than $I+P$ in all states and $x(s)$ will be zero in all states. The firm will be worthless because its growth option will expire unexercised.

The creditors will receive nothing at all if the growth option is not exercised. If it is exercised, then $V(s)$ must exceed P, so $\min(V(s), P) = P$. Thus,

$$V_D = \int_{s_b}^{\infty} Pq(s)\,ds. \tag{6}$$

Clearly $V_D < V$, except in the limit where $P \to \infty$, $s_b \to \infty$ and $V \to 0$. Also, V must be less than its all-equity value [given by eq. (3)] whenever P is positive. Consequently, the relationship of V_D to P must be as shown in fig. 3. There is a definite limit, $V_D(\max)$, to the amount the firm can borrow (assuming it wants

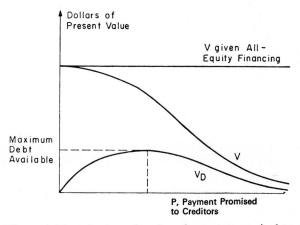

Fig. 3. Firm and debt values as a function of payment promised to creditors.

to). This limit is less than V and falls even further short of what V would be under all-equity financing. This is an interesting result because it shows one way in which credit rationing can occur even in perfect capital markets. After a point the firm cannot borrow more by offering to pay a higher interest rate. In fact, it may find that an offer to pay more *reduces* the amount of credit available to it.

Since the shareholders' objective is to maximize V, the market value of the firm, the optimal policy in the case described by fig. 3 is to issue no debt at all. Any promised payment will lead the firm to abandon a project with positive net present value in some future states. Thus V is a monotonically decreasing function of P, and it is maximized when P and V_D equal zero.

2.3. Comments

The example shows how the existence of corporate debt *can* reduce the present market value of the firm by weakening the corporation's incentive to undertake good future investments. I have not yet argued that the incentive *will* actually lead to the result just described. The incentive problem could be easily avoided in the simple world postulated for the example. For example, creditors could be given the right to exercise the investment option (with their own money) if stockholders get cold feet. But I argue below that the problem is not so easily evaded in reality.

Of course, the example leads to an extreme result: firms with valuable growth opportunities would never issue risky debt. But, as Jensen and Meckling (1976) point out, there are incentive problems – agency costs – associated with equity as well as debt issues. Debt may be the lesser evil. Also there may be tax advantages to debt. The appendix shows how taxes affect optimal borrowing in the case just discussed.

3. Discussion

3.1. Assets as call options

What are the essential characteristics of the 'growth opportunity' discussed in the previous section? They flow from the fact that it can be regarded as a call option on a real asset. The option's exercise price is the future investment needed to acquire the asset. Whether the option has any value when it expires depends on the asset's future value, and also on whether the firm chooses to exercise. The decision to exercise is not trivial and automatic, as it is for options written on securities, because it depends on the magnitude of promised payments to bondholders.

Thus the most fundamental distinction is not between 'growth opportunities' and 'assets in place', but between (1) assets that can be regarded as call options, in the sense that their ultimate values depend, at least in part, on further discretionary investment by the firm and (2) assets whose ultimate value does not depend on further discretionary investment.

In reality, the difference between 'assets in place' and 'growth opportunities' is more of degree than kind. The market value of almost all real assets can be partly attributed to associated call options. That is, the ultimate payoff of almost all assets depends on future discretionary investment by the firm. The discretionary investment may be maintenance of plant and equipment. It may be advertising or other marketing expenses, or expenditures on raw materials, labor, research and development, etc. All variable costs are discretionary investments.

For most lenders the relevant asset is the firm itself. Their loans' values depend on the value of the firm as a going concern, not on the value of any specific physical asset. (It is true that lenders often protect themselves by obtaining security in the form of specific assets for which secondary markets exist. But that is an attempt to avoid the problems analyzed in this paper.) The value of a going concern can be maintained only by positive action; in a competitive industry the firm should have to work hard to simply keep up. This is not simply a matter of maintaining plant and equipment. There is continual effort devoted to advertising, sales, improving efficiency, incorporating new technology, and recruiting and training employees. All of these activities require discretionary outlays. They are options the firm may or may not exercise; and the decision to exercise or not depends on the size of payments that have been promised to the firm's creditors.

Thus the issues introduced in the discussion of growth opportunities are really very general ones. The heart of the matter is that the existence of debt changes the firm's actions in some circumstances. It creates situations ex post in which management can serve shareholders' interests only by making sub-optimal decisions. Ex ante, this reduces the value of the firm (other things equal) and reduces shareholders' wealth.

3.2. The costs of avoiding the problem

Why not eliminate this problem by adding a clause to the debt contract? That is, the contract could include a specific requirement that the firm take on each investment project in all states where its net present value is positive.

Rewriting the contract is not the only alternative. For example, the initial contract could be accepted with the expectation that it would be renegotiated if a favorable investment opportunity would otherwise be passed up.

These are two of the several possible solutions discussed below in the context of the simple case of section 2. The discussion also applies to the general case to be presented in section 4.

All the possible solutions I have been able to identify are costly, in some cases so costly that they seem infeasible. The costs reflect primarily the costs of monitoring and contract enforcement. I am also assuming imperfect markets for growth options and other intangible real assets. That is discussed further in section 4.

3.2.1. Rewriting the debt contract

The firm could accept a debt contract requiring it to undertake all future investments having positive net present value, but that would be an empty promise. There are several reasons. First, the contract could not be enforced when it counts, because limited liability protects shareholders from mandatory future assessments. To make the contract work, the firm's owners would all have to sign contracts as individuals, with each shareholder bearing a pro rata share of the possible assessment. The difficulties of obtaining such an agreement go beyond the costs of paperwork, distributing information, and monitoring.[14] Consider an individual who accepts, in principle, that shareholders ought to forfeit part of their right to limited liability. (Presumably, the possible assessment would be limited to some maximum amount.) It is not in his interest, acting individually, to guarantee his share of the potential assessment. The resulting increase in firm value accrues to all shareholders, not to him alone. In other words, the commitment to advance funds is, from the individual shareholder's viewpoint, a public good.

Second, even if such a contract were laboriously constructed, there would rarely be any objective basis for judging whether it is breached. In the example discussed in section 2, bondholders could press for specific performance only by showing that $V(s) > I$. But for most corporate investments $V(s)$ is not objectively observable. Instead it is estimated by management, who will no doubt be appropriately pessimistic if their unbiased estimate of $V(s)$ is greater than I but less than $I+P$. Even if $V(s)$ is observable, its magnitude is typically under management control. If it turns out that $V(s)$ is potentially between I and $I+P$, a management that acts in the shareholders' interests will surely be able to find some suboptimal policy that dissipates the opportunity, forcing its actual value below I. No sane lawyer attempts to write a contract requiring management to 'abstain from suboptimal decisions'.

In most cases the only enforceable contract would be a promise by the firm, backed up by the present value of I in escrow, to take the investment opportunity *whatever happens*. Then the value of the firm, including the escrow, is

$$V = \int_0^\infty V(s)\,\mathrm{d}s. \tag{7}$$

Since the investment in this case is not discretionary, the existence of debt does affect it, and the firm can go to 100 percent debt if it wishes.

Why do we not observe firms committing themselves to future investments? Evidently this action has offsetting costs. The firm's net debt position under such a contract is V_D less the value of the escrow. If the escrow exceeds V_D, the firm ends up as a net lender rather than a net borrower. In that case, what is the point?

More important, the debt contract forces the firm to accept projects with negative net present values in unfavorable states of nature. Thus the value of the firm declines by

$$\Delta V = \int_0^{s_a} [V(s)-I]q(s)\,\mathrm{d}s < 0.$$

Note that $V(s) < I$ in states $0 < s < s_a$.

---

[14]There are many things creditors would have to guard against. For example, shareholders can protect themselves against possible assessment by setting up a thinly capitalized, intermediate corporation to hold the firm's shares.

Thus there is a tradeoff between the loss ΔV and the gain created by the commitment to invest. Of course, if it is unlikely that $V(s)$ will be less than I, then the cost ΔV is small and the commitment to invest in all states may be worthwhile. Nevertheless this exception proves the rule. The lower the probability that $V(s)$ will be less than I, the less the asset has of the essential characteristics of a growth opportunity, and the more it is like an asset in place.

3.2.2. Renegotiating the debt contract

Thus it seems extremely difficult to write and enforce a debt contract which requires optimal (i.e., firm value maximizing) capital budgeting decisions. But if the problem cannot be solved ex ante, perhaps it can be solved ex post. If creditors and shareholders find themselves in a position where the net present value of an investment project is positive, but less than the payment promised to creditors, then it is in both sides' interest to renegotiate the debt contract. Renegotiation may lead to an arrangement in which creditors accept less than the face amount of their securities in exchange for the owners' commitment to put up funds for further investment. The arrangement may call for either party to buy out the other, or for a third party to buy out the first two.

Renegotiation is not impossible, merely costly. There are the direct costs of renegotiating, perhaps magnified by the mutual suspicion which tends to arise in situations of financial distress. Second, the creditors cannot renegotiate intelligently without an estimate of the net present value of the project in question. They cannot depend on management's estimate, since the shareholders' interest is served by downplaying the opportunity's value.[15] Yet it is doubtful that creditors could obtain an adequate estimate of this value without continual monitoring of the firm's actions and prospects – a costly duplication of one important aspect of the management function.

These monitoring and renegotiation costs are worthwhile to the extent that the incidence of suboptimal investment decisions is reduced, but the prospect of these costs nevertheless reduces the present market value of the firm. Moreover, the reduction is an increasing function of the amount of debt the firm carries.

3.2.3. Shortening debt maturity

One apparently easy way out is to shorten the maturity of outstanding debt. Debt that matures *before* an investment option is to be exercised does not

---

[15]The firm may even 'demand' renegotiation when $V(s) > I + P$. After all, they can always claim that $V(s) < I + P$. Without monitoring creditors cannot know which is the truth. This may be one reason why conditions of financial distress often are resolved by a third party buying out all security holders – via a merger, for example. Of course this simplifies capital structure and removes many of the conflicts of interest that would otherwise lead to good opportunities being passed up. But the possibility of a third party offer also assists debtor-creditor negotiations, since debtors are less tempted to downplay the firm's investment prospects.

induce suboptimal investment decisions. Thus it seems that permanent debt capital is best obtained by a policy of rolling over short maturity debt claims.

The roll-over cannot be automatic however. If it is, we are back to the problem described in section 2. Borrowing short does not, in itself, reduce monitoring costs. What it does offer is the setting for continuous and gradual renegotiation, in which the firm can in principle shift at any time back to all-equity financing, or to another source of debt capital. This seems to be a good solution, but there are costs of maintaining such a continuous, intimate and flexible relationship.

3.2.4. Mediation

There is still another possibility. Creditors could reserve the right to bring in an independent fact-finder and mediator *ex post* when there are symptoms of financial distress and suspicion that a suboptimal investment policy is being followed. Both creditors and debtors may be better off placing their fate in the hands of an impartial third party than attempting to negotiate bilaterally.

The major disadvantage of this approach is the difficulty of defining when the mediator is to be called in. The firm would not give its creditors an open option to force artibration, yet there seems no fully objective way of defining the degree of 'financial distress' or 'suboptimal investment policy' that justifies calling the mediator.

The potential advantage of the approach is that creditors may be willing to cut back on routine monitoring if the option of mediation is available. This saves money and makes the firm more valuable than it would be otherwise. Monitoring by creditors cannot be eliminated though. If it were the creditors would have no way of knowing when to call the mediator!

In many cases the process of bankruptcy or reorganization is really a mediation and fact finding service provided by society at large. Sometimes debt contracts are tightly construed in this process, but often creditors' absolute priority over stockholders is sacrificed in the search for a reorganization plan that can be accepted by all parties. This makes sense: *Ex post* fact finding and mediation are needed to reduce routine monitoring costs and reduce the conflicts of interest and incentives for deception that inevitably arise in conditions of financial distress. Bankruptcy law provides for these services. But the services have little value if reserved exclusively for terminal cases. Thus the law holds out some hope for debtors as well as creditors.

3.2.5. Restrictions on dividends

Jeffrey Halis, in his comments on an earlier verion of this paper, has described how restricting dividend payments can protect against the suboptimal investment decisions induced by risky debt.

In the simple case discussed in section 2, I assumed that the investment I was fresh equity capital, raised by issuing stock. But suppose the firm has plenty of cash on hand. It can either invest the cash or pay it out to the stock-holders. In that case the investment is financed not by a stock issue, but by forgoing a dividend. The firm's investment decision is unchanged.

But if dividends are restricted, the firm must invest in *something*. If funds can be placed either in cash or a real asset offering $V(s) > I$, the real asset will be chosen and the value of the firm will be maximized.

I regard this as a strong rationale for restrictive covenants on dividends, and a *partial* solution to the warped investment incentives created by risky debt. The reasons it is only a partial solution include the following:

(1) There are still monitoring costs, since there are so many possible channels for transferring capital to the firm's owners. This is particularly difficult when owners are also managers. As Jensen and Meckling (1976) point out, transfers can take a variety of non-pecuniary forms.

(2) The investment incentives are still not exactly right. That is, the best investment policy from the shareholders' viewpoint is not the one which maximizes the market value of the firm. Shareholders will prefer risky assets to safe ones, other things equal. Thus they may reject valuable safe assets in favor of riskier assets with lower, or even negative net present value. This has been discussed by Jensen and Meckling (1976) and Galai and Masulis (1976).

(3) The dividend restriction, if binding, may force the firm to invest in assets with negative net present values in unfavorable states of nature. That is, it may force firms to retain cash that really should be distributed to the firm's owners.[16]

(4) A dividend constraint is helpful only when cash is actually available for payout. Consider the following scenario. Firm X issues what seems a moderate amount of long-term bonds. It accepts a covenant restricting dividend payments if retained earnings fall below a certain threshold.[17] Additional debt is also restricted in these circumstances. But the firm falls on bad times, and losses accumulate to the point where the dividend con-straint is binding. In this situation there is little cash for dividends or plowback. The shortage of cash does not matter if there are no good investment opportunities. But it may make economic sense to spend money to save the firm. If so, the funds will have to be raised by stock issue, unless the debt contract is renegotiated. But here the analysis of section 2 applies directly. Moreover, the firm's financial distress has made its bonds riskier

---

[16]If there is a tax advantage to corporate borrowing, there is a tax disadvantage to lending. The purchase of marketable securities is a negative net present value investment.

[17]It would not make sense for the firm to forfeit the right to pay dividends in all circum-stances – see paragraph (3) just above. Nor would the firm allow creditors to say when divi-dends could be paid, since creditors are better off any time earnings are retained, regardless of whether the firm has valuable investment opportunities.

than they were when issued. As is shown below, the riskier the debt, the weaker is shareholders' incentive to commit additional capital to the firm.

3.2.6. Honesty is the best policy

This paper is about a game that stockholders can play at the short-run expense of creditors. But in the longer run, stockholders bear the costs – the costs of inappropriate investment decisions and the cost of playing the game itself, particularly the costs of monitoring and contract enforcement by creditors.

We would expect society to work out contractual, legal and institutional arrangements which minimize the overall cost of the game, assuming that there are valid reasons to issue risky debt. Yet totally eliminating the cost of the game seems impossible so long as the firm is tempted to play it.

Voluntary forbearance would be the simplest and best solution to the investment incentive problem. An announced policy of taking all future investment opportunities with positive net present values is the best policy if believed by creditors and capital markets. But a reputation for honesty is acquired mainly by performance. It is therefore most often pursued by firms that expect to stay in business for a long time. It is also easier to acquire for firms which do *not* borrow heavily against the value of growth opportunities. The truly honest man avoids temptation.

3.2.7. Monitoring and protective covenants

It is important to remember that monitoring costs are borne by stockholders. In well-functioning capital markets lenders foresee the costs, which are therefore reflected in the equilibrium promised interest rates for various debt contracts. When debt is issued, the costs' present value is reflected in the market value of the firm and absorbed by stockholders, who have the residual claim on firm value. It is up to shareholders to decide whether to accept these costs. They could borrow on terms which exclude renegotiation and monitoring. They may not be able to borrow as much,[18] and they may have to pay an extremely high promised interest rate, but they can do it.

The reason why firms accept loan terms which compensate lenders for monitoring and renegotiation is that the costs thus incurred are offset by the increase in firm value due to a lower incidence of suboptimal investment decisions or other agency costs.

It is the same with loan covenants. Managers complain about 'restrictive covenants' but they are rational from the debtors' point of view as well as the creditors'. It is true that lenders may demand such covenants before lending money *at a given interest rate,* but the choice of covenants is fundamentally the shareholders'. Where covenants exist, we must conclude that managers and shareholders have found that it pays to accept them. They freely choose to

---

[18]See section 2.

accept constraints today which rule out behavior which *seems* rational tomorrow. The resulting arrangement is an exact financial analogue to a situation described by Homer (c. −900, pp. 227–228):

> I carved a massive cake of beeswax into bits and rolled them in my hands until they softened – no long task, for a burning heat came down from Hêlios, lord of high noon. Going forward I carried wax along the line, and laid it thick on their ears. They tied me up, then, plumb amidships, back to the mast, lashed to the mast, and took themselves again to rowing. Soon, as we came smartly within hailing distance, the two Seirênês, noting our fast ship off their point, made ready, and they sang ... The lovely voices in ardor appealing over the water made me crave to listen, and I tried to say 'Untie me!' to the crew, jerking my brows; but they bent steady to the oars.

3.3. Secondary markets for real assets

Consider a firm which is holding a real asset for which there is a secondary market. In each period the firm will compare the present value of using the asset (for at least one more period) with the cash it could obtain by selling it. If it decides to use the asset, it is in effect investing the secondary market value.

Fig. 1 depicts this case exactly, if we interpret $V(s)$ as the value in use by the firm, given state s, and I as the secondary market value. (I could also depend on the state occurring.) The rational decision is to sell if $V(s) < I$.

However, if the firm has debt outstanding, having promised to pay the amount P, the rational move from the shareholders' point of view is to sell if $V(s) < I+P$. When this condition holds, selling generates the amount I, whereas not selling generates only $V(s)-P$, which is less than I. The shareholders should attempt to liquidate and run, leaving the creditors holding the empty bag.

If this option is open, then all of the analysis presented in section 2 applies exactly. The fact that we were there concerned with possible future investment, and here with possible disinvestment, is immaterial. The two cases are exactly symmetrical. Holding I, the set of contingent values $V(s)$, and other parameters equal, we can say that the 'debt capacity' of an asset in place is exactly the same as that of a growth opportunity.

This pleasant symmetry does not carry over into real life however. For one thing, it is illegal (specifically, fraudulent) to liquidate assets and distribute the proceeds to shareholders if bankruptcy is imminent. More important, it is relatively easy to write a clause in the debt contract prohibiting this maneuver. So long as the creditors have veto power over dividends or any form of return of capital under conditions of financial distress, they are protected.[19]

---

[19]They do not care if the asset is liquidated and the proceeds put in cash or securities. Normally these assets will provide better security than the original ones.

The existence of a secondary market for an asset will, in general, increase the present market value of the firm, providing that the appropriate restrictive covenants can be written. That is, the option to abandon is valuable. This is directly evident from fig. 1. The existence of a secondary market allows a higher payoff ($I > V(s)$) for states $s < s_a$, while the payoff for states $s > s_a$ is the same. However, if the appropriate restrictive covenants for some reason cannot be written or enforced, then the existence of a secondary market may actually reduce the value of the firm, and reduce the amount of debt that can be issued against any promised payment P.

4. Generalization

4.1. Restatement of the problem: Imperfections in real asset markets

The value of the firm as a going concern depends on its future investment strategy. Thus it is useful for expositional purposes to think of the firm as composed of two distinct asset types: (1) *real assets*, which have market values independent of the firm's investment strategy, and (2) *real options*, which are opportunities to purchase real assets on possibly favorable terms.

The existence of valuable real options presumes some adjustment costs, market power, or other imperfections in the real sector. There are no investment opportunities offering positive net present value if product and factor markets are perfectly competitive and in continuous, long-run equilibrium. The value of real options reflects the possibility of rents or quasi-rents.

Moreover, the theory presented here rests not only on costs of monitoring and enforcement of contracts, but also on certain specific imperfections in the market for real options. It is necessary that the value of a growth option vanishes or declines if it is not exercised by the firm. This assumption may be justified in several ways:

(1) The real options may be firm-specific, having no value to any other firm. This could occur if real options are to some extent embodied in real assets, so that the options cannot be purchased separately. Real options may also be firm-specific if generated by experience curves, leaning-by-doing, or other similar phenomena.

(2) If real options are not firm-specific they may nevertheless be traded in thin and imperfect secondary markets. If so, the real option's 'liquidation value' is less than its value as part of a going concern. This limits the extent to which a real option can be used as specific security for a debt claim. Even if a clear and enforceable contract could be written, permitting creditors to claim a specific real option if not exercised by the firm at the optimal time, creditors would face a costly and lengthy task in recovering the value of

their security. By the time they sue, recover the option, and resell it or exercise it themselves, the value of the opportunity may vanish.

One can think of real options that are separable, objectively identifiable, relatively long-lived, and for which reasonable secondary markets exist. Examples are patents, certain trademarks, franchises and operating licenses. Such options should 'support' debt to the same extent as otherwise similar real assets.

This paper takes the existence of real options as given. It does not ask whether they are acquired via purchase of real assets, via learning-by-doing, or via direct expenditure in research, advertising, training or some other activity. The development of a theory of the firm which treats real options as endogenous is a challenging subject for future research.

The immediate problem is to extend the arguments given in section 2 to cases in which investment occurs in more than one period, and in which firms hold more than one type of asset.

4.2. Long-term borrowing

A detailed dynamic model of the firm's investment and borrowing behavior is beyond the scope of this paper. But it is not hard to predict the qualitative effects of debt financing on the firm's investment policy and market value.

We consider a firm holding options on real assets, one of which should be partially or wholly exercised at time t. Exercising the option requires a fresh commitment of equity capital by shareholders.[20] The firm may have assets in place at t. It also has bonds outstanding which mature at some point beyond t.[21]

Since $V_t = V_{E,t} + V_{D,t}$, the effect of an incremental discretionary investment on the market value of equity is $dV_E/dI = dV/dI - dV_D/dI$. The investment policy which maximizes the value of the firm is to continue investing as long as $dV/dI > 1$. This means exercising all options which (1) have positive net present value and for which (2) period t is the expiration date or the optimal time for exercise. But options having positive net present value are not necessarily attractive to the firm's owners. Whether they are depends on the sign and magnitude of dV_D/dI.

At any point in time the value of outstanding bonds is related to the value of the firm and to the uncertainty about the firm's future value,[22]

$$V_{D,t} = f_t[V_t, \sigma^2(\tilde{V}_{t+1}/V_t)],$$

[20] The commitment can be a dividend forgone.

[21] There may or may not be a cash payment P_t due to bondholders. I assume, however, that any such payment is made after the firm decides whether to exercise its investment option. Any payment made before this decision is a sunk cost.

[22] Discussions with Jeffrey Halis were helpful in simplifying the following exposition.

where $\sigma^2(\tilde{V}_{t+1}/V_t)$, henceforth σ^2, is the variance rate of overall market value. Therefore,

$$\frac{dV_{E,t}}{dI_t} = \frac{dV_t}{dI_t}\left(1 - \frac{\delta f_t}{\delta V_t}\right) - \frac{\delta f_t}{\delta \sigma_t^2}\left(\frac{\delta \sigma_t^2}{\delta I_t}\right). \tag{8}$$

In other words, there is a transfer of value from stockholders, who make the investment, to bondholders, who contribute nothing. Call this transfer Z,

$$\begin{aligned} Z_t &\equiv \frac{dV_t}{dI_t} - \frac{dV_{E,t}}{dI_t} \\ &= \frac{dV_t}{dI_t} \cdot \frac{\delta f_t}{\delta V_t} + \frac{\delta f_t}{\delta \sigma^2} \cdot \frac{\delta \sigma^2}{\delta I_t}. \end{aligned} \tag{9}$$

Appropriate investment incentives exist only when $Z_t = 0$.

First take the case where $\delta \sigma_t^2/\delta t = 0$, so that the firm's 'risk class' is unaffected by the decision to exercise. Now $\delta f_t/\delta V_t$ will always be positive except in the limiting case where the debt is default risk free. Thus $Z_t > 0$. The existence of risky debt in period t weakens the incentive to invest, induces a suboptimal investment strategy, and reduces the market value of the firm in all periods prior to t.

This result rests on no assumption about the firms' other assets or opportunities. The only assumption made about the debt is that there is some risk of default in t or afterwards, so that changes in the market value of risky debt are positively related to changes in the market value of all the firm's assets.

Eqs. (8) and (9) assume a continuous investment schedule (with decreasing returns to scale) rather than discrete projects which have to be accepted or rejected. In this situation the firm invests less than the optimal amount. The discrete case is shown in fig. 4. In the figure $\Delta V(s) - I(s)$ is the net present value of the investment option if exercised. It is positive for all states $s > s_a$. ΔV_D is the capital gain to bondholders if the option is exercised – but exercise will not occur unless $\Delta V(s) \geq \Delta V_D(s) + I(s)$. Thus a valuable option is forgone in some states of nature.

The shaded area in figure 4 indicates the loss of value in a range of states at time t. The implications are just as shown in fig. 3.

4.2.1. Target debt ratios

What happens if the incremental investment I is partially or wholly debt financed? There is no way for the firm to gain at the expense of the new bond-holders, but the increase in the firm's debt ratio erodes the old bondholders' position. Therefore ΔV_D, the capital gain to old bondholders, is reduced and possibly eliminated.

This presumes that the additional borrowing is tied to the incremental investment, as it would be by a covenant restricting total borrowing to a certain proportion of the value of assets in place. Here we have one rationale for target debt ratios. A simple debt ratio constraint is unlikely to eliminate the incentive problem discussed in this paper, but it helps.

4.2.2. Spillover effects

The fact that too little will be invested in some or all states of nature at time t reduces the value of the firm prior to t. Consider how this affects investment strategy in $t-1$. The suboptimal strategy at t reduces V_{t-1}. This, in turn, reduces the market value of outstanding debt at $t-1$, assuming the debt matures after t's investment decision. It also makes the debt riskier: $\delta f_{t-1}/\delta V_{t-1}$ increases.[23] Therefore, Z_{t-1} increases, and investment incentives are weakened in period $t-1$ as well as t.

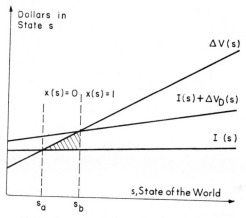

Fig. 4. The firm's investment decision with prior debt financing – multiperiod case. $I(s)$ = discretionary outlay; $\Delta V(s)$ = increase in firm value if outlay is made $(x(s) = 1)$; $\Delta V_D(s)$ = increase in debt value if outlay is made, including debt service in t.

A similar effect may occur after period t, if the existence of risky debt in t leads the firm to pass up valuable investment opportunities. If this happens, the value of the firm is less in $t+1$, debt in $t+1$ is less valuable and riskier, and investment incentives are weakened.

Thus, if the existence of risky debt in t causes an inappropriate investment strategy in t, it will also cause an inappropriate strategy both before and after t. This strengthens the negative link between the existence of risky debt and the present market value of the firm.

[23]I assume that $\delta^2 f/\delta V^2 < 0$. See Merton (1974).

4.2.3. Shifts in asset risk

Up to this point I have assumed that discretionary investment does not affect σ_t^2, the variance rate of market value. But the effects of a shift in risk are easily seen from eqs. (8) or (9). If investment decreases σ_t^2 then Z_t, the transfer to bondholders, is greater than was assumed above, and the incidence and extent of suboptimal investment choices increases.[24] An increase in σ_t^2, on the other hand, is favorable. In fact, as Jensen and Meckling (1976) have emphasized, the increase in σ_t^2 could be so great that Z_t is negative, leading the firm to exercise investment options with negative net present values.

We have an interesting, perhaps surprising, conclusion. The impact of risky debt on the market value of the firm is less for firms holding investment options on assets that are risky relative to the firms' present assets.[25] In this sense we may observe risky firms borrowing more than safe ones.

4.3. Borrowing against a portfolio of assets

One alleged advantage of corporate diversification is that diversified firms can borrow more. A combination of assets with less than perfectly correlated returns gives a variance rate for the combination's value that is less than the average rate of the assets considered separately. The usual conclusion is that this increases the amount the firm can or should borrow.[26]

The conclusion does *not* follow from the theory presented here. The following preliminary analysis indicates that there should be no consistent relationship between 'diversification' and 'debt capacity'.

We return to the simple world analyzed in section 2. Now there are two firms holding two real options. We simplify notation by redefining $V_i(s)$ as the *net* value (at $t = 1$) of firm i's option contingent on s. Previously net value was $V_i(s) - I_i$. Present value is

$$V_i = \int_{S_i} q(s) V_i(s) \, \mathrm{d}s, \tag{10}$$

where S_i is the set of all states for which i exercises its option. It will do so when $V_i(s) > P_i$, where P_i is the amount it has promised to creditors. P_i is a positive constant, but the debt is risky: $V_i(s) < P_i$ in some states.

Now suppose firms i and j merge. The new firm holds a portfolio of the two options. The original debt of the two firms is merged into one class with a promised payoff $P_i + P_j$. Is the present market value of the merged firm greater

---

[24]The risk of the real asset acquired is taken into account in its net present value. Thus $\mathrm{d}V_t/\mathrm{d}I_t$ already reflects the effects of a shift in σ^2 on firm value.

[25]A special case of this result can be derived from fig. 2. Greater uncertainty about the value $V(s)$ corresponds to a steeper slope of $V(s)$ plotted against s. The steeper the slope, the smaller the area of the shaded triangle representing lost value.

[26]Lewellen (1971). See also Higgins and Schall (1975).

than the sum of the separate market values of i and j? Does diversification ameliorate the investment incentive problem created by the existence of risky debt?

The present value of option i in portfolio with the other option j is

$$V_i(j) = \int_{S_i(j)} q(s) V_i(s) \, ds, \tag{11}$$

where $S_i(j)$ is the set of states in which option i is exercised. $S_i(j)$ includes states s for which $V_i(s) \geq P_i + P_j - \max[V_j(s), 0]$ *and* for which $V_i(s) \geq 0$.

The conditions defining $S_i(j)$ need a word of further explanation. First, there is no incentive to exercise an option with negative net present value. $V_i(s)$ must be positive to justify investment. Suppose both options have positive net present value. Then the firm will accept both or neither, depending on whether $V_i(s) + V_j(s)$ exceeds $P_i + P_j$. However, suppose $V_j(s)$ is negative. In this case i is exercised only if it can carry the burden of j's debt, that is, if $V_i(s) > P_i + P_j$.

The problem can now be stated as follows. What is the relationship of $V_i(j) + V_j(i)$ to $V_i + V_j$? Alternatively, is $DV_i + DV_j > 0$, where $DV_i \equiv V_i(j) - V_i$ and $DV_j \equiv V_j(i) - V_j$? DV_i can be loosely interpreted as 'diversification value' – more precisely, as the change in the present value of option i due to the co-existence of j and its associated debt burden.[27]

Under general assumptions we cannot say whether $DV_i + DV_j$ is positive. Consider box (2) in table 1. In this case both options are valuable ($V_i(s) > 0$ and $V_j(s) > 0$) but firm i would not have exercised its option absent the merger, because the promised payment to i's creditors exceeds the net present value of exercise ($V_i(s) < P_i$).

The new firm may confront an all-or-nothing decision. It may take both projects if

$$V_i(s) + V_j(s) - P_i - P_j \geq 0.$$

Otherwise it may take neither one.

Here is a numerical example:

Case	V_i	P_i	V_j	P_j
A	50	100	80	20
B	50	100	60	20

[27]Note I am asking whether the present value of the *firm* increases at $t = 0$ when i and j are combined. $DV_i + DV_j$ will be fully captured by equity if debt with a promised payment $P_i + P_j$ is issued *after* assets i and j are combined. However, if two separate debt issues are made, promising P_i and P_j and secured by V_i and V_j, respectively, and if i and j are then combined (a surprise to the two creditor groups), then creditors may receive a capital gain at the expense of equity.

Table 1

Investment decisions which maximize equity value when two real options and their associated debt are combined into one firm.

Net present value of option j, $V_j(s)$, relative to promised payment, P_j, on debt issued against project j	Net present value of option i, $V_i(s)$, relative to promised payment, P_i, on debt issued against project i		
	$V_i(s) \geqq P_i$	$P_i > V_i(s) \geqq 0$	$V_i(s) < 0$
$V_j(s) \geqq P_j$	(1) Take both $DV_i = 0$ $DV_j = 0$	(2) Take both if $V_i(s) + V_j(s) - P_i - P_j \geqq 0$. Otherwise reject both. X_i may = 1 (0 before); $DV_i \geqq 0$, X_j may = 0 (1 before); $DV_j \leqq 0$.	(3) Reject i, take j if $V_j(s) - P_i - P_j \geqq 0$. $DV_i = 0$, X_j may = 0 (1 before); $DV_j \leqq 0$.
$V_j(s) < P_j$, $V_j(s) \geqq 0$	(4) Take both if $V_i(s) + V_j(s) - P_i - P_j \geqq 0$. Otherwise reject both. X_i may = 0 (1 before); $DV_i \leqq 0$, X_j may = 1 (0 before); $DV_j \geqq 0$.	(5) Reject both. $DV_i = 0$, $DV_j = 0$.	(6) Reject both. $DV_i = 0$, $DV_j = 0$.
$V_j(s) < 0$	(7) Reject j, take i if $V_i(s) - P_i - P_j \geqq 0$. X_i may = 0 (1 before); $DV_i \leqq 0$, $DV_j = 0$.	(8) Reject both. $DV_i = 0$, $DV_j = 0$.	(9) Reject both. $DV_i = 0$, $DV_j = 0$.

Note: 'Before' refers to the decisions that would be made by firms i and j acting separately.

In case A the merger rescues project i. Both projects are taken because $V_i + V_j - P_i - P_j = +10$. (Note that the firm is liable for the full promised payment to bondholders regardless of whether project i is taken.) In case B project i is rejected and it drags j down with it: $V_i + V_j - P_i - P_j = -10$. In case A, $DV_i > 0$ and $DV_j = 0$, so the merger increases value. In case B, $DV_i = 0$ and $DV_j < 0$, so value is reduced.

Table 1 displays all possible outcomes. In boxes (2) and (4) the merger may or may not help. In boxes (3) and (7) it cannot help but may hurt. In the other boxes there is no effect. Overall one cannot say.

It may be possible to reach more specific conclusions by making stronger assumptions about the joint distributions of $V_i(s)$ and $V_j(s)$.[28]

5. Conclusions

The analysis presented in this paper adds up to a partial theory of the corporate borrowing decision. The theory does not rely on imperfect or incomplete *financial* markets. Although I have dealt only with certain simple cases, it still leads to testable propositions.

According to the theory, the amount of debt issued by the firm should be set equal to V_D^*, that amount which maximizes the market value of the firm. It has no direct relationship to the probability of default or the amount lenders are willing to advance.

The theory predicts that V_D^* will be inversely related to the ratio of V_G to V, where V_G is the part of firm value V accounted for by growth opportunities, or, more generally, the part of V that is contingent on discretionary future expenditure by the firm. In the broader interpretation discretionary expenditures include all future investment and variable costs, which, if undertaken, increase the end-of-period value of the firm. Although a general measure of this concept is difficult to derive from accounting data, the following specific propositions should hold, other things equal, if the theory is right:

(1) Assets-in-place should be financed with more debt than growth opportunities. The investment in assets-in-place is a sunk cost and, by definition, not discretionary. (I assume that secondary markets for assets-in-place do not exist or that sale in secondary markets can be regulated by the debt contract.)

---

[28]However, examination of table 1 prompts the suspicion that $DV_i + DV_j$ will be more often negative than positive, particularly if $V_i(s)$ and $V_j(s)$ lack strong positive correlation. Observe that in box (2) $DV_i \geqq 0$ is offset by $DV_j \leqq 0$. Similarly in box (4) $DV \geqq 0$ and $DV_i \leqq 0$. But in boxes (3) and (7) the only possibilities are $DV_j \leqq 0$ and $DV_i \leqq 0$, respectively. If $V_i(s)$ and $V_j(s)$ are negatively correlated, so that boxes (3) and (7) are likely cases, the present value of $DV_i + DV_j$ will probably be negative. But this is the case in which intuition tugs us to say that 'diversification value' ought to be largest!

(2) For assets-in-place, the following factors should be associated with heavy debt financing: (a) capital-intensity and *high* operating leverage, and, of course, (b) profitability, ideally measured in terms of expected future value of the firm's assets.

The theory also provides a rationalization for certain aspects of the operations of bond markets. I have already explained why firms are not observed borrowing against the present value of future growth opportunities. Sinking funds can be interpreted as a device to reduce creditors' exposure in parallel with the expected decline in the value of assets in place when the loan is made. It is also some protection against the debtors running off with the cash flow that these assets produce.

This same argument explains why firms attempt to match the maturities of their assets and liabilities. As far as I can see, standard finance theory gives no reason why firms should not finance long-lived assets with short-term debt, or conversely, short-lived assets with long-term debt. But we can interpret matching maturities as an attempt to schedule debt repayments to correspond to the decline in future value of assets currently in place.

Of course, these predictions are not a complete statement of the theory's implications. Others were noted in the main text of the paper. No doubt there are still others that I haven't grasped yet.

5.1. Areas for further research of real asset valuation

All of this paper's interesting results stem from the idea of regarding real assets as options whose ultimate value depends on future discretionary investment by the firm. It may be that this idea's most important application will turn out to be the valuation of real assets. Let me conclude by stating one important theorem.

Following MM [Miller and Modigliani (1961)], we can regard the market value of the firm as representing two components, the present value of (earnings generated by) assets-in-place, and the present value of growth opportunities. In MM's model, growth opportunities have value if investors expect the rate of return earned on future investments to exceed the firm's cost of capital. No distinction is drawn between the cost of capital for assets-in-place versus future investment.[29]

This model can be given an interesting reinterpretation in terms of option theory. At any point in time the firm is a collection of tangible and intangible assets. Assume the tangible assets are accumulated units of productive capacity – i.e. real assets – all drawn from the same risk class. The intangible assets are options to purchase additional units in future periods. The sum of these option

[29]See, in particular, Miller and Modigliani (1966).

values is clearly what MM mean by the present value of growth. A similar interpretation can be put on going concern value.

We immediately have the question of whether growth options arrive randomly or systematically, whether they are 'free' or must be purchased by the firm, and whether they have value if split off from the assets the firm already holds. It may be that real options are acquired only through the purchase of real assets in place – i.e., exercising options today may create more options for possible exercise tomorrow. This paper has barely begun to consider how corporate investment decisions might be modelled.

But back to MM. Note that stock options are riskier than the stocks they are written on. Suppose that is true for real options also.[30] Consequently, the observed risk of a common stock (e.g., its beta) will be a positive function of the proportion of the stock's value accounted for by growth in MM's sense. Two implications are immediately obvious.

(1) Neoclassical valuation models, like MM's, which use the same 'cost of capital' to evaluate earnings from present versus future investment, are mis-specified. (Whether this is empirically serious is, of course, unclear.)
(2) One cannot measure the equilibrium capitalization rate for a firm's stock (e.g., by measuring its beta and calculating $E[R]$ from the capital asset pricing model) and then use it as a hurdle rate for capital budgeting. This will be an overestimate of the correct rate for any firm having valuable growth opportunities.

Appendix

This appendix analyzes the link between debt financing and firm value when interest is a tax-deductible expense. Only corporate taxes are considered. The effects, if any, of *investors'* income tax liabilities on the firm's debt–equity choice are ignored. The analysis is restricted to the simple case discussed in section 2.

As the firm substitutes debt for equity in its initial capital structure, it finds that the present value of tax shields generated by debt at first outweighs the decline in firm value due to loss of valuable investment opportunities. At some point the two effects just balance. Beyond that point further borrowing decreases the value of the firm.

The optimum borrowing level depends on whether the interest tax shields retain their value if the firm goes bankrupt and on whether there is a limit to the amount of interest allowed as a tax-deductible expense. Suppose the firm can deduct the full *promised* interest payment $P - V_D$ in all states. The tax rate

---

[30]It is not necessarily true, as Michael Brennan has pointed out. See the discussion in Myers and Turnbull (1977).

is T. Then the value of the firm is

$$V = \int_{s_b}^{\infty} [V(s) - I]q(s)\,ds + T(P - V_D)\int_0^{\infty} q(s)\,ds, \tag{A.1}$$

where s_b is defined by $V(s_b) = I + P - T(P - V_D)$, and the debt value V_D is given by

$$V_D = \int_0^{s_b} T(P - V_D)q(s)\,ds + \int_{s_b}^{\infty} Pq(s)\,ds. \tag{A.2}$$

But an examination of eq. (A.1) reveals a quite unreasonable feature: V can be made arbitrarily large by choosing a large enough value for P. It is more reasonable to suppose that the tax authorities allow deductions based on some maximum promised interest rate R, so that the maximum attainable tax shield is RTV_D. The tax shield actually attained is $\min(RTV_D, T(P - V_D))$. The firm's value is

$$V = \int_{s_b}^{\infty} [V(s) - I]q(s)\,ds + \min(RTV_D, T(P - V_D))\int_0^{\infty} q(s)\,ds. \tag{A.3}$$

As $P \to \infty$, $V \to RTV_D\int q(s)\,ds$. But as this happens $V_D \to V$. At the limit, therefore, $V_D = RTV_D\int q(s)\,ds$, which is satisfied only if $V_D = 0$.[31] Thus we have the sensible result that V and V_D each approach zero if P is set high enough. Moreover, there is a definite maximum amount of debt that firms can raise if they attempt to do so. This amount is less than the market value of the firm.

The behavior of V and V_D as a function of P is shown in fig. 5. This figure is drawn so that the maximum value of V occurs before that of V_D. That is, the firm does not attempt to borrow as much as it can. This is always true providing that eq. (A.3) holds, and that P is high enough that the tax shield is RTV_D rather than $T(P - V_D)$.[32] To show this, we calculate $\delta V / \delta P$,

$$\frac{\delta V}{\delta P} = -\left(\frac{\delta s_b}{\delta P}\right)[V(s_b) - I]q(s)) + RT\left(\frac{\delta V_D}{\delta P}\right)\int_0^{\infty} q(s)\,ds.$$

Evaluating the derivative at $\delta V_D / \delta P = 0$, we find that $\delta V / \delta P$ must be negative Thus the firm must go beyond the point of maximum firm value in order to borrow the maximum amount. This is not in the shareholders' interest, so the firm will stop at the point where V is maximized.

---

[31]Note that $\int RTq(s)\,ds$ is on the order of 0.05 – that is substantially less than 1.0.
[32]Kim (1976) has obtained a similar result.

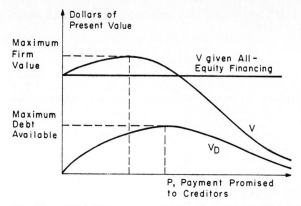

Fig. 5. Firm and debt values when debt interest is tax-deductible.

A second case occurs when the tax shield is lost as the firm goes bankrupt. Then,

$$V = \int_{s_b}^{\infty} [V(s) - I + T(P - V_D)]q(s)\,\mathrm{d}s,\tag{A.4}$$

and V_D is given by eq. (6).

The general behavior of V and V_D is again as shown by fig. 5, although in this case it cannot be guaranteed that the maximum value of V is reached before the maximum value of V_D. This result holds generally only if the tax shield is restricted to TRV_D (or to any amount that is independent of P). But this is not crucial. The essential point is that the firm will choose P to maximize V, not V_D. Only by coincidence will these two functions reach their maximum levels at the same point. The firm should not attempt to borrow as much as possible.

References

Donaldson, G., 1963, Financial goals: Management vs. stockholders, Harvard Business Review 41, 116–129.

Durand, D., 1959, The cost of capital, corporation finance, and the theory of investment: Comment, American Economic Review 49, 639–655.

Fama, E.F., 1976, The effects of a firm's investment and financing decisions on the welfare of its security holders, Working Paper (European Institute for Advanced Studies in Management, Brussels).

Fama, E.F. and M.H. Miller, 1973, The theory of finance (Holt, Rinehart and Winston, New York).

Farrar, D.E. and L.L. Selwyn, 1967, Taxes, corporate financial policy and the return to investors, National Tax Journal 20, 444–454.

Galai, D. and R.W. Masulis, 1976, The option pricing model and the risk factor of stock, Journal of Financial Economics 3, 53–82.

Halis, J., 1976, Should companies issue warrants?, Unpublished M.S. Thesis (M.I.T., Cambridge, MA).

Higgins, R.C. and L.D. Schall, 1975, Corporate bankruptcy and conglomerate merger, Journal of Finance 30, 93–114.

Hirshleifer, J., 1966, Investment decision under uncertainty: Applications of the state-preference approach, Quarterly Journal of Economics 80, 252–277.

Homer, c. −900, The Odyssey, tr. R. Fitzgerald (Anchor Press/Doubleday, Garden City, NJ).

Ingersoll, J., 1976, A contingent-claims valuation of convertible bonds and the optimal policies for call and conversion, Unpublished Ph.D. Dissertation (M.I.T., Cambridge, MA).

Jaffee, D.M., 1971, Credit rationing and the commercial loan market (Wiley, New York).

Jaffee, D.M. and F. Modigliani, 1969, A theory and test of credit rationing, American Economic Review 59, 850–872.

Jaffee, D.M. and T. Russell, 1976, Imperfect information, uncertainty, and credit rationing, Quarterly Journal of Economics 90, 651–666.

Jensen, M.C. and W.H. Meckling, 1976, Theory of the firm: Managerial behavior, agency costs and capital structure, Journal of Financial Economics 3, 305–360.

Kim, E.H., 1976, A mean-variance theory of optimal capital structure, Working Paper (Ohio State University, Columbus, OH).

Leland, H.E. and D.H. Pyle, 1976, Informational asymmetries, financial structure and financial intermediation, Working Paper (University of California, Berkeley, CA).

Lewellen, W., 1971, A pure financial rationale for the conglomerate merger, Journal of Finance 26, 521–537.

Merton, R., 1974, On the pricing of corporate debt: The risk structure of interest rates, Journal of Finance 29, 449–470.

Miller, M.H., 1977, Debt and taxes, Journal of Finance 32, 261–275.

Miller, M.H. and F. Modigliani, Dividend policy, growth and the valuation of shares, Journal of Business 34, 411–433.

Miller, M.H. and F. Modigliani, 1966, Some estimates of the cost of capital to the electric utility industry, 1954–57, American Economic Review 56, 333–391.

Modigliani, F. and M.H. Miller, 1963, Corporate income taxes and the cost of capital: A correction, American Economic Review 53, 433–443.

Myers, S.C., 1975, A note on the determinants of corporate debt capacity, Working Paper (London Graduate School of Business Studies, London).

Myers, S.C. and S.M. Turnbull, 1977, Capital budgeting and the capital asset pricing model: Good news and bad news, Journal of Finance 32, 321–333.

Robichek, A.A. and S.C. Myers, Problems in the theory of optimal capital structure, Journal of Financial and Quantitative Analysis 1, 1–35.

Ross, S.A., 1977, The determination of financial structure: The incentive-signalling approach, Bell Journal of Economics 8, 23–40.

Stiglitz, J.E., 1972, On some aspects of the pure theory of corporate finance, bankruptcies and takeovers, Bell Journal of Economics 3, 458–482.

Stiglitz, J.E., 1974, On the irrelevance of corporate financial policy, American Economic Review 64, 851–866.

Warner, J.B., 1977, Bankruptcy costs, absolute priority and the pricing of risky debt claims, Journal of Financial Economics 4, 239–276.

ON FINANCIAL CONTRACTING

An Analysis of Bond Covenants*

Clifford W. SMITH, Jr. and Jerold B. WARNER

University of Rochester, Rochester, NY 14627, USA

Received September 1978, revised version received May 1979

With risky debt outstanding, stockholder actions aimed at maximizing the value of their equity claim can result in a reduction in the value of both the firm and its outstanding bonds. We examine ways in which debt contracts are written to control the conflict between bondholders and stockholders. We find that extensive direct restrictions on production/investment policy would be expensive to employ and are not observed. However, dividend and financing policy restrictions are written to give stockholders incentives to follow a firm-value-maximizing production/investment policy. Taking into account how contracts control the bondholder-stockholder conflict leads to a number of testable propositions about the specific form of the debt contract that a firm will choose.

1. Introduction and summary

The conflict of interest between the firm's bondholders and its stockholders has been discussed by a number of authors. For example, Fama/Miller (1972, p. 179) indicate that under certain circumstances 'it is easy to construct examples in which a production plan that maximizes shareholder wealth does not maximize bondholder wealth, or vice versa'.[1] Citing an extreme case of the bondholder–stockholder conflict, Black (1976) points out that 'there is no easier way for a company to escape the burden of a debt than to pay out all of its assets in the form of a dividend, and leave the creditors holding an empty shell'.

In this paper, we examine how debt contracts are written to control the bondholder–stockholder conflict. We investigate the various kinds of bond covenants which are included in actual debt contracts. A bond covenant is a provision, such as a limitation on the payment of dividends, which restricts the firm from engaging in specified actions after the bonds are sold.

*This research is supported by the Managerial Economics Research Center, Graduate School of Management, University of Rochester. We are indebted to numerous colleagues, both those at the University of Rochester and elsewhere, for their help on this paper. We are especially grateful to Michael C. Jensen for his assistance.

[1]See also, Modigliani/Miller (1958, p. 293), Black/Cox (1976), Jensen/Meckling (1976), Miller (1977a), and Black/Miller/Posner (1978).

Journal of Financial Economics 7 (1979) 117–161. © North-Holland Publishing Company

Our description of the specific provisions in debt contracts is based primarily on an American Bar Foundation compendium entitled *Commentaries on Indentures*. This volume contains both the standardized provisions which are included in the debt contract (the 'boilerplates') and a practitioner-oriented discussion of their use.

1.1. Sources of the bondholder–stockholder conflict

Corporations are 'legal fictions which serve as a nexus for a set of contracting relationships among individuals'.[2] To focus on the contract between the bondholders and the corporation, we assume that costs of enforcing other contracts are zero. For example, we assume that contracts between stockholders and managers costlessly induce managers to act as if they own all the firm's equity.

The corporation has an indefinite life and the set of contracts which comprise the corporation evolves over time: as the firm's investment opportunity set changes decisions are made about the real activities in which the firm engages and the financial contracts the firm sells. With risky bonds outstanding, management, acting in the stockholders' interest, has incentives to design the firm's operating characteristics and financial structure in ways which benefit stockholders to the detriment of bondholders. Because investment, financing, and dividend policies are endogenous, there are four major sources of conflict which arise between bondholders and stockholders:

Dividend payment. If a firm issues bonds and the bonds are priced assuming the firm will maintain its dividend policy, the value of the bonds is reduced by raising the dividend rate and financing the increase by reducing investment. At the limit, if the firm sells all its assets and pays a liquidating dividend to the stockholders, the bondholders are left with worthless claims.

Claim dilution. If the firm sells bonds, and the bonds are priced assuming that no additional debt will be issued, the value of the bondholders' claims is reduced by issuing additional debt of the same or higher priority.

Asset substitution. If a firm sells bonds for the stated purpose of engaging in low variance projects[3] and the bonds are valued at prices commensurate

---

[2]Jensen/Meckling (1976, p. 310).

[3]The importance of the variance rate is derived from the option pricing analysis of Black/Scholes (1973). In section A.1 of the appendix we discuss the determinants of the value of a bond issue where the bonds are single-payment contracts, and the market is efficient and competitive, without transactions costs, information costs, other agency costs, or taxes. The option pricing analysis assumes that the value of the firm will be independent of its financial structure. Our concern in this paper is with a world in which covenants can change the value of the firm. Hence a critical assumption of the option pricing analysis is violated; the value of the firm will, in general, be a function of the covenants which are offered. The option pricing

with that low risk, the value of the stockholders' equity rises and the value of the bondholders' claim is reduced by substituting projects which increase the firm's variance rate.[4]

Underinvestment. Myers (1977) suggests that a substantial portion of the value of the firm is composed of intangible assets in the form of future investment opportunities. A firm with outstanding bonds can have incentives to reject projects which have a positive net present value if the benefit from accepting the project accrues to the bondholders.

The bondholder–stockholder conflict is of course recognized by capital market participants. Rational bondholders recognize the incentives faced by the stockholders. They understand that after the bonds are issued, any action which increases the wealth of the stockholders will be taken. In ricing the bond issue, bondholders make estimates of the behavior of the stockholders, given the investment, financing, and dividend policies available to the stockholders. The price which bondholders pay for the issue will be lower to reflect the possibility of subsequent wealth transfers to stockholders.[5] The pricing of the bond issue is discussed in more detail in the appendix.

1.2. Control of the bondholder–stockholder conflict: The competing hypotheses

There seems to be general agreement within the finance profession that the bondholder–stockholder relationship entails conflict and that the prices in security markets behave as if all security-holders form rational expectations about the stockholders' behavior after the bonds are issued. However, there is disagreement about whether the total value of the firm is influenced by the way in which the bondholder–stockholder conflict is controlled. There are

---

analysis does not address the issue of the endogeneity of the stockholders' behavior because variables such as the value of the firm's assets or the variance rate are treated as fixed rather than as decision variables. Therefore, the implications drawn from the option pricing model are only suggestive. In section A.2 of the appendix, we suggest how the endogeneity of investment policy affects the optimal choice of financial structure and the value of the firm's financial claims.

[4]The mere exchange of low-risk assets for high-risk assets does not alter the value of the firm if both assets have the same net present values. However, stockholders will have incentives to purchase projects with negative net present values if the increase in the firm's variance rate from accepting those projects is sufficiently large. Even though such projects reduce the total value of the firm, the value of the equity rises.

[5]Similarly, the value of the common stock at the time the bonds are issued will be higher to reflect possible transfers which shareholders will be able to effect. However, this is not to suggest that there is always a positive price at which the bonds can be sold. If the probability of a complete wealth transfer to stockholders prior to required payments to bondholders is 1, then the bonds will sell for a zero price.

two competing hypotheses. We call them the Irrelevance Hypothesis and the Costly Contracting Hypothesis.

1.2.1. The Irrelevance Hypothesis

The Irrelevance Hypothesis is that the manner of controlling the bondholder–stockholder conflict does not change the value of the firm.

Irrelevance under a fixed investment policy. In the Modigliani/Miller (1958) or Fama/Miller (1972) models the firm's investment policy is assumed fixed.[6] As long as the firm's total net cash flows are fixed, the value of the firm will not be changed by the existence or non-existence of protective covenants; with fixed cash flows, any gain which covenants give bondholders is a loss to stockholders, and vice versa. Covenants merely alter the distribution of a set of payoffs which is fixed to the firm's claimholders as a whole, and the choice of specific financial contracts is irrelevant to the value of the firm.

Irrelevance when investment policy is not fixed. Dividend payout, asset substitution, and underinvestment all represent potential opportunities for wealth transfer to stockholders. When these opportunities are available, the firm's investment policy cannot be regarded as fixed because it is likely to be altered by the presence of risky debt. The total value of the firm could be reduced if stockholders engage in actions which maximize the value of their own claims, but not the total value of the firm. However, even if investment policy cannot be regarded as fixed, mechanisms other than covenants exist which could be sufficient to induce the firm's stockholders to choose a firm-value-maximizing production/investment policy.

The forces exerted by external markets could induce the stockholders to maximize the value of the firm. Long (1973) suggests that the firm will accept all projects with a positive net present value if recapitalization is costless. Fama (1978a) argues that if takeovers are costless, the firm's owners always have an incentive to maximize the value of the firm. Additionally, ongoing firms have other incentives to follow a value-maximizing policy. Cases can be constructed in which a firm with a long history of deviating from such a policy in order to maximize only shareholder wealth will be worth less than it would have, had a value-maximizing policy been followed and expected to continue.

Ownership of the firm's claims could be structured in a way which controls the stockholders' incentive to follow a strategy which does not maximize the total value of the firm. Galai/Masulis (1976) suggest that if all investors hold equal proportions of both the firm's debt and the firm's equity

[6]The mechanism by which this fixity occurs is not well specified. However, the assumption of zero transactions costs in these models suggests that contractual provisions which fix investment policy and control the bondholder–stockholder conflict can be costlessly written and enforced.

issues, wealth redistributions among claimholders leave all investors indifferent. In such a case, bondholder–stockholder conflict arising over investment policy is costlessly controlled, and, even with risky debt, the stockholders will still follow a firm-value-maximizing strategy.

Thus, even when the firm's investment policy is not fixed, under the Irrelevance Hypothesis the stockholders' behavior is not altered by the presence of the bondholder–stockholder conflict. The influence of external markets or the possibility of restructuring the firm's claims implies that the choice of financial contracts is irrelevant to the value of the firm.

1.2.2. The Costly Contracting Hypothesis

The Costly Contracting Hypothesis is that control of the bondholder–stockholder conflict through financial contracts can increase the value of the firm. Like the Irrelevance Hypothesis, the Costly Contracting Hypothesis recognizes the influence which external markets and the possibility of recapitalization exert on the firm's choice of investment policy. However, this hypothesis presupposes that those factors, while controlling to some extent the bondholder–stockholder conflict, are insufficient to induce the stockholders to maximize the value of the firm rather than maximizing the value of the equity. The Costly Contracting Hypothesis underlies the work of Jensen/Meckling (1976), Myers (1977), and Miller (1977a).

Financial contracting is assumed to be costly. However, bond covenants, even if they involve costs, can increase the value of the firm at the time bonds are issued by reducing the opportunity loss which results when stockholders of a levered firm follow a policy which does not maximize the value of the firm. Furthermore, in the case of the claim dilution problem (which involves only a wealth transfer), if covenants lower the costs which bondholders incur in monitoring stockholders, the cost-reducing benefits of the covenants accrue to the firm's owners. With such covenants, the firm is worth more at the time the bonds are issued.

Under the Costly Contracting Hypothesis, there is a unique optimal set of financial contracts which maximizes the value of the firm. Note, however, that the bondholder–stockholder conflict would be resolved and its associated costs driven to zero without bond covenants if the firm never issued any risky debt. But for the firm to follow such a policy is costly if it is optimal to have risky debt in the firm's capital structure. Thus, the Costly Contracting Hypothesis presupposes that there are benefits associated with the inclusion of risky debt. Others have suggested benefits associated with issuance of risky debt which relate to, for example, (1) information asymmetries and signalling [Stiglitz (1972) and Ross (1977)], (2) taxes [Modigliani/Miller (1958, 1966)], (3) agency costs of equity financing [Jensen/Meckling (1976)], (4) differential transactions and flotation costs, and (5) unbundling of riskbearing and capital ownership [Fama (1978b)]. We do not address the issue of the exact nature of the benefit from the issuance of risky debt.

1.3. Evidence provided by an examination of bond covenants

In this paper, we use the data base provided by the *Commentaries* to distinguish between the Irrelevance and the Costly Contracting Hypotheses. Much of our evidence is qualitative rather than quantitative. Many social scientists are reluctant to consider such observations as evidence. However, qualitative evidence such as that provided by the *Commentaries* is frequently employed in the social sciences and in particular the property rights/economic analysis of law literature [see Alchian/Demsetz (1972), Cheung (1973), Coase (1960), Demsetz (1967), Manne (1967), and Posner (1972)]. Furthermore, qualitative evidence appears to have been instrumental in the development of the natural sciences [e.g., Darwin (1859)].[7]

Observation of persisting institutions represents important empirical evidence. However, we must specify precisely the nature of the evidence afforded by the observations under a particular hypothesis. After all, evidence (whether qualitative or quantitative) is useful only if it distinguishes among competing hypotheses;[8] what separates good empirical evidence from bad is not whether it can be reduced to numbers, but whether it increases our knowledge of how the world functions.

Debt covenants are a persistent phenomenon. They have been included in debt contracts for hundreds of years,[9] and over time the corporate debt contract which contains them has evolved into 'undoubtedly the most involved financial document that has been devised'.[10] The covenants discussed in *Commentaries* are representative of the covenants found in actual practice. As discussed by Rodgers (1965) and in the preface to the *Commentaries*, specific sections of the *Commentaries* were written by those considered to be the leading practitioners in their field. To check the correspondence between *Commentaries* and observed contractual provisions, we selected a random sample of 87 public issues of debt which were

---

[7]Darwin is perhaps the most familiar example; however, it is not the best. Although Darwin presents no quantitative evidence to support his hypotheses, his discussions are typically phrased in quantitative terms, referring to testable propositions about population sizes, etc. However, other areas of biology were developed totally without quantitative evidence. For example, see von Baer's work on embryology, Barnard's work in physiology, and Cuvier's work on taxonomy. For a general description of the development of the science of biology, see Coleman (1971).

[8]This proposition is well established in the philosophy literature. See Kuhn (1970), Nagel (1961), and Popper (1959).

[9]Rodgers (1965) discusses the evolution of debt contracts; he also discusses the history of the American Bar Foundation's Corporate Trust Indenture Project, under which the *Commentaries* were written.

[10]Kennedy (1961, p. 1).

registered with the Securities and Exchange Commission between January, 1974 and December, 1975. The standardized provisions of the type discussed in *Commentaries* are used frequently: 90.8 percent of the bonds contain restrictions on the issuance of additional debt, 23.0 percent have restrictions on dividend payments, 39.1 percent restrict merger activities, and 35.6 percent constrain the firm's disposition of assets. Furthermore, we found that when a particular provision is included, a boilerplate from *Commentaries* is used almost exclusively.

It seems reasonable that the covenants discussed in *Commentaries* have not arisen merely by chance; rather, they take their current form and have survived because they represent a contractual solution which is efficient from the standpoint of the firm.[11] As Alchian (1950) indicates, 'success (survival) accompanies relative superiority';[12] and 'whenever successful enterprises are observed, the elements common to those observed successes will be associated with success and copied by others in their pursuit of profits or success'.[13] Hence the *Commentaries* represents a powerful piece of evidence on efficient forms of the financial contract.

However, Miller (1977b, p. 273) indicates an important constraint on the use of this evidence: 'The most that we can safely assert about the evolutionary process underlying market equilibrium is that harmful heuristics, like harmful mutations in nature, will die out. Neutral mutations that serve no function, but do no harm, can persist indefinitely.' In addition to observing the persistence of covenants, we must demonstrate that the covenants involve out-of-pocket or opportunity costs for the firm, since the mere existence of covenants is consistent with both the Irrelevance and the Costly Contracting Hypotheses. But if covenants are costly, as we find in this paper, we must reject the Irrelevance Hypothesis. Similarly, the existence of the costly incentive-related covenants we discuss is inconsistent with the argument that external market forces and the possibility of restructuring the firm's claims provide a sufficient incentive for stockholders to follow a firm-value-maximizing policy. On the other hand, costly incentive-related covenants are exactly what would be expected under the Costly Contracting Hypothesis.

Given that the costs of restrictive covenants are positive, an important question is whether those costs are economically significant. The costs of particular covenants cannot easily be measured, and we present no direct evidence on the dollar magnitude of the costs. In a number of instances we use the assumption that such costs are important to generate testable propositions about the firm's capital structure. Although the evidence on the

---

[11]See Alchian (1950) and Stigler (1958) for a discussion of the survivorship principle.
[12]Alchian (1950, p. 213).
[13]Alchian (1950, p. 218).

importance of the bondholder–stockholder conflict is by no means conclusive, in several cases where the predictions of the analysis have been
tested, the evidence is consistent with the theory. It appears that the Costly
Contracting Hypothesis, which explains how firms reduce the costs of the
bondholder–stockholder conflict, helps to account for the variation in debt
contracts across firms. In contrast, the Irrelevance Hypothesis, while consistent with any observed set of contracts, yields no predictions about the
form of the debt contract.

1.4. Overview of the paper

Observed debt covenants are discussed in section 2. To facilitate the
discussion, observed covenants are grouped into four categories: produc-
tion/investment covenants, dividend covenants, financing covenants, and
bonding covenants. We use a common format for the discussion of each
covenant; a particular type of covenant is first described, and its impact then
analyzed.

Covenants which directly restrict the shareholders' choice of production/in-
vestment policy, are discussed in section 2.1. These covenants impose restrictions on the firm's holdings of financial investments, on the disposition of
assets, and on the firm's merger activity. The observed constraints place few
specific limitations on the firm's choice of investment policy. However, it is
important to realize that, because of the cash flow identity, investment,
dividend, and financing policy are not independent; they must be determined
simultaneously. Thus, covenants which restrict dividend and financing policy
also restrict investment policy.

Bond covenants which directly restrict the payment of dividends are
considered in section 2.2. The dividend restriction does not take the form of
a constant dollar limitation. Instead, the maximum allowable dividend
payment is a function of both accounting earnings and the proceeds from the
sale of new equity. The analysis suggests that the dividend covenant places
an implicit constraint on the investment policy of the firm and provides the
stockholders with incentives to follow a firm-value-maximizing produc-
tion/investment policy.

Financing policy covenants are discussed in section 2.3. These covenants
restrict not only the issuance of senior debt, but the issuance of debt of any
priority. In addition, the firm's right to incur other fixed obligations such as
leases is restricted. These restrictions appear to reduce the underinvestment
incentives discussed by Myers (1977). In section 2.4, convertibility, callability,
and sinking fund provisions are also examined. These provisions appear to
specify payoffs to bondholders in a way which also controls bondholder–
stockholder conflict.

In section 2.5, we analyze covenants which specify bonding activities –

expenditures made by the firm which control the bondholder–stockholder conflict. These bonding activities include the provision of audited financial statements, the specification of accounting techniques, the required purchase of insurance, and the periodic provision of a statement, signed by the firm's officers, indicating compliance with the covenants.

Just as the covenants described in section 2 are persistent phenomena, so are the institutions for enforcing these contractual restrictions. The enforcement of bond covenants within the existing institutional arrangements is the subject of section 3. The Trust Indenture Act of 1939 restricts the provisions of the debt contract for public issues in a way which makes the enforcement of tightly restrictive covenants very expensive. Another enforcement cost emanates from the legal liability which bondholders incur when they exercise control over the firm. Default remedies which are available to the firm, and their associated costs, are also discussed.

Our conclusions are presented in section 4.

2. A description and analysis of bond covenants

We group observed covenants into four categories: production/investment covenants, dividend covenants, financing covenants, and bonding covenants. Our discussion of the covenants covers all the restrictions reported in *Commentaries*; we have not singled out only particular types of covenants for discussion.[14]

2.1. Restrictions on the firm's production/investment policy

The stockholders' production/investment decisions could be directly constrained by explicitly specifying the projects which the firm is allowed to undertake. Alternatively, if it were costless to enforce, the debt contract could simply require the shareholders to accept all projects (and engage in only those actions) with positive net present values. Although certain covenants directly restrict the firm's investment policy, debt contracts discussed in *Commentaries* do not generally contain extensive restrictions of either form.

2.1.1. Restrictions on investments

Description. Bond covenants frequently restrict the extent to which the firm can become a claimholder in another business enterprise. That restriction, known as the 'investment' restriction, applies to common stock investments, loans, extensions of credit, and advances.[15] Alternative forms of this cov-

---

[14]However, note that we do not discuss the standard contractual provisions governing procedural matters (e.g., face amount, redemption procedure) which are necessary to define the firm's obligations as debt.

[15]Investments in direct obligations of the United States of America, prime commercial paper, and certificates of deposit are frequently excepted. *Commentaries* (p. 461, sample covenant 1A).

enant suggested in *Commentaries* either (1) flatly prohibit financial investments of this kind, (2) permit these financial investments only if net tangible
assets meet a certain minimum, or (3) permit such investments subject to
either an aggregate dollar limitation or a limitation representing a prespecified percentage of the firm's capitalization (owners' equity plus long-
term debt).

Analysis. We suggest that stockholders contractually restrict their ability to
acquire financial assets in order to limit their ability to engage in asset
substitution after the bonds are issued.[16,17] However, the inclusion of the
investment covenant imposes opportunity costs. First, if there are economies
of scale in raising additional capital, or costs associated with changing
dividends, then allowing the purchase of financial assets can reduce these
costs.[18] Second, if a firm is involved in merger activities, the purchase of
equity claims of the target firm prior to the merger can also provide benefits.
Thus, the Costly Contracting Hypothesis predicts that bond contracts of
firms involved in merger activities, for which the opportunity cost of
restricting 'investments' is therefore high, will contain less restrictive investment covenants. However, our analysis does not predict which of the above
forms the investment restriction will take.

2.1.2. Restrictions on the disposition of assets

Description. 'The transfer of the assets of the obligor substantially as an
entirety' can be restricted by a standard boilerplate.[19] The contract can also
require that the firm not 'otherwise than in the ordinary course of business,
sell, lease, transfer, or otherwise dispose of any substantial part of its
properties and assets, including...any manufacturing plant or substantially
all properties and assets constituting the business of a division, branch, or
other unit operation'.[20] Another restriction is to permit asset disposition only

---

[16]Given that stockholders of most corporations are subject to double taxation of their returns,
financial assets are negative net present value projects whose acquisition reduces the value of the
firm. However, shareholders will have an incentive to purchase such assets if acquiring them
increases the variability of the firm's cash flows by enough to offset the reduction in the value of
the firm. Thus, the investments covenant raises the price to the stockholders of increasing the
variability of the firm's cash flows.

[17]An alternative explanation for the investment restriction is that it reduces the conflict
between managers and stockholders. The investment restriction typically applies to 'any person'.
Hence managers are restricted from making loans to themselves, as well as from investing the
firm's resources in firms which the managers own. We cannot reject this explanation for the
investment restriction. However, it is not clear why bondholders have a comparative advantage
(over stockholders) in policing managerial behavior of this form.

[18]That the purchase of short-term riskless assets is often allowed under the investments
restriction is consistent with this explanation. Stockholders cannot increase the variability of
cash flows with riskless assets. Furthermore, Treasury Bills dominate cash, which has a zero
pecuniary return.

[19]*Commentaries* (p. 423).

[20]*Commentaries* (p. 427, sample covenant 2).

up to a fixed dollar amount, or only so long as (1) the proceeds from the sale are applied to the purchase of new fixed assets, or (2) some fraction of the proceeds is used to retire the firm's debt.[21]

Analysis.   The Costly Contracting Hypothesis suggests that restrictions on the sale of substantial units of the firm's assets are observed because, in general, the proceeds if assets are sold piecemeal will be less than if sold as a going concern.[22] By imposing the higher cost of piecemeal sale, this covenant also raises the cost to stockholders of substituting variance increasing assets for those currently owned by the firm.

One cost associated with flat prohibitions on the sale of particular assets rises from the fact that the firm is not permitted to divest itself of those assets whose value to others is greater than the value to itself. Thus the restriction which permits asset sale if the proceeds are applied to the purchase of new fixed assets lowers this opportunity cost. However, a provision which permits such asset exchange is costly because it allows for the possibility of obtaining variance increasing negative net present value assets in the exchange. The stipulation that a fraction of the proceeds from the sale of assets be used for the retirement of the firm's debt makes asset substitution more expensive for stockholders by requiring a concurrent increase in the coverage on, and thus the value of, the outstanding debt.

2.1.3. Secured debt

Description.   Securing debt gives the bondholders title to pledged assets until the bonds are paid in full. Thus, when secured debt is issued the firm cannot dispose of the pledged assets without first obtaining permission of the bondholders.

Analysis.   We suggest that the issuance of secured debt lowers the total costs of borrowing by controlling the incentives for stockholders to take projects which reduce the value of the firm; since bondholders hold title to the assets, secured debt limits asset substitution. Secured debt also lowers administrative costs and enforcement costs by ensuring that the lender has clear title to the assets and by preventing the lender's claim from being jeopardized if the borrower subsequently issues additional debt. In addition, collateralization

---

[21]Such provisions typically apply to the retirement of the firm's funded (i.e., long-term) debt. The covenant in a particular bond issue requires that *all* the firm's debt be retired on a prorated basis. To require that only the particular bond issue containing the covenant be retired might well violate the firm's other debt agreements.

[22]Given that selling substantial portions of the firm's assets can be illegal under, for example, the Uniform Fraudulent Conveyance Act, the standard boilerplate would seem redundant. Our theory does not explain the redundancy of the terms of the bond contract and the constraints implied by the legal system. But in the case of this boilerplate, we suggest that, should the assets of the firm be sold, subjecting the firm's managers to civil and criminal liability alone is a more costly remedy than allowing the bondholders to put the firm in default.

reduces expected foreclosure expenses because it is less expensive to tsae possession of property to which the lender already has established title.

However, secured debt involves out of pocket costs (e.g., required reports to the debt-holders, filing fees, and other administrative expenses). Securing debt also involves opportunity costs by restricting the firm from potentially profitable dispositions of collateral.

The Costly Contracting Hypothesis leads to two predictions about the use of secured debt. First, if the firm goes into bankruptcy proceedings and the collateral is judged necessary for the continued operation of the firm, the bankruptcy judge can prohibit the bondholders from taking possession of the property. Thus for firms where liquidation is more likely than re-organization (e.g., for smaller firms), the issuance of secured debt will be greater. Second, we would expect more frequent use of secured debt the less specialized the firm's resources. To the extent that assets (such as a patent right) are highly specialized and firm-specific, their value is greater to the firm than in the market place. Consequently, it will be costly to the stockholders if they dispose of such assets in order to engage in asset substitution. The more specialized the assets, the more costly is asset substitution to stockholders, the tighter the implicit constraint on asset sale, and thus the less likely is the use of secured debt.[23]

2.1.4. Restrictions on mergers

Description. Some indenture agreements contain a flat prohibition on mergers. Others permit the acquisition of other firms provided that certain conditions are met. For example, *Commentaries* suggests restrictions in which the merger is permitted only if the net tangible assets of the firm, calculated on a post-merger basis, meet a certain dollar minimum, or are at least a certain fraction of long-term debt. The merger can also be made contingent on there being no default on any indenture provision after the transaction is completed.

The acquisition and consolidation of the firm into another can be permitted subject to certain requirements. For example, the corporation into which the company is merged must assume all of the obligations in the initial indenture. Article 800 of the American Bar Foundation *Model Debenture Indenture Provisions* also requires that there be no act of default after completion of the consolidation, and that the company certify that fact through the delivery to the trustee of an officer's certificate and an opinion of counsel.

Analysis. Since the stockholders of the two firms must approve a merger, the market value of the equity claims of both the acquired and acquiring firm must be expected to rise or the merger will not be approved by

---

[23]For a further discussion of secured debt, see Scott (1977) and Smith/Warner (1979).

stockholders of the respective firms.[24] A merger between two firms usually results in changes in the value of particular classes of outstanding claims because both the asset and liability structure of the resulting firm differ from that of the predecessor firms. The effects of a merger on the value of particular claims depend upon: (1) the degree of synergy brought about by the merger, (2) the resources consumed in accomplishing the merger, (3) the variance rates of the pre-merger firms' cash flows, (4) the correlation coefficient between the merged firms' cash flows, and (5) the capital structure (i.e., ratio of face value of debt to market value of all claims) of the respective firms. A merger leaves the value of outstanding debt claims unaffected if (1) the merger involves no synergy, (2) there are no transactions costs, (3) the pre-merger firm's cash flows have equal variance rates, (4) the correlation coefficient between the merged firms' cash flows is $+1$, and (5) the pre-merger firms have the same capital structure.

With no contractual constraints against mergers, the value of the bondholders' claims can be reduced due to the effect of a difference in variance rates or a difference in capital structures. Our analysis implies, then, that merger restrictions limit the stockholders' ability to use mergers to increase either the firm's variance rate or the debt to asset ratio to the detriment of the bondholders. Note that to the extent that synergistic mergers are prevented by this covenant, the firm suffers an opportunity loss.[25]

2.1.5. Covenants requiring the maintenance of assets

Description. The covenants we have discussed constrain production/investment policy by prohibiting certain actions. However, the firm's operating decisions can also be limited by *requiring* that it take certain actions, that it invest in certain projects, or hold particular assets. Examples of such covenants are those requiring the maintenance of the firm's properties and maintenance of the firm's working capital (i.e., current assets less current liabilities).[26] *Commentaries* offers covenants which require the firm to maintain working capital above a certain minimum level. Frequently, activities

---

[24]This is consistent with the evidence of Dodd/Ruback (1977) and Bradley (1978). They find that, on average, there is positive abnormal performance for common stocks of both acquiring and acquired firms.

[25]As we discuss in section 2.3, the indenture agreements typically require that the firm comply with one or more tests (such as minimum ratios of net tangible assets to funded debt) in order to issue additional debt. According to *Commentaries*, when additional debt obligations are incurred through a merger, for purposes of the tests, the debt incurred can be treated as having been issued as of the merger. Thus, financing policy covenants can be employed to control mergers.

[26]Another restriction on increases in the risk of the firm's activities is a covenant requiring that the firm stay in the same line of business. For example, the Associated Dry Goods Credit Corporation Notes of 1983 require that the firm 'not engage in any business other than dealing in Deferred Payment Accounts'. This covenant thus makes it more costly to engage in asset substitution.

such as mergers are made contingent upon the maintenance of working capital

Analysis. While a covenant can require that the firm maintain its properties, such a covenant will not have much impact if it is expensive to enforce. However, if the maintenance is performed by an independent agent, enforcement costs are expected to be lower and such a restriction will be effective. For example, in the shipping industry, where maintenance services are typically provided through third parties, bond covenants frequently explicitly include service and dry-docking schedules in the indenture.

We suggest that the working capital requirement is included because any violation of the covenant provides a signal to the lender. This signal can result in renegotiation of the debt contract, an alternative preferable to default when bankruptcy is more costly than renegotiation. This hypothesis is consistent with the interpretation of the working capital covenant in *Commentaries* (p. 453): 'If a breach of the covenant occurs, the lender is in a position to use this early warning to take whatever remedial action is necessary.'

2.1.6. *Covenants which indirectly restrict production/investment policy*

Stockholder use (or misuse) of production/investment policy frequently involves not some action, but the failure to take a certain action (e.g., failure to accept a positive net present value project). Because of this, investment policy can be very expensive to monitor, since ascertaining that the firm's production/investment policy does not maximize the firm's market value depends on magnitudes which are costly to observe. Solutions to this problem are not obvious. For example, if the indenture were to require the bondholders (rather than the stockholders) to establish the firm's investment policy, the problem would not be solved; the bondholders, acting in their self interest, would choose an investment policy which maximized the value of the bonds, not the value of the firm.[27] In addition, there are other costs associated with giving bondholders a role in establishing the firm's investment policy. For instance, as we discuss in section 3, legal costs can be imposed on bondholders if they are deemed to have assumed control of the corporation.

However, direct restrictions on the stockholder's choice of production/investment policy are only one way to limit the projects in which the firm can engage. Covenants constraining the firm's dividend and financing policies can also be written in a way which serves a similar function, since the firm's production/investment, dividend, and financing policies are linked through the cash flow identity. If direct restrictions on production/investment policy

---

[27]Jensen/Meckling refer to this as the symmetry property.

were sufficiently expensive to enforce, dividend and financing policy covenants would be the only efficient way of constraining the firm's actions.

2.2. Bond covenants restricting the payment of dividends

Description. Cash dividend payments to stockholders, if financed by a reduction in investment, reduce the value of the firm's bonds by decreasing the expected value of the firm's assets at the maturity date of the bonds, making default more likely. Thus, it is not surprising that bond covenants frequently[28] restrict the payment of cash dividends to shareholders.[29] Since the payment of dividends *in cash* is just one form which distributions to stockholders can take, actual dividend covenants reflect alternative possibilities. For example, if the firm enters the market and repurchases its own stock the coverage on the debt decreases in exactly the same way as it would if a cash dividend were paid. The constraints discussed in *Commentaries* relate not only to cash dividends, but to 'all distributions on account of or in respect of capital stock...whether they be dividends, redemptions, purchases, retirements, partial liquidations or capital reductions and whether in cash, in kind, or in the form of debt obligations of the company'.[30]

The dividend covenant usually establishes a limit on distributions to stockholders by defining an inventory of funds available for dividend payments over the life of the bonds.[31] The inventory is not constant; rather, it is allowed to change as a function of certain variables whose values can be influenced by the stockholders. Typically, the inventory of funds available for the payment of dividends in quarter τ, D_τ^*, can be expressed as

$$D_\tau^* = k\left(\sum_{t=0}^{\tau} E_t\right) + \left(\sum_{t=0}^{\tau} S_t\right) + F - \left(\sum_{t=0}^{\tau-1} D_t\right), \tag{1}$$

[28]Kalay (1979) reports that in a sample of 150 randomly selected industrial firms, every firm had a dividend restriction in at least one of its debt instruments.

[29]According to Henn (1970, pp. 648–656) most states have also limited the source of dividends to legally prescribed funds. Various laws define the funds legally available for dividends in terms of (1) earned surplus, (2) net profits or net earnings, (3) non-impairment of capital, (4) insolvency, or some combination. Directors are often made liable by statute (and possibly subject to criminal penalties) for dividends paid out of funds not legally available. Even apart from statutes expressing such limitation, distribution of dividends which would render the corporation insolvent is probably wrongful in most jurisdictions on principles of the law of creditors' rights.

[30]*Commentaries* (p. 405). It should be noted that the problem of constraining the firm's investment in financial assets, which we discussed in section 2.1, is sometimes handled within the dividend covenant. Distributions restricted under the dividend covenant can be defined to include purchases of securities by the firm. Under this definition, the stockholders of the firm can choose to hold any amount of financial investments so long as they give up an equal amount of dividends.

[31]Kennedy (1961, p. 137). In his study of dividend covenants, Kalay (1978) finds that most of them take the form discussed here.

where, for quarter t,

E_t is net earnings,
S_t is the proceeds from the sale of common stock net of transactions costs,
F is a number which is fixed over the life of the bonds, known as the 'dip',
k is a constant, $0 \leq k \leq 1$.

Hence the inventory of funds is a positive function of the earnings which the firm has accumulated, a positive function of the extent to which the firm has sold new equity claims, and a negative function of the dividends paid since the bonds were issued at $t=0$.

The payment of a dividend is not permitted if its payment would cause the inventory to be drawn below zero. The inventory can become negative if the firm's earnings are negative. In that case, no dividend is permitted. However, stockholders are not required to make up the deficiency.[32] Thus the dividend payment in quarter τ, D_τ, must satisfy the constraint

$$D_\tau \leq \max[0, D_\tau^*]. \tag{2}$$

Analysis. This form of dividend covenant has several interesting features. The dividend restriction is not an outright prohibition on the payment of dividends. In fact, the stockholders are permitted to have any level of dividends they choose, so long as the payment of those dividends is financed out of new earnings or through the sale of new equity claims. The dividend covenant acts as a restriction not on dividends *per se*, but on the payment of dividends financed by issuing debt or by the sale of the firm's existing assets, either of which would reduce the coverage on, and thus the value of, the debt.

The dividend covenant described in eqs. (1) and (2) coupled with the cash-flow identity that inflows equal outflows constrain investment policy.[33] The cash-flow identity for the firm can be expressed as

$$D_t + R_t + P_t + I_t \equiv \phi_t + S_t + B_t, \tag{3}$$

where, for quarter t,

D_t is the dividend paid,
R_t is interest paid,
P_t is debt principal paid,
I_t is new investment,
ϕ_t is the firm's cash flow.

---

[32]Given limited liability, a covenant requiring that a positive balance be maintained in the inventory and that individual shareholders be assessed for deficiencies is probably not enforceable without considerable cost.

[33]We would like to thank John Long for suggesting this expositional model and for helpful discussions on this point.

S_t is the proceeds from the sale of equity net of transactions cost,
B_t is the proceeds from the sale of bonds net of transactions cost.

The firm's cash flow, ϕ_t, can be expressed as [34]

$$\phi_t \equiv E_t + d_t + R_t + L_t, \tag{4}$$

where, for quarter t,

E_t is the firm's net earnings,
d_t is depreciation,
L_t is the book value of any assets liquidated. [35]

Substituting (3) into (4) and solving for D_t yields

$$D_t \equiv E_t + d_t + R_t + L_t - I_t + S_t + B_t - R_t - P_t. \tag{5}$$

To see how the dividend covenant constrains investment policy, consider the simplest case. Assume that an all equity firm sells bonds at par with a covenant that it will issue no additional debt over the life of the bonds (i.e., $B_t = 0$ for $t \neq 0$, and $P_t = 0$ for $t \neq T$). If we also assume that $F \equiv 0$, and $k \equiv 1$, then substituting (5) and (1) into (2) yields the condition for dividends in quarter τ to be positive,

$$B_0 \leq \sum_{t=0}^{\tau} (I_t - L_t - d_t). \tag{6}$$

The right-hand side of (6) is simply the cumulative change in the book value of the firm's assets since the bonds were sold. Thus in this simple case, the dividend covenant requires that for dividends to be paid in the quarter the bonds are issued, investment must be large enough that the net change in the book value of the firm's assets be no less than the net proceeds from the sale of the debt – the firm cannot borrow to pay dividends. The constraint also requires that in subsequent quarters investment be large enough for the book value of the firm's assets to be maintained at that level.

If the assumptions that $k = 1$ and $F = 0$ are now relaxed, then eq. (6) becomes

$$B_0 + (1 - k)\left(\sum_{t=0}^{\tau} E_t \right) - F \leq \sum_{t=0}^{\tau} (I_t - L_t - d_t). \tag{7}$$

[34]For purposes of illustration we assume that the accrual is depreciation and that all items other than depreciation, interest payments, and liquidations affect cash flows and earnings in the same way.
[35]L_t is defined as the book value of assets liquidated when earnings includes gains or losses on the sale of assets. If such gains or losses are not included in earnings, then L_t is the proceeds from the liquidation.

Setting k between zero and one requires that if the firm has positive earnings, the book value of the assets of the firm must actually increase in order for dividends to be paid.[36]

By placing a maximum on distributions, the dividend covenant effectively places a minimum on investment expenditures by the owners of the firm, as Myers and Kalay (1979) argue. This reduces the underinvestment problem discussed by Myers, since so long as the firm *has* to invest, profitable projects are less likely to be turned down.

While having a tight dividend constraint controls the stockholders incentives associated with the dividend payout problem, there are several associated costs. An outright prohibition on dividends or allowing dividends but setting k less than one increases the probability that the firm will be forced to invest when it has no available profitable projects. Investment in securities of other firms is not always possible, since purchases of capital market instruments (which in the absence of corporate taxes have zero net present value) are frequently prohibited by the investments covenant we discussed in section 2.1. Even if financial investments are not restricted, Kalay argues that if the firm pays income taxes on its earnings, the taxation of the returns from the financial assets makes them negative net present value projects.[37]

The tighter restriction on dividends implied by a lower k also increases the stockholders' incentives to engage in asset substitution, and increases the gain to the firm's shareholders from choosing high variance, negative net present value projects. Assume that negative net present value projects generate negative accounting earnings. Then from the first term of eq. (1), the inventory available for dividends will be reduced by taking such a project. The lower the value of k, the smaller the reduction in the inventory. To the extent that dividends transfer wealth to stockholders, the marginal impact of lowering k is thus to increase the gain (or decrease the loss) to shareholders from accepting such projects. However, as we discuss below, a lower k also confers benefits, since it reduces the stockholders' incentive to engage in 'creative accounting' to increase reported earnings.

If it is costly to restrict dividends, not all debt agreements will include a dividend restriction. Dividend covenants would be expected only if there are offsetting benefits. One prediction of our analysis is that the presence of a dividend covenant should be related to the maturity of the debt. Thus, short-

---

[36]The value of k is less than 1 in about 20 percent of the dividend covenants which Kalay (1979) examines. According to *Commentaries* (p. 414), the 'dip', F, is equal to about a year's earnings. Kalay finds that the mean value of the dip, as a fraction of earnings, is indeed approximately 1.

[37]We conjecture that the specification of a positive F in the debt contract is directed at reducing the costs of temporarily having no profitable investment projects and being unable to pay dividends. In spite of the increased payouts it allows, the dip permits a dividend to be paid to shareholders even when earnings are negative and the firm has not sold new equity.

term debt instruments (such as commercial paper) are less likely to contain dividend restrictions than long-term debt; if liquidation of the firm's assets within a short period of time is sufficiently costly to the shareholders, they are better off not selling the firm's assets for cash in order to pay themselves a dividend. This implicit constraint on dividend payout becomes less restrictive the longer the time to maturity of the debt, and the cost-offsetting benefits of an explicit dividend constraint thus become greater as a function of maturity.

Evidence. Kalay develops and tests a number of propositions about how the dividend constraint will be set. He argues that the shareholders' incentive to sell assets for cash is greater the higher the fraction of the firm consisting of debt: the higher that fraction, the greater the potential wealth transfer to stockholders. Consistent with the argument that the dividend constraint involves costs, he finds a significant negative cross-sectional relationship between the dividends which can be paid out under the constraint and the firm's debt/equity ratio.[38]

Kalay also reports that firms do not always pay out all of the dividends to which they are entitled under the indenture agreement. He argues that firms maintain such an 'inventory of payable funds' because having an inventory reduces the probability that the firm will be unable to pay dividends and thus be forced to invest when there are temporarily no profitable investment projects. However, if stockholders maintain an inventory and fail to pay out all funds available for dividends, wealth transfers from bondholders are foregone. On this basis, Kalay posits that the shareholders' incentive to maintain an inventory is lower the higher the firm's leverage. That proposition is consistent with his finding that there is a significant negative relationship between the firm's debt/equity ratio and the (size adjusted) 'inventory of payable funds'.

2.2.1. Control of investment incentives when the inventory is negative

Throughout the above analysis we have assumed that the inventory of funds available for the payment of dividends, D_τ^*, is positive. If the firm has been experiencing negative earnings, the inventory can become negative; with a negative inventory, no dividends can be paid. The negative earnings which lead to a dividend prohibition are likely to be associated with a fall in the value of the firm, and an increase in both its debt/equity ratio and the probability of default on its debt. Hence at the times when a dividend

---

[38]The effective constraint on dividends cannot be determined without considering dividend covenants across all the firm's bond issues. Kalay treats the tightness of the dividend constraint with this in mind; the negative relationship he postulates is between the amount which can be paid out (adjusted for firm size) under the firm's *most* restrictive dividend constraint and its leverage.

prohibition comes into play, the firm is also likely to be faced with greater incentives to engage in asset substitution and claim dilution.

When the firm is doing poorly, the dividend constraint is not capable of controlling the investment and financing policy problem induced by the presence of risky debt. But the direct limitations on production/investment policy we discussed in section 2.1 can limit the stockholders' actions when the inventory for payment of dividends is negative. In addition, financing policy covenants not only address the claim dilution problem, but independently reinforce the effect of the dividend covenant in restricting production/investment policy.

2.3. Bond covenants restricting subsequent financing policy

2.3.1. Limitations on debt and priority

Description.   In section 1 we discussed the stockholders' incentives to reduce the value of the outstanding bonds by subsequently issuing additional debt of higher priority, thereby diluting the bondholders' claim on the assets of the firm. Covenants suggested in *Commentaries* limit stockholders actions in this area in one of two ways: either through a simple prohibition against issuing claims with a higher priority, or through a restriction on the creation of a claim with higher priority unless the existing bonds are upgraded to have equal priority. The latter restriction requires, for example, that if secured debt is sold after the issuance of the bonds, the existing bondholders must have their priority upgraded and be given an equal claim on the collateral with the secured debtholders.

In addition to restricting the issuance of debt of higher priority, there are sample covenants in *Commentaries* restricting the stockholders' right to issue *any* additional debt. Issuance of new debt can be subject to aggregate dollar limitations. Alternatively, issuing debt can be prohibited unless the firm maintains minimum prescribed ratios between (1) net tangible assets and funded (i.e., long-term) debt, (2) capitalization and funded debt, (3) tangible net worth[39] and funded debt, (4) income and interest charges (referred to as earnings tests), or (5) current assets and current debt (referred to as working capital tests). There are also provisions requiring the company to be free from debt for limited periods (referred to as 'clean-up' provisions). Combinations of two or more of these limitations are sometimes included in the indenture agreement.

It is important to note the scope of the restrictions imposed through the

---

[39]Some definitions of net worth include subordinated debt and thus treat it as equity. Thus the issuance of debt of equal priority is limited, and the constraint on the issuance of junior debt is relaxed. Our theory does not explain which alternative definition of net worth will be appropriate for a given firm.

covenants limiting the issuance of additional debt. In addition to money borrowed, the covenants also apply to other liabilities incurred by the firm. Other debt-like obligations which can be limited by the covenants are: (1) assumptions or guarantees of indebtedness of other parties,[40] (2) other contingent obligations which are analogous to, but may not technically constitute, guarantees; (3) amounts payable in installments on account of the purchase of property under purchase money mortgages, conditional sales agreements or other long-term contracts; (4) obligations secured by mortgage on property acquired by the company subject to the mortgage but without assumption of the obligations.

Since the claims of the firm in subsidiary corporations are like that of a stockholder, if a subsidiary issues debt or preferred stock the coverage afforded the bondholders of the parent firm is reduced. Thus the limitations on debt usually apply to the debt of the consolidated firm.[41]

Analysis. Our analysis suggests that it is generally not optimal to prevent all future debt issues. If, as the firm's opportunity set evolves over time, new investments must be financed by new equity issues or by reduced dividends, then with risky debt outstanding part of the gains from the investment goes to bondholders, rather than stockholders. Those investments increase the coverage on the debt, and reduce the default risk borne by the bondholders. To the extent such reductions are unanticipated, they result in an increase in the value of outstanding bonds at the expense of the stockholders. So a prohibition of all debt issues would reduce the value of the firm because wealth maximizing stockholders would not take all positive net present value projects. The possibility of asset substitution increases the costs of outright prohibition on debt issues and makes variance reducing positive net present value projects less attractive. However, our analysis suggests that contractually agreeing to have *some* degree of restriction on future debt issues is in the interests of the firm's owners. By merely restricting the total amount of *all* debt which can be issued, the perverse investment incentives associated with debt discussed by Myers (1977) are limited.

---

[40]The third edition of Dewing (1934, p. 105) discusses the Denver Rio Grande Railroad, which is the 'classic case' of a guaranteed bond which brought a severe test of the strength of the guarantor:

> 'The old Western Pacific Railway was built for strategic reasons in order to complete a Pacific coast extension for the Denver and Rio Grande Railroad – all a part of Gould's contemplated transcontinental railway system. The bonds of the Western Pacific were guaranteed, principal and interest, by the Denver and Rio Grande. When it developed that the Western Pacific failed to earn the interest charges, default occurred, and the Western Pacific passed into the hands of receivers.
> The Denver and Rio Grande Railroad, having failed to meet the guarantees, was ordered to pay over to the trustees of the Western Pacific bonds the sum of $38,000,000. Thereupon the Denver and Rio Grande itself failed.'

[41]Borrowing by a subsidiary from the company or another subsidiary is excluded.

Financing-policy covenants also impact on investment incentives in other ways. In section 2.1, we discussed the direct limitations on financial investments included in bond covenants. Financial investments can also be restricted through the debt covenant. For example, when debt is limited to a specific percentage of net tangible assets, financial investments are sometimes excluded from the definition of net tangible assets for purposes of the covenant. This definition allows the firm to hold a portion of its assets as financial investments, but requires the firm to reduce the debt and its capital structure to do so, thus controlling the asset substitution problem associated with financial investments.

Financing policy impacts on production/investment policy through the dividend covenant. If the level of outstanding debt changes over the life of the bonds, eq. (6) (which presumes that no additional debt is either issued or repaid) must be modified,

$$\sum_{t=0}^{\tau} (B_t - P_t) \leqq \sum_{t=0}^{\tau} (I_t - L_t - d_t), \tag{8}$$

where

B_t is the proceeds from the sale of bonds net of transactions costs,
P_t is debt principal paid,
I_t is new investment,
L_t is the book value of any assets liquidated,
d_t is depreciation.

The left-hand side of eq. (8) is simply the cumulative change in the book value of the firm's debt since the sale of this bond issue at $t=0$. For dividends to be paid the cumulative change in the book value of the assets must be no less than the cumulative change in the book value of the debt. Thus the stockholders cannot borrow to finance dividend payments.

2.3.2. Limitations on rentals, lease, and sale-leasebacks

Description. Commentaries offers alternative restrictions on the stockholders' use of lease or rental contracts. The covenant typically restricts the firm from the sale-leaseback of property owned prior to the date of the indenture.[42] Some covenants also exclude individual leases or sale-leasebacks below a specified dollar total. Lease payments can also be limited to a fraction of net income. Finally, leasing and renting can be controlled through the debt covenant by capitalizing the lease liability and including it in both

---

[42]This restriction sometimes applies only to specific property (e.g., manufacturing property or heavy equipment) or applies except for items specifically exempted (e.g., office space, warehouses, or automobiles). Alternatively, only long-term leases are covered, with a condition that for short-term leases the company discontinue the use of the property after the term of the lease.

the long-term debt definition and asset definitions. In this case, the covenant specifies the procedure for computing the capitalized value of the asset and liability.[43]

Analysis. Continued use of leased or rented assets by the firm is contingent on making the lease or rental payments. These payments represent liabilities to the firm, and are a claim senior to that of the debtholders: such obligations reduce the value of the outstanding bondholders' claim. For this reason, the Costly Contracting Hypothesis predicts restrictions on the stockholders' subsequent use of leases in the indenture agreement. However, we are unable to explain the specific form which the restriction will take for a particular set of firm characteristics.

2.4. Bond covenants modifying the pattern of payoffs to bondholders

There are several provisions which specify a particular pattern of payoffs to bondholders in a way which controls various sources of stockholder–bondholder conflict of interest.

2.4.1. Sinking funds

Description. A sinking fund is simply a means of amortizing part or all of an indebtedness prior to its maturity. A sinking fund bond is like an installment loan.[44] In the case of a public bond issue, the periodic payments can be invested either in the bonds which are to be retired by the fund or in some other securities. The sinking fund payments can be fixed, variable or contingent. For the years 1963–1965, 82 percent of all publicly-offered issues included sinking fund provisions.[45]

Analysis. A sinking fund affects the firm's production/investment policy through the dividend constraint. From eq. (8) we see that if a sinking fund is included in the indenture, principal repayment, P_t, will be positive prior to the maturity date of the bond; the book value of the assets of the firm can decline over the life of the bond issue without violating the dividend constraint. A sinking fund reduces the possibility that the dividend constraint will require investment when no profitable projects are available. One potential cost associated with the dividend constraint is thus reduced.

Myers (1977) has suggested that sinking funds are a device to reduce

---

[43]See *Commentaries* (p. 440).

[44]In a private placement, the amortization may simply require periodic partial payments to the holder. An alternative to a sinking fund it to provide for serial maturities with part of the issue maturing at fixed dates. This practice is rarely used in the corporate bond market presumably because with fewer identical contracts, maintenance of a secondary market in the bond contracts is more expensive.

[45]See Norgaard/Thompson (1967, p. 31). Note also that in enforcing the Public Utilities Holding Company Act, the SEC requires a sinking fund to be included.

creditors' exposure in parallel with the expected decline in the value of the assets supporting the debt. Myers' analysis implies that sinking funds would be more likely to be included in debt issues (1) the higher the fraction of debt in the capital structure, (2) the greater the anticipated future discretionary investment by the firm and (3) the higher the probability that the project will have a limited lifetime. One industry which illustrates an extreme of the last of these characteristics is the gas pipeline industry. The sinking fund payments required in some gas pipeline debentures are related to the remaining available gas in the field.[46]

Not all debt issues have sinking funds; their exclusion from some contracts can be explained by anticipated costs which sinking funds can impose on the trustee if there is a default. Although the application of sinking fund monies is set forth in the covenant, should default occur the applicable law is not clear.[47] Even where only one series of bonds is involved, application of funds to the retirement of specific bonds with knowledge of a default might involve participation by the trustee in an unlawful preference for which the trustee might be held liable.

2.4.2. Convertibility provisions

Description. A convertible debenture is one which gives the holder the right to exchange the debentures for other securities of the company, usually shares of common stock and usually without payment of further compensation. The convertible must contain provisions specifying:

[46]The model indenture provision on this point from the American Bar Foundation (1971) states:

'The Company will file with the Trustee on or before..., and on or before each [insert month and day] thereafter so long as the Debentures shall remain Outstanding, a Certificate of Available Gas Supply. In the event that any such Certificate shall show that the date of exhaustion of available gas supply of the Company is a date earlier than..., the aggregate of the Sinking Fund installments due on the next succeeding Sinking Fund Date and each Sinking Fund Date thereafter up to and including the Sinking Fund Date immediately preceding a date (herein called the Margin Date) two years prior to said date of exhaustion of available gas supply shall be increased by an amount equal to the aggregate of the Sinking Fund instalments due on and after the Margin Date, each such Sinking Fund Instalment coming due between the date of such Certificate and the Margin Date being increased proportionately, as nearly as may be, so that each increased installment shall be multiple of $1,000 and the Sinking Fund installments due on and after the Margin Date shall be eliminated and the schedule of Sinking Fund installments thus revised shall constitute the schedule of Sinking Fund installments under this Indenture until further revised as hereinafter provided.'

[47]If specific bonds have been selected for purchase or redemption by the sinking fund, and all necessary steps have been taken except the actual surrender of the bonds, the funds in the hands of the trustee become specifically allocated to the selected bonds. In the event of subsequent default the holder is entitled to payment upon surrender of the bonds, regardless of the payoff to the other bondholders. If default occurs before all steps necessary for retirement of a specific bond have been concluded, all further action is typically suspended. Any preliminary steps taken are revoked, and the funds are retained by the trustee until the default is cured or the trustee receives judicial direction as to the disposition of the funds.

(1) The type of security issuable upon conversion. This is usually common stock of the company, but occasionally it has been stock of a parent or affiliated corporation.
(2) The duration of the conversion period. This may start at the time of issuance or after a specified date, and run until maturity, redemption, or some specified earlier date. The New York Bond Exchange will not permit the designation 'convertible' on the issue unless the privilege extends for the life of the debenture. The exchange will permit the formal designation to be followed by '(convertible prior to ...)'.
(3) The conversion price at which the stock can be acquired. The conversion price may be the same for the entire period or increase at stated intervals. The conversion price is normally payable only by surrender of a like principal amount of the debentures but occasionally the payment of cash in a fixed ratio to debentures is also required.
(4) Additional Procedural Points. E.g., where must the issue be surrendered for conversion? Does the debenture holder receive accrued interest upon conversion? Will the firm issue fractional shares?
(5) Antidilution Provisions. Provisions which protect the conversion privilege against certain actions by the stockholders such as stock splits, stock dividends, rights offerings, issuance of other convertible securities, mergers, and the distribution of assets.

Analysis. Jensen/Meckling (1976) and Mikkelson (1978) discuss the use of convertible debt as a way to control aspects of the bondholder–stockholder conflict of interest. With non-convertible debt outstanding, the stockholders have the incentive to take projects which raise the variability of the firm's cash flows. The stockholders can increase the value of the equity by adding a new project· with a negative net present value if the firm's cash flow variability rises sufficiently. The inclusion of a convertibility provision in the debt reduces this incentive. The conversion privilege is like a call option written by the stockholders and attached to the debt contract. It reduces the stockholders' incentive to increase the variability of the firm's cash flows, because with a higher variance rate, the attached call option becomes more valuable. Therefore the stockholders' gain from increasing the variance rate is smaller with the convertible debt outstanding than with non-convertible debt.

However, not all debt contracts include a convertibility provision since it is costly to do so.[48] For example, the underinvestment problem is exacerbated with convertible debt outstanding.

---

[48]If part of the incentive for issuing debt comes from the tax deductibility of interest payments, then the tax treatment of interest payments by the Internal Revenue Service can be important and is affected by whether the debt is convertible. Where the capitalization of a corporation is largely debt, the IRS under Section 385 of the Tax Code can contend that some of the 'loans' are in fact capital contributions, and will deny the deduction of 'interest' on the loans. While debt-equity ratios of as much as 700 to 1 have been allowed for tax purposes, the

Evidence. Mikkelson (1978) presents cross-sectional evidence that the probability of the inclusion of the conversion privilege is positively related to (1) the firm's debt/equity ratio, (2) the firm's level of discretionary investment expenditure, and (3) the time to maturity of the debt. Each of these relationships is consistent with the Costly Contracting Hypothesis, and the hypothesis that the benefits of convertible debt are related to a reduction in the bondholder–stockholder conflict.

2.4.3. Callability provisions

Description.   The firm's right to redeem the debentures before maturity at a stated price is typically included in the indenture agreement. Without the inclusion of the callability provision in the indenture agreement, a debenture holder cannot be compelled to accept payment of his debenture prior to its stated maturity date. In the usual case, the call price is not constant over the life of the bonds. The redemption price in a callable bond normally is initially set equal to the public offering price plus one year's interest on the bond. The schedule of call prices then typically scales the call premium to zero by a date one year prior to the maturity of the bonds, although it is sometimes as early as two to five years prior to maturity.

Analysis. We have suggested that if agency costs of equity are zero and recapitalization of the firm is costless, the firm will accept all projects with positive net present values and thus the stockholder–bondholder conflict of interest will be solved. One cost of buying out bondholders in a recapitalization results from the additional premium the bondholders demand for the firm to repurchase the bonds. Since the firm cannot vote bonds which it repurchases, a bilateral monopoly results from the attempt to repurchase

---

Treasury is inclined to look askance at 'loans' by stockholders in proportion to their stockholdings to a corporation with a high debt-equity ratio.

Whether stockholder advances to a corporation are loans or equity is a question of fact under the Tax Code. The taxpayer has the burden of proof as to this fact. The Treasury has issued guidelines for determining whether a corporate obligation is equity or debt. The major factors are: (1) the ratio of debt to equity of the corporation; (2) the relationship between holdings of stock and holdings of debt; (3) whether the debt is convertible into the stock of the corporation; (4) whether there is a subordination to or preference over any indebtedness of the corporation; and (5) whether there is a written, unconditional promise to pay on demand, or on a specified date a sum of money in return for adequate compensation, and to pay a fixed rate of interest.

If the IRS determines that the 'debt' is really equity there are a number of tax consequences. (1) The 'interest' deduction to the corporation is disallowed. (2) All payments of 'interest' and 'principal' are treated as dividend income to the shareholder/lender. (3) The shareholder/lender is denied a bad debt deduction if the corporation is unable to pay the principal.

The guidelines point out a potential cost in making all debt convertible. Even if the agency costs of debt are reduced to zero when stockholders and bondholders are the same, there can be an associated increase in taxes paid by the firm and its claimholders. It should be kept in mind, however, that factors other than taxes are necessary to explain why, prior to the corporate income tax, firms typically did not issue proportional claims, and not all debt was convertible.

the outstanding bonds. With a bilateral monopoly it is indeterminate how the gains will be divided between stockholders and bondholders. As Bodie/Taggart (1978) and Wier (1978) argue, a call provision places an upper limit on the gains which the bondholders can obtain. Wier notes further that if side payments can be negotiated costlessly, then the bondholder monopoly is unimportant from the standpoint of the value of the firm; the callability provision merely redistributes the property rights to the monopoly from bondholders to stockholders. Implicit in the argument that the call provision affects the total value of the firm is the notion that the bilateral monopoly implies real resource expenditures on negotiation.

It should also be noted that our argument cannot represent the only reason for callable bonds: after all, government bonds are often callable but there is no obvious investment incentive problem which such a provision addresses.[49]

2.5. Covenants specifying bonding activities by the firm

Potential bondholders estimate the costs associated with monitoring the firm to assure that the bond covenants have not been violated, and the estimate is reflected in the price when the bonds are sold. Since the value of the firm at the time the bonds are issued is influenced by anticipated monitoring costs, it is in the interests of the firm's owners to include contractual provisions which lower the costs of monitoring. For example, observed provisions often include the requirement that the firm supply audited annual financial statements to the bondholders. Jensen/Meckling call these expenditures by the firm bonding costs.

2.5.1. Required reports

Description. Indenture agreements discussed in *Commentaries* normally commit the company to supply financial and other information for as long as the debt is outstanding. Typically, the firm agrees to supply the following types of information: (1) all financial statements, reports, and proxy statements which the firm already sends to its shareholders; (2) reports and statements filed with government agencies such as the SEC or Public Utility Commissions; (3) quarterly financial statements certified by a financial officer of the firm and (4) financial statements for the fiscal year audited by an independent public accountant.

Analysis. Our analysis suggests that bondholders find financial statements to be useful in ascertaining whether the provisions of the contract have been (or are about to be) violated. If the firm can produce this information at a

---

[49]In addition, since virtually all debt is callable, there is little cross-sectional variation in its use. For a discussion of the empirical testability of arguments for callable debt, see Wier (1978).

lower cost than the bondholders (perhaps because much of the information is already being collected for internal decision making purposes), it pays the firm's stockholders to contract to provide this information to the bondholders. The market value of the firm increases by the reduction in agency costs.[50]

Jensen/Meckling (1976) and Watts (1977) point out that firms have the incentive to provide financial statements which have been audited by an external accounting firm if the increase in the market value of the bonds is greater than the present value of the auditing fees, net of any nominal benefits which accrue in internal monitoring. If bonding activities which are related to the bondholder–stockholder conflict involve incremental costs, then since the conflict increases with the debt in the firm's capital structure, the use of externally audited financial statements should be positively related to the firm's debt/equity ratio. Auditing expenditures should be associated with the extent to which covenants are specified in terms of accounting numbers from financial statements.[51,52]

2.5.2. Specification of accounting techniques

Description. As indicated, covenants restricting dividend, financing, and production/investment policy are frequently specified in terms of income or balance sheet numbers.[53] For public debt issues, other than stating that they should be consistent with generally accepted accounting principles (GAAP), covenants frequently do not specify how the accounting numbers will be computed.

Analysis. Restrictions on the shareholders' behavior can be relaxed by manipulating the accounting numbers which define the constraints.[54] For example, the impact of a change in accounting techniques on dividend and investment policy can be seen by referring to eq. (1) defining the inventory of funds for payment of dividends. The change in allowed dividend payments in quarter τ resulting from a change in earnings in quarter τ is proportional to k (i.e., $\partial D_\tau^* / \partial E_\tau = k$). If accounting earnings are overstated, then required current investment is increased by $(1 - k)$ times the change in reported earnings. After the bonds have been sold, shareholders have an incentive to use whichever method of calculation inflates stated earnings. However, this

---

[50]See Jensen/Meckling (1976, p. 338) and Watts (1977).

[51]For a further discussion of the incentives to employ external auditors, see Watts (1977).

[52]Furthermore, this analysis leads Leftwich/Watts/Zimmerman (1979) to predict that voluntary public disclosure of financial statements prior to required provision by the exchanges or regulation should be associated with the level of debt in the firm's capital structure.

[53]See Holthausen (1979) and Leftwich (1979) for more comprehensive analyses of the use of accounting definitions in bond covenants.

[54]One case where accounting manipulations may have been made to prevent the firm from violating its debt covenants is that of Pan American World Airways. See Foster (1978, p. 354).

argument overstates the incentive to manipulate accounting earnings if current earnings can only be increased by reducing future earnings. To illustrate, since the total amount of depreciation on a machine is fixed, taking less depreciation now implies that future accounting earnings will be reduced. In this case the shareholders can only lower required current investment by increasing required future investment. The magnitude of the gain to the shareholders from manipulation of accounting numbers is on the order of the discount rate multiplied by k times the change in reported earnings and this is likely to be relatively small.

It is expensive to specify the accounting procedure by contract and, if the specified procedure differs from GAAP, it is expensive to prepare an additional set of accounting statements for the bondholders. Such detailed procedures can be a more costly mechanism for the bondholders to protect themselves against 'creative accounting' than by requiring external auditing and reflecting any risk of accounting manipulations in the price paid for the bonds.

Holthausen (1979) argues that the firm's decision to change depreciation methods could result in a change in reported earnings which relaxes contractual constraints and results in a transfer of wealth to stockholders. Furthermore, Leftwich (1979) argues that restricting stockholders to GAAP involves costs since over time, accounting principles change. Mandated changes in GAAP can cause the constraints on the stockholders' behavior to change and in some cases to be violated.[55] Leftwich's analysis predicts that certain changes in GAAP should be associated with wealth losses to the firm's claimholders. Moreover, the extent of the loss should be related to the extent to which the contracts are specified in terms of GAAP.

2.5.3. Officers' certificate of compliance

Description. *Commentaries* suggests that in addition to submitting the reports indicated above, the firm usually promises to provide an annual certificate as to whether there has been any default under the indenture. The Certificate of Compliance must be signed both by the president or vice-president, and by either the treasurer, assistant treasurer, controller or assistant controller of the company. The statement indicates that the signing officer has reviewed the activities of the company for the year, and that to the best of his knowledge the firm has fulfilled all of its obligations under the indenture. If there has been a default, the nature and status of the default must be specified. Some indentures also call for certificates or opinions as to compliance to be supplied by independent accountants. Normally it is provided that the accountants' statement certify that during the examination the accountants 'obtained no knowledge' of any default. The accountants are

---

[55] Fogelson (1978) discusses several cases where this has occurred.

often expressly relieved of all liability for failure to obtain knowledge of a default.

Analysis.   The Costly Contracting Hypothesis suggests that the certificate of compliance is a way of reducing the monitoring costs of the bondholders. It is less expensive to have officers of the firm or the firm's accountants, who already will be knowledgeable of any defaults, contract to call such defaults to the attention of the bondholders than to let bondholders themselves ascertain if a default has occurred.

2.5.4. *The required purchase of insurance*

Description.   Indenture agreements frequently include provisions requiring the firm to purchase insurance. The sample covenants in *Commentaries* specify that the firm will purchase insurance 'to substantially the same extent as its competitors'. The stockholders sometimes retain the right to self-insure if the plan is certified by an actuary. Typically, the indenture requires the firm to maintain liability insurance.

Analysis.   In a world with perfect markets, there is no corporate demand for insurance; the corporate form effectively hedges insurable risk.[56] Our analysis suggests that the corporate purchase of insurance is a bonding activity engaged in by firms to reduce agency costs between bondholders and stockholders (as well as between the managers and the owners of a corporation). If insurance firms have a comparative advantage in monitoring aspects of the firm's activities, then a firm which purchases insurance will engage in a different set of activities from a firm which does not.

For example, a frequently purchased line of corporate insurance is boiler insurance. Insurance companies hire and train specialized inspectors to monitor the operation and maintenance of boilers, and the loss control program which is provided by the insurance company constrains the actions of the stockholders and managers of the firm. A covenant requiring the purchase of insurance gives stockholders the incentive to engage in the optimal amount of loss control projects. If the purchase of a sprinkler system were a positive net present value project it could still be rejected by stockholders of a levered firm because it reduces the variance rate of the firm's cash flows and thereby increases the value of the debt. But if the firm is contractually required to purchase insurance and if the insurance industry is competitive, the firm has the incentive to take any loss control project where the present value of the premium reductions is greater than the cost of the project. With the purchase of insurance the corporation's cash flow variability is unaffected by the purchase of loss control projects.

---

[56]See Mayers/Smith (1978).

3. The enforcement of bond covenants

The covenants we have discussed do not completely control the conflict between bondholders and stockholders; they do not go nearly so far as they could in restricting the firm's actions. The covenants could require that the firm secure permission of the bondholders for each action it takes, or that the firm 'accept all profitable projects, and only those projects'. However, as Jensen/Meckling (1976, p. 338) and Myers (1977, p. 158) argue, if such covenants are sufficiently expensive to enforce, it will not be in the interests of the firm's owners to offer them.

To specify types of enforcement costs, we must examine the institutional framework within which covenant enforcement takes place for further insight into why certain kinds of covenants are observed – and others not. Our analysis takes the institutional arragements as given. A deeper issue relates to the endogeneity of the institutions themselves. To the extent that the existing legal institutions represent an efficient solution to the problem of financial contracting, enforcement costs are lowered. But regardless of whether or not existing institutions imply 'minimum' costs, the types of contracts we observe depend on the level of these institutionally-related costs.

3.1. The legal liability of bondholders

Description. When bondholders exercise a significant degree of 'control' over the firm, they become legally liable to both the firm (i.e., the shareholders) and to third parties for losses incurred as a result of certain of their actions.[57] Although acts such as the seizure of collateral do not, in general, subject the creditor to liability,[58] creditor liability still occurs under a variety of conditions. For example, it can arise when a creditor who controls the firm is responsible for mismanagement. One of the leading cases is *Taylor versus Standard Gas Company*,[59] in which the court held the firm's creditor responsible for abuses which resulted from the exercise of control.

Creditors whose debt contracts contain restrictions which cause the firm to breach its contract with third parties, such as suppliers, employees, and other creditors, can also be held liable. One notable case in which a covenant

---

[57]Much of the discussion of the liability issue is based on the survey article of Douglas-Hamilton (1975). The liability of bondholders depends critically on the definition of 'control'. In the case of liability for securities law violations, 'a creditor would be considered in control of a corporate debtor even it if only indirectly possessed the power to direct the management or the policies of the debtor'. See Douglas-Hamilton (pp. 346–347).

That the courts frown upon bondholder control is not a new notion. Dewing (1953, pp. 188–189) indicates that the 'exclusion of bondholders from all voice in the management of the corporation...has been sanctioned by centuries of legal authority' and is a 'time honored legal theory'.

[58]Douglas-Hamilton (p. 364).

[59]306 U.S. 307 (1939). See Douglas-Hamilton (p. 348).

violated the rights of third parties is that of *Kelly versus Central Hanover Bank and Trust Company*.[60] There, the bondholders of the debtor corporation brought suit against another class of claimants, namely the creditor banks of the debtor. The bondholders charged that the banks, in obtaining a covenant pledging stock as security for their loans, violated the terms of the indenture agreement between the bondholders and the debtor. According to Douglas-Hamilton (1975, p. 364):

> 'It appears that the case against the banks was later settled on terms which included a payment of $3,435,008 by the banks to the bondholders and the withdrawal by the banks of claims aggregating $42,887,500 in the debtor corporation's bankruptcy proceedings.'

Creditors can also incur liability for Federal Securities Law violations. For example, under Rule 10b–5 of Section 10 of the Securities Act of 1934, which deals with fraud, a creditor incurs liability for failing to disclose material information about the firm. Creditor liability even arises in cases where there has been inadequate 'policing by a creditor of press releases of its troubled debtor to insure that they do not depict an inaccurate optimistic picture to the public'.[61]

Analysis. Covenants which have the effect of assigning legal liability to the bondholders represent a real cost to the firm's owners if bondholders, or their agent, are more likely than the firm's management to be held responsible for actions which result in losses and if the legal process which establishes liability is costly. In that case, giving bondholders control is a more costly way to run the firm simply because of the legal costs involved in the determination of bondholder liability. The firm's owners are better off simply not issuing those types of debt which are likely to result in such costs being incurred. While we have no direct evidence on the costs of creditor liability, one comment from the legal literature which suggests that those costs are not trivial is the warning that 'whenever a creditor contemplates taking a hand in the management of a financially troubled debtor, it should think of its deeper pockets and keep its hands there'.[62]

3.2. The role of the trust indenture and the trustee

Description. Debt contracts discussed in *Commentaries* typically appoint an independent 'trustee' to represent the bondholders and act as their agent in covenant enforcement. This is done under a device known as a corporate trust indenture, which specifies the respective rights and obligations of the

[60]85 F 2d 61 (2d Cir. 1936).
[61]Douglas-Hamilton (p. 354).
[62]Douglas-Hamilton (p. 364).

firm, the individual bondholders, and the trustee. Although the trustee is an agent of the bondholders, in practice he is actually compensated by the firm.[63]

Analysis. If the firm's debt is not held by a single borrower, then a number of problems related to enforcement of the debt contract arise. For example, any individual's holdings of the firm's debt may be so small that no single bondholder has much incentive to expend resources in covenant enforcement. But it is not the case that individual bondholders necessarily expend 'too few' resources in covenant enforcement. If the number of bondholders is small, then there can actually be overinvestment in enforcement in the sense that there is either a duplication of effort, or that creditors expend resources which simply result in change in the distribution of the proceeds. Our analysis implies that the firm's owners offer a contract which appoints a trustee to help assure that the optimal amount of covenant enforcement will take place.

Having the firm pay the trustees directly solves the 'free-rider' problem which would be inherent in making individual bondholders pay the trustee for enforcing the covenants. However after the bonds have been sold, the stockholders have an incentive to bribe the trustee so that they can violate the debt covenants. There are several factors which prevent such bribery from taking place.

Bribing the trustee is expensive if the trustee's reputation has significant value in the marketplace. *Ex ante*, it is in the interests of the firm's owners to choose an 'honest' trustee – that is, one who is expensive to bribe. This is because the value of the firm at the time it issues the debt contract reflects the probability of covenant enforcement. To the extent that enforcement by an 'honest' trustee reduces the problems of adverse borrower behavior induced by risky debt, the value of the firm is higher. Our analysis therefore implies that those chosen as trustees stand to lose much if they are caught accepting bribes. In fact, the indenture trustee is 'generally a large banking institution',[64] which has significant revenues from activities unrelated to being a trustee and which also depend on the market's perception of its trustworthiness. Furthermore, the behavior of the trustee is restricted by both trust and contract law.[65]

3.2.1. The Trust Indenture Act of 1939

Description. Publicly issued debt obligations must comply with the requirements of the Trust Indenture Act of 1939 (TIA).[66] Although the TIA does

[63]For a further discussion of the trustee's compensation, see Kennedy (1961, p. 49).
[64]Obrzut (1976, p. 131).
[65]For a further discussion, see Kennedy, especially chapter 2.
[66]There are minor exceptions. For example, issues of less than $1 million are exempted. The TIA is enforced by the Securities and Exchange Commission. For the bonds to be sold, the terms of the indenture must be 'qualified' by the SEC.

not explicitly regulate the restrictive covenants which the bond contract can include, the TIA does impose certain standards of conduct on the trustee. The trustee must meet certain minimum capital requirements. The trustee is not permitted to have a serious conflict of interest; with some minor exceptions, he may not act as the agent for two different classes of bondholders of the same firm, and he may not himself be a creditor in the firm for whose debt contract he acts as trustee.[67]

Analysis. In spite of these restrictions on the behavior of the trustee, it can still be very costly to write a contract where the bondholders are represented by such an agent. The trustee will still not act entirely in the bondholders' interest. This is particularly true because the extent to which the trustee can be held negligent is limited: while the trustee must act in good faith, his responsibilities often go no further unless there is a default. Under the TIA, when a default has occurred the trustee is only required to 'use the same degree of care and skill...as a prudent man would exercise' in enforcing the covenants. Furthermore it is not clear whether, prior to the TIA, the legal standards for either pre- or post-default conduct of trustees were significantly different.[68]

3.2.2. *Public versus private placements*

Description. Section 4(2) of the Securities Act of 1933 provides that a sale of securities not involving any public offering is exempt from registration. Such exempt issues are referred to as private placements or direct placements. Private placements are not typically subject to the TIA. They represent an alternative to publicly placed debt.

Analysis. Since the enforcement of tightly restrictive covenants through a trustee is difficult, the benefit from private (rather than public) placement of the firm's debt issues can be substantial. Our analysis suggests that private placements will contain more detailed restrictions on the firm's behavior than do public issues.[69] In addition, we would expect that the riskier the debt, the more likely that it will be privately placed. Because of the costs associated with the enforcement of trust indentures, the covenants in debt issues are not likely to eliminate the problems induced by the presence of risky debt.

---

[67]Kennedy (p. 35) claims that the standards of conduct contained in the TIA 'had been accepted and followed by the more responsible trust companies for a long time prior to the enactment of the legislation, so that no abrupt or sudden change was effected'. A major proponent of the legislation which resulted in the TIA was the Securities and Exchange Commission [Obrzut (1976, p. 133)].

[68]For a further discussion, see Johnson (1970).

[69]That private issues contain more restrictive covenants than public issues is consistent with the observations of the authors of *Commentaries* (p. 11 and p. 14). Note that private issues may also have trustees, even though the number of claimholders is typically small.

Evidence. Consistent with the hypothesis that privately placed debt contracts contain more extensive provisions than public, Leftwich (1979) presents evidence that variations from generally accepted accounting procedures occur more frequently in private than public debt issues. The adjustments to GAAP are systematic; they generally eliminate non-cash gains. However they do not restrict non-cash losses. For example, restatement of asset values which result in gains are typically eliminated from computed earnings while those resulting in losses are not.

Cohan (1967, p. 1) finds evidence of a shift to private placements during the 1930s: 'In the thirty-four years from 1900 to 1934, about 3 percent of all corporate debt cash offerings, or approximately $1 billion were directly (privately) placed. However, in the ensuing thirty-one years, from 1935 to 1965, 46 percent, or $85 billion, were directly placed.' While our analysis does predict such a shift to private placements after the TIA, this shift is also consistent with Benston's (1969) suggestion that the inception of the SEC in 1934 increased the cost of public versus private issues.

3.3. Default remedies

The debt contract typically gives the firm a strong incentive to live up to the restrictive covenants: any breach of the covenants is considered an act of default. Not only is the firm normally required to report any such breach, but the lender is given the right to engage in certain actions (e.g., seizure of collateral, acceleration of the maturity of the debt) to protect his interest.

3.3.1. Renegotiation

Description. Since actions such as the seizure of collateral consume real resources, the debt contract is often renegotiated in order to eliminate the default. In public debt issues the contract can be changed by the use of a 'supplemental indenture'. The supplement must be approved by the bondholders, and must meet the requirements of the TIA.

Changes in the specific covenants cannot usually be made without the consent of the holders of two-thirds in principal amount of the outstanding debt[70] (the firm itself is not allowed to vote any debt it holds). Moreover, the consent of 100 percent of the debtholders is required in order to change the maturity date or principal amount of the bonds. In private placements involving few lenders, renegotiation is typically easier.[71]

[70]See *Commentaries* (p. 307) and Section 902, American Bar Foundation Model Debenture Indenture Provisions – All Registered Issues.

[71]According to Zinbarg (1975): 'My own institution's experience [Prudential Insurance Co. of Am] may serve as an illustration. In any given year, we will, on average, receive one modification request per loan on the books. In no more than five per cent of these cases will we refuse the request or even require any quid pro quo, because the vast majority of corporate requests are perfectly reasonable and do not increase our risk materially.'

Analysis. The seemingly lower renegotiating costs of privately placed debt issues further re-inforce our earlier prediction that such private placements will contain tighter restrictions on the firm's behavior than will public issues.

3.3.2. Bankruptcy

Description. Should renegotiation fail, a default also gives the lender the right to put the firm into legal bankruptcy proceedings. Several features of the bankruptcy process bear on the enforcement of debt contracts. For example, since the bankruptcy process gives the firm temporary protection from acts of foreclosure and lien enforcement, some enforcement mechanisms are no longer available to the lender.

Analysis. Our theory suggests that it is more efficient to have some ambiguities in the initial debt contract, and to let them be resolved in bankruptcy should default ever occur. Since it is the firm's owners who bear the total costs associated with enforcing the debt contract, it is in their interests to find the most efficient balance between expenditures on drafting the debt contract and expected legal expenditures in bankruptcy. In a world where contracting is costly, that balance will imply less than complete specification of the payoff to be received by claimholders in every possible future state of the world.

As Warner (1977) discusses, bankruptcy courts recognize the priorities specified in the firm's debt agreements in only a limited sense. There are many cases where 'junior' claimants are compensated before claimants 'senior' to them are paid in full. Since 'priorities' are not always enforced, it will not always pay the firm to indicate the priority of a given debt issue with much specificity (e.g., creditor A is forty-seventh in line).

4. Conclusions

4.1. The role of bond covenants

We have examined the specific provisions which are included in corporate debt contracts. Since covenants are a persistent phenomena, we can therefore assume that these provisions are efficient from the standpoint of the firm's owners, and thus we can draw inferences about the role of these contractual forms in the firm's capital structure.

Observed debt covenants reduce the costs associated with the conflict of interest between bondholders and stockholders; the ingenuity with which debt contracts are written indicates the strong economic incentives for the firm's owners to lower the agency costs which can result from having risky debt in the firm's capital structure.

The existence of standardized debt contracts such as those found in

Commentaries suggests that the out-of-pocket costs of drafting observed bond contracts are small indeed. However, the direct and opportunity costs of complying with the contractual restrictions appear to be substantial. We have presented no evidence on the precise dollar magnitudes, and we emphasize that a particular covenant included in a given debt contract will not impose opportunity costs with probability one. But our analysis indicates that observed bond covenants involve expected costs which are large enough to help account for the variation in debt contracts across firms. This is consistent with the Costly Contracting Hypothesis. On the other hand, it is inconsistent with the Irrelevance Hypothesis, which predicts that total resource expenditures on control of the bondholder–stockholder conflict will be negligible.

Our analysis also sheds some light on the relative costs of the alternative types of restrictions which can be written into the debt contract. We conclude that production/investment policy is very expensive to monitor. Stockholder use (or misuse) of production/investment policy frequently involves not some explicit act, but the failure to take a certain action (e.g., failure to accept a positive net present value project). It is expensive even to ascertain when the firm's production/investment policy is not optimal, since such a determination depends on magnitudes which are difficult to observe. The high monitoring costs which would be associated with restrictive production/investment covenants, including the potential legal costs associated with bondholder control, dictate that few production/investment decisions will be contractually proscribed. For the firm's owners to go very far in directly restricting the firm's production/investment policy would be inefficient.

On the other hand, we conclude that dividend policy and financing policy involve lower monitoring costs. Stockholder use of these policies to 'hurt' bondholders involves acts (e.g., the sale of a large bond issue) which are readily observable. Because they are cheaper to monitor, it is efficient to restrict production/investment policy by writing dividend and financing policy covenants in a way which helps assure that stockholders will act to maximize the value of the firm.

4.2. Implications for capital structure

With more fixed claims in the capital structure, the benefits to the stockholders from asset substitution, claim dilution, underinvestment, and dividend payout increase; with higher benefits, the stockholders will expend more real resources 'getting around' any particular set of contractual constraints. This, in turn, will increase the benefits of increased tightness of the covenants. Accordingly, the costs associated with the bondholder–stockholder conflict rise with the firm's debt/equity ratio. Simply limiting the debt in the capital structure is an efficient mechanism for controlling this conflict. Because of this, the costs associated with writing and enforcing covenants influence the level of debt the firm chooses.

Since observed debt covenants involve real costs, there must be some benefit in having debt in the firm's capital structure; otherwise, the bondholder–stockholder conflict can be costlessly eliminated by not issuing debt. Hence our evidence indicates not only that there is an optimal form of the debt contract, but an optimal *amount* of debt as well. The benefits from issuing risky debt are not well understood, and even though the costs we have discussed in this paper provide a lower bound on their magnitude, our analysis has not permitted us to distinguish between alternative explanations of the benefits: (1) information asymmetries and signalling, (2) taxes, (3) agency costs of equity financing, (4) differential transactions and flotation costs, and (5) unbundling of riskbearing and capital ownership.

4.3. Some possible extensions

While our analysis of debt covenants is a useful start at explaining certain aspects of the firm's capital structure, there are a number of issues which have not been explored here which, we believe, merit further attention. We have attempted to indicate the interrelationship between covenants restricting dividend, financing, and production/investment policy. However, we have not developed a theory which is capable of explaining how, for a given debt issue, the total 'package' of covenants is determined. Further work on the substitutability or complementarity of the specific contractual provisions is necessary before it is possible to predict, for any set of firm-specific characteristics, the form which the debt contract will take.

Second, we emphasize that bond covenants are but one way in which the behavior of the stockholders is constrained. For example, both the legal system and the possibility of takeovers are factors which make it more expensive for stockholders to engage in actions aimed at maximizing the value of their own claim but not the total value of the firm. The relative importance of these factors, and how they affect the firm's choice of debt covenants, is not yet well understood.

Finally, it is important to remember that in focusing on the bondholder–stockholder conflict, we have ignored other conflicts, such as that between managers and stockholders, which also exist. To the extent that the contracts comprising the firm are interdependent and simultaneously determined, the bondholder–stockholder conflict should not be viewed in isolation. The impact of the bondholder–stockholder conflict on the firm's total contracting costs cannot be fully understood until the nature of these contractual interdependencies is explored.

Appendix

In this appendix, we consider in more detail the results presented in section 1. First, we discuss the valuation of the debt of a levered firm when the relevant variables in the valuation equations can be specified parametrically over the life of the bonds. We then expand the analysis to the case where stockholders can change these variables after they obtain the proceeds from the sale of the debt, and where both the stockholders and bondholders are aware of this possibility when the bonds are originally issued.

A.1. Option pricing valuation of the firm's financial claims

The valuation of the equity and debt of a levered firm is examined by Black/Scholes (1973) and Merton (1974). Where the bonds are single-payment contracts and the market is efficient and competitive, without transactions costs, information costs, other agency costs, or taxes, the analysis is straightforward. Consider a bond contract which promises to repay a lump sum, X, covering both principal and interest at a specified date in the future, t^*. When the bond issue is sold, the proceeds from the sale equal the current value of the bondholders' claim, B, on the firm's assets. Assume that the firm's financial claims consist of this bond issue and common stock. Thus, the current value of the stock, S, is the difference between the current value of the firm's assets, V, and the value of the bonds, B,

$$S \equiv V - B. \tag{A.1}$$

Given this contract, the optimal strategy for the firm's shareholders at the maturity date of the bonds can be specified: if the value of the firm's assets at the maturity date, V^*, is greater than the face value of the bonds, X, then repay the bonds; the stockholders equity at that date, S^* will be the difference between the value of the firm's assets and the face value of the bonds, $V^* - X$. On the other hand, if at the maturity date of the bonds the value of the firm's assets is less than the face value of the bonds, then default on the bonds; the bondholders do not receive the face value of the bonds, they receive only the firm's assets, V^*. Given limited liability, the shareholders' equity is zero. Thus, at t^* the value of the stock, S^*, is

$$S^* = \max[0, V^* - X], \tag{A.2}$$

and the value of the bonds is

$$B^* = \min[V^*, X]. \tag{A.3}$$

This bond issue is equivalent to the sale of the firm's assets to the bondholders for a package containing: (1) the proceeds from the sale of the bonds, B, (2) a claim which allows the stockholders to receive the dividends paid by the firm over the life of the bonds, and (3) a European call option[72] to repurchase the assets at the maturity date of the loan T time periods later $(T = t^* - t)$, with an exercise price equal to the face value of the bonds, X. Those variables which affect the value of call options are also important in valuing the financial claims of firms.

To derive an explicit solution for the market value of the bonds given the other variables, make the following assumptions:

(1) There are homogeneous expectations about the dynamic behavior of the value of the firm's assets. The distribution at the end of any finite time interval is lognormal. The variance rate, σ^2, is constant.

(2) The dynamic behavior of the value of the assets is independent of the face value of the bonds, X.

(3) There are no transactions costs associated with default.

(4) The firm pays a continuous flow of dividend payments to the share-holders. The dividend payment, per unit time D, is a constant fraction, δ, of the market value of the assets: $\delta = D/V$.

(5) Capital markets are perfect. There are no transactions costs or taxes. All participants have free access to all available information. Participants are price takers.

(6) There is a known constant riskless rate of interest, r.[73]

Under these assumptions, Merton (1974) has shown that the value of the bonds, B, can be written as

$$B = V e^{-\delta T} N \left\{ \frac{-\ln(V/X) - (r - \delta + \sigma^2/2)T}{\sigma\sqrt{T}} \right\}$$

$$+ X e^{-rT} N \left\{ \frac{\ln(V/X) + (r - \delta - \sigma^2/2)T}{\sigma\sqrt{T}} \right\}, \tag{A.4}$$

---

[72] A European call option is a contract which gives the owner the right to purchase a specified asset at a specified price, called the exercise price, on a specified date, called the maturity date. Since the option is only exercised if it is in the best interest of the owner, it will be exercised only if the value of the asset is above the exercise price at the maturity date; otherwise it will expire worthless.

[73] Merton (1973) has modified the Black/Scholes contingent claims analysis to account for time series variability in interest rates. His solution retains the basic form of this analysis. Since the effects of the variability of the riskless rate and term structure are not of primary concern here, this simpler assumption will be maintained.

where $N\{\ \}$ is the cumulative standard normal distribution function. In general form,

$$B = B(V, X, T, \delta, \sigma^2, r),\tag{A.5}$$

where

$$\frac{\partial B}{\partial V}, \frac{\partial B}{\partial X} > 0 \quad \text{and} \quad \frac{\partial B}{\partial T}, \frac{\partial B}{\partial \delta}, \frac{\partial B}{\partial \sigma^2}, \frac{\partial B}{\partial r} < 0.$$

A.2. The nature of the covenants to be included in the debt contract

As we discussed in section 1, in pricing the bonds the bondholders must ascertain the values of the variables in eq. (A.5). These variables can be changed after the bonds are issued; the bondholders make assessments of likely stockholder actions, given whatever restrictions the debt contract places on the stockholders. The particular covenants written are those which maximize the wealth of the firm's current owners. This is the set of covenants which maximizes the with-dividend value of the firm when the bonds are issued.

For explicit analysis of the incentives faced by the shareholders and bondholders in drafting the debt contract, the analysis of the valuation of claims must be expanded.[74] The firm's objective is assumed to be the maximization of current equity, S, and the current dividend, D,

$$W \equiv S + D.\tag{A.6}$$

For an all equity firm which has decided to sell bonds, the value of the stock, S, can be expressed as the total ex-dividend value of the firm, V, minus the value of the claim sold to the new bondholders, B,

$$S \equiv V - B.\tag{A.7}$$

The value of the claim sold to the new bondholders is a function of the projects chosen, and the terms of the contract. More specifically, let the firm choose a vector of activities, α, and a vector of provisions in its financial contracts, f (e.g., f includes the face value of the debt, X, and the time to maturity of the bonds, T, as well as covenants such as restrictions on dividend payments). In general, the value of the firm's assets, the variance rate, and the dividend payments area function of the activities and contractual provisions chosen. Thus the value to the stockholders of the claim sold to the bondholders can be expressed as

$$B = B(\alpha, f).\tag{A.8}$$

[74]The following analysis was suggested by John Long.

The cash flow identity that inflows equal outflows can be used to re-express the dividend payment, D, as the sum of the internally generated cash flow before interest expense, ϕ, plus the net proceeds from the sale of the new bonds, B, minus the new investment expenditures, I,

$$D \equiv \phi + B - I. \tag{A.9}$$

The proceeds from the sale of the new bonds will depend on the financial covenants, f, chosen. Let $\alpha(f)$ represent the activity that, given the choice of financial contract, f, maximizes the with-dividend value of the shareholder's equity. The bondholders will assume that if the contractual provisions are f, then the stockholders will act in their own self-interest and choose the vector of activities, $\alpha(f)$. Thus, the proceeds from the sale of the new bonds will be

$$B = B(\alpha(f), f). \tag{A.10}$$

Substituting (A.7), (A.8), (A.9) and (A.10) into (A.6) allows us to re-express shareholder wealth as

$$W = V(\alpha, f) - B(\alpha, f) + B(\alpha(f), f) + \phi(\alpha, f) - I(\alpha, f). \tag{A.11}$$

Thus, for a given financial structure, f, the optimal activity choice, α, to maximize shareholder wealth is

$$W(\alpha(f), f) = V(\alpha(f), f) + \phi(\alpha(f), f) - I(\alpha(f), f). \tag{A.12}$$

From (A.12) it is clear that the optimal financial structure, f^*, will be that structure for which the with-dividend value of the firm is maximized subject to the available set of financial structures; i.e.,

$$V[\alpha(f^*), f^*] + \phi[\alpha(f^*), f^*] - I[\alpha(f^*), f^*]$$
$$\geq V[\alpha(f), f] + \phi[\alpha(f), f] - I[\alpha(f), f],$$

for all feasible f.

This can be illustrated graphically. Let (α^{**}, f^{**}) be the point where the with-dividend value of the firm is maximized; i.e., where

$$V(\alpha^{**}, f^{**}) + \phi(\alpha^{**}, f^{**}) - I(\alpha^{**}, f^{**})$$
$$\geq V(\alpha, f) + \phi(\alpha, f) - I(\alpha, f),$$

for all choices of financial structure and activities, assuming that the magnitudes could be independently set. We call this point the 'idealized' capital structure/activity choice for the firm. In fig. 1 the with-dividend value of the firm is represented in (α, f) space as level sets. The set of optimal activity choices as a function of financial structure, $\alpha(f)$, is also represented. The agency costs described by Jensen/Meckling (1976) are $[V(\alpha^{**}, f^{**}) + \phi(\alpha^{**}, f^{**}) - I(\alpha^{**}, f^{**})] - [V(\alpha(f^*), f^*) + \phi(\alpha(f^*), f^*) - I(\alpha(f^*)f^*)]$, i.e., the difference between the with-dividend value of the firm given the idealized capital structure and the idealized activity choice minus the value of the firm given the optimum (feasible) choice of activities and capital structure.

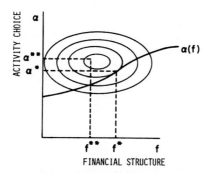

Fig. 1. Determination of the optimal financial structure, f^*, and activity choice, α^*. The collection of level sets represent different with-dividend market values of the firm, assuming the activity choice, α, and financial structure, f, can be set independently. The point (α^{**}, f^{**}) is the maximum with-dividend firm market value. The function $\alpha(f)$ represents the choice of activity which maximizes shareholder wealth for a given financial structure. Agency costs are $\{[V(\alpha^{**}, f^{**}) + \phi(\alpha^{**}, f^{**}) - I(\alpha^{**})] - [V(\alpha(f^*), f^*) + \phi(\alpha(f^*), f^*) - I(\alpha(f^*), f^*)]\}$.

References

Alchian, Armen, 1950, Uncertainty, evolution, and economic theory, Journal of Political Economy 58, 211–221.

Alchian, Armen and Harold Demsetz, 1972, Production, information costs, and economic organization, American Economic Review 62, 777–795.

American Bar Foundation, 1971, Commentaries on model debenture indenture provisions 1965, Model debenture indenture provisions all registered issues 1967, and Certain negotiable provisions which may be included in a particular incorporating indenture (Chicago, IL).

Benston, George J., 1969, The effectiveness and effects of the SEC's accounting disclosure requirements, in: Henry G. Manne, ed., Economic policy and the regulation of corporate securities (American Enterprise Institute, Washington, DC), 23–79.

Black, Fischer, 1976, The dividend puzzle, Journal of Portfolio Management 2, 5–8.

Black, Fischer and John C. Cox, 1976, Valuing corporate securities: Some effects of bond indenture provisions, Journal of Finance 31, 351–367.

Black, Fischer, Merton H. Miller and Richard A. Posner, 1978, An approach to the regulation of bank holding companies, Journal of Business 51, 379–412.

Black, Fischer and Myron Scholes, 1973, The pricing of options and corporate liabilities, Journal of Political Economy 81, 637–659.

Bodie, Zvi and Robert Taggart, 1978, Future investment opportunities and the value of the call provision on a bond, Journal of Finance 23, 1187–1200.

Bradley, Michael, 1978, An analysis of interfirm cash tender offers, Unpublished manuscript (University of Chicago, Chicago, IL).

Cheung, Steven, 1973, The fable of the bees: An economic investigation, Journal of Law and Economics 16, 11–33.

Coase, Ronald, 1960, The problem of social cost, Journal of Law and Economics 3, 1–44.

Cohan, Avery G., 1967, Yields on corporate debt directly placed (National Bureau of Economic Research, New York).

Coleman, William, 1971, Biology in the nineteenth century: Problems of form, function, and transformation (Wiley, New York).

Darwin, Charles, 1859, The origin of species by means of natural selection or the preservation of favoured races in the struggle for life. Reprinted in 1962 (Collier Books, New York).

Demsetz, Harold, 1967, Toward a theory of property rights, American Economic Review 57, 347–359.

Dewing, Arthur, 1934, 1953, The financial policy of corporations (Ronald Press, New York).

Dodd, Peter and Richard Ruback, 1977, Tender offers and stockholder returns: An empirical analysis, Journal of Financial Economics 5, 351–373.

Douglas-Hamilton, Margaret H., 1975, Creditor liabilities resulting from improper interference with the management of a financially troubled debtor, Business Lawyer 31, 343–365.

Fama, Eugene F., 1978a, The effect of a firm's investment and financing decisions on the welfare of its security holders, American Economic Review 68, 272–284.

Fama, Eugene F., 1978b, Agency problems and the theory of the firm, Unpublished manuscript (University of Chicago, Chicago, IL).

Fama, Eugene F. and Merton Miller, 1972, The theory of finance (Holt, Rinehart and Winston, New York).

Fogelson, James H., 1978, The impact of changes in accounting principles on restrictive covenants in credit agreements and indentures, Business Lawyer 73, 769–787.

Foster, George, 1978, Financial statement analysis (Prentice-Hall, Englewood Cliffs, NJ).

Galai, Dan and Ronald W. Masulis, 1976, The option pricing model and the risk factor of stock, Journal of Financial Economics 3, 53–81.

Henn, Harry H., 1970, Handbook of the law of corporations and other business enterprises (West Publishing Company, St. Paul, MN).

Holthausen, Robert, 1979, Toward a positive theory of choice of accounting techniques: The case of alternative depreciation methods, Unpublished manuscript (University of Rochester, Rochester, NY).

Jensen, Michael C. and William H. Meckling, 1976, Theory of the firm: Managerial behavior, agency costs, and capital structure, Journal of Financial Economics 3, 305–360.

Johnson, William A., 1970, Default administration of corporate trust indentures: The general nature of the trustee's responsibility and events of default, St. Louis University Law Journal 15, 203–236.

Kalay, Avner, 1979, Toward a theory of corporate dividend policy, Unpublished Ph.D. thesis (University of Rochester, Rochester, NY).

Kennedy, Joseph C., 1961, Corporate trust administration (New York University Press, New York).

Kuhn, Thomas S., 1970, The structure of scientific revolutions (University of Chicago Press, Chicago, IL).

Leftwich, Richard, 1979, Accounting principles and bond indentures: The role of private contracts, Unpublished manuscript (University of Rochester, Rochester, NY).

Leftwich, Richard, Ross Watts and Jerold L. Zimmerman, 1979, A theory of voluntary corporate disclosure, Unpublished manuscript (University of Rochester, Rochester, NY).

Long, John B., 1973, Book review of the theory of finance by Eugene Fama and Merton Miller, Journal of Money, Credit and Banking 5, 229–235.

Manne, Henry, 1967, Our two corporation systems: Law and economics, Virginia Law Review 53, 259–284.

Mayers, David and Clifford W. Smith, 1978, Towards a positive theory of insurance, Unpublished manuscript (University of Rochester, Rochester, NY).

Merton, Robert C., 1973, Theory of rational option pricing, Bell Journal of Economics and Management Science 4, 141–183.

Merton, Robert C., 1974, On the pricing of corporate debt: The risk structure of interest rates, Journal of Finance 29, 449–470.

Mikkelson, Wayne, 1978, An examination of the agency cost rationale for convertible bonds, Unpublished manuscript (University of Rochester, Rochester, NY).

Miller, Merton, 1977a, The wealth transfers of bankruptcy: Some illustrative examples, Special issue on the economics of bankruptcy reform, Law and Contemporary Problems 41, Autumn, 39–46.

Miller, Merton, 1977b, Debt and taxes, Journal of Finance 22, 261–275.

Miller, Merton and Franco Modigliani, 1966, Some estimates of the cost of capital to the electric utility industry, American Economic Review 56, 334–391.

Modigliani, Franco and Merton Miller, 1958, The cost of capital, corporation finance, and the theory of investment, American Economic Review 48, 261–297.

Myers, Stewart C., 1977, Determinants of corporate borrowing, Journal of Financial Economics 5, 147–175.

Nagel, Ernest, 1961, The structure of science: Problems in the logic of scientific explanation (Harcourt, Brace & World, New York).

Norgaard, Richard L. and F. Corine Thompson, 1967, Sinking funds: Their use and value (Financial Executives Research Foundation, New York).

Obrzut, Frederica R., 1976, The trust indenture act of 1939: The corporate trustee as creditor, UCLA Law Review 24, 131–159.

Popper, Karl, 1959, The logic of scientific discovery (Hutchinson, London).

Posner, Richard A., A theory of negligence, Journal of Legal Studies 1, 29–96.

Rodgers, Churchill, 1965, The corporate trust indenture project, Business Lawyer 20, 551–571.

Ross, Stephen A., 1977, The determination of financial structure: The incentive signalling approach, Bell Journal of Economics 8, 23–40.

Scott, James H., Jr., 1977, Bankruptcy, secured debt, and optimal capital structure, Journal of Finance 32, 1–19.

Smith, Clifford W., 1976, Option pricing: A review, Journal of Financial Economics 3, 3–51.

Smith, Clifford W. and Jerold B. Warner, 1979, Bankruptcy, secured debt, and optimal capital structure: Comment, Journal of Finance 34, 247–251.

Stigler, George J., 1958, The economies of scale, Journal of Law and Economics 1, 54–71.

Stiglitz, Joseph E., 1972, Some aspects of the pure theory of corporate finance: Bankruptcies and takeovers, Bell Journal of Economics 3, 458–482.

Warner, Jerold B., 1977, Bankruptcy, absolute priority, and the pricing of risky debt claims, Journal of Financial Economics 4, 239–276.

Watts, Ross, 1977, Corporate financial statements, a product of the market and political processes, Australian Journal of Management 2, 53–75.

Wier, Peggy, 1978, Callable debt, Unpublished manuscript (University of Rochester, Rochester, NY).

Zinbarg, Edward, 1975, The private placement loan agreement, Financial Analysts Journal 31, July/Aug., 33–52.

THREE

CORPORATE PAYOUT POLICY

The Dividend Puzzle

Fischer Black

Why do corporations pay dividends?

Why do investors pay attention to dividends?

Perhaps the answers to these questions are obvious. Perhaps dividends represent the return to the investor who put his money at risk in the corporation. Perhaps corporations pay dividends to reward existing shareholders and to encourage others to buy new issues of common stock at high prices. Perhaps investors pay attention to dividends because only through dividends or the prospect of dividends do they receive a return on their investment or the chance to sell their shares at a higher price in the future.

Or perhaps the answers are not so obvious. Perhaps a corporation that pays no dividends is demonstrating confidence that it has attractive investment opportunities that might be missed if it paid dividends. If it makes these investments, it may increase the value of the shares by more than the amount of the lost dividends. If that happens, its shareholders may be doubly better off. They end up with capital appreciation greater than the dividends they missed out on, and they find they are taxed at lower effective rates on capital appreciation than on dividends.

In fact, I claim that the answers to these questions are not obvious at all. The harder we look at the dividend picture, the more it seems like a puzzle, with pieces that just don't fit together.

THE MILLER-MODIGLIANI THEOREM

Suppose you are offered the following choice. You may have $2 today, and a 50-50 chance of $54 or $50 tomorrow. Or you may have nothing today, and a 50-50 chance of $56 or $52 tomorrow. Would you prefer one of these gambles to the other?

Probable you would not. Ignoring such factors as the cost of holding the $2 and one day's interest on $2, you would be indifferent between these two gambles.

The choice between a common stock that pays a dividend and a stock that pays no dividend is similar, at least if we ignore such things as transaction costs and taxes. The price of the dividend-paying stock drops on the ex-dividend date by about the amount of the dividend. The dividend just drops the whole range of possible stock prices by that amount. The investor who gets a $2 dividend finds himself with shares worth about $2 less than they would have been worth if the dividend hadn't been paid, in all possible circumstances.

This, in essence, is the Miller-Modigliani theorem.[1] It says that the dividends a corporation pays do not affect the value of its shares or the returns to investors, because the higher the dividend, the less the investor receives in capital appreciation, no matter how the corporation's business decisions turn out.

When we say this, we are assuming that the dividend paid does not influence the corporation's business decisions. Paying the dividend either reduces the amount of cash equivalents held by the corporation, or increases the amount of money raised by issuing securities.

IF A FIRM PAYS NO DIVIDENDS

If this theorem is correct, then a firm that pays a regular dividend equal to about half of its normal earnings will be worth the same as an otherwise similar firm that pays no dividends and will never pay any dividends. Can that be true? How can a firm that will never pay dividends be worth anything at all?

Actually, there are many ways for the stockholders of a firm to take cash out without receiving dividends. The most obvious is that the firm can buy back some of its shares. This has the advantage that most investors are not taxed as heavily on shares sold as they are on dividends received.

If the firm is closely held, it can give money to its shareholders by giving them jobs at inflated salaries, or by ordering goods from other firms owned by the shareholders at inflated prices.

If the firm is not closely held, then another firm or individual can make a tender offer which will have the effect of making it closely held. Then the same methods for taking cash out of the firm can be used.

Under the assumptions of the Modigliani-Miller theorem, a firm has value even if it pays no dividends. Indeed, it has the same value it would have if it paid dividends.

TAXES

In a world where dividends are taxed more heavily (for most investors) than capital gains, and where capital gains are not taxed until realized, a corporation that pays no dividends will be more attractive to taxable individual investors than a similar corporation that pays dividends. This will tend to increase the price of the non-dividend-paying corporation's stock. Many corporations will be tempted to eliminate dividend payments.

Of course, corporate investors are taxed more heavily on realized capital gains

---

[1]See Merton H. Miller and Franco Modigliani, "Dividend Policy, Growth, and the Valuation of Shares." *Journal of Business* 34 (October, 1961): 411–433. Also Franco Modigliani and Merton H. Miller, "The Cost of Capital, Corporation Finance, and the Theory of Investment: Reply."*American Economic Review* 49 (September, 1959): 655–669.

than on dividends. And tax-exempt investors are taxed on neither. But it is hard to believe that these groups have enough impact on the market to outweigh the effects of taxable individuals.

Also, the IRS has a special tax that it likes to apply to companies that retain earnings to avoid the personal taxation of dividends. But there are many ways to avoid this tax. A corporation that is making investments in its business usually doesn't have to pay the tax, especially if it is issuing securities to help pay for these investments.

If a corporation insists on paying out cash, it is better off replacing some of its common stock with bonds. A shareholder who keeps his proportionate share of the new securities will receive taxable interest but at least the interest will be deductible to the corporation. Dividends are not deductible.

With taxes, investors and corporations are no longer indifferent to the level of dividends. They prefer smaller dividends or no dividends at all.

TRANSACTION COSTS

An investor who holds a non-dividend-paying stock will generally sell some of his shares if he needs to raise cash. In some circumstances, he can borrow against his shares. Either of these transactions can be costly, especially if small amounts of money are involved. So an investor might want to have dividend income instead.

But this argument doesn't have much substance. If investors are concerned about transaction costs, the corporation that pays no dividends can arrange for automatic share repurchase plans, much like the automatic dividend reinvestment plans that now exist. A shareholder would keep his stock in trust, and the trustee would periodically sell shares back to the corporation, including fractional shares if necessary. The shareholder could even choose the amounts he wants to receive and the timing of the payments. An automated system would probably cost about as much as a system for paying dividends.

If the IRS objected to the corporation's buying back its own shares, then the trustee could simply sell blocks of shares on the open market. Again, the cost would be low.

Thus transaction costs don't tell us much about why corporations pay dividends.

WHAT DO DIVIDEND CHANGES TELL US?

The managers of most corporations have a tendency to give out good news quickly, but to give out bad news slowly. Thus investors are somewhat suspicious of what the managers have to say.

Dividend policy, though, may say things the managers don't say explicitly. For one reason or another, managers and directors do not like to cut the dividend. So they will raise the dividend only if they feel the company's prospects are good enough to support the higher dividend for some time. And they will cut the dividend only if they think the prospects for a quick recovery are poor.

This means that dividend changes, or the fact that the dividend doesn't change, may tell investors more about what the managers really think than they can find out from other sources. Assuming that the managers' forecasts are somewhat reliable, dividend policy conveys information.

Thus the announcement of a dividend cut often leads to a drop in the company's stock price. And the announcement of a dividend increase often leads to an increase in the company's stock price. These stock price changes are permanent if the company in fact does as badly, or as well, as the dividend changes indicated.

If the dividend changes are not due to forecasts of the company's prospects, then any stock price changes that occur will normally be temporary. If a corporation eliminates its dividend because it wants to save taxes for its shareholders, then the stock price might decline at first. But it would eventually go back to the level it would have had if the dividend had not been cut, or higher.

Thus the fact that dividend changes often tell us things about the corporations making them does not explain why corporations pay dividends.

HOW TO HURT THE CREDITORS

When a company has debt outstanding, the indenture will almost always limit the dividends the company can pay. And for good reason. There is no easier way for a company to escape the burden of a debt than to pay out all of its assets in the form of a dividend, and leave the creditors holding an empty shell.[2]

While this is an extreme example, any increase in the dividend that is not offset by an increase in external financing will hurt the company's creditors. A dollar paid out in dividends is a dollar that is not available to the creditors if trouble develops.

If an increase in the dividend will hurt the creditors, then a cut in the dividend will help the creditors. Since the firm is only worth so much, what helps the creditors will hurt the stockholders. The stockholders would certainly rather have $2 in dividends than $2 invested in assets that may end up in the hands of the creditors. Perhaps we have finally found a reason why firms pay dividends.

Alas, this explanation doesn't go very far. In many cases, the changes in the values of the stock and bonds caused by a change in dividend policy would be so small they would not be detectable. And if the effects are large, the company can negotiate with the creditors. If the company agrees not to pay any dividends at all, the creditors would presumably agree to give better terms on the company's credit. This would eliminate the negative effects of cutting the dividend on the position of the stockholders relative to the creditors.

---

[2]This issue is discussed in more detail in Fischer Black and Myron Scholes, "The Pricing of Options and Corporate Liabilities." *Journal of Political Economy* 81 (May/June, 1973): 637–654.

DIVIDENDS AS A SOURCE OF CAPITAL

A company that pays dividends might instead have invested the money in its operations. This is especially true when the company goes to the markets frequently for new capital. Cutting the dividend, if there are no special reasons for paying dividends, has to be one of the lowest cost sources of funds available to the company.

The underwriting cost of a new debt or equity issue is normally several percent of the amount of money raised. There are no comparable costs for money raised by cutting the dividend.

Perhaps a company that has no profitable investment projects and that is not raising money externally should keep its dividend. If the dividend is cut, the managers may lose the money through unwise investment projects. In these special cases, there may be a reason to keep the dividend. But surely these cases are relatively rare.

In the typical case, the fact that cutting the dividend is a low cost way to raise money is another reason to expect corporations not to pay dividends. So why do they continue?

DO INVESTORS DEMAND DIVIDENDS?

It is possible that many, many individual investors believe that stocks that don't pay dividends should not be held, or should be held only at prices lower than the prices of similar stocks that do pay dividends. This belief is not rational, so far as I can tell. But it may be there nonetheless.

Add these investors to the trustees who believe it is not prudent to hold stocks that pay no dividends, and to the corporations that have tax reasons for preferring dividend-paying stocks, and you may have a substantial part of the market. More important, you may have a part of the market that strongly influences the pricing of corporate shares. Perhaps the best evidence of this is the dominance of this view in investment advisory publications.

On the other hand, investors also seem acutely aware of the tax consequences of dividends. Investors in high tax brackets seem to hold low dividend stocks, and investors in low tax brackets seem to hold high dividend stocks.[3]

Furthermore, the best empirical tests that I can think of are unable to show whether investors who prefer dividends or investors who avoid dividends have a stronger effect on the pricing of securities.[4]

If investors do demand dividends, then corporations should not eliminate all dividends. But it is difficult or impossible to tell whether investors demand dividends or not. So it is hard for a corporation to decide whether to eliminate its dividends or not.

[3]See Marshall E. Blume, Jean Crockett, and Irwin Friend, "Stockownership in the United States: Characteristics and Trends." *Survey of Current Business* 54 (November, 1974): 16–40.

[4]See Fischer Black and Myron Scholes, "The Effects of Dividend Yield and Dividend Policy on Common Stock Prices and Returns." *Journal of Financial Economics* 1 (May, 1974): 1–22.

PORTFOLIO IMPLICATIONS

Corporations can't tell what dividend policy to choose, because they don't know how many irrational investors there are. But perhaps a rational investor can choose a dividend policy for his portfolio that will maximize his after-tax expected return for a given level of risk. Perhaps a taxable investor, especially one who is in a high tax bracket, should emphasize low dividend stocks. And perhaps a tax-exempt investor should emphasize high dividend stocks.

One problem with this strategy is that an investor who emphasizes a certain kind of stock in his portfolio is likely to end up with a less well-diversified portfolio than he would otherwise have. So he will probably increase the risk of his portfolio.

The other problem is that we can't tell if or how much an investor will increase his expected return by doing this. If investors demanding dividends dominate the market, then high dividend stocks will have low expected returns. Even tax-exempt investors, if they are rational, should buy low dividend stocks.

On the other hand, it seems that rational investors in high brackets will do better in low dividend stocks no matter who dominates the market. But how much should they emphasize low dividend stocks? At what point will the loss of diversification offset the increase in expected return?

It is even conceivable that investors overemphasize tax factors, and bid low dividend stocks up so high that they are unattractive even for investors in the highest brackets.

Thus the portfolio implications of the theory are no clearer than its implications for corporate dividend policy.

What should the individual investor do about dividends in his portfolio? We don't know.

What should the corporation do about dividend policy? We don't know.

Two Agency-Cost Explanations of Dividends

By Frank H. Easterbrook*

The economic literature about dividends usually assumes that managers are perfect agents of investors, and it seeks to determine why these agents pay dividends. Other literature about the firm assumes that managers are imperfect agents and inquires how managers' interests may be aligned with shareholders' interests. These two lines of inquiry rarely meet.[1] Yet logically any dividend policy (or any other corporate policy) should be designed to minimize the sum of capital, agency, and taxation costs. The purpose of this paper is to ask whether dividends are a method of aligning managers' interests with those of investors. It offers agency-cost explanations of dividends.

I. The Dividend Problem

Businesses find dividends obvious. Boards declare them regularly and raise them from time to time or face disquiet from investors, or so they think. Many managers are sure that higher dividends mean higher prices for their shares. There is a substantial body of law that controls when boards may (sometimes must) declare dividends, in what amount, and using what procedures.[2] Firms enter into complicated contracts with creditors and preferred stockholders that govern the permissible rates of payouts.[3] Dividends are paid (and regulated) at considerable cost to the firms involved.

Economists find dividends mysterious. The celebrated articles by Merton Miller and Franco Modigliani declared them irrelevant because investors could home brew their own dividends by selling from or borrowing against their portfolios. Meanwhile the firms that issued the dividends would also incur costs to float new securities to maintain their optimal investment policies.[4] Dividends are, moreover, taxable to many investors, while firms can reduce taxes by holding and reinvesting their profits. Although dividends might make sense in connection with a change in investment policy—when, for example, the firms are disinvesting because they are liquidating or, for other reasons, shareholders can make better use of the money than managers—they are all cost and no benefit in the remaining cases of invariant investment policies.[5]

Dividends are hard enough to explain when they occur in isolation; a combination of dividends and simultaneous raising of new capital is downright inexplicable.[6] Yet the simultaneous or near-simultaneous payment of dividends and raising of new capital are common in business. Sometimes firms issue new stock at or around the time they pay

---

*University of Chicago Law School, 1111 East 60th Street, Chicago, IL 60637. I thank Douglas Baird, Walter Blum, Dennis Carlton, Harry DeAngelo, Eugene Fama, Daniel Fischel, Michael Jensen, William Landes, Saul Levmore, Merton Miller, Myron Scholes, and Alan Schwartz for helpful comments on earlier drafts.

[1] One meeting place is Michael Rozeff (1982), who suggests that dividends and agency costs are related and offers a test showing that dividends depend in part on the fraction of equity held by insiders. He does not provide any mechanism, however, by which dividends and the consequent raising of capital control agency costs. I discuss some mechanisms of this sort below.

[2] See Bayless Manning (1981), for a description of the legal rules. Compare Victor Brudney (1980) calling for more legal regulation with Daniel Fischel (1981) offering economic support for current legal rules.

[3] See Clifford Smith and Jerold Warner (1979); Kose John and Avner Kalay (1982).

[4] See Miller and Modigliani (1961); also Modigliani and Miller (1958); Joseph Stiglitz (1974).

[5] See Modigliani (1982), for an argument to this effect that modifies the M-M irrelevance model by considering taxes and uncertainty. Compare Miller and Myron Scholes (1982), applying their earlier analysis (1978) to extend the irrelevance hypothesis to a world with taxes. Miller and Scholes argue that taxes need not, and do not appear to, determine dividend policy; all the same, their analysis does not show why there are dividends in a world of costly flotation.

[6] For example, Miller and Kevin Rock: "It would be uneconomic as well as pointless" for firms to pay dividends and raise capital simultaneously (1982, p. 13).

221

dividends. More frequently they issue new debt, often in the form of bank loans that are almost invisible to finance economists. Why does this occur?

The problem with the irrelevance proposition is that dividends are costly yet ubiquitous. Something causes them. Even if most investors are irrational most of the time, dividends would go away if their costs exceeded their benefits to investors. Firms that reduced payouts would prosper relative to others; investors who figured out the truth also would prosper relative to others; and before long—certainly before now in light of the large costs of floating new capital issues and the large differences between income and capital gains tax rates—dividends would be infrequent occurrences characterizing failing or disinvesting firms.

The existence of dividends despite their costs has inspired a search for explanations. Some of the efforts have been obvious failures. Take the argument that investments are risky and that dividends hedge against the possibility that the firms will go bankrupt before distributing the saved-up assets to the shareholders. The argument goes: investors value a steady stream of dividends over the uncertain prospect of a large return when the firms liquidate or are sold as going concerns and the investors are cashed out, and firms pay dividends to cater to that preference. The problem here is that dividends are matched by reinvestments: so long as dividends do not affect firms' investment policies, they do not represent any withdrawal of capital from risky ventures. New investors bear the risk that the dividend-receiving investors avoid, and these new investors must be compensated. The new investors may well turn out to be the old ones; shareholders do not usually use the dividends for consumption or to purchase Treasury bills. If they reinvest the proceeds in the same or a different firm, they commit their cash (less taxes paid) to the same risks as if there had been no dividends. In sum, there is no bird-in-the-hand effect unless the firm also changes its investment policy.[7]

Other arguments are only slightly more plausible. Consider the argument that dividends "signal" the well-being of the firm to investors and so promote confidence (and, one supposes, higher stock prices and a flow of investment capital).[8] The problem here is that it is unclear just what dividends signal, how they do so, or why dividends are better signals than apparently cheaper methods. Firms could and do issue disclosures of their prospects and profits. True, investors may be disinclined to believe the self-serving statements of managers about the firms' endeavors, but managers' usual response to this is to hire outsiders who examine the firms' books and other materials and opine on whether the managers are telling the truth. These outsiders work for many firms and acquire reputational capital so large that they become unbribable. No firm could offer them enough for a false (or slipshod) verification to make up for their losses on business with other firms. Auditors serve this function yearly or more often;[9] even judges may serve this function in suits charging the managers with making false statements or omitting material facts.

Dividends would be desirable only if they added to the efficacy of these methods of disclosure. The beauty of a "signal" is that it is self-verifying. People believe the signal because sending the message is rational for the signaller only if the message is or is believed to be accurate. Thus one could say that a Ph.D. from the University of Chicago is a good signal of intelligence and diligence (two notoriously hard-to-verify qualities) be-

---

[7]Compare M. J. Gordon (1959), with Michael Brennan (1971) and Sudipto Bhattacharya (1979). It is some-

times said that the bird-in-the-hand argument fails because one may get cash for consumption (or to put in the bank) by selling stock as well as by waiting for dividends. This is not a good refutation, because if the lack of dividends puts invested dollars at unacceptable risk, shares will fetch less in the market on a no-dividend policy than otherwise, and investors will be poorer than they would be if dividends were plentiful.

[8]See, for example, Bhattacharya; Nils Hakansson (1982); Steven Ross (1977). Compare Miller and Rock: in this model, dividends may permit inference of sources and uses of funds; this achieves many of the effects of a signalling model but by direct revelation or inference.

[9]See Linda DeAngelo (1981): using the auditor's "reputational bond" to show that larger auditors provide better quality.

cause persons of inferior intellect could not obtain one. But dividends do not directly reveal the prospects of the firms, so the message they convey may be ambiguous.[10] Unless the cost of issuing dividends is uniformly lower for prosperous firms, no signal is possible.

Prosperous firms may withhold dividends because internal financing is cheaper than issuing dividends and floating new securities. Worse, dividends do not distinguish well-managed, prospering firms from others. They are not irrational for poorly managed or failing firms. Quite the contrary, such firms should disinvest or liquidate, and their managers may choose dividends as a method of accomplishing this. Someone who observes an increase in the dividend has no very good way to tell whether this signals good times or bad. (This is consistent with both the finding that dividends are poor predictors of future net earnings and the finding that stock prices are poor predictors of future dividends.)[11] Doubtless only a prospering firm can continue to pay dividends year in and year out, but a firm with a long record of prosperity also would not need the verification available from the dividend signal. The persistent reports of auditors and securities dealers, its securities' prices, and the apparent marketing success of the firm would do as well in verifying the managers' tales.

The explanations based on clientele effects also are unsatisfactory. It is easy enough to see that if some investors are in different tax positions from others (for example, some hold tax-sheltered funds while others are taxed at ordinary rates), the different groups will have different preferences for dividends. The taxed group would prefer to take profits as capital gains; the untaxed group would be indifferent. Some equilibrium would develop in which firms adopted different payout policies to cater to the different clienteles.[12] It is much harder, though, to use clientele effects to demonstrate why the current dividend structure exists. Why do most firms pay significant dividends, given the costs of paying them (and raising new capital), and given that all investors either prefer capital gains or are indifferent between dividends and capital gains?[13]

II. Two Explanations

The dividend puzzle has been stated as: "what is the effect of a change in cash dividends paid, *given the firm's capital-budgeting and borrowing decisions?*"[14] This statement of the problem makes it insoluble, because the irrelevance hypothesis and the growing body of evidence say that dividends do not matter so long as the firm's financing and investment policy is unaffected. The existence of dividends in the face of this, and despite the costs of paying them out and raising new money, suggest that it is appropriate to ask a different question: "what is the effect of a *consistent* policy of paying dividends?" This question leads to what could be called a naive explanation of dividends. Dividends exist *because* they influence the firms' financing policies, *because* they dissipate cash and induce firms to float new securities.

Let us suppose that managers are not perfect agents of the other participants in the corporate venture, but that they pursue their own interests when they can. Because the managers are not the residual claimants to the firm's income stream, there may be a substantial divergence between their interests and those of the other participants. Man-

10 Only "may be" instead of "is" because the message may be self-justifying, as in the Miller and Rock model.

11 Stephen Penman (1983) finds that knowledge of dividends adds little or nothing to earnings forecasts as predictors of future earnings. See also, for example, Robert Shiller (1981).

12 See Fischer Black and Scholes (1974) and Alan Auerbach (1982). But see Miller and Scholes (1982).

13 Martin Feldstein and Jerry Green (1983) do not overcome this problem with clientele models. They use a two-firm, two-holder model in which portfolio diversification, without steady trading, depends on differential dividend policies. The two-firm assumption drives the model. With large numbers of firms an investor can get plenty of diversification without differential dividend policies.

14 Richard Brealey and Stewart Myers (1981, p. 324, italics in original).

agers, investors, and other participants will find it advantageous to set up devices, including monitoring, bonding, and *ex post* readjustments that give managers the incentive to act as better agents. The costs of monitoring, bonding, and the residual losses from slippage are agency costs borne by investors.[15]

One form of agency cost is the cost of monitoring of managers. This is costly for shareholders, and the problem of collective action ensures that shareholders undertake too little of it.[16] Although a monitor-shareholder would incur the full costs of monitoring, he would reap gains only in proportion to his holdings. Because shares are widely held, no one shareholder can capture even a little of the gain. Shareholders would be wealthier if there were some person, comparable to the bondholders' indenture trustee, who monitored managers on shareholders' behalf.

A second source of agency costs is risk aversion on the part of managers.[17] The investors, with diversified portfolios of stocks, will be concerned only about any nondiversifiable risk with respect to any one firm's ventures. Managers, though, have a substantial part of their personal wealth tied up in their firms. If the firms do poorly or, worse, go bankrupt, the managers will lose their jobs and any wealth tied up in their firms' stock. Managers therefore will be concerned about total risk, and their personal risk aversion will magnify this concern.

The risk-averse managers may choose projects that are safe but have a lower expected return than riskier ventures. Shareholders have the opposite preference. Riskier ventures enrich shareholders at the expense of creditors (because shareholders do not pay any of the gains to bondholders, yet bondholders bear part of the risk of failure), and shareholders would want managers to behave

as risk preferrers.[18] Of course, creditors recognize this and try to control it in advance through bond indentures and other instruments; they also adjust the rate of interest they demand. Debtholders assume that given the limits set by their contracts, shareholders prefer to take the maximum advantage. But the question is not whether the riskiness of projects can be controlled through indentures or other legal devices. It is, rather, whether costs of control (including the costs of control and residual agency costs) can be reduced by a method that includes dividends.

Managers can change the risk of the firm not only by altering its mix of projects, but also by altering its debt-equity ratio. The lower the ratio of debt to equity, the lower the chance of bankruptcy of the firm. Once again, debtholders consider this in deciding what rate of interest to demand. Once again, given the existence of debt, managers can control the amount of risk. One way they can do this is by picking a dividend policy. If managers first issue debt and then finance new projects out of retained earnings, the debt-equity ratio will fall. The lower it falls, the lower the managers' risk and the greater the boon bestowed on the debtholders, who receive their contracted-for interest but escape the contracted-for risk. Financing projects out of retained earnings—if unanticipated by bondholders—transfers wealth from shareholders to debtholders. Just as bondholders want to limit dividends, to prevent advantage-taking by shareholders once a rate of interest has been set, so shareholders want to increase dividends to the extent possible in order to avoid being taken advantage of by bondholders.[19]

Shareholders therefore would like to induce managers to take more risks, so that

[15]Michael Jensen and William Meckling (1976); Eugene Fama (1980); Bengt Holmstrom (1982); *JLE* Symposium (1983).

[16]See my articles with Fischel (1982, 1983a) for discussions of the extent to which legal rules address this problem.

[17]See Jensen and Meckling (pp. 349–50, 352–53), Steven Shavell (1979), and Alan Marcus (1982).

[18]This is one possible argument for permitting insider trading, if other compensation schemes are too costly. Compare Henry Manne (1966) and Dennis Carlton and Fischel (1983), with my article (1981, pp. 330–38).

[19]John and Kalay also stress this, See also George Handjinicolaou and Kalay (1982): stressing role of dividends in adjusting risk between bondholders and stockholders; concluding that dividends do not appear to cause unanticipated losses to bondholders.

they do not give away wealth to bond-holders. The shareholders would prefer that managers go to the limit authorized by contract in imposing risks on the firm's creditors. Yet it is hard to give managers the right incentives to do this. There is little one can do to get rid of their risk aversion. They will remain undiversified, because of the nature of their human capital, no matter what; indeed, the lack of diversification in managers' holdings has other benefits.[20] Unless there is some form of *ex post* settling up with managers, which will be difficult (costly) to achieve, shareholders' payoffs will be lower, with consequences for the level of investment.

Both the monitoring problem and the risk-aversion problem are less serious if the firm is constantly in the market for new capital. When it issues new securities, the firm's affairs will be reviewed by an investment banker or some similar intermediary acting as a monitor for the collective interest of shareholders, and by the purchasers of the new instruments. The same occurs when the firm issues new debt, including bonds, commercial paper, and syndicated bank loans. Managers who need to raise money consistently are more likely to act in investors' interests than managers who are immune from this kind of scrutiny. Moreover, when it issues new securities, the firm can adjust the debt-equity ratio (and obtain a new rate of interest for its debt) so that neither shareholders nor bondholders are taking advantage of the other group. (It can, of course, make this adjustment in other ways, including making more frequent trips to financial markets for smaller sums of new cash, but because flotation costs decrease with the size of the offering, such alternatives may be more costly than combining infrequent flotation with dividends.)

The principal value of keeping firms constantly in the market for capital is that the contributors of capital are very good monitors of managers. The firm's existing investors can influence the managers' actions only by voting (which suffers from a collective choice problem) and by selling. Purchasers of stock will pay no more than the value of future profits under current management unless they are prepared to wage a takeover contest of some sort, which can be very costly. Managers of firms with fixed capital structures may well have substantial discretion to be slothful, consume perquisites, or otherwise behave in their own interests rather than the investors' interests.

New investors do not suffer under the collective choice disabilities of existing investors. They can examine managers' behavior before investing, and they will not buy new stock unless they are offered compensation (in the form of reduced prices) for any remediable agency costs of management. Managers who are in the capital market thus have incentives to reduce those agency costs in order to collect the highest possible price for their new instruments. New investors are better than old ones at chiseling down agency costs.

Of course, new investors need information, and that may be hard to come by. Neither auditors nor the managers themselves are perfectly reliable unless there is a foolproof legal remedy for fraud.[21] Other forms of information gathering, such as shareholders' inquiries and stock brokers' studies, suffer from the problem that none of the persons making inquiry can capture very much of the gain of this endeavor, and thus there will be too little information gathered. There would be savings if some information gatherers had larger proportionate stakes, and if the verification of information could be accomplished at lower cost. Underwriters of stock and large lenders may supply the lower-cost verification. These firms put their own money on the line, and any information inferred from this risk-taking behavior by third parties may be very valuable to other investors. This form of verification by acceptance of

---

[20] Douglas Diamond and Robert Verrecchia (1982). Fama and Jensen (1983a) offer a substantially different treatment, in which they do not employ the artifact of the firm as risk-averse "principal." Managers then bear risk in the form of undiversified portfolios in order to induce reductions in other agency costs.

[21] See Stanford Grossman (1981); myself and Fischel (1983b).

risk is one of the savings that arise when dividends keep firms in the capital market.[22]

The role of dividends in starting up the monitoring provided by the capital market is easy to see. An example of the role of dividends in making risk adjustments may help. Suppose a firm has an initial capitilization of 100, of which 50 is debt and 50 equity. It invests the 100 in a project. The firm prospers, and earnings raise its holdings to 200. The creditors now have substantially more security than they started with, and correspondingly the residual claimants are paying the creditors a rate of interest unwarranted by current circumstances. They can correct this situation by paying a dividend of 50 while issuing new debt worth 50. The firm's capital continues to be 200, but the debt-equity ratio has been restored, and the interest rate on the original debt is again appropriate to the creditors' risk.[23]

Expected, continuing dividends compel firms to raise new money in order to carry out their activities. They therefore precipitate the monitoring and debt-equity adjustments that benefit stockholders. Moreover, even when dividends are not accompanied by the raising of new capital, they at least increase the debt-equity ratio so that shareholders are not giving (as much) wealth away to bondholders. In other words, dividends set in motion mechanisms that reduce the agency costs of management and that prevent one group of investors from gaining, relative to another, by changes in the firm's fortunes after financial instruments have been issued.[24] The future is always anticipated imperfectly in these contracts, so there will always be some need for *ex post* adjustments and supervision, and dividends play a role in these adjustments.

This obviously is not altogether different from information or signalling explanations of dividends. One could recharacterize part (but not all) of this treatment as an assertion that investment bankers and other financial intermediaries send signals to investors by putting their reputations (and, in underwritten offerings, money) on the line and certifying that the new securities are backed by the represented earnings potential. The information interpretation of this agency-cost treatment at least offers a plausible explanation why dividends (rather than, say, earnings announcements) carry essential information.

There is a further problem because the explanations I have offered are not unique explanations *of dividends*. Nothing here suggests that repurchases of shares would not do as well as or better than dividends. The issuance of debt instruments in series, so that payments and refinancings are continuous, serves the same function as dividends. I have "explained" only mechanisms that keep firms in the capital market in ways that instigate consistent monitoring and consistent readjustment of the risk among investors.

The explanation I have offered also is open to the objection, along the lines of Fischer Black (1976), that shareholder-creditor conflicts may be resolved by negotiation after any change in the fortunes of the firm. After investors could agree to new payoffs or shares of control rather than to a dividend policy. This may well be true, but such *ex post* negotiation raises a bilateral monopoly problem, and the costs of the negotiation could be substantial even if (contrary to my assumption) there were no agency problems. Unless *ex post* negotiation is very costly, the

---

[22] One thus cannot treat it as paradoxical that in raising capital firms use investment bankers at a cost greater than the firm would incur in raising capital via rights offerings or other non-intermediated devices. Compare Robert Hansen and John Pinkerton (1982).

[23] Some cases contain an implicit recognition of this function of dividends. For example, *Randall v. Bailey*, 23 N.Y.S.2d 173 (N.Y. Sup. Ct. 1940), aff'd mem., 262 App. Div. 844, 29 N.Y.S.2d 512 (1st Dep't 1941), aff'd, 288 N.Y. 280, 43 N.E.2d 43 (1942) (permitting dividend out of unrealized appreciation, financed by new debt).

[24] This explanation of dividends is closely related to the one Grossman and Oliver Hart (1982) offer for debt. They say that debt is desirable to equity holders precisely because it creates bankruptcy costs, thus inducing managers to take extra care. I say, in parallel fashion,

that dividends are beneficial to equity holders because they force managers constantly to obtain new capital in competitive markets. Fama and Jensen (1983b, pp. 13–15) also treat debt as a mechanism for regulating agency costs, although their argument is not the same as that of Grossman and Hart. See also Saul Levmore (1982, pp. 70–71). There is a family resemblance among all of these arguments.

existing pattern of complex bond indentures that provide for most contingencies makes little sense. I therefore think we must assume that in some decently large number of cases, accommodation through dividends and financing decisions set by the residual claimants is cheaper than accommodation through *ex post* negotiation. This is, however, an empirical matter, which raises the question whether the agency-cost explanations are testable.

III. Possible Tests

There have been a flurry of tests on the consequences of dividends. Some show that dividend changes are not related to the price of shares; others claim that increases in dividends are associated with decreases in the prices of shares.[25]

These are hard to evaluate, for it is hard to obtain a measure of unanticipated changes in the level of dividends, and only unanticipated changes could change the prices of shares. The "level of dividends" is itself difficult to calculate for purposes of these studies. Earlier treatments of dividends seek to explain *net* dividends (payouts in excess of new flotation), and it is almost impossible to obtain data on net dividends. Moreover, because an increase in dividends could be caused either by an increase in the firm's profits (implying higher stock prices) or by the commencement of disinvestment as the firm has fewer profitable opportunities (implying lower stock prices), studies that aggregate dividend increases across the classes could show small effects even when studies separating the two reasons for increase would show large ones. The studies have other problems as well.

It is not my purpose to offer a critique of the available work. Any study of the implications of the hypotheses I offer here would be beset by many of the same difficulties. Because of the agency-cost explanations of dividends focus on constant payout policies rather than changes in dividends, new tests will raise difficult questions of anticipation.

[25]For example, Robert Litzenberger and Krishna Ramaswamy (1982); Miller and Scholes (1982); Miller and Rock; all discussing earlier studies.

It should be possible to reexamine the data using as a new independent variable whether the firm had been in the capital market raising new money (whether debt or equity) at much the same time as it was paying dividends. The presence of new fund raising would indicate that dividends did not represent disinvestment. It also would isolate the set of firms whose managers were not able to rely wholly on internally generated funds and for which, therefore, dividends might reduce agency costs. The hypotheses I offer here suggest that the securities of firms simultaneously paying dividends and raising new money will appreciate relative to other securities. A test, however, will encounter substantial difficulty in identifying the time at which new capital is raised. Some syndicated loans are not announced to the public, and what is one to make of a firm's drawing against a line of credit arranged at an earlier time? A test also would face the problem of determining which payout policies were anticipated and which were not.

Finding a significant number of firms simultaneously (another problem of interpretation!) paying dividends and raising new money should offer substantial support for the agency-cost explanations, because other approaches to dividends imply that firms raise capital or pay dividends but do not do both. The agency-cost explanations also offer a plausible reason, other than clientele effects, why changes in dividend or financing policy may be associated with price reductions. It would be interesting to find out whether simultaneous dividend and financing changes produce the same negative residuals sometimes found when one changes but the other does not. One also could attempt to distinguish firms with high dividend/financing-to-asset ratios from firms with low dividend/financing-to-asset ratios. The hypotheses offered here suggest that there is some optimal ratio for each firm or set of firms.[26]

The difficulty of designing an empirical test is formidable, which suggests resorting

[26]Existing findings that new financings are associated with price reductions do not account for the possibility that rights offerings and below-market underwritten offerings will reduce the price of stock without diluting the current investors' interests (and thus without making them worse off).

to some less formal inquiries. The agency-cost explanations of dividends imply that dividends are worthless in themselves. Thus if firms are driven to the capital market by other conditions, we would expect to see less paid out in dividends. This is consistent with the observation that no-dividend (or low-dividend) stocks are usually "growth" firms, which are regularly in the capital market, and with the impression that such firms start paying dividends only when the rate of their growth (and thus the frequency of their trips to the capital market) has been reduced. The need to find some agency-cost control device increases as a firm becomes older and the original devices are less well adapted to the current form of business, and the initiation of dividends may supply such a device from the capital market.[27]

The agency-cost explanations have implications for the stability of dividends over time as well. Because the first function of dividends is to keep firms in the capital markets, we would not expect to see a very strong correlation between short-term profits and dividends. This implication cries out for testing, but it is certainly consistent with the fact that most firms have consistent policies (for example, 20 cents per share per quarter) that are not changed very often. A consistent policy uncouples dividends from profits while maintaining a link to the capital market. One indirect way to examine whether consistent dividends are valued for their effect on agency costs is to examine whether prices appreciate more on an increase in the "regular" dividend than on an increase of the same present value in "extraordinary" dividends. Shareholders concerned only about payouts in hand value the two equally; if dividends contain agency costs, regular payouts are more valuable. Evidence indicates that the regular dividend is associated with greater increases in price (see James Brickley, 1983).

Profits would have some effect on the risk-adjustment function, but past profits (which inure to debtholders' benefit unless dividends are increased) would be more important explanatory variables than current or anticipated profits. Anticipated profits can be handled by an adjustment of the terms on which money is raised; unanticipated past profits must be paid out to avoid windfalls to debtholders. The agency-cost treatment predicts that increases in dividends lag increases in profit and are uncorrelated with future profits. The lag may be substantial, because small increases (small changes of all sorts) in profits will be anticipated by debtholders, and there will be no need to make adjustments for these changes. Only the unanticipated (relatively large) changes call for adjustments in dividend policy.

Finally, because all forms of controlling agency costs are themselves costly, we would expect to see substitution among agency-cost control devices. One method of dealing with agency costs is for the managers to hold substantial residual claims in the firm. As such managers' claims increase, other things equal, dividends would be less valuable to investors and would decrease. Michael Rozeff suggests that this occurs. The same sort of substitution should accompany use of other devices.

The agency-cost explanations do not, however, yield unambiguous predictions about how bond prices will react to dividends. On the one hand, dividends favor investors and expose bondholders to more risk, thereby depressing bond prices. Of course, bondholders anticipate the use of dividends and the ensuing adjustment of risk, so it is not clear whether any price effects will be large. On the other hand, dividends keep managers' noses to the grindstone, conferring benefits on all investors. The net effect may be a wash, or it may not.[28]

IV. Conclusion

The economics literature has yet to integrate the study of corporate finance and the theory of the firm. This paper is a small step toward understanding whether, and how, dividends may be useful in reducing the agency costs of management. I suggest that dividends may keep firms in the capital

[27]Paul Asquith and David Mullins (1983) find that there is a significant appreciation in the price of stock when a firm initiates dividend payments. This offers some support for the thesis in the text. (Asquith and Mullins treat the increase as an information effect; they do not consider other explanations for their findings.)

[28]Handjinicolaou and Kalay show ambiguous effects.

market, where monitoring of managers is available at lower cost, and may be useful in adjusting the level of risk taken by managers and the different classes of investors. Such an explanation offers a hope of understanding why firms simultaneously pay out dividends and raise new funds in the capital market. It does not, however, explain dividends (as opposed to the set of all devices that have the effect of keeping firms in the capital market), and it will be difficult to test.

REFERENCES

Asquith, Paul and Mullins, David W., "The Impact of Initiating Dividend Payments on Shareholders' Wealth," *Journal of Business*, January 1983, *56*, 77–96.

Auerbach, Alan J., "Stockholder Tax Rates and Firm Attributes," Working Paper No. 817, National Bureau of Economic Research, 1982.

Bhattacharya, Sudipto, "Imperfect Information, Dividend Policy, and 'The Bird in the Hand Fallacy'," *Bell Journal of Economics*, Spring 1979, *10*, 259–70.

Black, Fischer, "The Dividend Puzzle," *Journal of Portfolio Management*, Winter 1976, *2*, 5–8.

_____ and Scholes, Myron S., "The Effects of Dividend Yield and Dividend Policy on Common Stock Prices and Returns," *Journal of Financial Economics*, May 1974, *1*, 1–22.

Brealey, Richard and Myers, Stewart, *Principles of Corporate Finance*, New York: McGraw-Hill, 1981.

Brennan, Michael J., "A Note on Dividend Irrelevance and the Gordon Valuation Model," *Journal of Finance*, December 1971, *26*, 1115–22.

Brickley, James A., "Shareholder Wealth, Information Signalling, and the Specially Designated Dividend: An Empirical Study," *Journal of Financial Economics*, August 1983, *12*, 187–209.

Brudney, Victor, "Dividends, Discretion, and Disclosure," *Virginia Law Review*, November 1980, *66*, 85–129.

Carlton, Dennis W. and Fischel, Daniel R., "The Regulation of Insider Trading," *Stanford Law Review*, May 1983, *35*, 857–95.

DeAngelo, Linda E., "Auditor Size and Audit Quality," *Journal of Accounting and Economics*, July 1981, *3*, 183–99.

Diamond, Douglas W. and Verrecchia, Robert E., "Optimal Managerial Contracts and Equilibrium Security Prices," *Journal of Finance*, May 1982, *37*, 275–87.

Easterbrook, Frank H., "Insider Trading, Secret Agents, Evidentiary Privileges, and the Production of Information," *Supreme Court Review*, *1981*, 309–65.

_____ and Fischel, Daniel R., "Auctions and Sunk Costs in Tender Offers," *Stanford Law Review*, November 1982, *35*, 1–21.

_____ and _____, (1983a) "Voting in Corporate Law," *Journal of Law and Economics*, June 1983, *26*, 395–425.

_____ and _____, (1983b) "Mandatory Disclosure and the Protection of Investors," Working Paper No. 17, Law and Economics Program, University of Chicago, October 1983 (*Virginia Law Review*, May 1984).

Fama, Eugene F., "Agency Problems and the Theory of the Firm," *Journal of Political Economy*, April 1980, *88*, 288–307.

_____ and Jensen, Michael C., (1983a) "Agency Problems and Residual Claims," *Journal of Law and Economics*, June 1983, *26*, 327–49.

_____ and _____, (1983b) "Organizational Forms and Investment Decisions," Working Paper No. MERC 83-03, Managerial Economics Research Center, University of Rochester, June 1983.

Feldstein, Martin and Green, Jerry, "Why Do Companies Pay Dividends?," *American Economic Review*, March 1983, *73*, 17–30.

Fischel, Daniel R., "The Law and Economics of Dividend Policy," *Virginia Law Review*, May 1981, *67*, 669–726.

Gordon, M. J., "Dividends, Earnings, and Stock Prices," *Review of Economics and Statistics*, May 1959, *41*, 99.

Grossman, Sanford J., "The Informational Role of Warranties and Private Disclosure About Product Quality," *Journal of Law and Economics*, December 1981, *24*, 461–83.

_____ and Hart, Oliver, "Corporate Financial Structure and Managerial Incentives," in J. J. McCall, ed., *The Economics of*

Information and Uncertainty, Chicago: University of Chicago Press, 1982.

Hakansson, Nils H., "To Pay or Not to Pay Dividend," *Journal of Finance*, May 1982, *37*, 415–28.

Handjinicolaou, George and Kalay, Avner, "Wealth Redistribution or Informational Content: An Analysis of Returns to the Bondholders and to the Stockholders," draft, July 1982.

Hansen, Robert S. and Pinkerton, John M., "Direct Equity Financing: A Resolution of a Paradox," *Journal of Finance*, June 1982, *37*, 651–65.

Holmstrom, Bengt, "Moral Hazard in Teams," *Bell Journal of Economics*, Autumn 1982, *13*, 324–40.

Jensen, Michael C. and Meckling, William, "Theory of the Firm: Managerial Behavior, Agency Costs, and Capital Structure," *Journal of Financial Economics*, October 1976, *3*, 305–60.

John, Kose and Kalay, Avner, "Costly Contracting and Optimal Payout Constraints," *Journal of Finance*, May 1982, *37*, 457–70.

Levmore, Saul, "Monitors and Freeriders in Commercial and Corporate Settings," *Yale Law Journal*, November 1982, *91*, 49–83.

Litzenberger, Robert H. and Ramaswamy, Krishna, The Effects of Dividends on Common Stock Process: Tax Effects or Information Effects?," *Journal of Finance*, May 1982, *37*, 429–43.

Manne, Henry G., *Insider Trading and the Stock Market*, New York: Free Press, 1966.

Manning, Bayless, *Legal Capital*, St. Paul: West Publishing, 1981.

Marcus, Alan J., "Risk Sharing and the Theory of the Firm," *Bell Journal of Economics*, Autumn 1982, *13*, 369–78.

Miller, Merton H. and Modigliani, Franco, "Dividend Policy, Growth, and the Valuation of Shares," *Journal of Business*, October 1961, *34*, 411–13.

_____ and Rock, Kevin, "Dividend Policy Under Asymmetric Information," draft, November 1982.

_____ and Scholes, Myron S., "Dividends and Taxes," *Journal of Financial Economics*, December 1978, *6*, 333–64.

_____ and _____, "Dividends and Taxes: Some Empirical Evidence," *Journal of Political Economy*, December 1982, *90*, 1108–42.

Modigliani, Franco, "Debt, Dividend Policy, Taxes, Inflation and Market Valuation," *Journal of Finance*, May 1982, *37*, 255–73.

_____ and Miller, Merton H., "The Cost of Capital, Corporation Finance and the Theory of Investment," *American Economic Review*, June 1958, *48*, 261–97.

Penman, Stephen H., "The Predictive Content of Earnings Forecasts and Dividends," *Journal of Finance*, September 1983, *38*, 1181–99.

Ross, Steven S., "The Determination of Financial Structure: The Incentive Signalling Approach," *Bell Journal of Economics*, Spring 1977, *8*, 23–40.

Rozeff, Michael S., "Growth, Beta and Agency Costs as Determinants of Dividend Payout Ratios," *Journal of Financial Research*, Fall 1982, *5*, 249–59.

Shavell, Steven, "Risk Sharing and Incentives in the Principal and Agent Relationship," *Bell Journal of Economics*, Spring 1979, *10*, 55–73.

Shiller, Robert H., "Do Stock Prices Move Too Much to be Justified by Subsequent Changes in Dividends?," *American Economic Review*, June 1981, *71*, 421–36.

Smith, Clifford W. and Warner, Jerold B., "On Financial Contracting: An Analysis of Bond Covenants," *Journal of Financial Economics*, June 1979, *7*, 117.

Stiglitz, Joseph, "On the Irrelevance of Corporate Financial Policy," *American Economic Review*, September 1974, *64*, 851–66.

Symposium (on the Theory of the Firm, various authors), *Journal of Law and Economics*, June 1983, *26*, 237–427.

SHAREHOLDER WEALTH, INFORMATION SIGNALING AND THE SPECIALLY DESIGNATED DIVIDEND

An Empirical Study*

James A. BRICKLEY

University of Utah, Salt Lake City, UT 84112, USA

Received June 1982, final version received October 1982

This paper examines common stock returns and dividend and earnings patterns surrounding specially designated dividends labeled by management as 'extra', 'special' or 'year-end' and compares them to those surrounding regular (unlabeled) dividend increases. The results support the notion that management uses the labeling of dividend increases to convey information to the market about the future potential of the firm. Unlabeled increases appear to contain the most positive information. Contrary to the sometimes suggested view, specially designated dividends appear to convey positive information about future dividends and earnings beyond that relating to the current period.

1. Introduction

A major area of controversy and interest is the effect of dividend policy on shareholder wealth. While empirical studies generally have supported the hypothesis that dividend changes convey information to the market and affect common stock prices, our undertanding of dividends as 'information signaling devices' is limited. Theoretical models for dividend signaling are still in the pioneering stage and empirical studies essentially have documented only that the market appears to react favorably to dividend increases and negatively to decreases.[1]

This study examines common stock returns and dividend and earnings patterns surrounding 'specially designated dividends' (SDDs) labeled by

---

*This paper is based on my Ph.D. dissertation at the University of Oregon. I would like to thank George Racette, my Chairman, and other members of my committee, Larry Dann, Michael Hopewell and Alden Toevs for their support and encouragement. Also, I would like to thank Sanjai Bhagat, Ken Eades, John McConnell, Wayne Mikkelson, Chris Muscarella, Michael Pinegar, James Schallheim, Samuel Stewart and especially Ronald Lease for numerous helpful comments. I have also benefited from the suggestions of Ross Watts, the referee for this journal. All remaining errors are mine.

[1]Theoretical works on dividend signaling include Bhattacharya (1979, 1980), Eades (1982), Hakansson (1982), and Kalay (1980). Empirical studies include Aharony and Swary (1980), Asquith and Mullins (1982), Charest (1978), Eades (1982), Gonedes (1978), Kalay (1980), Laub (1976), Penman (1980), Pettit (1972, 1976) and Watts (1973, 1976).

Journal of Financial Economics 12 (1983) 187–209. © North-Holland Publishing Company.

management as either 'extra', 'special' or 'year-end' and compares them to those surrounding regular (unlabeled) dividend increases. The study is important for at least three reasons. First, the paper improves our understanding of the motivations for dividend changes and the role of these changes as information signaling devices. Second, the paper provides insights into the role of SDDs in corporate finance. Third, the study has broader implications relating to the general topic of financial signaling. There is a growing number of empirical studies which suggest that certain financial decisions may be interpreted by the market as signals about the firm's prospects.[2] While these studies are consistent with an information signaling hypothesis, no direct evidence exists that management consciously uses financial decisions for signaling the firm's outlook. Regular dividend increases and SDDs are both dividend decisions which represent cash disbursements to shareholders with identical tax consequences. Thus regular dividend increases and SDDs provide an opportunity to compare two financial events which differ ostensibly only in the label chosen by management. Any difference in the market reaction to the labeling of a dividend increase presumably is attributable to a difference in the signal or 'message' conveyed by management through the label. Evidence of such a differential market reaction would support the notion that management consciously is aware of the signaling implications of financial decisions (at least for dividend increases).[3]

2. Overview of the study and preview of the results

Each year there are about 2,000 to 4,000 increases in the quarterly dividend by U.S. firms.[4] Approximately 1,000 of these increases each year are given special labels by management. The most frequent label is the word 'extra' (used about 80% of the time).[5] The second most frequent designation is 'special' (about 14%). Occasionally management will label the increase 'year-end' (about 6%). In this study all three labels are grouped into the general category of 'specially designated dividends'.

Some firms such as Dupont, Eastman Kodak and Sears Roebuck declare SDDs in the same quarter almost every year. Other firms declare SDDs on a much less frequent basis, if at all. For example, American Can declared only one SDD in the 15 years from 1966 through 1980. Presumably management's

---

[2]Relevant studies include Aharony and Swary (1980), Asquith and Mullins (1982), Dann (1981), Masulis (1980), McConnell and Schlarbaum (1981), Pettit (1972, 1976) and Vermaelen (1981).

[3]A question which immediately arises is: Why would management use financial decisions such as dividend policy to signal the firm's outlook instead of simply making a public announcement of its forecasts? This question is not addressed in this paper.

[4]Based on *Moody's Annual Dividend Record*, 1969–1979.

[5]Percentage figures on the frequency of the various labels come from Brickley (1982).

intent and the subsequent market reaction to these latter 'infrequent SDDs' may vary from SDDs which are declared routinely.[6] This study focuses on 'infrequent SDDs' (hereafter simply referred to as SDDs).

The conventional explanation for the function of SDDs is set in the context of dividend changes conveying information.[7] Traditionally, it is argued that management increases the regular dividend only when it is confident that the new dividend can be maintained over time. Following this argument, the announcement of a regular dividend increase may convey positive information about the firm's prospects. In this setting, an SDD can be viewed as a distribution of cash to shareholders which may not convey as bright a message as an increase in the regular dividend. Sometimes it is suggested that the SDD contains the message that the SDD is a temporary increase in the dividend and will not be repeated.[8] Other times it is claimed that the SDD simply implies that the likelihood of repeating the higher dividend is less than when the regular dividend is increased.[9]

While dividend changes have provided the focus for considerable empirical research, the distinction between labeled and unlabeled increases has been ignored.[10] This paper provides empirical evidence relating to three major questions relating to the labeling of dividend increases. These include:

(1) Do SDDs convey information?
(2) Are SDDs only temporary dividend increases or do they imply more positive information about future dividends and earnings?
(3) Is different information conveyed by SDDs and regular dividend increases?

The remainder of this section describes the organization of the paper and previews the results of the empirical analysis.

After the sample design is described in section 3, section 4 examines the common stock returns around the announcements of SDDs and compares them to the returns surrounding regular dividend increases. To focus on 'infrequent SDDs' only SDDs which are the first SDDs to be announced in at least two years by the firms in question are used in the analysis. A significant positive market reaction to the announcements of SDDs suggests that these announcements convey new positive information to the market. The size of the SDD compared to the magnitude of the announcement period common stock return indicates that SDDs convey information beyond that relating to the immediate higher dividend. The comparative

---

[6]For example, Van Horne (1977, p. 303) writes: 'As soon as a certain level of dividends is recurrent, investors begin to expect that level regardless of the distinction between 'regular' and 'extra' dividends.'

[7]Found in most managerial finance textbooks.

[8]See, for example, Archer et al. (1979, p. 275).

[9]See, for example, Brealey and Myers (1981, p. 325–326).

[10]See footnote 1 for citation of the relevant studies.

market reactions to SDDs and regular dividend increases indicates that regular dividend increases convey more positive information than do SDDs.

In section 5 we examine dividend payouts in the year following the announcements of SDDs and regular dividend increases. The purpose of this analysis is to determine if these payouts support the conclusions made in section 4 about the informational content of labeled and unlabeled dividend increases. Assuming that the market does not change its assessment of the risk of a firm when a firm declares an SDD or increases its regular dividend, the positive market reactions found in section 4 should relate to an altering of expectations about future dividends and earnings. Further, the differential market reactions to SDDs and regular dividend increases implies that the market expectations about future dividends and earnings depend on the label attached to a dividend increase. First, we compare tha dividend payouts following SDDs to the payouts following decisions not to change the dividend. Consistent with the conclusion in section 4 that SDDs are more than a transitory increase in the dividend, we find that the payout following an SDD is 'above average' when compared to firms which do not change their dividend. Second, we compare dividend payouts following SDDs with payouts following regular dividend increases. Consistent with the differential market reactions to SDDs and regular dividend increases, dividend payouts following regular dividend increases are shown to be larger than the payouts following SDDs.

Section 6 examines earnings patterns around SDDs and compares them to the earnings patterns around regular dividend increases. The examination reveals that both regular dividend increases and SDDs tend to be declared by firms experiencing good earnings over the previous year. Further there is no significant difference in the earnings performances in this prior year between firms declaring SDDs and firms increasing their regular dividend. However, consistent with the notion that the labeling of a dividend increase conveys information about the future potential of the firm, the firms declaring regular dividend increases have statistically significant larger earnings changes in the year after the dividend increase than the firms declaring SDDs. Section 7 summarizes the study.

3. Data sources and sample design

Three samples are utilized in the empirical analysis. These include a sample of firms announcing SDDs and two control samples consisting of firms announcing regular dividend increases and firms announcing no change in the dividend, respectively. To minimize the likelihood that the common stock price impacts on the dividend announcement date are confounded with other contemporaneous firm-specific events, the samples are limited to firms with no other firm-specific announcements reported in the *Wall Street*

Journal within five trading days (plus or minus) of the dividend announcement. This section describes each sample and the data sources.

3.1. Sample of SDDs

The basic sample used in this study consists of 165 SDDs declared from 1969 through 1979 on common stock listed on the New York or American Stock Exchange. The sample is designed to contain SDDs of firms which do not declare them on a routine basis. To qualify for inclusion in the sample:

(1) the dividend must be reported in *Moody's Annual Dividend Record* as an SDD;

(2) the SDD must be the first SDD declared by the firm in at least a two-year period; and

(3) the SDD must not be a resumption of interrupted dividends, i.e., the firm must have paid a dividend the quarter before.

3.2. Control sample of regular increases

To compare market reactions and subsequent dividend and earnings performance for SDDs and regular dividend increases, it is necessary to develop a control sample of firms announcing increases in their regular dividends. To meet *ceteris paribus* conditions, it is desirable to try to match as closely as possible the characteristics of the control sample with the sample of SDDs. Obviously, it is impossible to develop a control sample which is identical to the sample of SDDs in all aspects except for the designation of the increased dividend (e.g. timing, amount, type of industry, and type of firm).

In this analysis, timing is viewed as of primary importance for three reasons. First, in analyzing dividend and earnings patterns after a dividend announcement, timing is extremely important. As the strength of the national economy is likely to affect a firm's ability to generate earnings and to pay dividends and as this strength varies over time, biases could be imparted if the control sample observations occur at different times than the sample SDDs. Second, it is possible that the market may react differently to dividend changes during certain subperiods of the overall sample period, or during different times during the year. Third, if the control observations and the sample SDDs are declared on the same day, market effects can be controlled easily.[11]

---

[11]For instance, a difference of means test for paired observations involves subtracting the return of one member of the pair from the other. As both members are for the same dates, the market effect is taken into account. Note that this is based on the presumption that any differences in the betas and thus expected returns of the control firms and SDD firms given

Another aspect which we consider important to control is the size of the dividend increase. The size measure used for control purposes is the SDD or dividend increase expressed as a percentage of the regular dividend paid prior to the increase. This measure we refer to as 'relative size'. Evidence presented by Pettit (1972) supports the belief that 'relative size' is important in explaining reactions to regular dividend increases. Also, evidence presented below suggests that this variable is important in explaining market reactions to SDDs.

The selected control sample consists of 100 observations where the regular dividend is increased from the previous quarter by a firm listed on either the New York or American Stock Exchange.[12] To be included in the sample, a firm must not have declared an SDD in the year prior to the decision to increase the regular dividend. Control observations are chosen to match as closely as possible the timing and secondarily the 'relative size' of 100 SDDs selected from the sample of 165. This process yields a paired comparison sample of SDDs and regular dividend increases of 100 observations.[13]

The SDDs used in the paired comparison are chosen so that the distribution for this subsample in terms of year and month declared is representative of the distribution for the overall sample of 165 SDDs. As 100 represents 60% of 165, the 100 SDDs are chosen by selecting randomly 60% of the observations within each month of each year from the larger sample. This procedure yields a subsample of SDDs with a very similar distribution of the dates declared as that of the larger sample.

In developing the paired sample, when possible a regular dividend increase occurring on the same date as its paired SDD is chosen (possible in 68 cases). When this is not possible an observation is selected from the next business day containing an appropriate observation.[14] When choices are available, the regular dividend increase with the 'relative size' closest to the paired SDD is selected.

---

market returns are offset through the averaging process. It is important to note also that the advantage of controlling for market effects is viewed as only of secondary importance. As the events are not clustered in calendar time, it is unlikely that the adjustment of raw returns for market effects will alter the results materially. See Brown and Warner (1980), Dann (1981), and Kraus and Stoll (1972).

[12]The definition of a dividend increase as an increase in the dividend from the previous quarter is used by Pettit (1972) and Aharony and Swary (1980). Both studies found informational content in dividend changes.

[13]A paired sample of 100 (instead of 165) was chosen in light of the tradeoff between the cost of collecting control observations and the desire to have a large sample.

[14]In 20 of the 32 cases where it was not possible to obtain a paired observation on the same date, it was possible to obtain one on the next day. In 12 cases, it was necessary to obtain observations from days beyond the day following the announcement of the SDD. In cases where the next day is used, common market effects are likely to exist for the increased regular and its paired comparison. First, as two-day returns are used, these observations share one day in common. Second, researchers have found some serial correlation in daily stock returns. See Fama (1976).

Unfortunately, given the timing constraints, it is not possible in most cases to match closely the size of the regular increase in the dividend with that of the SDD. SDDs tend to be large both in dollar size and 'relative size' compared to regular dividend increases. It is common for an SDD to equal or even exceed the regular quarterly dividend. It is very uncommon for a regular dividend to be doubled. Tables 1 and 2 compare the distributions of the control observations and their paired SDDs in terms of dollar size and 'relative size'. The SDDs clearly dominate in size using either measure. Fortunately, it is possible to control for size using various statistical techniques employed below.

Table 1

Distribution by dollar size; Regular dividend increases and SDDs in the paired sample (100 paired observations; sample period 1969–1979).

Dollar size	Number of regular increases	Number of paired SDDs
0–1 cent	30	5
2–5 cents	64	36
6–10 cents	6	32
> 10 cents	0	27
Total	100	100
Median size	2.5 cents	9.5 cents
Range	1/3–10 cents	1 cent–$1.00

Table 2

Distribution by 'relative size';[a] regular dividend increases and SDDs in the paired sample (100 paired observation's; sample period 1969–1979).

Relative size	Number of regular increases	Number of paired SDDs
0%–5%	16	0
6%–10%	16	0
11%–19%	27	17
20%–39%	26	20
40%–99%	14	27
100%–200%	1	23
> 200%	0	13
Total	100	100
Median size	15%	56%
Range	2.9%–100%	10.8%–1200%

[a]Relative size is defined as the SDD or regular dividend increase expressed as a percentage of the regular dividend paid prior to the increase.

3.3. Control sample of firms announcing no change in the dividend

To compare dividend payouts following SDDs and decisions not to change the dividend, a control sample of 100 firms not changing their quarterly dividend is developed. The 100 SDDs used to obtain the paired comparison sample of SDDs and increased regular dividends are used to develop a paired comparison sample of firms announcing SDDs and firms announcing no change in the dividend. For each announcement date for the SDDs in the comparison sample, an observation of a firm not changing its quarterly dividend is selected randomly from *The Wall Street Journal*. To be included, a control firm must not have declared an SDD in the year prior to the decision not to change the dividend. It was possible in all cases to match exactly the date of the no change in the dividend with the date of its paired SDD.

4. Common stock returns around the announcements of SDDs and regular dividend increases

This section examines common stock returns surrounding the announcements of SDDs and regular dividend increases. The purposes of this analysis are: (1) to investigate if SDDs disclose information to the market; (2) to examine the nature of this information (if any); and (3) to investigate whether SDDs and regular dividend increases convey different information. First, the common stock returns surrounding SDDs are analyzed. Second, the magnitude of the common stock return surrounding the announcement of an SDD is compared to the size of the SDD. Third, the common stock returns around the announcement of SDDs are compared to the common stock returns around the announcements of regular dividend increases.

4.1. Market reactions to SDDs

A time series of daily common stock returns for 121 trading days centered around the declaration date of the SDD is taken from the CRSP Daily Returns File for each of the 165 SDDs. Average returns for each of the 121 trading days relative to the declaration day (day 0) are calculated as the arithmetic mean of the individual securities' raw returns on their common dates in event time. For example, the average return on day 0 is the arithmetic mean of the daily returns on the date of the SDD announcement for the 164 observations in our sample which have returns on CRSP for that day. Like other recent event studies using daily returns, raw returns rather than market- or risk-adjusted returns are used in the analysis.

Table 3 presents the time series of average returns for the 121 trading days. Column 1 shows the trading day relative to the declaration date (day 0). Column 2 presents the average daily return on each of these days. The

Table 3

Common stock rates of return over 121-day period around announcement of specially designated dividends (165 events; sample period 1969–1979).

(1) Trading day	(2) Mean rate of return (%)	(3) Sample size	(4) # Positive: # Negative: # Zero
−60	0.291	162	61:56:45
−50	−0.208	162	56:76:30
−40	0.162	164	58:63:43
−30	−0.014	164	70:60:34
−25	−0.346	164	54:78:32
−20	0.148	164	63:70:31
−19	−0.033	163	59:62:42
−18	0.087	164	59:65:40
−17	−0.044	164	61:72:31
−16	0.227	164	59:71:34
−15	−0.014	164	61:74:29
−14	0.585	163	66:57:40
−13	−0.224	164	46:70:48
−12	0.172	163	65:56:42
−11	0.041	163	61:71:31
−10	0.147	163	67:66:30
−9	0.046	164	61:68:35
−8	0.184	164	69:65:30
−7	0.335	163	68:55:40
−6	−0.077	164	67:65:32
−5	0.193	164	63:62:39
−4	−0.014	164	66:61:37
−3	−0.082	162	53:78:31
−2	0.551	163	77:59:27
−1	0.213	164	63:66:35
0	0.905	164	84:38:42
1	1.211	164	93:39:32
2	0.421	164	68:57:39
3	0.066	164	69:58:37
4	0.335	163	67:62:34
5	0.293	164	70:61:33
6	−0.102	164	61:75:28
7	0.462	164	72:56:36
8	0.078	164	70:63:31
9	−0.002	164	62:73:29
10	0.172	164	64:64:36
11	−0.281	164	57:76:31
12	0.214	165	63:69:33
13	0.096	165	57:70:38
14	0.043	164	63:59:42
15	−0.004	165	62:71:32
16	−0.076	165	57:78:30
17	0.413	165	69:54:42
18	−0.102	165	68:66:31
19	−0.175	165	64:67:34
20	0.064	164	67:64:33
25	0.186	164	62:60:42
30	0.286	165	64:64:37
40	−0.088	164	57:65:42
50	0.119	164	72:58:34
60	0.248	165	73:60:32

last two columns report the number of valid returns contained on CRSP for each of the trading days and the number of those returns which are positive, negative and zero.[15]

Day 0 and day $+1$ are designated as the 'announcement period'.[16] The day 0 average return is 0.91% and the day $+1$ return is 1.2%. In contrast, the average return for the 50-day period beginning 60 days prior to the announcement period and ending on day -11 is 0.05%. This period which we designate as the 'pre-announcement comparison period' is used as a standard to judge whether the announcement period returns are 'abnormal'.[17]

The statistical significance of the two-day announcement period average common stock return is tested formally by a t-test. The null hypothesis is that the two-day announcement period average return ($\bar{R}_{2a}$) equals the mean of the non-overlapping two-day average returns from the comparison period ($\bar{R}_{2c}$). The t-statistic is given by

$$t = (\bar{R}_{2a} - \bar{R}_{2c})/(\hat{s}\sqrt{1 + 1/N}), \tag{1}$$

where the estimate of the standard deviation ($\hat{s}$) of two-day portfolio returns is obtained from the time series of comparison period two-day portfolio resturns.[18] Given that $\bar{R}_{2a} = 2.11\%$, $\bar{R}_{2c} = 0.10\%$, $\hat{s} = 0.34\%$ and $N = 25$, the t-value for the difference in two-day returns is 5.9 (24 degrees of freedom), and the null hypothesis can be rejected at the 0.01 level of significance.

Additional evidence on the abnormality of the announcement period returns is contained in the signs of the individual two-day security returns during the announcement period. The number of positive two-day returns during the announcement period is larger than for any of the non-overlapping two-day intervals in the comparison period. One hundred-ten of the two-day returns for the announcement period are positive, compared to 54 which are either negative or zero. The number of positive two-day returns in the comparison period ranges from a low of 63 to a high of 93. If we assume independence, the probability is only 0.04 that the largest number of positive returns will occur in the announcement period given both periods have the same return distribution. Therefore, based on the signs of the

---

[15]The number of 'valid returns' may vary because of missing values on the CRSP tapes.

[16]For some firms, the announcement of the SDD may occur too late in the day to affect the day 0 stock return, but instead will be impounded in the day 1 stock return. Day 1 is the date the event is reported in the *Wall Street Journal*.

[17]This period is chosen for comparison because it is close to the announcement period, but enough before it to enhance the probability that security returns in the comparison period are not contaminated by leakages relating to the forthcoming dividend announcement. It is desirable to have a comparison period close to the announcement period to minimize the probability that there are significant differences in the firm's economic characteristics between the two periods.

[18]This test assumes normality and equal variances for the distributions generating announcement period and comparison period two-day portfolio returns.

returns, we can reject the hypothesis that the return distributions are identical for the comparison and announcement periods at the 4% level.[19]

The evidence in this section of abnormal positive returns around the announcement of SDDs is consistent with the hypothesis that SDDs convey positive information to the market. It is not possible to tell from this analysis whether the SDD is simply a temporary but unanticipated dividend or whether SDDs convey a more positive message. We address this issue in the next section which compares the size of the SDD with the size of the accompanying common stock return.

4.2. *A comparison between the size of the SDD and the size of the announcement period stock return*

If the SDD is simply a temporary but unanticipated increased payout, one would expect (*ceteris paribus*) that the common stock return accompanying the announcement of an SDD would be approximately equal to the SDD expressed as a percentage of the common stock price. This measure of an SDD we call '*percentage size*'. For example, if a stock is selling for $30 and it is announced by declaring an SDD that the stockholders are to receive an unanticipated, but one time increased payout of 10¢ in the near future, stock price would be expected to increase approximately 0.3% (the 'percentage size'). On the other hand, if the announcement of an SDD conveys additional positive information, one would expect a larger common stock return than the 'percentage size' of the SDD.

In this section we test formally whether there is a significant difference between the magnitude of the announcement period common stock return and the 'percentage size' of the SDD. The closing price of the common stock on the Friday before the announcement of the SDD is used for calculating the 'percentage size'. The *t*-statistic for testing the null hypothesis that the announcement period return is equal to the percentage size of the SDD is given by

$$T = M_d/(S_d | \sqrt{N}),$$ (2)

where M_d is the mean for our sample of the 'percentage size' of the SDD subtracted from the accompanying announcement period return, S_d is the estimated cross-sectional standard deviation of this difference and N is the sample size. Given values of 1.2%, 4.2% and 164 for M_d, S_d and N, respectively, the *t*-value is 3.65. This *t*-value allows us to reject the null hypothesis at the 1% level. The positive sign of M_d and the results of the statistical test are consistent with the notion that the SDD is more than a

---

[19]The test procedure used here is the same as a Mann–Whitney test.

temporary increase in the dividend. The average market reaction is too large to be explained by the immediate higher dividend represented by the SDD. This issue is examined in more detail later in the paper.

4.3. A comparison of common stock returns surrounding SDDs and regular dividend increases

The conventional view of the SDD is that more positive information is disclosed to the market by regular dividend increases than by SDDs (*ceteris paribus*). This view implies that the common stock return accompanying a regular dividend increase will be larger than the return accompanying the announcement of an SDD (*ceteris paribus*). In this section we compare the stock returns around these two types of dividend announcements.

The first test of differential market reactions to SDDs and regular dividend increases does not control for the size of the dividend increase. The test consists of a standard difference in means t-test for paired comparisons (see eq. 2). The null hypothesis is that the mean of the announcement period return for an SDD subtracted from the announcement period return for its companion regular dividend increase is zero. This test produces a t-value of -1.94. This t-value is not only insignificant at the 5% level but the sign is opposite that predicted by conventional wisdom. The p-value of 0.06, if anything, suggests that the market reaction to an SDD dominates the reaction to a regular increase. However, this result may be misleading in the absence of any control for size. The result may simply suggest that the market prefers a larger SDD to a small regular dividend increase.

To control for size, the following regression model is used:

$$RET2D = \delta_0 + \delta_1 REGINC + \beta SZREL + u, \tag{3}$$

where $RET2D$ is the announcement period return relative, $REGINC = 1$ if the observation is a regular dividend increase, 0 if it is an SDD, $SZREL$ is the SDD or regular dividend increase divided by the regular dividend declared in the previous quarter ('relative size') and u is a random error term.[20]

Because the relative sizes ($SZREL$) of the SDDs and the control observations are so radically different, the regression model is estimated using only observations that have a 'relative size' of at least 20% and less

---

[20]With this formulation the observations are no longer paired, but are simply single observations in a larger sample. The correlation between the two-day returns for the control sample and the paired comparison sample is very low and is unlikely to cause any statistical problems. The square of the estimated correlation coefficient (R^2) between the two-day returns of the control sample and their paired SDDs is only 0.028 (p-value of 0.10 for the standard F-test). This result suggests no significant linear dependence.

than 100%. The use of this criterion has the advantage of limiting the focus of analysis to a size range in which observations from both categories exist. The criterion further screens out small dividend increases which are more likely than larger increases to have any information disseminated swamped by random error. As the observations are no longer treated as paired comparisons, it is not necessary to limit the observations to SDDs contained in the paired comparison sample. Therefore, any SDD in the larger sample of 165 that meets the size criterion is used.

Using the 40 control observations and 65 SDDs that meet the size criterion, the estimated model using ordinary least squares (OLS) is

$$\cdot RET2D = 0.99 + 0.016 \; REGINC + 0.048 \; SZREL, \quad R^2 = 0.05. \qquad (4)$$
$$(79.0) \quad (1.9^*) \qquad\qquad (2.0^*)$$

where the asterisks indicate a one-tailed p-value of 3% (102 degrees of freedom).

The positive sign on the coefficient for *REGINC* and the t-value of 1.9 allow us to reject at the 3% level the null hypothesis that the market reaction to SDDs is greater than or equal to the market reactions to regular dividend increases of similar 'relative size'.[21] This result is consistent with the traditional notion that regular increases convey more positive information than SDDs (*ceteris paribus*).

The plots of residuals from this regression indicate the error term is not of constant variance. Given this violation of OLS assumptions, the resulting estimates are unbiased, but are not minimum variance. To correct for this problem, we re-estimate the parameters of the model using weighted least squares. The technique used requires dividing each variable in the regression by *SZREL* and then re-estimating the model with OLS.[22] The resulting coefficient for *REGINC* is again 0.016, but its one-tail p-value is lower at 1.25% (increased significance). Plots of the residuals from this regression showed no evidence of heteroscedasticity.

The results in this section support the contention that the labeling of a dividend increase conveys information to the market. Apparently, the market perceives that an unlabeled dividend increase conveys more positive information than an SDD of similar relative size.

---

[21]One must be cautioned that the error term of this regression does not appear to be normally distributed. Using the Kolmogorov–Smirnov test, the hypothesis that the error term is normally distributed can be rejected at the 1% level. However, statistical tests of the type used are generally quite robust to departures from normality with samples of our size. See Box and Anderson (1955), Hotelling (1961), Kendall and Stuart (1973) and Box and Watson (1962).

[22]This model assumes that the standard deviation of the error term is directly proportional to *SZREL*.

5. Dividend performance following an SDD

The evidence reported in section 4 suggests that the announcement of an SDD conveys positive information about the firm beyond that relating to an unanticipated but only temporary increase in cash to shareholders. The evidence further indicates that this information is less positive than that conveyed by a regular dividend increase of similar magnitude. Assuming that the market does not change its assessment of the risk of a firm when a firm increases its dividend, the information conveyed by SDDs and regular dividend increases presumably relates to future dividends and earnings. In this section we examine dividend patterns following the announcements of SDDs. In section 6 we examine the earnings patterns around SDDs.

In this section we first present descriptive data on the dividend actions taken in the year following the announcement of the SDD. The dividend payouts following SDDs are then compared to the payouts for firms not changing their dividend. The purpose of this analysis is to examine if dividend payouts following SDDs are 'above average' as suggested by section 4. The dividend payouts following SDDs are then compared to those patterns observed for firms with regular dividend increases. The common stock returns reported in section 4 suggest that payouts following regular dividend increases will be larger than those following SDDs.

5.1. Descriptive overview of the dividend performance following an SDD

Table 4 summarizes by quarter the dividend actions taken by the sample SDD firms in the year following the announcement of the initial SDD. One striking feature is that very few of the firms lowered their regular dividend (from the previous quarter) during the year. Only one percent of the sample firms decreased their regular dividend in any given quarter. On the other hand, in each quarter at least 20 percent of the firms made larger dividend payouts than their regular dividend in the previous quarter. In the anniversary quarter of the SDD, 66 percent of the firms took such action. Forty-one percent of the firms in the anniversary quarter declared another SDD.

While the sample firms tended to increase their dividends in the year after the SDD, it is not possible to discern from this data alone whether these firms had 'above average' dividend performance. The reason for this is that firms in general appear to be reluctant to lower their regular dividend and so one would expect more dividend increases than decreases for any randomly selected group of firms.[23] The issue of whether or not the average dividend performance following an SDD is abnormally positive is addressed in the following section.

[23]Lintner (1956) and Fama and Babiak (1968) provide evidence on the managerial reluctance to cut dividends.

Table 4

Dividend actions taken in the four quarters following the announcement quarter of the specially designated dividend (SDD) (% of sample firms taking the action).[a]

	Quarter 1	Quarter 2	Quarter 3	Quarter 4
1. Increased regular dividend from the previous quarter	24%	17%	13%	15%
2. Declared the same regular dividend as in the previous quarter plus paid an SDD	5%	1%	7%	32%
3. Increased the regular dividend from the previous quarter and declared an SDD	0%	2%	1%	9%
Larger payout than the previous quarter's regular dividend (sum of #'s 1, 2, 3)	29%	20%	21%	66%
Same payout as the previous quarter's regular dividend	70%	79%	78%	43%
Lower payout than the previous quarter's regular dividend	1%	1%	1%	1%
Average total payout as a percent of the regular dividend paid prior to the initial SDD	109%	116%	124%	168%

[a]This table is based on the full sample of 165 firms declaring SDDs in 1969–1979. Sample size may vary slightly from quarter to quarter as firms merge with other firms and so have no dividend records.

5.2. Dividend payouts following SDDs vs. decisions not to change the dividend

At least two alternative methodologies exist that could be used to examine whether or not dividend payouts following SDDs are abnormally positive. One is a time series approach in which trends of dividend payouts for firms declaring SDDs are examined for possible shifts after the SDDs. Alternatively, dividend payouts following SDDs can be compared to the dividend payouts following decisions by other firms not to increase their dividends. This cross-sectional approach assumes the average trend in dividend payouts for the 'no change' firms is the same as the trend for the comparison firms prior to their declaring SDDs. Given this assumption, one can test whether the dividend performance following an SDD is 'above average'. In this study we employ this cross-sectional approach. For the analysis the control sample of 100 no change firms described in section 3 is used.

Three measures of subsequent dividend payout per share are used in this study. All measures are adjusted for stock splits and stock dividends. All the measures are relative measures, i.e., total payout per share for a given time period divided by some base payout. Relative measures make it possible to compare dividend performance of firms which start with different dollar amounts per share being paid as dividends. The measures include:

Following quarter measure (FQM)

    The total dividend payment per share (regular and SDD) declared in the quarter after the announcement quarter (of the SDD, regular dividend increase or no change in the dividend) divided by the regular quarterly dividend declared in the quarter prior to the announcement quarter. This measures the relative dividend level in the quarter immediately following the announcement of the SDD, regular dividend increase, or no change in the dividend.

Anniversary quarter measure (AQM)

    The total dividend declared in the anniversary quarter of the initial announcement divided by the regular quarterly dividend declared in the quarter before the initial announcement. This measures the relative dividend level in the anniversary quarter of the SDD, regular dividend increase, or no change in the dividend.

Following year measure (FYM)

    The total dividends declared in the four quarters following the initial announcement divided by four times the regular quarterly dividend declared in the quarter prior to announcement. This measures the relative dividend level over the 12-month period following the initial announcement.

    Table 5 displays the means for each dividend performance measure for the SDD firms and no change firms in the comparison sample. The table also includes the results for each performance measure of a standard difference in means t-test for paired comparisons.[24] The firms in both groups, on the average, increased their dividend payouts over their previous regular dividend during the year after the initial dividend announcement. However, the mean for all performance measures is larger for the SDD group. The results of the t-test support the hypothesis that dividend performance following an SDD dominates that following a decision not to change the dividend. The null hypothesis that the dividend payout following an SDD is the same or worse than following a decision not to change the dividend is rejected at the 5% level (or better) for all three measures.

---

[24]See eq. (2) for a specification of the test. Also, note that the sample size is 90 instead of 100. This is because 10 out of the 200 firms merged with other firms and so did not have complete dividend records for the full year.

Table 5

Mean dividend performance measures for the paired comparison sample of firms not changing their dividend and firms declaring specially designated dividends and a t-test for paired comparisons for each measure (sample period 1969–1979).

	FQM[a]	AQM[b]	FYM[c]
Mean for SDDs	1.07	1.50	1.23
Mean for no changes	1.02	1.10	1.06
Mean difference[d]	0.056	0.407	0.182
Sample size	90	90	90
Standard error of mean	0.0297	0.0869	0.0468
t-value for difference of means test	1.88[e]	4.68[f]	3.89[f]

[a]FQM is the total dividend per share declared in the quarter following the SDD or no change in the dividend divided by the regular dividend declared prior to the SDD or no change in the dividend.

[b]AQM is the total dividend per share declared in the anniversary quarter of the SDD or no change in the dividend divided by the regular dividend declared prior to the SDD or no change in the dividend.

[c]FYM is the total dividend per share declared in the year after the SDD or no change in the dividend divided by four times the regular dividend declared prior to the SDD or no change in the dividend.

[d]The reported number is the mean difference of the performance measure for each no change observation subtracted from the performance measure for the paired SDD. The null hypothesis of the t-tests is that this mean difference is less than or equal to zero.

[e]One-tailed p-value of 0.04.

[f]One-tailed p-value of less than 0.01.

Two possible biases may exist in the above analysis. First, the no change firms may include firms which are reluctant to increase their dividend and have a long history of paying the same dividend. The SDD firms, on the other hand, may be less likely to follow such a conservative policy as they have demonstrated a willingness to increase their payout. Second, as shown in section 6, firms tend to declare SDDs after periods of good earnings performances. The control sample of no change firms contains firms with both positive and negative earnings performances. As firms which experienced earnings decreases may be less likely to increase their dividend in the future than those experiencing earnings increases, a bias may exist in the above analysis, making rejection of the null hypothesis more likely. To help correct for these possible biases, we examine a subsample of 36 no change firms which had earnings increases and which also increased their dividend sometime in the two-year period before the announcement date of their decision not to change the dividend. A no change firm is classified as having an earnings increase if the earnings reported during the announcement quarter are greater than the earnings reported four quarters before (adjusted for stock splits and stock dividends).[25] If any bias existed in the original specification, use of this subsample should reduce the mean difference in the performance measures and make acceptance of the null hypothesis more likely.

The results of the paired comparison *t*-tests for this subsample of 36 no change firms are very similar to those for the entire sample. The *t*-values of 3.37 and 2.50 for the measures *AQM* and *FYM* allow us to reject the null hypothesis at the 1% level. The *t*-value of 2.04 allows us to reject the null hypothesis at the 2.5% level of significance, using the measure *FQM*.

The results of this section support the notion that the SDD is more than a temporary increase in the dividend. The evidence supports the contention that firms declaring SDDs are likely to experience superior dividend performance in the future relative to a firm which does not increase its dividend. The next section compares the dividend payouts following SDDs with those following regular dividend increases.

5.2. Dividend payouts following SDDs vs. regular dividend increases

Table 6 presents an analysis of variance for each of the performance measures classified by SDD or regular dividend increase. Consistent with section 4 only observations having a relative size between 20% and 100% are used. The statistical results support the hypothesis that the dividend performance following a regular dividend increase dominates that following an SDD. The *F*-tests for each dividend measure are significant at the 2% level or better (one-tailed test). Further, three additional non-parametric tests are performed for each measure and all tests are significant at the 1% level.[26] These results are consistent with the evidence presented above that the stock price response to regular dividend increases is more positive than to SDDs.

6. Earnings performance surrounding SDDs

The common stock returns reported in section 4 are consistent with the hypothesis that management uses the labeling of dividend increases to

---

[25]The method of choosing the subsample yielded paired observations with approximately equivalent earnings changes from the previous year. The mean change in earnings from the corresponding quarter in the previous year is 55 percent for the SDD observations compared to 47 percent for the paired no change observations. A standard difference in means *t*-test for paired comparisons does not allow us to reject the null hypothesis that the mean difference in the percentage earnings changes for the paired observations is equal to zero.

[26]Tests for each measure include the Wilcoxon test, the Median test for two samples and the Van der Waerden test.

Table 6

Analysis of variance; dividend performance measures classified by specially designated dividend (SDD) and regular dividend increase $(20\% \leqq SZREL < 100\%)$.[a]

	N[b]	Mean	F-value	P-value[c]
(1) *FQM*[d]				
SDD	65	1.06	45.82	0.0001
Regular dividend increase	40	1.40		
(2) *AQM*[e]				
SDD	63	1.39	5.22	0.0250
Regular dividend increase	35	1.75		
(3) *FYM*[f]				
SDD	63	1.20	13.84	0.0003
Regular dividend increase	35	1.52		

[a]*SZREL* is defined as the SDD or regular dividend increase divided by the regular dividend paid prior to the dividend increase.

[b]Sample size may vary as firms merge into other firms after the announcement date.

[c]The appropriate *p*-value for testing the null hypothesis that a dividend performance measure for the SDD group is greater than that for the regular dividend increase group is this value divided by two.

[d]*FQM* is the total dividend per share declared in the quarter following the SDD or regular dividend increase divided by the regular dividend declared prior to the increase.

[e]*AQM* is the total dividend per share declared in the anniversary quarter of the SDD or regular dividend increase divided by the regular dividend declared prior to the increase.

[f]*FYM* is the total dividend per share declared in the year after the SDD or regular dividend increase divided by four times the regular dividend declared prior to the dividend increase.

convey information about future dividends and earnings. In section 5 dividend payouts following SDDs and regular dividend increases were found to be consistent with this hypothesis. In this section we examine earnings patterns surrounding SDDs and regular dividend increases.

First we compare the SDD and regular dividend increase firms based on the change in earnings per share between the fiscal year prior to the dividend increase (FY -1) and the fiscal year of the increase (FY 0). To the extent that the two groups cannot be distinguished based on their earnings changes over this period, the potential for dividend labeling to convey new information is increased. If the two groups have substantially different earnings changes between FY -1 and FY 0, information about differences in future earnings (and dividends) of the two groups may in part be conveyed by earnings announcements over this period instead of being conveyed primarily through the dividend label. Second we compare the two groups based on the earnings change between the fiscal year of announcement and the following fiscal year (FY $+1$). The evidence in section 4 and 5 suggests that the regular dividend increase group would have a more positive earnings change over this period than the SDD group.

6.1. Earnings changes from the fiscal year prior to announcement to the fiscal year of announcement

Table 7 presents an analysis of variance for the change in earnings per share (adjusted for stock splits and stock dividends) between FY -1 and FY 0 classified by SDD or regular dividend increase. Consistent with the earlier analysis only observations having a 'relative size' between 20% and 100% are included. The table indicates that both groups on the average experienced relatively large increases in earnings per share during the year (58% for the SDD group and 51% for the regular dividend increase group). Over 90% of the firms in each group had non-negative earnings changes. The low F-value of 0.078 does not allow us to reject the null hypothesis that the average earnings change over this period is the same for both groups.[27] As the two groups have indistinguishable earnings changes from the year prior to the dividend increase to the year of the increase, the potential for dividend signaling is enhanced.

Table 7

Analysis of variance; percentage change in earnings per share from the fiscal year before the dividend increase to the fiscal year of the increase $(20\% \leqq SZREL < 100\%)$.[a]

	N	Mean	% non-negative	F-value
Specially designated dividend	63	58%	92%	0.078
Regular dividend increase	35	51%	94%	

[a]*SZREL* is the SDD or regular dividend increase divided by the regular dividend paid prior to the increase.

6.2. Earnings changes from the fiscal year of announcement to the fiscal year after the announcement

Table 8 presents an analysis of variance for the change in earnings per share between FY 0 and FY $+1$ classified by SDD and regular dividend

[27]The Wilcoxon test, the Median test for two samples and the Van der Waerden test also do not allow rejection of the null hypothesis.

Table 8

Analysis of variance; percentage change in earnings per share *(EPS)* from the fiscal year of the dividend increase to the following fiscal year $(20\% \leqq SZREL < 100\%)$.[a]

	N	Mean	% non-negative	F-value
Specially designated dividend	63	−1%	66%	2.89[b]
Regular dividend increase	35	30%	77%	

[a]*SZREL* is the SDD or regular dividend increase divided by the regular dividend paid prior to the increase.

[b]One-tail *p*-value of 0.0462. Null hypothesis is that the percentage increase in *EPS* from the fiscal year of announcement to the following fiscal year is the same between groups or greater for the SDD group.

increase. The table indicates that the earnings for the SDD group did not tend to fall back to the pre-SDD level. The average change in earnings for this group is −1% compared to the 58% average increase for the previous year. Sixty-six percent of the SDD firms had non-negative earnings changes between FY0 and FY+1. This data is consistent with the evidence presented previously, suggesting that the SDD represents more than a transitory increase in the earnings and dividend potential of the firm.

On the average the regular dividend increase group faired better between FY0 and FY+1 than the SDD group. The regular dividend increase group averaged a 30% increase in earnings over this year with 77% of the firms having non-negative earnings changes. The *F*-value of 2.89 allows us to reject the null hypothesis that the earnings change between FY0 and FY+1 is the same or greater for the SDD group than for the regular dividend increase group at the 5% level of significance (one-tailed *p*-value of 0.046.)[28] This result is consistent with the evidence presented previously that a regular dividend increase conveys more positive information than an SDD of similar magnitude.

7. Summary

Common stock returns around the announcements of specially designated dividends (SDDs) and regular (unlabeled) dividend increases support the notion that management uses the labeling of dividend increases to convey information to the market about future dividends and earnings. Both SDDs and regular dividend increases appear to convey positive information with the regular dividend increase providing a more positive message.

[28]The Wilcoxon test, the Median test for two samples and the Van der Waerden test also all allow us to reject the null hypothesis with *p*-values (one-tailed) of less than 5%.

A comparison of the size of the market reaction to the size of the SDD suggests, contrary to the sometimes stated view, that the SDD represents more than a transitory increase in dividends and earnings. An analysis of dividend payouts and earnings in the year following the announcement of the SDD supports this conclusion.

The notion that a regular dividend increase conveys more positive information than an SDD is reinforced by the dividend payouts in the year following the dividend increases. Payouts following regular dividend increases are shown to be significantly larger than those following SDDs. The notion of differential information between labeled and unlabeled increases also is supported by the earnings performances of the two groups. Both SDDs and regular dividend increases tend to be declared after a period of good earnings. Further there is no significant difference between the two groups based on earnings changes between the fiscal year of declaration and the prior fiscal year. However, consistent with the signaling notion, the regular dividend increase group has statistically larger earnings changes in the fiscal year after the dividend announcement.

References

Aharony, J. and I. Swary, 1980, Quarterly dividend and earnings announcements and stockholder returns, Journal of Finance 35, 1–12.
Archer, S., G.M. Choate and G. Racette, 1979, Financial management: An introduction (Wiley, New York).
Asquith, P. and D.W. Mullins, Jr., 1982, The impact of initiating dividend payments on shareholder's wealth, Journal of Business, forthcoming.
Bhattacharya, S., 1979, Imperfect information, dividend policy and 'the bird in the hand' fallacy, Bell Journal of Economics 10, 259–270.
Bhattacharya, S., 1980, Nondissipative signaling structures and dividend policy, Quarterly Journal of Economics 95, 1–24.
Box, G.E.P. and S.L. Anderson, 1955, Permutation theory in the derivation of robust criteria and the studies of the departures from assumption, Journal of the Royal Statistical Society B 17, 403–415.
Box, G.E.P. and G.S. Watson, 1962, Robustness to nonnormality of regression analysis, Biometrika 49, 93–106.
Brealey, R. and S. Myers, 1981, Principles of corporate finance (McGraw-Hill, New York).
Brickley, J., 1982, Shareholder wealth, information signaling, and the specially designated dividend, Unpublished dissertation (University of Oregon, Eugene, OR).
Brown, S.J. and J.B. Warner, 1980, Measuring security price performance, Journal of Financial Economics 8, 205–258.
Charest, G., 1978, Dividend information, stock returns and market efficiency-II, Journal of Financial Economics 6, 205–208.
Dann, L.Y., 1981, Common stock repurchases: An analysis of returns to bondholders and shareholders, Journal of Financial Economics 9, 113–138.
Eades, K.M., 1982, Empirical evidence on dividends as a signal of firm value, Journal of Financial and Quantitative Analysis, forthcoming.
Fama, E.F., 1976, Foundations of finance (Basic Books, New York).
Fama, E.F. and H. Babiak, 1968, Dividend policy: An empirical analysis, Journal of the American Statistical Association 63, 1132–1161.

Gonedes, N.J., 1978, Corporate signaling, external accounting, and capital market equilibrium: Evidence on dividends, income, and extraordinary items, Journal of Accounting Research 16, 26–79.

Hakansson, N., 1982, To pay or not to pay dividends, Journal of Finance 37, 415–428.

Hotelling, H., 1961, The behavior of some standard statistical tests under nonstandard conditions, Proceedings of the fourth Berkeley symposium (University of California Press, Berkeley, CA) 314–359.

Kalay, A., 1980, Signaling, information content, and the reluctance to cut dividends, Journal of Financial and Quantitative Analysis 15, 855–863.

Kendall, M.G. and A. Stuart, 1973, The advanced theory of statistics, Vol. 2 (Hafner, New York).

Kraus, A. and H. Stoll, 1972, Price impacts of block trading on the New York Stock Exchange, Journal of Finance 27, 569–588.

Laub, P.M., 1972, Some aspects of the aggregation problem in the dividend earnings relationship, Journal of the American Statistical Association 67, 552–559.

Laub, P.M., 1976, On the informational content of dividends, Journal of Business 49, 73–80.

Lintner, J., 1956, Distribution of income of corporations among dividends, retained earnings, and taxes, American Economic Review 46, 97–113.

Masulis, R.W., 1980, Stock repurchases by tender offer: An analysis of the causes of common stock price changes, Journal of Finance 35, 305–319.

McConnell, J.J. and G.G. Schlarbaum, 1981, Evidence on the impact of exchange offers on security prices, Journal of Business 54, 65–85.

Mikkelson, W.H., 1981, Convertible calls and security returns, Journal of Financial Economics 9, 237–264.

Miller, M.H. and F. Modigliani, 1961, Dividend policy, growth, and the valuation of shares, Journal of Business 34, 411–413.

Modigliani, F. and M.H. Miller, 1959, The cost of capital, corporation finance and the theory of investment: A reply, American Economic Review 49, 655–669.

Penman, S.H., 1980, Tests of dividend-signaling: A comparative analysis, Unpublished manuscript (University of California, Berkeley, CA).

Pettit, R.R., 1972, Dividend announcements, security performance, and capital market efficiency, Journal of Finance 27, 993–1007.

Pettit, R.R., 1976, The impact of dividend and earnings announcements: A reconciliation, Journal of Business 49, 86–96.

Van Horne, J.C., 1977, Financial management and policy, Fourth edition (Prentice-Hall, Englewood Cliffs, NJ).

Vermaelen, T., 1981, Common stock repurchases and market signalling: An empirical study, Journal of Financial Economics 9, 139–183.

Watts, R., 1973, The information content of dividends, Journal of Business 46, 191–211.

Watts, R., 1976, Comments on 'On the informational content of dividends', Journal of Business 46, 81–85.

Watts, R., 1976, Comments on 'The impact of dividend and earnings announcements: A reconciliation', Journal of Business 49, 97–106.

STOCKHOLDER–BONDHOLDER CONFLICT
AND DIVIDEND CONSTRAINTS

Avner KALAY*

New York University, New York, NY 10003, USA

Received July 1981, final version received February 1982

This paper examines a large, randomly chosen, sample of bond indentures focusing on the constraints they set on dividend payments that have the potential to transfer wealth from the bondholders (i.e., payments which are financed by a new debt issue or reduced investment). The nature of these restrictions support the hypothesis that bond convenants are structured to control the conflict of interest between stockholders and bondholders. Further, the empirical evidence suggests that these constraints are not binding — i.e., stockholders do not pay themselves as much dividends as they are allowed to. Explanations of this puzzling empirical regularity are suggested.

1. Introduction and summary

Corporate dividend policy has long been an issue of interest in the financial literature. Thus far, this issue has been examined under the assumption that the firm is one homogeneous unit whose clear objective is to maximize its market value [Brennan (1970), Miller–Modigliani (1961), Miller–Scholes (1978)]. However, in a growing body of recent literature [Black (1976), Fama (1978), Fama–Miller (1972), Galai–Masulis (1976), Jensen–Meckling (1976), Kalay (1979a, b), Myers (1977), Smith–Warner (1979)] researchers have recognized that the firm is a collection of groups whose interest can, and do, conflict. Thus, the renewed interest in corporate dividend policy expressed in this paper stems from their important role in this conflict.

Of the groups comprising the firm, the largest and perhaps the most important two are the bondholders and the stockholders. The stockholders, who control the firm, are expected to choose investment and financial decisions that maximize their own wealth. In particular, they could, if permitted, attempt to transfer wealth from bondholders by choosing policies which increase the risk of the outstanding bonds. The stockholders can effect

---

*I would like to thank Ernest Bloch, Kenneth Garbade, Kose John, Richard Leftwich, William Schwert, Ronald Singer, Marti Subrhamanyam, Jerold Warner, Ross Watts, the referee, Clifford Smith, and especially John Long and Michael Jensen for their helpful comments.

Journal of Financial Economics 10 (1982) 211–233. North-Holland Publishing Company

such a transfer by utilizing two dividend related mechanisms.[1] First, stockholders can reduce planned investment or deplete existing assets and pay the 'saved' outlays as dividends (hereafter pay 'investment financed dividends'). Secondly, stockholders can pay out the proceeds of a new issue of senior debt as dividends (hereafter pay 'debt financed dividends'); thereby, increasing the risk of the outstanding bonds. If these payments were not anticipated by the bondholders, wealth would be transferred from them to the stockholders. Clearly, these two wealth transfer mechanisms depend on stockholders' ability to pay out funds.[2] Moreover, as Jensen and Meckling (1976) and Myers (1977) demonstrate, stockholders can choose to finance dividend payments by rejecting investment projects with positive net present value (NPV). These potential costs associated with the conflict can be reduced (or avoided) by stockholders' precommitment to limit the level of future dividend[3] payments.

The above rationale for the existence of dividend constraints is suggested in the financial literature [see Jensen–Meckling (1976), Myers (1977), Smith–Warner (1979), Kalay (1979a, b)], although the exact form of the constraint, the details of its properties, its variations across firms and the extent to which it is likely to be binding, are yet to be documented. This paper addresses these issues by examining limitations on dividend payments in a large, randomly chosen, sample of bond indentures.

Overview of the paper

Examination of the bond indentures reveals that the dividend decisions of levered firms are constrained. Section 2 contains a documentation and analysis of the typical direct dividend constraint. Most of the firms in the sample choose a constraint of the same form in which the limitations apply to all forms of payout — i.e., share repurchases and other distributions to the stockholders are treated as cash dividends. Most importantly, the typical direct dividend constraint limits only dividend payments that have the potential to cause a wealth transfer, i.e., it limits debt and investment financed dividends while allowing for unlimited amounts of dividend

---

[1]As Black and Scholes (1973) suggest, stockholders of a levered firm can be viewed as holders of an European call option on their firm whose exercise price is equal (in the case of a pure discount bond) to the face value of the debt. Thus, by increasing the investment's risk (other things constant) the value of this call option — i.e., the value of the equity — increases. The availability of this wealth transfer mechanism, however, is not related to the dividends and therefore is not investigated here.

[2]If dividend payments are constrained, the proceeds of any new debt issue must be invested. In this case the market value of the old bonds is affected favorably by the increment in the investment and negatively by the increment in the leverage ratio. The net effect is unclear.

[3]Since we expect the payout constraints to apply to all forms of cash distributions to the stockholders, we use the words 'payout' and 'dividends' interchangeably. In other words, 'dividends' are defined to be the sum of all cash distributions to the stockholders.

payments which are financed by new issues of equity (hereafter 'equity financed dividends'). Finally, the constraint is cumulative; namely, stockholders' legal ability to pay dividends can be postponed into the future.

The sample of bond indentures studied in this paper reveals that dividend payments are constrained indirectly as well — for example, through stockholders' precommitment to maintain a minimum level of working capital or a minimum ratio of assets to liabilitites. Similar to the direct dividend constraint, the indirect constraints are cumulative and place additional restrictions *only* on the payment of debt and investment financed dividends. Usually, firms are subject to several direct and indirect constraints. This makes the estimation of the effective dividend constraint — i.e., the amount of debt or investment financed dividends that can be paid under the most restrictive constraint — difficult. Fortunately, *Moody's Industrial Manual* contains corporate reports as to what we shall call their 'reservoir of payable funds'. This reservoir is defined to be the maximum amount of debt or investment financed dividends that stockholders can pay under the most restrictive direct or indirect dividend constraint at a given point in time. Hence, at a given point in time the reservoir measures a deviation from a preimposed constraint. When the reservoir becomes zero the effective constraint can be said to be binding.

As reported in section 3, all the firms in the sample maintain positive reservoirs continuously for periods of ten to twenty years. These reservoirs are of non-trivial magnitude. They can, therefore, be used to increase the risk of the outstanding bonds by increasing the existing leverage ratio substantially. If the bonds are priced expecting no reservoirs to be maintained, any positive level of reservoir would transfer wealth from the stockholders *to* the bondholders. It is, therefore, surprising to find that the stockholders do not pay themselves the maximum allowed debt or investment financed dividends. Moreover, a precommitment by stockholders to pay no dividends would ensure that no reservoirs would be maintained and eliminate any possible tax related costs of paying dividends. The question which naturally arises is why would stockholders choose a constraint which allows for future dividend payments and, given that they do, why would they maintain reservoirs?

Section 4 contains an examination of possible explanations for these puzzling empirical regularities. It is suggested that if the corporation has a limited supply of non-negative net present value projects, a precommitment to pay no dividends in the future and therefore to maintain no reservoirs can result in *overinvestment* (i.e., forced acceptance of projects with negative net present value). The choice of a constraint that allows for investment financed dividends, and, consequently, for the existence of reservoirs reduces the likelihood of overinvestment. In periods in which the dividend constraint implies a minimum investment that would cause overinvestment, stockholders can use the reservoir to pay investment financed dividends, thereby avoiding the losses associated with overinvestment.

2. The typical direct dividend constraint

To investigate the form and potential uniformity of the dividend constraints, the debt indentures of 150 corporations as reported in *Moody's Industrial Manual* were randomly selected. All of them include restrictions on stockholders' future ability to pay dividends. The direct dividend constraint is reported for 135 firms of which 128 have the following form:

$$D_t \leq \max\left\{0, \sum_{j=0}^{t} S_j + \sum_{j=0}^{t} \alpha NE_j + F - \sum_{j=0}^{t-1} D_j\right\}, \tag{1}$$

where

$j \quad = 0, 1, \ldots, T$ ($j=0$ is the bond's issue date, $j=T$ is the debt maturity),

$D_j \quad =$ dividends (defined to be the sum of cash dividends, share repurchase and all other distribution to the stockholders) at j,

$S_j \quad =$ proceeds from sales of stock at j,

$NE_j =$ net earnings at j,

α and F are constant over the life of the bond.

2.1. Analysis

The direct dividend constraint has several interesting features. First, it constrains all forms of payments and does not distinguish between cash dividends and share repurchase. Second, as the formulation of the direct dividend constraint into eq. (1) indicates, corporations are not forced to pay negative dividends (i.e., issue new equity) in periods of successive negative earnings. In such periods the dividends would be zero. However, dividends cannot be paid unless the right-hand side of eq. (1) is positive. It is interesting to note that the constraint is cumulative; namely, the legal ability to pay dividends can be postponed into the future. In other words, under this constraint stockholders can maintain a reservoir of funds which are legally available for dividend payments. The direct dividend constraint not only enables the maintenance of a reservoir but also defines the initial reservoir which is the dip [F in eq. (1)].

The direct dividend constraint limits only investment and debt financed dividends while allowing unlimited amounts of equity financed dividends. This can be shown by an examination of the firm's cash flow identity.[4] The firm's cash inflows at time t are

$$NE_t + \Delta_t + L_t + S_t + B_t, \tag{2}$$

[4]I am indebted to John Long for suggesting this expositional model to me.

where NE_t is net earnings, Δ_t is depreciation, L_t is proceeds from sale of assets, S_t is proceeds from sale of new equity, and B_t is proceeds from sale of new debt. The firm's outflows at time t are

$$D_t + I_t + P_t, \tag{3}$$

where I_t is new investment, P_t is repayment of debt principal, and D_t is the dividend (defined to include all payments to the stockholders). At time t the firm's inflows must equal its outflows. Hence, the cash flow identity can be rewritten as

$$D_t = NE_t + \Delta_t + L_t + S_t + B_t - I_t - P_t. \tag{4}$$

Alternatively,

$$D_t = \sum_{j=0}^{t} (NE_j + \Delta_j + L_j + S_j + B_j - P_j - I_j) - \sum_{j=0}^{t-1} D_j. \tag{5}$$

Substituting the right-hand side of eq. (1) for D_t yields

$$\sum_{j=0}^{t} (NE_j + \Delta_j + L_j + S_j + B_j - P_j - I_j) - \sum_{j=0}^{t-1} D_j$$

$$\leq \max \left\{ 0, \sum_{j=0}^{t} (S_j + \alpha NE_j) + F - \sum_{j=0}^{t-1} D_j \right\}. \tag{6}$$

If the right-hand side of (6) is positive,[5] the inequality simplifies to

$$\sum_{j=0}^{t} (I_j + \Delta_j - L_j) \geq \sum_{j=0}^{t} [(1-\alpha)NE_j + B_j - P_j] - F. \tag{7}$$

The left-hand side of (7) is the firms' cumulative net investment; namely, the cumulative amount by which new investments exceeds the sum of depreciation and proceeds from sale of assets. Hence, the direct dividend constraint can be viewed as a minimum investment constraint. To illustrate this point, assume the firm issues a pure discount bond (i.e., $P_t = 0$ for any t which is less than the maturity date T, and $B_t = 0$ for any positive t) which includes a direct dividend constraint with $\alpha = 1$. In this case eq. (7) simplifies to

$$\sum_{j=0}^{t} (I_j - \Delta_j - L_j) \geq B_0 - F, \tag{8}$$

[5]If the right-hand side of eq. (6) is zero, the proceeds of new equity or debt issued as well as net earnings must be invested. Clearly, in this case the firm cannot pay any debt or investment financed dividends.

where B_0 is the market value of the debt on the contracting date. Thus, the firm can pay dividends if and only if the net cumulative investment, during the life of the bond, exceeds the proceeds from the sale of the debt minus the initial reservoir, F. The implications of eqs. (7) or (8) are obvious. On the contracting date, debt financed dividends are constrained[6] to F and the minimum investment to be maintained is restricted to $B_0 - F$.

Finally, note that if the right-hand side of eq. (1) is positive, the firm can pay out its proceeds from sale of new equity. Hence, anticipating non-negative cumulative earnings, the direct dividend constraint limits only dividend payments that have the potential to cause a wealth transfer — debt and investment financed dividends.

2.2. Empirical characteristics of the direct dividend constraints

A sample of 150 firms, all of which are included in *Moody's Industrial Manual*, were chosen randomly. For each firm, the details of the direct dividend constraint, as reported in *Moody's Industrial Manual* for the period 1956–1975, were collected. Of these firms the direct dividend constraint of 128 is of the form quantified by eq. (1).[7] This section contains the cross-sectional description of the two parameters α and F. Table 1 depicts the cross-sectional distribution of the unconstrained portion of net earnings, α, reported by the firms. I found 106 firms to have α equal to 1, and the lowest α is 0.5. The sample mean is 0.95 and its standard deviation is 0.1. This evidence indicates that in most cases stockholders maintain the ability to pay a large fraction of future net earnings.

To estimate the magnitude of F, the initial reservoir, the 80 firms in the sample for which net annual earnings (at the year the debt was issued) are available in the *Compustat Industrial File*, were examined. For each firm, the ratio $F/$(net annual earning at the year the debt was issued) was calculated, thereby obtaining a size adjusted measure of F. The histogram of the resulting 90 observations[8] is given in fig. 1. The sample mean is 1.235 and the ratio ranges in value from 0 to 8.7. The evidence suggests that firms choose F to be, on average, slightly greater than net annual earnings.[9]

---

[6]Since the new debt issued can include other and more restrictive constraints, the amount of funds available for debt or investment financed dividends on the contracting day can be smaller than F.

[7]The debt indentures of the other 22 firms contain dividend constraints as well. However, of them 15 firms do not report the form of the direct constraints and 7 report a form similar to eq. (1) — i.e., a cumulative constraint which restricts only debt and investment financed dividends and all methods of distribution.

[8]Some firms have more than one F in the period covered.

[9]It is interesting to note that the American Bar Foundation's *Commentaries on Indentures* (1971) contains a description of suggested restrictive covenants to be included in the debt indentures. It contains a suggestion for a dividend constraint identical to eq. (1). In it the suggested F is annual net earnings. For an analysis of these covenants, see Smith and Warner (1979).

Table 1

The distribution of α, the coefficient of net earnings in the direct dividend constraint, as reported in *Moody's Industrial Manual* for 128 corporations, in the period 1956 to 1975.

Number of firms	Value of α
106	1.00
1	0.85
4	0.80
8	0.75
7	0.7
1	0.6
1	0.5

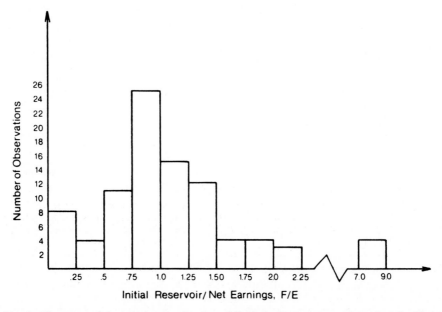

Fig. 1. Histogram of the initial reservoir of payable funds, F, to net annual earnings for 90 debt indentures issued in the period 1951 to 1976. F is the constant in the direct dividend constraint, and net annual earnings used are from the *Compustat Industrial File* tape for the year the debt was issued.

Since F is the initial reservoir of payable funds, F/B_0 is the fraction of the market value of the debt outstanding on the contracting date which can be paid out as investment or debt financed dividends. It is interesting to examine the magnitude of this ratio; however, this estimation involves several problems. First, almost all the firms in our sample have several issues of debt outstanding on the contracting date, and data on the market value of these issues of debt is unavailable. I therefore estimate B_0 as the sum of the book values of all outstanding debt issues on the contracting day as reported in the *Compustat Industrial File*. The resulting histogram of F/B_0 for the 128 firms in the sample is reported in fig. 2. The sample mean is 0.318 and the estimates range from 0 to 3.402. Hence, on average, the direct dividend constraint implies that roughly 68% of the book value of the debt could not have been paid out.

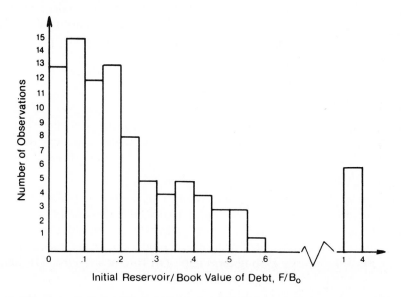

Fig. 2. Histogram of the initial reservoir of payable funds, F, to the book value of debt for 92 debt indentures issued in the period 1951 to 1976. F is the constant in the direct dividend constraint, and the book values of debt used are from the *Compustat Industrial File* tape for the year in which the debt which includes this constraint is issued.

3. The indirect dividend constraints and the reservoir of payable funds

3.1. The indirect dividend constraints

The sample of bond indentures reveals that dividend payments are constrained indirectly as well as directly. Indirect dividend constraints are restrictions generated by items such as the contractual obligations of stockholders to maintain a minimum level of working capital or net worth and a minimum ratio of assets to liabilities. The indirect dividend constraints place additional restrictions only on the payment of debt and investment financed dividends. For example, the obligation to maintain minimum net worth limits the allowed amount of debt and investment financed dividends, while a commitment to maintain a minimum ratio of current assets to current liabilities restricts only the allowed amount of investment financed dividends. Hence, depending on which of its indirect dividend constraints are binding, the maximum amount of debt financed dividends the firm is allowed to pay can differ from the allowed amount of investment financed dividends, even if the new debt issued to finance the dividends contains no new restrictions.

A complete documentation, quantification and analysis of the major forms the indirect dividend constraint takes is contained in the appendix where it is shown that the indirect dividend constraints differ from the direct dividend constraint in one important aspect — they can force the firm to pay *negative dividends* (i.e., to issue new equity).

3.2. The reservoir of payable funds

Moody's Industrial Manual contains corporate reports specifying their legal ability to pay dividends at a given point in time under the most restrictive dividend constraint. For example, the report of Kelsey–Hayes Company [*Moody's Industrial Manual* (1967, page 443)] is:

> 'Company may not pay cash dividends in excess of consolidated net income after September 1, 1963, plus $6,000,000; also agrees to maintain consolidated current assets of at least twice consolidated current liabilities and consolidated working capital of at least the greater of $17,000,000 or 140% of long term debt. On August 31, 1966, $16,400,000 of retained earnings were not so restricted.'

Note that Kelsey–Hayes Company can pay out unlimited amounts of equity financed dividends. However, as of August 31, 1966, this company can pay out $16,400,000 worth of debt *or* investment financed dividends, which is its reservoir of payable funds.

3.3. The sample

To document the magnitude of the reservoir, a subset of 100 firms, which are included in the sample and report their reservoirs in *Moody's Industrial Manual*, is selected. The reservoir is reported once a year. Thus, a time series of annual reservoirs was collected for each firm in this sample. Fig. 3 describes the sample. The number of reservoirs reported for the company is plotted on the horizontal axis and the number of firms is plotted on the vertical axis. For example, 34 firms in our sample had 10 years of reservoirs reported. As can be seen in fig. 3 the number of observations (i.e., reservoirs) varies from 5 to 20. Six firms have as little as 5 observations, while 20 firms report 20 reservoirs.

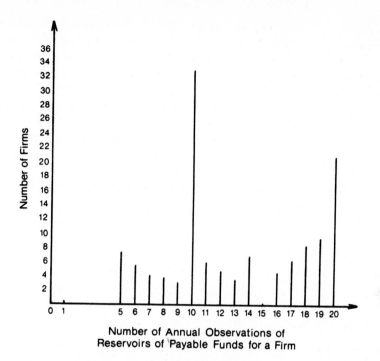

Fig. 3. Frequency distribution of the number of annual observations on reservoirs of payable funds maintained by 100 firms and reported in *Moody's Industrial Manual* for the period 1955 to 1976.

3.4. The cross-sectional description

The magnitude of the reservoir is estimated by standardizing it by an estimate of the market value of the firm. This size adjusted reservoir is estimated for each firm in the sample in the following way:

$$R_j = (1/T_j) \sum_{t=1}^{T_j} (RPF_{j,t}/PMV_{j,t}), \qquad j = 1, 2, \ldots, 100,$$

where

$RPF_{j,t}$ = reservoir of payable funds for firm j at time t,
$PMV_{j,t}$ = market value of the equity plus book value of debt for firm j at time t,
T_j = number of observations available for firm j,

and the data on the standardizing variables is from the *Compustat Industrial File*.

These ratios were sorted from low to high and divided into deciles. Decile 1 contains the lowest ratios and decile 10 contains the highest. An equally weighted average of the corporate ratios was calculated in each decile. Table 2 depicts the results. The average ratio in the ith decile, $\bar{R}_i$, is as low as 0.031 for decile 1 and as high as 0.273 for decile 10. These ratios vary from about 0.02 (see column 4) to about 0.44 (see column 5). Thus, the size adjusted reservoir exhibits large cross-sectional variability.[10] The overall mean of these ratios is 0.117, i.e., firms hold, on average, a reservoir equal to 11.7% of their market value (as estimated by the proxy employed). Hence, the magnitude of the reservoir is a non-trivial fraction of total firm value.

Table 2

Distribution of the average ratios of reservoir of payable funds to market value of the firm for 100 corporations.

Decile	Average size adjusted reservoir[a]	Standard deviation	Minimum size adjusted reservoir	Maximum size adjusted reservoir
1	0.031	0.008	0.017	0.041
2	0.050	0.003	0.043	0.057
3	0.066	0.005	0.059	0.075
4	0.081	0.004	0.076	0.087
5	0.099	0.003	0.091	0.102
6	0.112	0.005	0.103	0.120
7	0.130	0.006	0.121	0.137
8	0.148	0.007	0.138	0.159
9	0.176	0.012	0.161	0.190
10	0.273	0.076	0.198	0.437
Total sample	0.117	0.071	0.107	0.437

[a]The average size adjusted reservoir in the ith decile, $\bar{R}_i$, is an equally weighted average of the individual size adjusted reservoirs, R_j, in that decile. R_j is estimated as follows:

$$R_j = (1/T_j) \sum_{t=1}^{T_j} (RPF_{j,t}/MVF_{j,t}),$$

where $RPF_{j,t}$ is the reservoir of payable funds of firm j at time t, $MVF_{j,t}$ is the market value of equity plus the book value of debt of firm j at time t, and T_j is the number of reservoirs available for firm j.

3.5. Time series description

To describe the time series profile of the RPF's the sample was limited to firms having at least 16 observations. This requirement reduces the sample of 100 firms, described in fig. 3, to 40 firms, and the period covered to 1956–

---

[10]An alternative measure of size adjusted reservoir — a ratio of the average RPF divided by the average of the standardizing variable — resulted in similar cross-sectional variability. Furthermore, the adjustments of the reservoir for size with net earnings and cash dividends resulted in a similar large cross-sectional variability.

1975. For any given year the average *RPF*, I_t, is calculated as follows:

$$I_t = (1/N_t) \sum_{j=1}^{N_t} RPF_{j,t},$$

where N_t is the number of firms reporting their reservoirs for year t.

Fig. 4 describes the time series profile of I_t. The evidence suggests that the average *RPF* increases with time. The average size adjusted *RPF* at year t, IM_t, is estimated by

$$IM_t = (1/N_t) \sum_{j=1}^{N_t} (RPF_{j,t}/PMV_{j,t}).$$

Fig. 5 describes its time series profile which suggests that the average size adjusted *RPF* is around 12% per year. Additionally, the size adjusted *RPF* does not exhibit an upward trend.

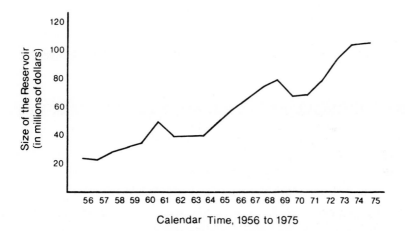

Fig. 4. Time series behavior of the average reservoir of payable funds (in millions) for 40 firms over the period 1956 to 1975.

3.6. The behavior of the reservoir around new debt issues

Frequently firms issue new debt while the old debt is still outstanding. The new issue can contain a different set of constraints thereby changing the magnitude of the reservoir maintained. To address this issue a subset of 61 firms, each having a new debt issue and at least 8 annual reservoirs reported for the period 1957–1975, was selected. Since the reservoirs are reported once a year, the date of the new issue is rounded to the nearest calendar year. For

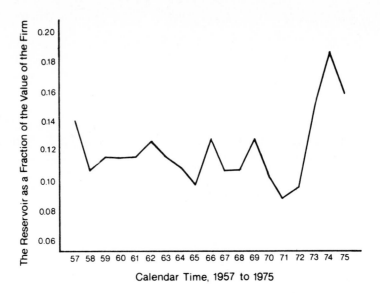

Fig. 5. The time series behavior of the average reservoir of payable funds as a fraction of the market value of the firm for 40 firms over the period 1957 to 1975.

example, July 1975 is changed to 1976 while May 1975 is changed to 1975. Defining the issue date as time 0, I calculate

$$I_t = (1/N_t) \sum_{j=1}^{N_t} RPF_{j,t},$$

where

t = number of years before and after the new issue (t ranges in value from −9 to 10),

N_t = number of firms reporting their reservoirs for year t.

Table 3 depicts the results. The average reservoir around the new debt issue seems to be similar to that usually maintained.

3.7. Potential increments in the risk of the outstanding bond

The reservoir of payable funds could be utilized to pay debt or investment financed dividends. These payments would, in turn, increase the leverage ratio and therefore the risk of the outstanding bonds. To estimate these potential increments of the leverage ratio it is assumed that the stockholders can eliminate the *RPF* by paying debt financed dividends.[11] The potential

---

[11]Assuming that the reservoir can be eliminated only by the payment of investment financed dividends would result in a similar potential change in the leverage ratio. This method will be used if the existing debt is protected by a 'me first' rule.

Table 3

The average reservoir of payable funds for 61 firms for the period 1957 to 1975 during which each had issed new debt. The date of the new issue is denoted as zero. The average reservoir is the cross-sectional average of the reservoirs available at time t for the relevant firms.

Number of years relative to the date of the new debt issue, t	Average reservoir (in millions)	Number of firms
-9	$29.25	13
-8	51.18	19
-7	33.58	22
-6	34.42	22
-5	24.29	26
-4	34.15	36
-3	33.17	44
-2	35.98	45
-1	46.75	44
0	45.76	61
1	42.36	55
2	53.66	53
3	57.81	56
4	64.04	55
5	71.33	51
6	71.82	44
7	91.98	43
8	80.05	30
9	82.88	26
10	95.13	23

change in the leverage ratio is therefore estimated by

$$PL_j - L_j = \left((1/T_j) \sum_{t=1}^{T_j} RPF_{j,t} \right) \bigg/ \left((1/20) \sum_{t=1}^{20} PMV_{j,t} \right),$$

and

$$L_j = \sum_{t=1}^{20} (\text{Book value of debt})_{j,t} / PMV_{j,t},$$

where

L_j = estimated leverage ratio of the jth firm ($j = 1, 2, \ldots, 100$),
PL_j = estimated leverage ratio the firm can achieve by eliminating the RPF.

T_j and $PMV_{j,t}$ are the number of observations for firm j and the sum of the market value of equity and the book value of debt as defined above. The period covered is from 1956 (i.e., $t = 1$) to 1975 (i.e., $t = 20$). Both PL_j and L_j were estimated for each firm in the sample. The results are reported in table 4.

Table 4

The estimated average leverage ratio of 100 corporations and the average of their potential leverage ratios.

Variable[a]	Average	Standard deviation	Lowest	Highest
(1) Leverage ratio	0.299	0.142	0.051	0.852
(2) Potential leverage	0.425	0.144	0.115	0.859
(3) Difference [(2)−(1)]	0.126	0.081	0.006	0.547

[a]The Spearman rank correlation between (1) and (3) is −0.213 whose z value is −2.128, i.e., significant at the 5% level.

The estimated leverage ratios of the 100 firms examined ranged from 0.051 to 0.852 with a mean of 0.299. The high ratio indicates that the sample of firms investigated contains firms which have risky bonds outstanding. These ratios can be increased on the average by 12.6 percentage points to 0.425 by the elimination of the reservoirs. These potential increments range from 0.006 to 0.547, and are larger for firms with low leverage ratios. The histogram of the potential increments in the leverage ratios is depicted in fig. 6. Clearly, the levels of the reservoirs maintained imply that the leverage ratios, and therefore the risk of the outstanding bonds, can be increased substantially.

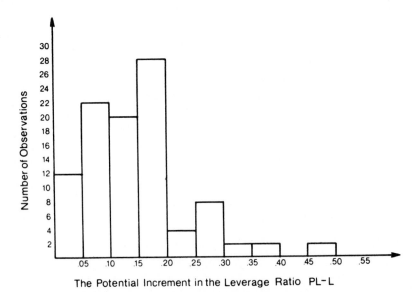

The Potential Increment in the Leverage Ratio PL−L

Fig. 6. Histogram of the potential increments in the leverage ratio, $PL_j - L_j$, for 100 firms. PL_j is the potential leverage ratio, i.e., the leverage ratio firm j can achieve if it eliminates its reservoir by paying debt financed dividends. L_j is the current leverage ratio of firm j.

4. The *RPF*'s, wealth transfers and potential explanations

As the sample of bond indentures reveals, stockholders impose restrictions on themselves by constraining their future ability to pay debt and investment financed dividends. At the time of issuance of the bonds, the potential bondholders would expect a certain level of future dividend payments. Obviously, bondholders' wealth is unaffected if actual dividend payments coincide with their expectations. However, if stockholders pay themselves less than the expected dividends, wealth is transferred from them to the bondholders. It is, therefore, surprising to find that stockholders do not pay themselves as much debt or investment financed dividends as they are allowed to. If the bonds are priced at issue under the expectation that no reservoir will be maintained, any positive level of reservoir maintained through the life of the bond transfers wealth *to* the bondholders. The obvious question is: Why do stockholders maintain these reservoirs?

Moreover, the existence of these reservoirs stems from stockholder's choice of dividend constraints which allow for positive payment of future dividends. In other words, stockholders can ensure that no reservoir would be maintained by precommitting themselves to pay no dividends. By doing that they would also avoid any possible tax related costs of paying dividends. In this case bonds are priced expecting no reservoir to be maintained and no dividends to be paid. The question which therefore arises is: Why do stockholders choose a constraint which allows for some dividend payments?[12]

If the typical corporation faces an unlimited supply of investment projects with non-negative net present value, stockholders can resolve these issues costlessly by precommitting themselves to pay no dividends. Indeed, investment in financial instruments trading in a perfect capital market provides the firm with unlimited supply of projects with zero net present value. However, when taxes are introduced, investment in the financial market by the corporations for the stockholders is subject to double taxation.[13] This investment, therefore, can impose negative net present value

---

[12]Notice that the reservoir is the maximum amount of debt *or* investment financed dividends that can be paid under the most restrictive dividend constraint. Thus, one cannot rule out the possibility that the reservoirs documented here are of funds available only for the payment of investment financed dividends. These payments, in turn, could require the rejection of projects with positive net present value. In this case the costs of eliminating the reservoir can exceed the benefits from increasing the risk of the outstanding bonds. Furthermore, in pricing the bonds the potential bondholders would rationally anticipate that such a reservoir would be maintained and price the debt accordingly. Therefore, the ex-post maintenance of such a reservoir would not involve any wealth transfer.

Unfortunately, due to data limitations, we are unable to determine what kinds of dividends can be paid under the maintained reservoir. However, all the firms in our sample have maintained reservoirs continuously over periods of ten to twenty years. Is it possible that *all* of them have found it *always* too costly to pay investment financed dividends?

on the stockholders. In this case the corporation has a limited supply of non-negative NPV projects and its precommitment to pay no dividends and therefore to maintain no reservoirs can result in *overinvestment* (i.e., forced acceptance of projects with negative NPV) in the future. To avoid such costs, stockholders would choose a constraint which allows for dividend payments and consequently they would maintain reservoirs. For in periods in which the minimum investment implied by the dividend constraint would have caused overinvestment, stockholders would avoid it by using the reservoirs.[14]

5. Conclusions and implications

This paper investigates a large sample of bond indentures focusing on the effects of the conflict of interests between the bondholders and the stockholders on the dividend decision of levered firms. The traditional examination of corporate dividend policy assumes that the firm is one homogeneous unit. The examination of dividend policy has therefore centered around stockholders' choice of the level of payout and the method of payout (i.e., cash dividends versus share repurchase). However, when dividends are examined in the context of their role in the bondholders–stockholders conflict, they are distinguished by their method of financing (i.e., debt, investment or equity). Indeed, the evidence presented here indicates that the stockholders of levered firms choose to limit the ability to pay *only* dividends which are financed in a way that has the potential to generate a wealth transfer from the bondholders — i.e., debt and investment financed dividends. Furthermore, these restrictions of future payouts do not distinguish between dividends and share repurchases.

My evidence indicates that the stockholders do not pay out all the allowed amount of debt and investment financed dividends. All the firms in my

---

[13]In addition to the issue of double taxation the tax on 'improper profit accumulation' [see Bittker and Eustice (1971, pp. 8-3, 8-18)] can affect the supply of zero net present value projects. By retaining earnings beyond the 'reasonable needs of the business' the corporation is providing evidence of its intent to avoid income tax paid by its stockholders. Among the major elements determining whether the tax avoidance purpose is present, are the corporation's dividend history and investment of undistributed earnings in assets unrelated to the corporation's business. Investment in the financial market is viewed as investment not related to the purpose of the business. Hence, including the expected costs due to the accumulated earnings' tax, those projects can have negative net present value. Admittedly, very few publicly held corporations have been prosecuted under this law. However, this can be an equilibrium result; firms can avoid this cost by paying dividends. Moreover, investing in assets having no reasonable connection with the purpose of the business can bring on a searching inquiry. Thus, costs can be imposed even if investigation is not followed by an actual prosecution.

[14]This potential explanation for the choices of the level of the dividend constraint and the magnitude of the reservoir maintained is developed in Kalay (1979a, b). In it the analysis is extended, a model is developed, and its empirical implications are found to be consistent with the empirical evidence.

sample maintain reservoirs of substantial magnitude. The existence of these reservoirs stems from a choice of a dividend constraint which allows for future dividend payouts. If the corporation faces a limited supply of non-negative NPV projects a precommitment to pay no dividends would result in overinvestment. In this case the choice of a constraint which allows for future payouts and the maintenance of the reservoirs reduces this cost. Hence firms can find it optimal to pay out funds, even if these payments involve tax and transaction related costs.

The analysis does not provide an answer to the 'dividend puzzle' — i.e., an explanation for the payment of cash dividends which are taxed more heavily than realized capital gains. The argument is that some form of payment should be used to avoid taking negative net present value projects. Since the dividend constraint allows for both share repurchase and cash dividends, corporations should only use share repurchase as a method of distribution if the effective tax on cash dividends is always higher than that on realized capital gains.

The effective tax on cash dividends, however, is not always higher than that on *realized* capital gains. Miller and Scholes (1978) point out a way in which investors can avoid the tax payments on dividends by converting them to tax deferred capital gains. In this case the effective tax on dividends would be *lower* than that on realized capital gains. Furthermore, the use of share repurchases as a method of distribution is subject to limiting regulation (SEC rule 13 e-2) and can lead to charges of violations of the insider trading rules. Hence, it is not necessarily a less costly method of distribution than cash dividends. It can, therefore, be optimal for the corporation to use both. Extending this argument, it can be optimal for the corporation to pay cash dividends even if these payments involve tax related costs as long as the alternative method of distribution is not less costly.

Finally, the empirical evidence presented in this paper is encouraging in several respects. It is consistent with rational maximizing behavior and constitutes powerful evidence in support of the importance of the control of the conflict of interest between the bondholders and the stockholders to corporate financial policies. But perhaps more importantly, it details sophisticated solutions discovered long ago by the financial community to problems that have attracted attention in the academic literature only recently.

Appendix: The indirect dividend constraints

This appendix details and quantifies the various forms the indirect dividend constraints take. For ease of exposition I will focus my analysis on a firm with a simplified balance sheet as shown in table 5.

Table 5[a]

Assets	Liabilities
$CA_t =$ 740	$CL_t = 300$
	$LD_t = 700$
$FA_t = 1,300$	
	$TL_t = 1,000$
$TA_t = 2,000$	$NW_t = 1,000$
	$TCF_t = 2,000$

[a]CA_t = current assets at time t,
FA_t = fixed assets at time t,
TA_t = $CA_t + FA_t$ = total assets at time t,
CL_t = current liabilities at time t,
LD_t = long-term debt at time t,
TL_t = $CL_t + LD_t$ = total liabilities at time t,
NW_t = net worth at time t,
TCF_t = $TL_t + NW_t$ = total claims on the firms' assets at time t.

Furthermore, throughout this appendix I assume (without loss of generality):

Assumption 1. The book values of this firm's assets and liabilities are equal to their respective market values.

Assumption 2. In paying investment financed dividends, stockholders forego projects with zero net present value (or deplete assets and pay out their proceeds without any liquidation costs).

Assumption 3. When new debt is issued to finance dividend payments it is issued at par and the coupon payments are equal to the required rate of return on that debt.

Assumption 4. The firm will not buy back all or parts of its outstanding debt.

As revealed by the examination of our sample, the indirect dividend constraints place additional restrictions only on the payment of debt and investment financed dividends. These constraints, in turn, can be grouped into five categories.

First, stockholders often precommit themselves to maintain a minimum level of net worth during the life of the outstanding debt. This restriction can be quantified as

$$NW_t > a, \qquad \forall t < T, \tag{A.1}$$

where T is the debt maturity and a is the minimum net worth.

This constraint specifies the maximum allowed amount of investment financed dividend, D_t^I, to be

$$D_t^I \leqq NW_t - a = TA_t - TL_t - a. \tag{A.2}$$

If, for example, (A.2) is the most binding dividend constraint and $a = 400$, the stockholders of our firm can pay 600 dollars worth of investment financed dividends. Similarly, under Assumptions 1–4 they can pay 600 dollars worth of debt financed dividends. Note that this constraints and, as will be shown shortly, each of the other indirect dividend constraints can force the firm to issue new equity. If the net worth falls below the promised minimum, stockholders must issue new equity to meet their obligation. Hence, the indirect dividend constraints differ from the direct dividend constraint in that they can imply negative dividends.

The second type of indirect dividend constraint found is stockholder's obligation to maintain a minimum level of working capital throughout the life of the bonds. Formally,

$$WC_t = CA_t + CL_t \geqq b, \qquad \forall t < T, \tag{A.3}$$

where WC_t is the working capital at time t.

Hence,

$$D_t^I \leqq TA_t - (b + CL_t). \tag{A.4}$$

If (A.4) is the most binding investment financed dividend constraint and $b = 400$, our stockholders can pay 1300 dollars worth of investment financed dividends, D_t^I. This constraint, however, allows for unlimited payments of debt financed dividends, D_t^D, as long as these payments are financed by the issue of long-term debt.

The third form the indirect dividend constraint takes is similar to the second. In it stockholders precommit to maintain a minimum level of working capital which is no less than the greater of a given constant or some fraction of long-term debt. Formally,

$$WC_t = CA_t - CL_t \geqq \max[c, \gamma LD_t], \tag{A.5}$$

where γ and c are constants. We can rewrite (A.5) as

$$CA_t \geq \max\,[c + CL_t, \gamma LD_t + CL_t].\qquad\text{(A.6)}$$

Thus the allowed amount of investment financed dividends is

$$D_t^I \leq TA_t - \max\,[c + CL_t, \gamma LD_t + CL_t].\qquad\text{(A.7)}$$

If (A.7) is the most binding investment financed dividend constraint and $\gamma = 2$, $D_t^I \leq 300$. Moreover, an identical amount of debt financed dividends can be paid if it is financed by an increase in current liabilities. However, only 150 dollars of dividends financed by the issue of long-term debt can be paid.

The fourth indirect dividend constraint is stockholders' precommitment to maintain the ratio of total liabilities to total assets below an agreed upon maximum. Formally,

$$TL_t / TA_t \leq L^*.\qquad\text{(A.8)}$$

Thus, for a given level of TL_t, the investment financed dividends the stockholder can pay are restricted by

$$D_t^I \leq TA_t - TL_t / L^*.\qquad\text{(A.9)}$$

Hence, if (A.9) is the most restrictive dividend constraint, the stockholders of our firm can pay $2000 - 1000/0.7 = 571$ dollars of investment financed dividends, D_t^I. On the other hand, for a given level of total assets, TA_t, debt financed dividends, D_t^I, are restricted by

$$D_t^D \leq TA_t(L^* - TL_t / TA_t).\qquad\text{(A.10)}$$

The stockholders of our firm can therefore pay themselves 400 dollars worth of D_t^D.

Finally, the fifth indirect dividend constraint is similar to the fourth. It contains the stockholders' obligation to maintain a ratio of current liabilities to current assets that will not exceed an agreed upon maximum during the life of the bond. This restriction can be quantified as follows:

$$CL_t / CA_t \leq e^*.\qquad\text{(A.11)}$$

Thus, for a given level of CL_t, stockholders can pay

$$D_t^I \leq TA_t - CL_t / e^*.\qquad\text{(A.12)}$$

Hence, if (A.12) is the most binding dividend constraint and $e^* = 0.5$, our firm can pay $2000 - 300/0.5 = 1,400$ dollars worth of D_t^i. This constraint, however, allows for unlimited payment of debt financed dividends as long as these payments are financed by the issue of a new long-term debt.

In summary, like the direct dividend constraint, the documented indirect dividend constraint places restrictions only on the payment of investment and debt financed dividends. Moreover, under these constraints, stockholders can postpone the payment of dividends into the future without 'losing' their right to pay them — i.e., these indirect dividend constraints (like the direct) are cumulative. Hence, they enable the creation and the maintenance of a reservoir of payable funds. Unlike the direct dividend constraint, the indirect constraint can force the stockholders to pay negative dividends. Finally, under the same indirect dividend constraint the maximum allowed amount of debt financed dividends can differ from the allowed amount of investment financed dividends.

References

American Bar Foundation, 1971, Commentaries on indentures, (American Bar Foundation, Chicago, IL).

Black, F. and M. Scholes, 1973, The pricing of options and corporate liabilities, Journal of Political Economy 81, 637–659.

Black, F., 1976, The dividend puzzle, Journal of Portfolio Management 2, 5–8.

Brennan, M.J., 1970, Taxes, market valuation and corporate financial policy, National Tax Journal 23, 417–427.

Bittker, B.I. and J.S. Eustice, 1971, Federal income taxation of corporations and shareholders (Warren, Gorham and Lamont, Boston, MA).

Fama, E.F. and M.H. Miller, 1972, The theory of finance (Holt, Rinehart and Winston, New York).

Fama, E.F., 1978, The effects of a firm's investment and financing decisions on the welfare of its security holders, American Economic Review 68, 272–284.

Galai, D. and R.W. Masulis, 1976, The option pricing model and the risk factor of stocks, Journal of Financial Economics 3, 53–81.

Jensen, M.C. and W.H. Meckling, 1976, Theory of the firm: Managerial behavior, agency costs, and capital structure, Journal of Financial Economics 3, 305–360.

Kalay, A., 1979a, Corporate dividend policy: A collection of related essays, Ph.D. dissertation (University of Rochester, Rochester, NY).

Kalay, A., 1979b, Towards a theory of corporate dividend policy, Unpublished paper (New York University, New York).

Long, J.B., Jr., 1973, Book review of the theory of finance by Eugene Fama and Merton Miller, Journal of Money, Credit and Banking 5, 229–235.

Long, J.B., Jr., 1978, The market valuation of cash dividends: A case to consider, Journal of Financial Economics 6, 235–264.

Mikkelson, W., 1981, Convertible calls and security returns, Journal of Financial Economics 9, 237–264.

Miller, M.H. and F. Modigliani, 1961, Dividend policy, growth and the valuation of shares, Journal of Business 34, 411–433.

Miller, M.H. and M. Scholes, 1978, Dividends and taxes, Journal of Financial Economics 6, 333–364.

Miller, M.H., 1977, Debt and taxes, Journal of Finance 32, 261–275.

Modigliani, F. and M.H. Miller, 1958, The cost of capital, corporation finance and the theory of investment, American Economic Review 48, 261–297.

Myers, S.C., 1977, Determinants of corporate borrowing, Journal of Financial Economics 4, 147–175.

Ross, S., 1977, The determination of financial structures: The incentive-signalling approach, The Bell Journal of Economics 8, 23–40.

Smith, C.W. and J.B. Warner, 1979, On financial contracting: An analysis of bond convenants, Journal of Financial Economics 7, 117–161.

COMMON STOCK REPURCHASES

An Analysis of Returns to Bondholders and Stockholders

Larry Y. DANN*

University of Oregon, Eugene, OR 97403, USA

Received March 1980, final version received September 1980

This paper examines the effects of a common stock repurchase on the values of the repurchasing firm's common stock, debt and preferred stock, and attempts to identify the dominant factors underlying the observed value changes. The evidence indicates that significant increases in firm values occur within one day of a stock repurchase announcement. These value changes appear to be due principally to an information signal from the repurchasing firm. Common stockholders are the beneficiaries of virtually all of the value increments, but no class of securities examined declines in value as a result of the repurchase.

1. Introduction

In a common stock repurchase, the repurchasing firm distributes cash to some of its shareholders and in exchange acquires a fraction of its outstanding equity. This paper examines the effects of a corporate share repurchase on the values of the repurchasing firm's securities. Investigation of the valuation impacts for all classes of securityholders is an important element in determining why firms repurchase their shares.

A cash repurchase of common shares in general changes the composition of assets held by the firm, alters the firm's financing mix, revises the ownership proportions of each of its shareholders, and distributes cash to shareholders by means of a transaction that is taxed differently than an

*This paper is based on my Ph.D. dissertation at UCLA. I would like to thank David Mayers, my dissertation chairman, for his support and encouragement. I am also indebted to the other members of my committee: Harold Demsetz, Michael Intriligator, Clement Krouse and J. Fred Weston. I have benefited greatly from the helpful comments and suggestions of Harry DeAngelo, Michael Hopewell, Christopher James, Michael Jensen, Ronald Masulis, Wayne Mikkelson, George Racette, Edward Rice, Larry Richards, Bert Steece, the participants at Finance Workshops at the University of Oregon and the University of Washington, and Eugene Fama, the referee for this journal. All remaining errors are mine.

Journal of Financial Economics 9 (1981) 113–138. North-Holland Publishing Company

equivalent dollar amount distributed as a dividend.[1] A repurchase may also signal information about firm value to investors. As a result, security price changes associated with a repurchase can result from several factors or combination of factors. We attempt to identify the dominant factors underlying the observed value changes.

In addition, an examination of stock repurchases provides evidence that potentially has implications for several major issues in corporate finance, including (1) the valuation impact of differences in taxability of a firm's cash distributions, (2) the effects of altering a firm's investment and/or financing decisions, (3) the means by which new information is disseminated to investors, and (4) the conflict of interest between a firm's stockholders and the owners of other classes of securities.

The next section of the paper describes the basic features and institutional arrangements of the principal ways in which firms repurchase their shares. In section 3, explanations of stock repurchase that are consistent with received finance theory are examined, and predictions of their respective price impacts on the major classes of outstanding securities are presented. Section 4 describes the sample of repurchasing firms and the principal sources of data. The empirical analysis of the impact of a common stock repurchase is presented in section 5. Section 6 summarizes the results of the investigation.

2. Methods of cash repurchase

A corporation can repurchase its own common shares in the open market,[2] through a privately negotiated transaction or via a tender offer. In a tender offer, the company usually specifies the number of shares it is offering to purchase, the tender offer price at which it will repurchase shares,[3] and the period of time during which the offer is in effect. Additionally, the company frequently reserves the right to extend the offer beyond the initially announced expiration date and to purchase shares tendered in excess of the amount specified. The offer may be conditional on receiving tenders for a minimum number of shares, and may permit the withdrawal of tendered shares prior to the expiration of the offer.

---

[1]Although these effects will generally arise, they may not in all cases. A firm that replaces the distributed funds with another source of financing may not change its asset composition. If the firm repurchases from each shareholder a uniform fraction of their pre-repurchase holdings, then ownership proportions will be unchanged. Other circumstances could be contrived so that the financing mix and taxability of the distribution are unaltered. Nevertheless, these circumstances are exceptional, not customary.

[2]Open market purchases of common stock by the issuing company are in substance identical to purchases of the stock made through a broker by an other investor.

[3]The tender offer price is usually higher than the market price at the time of the offer, and is almost always the net price received by the tendering shareholder. That is, the tendering shareholder pays no brokerage fees, and the company customarily pays any transfer taxes that are levied.

The number of shares specified in the offer usually represents the maximum number of shares that the company promises to repurchase. If the number of shares tendered by shareholders exceeds this maximum limit and if the company chooses to purchase less than all shares tendered, the purchases are generally made from each tendering shareholder on a pro rata basis.[4] Alternatively, if fewer shares are tendered during the initial offer period than are sought, the company may choose to extend the expiration date. If the offer is extended, the company will usually purchase all shares tendered before the initial expiration date, and may purchase shares tendered during the extension period on either a pro rata or first-come, first-served basis. The terms of the offer frequently preclude officers and directors of the repurchasing company from participation in the tender offer.

Open market repurchases occur more frequently than do tender offers to repurchase, but are generally of much smaller magnitude. Companies are not specifically required to publicly disclose their open market repurchase activities, but repurchase transactions must comply with the anti-manipulation and anti-fraud provisions of the Securities and Exchange Act of 1934 as Amended. Many companies do periodically announce board of directors' authorization to reacquire common stock, management intention to repurchase and/or completion of (sometimes) previously announced repurchase plans. In contrast to tender offers, which generally are completed within one month of the initial announcement date, open market repurchases frequently occur over several months or even years.

Private repurchases entail buying shares from a shareholder (usually having a sizable holding) via direct negotiation with the company. Either party may initiate the negotiations. Judging from the infrequency of announcements of private repurchases, this method of reacquiring common stock is less significant than either open market or tender offer repurchases.

Only the results of cash tender offers to repurchase are reported in detail in this study. Further analysis of the price impacts of open market repurchases is presented in Dann (1980). The empirical analysis focuses on tender offer repurchases for the following reasons:

(i)   with tender offer repurchases, the announcement date, the actual date of repurchase and the repurchase price are known, whereas with open market repurchases the repurchase dates and repurchase prices are infrequently reported;

(ii) because tender offer repurchases are substantially 'larger' than open market repurchases, the effects are likely to be more pronounced and therefore more readily observable in the tender offer sample;

---

[4]With the adoption of SEC Rule 13e-4 in September 1979, pro rata repurchase of shares in this situation became mandatory.

(iii) the extent of public disclosure of the terms of repurchase is significantly greater for tender offers than for open market buy-backs, which provides greater assurance that the full impact of the repurchase will be observed at the announcement date.

3. Explanations of repurchases and their predicted security price impacts

Several explanations and predicted effects of common stock repurchases appear in the finance literature. This study examines three of the most plausible and frequently mentioned hypotheses regarding repurchases.

The first hypothesis is that personal tax savings are generated from cash distributions by means of share repurchases in lieu of dividend payments.[5] The thrust of this argument is that, holding total cash payout fixed, personal taxes are reduced and hence share value is increased when stock repurchases are substituted for dividend distributions. The empirical implication of this hypothesis is that the stock price of the repurchasing firm increases following the unanticipated announcement of a forthcoming share repurchase.[6]

This proposition is identical to the argument frequently encountered in the dividend policy literature that a differential tax rate on dividends versus capital gains implies that a publicly held firm can affect the value of its shares by altering its dividend payout. However, Miller and Scholes (1978) theoretically develop conditions under which a change in the mix of an investor's dividend and capital gains wealth increments does not affect the investor's wealth or welfare. Moreover, a relaxation of the conditions necessary for this invariance proposition to obtain leads Miller and Scholes to conclude that '. . . the effects of taxes on the optimal financial policies of firms are far less obvious than the simple comparison of tax differentials might seem to suggest' (p. 348).

Along the same lines, Black and Scholes (1974) argue that since some investors are taxed more heavily on capital gains than on dividends (and consequently prefer dividends), firms will adjust their payout policies until the spectrum of policies offered by firms matches the spectrum of policies demanded by investors. Once this equilibrium is reached, no corporation will be able to increase the price of its shares simply by changing its payout policy. The Black–Scholes logic leads to the prediction that, based upon

---

[5]From the shareholder's perspective, the full amount of any dividend distribution received is taxable at ordinary income tax rates. In contrast, any distribution received as a result of a stock repurchase is taxable only to the extent that the repurchase price exceeds the shareholder's acquisition price, and then only at capital gains tax rates. Brigham (1964) and Bierman and West (1966) were among the first to mention this point.

[6]If a stock repurchase alters the repurchasing firm's investment decision as well as the form of its cash distribution, then the empirically observed stock price change will reflect the combined impact of the investment and payout changes.

personal tax considerations, a share repurchase announcement should not affect the price of the firm's shares.[7]

A second hypothesis is that the announcement of common stock repurchase constitutes a revelation by management of new information about the firm's future prospects. Disclosure of this information conceivably could either increase or decrease the value of the firm.[8] An empirical implication of the information disclosure or signalling hypothesis is that there generally will be price impacts on all of the firm's risky securities. However, the nature of the information (and a model of asset pricing) must be specified in order to predict unambiguously the magnitude and sign of the security price impacts. For instance, a simple mean shift in the probability distribution of the firm's future cash flows suggests that the price impacts on all of the firm's risky securities will be in the same direction. Alternatively, a mean-preserving increase in the variance rate of return on the firm produces an increase in the value of equity and a decrease in the value of debt.[9] Since at the time of repurchase most firms do not announce the explicit nature of the information to be inferred by investors, the impact of the information is not predictable.[10] However, a disclosure that decreases total firm value (for the reasons suggested in footnote 8) seems unlikely to occur for many of the firms announcing a repurchase, since in addition to internal productive investment opportunities, these firms also have the opportunity to purchase securities of other firms in the capital markets. Moreover, few incentives seem to exist for managements of these firms to make such unfavorable disclosures when there are readily available capital market investment opportunities.

[7]Extending the reasoning of the personal tax savings hypothesis, Elton and Gruber (1968) argue that share repurchases in lieu of cash dividends allow each stockholder to set his own current income, and that the ability to set current income increases the value of the firm's shares. However, opportunities to set current income by owning other securities with the desired (expected) dividend yield also exist. Moreover, it is far from obvious that stock repurchases in lieu of dividends economize on transaction costs and personal taxes for all shareholders. Consequently, the impact (if any) on share value of substituting a stock repurchase for a dividend is not clear.

[8]Most references to a value-increasing information signal cite management's belief that its firm's shares are undervalued as an important rationale for share repurchase [e.g., see Stewart (1976), Nantell and Finnerty (1974) and Coates and Fredman (1976)]. In addition, in a survey of repurchasing firms, Guthart (1967) reports that alleged undervaluation was a frequently mentioned reason for repurchase.

The value-decreasing interpretation of stock repurchase embodies the notion that management is signalling that the firm does not have desirable investment opportunities available in sufficient quantity to utilize all internally generated resources. This interpretation of stock repurchase appears in Ellis (1965), Guthart (1965, 1967), Woods and Brigham (1966) and Young (1967, 1969).

[9]Galai and Masulis (1976) demonstrate this result using the Black and Scholes (1973) option pricing model.

[10]For example, from a large sample of tender offer repurchases, the reason for repurchase most frequently cited at the repurchase announcement is management's belief that the stock is undervalued, yet this reason is offered for only about 10% of the cases.

A third hypothesis is that an unanticipated repurchase of stock represents a wealth transfer from the firm's senior claimants to the stockholders. The empirical implication of the wealth transfer or expropriation hypothesis is that the stock price increases and the market value of senior securities declines.[11] This implication is consistent with an information signal that conveys an increase in the firm's riskiness, which can also be viewed as an expropriation of debtholders' wealth brought about by imposing additional risk on the debt claims against the firm.

Table 1

Effects on security values of repurchasing firms predicted by alternative hypotheses.

Hypothesis	Predicted impact on value of:		
	Equity	Senior securities	Firm
Personal tax savings effect	Positive	Zero	Positive
Information effect	Positive	Positive or negative	Positive or unspecified[a]
	Negative	Positive or negative	Unspecified[a] or negative
Expropriation effect	Positive	Negative	Zero

[a]The sign of the impact on firm value depends on the relative magnitudes of the opposing value changes in equity and senior securities.

It is important to note that the personal tax savings, information and expropriation hypotheses are not mutually exclusive. Thus, the observed impacts must be interpreted as being possibly consistent with more than one hypothesis. Table 1 summarizes the empirical implications of each of the hypotheses. Note that the observation of certain results implies unambiguous support or lack of support for particular hypotheses. For instance, a negative common stock return at announcement is consistent only with a dominant information effect. Likewise, positive or zero senior security returns are not consistent with the expropriation hypothesis.

4. Data sources and sample design

Approximately 300 repurchase tender offers over the years 1962–1976 have been identified from a search of *The Wall Street Journal* and the *Investment*

---

[11]Galai and Masulis note this prospect. If the effect of the repurchase is purely expropriation, the firm's value is not affected.

Dealer's Digest. Of these offers initially identified, five additional criteria are required for a cash repurchase tender offer to enter the final sample:

(1) Common stock rates of return for the company around the repurchase announcement and expiration dates appear on the CRSP Daily Returns File; this restriction limits the sample to firms that were listed on either the New York Stock Exchange or American Stock Exchange at the time of their repurchase.[12]

(2) An announcement of the tender offer appears in *The Wall Street Journal,* or the initial public announcement date is reported in the 10-K or 8-K reports filed by the companies with the Securities and Exchange Commission.[13]

(3) Tender offers made specifically to reduce small holdings of stock (less than one hundred shares) are excluded, as are tender offers consisting of both cash and securities.

(4) The tender offer specifies a definite, single share price for repurchase.[14]

(5) Information regarding the number of shares outstanding, the maximum number of shares guaranteed to be repurchased and the number of shares acquired is available from published, reliable sources.

These additional restrictions reduce the final sample to 143 cash tender offers made by 122 different companies.

The announcement date of the tender offer is taken to be the earliest date at which the principal terms of the offer (maximum number of shares that the company guarantees to repurchase and tender offer price) are known to be publicly available. From published sources, the earliest reporting date for tender offers in this sample is without exception provided by *The Wall Street Journal.* In a handful of cases, an earlier public announcement date is obtained from SEC 8-K reports. As a result, for the purposes of this study the initial announcement date is defined to be the *trading day prior* to the appearance of the tender offer announcement in the eastern edition of *The*

---

[12]Nine companies whose stocks were listed on the New York Stock Exchange or American Stock Exchange at the announcement date but subsequently delisted (and therefore deleted from the CRSP Daily Returns File) at the expiration of the tender offer were dropped from the sample.

[13]*The Wall Street Journal* was found to represent the most reliable timely source of the earliest reported announcement date for those tender offers appearing in more than one published source.

[14]Of the original sample, four of the tender offers made in the early 1960's specified a maximum repurchase price, and allowed individual shareholders to specify the price at which they would tender shares. The company would then purchase shares in ascending order of tendering prices. Because the pricing regime of these offers differs markedly from the more customary practice of a uniform tender offer price, these observations were dropped from the sample.

Wall Street Journal or the date identified in the SEC reports, whichever is earlier.[15]

Use of the trading day prior to *The Wall Street Journal* reporting date allows for a one day lag between announcement and publication. However, in instances where the announcement is made after the close of trading on the day prior to appearance in *The Wall Street Journal*, the price impacts associated with the announcement will be embedded in the publication date rate of return. This will also be the case if *The Wall Street Journal* announcement is the first public announcement rather than a report of an earlier public announcement. Because it cannot be determined whether the actual announcement preceded or followed the close of trading on the designated announcement date, the initial post-announcement market transaction may occur on either the announcement date or the day following announcement. For this reason, we measure the response by observing the two-day announcement date return.

Expiration dates of the tender offers are obtained from reports appearing in *The Wall Street Journal* and from 8-K and 10-K reports to the Securities and Exchange Commission. The number of outstanding shares of the repurchasing firms is obtained from the Standard and Poor's Monthly *Stock Guide*. These figures are verified by cross-referencing with information contained in *The Wall Street Journal* articles which detail particulars of the offer, and 8-K and 10-K reports. The maximum number of shares that the company guarantees to repurchase (hereafter referred to as the number of shares sought) and the tender offer price are obtained from the initial *Wall Street Journal* announcement. The number of shares tendered and the number of shares acquired are obtained from published reports in either *The Wall Street Journal* or SEC 8-K, 10-Q and 10-K reports.

Publicly traded debt and preferred stock issues of the firm in the final tender offer sample are identified from *Moody's Industrial, Financial, Transportation and Public Utilities Manuals*. Closing prices on the days in which trading occurred in these securities for a 21-day period centered around the announcement date are obtained from *The Wall Street Journal*.

---

[15]Masulis (1980a) has obtained copies of offer letters and prospectuses for tender offers directly from repurchasing companies. In most cases these documents identify the date of first public announcement for the tender offer. A comparison of announcement dates for a subsample of the observations common to Masulis' study and this investigation reveals that 21 of 25 designated announcement dates are the same for both studies, i.e., the announcement date identified in company documents corresponds to the trading day prior to the day that the announcement appears in *The Wall Street Journal*. For two of the 25 offers the company-identified announcement date is the date that the announcement appears in *The Wall Street Journal*. In the other two cases, there were lags of 2 and 3 trading days between the company-identified announcement date and *The Wall Street Journal* report date. Both of these tender offers occurred in the early 1960's when *The Wall Street Journal* reports of tender offers were in general less extensive than reports in later years. It appears that *The Wall Street Journal* is a timely and reliable source of announcement dates for stock repurchase tender offers.

These prices are used to calculate daily rates of return. For preferred stocks, cash dividends are added to the percentage price change on the ex-dividend date. Bond rates of return include daily interest accruals. The amounts and dates of dividend and interest payments are obtained from Standard and Poor's *Stock Guide* and *Bond Guide*, respectively.

Many of these senior securities trade infrequently. For each security no return is calculated on days in which no trading is reported. Consequently, the rate of return reported on a trading day that follows a non-trading day constitutes a multiple day rate of return. This treatment of missing returns is consistent with the treatment of common stock returns in the CRSP Returns File. In total, 122 publicly traded preferred stock and debt issues for 51 of the tender offers have reported transactions prices that allow calculation of a rate of return for a time period that includes the tender offer announcement date.

Summary statistics describing the characteristics of the sample of tender offers are presented in table 2. The premia offered, percentage of equity sought and acquired, and common stock returns at announcement of the tender offers are sizable. According to row 1, the tender offer price is 22.46% higher on average than the closing market price on the day preceding announcement of the offer. Relative to market prices one month before the announcement, the mean premium is 20.85%. On average these firms have sought to acquire 15.3% of their outstanding shares. These proposed cash distributions represent almost 20% of the market value of equity one day prior to the announcement. The outcome of these offers is that the mean fraction of outstanding shares reacquired has been 14.64%. The market price of these targeted shares has responded with a mean two day rate of return of 15.41%. Varying degrees of positive skewness exist in the distributions of each of these parameters, but the medians of these distributions are of the same general magnitude as the means. Clearly, tender offers to repurchase common stock are significant events in the lives of the corporations which have undertaken them.[16] In addition, most firms undertaking cash tender offer repurchases have done so only once. Only 17 of the 122 firms have made more than one tender offer in the 1962–1976 time period.[17]

---

[16]Open market repurchases are considerably smaller in relative size and stock price impact than are tender offers to repurchase. Analysis of a sample of 121 open market repurchase announcements by Dann (1980) reveals that on average firms sought to acquire approximately 5% of their outstanding shares. The mean two-day announcement date rate of return for this sample was slightly more than 3%.

[17]Seventy-three of the 143 tender offers in the sample have announcement dates occurring in 1973 or 1974. Masulis (1978) finds a similar clustering of leverage-increasing exchange offers in these years. The concentration of these financial restructuring events in this two year period is a curious event for which no convincing explanation is readily apparent. Careful examination of the parameters of the repurchase tender offers announced in 1973 or 1974 fails to reveal any characteristics of this subsample that distinguish the subsample from the overall sample.

Table 2

Summary statistics for characteristics of the tender offer sample (143 observations).

Characteristic of offers	Mean	Median
1. Tender offer premium relative to closing market price one *day* prior to announcement.	22.46%	19.40%
2. Tender offer premium relative to closing market price one *month* prior to announcement.	20.85%	18.83%
3. Percentage of outstanding shares sought.	15.29%	12.57%
4. Percentage of outstanding shares acquired.	14.64%	11.93%
5. Percentage of outstanding shares tendered.	18.04%	14.27%
6. No. shares tendered ÷ No. shares sought.	142.30%	115.63%
7. No. shares acquired ÷ No. shares sought.	111.35%	100.00%
8. Value of proposed repurchase relative to pre-offer market value of equity (fraction sought times one plus the day-prior premium).	19.29%	15.28%
9. Value of actual repurchase relative to pre-offer market value of equity (fraction acquired times one plus the day-prior premium).	18.63%	13.90%
10. Two day announcement date common stock rate of return.	15.41%	12.40%
11. Duration of offer (number of trading days from announcement to expiration).	22 days	20 days

5. Empirical results

5.1. Common stock returns in response to tender offers

A time series of daily common stock returns for 121 trading days centered around the announcement date is taken from the CRSP Daily Returns File for each of the tender offers. Average returns for each of the 121 trading days relative to the announcement day (day 0) are calculated as the arithmetic mean of the individual securities' raw returns on their common dates in 'event time'. For example, the average return on day -5 is the arithmetic mean of the daily rates of return on all 143 securities five trading days prior to their respective announcement dates. This cross-sectional mean return can be interpreted as the return to an equally-weighted portfolio of the sample securities that is formed in event time.

A desirable feature of using a cross-sectional mean to measure security returns relative to a common event is that averaging across many observations mitigates the influence of other contemporaneous firm-specific or market-wide effects that are unrelated to the repurchase announcement.

However, relying exclusively on a cross-sectional mean or portfolio return can obscure important price impacts if the predicted impacts are of opposite sign for a subset of the sample observations. Since this possibility is suggested by the information disclosure hypothesis, the number of positive and negative returns each day are also reported. Observing the proportion of positive returns in conjunction with the mean return provides additional evidence regarding the uniformity of price impacts across the sample.

Raw returns rather than market or risk adjusted returns are used to measure the announcement date response to the tender offer for two principal reasons. First, for interpreting the economic importance of the event, the size of the average raw return is informative. Second, the magnitude of normal daily returns is on average sufficiently small that complicated market and risk adjustments are not likely to materially alter the results.[18] Moreover, recent evidence by Brown and Warner (1980) suggests that, unless the events are highly clustered in calendar time, the explicit adjustment of security returns for systematic risk and market returns does not increase the power of a statistical test to detect abnormal performance. Although the Brown–Warner results are derived using monthly returns data, there is no obvious reason to believe that the implications of their results would be altered by the use of daily data.[19]

Table 3 presents a time series of portfolio returns around the announcement date for the sample of 143 tender offers. Column 1 identifies the trading day relative to day 0, column 2 presents the portfolio daily return, and column 3 reports the cross-sectional standard deviation of the daily returns for each trading day. The fourth and fifth columns report the number of valid returns and the number of those returns which are positive and negative, respectively.[20] Fig. 1 portrays the cumulative portfolio returns

[18]Comparison of raw and market-adjusted returns in this study support the *a priori* belief that with daily data the form of adjustment to raw returns (including no adjustment whatsoever) does not materially alter the results. Consequently, market adjusted returns are not reported here.

[19]Brown and Warner do not examine raw returns directly. Instead, they analyze the difference between a security's realized return and its mean return (which is presumed to represent its 'normal' expected return) over a pre-event date control period. This difference is standardized by dividing by the standard deviation of the security's return over the control period.

Raw returns rather than Brown–Warner 'standardized differences' are reported in this study because whereas Brown and Warner are principally concerned with the power of a performance measure to detect statistically significant abnormal returns, the objective of this research is to disclose both the economic and statistical significance of the observed price impacts. The link between the magnitudes of the average return and the average 'standardized difference' is not straightforward.

[20]Security returns are not calculated for days when security prices are not available, or when no transactions occurred. The variation in the number of valid returns reported in column 4 reflects these trading discontinuities.

Table 3

Common stock rates of return over a 121-day period around announcement of common stock repurchase tender offer (143 events).

Trading day	Mean rate of return (%)	Cross-sectional standard deviation	Sample size	No. positive: No. negative
−60	0.217	3.050	141	52:48
−50	−0.034	3.366	142	50:48
−40	0.058	3.680	143	57:56
−30	−0.562	2.879	143	38:64
−25	−0.125	3.546	143	46:60
−20	−0.071	2.974	143	50:59
−19	0.026	3.081	143	51:56
−18	−0.346	3.127	143	46:63
−17	−0.317	3.264	143	41:61
−16	−0.413	3.415	143	42:69
−15	0.377	2.890	143	58:41
−14	−0.228	3.334	143	49:63
−13	−0.738	3.279	143	43:65
−12	0.051	4.664	143	46:64
−11	−0.424	3.703	143	47:67
−10	−0.578	4.132	143	44:66
−9	0.188	4.009	143	54:58
−8	−0.391	3.934	143	52:59
−7	0.107	3.690	142	54:58
−6	0.417	4.318	142	55:55
−5	−0.169	4.714	143	48:57
−4	0.943	4.261	143	62:45
−3	0.239	4.807	143	57:54
−2	0.490	3.762	142	62:43
−1	0.959	4.510	140	60:43
0	8.946	11.013	138	107:17
1	6.832	12.022	142	93:21
2	0.908	4.280	143	59:32
3	−0.041	2.192	143	40:48
4	0.133	2.123	143	50:35
5	0.158	1.968	143	45:34
6	0.230	2.054	143	41:38
7	0.129	2.060	143	47:29
8	0.051	1.700	143	43:40
9	−0.211	1.982	143	42:51
10	0.213	2.276	143	46:37
11	0.172	2.154	143	46:36
12	−0.024	3.089	143	40:48
13	0.181	2.264	143	49:45
14	−0.143	2.948	142	48:47
15	0.497	2.892	143	60:40
16	−0.105	3.133	142	44:50
17	−0.236	2.879	142	47:49
18	0.148	2.441	142	45:55
19	0.141	2.594	142	49:46
20	−0.057	3.588	142	43:58
25	−0.003	2.525	140	52:44
30	−0.025	3.443	141	46:62
40	0.133	3.175	141	56:53
50	−0.069	3.066	138	56:49
60	0.161	2.446	136	49:52

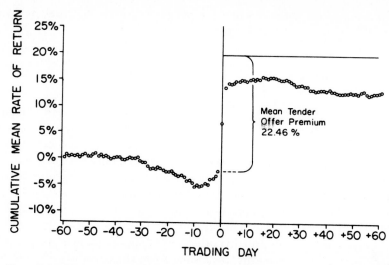

Fig. 1. Plot of cumulative mean rates of return for common stocks over a 121-day period around the announcement of a tender offer to repurchase common stock (143 observations). The tender offer premium is the percentage amount by which the tender offer price exceeds the closing market price on the trading day prior to the tender offer announcement.

graphically and identifies the mean of the premiums offered by firms relative to their respective closing market prices on day −1.[21]

Day 0 and day +1 are designated the announcement period.[22] The day 0 portfolio return for the entire sample of tender offer repurchases is 8.95%, and the day +1 return is 6.83%. In contrast, the mean portfolio daily return for the 50-day period beginning 60 days prior to the announcement date (hereafter referred to as the pre-announcement comparison period) is −0.09%.[23]

Two formulations of statistical tests are employed to determine whether announcement period returns are 'abnormal'. In the first, a standard difference of means t-statistic is utilized to test the null hypothesis that the mean daily announcement period portfolio return is not significantly different from the mean daily portfolio return during the pre-announcement

[21]The cumulative portfolio return is presented to demonstrate that the announcement date impact is not a 'temporary' price response. However, as Brown and Warner point out, one must be careful about inferring statistical significance from the cumulative returns.

[22]Returns for both day 0 and +1 are tested because the initial post-announcement transaction will occur on day 0 if the announcement precedes the close of trading on that day, but will occur on day +1 if the announcement occurs after the close of trading on day 0.

[23]Selection of a comparison period 'close' to the event date minimizes the probability that significant differences in the firm's economic characteristics between the comparison period and event date will exist. The period from day −60 through day −11 is chosen because it satisfies the above criterion, yet the security returns during this period are not likely to be contaminated by information leakages relating to the forthcoming repurchase announcement.

comparison period. This approach is identical to the one used by Masulis (1980a). The t-statistic for this test is given by

$$t = (\bar{R}_{pa} - \bar{R}_{pc}) \Big/ \left[\left(\frac{n_a s_a^2 + n_c s_c^2}{n_a + n_c - 2} \right) \left(\frac{1}{n_a} + \frac{1}{n_c} \right) \right]^{\frac{1}{2}}, \tag{1}$$

where $\bar{R}_{pa}$ and $\bar{R}_{pc}$ are the respective announcement period and comparison period mean daily portfolio returns, s_a^2 and s_c^2 are the respective sample variances of the announcement period and comparison period portfolio daily returns (computed from the time series of portfolio daily returns), and n_a and n_c are the respective numbers of daily portfolio returns in the announcement period and comparison period samples.[24] Given values of 7.889% and -0.09% for $\bar{R}_{pa}$ and $\bar{R}_{pc}$, respectively, and values of 1.057% and 0.252% for s_a and s_c respectively, the calculated t-value for this difference of means is 33.67. Consequently, the null hypothesis that announcement period (day 0 and day $+1$) portfolio returns are drawn from the same distribution as the portfolio returns in the pre-announcement comparison period (day -60 through day -11) is rejected at the 0.01 level of significance.[25]

An alternative specification of the test of statistical significance for announcement period portfolio returns analyzes the combined two-day

---

[24]The validity of this test relies on the assumptions of normally distributed portfolio daily returns and equal variances of the distributions generating announcement period and comparison period portfolio returns. Several researchers [Fama (1965), Officer (1971) and Blattberg–Gonedes (1974)] have examined the distributional properties of daily common stock rates of return. In general, they find that the returns exhibit negligible serial correlation, appear to be symmetrically distributed, and are leptokurtic ('fat-tailed') relative to a stationary normal distribution. Despite apparent departures from normality in individual security rates of return, as long as the second moment of the underlying distribution is finite, then the distribution of sample means of independent stock returns asymptotically converges to a normal distribution.

The assumption of equal variances for announcement period and comparison period returns is conventional in the finance literature. If we drop this assumption, then a test statistic that is approximately t-distributed can be utilized. However, for event studies utilizing daily returns and having a compact (two day) announcement period, this statistic has only one degree of freedom. Applying this test statistic to the returns in table 3, the null hypothesis of equal means can be rejected at the 0.05 level of significance (one-tailed test), but for event studies that document less dramatic announcement period returns, the use of a test statistic with only one degree of freedom makes rejection of the null hypothesis unlikely. The test of a difference in sample means with unequal variances is well known to statisticians as the Behrens–Fisher problem.

As an alternative to a parametric test of significance, we can employ Fisher's Method of Randomization to test the null hypothesis that announcement period returns and comparison period returns are identically distributed, without relying upon the assumptions of normally distributed portfolio returns or equal variances of the distributions generating announcement period and comparison period returns. Applying this distribution-free test, we reject the null hypothesis at the 0.0015 significance level. For a detailed discussion of Fisher's Method of Randomization, see Bradley (1968, pp. 78–85).

[25]Because there is reason to suspect that the comparison period mean daily portfolio return is not an unbiased estimate of the expected daily portfolio return, the null hypothesis that the mean daily announcement period portfolio return equals zero is also tested. The calculated t-value for this test is 33.29. This hypothesis is rejected at the 0.01 significance level.

return. Because we can only pinpoint the timing of the market response to the announcement to within a two day interval, a compelling argument can be made for using a two-day span as the basic measurement interval for testing the significance of returns. If the 'complete' price response to the announcement occurs on day 0 for some firms and day $+1$ for others,[26] then separate day 0 and day $+1$ mean returns, averaged across *all* sampled firms, are attenuated measures of the average response to the announcement. Following this line of reasoning, tests of the average of day 0 and day $+1$ portfolio returns, and tests of the separate day 0 and day $+1$ average returns such as those of Dodd (1980) and Mikkelson (1980), are potentially biased against rejecting the null hypothesis of no abnormal performance.

One solution to this problem is to contrast the two-day announcement period portfolio return with a comparison period sample of two-day returns. Accordingly, a set of 25 non-overlapping two-day portfolio returns from the pre-announcement comparison period were calculated. The null hypothesis that the announcement period two-day period portfolio return (R_{2a}) is equal to comparison period two-day portfolio returns is tested using the t-statistic given by

$$t = (R_{2a} - \bar{R}_{2c})/(\hat{s}\sqrt{1 + 1/N}), \qquad (2)$$

where $\bar{R}_{2c}$ is the comparison period mean two-day portfolio return, and where the estimate of the standard deviation ($\hat{s}$) of two-day portfolio returns is obtained from the time series of comparison period two-day portfolio returns.[27] Given that $R_{2a} = 15.41\%$, $\bar{R}_{2c} = -0.19\%$, $\hat{s} = 0.356\%$ and $N = 25$, the t-value for the difference in two-day returns is 42.97, which easily allows rejection of the null hypothesis at the 0.01 level of significance.[28]

Additional evidence that announcement period returns differ from returns in the comparison period is reported in columns 3 and 5 of table 3. Column 5 indicates that an overwhelming majority of the individual security returns are positive during the announcement period.[29] Despite this homogeneity of the sign of announcement period returns, column 3 indicates that the cross-sectional standard deviations on day 0 and day $+1$ are three to four times larger than their counterparts on a representative day from the surrounding time period. This dramatically higher dispersion of returns at announcement is in part induced by the cross-sectional variation in the magnitude of the premiums offered by the repurchasing firms. In addition, cross-sectional dispersion in day 0 and day $+1$ returns arises from the fact that the initial

---

[26]This pattern exists for the vast majority of firms in the sample investigated here.

[27]This test also assumes normality and equal variances for the distributions generating announcement period and comparison period two-day portfolio returns.

[28]Testing the null hypothesis that R_{2a} equals zero yields a t-value of 42.45.

[29]Only eight securities had negative two-day announcement period returns.

response to the tender offer announcement occurs on day 0 for some firms and on day +1 for other firms.

Careful scrutiny of table 3 suggests that the mean returns on day −1 and day +2 are also large relative to comparison period returns. While significant pre-announcement returns can always arise because of 'leakages' of the contents of forthcoming announcements or because of failure to properly specify the initial public disclosure date, significant returns subsequent to a known public disclosure date are less easily explained in the context of an efficient market. However, trading in four stocks in the sample was suspended for one day at the announcement, and for one stock trading was suspended for two days. Consequently this stock's first post-announcement return (of 45.45%) is reported on day +2. Additionally, the positive portfolio return on day +2 may be related to the fact that for some firms the effective date of the offer follows *The Wall Street Journal* announcement date. Although the announcement date is the relevant date of the disclosure of intent to repurchase, the effective date may be a significant one in the sense of confirming the intentions announced earlier. No evidence is offered in support of this conjecture. In any case, the portfolio returns on day 0 and day +1 are large relative to those surrounding days, implying that the principal impact on stock price occurs at the date of announcement.

Beyond day +2 we observe from fig. 1 a gradual upward movement in the cumulative portfolio return until day +20. However, this increase is not significantly different from zero.[30] We conclude that the 'complete' impact of the repurchase announcement is embodied in common stock returns within one trading day of the announcement. Moreover, the impact is not simply an artifact of the tender offer premium, since the positive cumulative portfolio return persists beyond the expiration of the tender offer. The mean duration of the tender offers in this sample is 22 trading days, yet the cumulative return on day +60 is not significantly different from the cumulative return as of day +2. The large positive announcement period return appears not to be a 'temporary' effect.

An additional observation of interest from fig. 1 is that the cumulative mean return for the entire 60-day period subsequent to the announcement is

---

[30]The cumulative portfolio return for days 3–20 is 1.236%. The sample standard deviation of daily portfolio returns over this period is 0.182%. Assuming that the portfolio returns over this period are independent and identically distributed, then the standard deviation of the sum of 18 returns is 0.773%. The *t*-value for the cumulative portfolio return for days 3–20 is therefore 1.60. This procedure is equivalent to testing whether the mean daily return over this period is equal to zero. Alternatively, to argue less than complete adjustment within one day of announcement is equivalent to claiming positive linear dependence in the time series of portfolio returns. If this is the case, then the standard deviation of the sum of 18 returns calculated above is understated, implying that the *t*-value of 1.60 is overstated. Either way, the cumulative portfolio return for days 3–20 is not significantly different from zero.

less than the mean tender offer premium.[31] The observed relationship between post-announcement price and tender offer price is consistent with the predictions of Dann (1980), Vermaelen (1980), and Bradley (1979) that the price prior to expiration is less than the tender offer price for tender offers that are fully subscribed or oversubscribed. When the sample is split into offers that are at least fully subscribed and offers that are undersubscribed, this prediction is confirmed. Since the majority of tender offers are at least fully subscribed, it is not surprising that the average post-announcement market price is below the average tender offer price for the overall sample.[32]

Positive returns resulting from the announcement of a tender offer to repurchase are apparently consistent with each of the hypotheses enumerated in table 1. However, the 'permanent' upward revision of stock prices implied by the returns presented in table 3 is implied by the personal tax savings hypothesis only if the repurchase of shares is perceived as a change in the firm's financial policies rather than a one time event. That is, once a tender offer has expired, the supposedly preferential tax treatment pertaining to the form of cash distributions by the firm is of value to the remaining shareholders only if the firm is expected to make future cash distributions by means of stock repurchase. The infrequency of repeat repurchasers in the sample casts doubt upon the plausibility of the personal tax savings hypothesis. Moreover, the evidence documenting large premia in repurchase tender offers seems inconsistent with the personal tax savings hypothesis, since offering to repurchase shares at a price above the pre-offer market price reduces any tax advantage gained by transforming cash distributions from ordinary income (dividends) to capital gains.[33]

---

[31]The market price remaining below the tender offer price should not be interpreted as evidence of a market inefficiency, since investors tendering shares to the company cannot be certain that all shares tendered will be accepted.

[32]An additional prediction of the theory in Dann pertains to differences in price impacts at the tender offer expiration date between offers that are at least fully subscribed and those that are undersubscribed. Fully subscribed (and oversubscribed) offers are predicted to register a price decline at the offer's expiration whereas no effect is expected to be observed for undersubscribed offers. This prediction is also confirmed. A statistically significant average return of -2.84% at expiration is found for fully subscribed tender offers, but no statistically significant expiration date returns are found for undersubscribed offers. In addition to confirming the theoretical prediction above, these results provide additional convincing evidence that the large positive announcement date returns to stockholders of repurchasing firms are not reversed when the tender offers expire. Masulis (1980b) reports negligible expiration date returns for undersubscribed offers, and significant negative returns for oversubscribed offers. However, he finds that the negative expiration date returns occur for the oversubscribed offers in which the firm repurchases less than all tendered shares.

[33]Further evidence contrary to the prediction of the personal tax savings hypothesis is reported in Dann (1980). He examines a sample of 22 announcements by firms disclosing completion of recent open market repurchase activity. For each of these 22 firms, no announcement pertaining to stock repurchase activity (actual or planned) by that firm appeared in *The Wall Street Journal Index* during the six months prior to the 'completed repurchase'

On the other hand, large positive lasting wealth increments to equityholders arising from stock repurchase are consistent with both the information and expropriation hypotheses. Examining value changes of senior securities of repurchasing firms at the repurchase announcement date has the potential to discriminate between these hypotheses. Analysis of announcement date rates of return to debtholders and preferred stockholders is presented in the next section.

5.2. Senior security returns in response to tender offers

Returns to 122 publicly traded debt and preferred stock issues around the announcement date are available for 51 of the tender offer events. The sample consists of 41 issues of straight debt, 34 issues of convertible debt, 9 issues of straight preferred stock and 38 issues of convertible preferred stock. Table 4 presents a breakdown of the number of securities by category and the number of events for which security rates of return in each of the categories are available.

The analysis of the returns to senior securities focuses on the immediate vicinity of the tender offer announcement date, since the examination of common stock returns suggests that the price impacts occur principally on day 0 and day +1. Daily returns from 10 days before announcement through 10 days after day 0 are reported. Many of these issues are convertible into common stock and thus also reflect common stock valuation changes. The expropriation hypothesis suggests that the impact of stock repurchase on convertible securities is likely to be different than the impact on securities which are not convertible into common stock. Moreover, Masulis (1980a) in his study of intra-firm exchange offers reports distinctly different price responses for straight versus convertible securities. Consequently, returns to straight debt, convertible debt, straight preferred stock and convertible preferred stock are reported and analyzed separately.

As with the common stock analysis, a time series of average daily raw (not market adjusted) returns for debt and preferred stock issues is generated. For each event represented by more than one senior security in the sample or subsample, an equally weighted portfolio of these securities is formed to generate a single return series for this event. These portfolio returns for each

---

announcement. The average rate of return in response to these repurchases with trailing announcements is 2.65%. This return is statistically significant at the 0.01 level.

Since open market repurchases occur at the prevailing auction market price, repurchasing shares in this fashion does not offer shareholders opportunities to sell their shares that are not already available. A significant positive average return in response to an announcement of completion of previously unannounced repurchase transactions is consistent with the expropriation hypothesis and the information hypothesis. But a positive return following announcement of the termination of repurchase activity is not consistent with the tax savings hypothesis.

Table 4

Debt and preferred stock issues for which announcement period rates of return are available — categorized by type of security and number of events.

Type of security (1)	Number of securities (2)	Number of events[a] (3)
Debt		
Straight (not convertible into common stock)	41	20
Convertible into common stock	34	28
Straight or convertible	75	40[b]
Preferred stock		
Straight (not convertible into common stock)	9	8
Convertible into common stock	38	25
Straight or convertible	47	32[b]
Debt or preferred stock (straight or convertible)	122	51

[a]Each tender offer announcement constitutes an event.
[b]For eight events rates of return for both straight and convertible debt are available. For one event rates of return for both straight and convertible preferred are available.

event are then averaged in event time to construct a mean or portfolio return series around the announcement date. The effect of this procedure is to equally weight each event rather than each security in the calculation of average returns to senior securities. Sample sizes for each subsample based on this weighting scheme are reported in column 3 of table 4.

In contrast with the sample of common stocks, many of the debt and preferred stock issues trade infrequently.[34] Infrequent trading poses potential difficulties for measurement of the impact of the tender offer announcement and interpretation of the time series of average returns. If there is a lag between the announcement date and the date of the next trade, then the average day 0 reported return will capture the impact on only those securities which traded that day. For securities not trading on the announcement day, the impact of the tender offer will be observed in the

[34]On average, instances in which no trades are reported on a day occurs approximately 35% of the time for this sample of securities.

next reported price (even if prices adjust 'instantaneously'). Moreover, if the lag between announcement and the next trade varies significantly across securities, then the post-announcement average returns series may portray an apparently gradual adjustment in security prices.

To overcome the probable incompleteness of the day 0 average return as a measure of the response to the tender offer, the initial post-announcement percentage rate of return for each security is also calculated, and an average of these rates of return is constructed. For each security, this return is based on the last price reported prior to day 0 and the first price reported subsequent to day 0. In constructing the average return, each event (not each security) is equally weighted.

Average rates of return on straight and convertible debt and preferred stock are reported in table 5. Table 5, part A presents mean daily percentage

Table 5

Debt and preferred stock percentage rates of return over a 21-day period around announcement of a tender offer to repurchase common stock.

Trading day	Straight debt		Convertible debt		Straight preferred		Convertible preferred	
	Mean return	Number of events	Mean return	Number of events	Mean return	Number of events	Mean return	Number of events
(A) Daily percentage rates of return								
−10	−0.22	7	−0.11	10	0.67	2	−0.25	8
−9	0.19	11	−0.01	14	−0.11	5	0.05	13
−8	0.24	15	−0.58	15	−0.63	5	0.41	17
−7	0.07	15	−0.01	15	1.53	2	0.30	16
−6	0.17	19	0.00	22	−0.55	4	−1.42	18
−5	−0.12	18	−0.16	19	1.32	3	0.30	19
−4	−0.24	16	0.29	17	−0.23	3	0.48	18
−3	0.19	15	0.66	21	−0.46	5	0.69	21
−2	−0.11	15	0.06	21	−0.65	5	0.04	19
−1	−0.01	15	0.05	18	0.63	4	0.80	19
0	0.13	16	2.41	22	−0.88	2	3.07	19
1	−0.46	17	1.21	23	1.64	4	0.94	21
2	0.76	18	0.56	21	−0.81	3	0.13	24
3	−0.34	16	−0.17	20	−0.82	3	0.29	20
4	0.40	16	0.09	23	−0.49	5	0.57	22
5	0.22	17	0.24	21	0.42	4	1.21	22
6	0.19	16	0.58	23	0.20	6	−0.19	20
7	−0.20	14	−0.15	24	0.11	6	0.34	23
8	−0.30	16	0.60	22	0.58	4	−0.01	18
9	0.44	13	0.09	24	0.15	4	0.22	19
10	0.45	17	−0.26	22	−0.17	4	0.64	17
(B) Initial post-announcement percentage rate of return								
	0.03	20	3.15	28	0.86	8	3.68	25

rates of return for a 21-day period surrounding the tender offer announcement date for each class of securities. The most important observation is that the combined returns for day 0 and day 1 are positive for convertible debt, straight preferred and convertible preferred, and slightly negative for straight debt. Moreover, the returns to convertible debt and preferred stocks are substantially greater than the returns to their non-convertible counterparts. The sum of day 0 and day 1 returns exceeds 3.5% for convertible debt and convertible preferred compared to percentage returns of -0.33% and 0.76% for straight debt and straight preferred, respectively.

Average initial post-announcement returns for each class of securities are presented in table 5, part B. These returns (which incorporate the impact on all securities in each security class) are generally consistent with the results reported in part A of table 5. Convertible debt and convertible preferred stock average announcement date returns each exceed 3%, while straight debt and straight preferred stock returns are much closer to zero than the returns to the convertibles.

Assessing the statistical significance of these percentage returns is less straightforward than the procedures applied to common stock returns, since little or no evidence documenting the distribution of daily returns for debt and preferred stock issues is available. For the samples utilized in this study, calculation of a Shapiro–Wilk W statistic leads to the conclusion that the individual daily returns are in most cases almost assuredly not generated by a normal distribution.[35] However, daily *portfolio* returns will approximate normality under the Central Limit Theorem. Therefore, a parametric test of means between announcement period and comparison period portfolio returns can be appropriate. Defining day -10 to day -1 as the comparison period, a t-statistic identical to the test statistic employed for single-day common stock returns is calculated for each class of security.[36] The null hypothesis that the mean announcement period portfolio return is not significantly different from the mean comparison period portfolio return is rejected at the 0.01 significance level for convertible debt and convertible preferred stock. For straight debt and straight preferred stock, we cannot reject the null hypothesis at the 0.20 significance level.[37]

The results presented in table 5 indicate that positive wealth effects are realized by owners of convertible securities at the time that a firm announces a tender offer to repurchase a fraction of its outstanding common stock.

[35]Shapiro and Wilk (1965) show that the W statistic generally provides the most powerful test for evaluating the assumption of normality against a wide range of non-normal alternatives.

[36]Two-day senior security portfolio returns are not tested for significance because of limitations on data availability.

[37]Similar results are obtained by using Fisher's Method of Randomization to test the null hypothesis that announcement period returns and comparison period returns are identically distributed.

Comparable wealth increments are not realized by owners of debt and preferred stock issues that are not convertible into common stock, but there is no evidence which suggests that owners of non-convertible securities suffer wealth losses as a result of tender offers to repurchase common stock.

Although the announcement period returns to each class of securities examined are on average either positive or zero, returns to some securities of some firms are negative. An inverse relationship between the returns to debt and preferred stockholders and the returns to common stockholders, or an inverse relationship between senior security returns and the magnitude of the proposed cash repurchase would be evidence consistent with the expropriation hypothesis. However, the correlation coefficients of announcement period two-day common stock returns with initial post-announcement returns to each of the senior security classes are positive. In addition, the proposed cash payout relative to equity value is positively correlated with returns to straight debt, convertible debt and convertible preferred stock and insignificantly negative with straight preferred stock. Although the correlation coefficients are not all statistically significant, the generally positive relationships of debt and preferred stock returns with common stock returns and with repurchase size represent further evidence contrary to the predictions of the expropriation hypothesis.[38]

5.3. Changes in firm value in response to tender offers

For each of the 51 firms, an estimate of the change in total firm value is obtained by summing the aggregate value changes for that firm's common stock and senior securities at announcement. For 50 of the 51 firms the estimated value change is positive, and the mean percentage change in estimated firm value is 8.9%. These value changes almost certainly over-estimate the actual percentage changes in firm values since virtually all firms have claims against their assets for which values and value changes are not observable. Nevertheless, the mean estimate of 8.9% is not a trivial figure. Moreover, the mean ratio of common stock value change to estimated firm value change is 94.9%, implying that firm value changes are captured almost exclusively by the common stockholders.

The value changes referred to in the previous paragraph are based upon percentage differences in firm value just prior to announcement and firm value immediately following announcement but before the distribution of cash (i.e., the post-announcement 'cum-distribution' value). Comparison of the pre-announcement firm value with the post-announcement 'ex-distribution' value (defined as the aggregate value of the firm's securities after announcement minus the product of the tender offer price and the number of

---

[38]For a more detailed presentation of this analysis, see Dann (1980).

shares sought) is also of interest. On average, pre-announcement firm value exceeds post-announcement 'ex-distribution' firm value by 2.4%. When compared with the relative size of the proposed payout, this is a modest decline in firm value, and may be one reason why senior claimholders do not suffer wealth losses at repurchase.

The announcement date senior security returns and the estimates of changes in firm values suggest that disclosure of favorable information is the dominant effect associated with tender offer repurchases. However, neither the nature of the information disclosed nor the reasons for its disclosure in this manner are readily apparent. Little evidence is found that is consistent with the expropriation hypothesis. On average, returns to straight debt and straight preferred stock are not significantly different from zero, and the relationship across firms between these returns and the size of repurchase is the opposite of what we would expect if expropriation were an important element of the repurchases. If expropriation of senior securityholders' wealth exists, it is only to the extent of what would have been (in the absence of the repurchase) their share of the value of the newly released information.

5.4. Relationship to other empirical research

Two other contemporaneous investigations of the security price impacts of stock repurchase are those of Masulis (1980b) and Vermaelen (1980). Both studies report sizable common stock returns at the time of the stock repurchase announcement. Moreover, Masulis, relying partially upon the results of the present study, reports returns on the senior securities of the repurchasing firms. Vermaelen does not examine returns to securities other than common stock.

Vermaelen's interpretation of his evidence is generally consistent with the evidence and interpretation presented here. He rejects tax and expropriation hypotheses and concludes that information signalling is the only hypothesis consistent with his results. While we concur that the information effect appears to be dominant, the senior security returns and other evidence presented in this study provide a stronger basis for questioning the importance of the expropriation and personal tax effects.

Although Masulis' announcement date returns are similar to the price behavior reported here, his interpretation of his evidence is substantially different. Based upon a partition of his overall sample into several subsamples and an examination of common stock returns at tender offer expiration dates, he concludes that the results are attributable to the combination of a personal tax savings effect, a reduction in corporate taxes due to increased leverage, and transfers of wealth across and within security classes. He does not explicitly consider an information effect.

Masulis' conclusion that tax effects are important is based primarily on his finding that firms seeking to reacquire relatively large fractions of their equity and financing the repurchase principally with debt (and thereby increasing corporate income tax deductions) have larger announcement period returns than the remainder of the sample. But if the fraction of equity sought is a proxy for the value of new information (as claimed by Vermaelen), then Masulis' finding does not discriminate between the tax savings and information hypotheses. The evidence reported here, that stock returns following announcements of completion of previously unannounced open market repurchases are positive, tilts the argument somewhat in favor of the information hypothesis.

Interestingly, another paper by Masulis (1980a) poses an opportunity to discriminate between the tax and information hypotheses upon intra-firm exchange offers, an event that is similar in many ways to a stock repurchase. For exchanges of preferred for common shares no tax implications exist, and thus changes in firm value resulting from these offers (where redistribution effects net out) presumably represent the value of new information. A reexamination of Masulis' data for aggregate firm value changes could shed some light on the information signalling hypothesis, at least insofar as it pertains to intra-firm exchange offers.

6. Summary and conclusions

Analysis of common stock returns, senior security returns and changes in aggregate firm value at the announcement of a tender offer to repurchase common stock yields several interesting conclusions. Sizable and significantly positive returns are realized by common stockholders of repurchasing firms within one day of the repurchase announcement. These positive value changes in common shares are permanent in that share prices do not return to their pre-announcement date levels following expiration of the opportunity for stockholders to tender shares.

Positive wealth changes are realized by owners of convertible debt and convertible preferred stock as well. However, the returns realized by these securityholders are considerably smaller than those accruing to common shareholders. Whereas the average common stock return at announcement is approximately 15%, the return to owners of convertibles is roughly 3%. In contrast with the returns to common stock and convertible senior securities, no significant announcement date returns are experienced by owners of straight debt and straight preferred stock. Aggregate firm values increase at announcement of the tender offer, but approximately 95% of these value increments are captured by common stockholders.

Overall, the results are consistent with the hypothesis that repurchase tender offer announcements constitute a revelation by management of favorable new information about the value of the firm's future prospects. The specific nature of the information conveyed to investors by means of the repurchase announcement is not readily apparent. Careful scrutiny of the rationale for repurchase proffered by management at the announcement fails to uncover concrete disclosures regarding improvements in the distribution of the firm's future cash flows.

The hypothesis that wealth losses for owners of senior securities arise from the repurchase of common stock by firms is not supported by the evidence presented in this study. For all classes of securities analyzed, announcement date returns are either significantly positive or insignificantly different from zero. Moreover, senior security rates of return at announcement are positively related to the size of repurchase and the wealth gain realized by stockholders, in contrast to the predictions of the expropriation hypothesis. This evidence does not rule out the prospect of offsetting information and expropriation effects for straight debt and preferred stock owners, but wealth levels of these securityholders are shown not to be reduced by announcement of a tender offer for repurchase.

The hypothesis that tender offer repurchases increase equity values because of personal tax savings is not directly refuted by the evidence presented here. But permanent stock price increases are consistent with a tax savings explanation only if the repurchase announcement conveys a change in the firm's policy regarding the form of future cash payouts. Since 86% of the sampled firms undertook only one cash repurchase tender offer between 1962 and 1976, the inference of a permanent policy change is at best implausible. Moreover, the positive stock price response to announcements of completion of previously unannounced open market repurchases is contrary to the predictions of the tax savings hypothesis.

The conclusion that disclosure of new information is the principal explanation of the firm value increments arising from common stock repurchases leaves at least two important questions unanswered. One is that the nature of the information producing sizable positive returns remains unidentified. The second question is why managers choose to convey the information by means of a costly common stock repurchase. These questions are fruitful subjects for future research.

References

Bierman, H. and R. West, 1966, The acquisition of common stock by the corporate issuer, Journal of Finance 21, 687–696.

Black, F. and M. Scholes, 1973, The pricing of options and corporate liabilities, Journal of Political Economy 81, 637–659.

Black, F. and M. Scholes, 1974, The effects of dividend yield and dividend policy on common stock prices and returns, Journal of Financial Economics 1, 1–22.

Blattberg, R.C. and N.J. Gonedes, 1974, A comparison of the stable and student distributions as statistical models for stock prices, Journal of Business 47, 244–280.

Bradley, J., 1968, Distribution-free statistical tests (Prentice-Hall, Englewood Cliffs, NJ).

Bradley, M., 1979, An analysis of interfirm cash tender offers, Unpublished manuscript (University of Rochester, Rochester, NY).

Brigham, E.F., 1964, The profitability of a firm's purchase of its own common stock, California Management Review 7, 69–76.

Brown, S.J. and J.B. Warner, 1980, Measuring security price performance, Journal of Financial Economics 8, 205–258.

Coates, C.R. and A.J. Fredman, 1976, Price behavior associated with tender offers to repurchase common stock, Financial Executive 44, 40–44.

Dann, L.Y., 1980, The effect of common stock repurchase on securityholder returns, Unpublished Ph.D. dissertation (University of California, Los Angeles, CA).

Dodd, Peter, 1980, Merger proposals, management discretion and stockholder wealth, Journal of Financial Economics 8, 105–137.

Ellis, C.D., 1965, Repurchase stock to revitalize equity, Harvard Business Review 43, 119–128.

Elton, E.J. and M.J. Gruber, 1968, The effect of share repurchase on the value of the firm, Journal of Finance 23, 135–149.

Fama, E.F., 1965, The behavior of stock market prices, Journal of Business 38, 34–105.

Galai, D. and R.W. Masulis, 1976, The option pricing model and the risk factor of stock, Journal of Financial Economics 3, 53–81.

Guthart, L.A., 1965, More companies are buying back their stock, Harvard Business Review 43, 41–53.

Guthart, L.A., 1967, Why companies are buying their own stock, Financial Analysts Journal 23, 105–110.

Masulis, R.W., 1978, The effects of capital structure change on security prices, Unpublished Ph.D. dissertation (University of Chicago, Chicago, IL).

Masulis, R.W., 1980a, The effects of capital structure change on security prices: A study of exchange offers, Journal of Financial Economics 8, 139–178.

Masulis, R.W., 1980b, Stock repurchase by tender offer: An analysis of the causes of common stock price changes, Journal of Finance 35, 305–319.

Mikkelson, Wayne, 1980, Convertible security calls and securityholder returns, Unpublished manuscript (Dartmouth College, Hanover, NH).

Miller, M.H. and M.S. Scholes, 1978, Dividends and taxes, Journal of Financial Economics 6, 333–364.

Nantell, T.J. and J.E. Finnerty, 1974, Effect of stock repurchase on price performance. Paper presented at the Financial Management Association Meeting (San Diego, CA).

Officer, R.R., 1971, A time series examination of the market factor of the New York stock exchange, Unpublished Ph.D. dissertation (University of Chicago, Chicago, IL).

Shapiro, S.S. and M.B. Wilk, 1965, An analysis of variance test for normality, Biometrika 52, 591–611.

Stewart, S.S., Jr., 1976, Should a corporation repurchase its own stock?, Journal of Finance 31, 911–921.

Vermaelen, T., 1980, Stock repurchases and market signalling: An empirical study, Unpublished manuscript (University of British Columbia, Vancouver).

Woods, D.H. and E.F. Brigham, 1966, Stockholder distribution decisions: Share repurchases or dividends?, Journal of Financial and Quantitative Analysis 1, 15–28.

Young, A., 1967, The performance of common stocks subsequent to repurchase, Financial Analysts Journal 23, 117–121.

Young, A., 1969, Financial, operating and security market parameters of repurchasing, Financial Analysts Journal 25, 123–128.

FOUR

CORPORATE LEASING POLICY

Determinants of Corporate Leasing Policy

CLIFFORD W. SMITH, JR. and L. MACDONALD WAKEMAN*

ABSTRACT

The existing finance literature assumes the real operating cash flows from leasing or owning are invariant to the ownership of the asset and focuses on tax-related incentives for corporate leasing policy. Our analysis suggests that taxes are important in identifying potential lessees and lessors, but are less important in identifying the specific assets leased. We provide a unified analysis of the various incentives affecting the lease-versus-purchase decision. We then show how these incentives explain the use of contractual provisions such as maintenance clauses, deposits, options to purchase the asset, and metering.

WHEN A FIRM BUYS AN ASSET, it obtains both the right to the services of that asset over the period it is owned plus the right to sell the asset at any future date. With a lease, the firm acquires only the right to the asset's services for a period specified in the contract.

The existing finance literature analyzing corporate leasing policy concentrates on the tax-related incentives to lease or buy (e.g., see Miller and Upton [19], Myers et al. [21], Lewellen et al. [13], Franks and Hodges [11], and Brealey and Young [4]). We believe that taxes play an important role in explaining certain dimensions of leasing policy, for example, the choice between manufacturer and third-party leasing. However, taxes provide only a limited explanation of why specific assets are leased rather than owned, and for the choice of provisions in lease contracts.

In this paper, we want to accomplish two things: (1) to provide a unified analysis of the various incentives affecting the lease-versus-buy decision and (2) to employ that analysis to explain observed variation in corporate leasing policy. In deriving testable hypotheses about the characteristics of lessees, lessors, the assets leased, and provisions in lease contracts, we extend the standard lease-versus-buy analysis found in corporate finance textbooks (e.g., Brealey and Myers [5]).

I. Tax Determinants of the Lease-Versus-Buy Decision

A. An Irrelevance Proposition

In Table I, we categorize the different cash-flow implications of leasing and purchasing. If the asset is purchased, the inflows are cash flows from the asset's

* Graduate School of Management, University of Rochester and Citicorp International Bank Limited. This research was partially supported by the Managerial Economics Research Center, Graduate School of Management, University of Rochester. We would like to thank L. Brown, H. Grieve, G. Hawkins, P. Healey, S. Liebowitz, J. Schallheim, W. Schwert, R. Stulz, J. Warner, and J. Zimmerman for helpful comments.

Reprinted from The Journal of Finance, Vol. XL, No. 3, July 1985.

Table I

Comparison of the Present Values of the Component Cash Flows from Purchasing an Asset with Those from Leasing the Asset

	Asset Purchased	Asset Leased	
	Buyer/User (b)	Owner/Lessor (o)	User/Lessor (u)
Description of Cash Flow	(1)	(2)	(3)
Nontax Cash Flows:[a]			
Initial investment in the asset	$-INV_b^{\text{b}}$	$-INV_o^{\text{b}}$	
Lease payments		$+LEASE_o^{\text{c}}$	$-LEASE_u^{\text{c}}$
Salvage value of asset	$+SALV_b^{\text{d,e}}$	$+SALV_o^{\text{d,e}}$	
Maintenance expenses	$-MAINT_b^{\text{d,f}}$	$-MAINT_o^{\text{d,f}}$	$-MAINT_u^{\text{d,f}}$
Cash flow from asset's operation	$+CFLOW_b^{\text{d}}$		$+CFLOW_u^{\text{d}}$
Out-of-pocket contracting costs	$-COSTS_b^{\text{g}}$	$-COSTS_o^{\text{g}}$	$-COSTS_u^{\text{g}}$
Tax-Related Cash Flows:[a,h]			
Investment tax credit	$+ITC_b$	$+ITC_o^{\text{i}}$	$+ITC_u^{\text{i}}$
Depreciation tax shield generated by asset	$+\tau_b(DEP_b)$	$+\tau_o(DEP_o)$	
Tax implications of lease payments		$-\tau_o(LEASE_o)$	$+\tau_u(LEASE_u)$
Tax on capital gains from disposal of asset	$-\tau_b(GAIN_b)$	$-\tau_o(GAIN_o)$	
Tax shield from maintenance	$+\tau_b(MAINT_b)$	$+\tau_o(MAINT_o)$	$+\tau_u(MAINT_u)$
Tax on cash flow from operations	$-\tau_b(CFLOW_b)$		$-\tau_u(CFLOW_u)$
Additional debt interest tax shield generated by asset	$+\tau_b(DEBT_b)^{\text{j}}$	$+\tau_o(DEBT_o)^{\text{j}}$	$+\tau_u(DEBT_u)^{\text{j}}$

[a] The entries in the table represent the present values of the cash flows associated with each component. Thus $\tau_b(DEP_b)$ is the present value of the tax shield provided to the buyer by depreciation over the asset's life.

[b] In a competitive market, $INV_b - INV_o$ (see Section II.B).

[c] If the lessor has market power, $LEASE_u$ may differ across different lessees (see Section II.B).

[d] If the value of the asset is sensitive to use or maintenance decisions, then $SALV_b > SALV_o$, $MAINT_b \neq MAINT_o + MAINT_u$, and $CFLOW_b \neq CFLOW_i$ (see Section II.A).

[e] If the lessor has a comparative advantage in asset disposal, $SALV_b < SALV_o$ (see Section II.B).

[f] Maintenance can be provided by the lessor as part of the contract (with a correspondingly higher lease rate) or by the lessee.

[g] For firm-specific assets or assets with short expected periods of use, $COSTS_b \neq COSTS_o + COSTS_u$ (see Section II.A).

[h] We assume that tax rates remain constant over time and income. See Mayers/Smith [15] or Smith/Stulz [22] for an analysis of variation in tax rates.

[i] The lessor can either take the tax credit or pass it through to the lessee and charge a higher lease price (see Section I.B).

[j] Incremental personal tax liabilities should be capitalized into the price of the debt when sold, and thus the net tax advantage of debt is related to the difference in effective marginal tax rates facing the corporation and the marginal individual in the bond market (see Miller [18] and DeAngelo/Masulis [8]).

operation ($CFLOW_b$) plus the asset's salvage value ($SALV_b$); the outflows are the initial investment (INV_b), maintenance expenditures ($MAINT_b$), out-of-pocket contracting costs ($COSTS_b$), plus incremental tax liabilities. When an asset is leased, the lessor (owner) receives the lease payments ($LEASE_o$) plus the asset's salvage value ($SALV_o$). The lessee (user) receives the cash flows from the asset's operations ($CFLOW_u$) in return for the lease payments ($LEASE_u$). Each party also incurs specific tax liabilities, maintenance expenditures, and out-of-pocket contracting costs.

Three conditions must be met for an asset to be leased: (1) for a lessor to offer to lease an asset, the net present value of the leasing operation must be nonnegative (the sum of the present values listed in column 2 of Table I must be greater than or equal to zero); for the user to lease the asset, the net present value of leasing must be (2) nonnegative (the sum in column 3 must be greater than or equal to zero); and (3) no less than that of purchasing (i.e., the sum in column 3 must be at least as large as the sum in column 1).

Given competitive markets (from Table I, $INV_b = INV_o$), no taxes (components in the lower panel of Table I = 0), no out-of-pocket contracting costs ($COSTS = 0$), and fixed real activity choices [$-INV_b + SALV_b - MAINT_b + CFLOW_b = -INV_o + SALV_o - (MAINT_o + MAINT_u) + CFLOW_u$], then the distribution of net cash flows from the use of an asset is independent of the set of financial contracts specifying the allocation of rights to the asset. Under these assumptions, the firm will be indifferent between owning and leasing it. This is simply a special case of the Modigliani and Miller [20] theorem. Conversely, the decision between leasing and buying will not be irrelevant if the lessor has market power or if taxes, contracting costs or production/investment incentives, are affected by the choice between buying and leasing.

B. Effective Marginal Tax Rates

If the lessor and lessee face different effective marginal tax rates, leasing can reduce the total tax bill. The lower panel of Table I sets out the present values of the tax-related cash flows from leasing and purchasing. To concentrate on these tax-related cash flows, we assume that the sum of the nontax items for owning and leasing in Table I are equal, and that the debt capacity of the asset is independent of its ownership (i.e., $DEBT_b = DEBT_o + DEBT_u$). The difference in total taxes paid between purchase and lease is the difference between the sum of the items in column (1) and the sum of the items in columns (2) and (3): ($\tau_o - \tau_b)[(DEP + DEBT_o + MAINT) - (LEASE + GAIN)]$. Note that for a given potential user, the tax rate for the potential buyer/user (τ_b) is equal to the tax rate for the potential lessee/user (τ_u). If the lessor and lessee face the same effective marginal tax rates, then the total tax liability is independent of the ownership structure. There is then no tax advantage to leasing.

C. Manufacturer Versus Third-Party Leasing

For some assets, leases are offered both by manufacturers and by third-party lessors. We believe that provisions in the tax code are important in explaining this variation. The tax-code provisions affecting the choice between manufacturer and third-party lessors are: (1) the basis for calculating both the investment tax credit and depreciation for manufacturer lessors is manufacturing cost, C, while for third-party lessors it is the sale price of the asset, S; and (2) for manufacturer lessors, the manufacturing profit, $S - C$, need not be immediately recognized for tax purposes. Since neither provision always dominates, tax-related incentives can flavor either manufacturer or third-party lessors, and generally the decision is affected by all the parameters in column 2 of Table I.

D. Allocation of the Investment Tax Credit

As noted in Table I, if a firm buys an asset, it receives the investment tax credit, but if it leases the asset either the lessor or the lessee can take the investment tax credit. Thus, the option to allocate the investment tax credit to the higher valued party provides a tax advantage to leasing. For the lessor to be indifferent on an after-tax basis between keeping the investment tax credit and giving it to the lessee, the net present value of the lease payments for a lease in which the credit is passed to the lessee must exceed the net present value of the lease payments for a lease in which the lessor retains it by $ITC/(1 - \tau_o)$. This difference is a function both of the net present value of the investment tax credit and the lessor's tax bracket, τ_o. Similarly, for a lessee to be indifferent, the difference in the present value of the lease payments must equal $ITC/(1 - \tau_u)$. Thus allocating the investment tax credit to the party in the higher tax bracket lowers the total tax bill. Furthermore, since it only applies to a subset of all assets, the investment tax credit provides a partial explanation for which assets will be leased, i.e., assets which generate investment tax credits are more likely to be leased.

II. Nontax Determinants of the Lease-Versus-Buy Decision

Examination of the tax code reveals that there are identifiable tax-related incentives for leasing. Yet most of the incentives only identify potential lessors and lessees. There is little guidance to which assets will be leased. The primary provisions which differ across assets are depreciation and the investment tax credit. Yet we observe systematically different leasing decisions within the same firm for assets with the same tax treatment. For example, office buildings appear to be leased with greater frequency than research-and-development or manufacturing facilities. Taxes alone do not appear to explain these aspects of corporate leasing policy. We now turn to nontax incentives affecting leasing policy. Our objective is to provide a managerial analysis of the observed variation in leasing practices. Thus, our analysis is organized to emphasize observable asset and firm characteristics which are important to the lease-or-buy decision.

A. User Characteristics Affecting the Leasing Decision

We first examine incentives established through financial contracts, compensation contracts, and ownership structure. While these three nontax incentives are not asset specific, and thus cannot explain which of the firm's assets will be leased, they do help identify firms that have special incentives to lease or buy. We then examine three nontax incentives for corporate leasing policy which do vary across different assets and thus help identify which of the firm's assets will be leased.

Financial Incentives of Leases. Smith and Warner [22] identify sources of conflict of interest between corporations' fixed and residual claimholders. They argue that a long-term, noncancellable lease commits the firm to use a particular set of assets over the life of the lease and thus controls the asset-substitution problem. However, the senior legal standing of leases implies that their use reduces the coverage on other, already outstanding, fixed claims. This induces corporations to limit leasing activities through provisions in corporate bond contracts. Stulz and Johnson (25) argue that the option to enter long-term, noncancellable leases also affects these incentive problems. They suggest that this option controls the underinvestment problem by allowing the firm to acquire a new project and segregate the claim on the project's cash flows. Thus, some new positive net present value projects will be undertaken if the use of the assets is acquired through long-term leases or if the project is financed with secured debt, but not with unsecured debt where the project's payoffs would accrue as a windfall to owners of previously issued fixed claims.

While a long-term lease is similar to secured debt in a number of dimensions, it differs in others. If the value of a pledged asset in bankruptcy is less than the face value of the associated secured debt claim, the secured creditor also has an unsecured claim on the firm's other assets for the remainder. The lessor's claim on the firm's other assets is limited to one year's lease payments (see Brealey and Myers [5, p. 544]). In a lease, the lessor retains title to the asset, and the lessee uses the asset only as long as there is no default on the lease payments. Should the lessee default on the lease payment, it is simpler for a lessor to regain physical possession of a leased asset either prior to or after the declaration of bankruptcy than for a secured debtholder to acquire the pledged asset.

Compensation-Related Incentives to Lease. Management compensation plans can create incentives to lease. For example, a manager whose bonus depends on the return on invested capital will argue strongly to lease rather than purchase office space. With a purchase, the denominator of the performance measure increases, perhaps dramatically. This incentive can be controlled by including the capitalized value of lease payments in the calculation of invested capital. (See Smith and Watts [23] for more detailed discussions of incentive effects of compensation plans.)

Specialization in Risk-bearing. For certain production processes (generally small and noncomplex operations), the gains from specialization in risk-bearing and management associated with the corporate form of organization are less than the concomitant agency costs caused by the separation of ownership and control. In these circumstances, as Fama and Jensen [9] note, the individual proprietorship is a more efficient form of organization than the corporation. However, ownership of the capital assets makes it more difficult for the proprietor to reduce risk through diversification. The proprietor can mitigate this problem by leasing the assets required. Leasing thus reduces the concentration of wealth in the one activity, and can facilitate a more efficient allocation of riskbearing.

Sensitivity to Use and Maintenance Decisions. Generally, an asset's value is affected by its history of use and maintenance. If an asset is owned and used by the same agent, then use and maintenance incentives are internalized—there are direct private incentives to maximize value since the owner/user bears the full cost of abuse. But a lessee does not have the right to an asset's residual value and hence has less incentive to care for the asset (see also Alchian/Demsetz [1]).

If the contractual provisions of a lease contract do not internalize effectively the incentive to provide maintenance, abuse of the asset by the lessee will be anticipated by the owner/lessor (in Table I, $SALV_b > SALV_o$) and reflected in the schedule of lease payments. That is, the lease payments must be set to offer the lessor a normal return given the expected salvage value which results from the forecasted use and maintenance decisions, conditional on the contractural provisions of the lease. Thus, the more sensitive the value of an asset to use and maintenance decisions, the higher the probability that the asset will be purchased rather than leased.

High forecasted abuse and the resulting high lease rates lead to the further problem of adverse selection by lessees. Specifically, if the lease payment is high relative to the purchase price, a lessee anticipating moderate use of the asset will tend to purchase the asset, and thus the fraction of lessees abusing the asset will increase. We therefore expect to observe a tendency to offer assets for lease whose value is less sensitive to abuse. For example, the furnishings in a rental unit are generally more durable than furnishings in an owner-occupied dwelling but rental units also make more extensive use of disposable cups, etc. In both cases, the forecasted value of the asset at the end of the lease is less sensitive to use decisions.

Within a corporation there is already a separation of the use rights to an asset from the claim to the asset's residual value. Thus, assets owned by corporations should be abused more and less well maintained than similar assets owned by individuals. However, we still expect a difference in use and maintenance decisions between leased and owned corporate assets because of the differential incentives of corporate managers to monitor the use and maintenance of the asset services acquired through lease versus purchase.

Firm-specific Assets. An asset highly specialized to a particular user is more highly valued by that organization than in its best alternative use. The lease of organization-specific assets generates agency costs in the form of significant additional negotiation, administration, and enforcement costs due to conflicts between lessor and lessee. These conflicts arise over the division of the value in excess of the alternative use value of the asset. Specifically, a bilateral monopoly is created between lessor and lessee when the lease on such an asset is negotiated (in Table I, $COSTS_b > COSTS_o + COSTS_u$). Klein et al. [12] note that this bilateral monopoly creates incentives to internalize these contracting problems by purchasing assets highly specialized to the firm. For example, we expect to observe corporations leasing office facilities with greater frequency than production or research facilities. Moreover, differential consequences of a production delay lead most newspaper publishers, but few book publishers, to own their presses.

Expected Period of Asset Use. The demand for firm-specific assets typically extends to most of the asset's useful life; however the demand for many general (nonfirm-specific) assets is relatively short. If the useful life of an asset is significantly longer than the period over which a particular firm expects to use the asset, and the costs of ownership transfer are significant, then there can be advantages to leasing rather than buying the asset (in Table I, $COSTS_b > COSTS_o + COSTS_u$). Miller and Upton [19] note that search costs can be reduced by selling the asset with a repurchase agreement. Yet legal fees and taxes are frequently higher to transfer ownership rather than lease an asset. Enforcement costs differ as well. Failure to return a rented asset is a criminal offense, while failure to honor a repurchase agreement is a civil offense.

Flath [10] notes that short-term leases reduce expenditures on information about quality. For example, a lessee of an automobile is less concerned about the condition of the motor, transmission, or cooling system than a potential purchaser of the vehicle. (Note, however, that the greater the certainty regarding quality and the lower the costs of transferring ownership in an asset, the less significant is the frequency of such transactions. For example, repurchase agreements between banks for bonds are transacted daily and exist in competition with overnight loans from the federal funds market.)

B. Lessor Characteristics Affecting the Leasing Decisions

We next examine two additional nontax incentives for corporate leasing policy. Since these incentives vary both across potential lessors and across assets, they also help identify which assets will be leased.

Price Discrimination Opportunities. If a manufacturer has some degree of market power in the market for a specific asset, then becoming a lessor can provide additional opportunities to extract rents by circumventing those provisions of the Robinson-Patman Act which prohibit differential pricing of the same good (see also, Burstein [6] and Liebowitz [14]). Specifically, if purchasers have less elastic demands and lessees have more elastic demands, then the firm can increase profits by setting the implicit purchase price to the lessee below the explicit price to the purchaser (in Table 1, $INV_b > INV_o$). Note that if the demand elasticities are reversed, the manufacturer's ability to price-discriminate is reduced by potential third-party lessors. A second method of price discrimination entails charging different prices to different leasing customers whose demands are correlated with one or more of the characteristics of the lease (for example, the term of the lease, the provision of maintenance services, or the intensity of use of the asset). In such cases the manufacturer/lessor may be able to use these characteristics to segment the relevant market by demand elasticity and thus to increase profits. In each of these cases, the effectiveness of the resulting second degree price discrimination is limited by the availability of close substitutes. Note also that because of the required market power, this argument only applies to manufacturer lessors. There is no obvious way for third-party lessors to exclude potential competitors.

If a manufacturer has a monopoly and thus can control the total supply of a durable asset, his ability to extract price above a marginal cost can still be restricted by customers' expectations. If the monopolist can only sell the asset, he will produce as long as price exceeds marginal cost. But potential customers, forecasting this behavior, have no incentive to pay more than marginal cost. Coase [7] argues that by leasing, the monopolist bears the cost of expanding the supply, and can thus more effectively exploit his monopoly position. Flath [10] argues similarly that leasing allows a manufacturer/lessor more effectively to bond quality.

Brealey and Myers [5] argue that if a manufacturer can affect the rate of technological obsolescence, that manufacturer has an incentive to offer to lease. By leasing some of its machines, the manufacturer signals to potential buyers that since it will suffer when obsolescent-leased equipment is returned, it has a reduced incentive to innovate quickly and thereby reduce the value of its current output. The value of this signal should be reflected in higher selling prices for the manufacturer's current generation of products. However, we doubt that this is an important incentive to lease because of both the value foregone by delaying innovation and the signal provided to potential competitors of the opportunities available to entrants.

Comparative Advantage in Disposing of the Asset. If the lessor has a comparative advantage in disposing of the asset, this provides an incentive to lease (in Table I, $SALV_o > SALV_b$). For example, Lewellen et al. [13] state: "The lessor may be more active or skillful in dealing in the associated second-hand asset market; his specialized knowledge may give him an edge." Three potential sources of this comparative advantage are: (1) the reduction in search, information, and transaction costs associated with the lessor's provision of a centralized marketplace for the asset (see Benston and Smith [3], p. 216]); (2) the reduction in service costs from reusing components of previously leased machines in the repair and maintenance of current machines; and (3) the reduction in production costs from reusing components of previously leased machines in the manufacture of new machines. (Note that the tax code limits the fraction of used parts that can be used in this manner if the new machine is to qualify for the Investment Tax Credit.) Yet we believe that this comparative advantage of lessor over user is, by itself, insufficient to provide an incentive to lease. In order to favor leasing, the cost reduction must not be available to buyers on similar terms. But manufacturers who take used assets in trade, offer purchasers access to this comparative advantage, thus eliminating a differential advantage to leasing.

III. Provisions in Lease Contracts

A. *Bonding Use and Maintenance*

Deposits and Penalty Clauses. Deposits and penalty clauses are frequently employed in lease contracts. The primary role of these provisions is to bond the lessee to compensate the lessor if the leased asset is either not returned on time or returned in an abused condition. If it is relatively inexpensive to detect undermaintenance or abuse which affects the value of the leased asset, we expect to observe bonding provisions in lease contracts. Conversely, if it is relatively expensive to detect undermaintenance or abuse, increased use of alternative methods for controlling this agency problem should be observed. For a particular asset, the more expensive the control of this agency problem, the more likely is the asset to be purchased. And if the asset is leased, the higher the fraction of the purchase price will be the lease rate (e.g., chain saw or ski rentals).

We do not expect the size of the deposit to be related to the market value of the asset, but rather to the forecasted distribution of damages to the asset over the period of the lease. If the damage can exceed this deposit amount, and if the lessor has no other recourse, the lease payment will implicitly include an insurance premium for a policy with a deductible equal to the amount of deposit.

Deposits appear to be used in conjunction with, rather than as alternatives to, penalty clauses in lease contracts. Deposits are, in fact, at one end of the spectrum of mechanisms that can bond the lessee to the liability established by a penalty clause. If it is relatively costly to obtain information about the lessee, and relatively expensive to enforce the penalty clause, we expect a bond to be posted when the asset is leased. Conversely, if it is relatively inexpensive to obtain information about the lessee and also relatively inexpensive to enforce the penalty clause, bonding through explicit deposits will be less frequently employed.

Restrictions on Subleasing and Use. A restriction on subleasing limits the ability of the lessee to transfer the right to use the asset to a third party. We expect to observe such restrictions in either of two situations: first, if the lessor has market power and uses leases to price-discriminate among customers; second, if the salvage value of the asset is sensitive to use and maintenance decisions, forecasted abuse differs among classes of potential lessees, and the characteristics of the actual lessee do not signal high abuse. Clauses can be included that limit the range of applications in which the asset can be employed. We expect to observe these restrictions when the salvage value of the asset depends on the activity in which the asset is used, and such differential use can either be monitored during the period of the lease or detected at its termination. These restrictions allow more effective bonding of a higher forecasted terminal value, resulting in a lower lease payment.

Service Versus Net Leases. In a net lease the lessee has the responsibility to maintain the asset. However, if the terminal value of an asset is affected by maintenance during the lease, the lessee has an incentive to undermaintain the asset. In a service lease, the lessor provides the maintenance. By bundling a maintenance contract and a lease contract, a service lease provides an effective bond that maintenance will be performed on an asset in a predictable manner. Thus, when an asset's value at the end of the lease is sensitive to maintenance decisions over the life of the lease, a service lease can reduce the costs of the conflict over maintenance policy. If deviations from an optimal maintenance program are easy to detect, other contractual provisions such as monitoring of user-provided maintenance and deposits can provide effective controls of the problem. But in the case of assets for which it is costly to monitor the provision of maintenance or costly to detect undermaintenance, service leases are especially valuable.

One cost associated with a service lease results from the fact that since maintenance expenditures are fixed in advance, the problem of asset abuse by the lessee is exacerbated. However, if the abuse is inexpensive to detect, service leases will be used which include penalty clauses controlling abuse.

If the lessor has a comparative advantage in disposing of the asset, then there is an additional incentive to negotiate a service lease: it lowers the information costs to the secondary market. A related but different argument is that service leases are observed because the lessor has a comparative advantage in maintaining the asset. However, since a maintenance contract can be provided separately, we do not believe such a comparative advantage is sufficient to explain service leases. As long as the demands for the two components are perfectly complimentary, the lessor cannot increase profits by bundling (see McGee and Bassett [17]). However, a small potential benefit would exist if out-of-pocket contracting costs were lower for a service lease than a separate net lease and maintenance contract.

As noted in Table I, lessor and lessee tax liabilities are affected by the allocation of maintenance expenditures. Yet as long as nontax cash flows are equal, there is no advantage to the allocation of maintenance expenditures even if the lessor and lessee face different effective marginal tax rates. Shifting maintenance responsibility from lessee (net lease) to lessor (service lease) will be accompanied by an increase in the present value of lease payments by the expected maintenance expenses. Since lease payments and maintenance expenditures by the lessee receive the same tax treatment, there is no tax incentive in the allocation. Thus taxes cannot explain the choice between service and net leases.

B. Capital Versus Operating Leases

For accounting purposes the definitions of operating and capital leases are set out in paragraphs 6 and 7 of the Financial Accounting Standards Board Standard No. 13. "Accounting for Leases," November 1976. Since 1976, only operating leases are accounted for as true leases; capital leases must be capitalized into the lessor's and lessee's balance sheets. Since capital leases are accounted for as if they were sales, incentives associated with bond contracts and executive compensation contracts discused in Section II. A. cannot explain the choice of capital leases.

While most leases are written to avoid the IRS "constructive sale" rule, certain leases have been structured to take advantage of this ruling. The removal of exchange controls by Britain in the early 1980's led to substantially increased lease activity by British banks to American companies. These leases are structured so that, under British tax law, the transaction is a lease and therefore the British bank can depreciate the asset, while under American tax law, the transaction is a constructive sale and therefore the American company can also depreciate the asset.

C. Metering and Tie-In Sales

Metering is a contractual provision that ties lease payments to some measure of the intensity of the asset's use. For example, automobile lease payments can be linked to elapsed mileage, computers to CPU cycles, copy machines to copies, and shopping center space to sales. A tie-in sale is the contractual requirement to use a specified nondurable input in the operation of the leased asset. For example, IBM required IBM cards to be used with IBM tabulating machines.

Metering and Price Discrimination. Burstein [6] argues that metering provisions and tie-in sales in leases provide opportunities for price discrimination. If lessees with different use intensities also have different demand elasticities, metering allows the firm to extract more rents. For example, American Can Company only leased their can-closing machines and required lessees to use their tin cans. The Court ruled that this practice was an illegal tying arrangement, and that the refusal to sell their products precluded competition by third-party lessors.

Metering and Asset Abuse. If it is relatively inexpensive to measure the intensity of use of the asset, metering can be effective in controlling use intensity. Without metering, the lessor must forecast the intensity of asset usage and charge accordingly. This leads to moral hazard and adverse selection problems. With metering, the lessor need only set a schedule of lease payments as a function of measured usage. This should more closely approximate marginal cost pricing of the leased asset. Thus, in a net lease, metering links lease payments more closely to changes in terminal value.

If alternate supplier's inputs are of lower quality and impose more rapid depreciation on the leased machine, a tie-in sale can control asset abuse. Without the tied sale, the lessor would forecast use of the less expensive input, lower salvage value, and set a higher lease rate. In this case, the tie-in sale allows the lessee to bond input quality.

Metering and Bonding. We expect to observe greater use of metering in service leases than in net leases, because metering also links lease payments more closely to expected maintenance expenditures. (Note that metering provisions are frequently used in pure maintenance contracts offered by manufacturers.) Moreover, this payment structure in service leases also allows the lessor to bond his obligation to provide timely maintenance services. For example, the lease payment on a copier is a function of the number of copies made, and thus the lessor's revenue is automatically lower if the machine is inoperative. Thus, we expect to observe service leases with metering provisions for assets impounding new technologies, a case where this incentive is especially important because of significant user uncertainty as to whether or not the asset will function.

A related incentive for metering occurs if the lessor owns and maintains common property such as malls parking facilities in the case of a shopping center. In this case, metering allows the lessor to bond the quality of the common property. Shopping center leases typically specify lease payments as a function of total revenues. Thus the lessor's receipts are reduced if the quality of maintenance of the common property (e.g., snow and litter removal or lighting in parking areas) is reduced. Moreover, since the demands facing specific shops tend to be interrelated, lease payments dependent on total revenues provide the lessor/developer with stronger incentives to coordinate the range of shops over the life of a shopping center to maximize joint profitability.

Metering and Risk Reduction. Liebowitz [14] argues that metering and tie-in sales reduce the volatility of the lessee's net cash flows by charging more when asset use is high and less when it is low. This hedging explanation is more forceful when the lessee is an individual, a partnership or a small, closely held corporation. Also, concavities in the tax function imply that the after-tax value of the firm is concave, and reduction in cash-flow volatility increases the expected after-tax value of the firm (see Smith/Stulz [24]). The hedging explanation seems more credible the higher the fraction of the lessee's total cash flows related to the use of the leased asset.

D. Options

Options to Extend and Options to Purchase. If the term of a noncancellable (financial) lease could be written to match the expected useful life of the asset, then the problem of undermaintenance and abuse would be largely controlled. While this approach has been disallowed by the Internal Revenue Service (which considers such a contract to be a "constructive sale"), we observe several provisions in leases which appear to be consistent with this principle. One approach is to set the term of the lease as long as possible under IRS guidelines (i.e., not exceeding 75 percent of the asset's estimated economic life).

A provision often observed in lease contracts specifies the conditions under which a lessee may either extend the life of the lease or purchase the leased assets. (McConnell and Schallheim [16] employ a compound option framework to value these options, treating the asset's expected rate of economic depreciation as an exogenous variable.) We expect these options to be used when the asset's terminal value is affected by use or maintenance decisions. Since the value of the option is a positive function of this terminal value, these options reduce the perverse use and maintenance incentives for the lessee.

Options to purchase or to extend the lease can also be effective in reducing the costs of the bilateral monopoly created by leases of firm-specific assets. If the lease contract contains options for the lessee to extend the lease or purchase the asset, then the lease payment for the initial lease period can be set high enough for the lessor to recover the extra investment required to "specialize" the leased asset, and the lessee is protected by being given an option to renew the lease, or purchase the asset, at a favorable price.

Cancellation and Noncancellation Clauses. A cancellation provision in a lease contract allows the lessee to terminate the contract prematurely. Examples of situations where the lessee might exercise the option are where the lessee's demand for the asset declines if the specific asset leased is below expected quality or if the leased asset becomes technologically obsolete. Therefore, the value of the cancellaiton option to the lessee is a positive function of uncertainty of the use-value of the asset. If the lessor has a comparative advantage in bearing these risks, we would expect contracts to include a cancellation option. Conditions under which this comparative advantage is likely to exist are: when demands for the asset are not perfectly positively correlated across lessees, where for a manufacturer lessor the leased assets impound new technology, or where the manufacturer lessor can affect the rate of technological change.

While the cancellation options focused on thus far are provided to the lessee, some lease contracts provide cancellation options to the lessor. One example is the lease of accommodations to "essential farm workers" throughout Europe. Contracts on these "tied cottages" often contain a clause which cancels the lease if labor is withheld.

If the cash flows from the use of a leased asset decline significantly over the life of the lease and the contract specifies level lease payments, we expect to observe a financial (noncancellable) lease. This provision precludes the lessee from cancelling the lease as soon as the asset's cash flow falls below the contracted lease payment. An alternative solution to this problem involves a schedule in which the lease payments decline over time.

Noncancellation clauses can also be an effective answer to abuse and under-maintenance problems. In this context, Brealey and Myers [4] note that most noncancellable leases are net leases. Our analysis suggests that noncancellation clauses will often be used in long-term net leases of assets where cash flows (and terminal values) are affected by use and maintenance decisions.

IV. Conclusions

The coexistence of both leased and purchased assets suggests that the net benefits of leasing are uniformly neither positive nor negative. The concentration of leases in certain industries and for certain assets implies that there are predictable cross-sectional differences in the net benefits of leasing. Yet most of the finance literature on leasing assumes that the real operating cash flows associated with leasing or owning are invariant to the financial contract chosen and focuses primarily on tax-related incentives to lease or buy. Our analysis suggests that taxes are important in determining the identity of lessor and lessee, but are less important in identifying specific assets to be leased. Finally, tax provisions offer little explanation for the choice of specific provisions in lease contracts such as metering, service provisions, or limitations on use.

We identify eight nontax incentives to lease or buy. Our analysis implies that leasing is more likely: (1) if the value of the asset is less sensitive to use and maintenance decisions; (2) if the asset is not specialized to the firm; (3) if the expected period of use is short relative to the useful life of the asset; (4) if corporate bond contracts contain specific financial policy covenants; (5) if man-agement compensation contracts contain provisions specifying payoffs as a function of the return on invested capital; (6) if the firm is closely held so that risk reduction is important; (7) if the lessor has market power; and (8) if the lessor has a comparative advantage in asset disposal. We also show how these incentives explain the use of standard contractual provisions such as maintenance clauses, deposits, penalty clauses, restrictions on use, options to extend, and metering.

We believe that our analysis also helps explain the results of studies such as Ang/Peterson [2] which examine trade-offs between leasing and debt. They find that the use of leases and debt are complimentary: firms which issue more debt tend to engage in more leasing. This result should not be surprising. Although leasing and debt are substitutes for a given firm, looking across firms, character-istics of firms' investment opportunity sets which provide high debt capacity also tend to provide more profitable leasing opportunities. In order to measure the extent of substitutability between leases and debt, the differences in the charac-teristics of the specific assets used by different firms must be controlled.

REFERENCES

1. Armen A. Alchian and Harold Demsetz. "Production, Information Costs, and Economic Organization." *American Economic Review* 62 (December 1972), 777–95.
2. James Ang and Pamela Peterson. "The Leasing Puzzle." *Journal of Finance* 39 (September 1984), 1055–65.
3. George Benston and Clifford Smith, "A Transactions Cost Approach to the Theory of Financial Intermediation." *Journal of Finance* 31 (May 1976), 215–31.
4. Richard Brealey and C. M. Young. "Debt, Taxes, and Leasing—A Note." *Journal of Finance* 35 (December 1980), 1245–50.
5. Richard Brealey and Stewart Myers. *Principles of Corporate Finance* New York: McGraw-Hill, 1984, 541–65.
6. M. L. Burstein. "The Economics of Tie-In Sales." *Review of Economics and Statistics* 42 (February 1960), 68–73.
7. Ronald Coase. "Durability and Monopoly." *Journal of Law and Economics* 15 (April 1972), 143–49.
8. Harry DeAngelo and Ronald Masulis. "Optimal Capital Structure Under Corporate and Personal Taxation." *Journal of Financial Economics* 8 (March 1980), 3–29.
9. Eugene F. Fama and Michael C. Jensen. "Agency Problems and Residual Claims." *Journal of Law and Economics* 26 (June 1983), 327–49.
10. David Flath. "The Economics of Short-Term Leasing." *Economic Inquiry* 18 (April 1980), 247–59.
11. Julian Franks and Stewart D. Hodges. "Valuation of Financial Lease Contracts: A Note." *Journal of Finance* 33 (May 1978), 657–69.
12. Benjamin Klein, Robert Crawford, and Armen A. Alchian. "Vertical Integration, Appropriable Rents and the Competitive Contracting Process." *Journal of Law and Economics* 21 (October 1978), 297–326.
13. Wilbur Lewellen, Michael Long, and John McConnell. "Asset Leasing in Competitive Capital Markets." *Journal of Finance* 31 (June 1976), 787–98.
14. Stanley J. Liebowitz. "Tie-In Sales and Price Discrimination." *Economic Inquiry* 21 (July 1983), 387–99.
15. David Mayers and Clifford Smith. "On the Corporate Demand for Insurance." *Journal of Business* 55 (April 1982), 281–96.
16. John J. McConnell and James S. Schallheim. "Valuation of Asset Leasing Contracts." *Journal of Financial Economics* 12 (August 1983), 237–61.
17. John S. McGee and Lowell R. Bassett. "Vertical Integration Revisited." *Journal of Law and Economics* 19 (April 1976), 17–38.
18. Merton Miller. "Debt and Taxes." *Journal of Finance* 32 (May 1977), 261–76.
19. ———— and Charles Upton. "Leasing, Buying, and the Cost of Capital Services." *Journal of Finance* 31 (June 1976), 761–86.
20. Franco Modigliani and Merton Miller. "The Cost of Capital, Corporation Finance and the Theory of Investment." *American Economic Review* 48 (June 1958), 261–97.
21. Stewart Myers, David Dill, and Alberto Bautista. "Valuation of Financial Lease Contract." *Journal of Finance* 31 (June 1976), 799–820.
22. Clifford Smith and Jerold Warner. "On Financial Contracting: An Analysis of Bond Covenants." *Journal of Financial Economics* 7 (June 1979), 117–61.
23. Clifford Smith and Ross Watts. "Incentive and Tax Effects of U.S. Executive Compensation Plans." *Australian Journal of Management* 7 (December 1982), 139–57.
24. Clifford Smith and René Stulz. "Determinants of Firm's Hedging Policies." Unpublished manuscript, University of Rochester, 1984.
25. René M. Stulz and Herb Johnson. "An Analysis of Secured Debt." *Journal of Financial Economics*, forthcoming, 1985.

THE DETERMINANTS OF YIELDS ON FINANCIAL
LEASING CONTRACTS*

James S. SCHALLHEIM and Ramon E. JOHNSON

University of Utah, Salt Lake City, UT 84112, USA

Ronald C. LEASE

Tulane University, New Orleans, LA 70118-5669, USA

John J. McCONNELL

Purdue University, West Lafayette, IN 47907, USA

Received June 1985, final version received November 1986

This study tests hypotheses about the valuation of leasing contracts. We examine the determinants of the yields of a relatively large, reasonably heterogeneous, and nationally representative sample of financial leases. We find lease yields to be significantly related to treasury bond yields and our proxies for the systematic risk of the leased asset's residual value and the transaction and information costs associated with the lease. There is also some evidence of a relationship between lease yields and the default-risk of the lessee.

1. Introduction

Theoretical developments in the valuation of corporate leasing contracts have proceeded at a more rapid rate than their empirical counterparts. The differential pace in the evolution of theory and evidence is readily explained by the lack of an easily accessible, large-scale data base containing the terms of corporate leasing arrangements. As a consequence, those few empirical studies that have been undertaken tend to be limited in their generality by the

*We are grateful for the cooperation of the American Association of Equipment Lessors, Western Association of Equipment Lessors, Kathy Scharf, and eight leasing companies that provided the data used in this study. Valuable comments on earlier drafts were provided by Sanjai Bhagat, James Brickley, and Rene Stulz. More recently, the paper has benefited from comments by Mark Bayless, Han Kim, Susan Chaplinsky, David Diltz, and Clifford Smith (the editor), and from presentations at Ohio State University, University of Michigan, University of Oklahoma, Tulane University, University of Iowa, University of Wisconsin, and Southern Methodist University. Lisa Borstadt and Kiyoshi Kato provided important assistance in data collection. John McConnell is grateful for financial support received from Eli Lilly and Company.

Journal of Financial Economics 19 (1987) 45–67. © North-Holland Publishing Company.

relatively small and/or regionally concentrated samples analyzed.[1] In addition, these initial empirical studies have advanced knowledge by reporting the descriptive characteristics of their samples rather than by examining the consistency between data and theory. While these studies have increased our understanding of the leasing market, they do not test specific hypotheses about the valuation of corporate leasing contracts.

In this paper we expand on earlier investigations of the terms of leasing contracts by analyzing the determinants of the yields of a relatively large, reasonably heterogeneous, and nationally representative sample of financial leases. We also test specific hypotheses about the valuation of leasing contracts.

Our investigation begins within the context of the theoretical models of Miller and Upton (1976) and McConnell and Schallheim (1983). Using the Sharpe–Lintner single-period capital asset pricing model, Miller and Upton (1976) demonstrate that the yield of a single-period lease is related positively to the current risk-free rate of return and negatively to the covariance between the market rate of return and the leased asset's rate of economic depreciation. McConnell and Schallheim (1983) combine the single-period results of Miller and Upton with the multi-period valuation techniques of Rubinstein (1976) and Geske (1977) to develop a multi-period model for the valuation of financial leases. Their analysis indicates that the equilibrium yield of a financial lease is related positively to the multi-period risk-free rate of interest and related negatively to the discounted value of the covariance between a 'market factor' and the logarithm of (one-minus) the leased asset's rate of economic depreciation. In our empirical analysis, the yields on financial leasing contracts are consistent with the predictions of the theoretical models of Miller and Upton and McConnell and Schallheim.

Miller and Upton and McConnell and Schallheim conduct their analyses within the confines of a perfect capital market setting in which leases are default-free. Once the assumptions of a perfect capital market and default-free leases are relaxed, the role of transaction costs, information/search costs, and default risk must be considered. As a consequence, we enter other possible explanatory variables iteratively into the regression analysis. Our proxies for transaction and information/search costs are statistically significant, whereas the results using our proxies for default risk are mixed. In addition, our analysis produces several interesting empirical by-products that support and complement earlier descriptive studies of the leasing market.

The paper is organized as follows. In sections 2 and 3 we recapitulate the essentials of the theoretical analysis of Miller and Upton and McConnell and

---

[1] The only two studies of lease yields that we know of are Sorenson and Johnson (1977) and Crawford, Harper and McConnell (1981). Both provide descriptive statistics for their samples and regress the lease yields against a number of independent variables.

Schallheim and spell out hypotheses to be tested. The data-collection procedure and the sample are described in section 4. Section 5 reports the results of our regression analysis. In the final section we summarize the results and provide some concluding remarks.

2. A model of financial lease valuation

In this paper we are concerned with the valuation of financial leasing contracts. Under a financial lease, the lessee is obligated to make all rental payments agreed upon under the terms of the lease. At the maturity date of the lease, the residual value of the leased asset reverts to the lessor, who can release or sell the asset to a third party, or, perhaps, use the asset internally. In a single-period capital asset pricing model framework, Miller and Upton (1976) demonstrate that the equilibrium rental payment on a single-period financial lease can be expressed as

$$L_{it} = \left[R_f - \beta_{it} \left[\overline{R}_m - R_f \right] + \overline{d}_{it} \right] A_{it},$$ (1)

where L_{it} is the equilibrium rental payment for the use of asset i over t; A_{it} is the beginning-of-period market value of asset i; R_f is the current risk-free rate of interest; $\overline{R}_m$ is the expected rate of return on the market portfolio; $\overline{d}_{it}$ is the expected rate of economic depreciation of asset i during period t; and $\beta_{it} = \mathrm{cov}(\tilde{d}_{it}, \tilde{R}_{mt})/\mathrm{var}(\tilde{R}_{mt})$ is the standard capital asset pricing measure of the relative non-diversifiable risk of asset i in period t. $\mathrm{Cov}(\tilde{d}_{it}, \tilde{R}_{mt})$ is the covariance between the asset's rate of economic depreciation and the market return in period t and $\mathrm{var}(\tilde{R}_{mt})$ is the variance of the market return in period t.

Thus, the equilibrium rental must compensate the owner of the asset (i.e., the lessor) for (1) the capital invested in the asset at the risk-free rate $(R_f \cdot A_{it})$, (2) the expected loss of capital due to expected depreciation $(\overline{d}_{it} \cdot A_{it})$, and (3) the non-diversifiable risk borne. Because the rental payment itself is risk-free, the risk borne by the lessor is the risk associated with the uncertain end-of-period residual value of the asset. This risk is captured by the term $-\beta_{it}[\overline{R}_m - R_f]A_{it}$. (The negative sign of β_{it} results because the change in asset value is measured as capital depreciation rather than capital appreciation.)

When (1) is converted to yield form, it is equivalent to the standard capital asset pricing model (CAPM) relationship

$$\overline{y}_{it} = R_f - \beta_{it} \left[\overline{R}_m - R_f \right].$$ (2)

The expected yield on the lease, $\overline{y}_{it}$, is a positive function of the current single period risk-free rate of interest and a negative function of the leased asset's non-diversifiable residual-value risk.

McConnell and Schallheim (1983) employ Rubinstein's technique for valuing risky cash flows to extend the Miller and Upton analysis to a multi-period framework. In this framework, the equilibrium yield of an N-period financial lease again is a function of the multi-period risk-free rate of interest and the non-diversifiable end-of-lease risk associated with the residual value of the asset. Because the lease is assumed to be default-free, however, only the discounted value of residual-value risk is relevant to the determination of the rental payment. To illustrate, the equilibrium condition for a multi-period non-cancellable financial lease can be written as

$$A_{i0} = \sum_{t=0}^{N-1} \frac{L_{it}}{(1 + R_f)^t} + S_{i0}^N, \tag{3}$$

where S_{i0}^N is the current market value of the residual value of the leased asset at the maturity date of the lease (i.e., at time N). From McConnell and Schallheim, the residual-value term can be rewritten as

$$S_{i0}^N = \frac{\lambda_i^N A_{i0}}{(1 + R_f)^N}, \tag{4}$$

where $\lambda_i = (1 - \bar{d}_i)e^{\text{cov}(l, y)}$, $\bar{d}_i$ is the expected rate of economic depreciation of leased asset i, and $\text{cov}(l, y)$ is the covariance between the log of one minus the random rate of economic depreciation of the asset l and a random 'market factor' y.[2] In this analysis, the risk-free rate, the expected rate of economic depreciation, and the covariance term are assumed to be constant over time, so the time subscript can be omitted. Thus, as in the single-period case, risk enters into the determination of the equilibrium rental rate of a financial lease only because the end-of-lease residual value of the asset is uncertain. Furthermore, only the non-diversifiable risk associated with the asset's residual value is relevant to the determination of the rental payments on the lease. However, because the lessor bears the residual-value risk only at the termination of the lease, only the discounted value of residual-value risk is relevant to the determination of the rental payment L_i.

To calculate the yield of a multi-period lease, (3) can be written as

$$A_{i0} = \sum_{t=0}^{N-1} \frac{L_i}{(1 + y)^t} + \frac{\bar{S}^N}{(1 + y)^N}, \tag{5}$$

---

[2] The term $\text{cov}(l, y)$ can be interpreted as $\text{cov}(l, y) \doteq \text{cov}(-\tilde{d}_i, -\tilde{R}_m) = \text{cov}(\tilde{a}_i, -\tilde{R}_m) = -\text{cov}(\tilde{a}_i, \tilde{R}_m)$, which is approximately equal to the negative of the traditional measure of an asset's systematic risk ($\tilde{a}$ represents random 'appreciation').

and solved iteratively for y, where $\bar{S}^N$ is the expected residual value of the leased asset at time N and the lease payment L_i is constant across time. Because L_i is a positive function of R_f, the yield on the lease is also a positive function of R_f. Furthermore, because L_i is a negative function of covariance risk, y is also a negative function of covariance risk. However, this term could have been stated in terms of capital appreciation, in which case L_i would be a positive function of non-diversifiable residual-value risk.

Our primary objective is to test the hypothesis of Miller and Upton and McConnell and Schallheim that yields of financial leases are a function of the risk-free interest rate and the discounted value of the covariance risk of the asset's residual value. However, other hypotheses are tested as well.

3. Other hypotheses

Two important assumptions underlie the Miller and Upton and McConnell and Schallheim analyses. The first is that capital markets are perfect. The second is that financial leases are default-free. Once these assumptions are relaxed, the role of transaction costs, information asymmetries, and default risk must be considered.

In a lease, transaction costs are the per-unit costs of writing the contract, specifying the security agreement, identifying the asset, negotiating the terms of the lease, and so forth. Most of these costs are fixed and independent of the characteristics of the lessee, the lessor, and the leased asset. Hence, transaction costs decline proportionately with the cost of the asset. These costs are recaptured over time by the lessor through periodic (level) rental payments. Thus, we hypothesize that lease yields are an inverse function of the value of the leased asset. To illustrate, assume a perpetual lease so that

$$y = \frac{L_i}{A_{i0}} \tag{6}$$

is the lease's yield in the absence of transaction costs. With a fixed transaction cost that is recaptured through periodic (level) rental payments over the life of the lease,

$$y = \frac{L_i^*}{A_{i0}} = \frac{L_i + c}{A_{i0}} = \frac{L_i}{A_{i0}} + \frac{c}{A_{i0}}, \tag{7}$$

where L_i^* is total periodic lease payment and c is the (unobservable) transaction cost recovered per period in the rental payment. L_i increases proportionately as A_{i0} increases, so L_i/A_{i0} remains constant. However, because c is fixed, c/A_{i0} declines as A_{i0} increases and, therefore, y declines as A_{i0} increases. Thus, we hypothesize that the lease yield is inversely related to the cost of the leased asset. Furthermore, because c/A_{i0} approaches zero as A_{i0} becomes large, for leases on higher-priced assets, transaction costs will be a less significant component of the lease yield, and, for leases on lower-priced assets, transaction costs will be a more significant component of the yield.

When the potential for default is admitted, information asymmetries also are relevant. When the lessor has perfect information about the financial condition of the lessee, lease yields accurately reflect lessees' default potential and lease yields will be related negatively to the lessee's financial condition. In the absence of perfect information, the lease yield will be a negative function of the lessee's financial condition and it also will be related negatively to the quality of information about the lessee. In the spirit of Akerlof (1970), in the absence of reliable information, the lessor will assume the worst and the lease yield will be commensurately high. Thus, we hypothesize that lease yields will be related negatively to the financial condition of the lessee and to the quality of information about the lessee.

In our empirical analysis, we do not have a precise measure of information quality. However, assuming that the 'size' of the firm is a reasonable proxy for 'prominence', we employ the book value of the lessee's assets as a proxy for the availability of reliable information. Thus, we conjecture that lease yields will be related inversely to the book value of the lessee's assets.

We also do not have an accurate measure of the lessee's financial condition. However, as a proxy for this information, we employ several measures of default risk that prior literature reports to have predictive power in identifying corporate bankruptcies.

4. Sampling procedure and data description

4.1. Sampling procedure

To gather data for this study we accessed the files of seven non-bank leasing companies and one bank-owned leasing company. Four of the companies have their headquarters in the Mountain West, two are located in the Midwest, one is located in the Southwest, and one is on the West Coast. These eight firms allowed their files to be inspected under the condition that their customers not be identified or contacted and that their names not be revealed. Both currently open (i.e., active) and closed (i.e., completed) leases were accessed.

A random sample of 453 contracts was drawn for evaluation. Because of certain data requirements, only 363 of these contracts are usable in our statistical analyses.[3] Of the 363 usable leases, 223 were open and 140 were closed contracts as of September 1982. All 363 usable leases are financial leases.

The information recorded for each lease includes the origination date of the contract, the geographic location of the lessee, the type and cost of the leased asset, the type and maturity of the lease, the date the lessor paid for the asset, the date and amount of any lease prepayments, the due dates and amounts of the periodic rental payments, the amount of any broker commissions paid to originate the lease, the residual value of the asset (as estimated by the lessor), and an indication as to whether the investment tax credit (*ITC*) was taken by the lessor or passed to the lessee. In addition, in those cases in which reliable financial information is available, various accounting data are taken from the lessee's application. Such data are available in reliable form for 82 of the 363 lease applications.

4.2. Data description

Data describing the sample are displayed in table 1. Panel A is a frequency distribution of the leases according to their contract initiation dates. The oldest lease was written in January 1973 and the most recent lease was written in June 1982. The lessees are located in at least 43 different states (for 41 leases, the state in which the lessee is located could not be identified). In each contract, the lessee is responsible for selection, acquisition, and maintenance of the asset and for paying associated property taxes and insurance premiums. All the leases are non-cancellable. At the maturity date of the lease, the residual value of the asset reverts to the lessor. If the lessee defaults, the lessor can repossess the asset, declare the remaining payments due and payable, and make claims for any deficiencies.

Frequency distributions of the leases categorized according to the cost of the leased asset and the term-to-maturity of the contract are contained in panels B and C, respectively. A frequency distribution of leases according to the general type of asset is contained in panel D. The assets are placed in 18 general categories. Panel E is a frequency distribution of the book values of the assets of the 258 lessee firms for which this statistic is available.

4.3. Covariance risk

According to the Miller and Upton and McConnell and Schallheim analyses, lease yields are a function of the covariance risk between the leased asset's

---

[3] Of the 453 contracts, 55 are deleted because we can not identify the industry type of the leased asset and 35 are deleted because they are not financial leases. Of the 35 that are not financial leases, 21 are conditional sales contracts.

Table 1

Descriptive statistics characterizing the sample of 363 financial leasing contracts originated over the period 1973–1982.

A. Frequency distribution by origination date of the lease contract

Year of origination	Number of leases	Percent of total
1973	9	2.5
1974	17	4.7
1975	7	1.9
1976	11	3.0
1977	46	12.7
1978	28	7.7
1979	65	17.9
1980	65	17.9
1981	82	22.6
1982	33	9.1

B. Frequency distribution by cost of leased asset

Cost of asset	Number of leases	Percent of total
$10,000 or Less	134	36.9
$10,001 to $50,000	109	30.0
$50,001 to $100,000	25	6.9
$100,001 to $250,000	35	9.7
$250,001 to $500,000	18	4.9
Over $500,000	42	11.6

Maximum = $63,000,000 Mean = $636,690
Minimum = $1,000 Median = $19,396

C. Frequency distribution by term-to-maturity of the lease

Term-to-maturity (in months)	Number of leases	Percent of total
24 or fewer	9	2.5
25 to 36	89	24.5
37 to 48	28	7.7
49 to 60	151	41.6
61 to 72	8	2.2
73 to 84	42	11.6
85 to 96	18	4.9
97 to 108	1	0.3
109 to 120	10	2.8
Over 120	7	1.9

Maximum = 300 months Mean = 61.3 months
Minimum = 11 months Median = 60 months

D. Frequency distribution by type of leased asset

Type of asset	Number of leases	Percent of total
Aircraft	10	2.8
Auto repair equipment	12	3.3
Computers and processors	43	11.8
Construction equipment	35	9.6
Copy machines	30	8.3
Farm machinery	17	4.7
Food preparation equipment	16	4.4

Table 1 (continued)

Industrial laundry machines	8	2.2
Machine tools	28	7.7
Marine equipment	4	1.1
Medical equipment	19	5.2
Misc. electronic equipment	21	5.8
Motel & hotel furnishings	6	1.7
Office equipment	15	4.1
Office furniture	23	6.3
Railroad rolling stock	6	1.6
Telephone systems	20	5.5
Trucks and trailers	50	13.8

E. Frequency distribution by book value of the assets of the lessee firm for 258 firms for which data are available

Book value of lessee's assets	Number of leases	Percent of total
$250,000 or less	76	29.5
$250,001 to $500,000	36	13.9
$500,001 to $1,000,000	24	9.3
$1,000,001 to $2,000,000	25	9.7
$2,000,001 to $5,000,000	24	9.3
$5,000,001 to $10,000,000	26	10.1
10,000,001 to $25,000,000	11	4.2
$25,000,001 to $100,000,000	17	6.6
Over $100,000,000	19	7.4

Maximum = $8,972,000,000   Mean = $135,800,000
Minimum = $5,000   Median = $845,000

F. Frequency distribution by leased asset's unlevered beta estimated with manufacturer firms

Asset beta	Number of leases	Percent of total
0.500 or less	48	13.2
0.501 to 0.600	61	16.8
0.601 to 0.700	61	16.8
0.701 to 0.800	60	16.5
0.801 to 0.900	69	19.0
0.901 to 1.000	29	8.0
1.001 to 1.100	23	6.3
1.101 to 1.200	7	1.9
1.201 to 1.300	5	1.4

residual value and a market factor. If the rate of change in the asset's market value is expressed in terms of the rate of capital appreciation, the relationship between residual-value covariance risk and lease yield is positive. Ideally, this measure of market-value risk would be estimated with a time series of market prices of the leased asset. Unfortunately, consistent time series data on these asset prices are not available. As a consequence, in this study, two proxies for systematic residual-value risk are employed.

The first proxy (and the one on which we rely most heavily) uses a representative sample of firms whose primary (or exclusive) activity is manufacturing assets of the same general type as the leased asset. For example, for leases covering construction equipment, the representative sample includes American Hoist, Caterpillar Tractor, Clark Equipment, and Harnischfeger. The use of data from firms manufacturing the asset to estimate systematic risk assumes that the risk of the asset producer is closely linked with the risk of the asset being produced.[4]

For each representative firm, a market model beta is estimated as of the origination date of the corresponding lease using 60 previous monthly stock market returns taken from the Center for Research in Security Prices (CRSP) returns file. The value-weighted market index from the CRSP file is used to represent the market return. The beta for each firm is then adjusted according to the procedure described by Hamada (1969) to remove the effect of financial leverage. Specifically, each levered beta is converted to an unlevered beta by dividing by one plus the debt/equity ratio as reported by *Value Line* for the year-end prior to the origination date of the relevant lease. Finally, for each asset in the sample, these unlevered betas are averaged across producer firms to obtain an estimate of the leased asset's systematic residual-value risk. This procedure yields one beta estimate for each lease in the sample. A frequency distribution of the unlevered betas is given in panel F of table 1.[5]

The second proxy measure of residual value covariance risk involves the estimation of a market model beta for a portfolio of asset-user firms whose primary line of business relies heavily on the use of a particular category of leased assets. The procedure involved in estimating this proxy is identical to the procedure used to estimate the first proxy, with the only difference being the representative firms employed. Further discussion of this proxy variable is contained in section 5.2.

4.4. The calculation of lease yields and the role of taxes

In our statistical analysis, the dependent variable is the lease yield. In a competitive leasing market, the relevant yield to the lessor firm is the after-tax yield that is comparable to after-tax yields on alternative investment opportunities. A pragmatic argument against the use of after-tax yields is that it is not possible to estimate accurately the marginal tax rates of either lessee or lessor

---

[4]A list of the representative firms in each category is available from the authors upon request.

[5]We recognize that our unlevered beta estimates are imperfect proxies for the asset's residual-value systematic risk. For example, we have not adjusted the unlevered beta for corporate taxes. We have not done so for two reasons. First, theoretically, the relationship between beta and taxes is unclear. Second, empirically, we are uncertain as to how to estimate each firm's marginal tax rate. Additionally, we have not adjusted unlevered beta for differing maturities of debt nor have we incorporated the lease liabilities of the representative firms. The imperfect nature of this proxy means that, barring some unknown source of spurious correlation, the tests are biased against rejecting the null hypothesis.

Table 2

Frequency distribution by lease yields for the sample of 363 leases originated over the period 1973–1982 computed according to the following equation:[a]

$$\frac{Cost - ITC}{(1+y)^{t_1}} = \frac{P(1-\tau)+SD}{(1+y)^{t_2}} - \frac{Com(1-\tau)}{(1+y)^{t_3}} + \sum_{x=4}^{np} \frac{L(1-\tau)}{(1+y)^{t_x}} + \sum_{t=q_1}^{q_n} \frac{D_t(\tau)}{(1+y)^{t}} + \frac{RV-SD}{(1+y)^{t_n}}.$$

Before-tax yield			After-tax yield		
Lease yield (% per year)	No. of leases	% of total	Lease yield (% per year)	No. of leases	% of total
9 or less	51	14.0			
9.1 to 12.0	37	10.2	6 or less	9	2.4
12.1 to 15.0	20	5.6	6.1 to 9.0	62	17.1
15.1 to 18.0	41	11.2	9.1 to 12.0	71	19.6
18.1 to 21.0	62	17.1	12.1 to 15.0	75	20.7
21.0 to 24.0	73	20.1	15.1 to 18.0	90	24.8
24.1 to 27.0	50	13.8	18.1 to 21.0	44	12.1
27.1 to 30.0	17	4.7	21.1 to 24.0	8	2.2
30.1 to 33.0	3	0.8	24.1 to 27.0	3	0.8
33.1 to 36.0	2	0.6	27.1 or more	1	0.3
36.1 to 39.0	3	0.8			
39.1 or more	4	1.1			
Minimum = 4.41%	Mean = 18.63%		Minimum = 3.49%	Mean = 13.40%	
Maximum = 45.30%	Median = 19.57%		Maximum = 29.0%	Median = 13.89%	

[a]Terms are defined as:

y: before-or after-tax lease yield,
$Cost$:   original cost of the leased asset,
ITC: investment tax credit if retained by the lessee in the after-tax yield calculations, zero in before-tax yield calculations,
P: prepayments made on the lease,
SD: security deposit on the lease,
Com: brokerage commission paid on the lease,
L: periodic lease payment,
D_t: depreciation on the leased asset in period t,
RV: residual value of the leased asset as estimated by the lessor,
τ: corporate tax rate in after-tax yield calculations, zero in before-tax yield calculations,
$t_1,\ldots,t_n$:   number of days between time zero and the date of the respective cash flow,
$q_1,\ldots,q_n$:   quarterly intervals,
np: the number of lease payments,
t_n: the number of days until the maturity date of the lease.

firms. Because of this limitation, each of the regressions is estimated with both a before- and an after-tax yield. The two yields are computed by solving the following equation iteratively for y:

$$\frac{Cost - ITC}{(1+y)^{t_1}} = \frac{P(1-\tau)+SD}{(1+y)^{t_2}} - \frac{Com(1-\tau)}{(1+y)^{t_3}} + \sum_{x=4}^{np} \frac{L(1-\tau)}{(1+y)^{t_x}}$$

$$+ \sum_{t=q_1}^{q_n} \frac{D_t(\tau)}{(1+y)^{t}} + \frac{RV-SD}{(1+y)^{t_n}}, \tag{8}$$

where *Cost* is the original cost of the leased asset; *ITC* is the investment tax credit if retained by the lessor; *P* is the amount of any prepayments made on the lease; *SD* is any security deposit required on the lease; *Com* is the amount of any broker commission paid on the lease;[6] *L* is the periodic lease payment; D_t is the depreciation on the leased asset in period *t*; *RV* is the residual value of the leased asset as estimated by the lessor; and τ is a corporate tax rate. The time components $t_1, \ldots, t_n$ are the number of days between time zero and the date of the respective cash flow. Time zero is either t_1 or t_2, depending on which cash flow occurs earliest. The time components $q_1, \ldots, q_n$ represent quarterly intervals. The symbol *np* represents the number of lease payments and t_n is the number of days until the maturity date of the lease.

In calculating the before-tax yield, *ITC* and τ are both set equal to zero. In calculating the after-tax yield, *ITC* is set equal to the amount of the *ITC* if the investment tax credit is retained by the lessor and τ is set equal to the maximum corporate tax rate in use when the lease was originated.[7] Frequency distributions of the annualized lease yields are displayed in table 2.

The final data used in the analysis are government bond yields. As of the origination date of the lease, for each lease in the sample, the yield of the treasury bond with a maturity date closest to the maturity date of the lease was collected. This yield is used as a proxy for the risk-free rate of return.

5. Empirical results

5.1. Yield regressions

The results of the regressions are reported in table 3. The two panels of the table contain parallel sets of regressions. Panel A contains the results when the dependent variable is the before-tax yield; panel B contains the results when the dependent variable is the after-tax yield. The statistical results across the two panels are remarkably consistent.

In the first regression reported in each panel, the two independent variables are the yield of the treasury bond of the same maturity as the lease contract and the leased asset's discounted beta estimated with asset-manufacturing-firm stock returns. The discounted beta is calculated by discounting the asset's estimated beta with the yield of the treasury bond of the same maturity as the

---

[6]Six of the lessor firms in the sample recorded some form of brokerage commissions. For those leases on which a brokerage commission was paid, the average commission (i.e., finder's fee) was 1.6% of the cost of the leased asset.

[7]For leases initiated before 1979, the maximum corporate tax rate of 48% is used. For leases originated after January 1, 1979, the maximum corporate rate of 46% is used. In addition, in computing after-tax yields it is necessary to make some assumption about the appropriate depreciation schedule. For leases beginning prior to 1981, double-declining balance depreciation for the life of the lease is used. For leases initiated after January 1, 1981, the accelerated cost recovery system is used. The tax benefits of depreciation are assumed to occur quarterly.

Table 3

Regressions of lease yields on various independent variables for a sample of 363 leases originated over the period 1973–1982; t-statistics in parentheses. [a]

	Intercept	T-bond	D-beta	Var	U-beta	1/Cost	1/BV	Profit	Lev	Liquid	R^2	F	N
A. Regression coefficients with the before-tax lease yield as the dependent variable													
1.	-2.89 (-1.76)	1.19 (11.45)	19.55 (9.05)								0.33	89.6	363
2.	-1.64 (-0.88)	1.16 (10.85)	20.38 (9.10)	-105.79 (-1.40)							0.34	60.5	363
3.	6.13 (3.64)	0.98 (8.67)			2.69 (1.53)						0.19	41.1	363
4.	-0.85 (-0.55)	1.09 (11.09)	14.01 (6.47)			133.51 (7.18)					0.42	85.3	363
5.	-0.96 (-0.54)	1.05 (9.31)	12.60 (5.05)			153.79 (6.05)	77.39 (3.46)				0.46	53.5	258
6.	-1.72 (-0.51)	1.12 (6.28)	14.31 (3.97)			183.09 (4.76)	347.35 (3.22)	1.09 (0.37)	-2.72 (-1.25)	-0.12 (-4.34)	0.65	19.2	82
B. Regression coefficients with the after-tax lease yield as the dependent variable													
1.	2.27 (2.20)	1.17 (9.99)	8.08 (6.45)								0.27	65.3	363
2.	1.92 (1.64)	1.19 (9.81)	7.85 (6.02)	30.44 (0.63)							0.27	43.6	363
3.	5.75 (5.72)	1.07 (8.64)			2.17 (2.03)						0.19	42.4	363
4.	3.24 (3.46)	1.08 (10.14)	5.20 (4.43)			100.99 (9.07)					0.40	80.8	363
5.	3.54 (3.30)	1.04 (8.49)	3.72 (2.71)			115.33 (7.49)	49.09 (3.56)				0.44	49.0	258
6.	4.34 (1.98)	1.08 (5.30)	4.49 (2.17)			144.10 (5.90)	212.74 (3.03)	0.79 (0.42)	-3.26 (-2.30)	-0.06 (-3.42)	0.61	16.3	82

[a]Independent variables are:

T-bond: yield of the treasury bond with a maturity date closest to the maturity date of the lease, as of the initiation of the lease,
D-beta: leased asset's estimated beta discounted at the corresponding treasury bond yield,
Var: variance of return estimated for each asset's representative firms,
U-beta: leased asset's undiscounted beta.

1/Cost: inverse of the purchase price of the leased asset,
1/BV: inverse of the book value of the lessee's assets,
Profit: lessee's net income divided by total assets,
Lev: lessee's total debt divided by total assets,
Liquid: lessee's current assets divided by current liabilities.

lease contract. In panel B, the treasury bond yield is an after-tax yield calculated by multiplying the before-tax yield by one minus the maximum statutory corporate tax rate applicable at the origination date of the lease. This after-tax yield also is used to calculate the asset's discounted beta.

In each panel, the coefficient of the treasury bond yield is positive and statistically significant at the 0.01 level, with t-statistics of 11.45 and 9.99. In addition, in each panel, the coefficient of discounted beta is positive and statistically significant at the 0.01 level, with t-statistics of 9.05 and 6.45. These results are consistent with the predictions of Miller and Upton and McConnell and Schallheim.

It is also possible that discounted beta reflects a general risk measure associated with leases rather than a specific measure of non-diversifiable risk. To investigate this possibility, the variance of return is estimated for each leased asset's representative firms. The variance of return is estimated using the 60 monthly returns immediately preceding the origination date of the relevant lease. The variance of return is then entered as a third independent variable in the regressions. The results are reported as the second regression in the two panels of table 3. In each case, the coefficients and t-statistics of the T-bond yield and discounted beta are virtually the same as those in the first regression. In no case, however, is the coefficient of the asset's estimated variance difference from zero at any reasonable level of significance.

It is also possible that the statistical significance of discounted beta is not due to the importance of beta, per se, but rather to the fact that the beta discounting function uses the treasury bond yield of the same maturity as the lease. Independently, this variable is significant in explaining lease yields, and it may be that the discounting function merely captures an additional element of the effect of interest rates on lease yields. To examine this possibility, the regressions are re-estimated with two independent variables: the treasury bond yield and undiscounted beta. The results are reported as the third regression in each panel.

In both regressions, the magnitudes of the coefficients of the treasury bond yield are approximately the same as in the previous regressions and they are significant at the 0.01 level. As might be anticipated, however, even if Miller and Upton and McConnell and Schallheim are correct, the coefficients and t-statistics of undiscounted beta are substantially attenuated in comparison with those estimated for discounted beta. However, in the two regressions, the coefficients continue to be positive and significant at the 0.15 and 0.05 levels, respectively. Although the statistics are not as strong as when discounted beta is employed, the evidence is consistent with the contention that residual-value covariance risk is a determinant of financial lease yields.

To this point, our results are consistent with the prediction that lease yields are a function of the risk-free rate of interest and the discounted value of the non-diversifiable residual-value risk of the leased asset. Beyond that, we have argued that once the assumptions of perfect capital markets and default-free leases are relaxed, lease yields also will be a function of the transaction costs associated with negotiating the lease, the availability of reliable information about the lessee, and the probability of default by the lessee. We further conjecture that the inverse of the value of the leased asset's purchase price can serve as a proxy for the transaction-cost effect in lease yields; that the inverse of the book value of the lessee firm's assets can serve as a proxy for the availability of reliable information about the lessee; and that various financial ratios of the lessee can serve as proxies for the probability of default by the lessee. The remaining regressions reported in table 3 are aimed at exploring these conjectures.

In the fourth regression in each panel, the independent variables are the treasury bond yield, discounted beta, and the inverse of the purchase price of the leased asset. In the fifth regression, the independent variables are the same as those in the fourth regression plus the inverse of the book value of the lessee's assets. (In the fifth regression, the sample size declines to 258 because we are not able to identify the book value of the assets of 105 of the lessees in the sample.)

In each regression, the coefficients of the treasury bond yield and discounted beta are positive and significant at the 0.01 level. In addition, the coefficients of the inverse of the purchase price of the leased asset and the inverse of the book value of the lessee's assets are positive and significant at the 0.01 level in each regression. If we assume that these variables capture the effects of transaction costs and asymmetric information in lease yields, the results are consistent with our hypotheses that the yields of risky leases are a function of the fixed cost of negotiating the lease and of the availability of reliable information about the lessee firm.

To test our hypothesis that the yields of risky leases are also a function of the financial condition of the lessee firm, three financial ratios – a profitability ratio, a leverage ratio, and a liquidity ratio – are added to the regressions. The profitability ratio is net income divided by total assets; the leverage ratio is total liabilities divided by total assets; and the liquidity ratio is current assets divided by current liabilities.

In a recent study, Ohlson (1980) reviews studies prior to his and uses variables identified by others in constructing a bankruptcy prediction model. He identifies four factors that are useful in predicting corporate bankruptcies: (1) the log of the total assets of the firm, (2) a leverage measure (total liabilities divided by total assets), (3) a measure of performance (either net income divided by total assets or funds provided by operations divided by total liabilities), and (4) a measure of liquidity (either working capital divided by total assets or working capital divided by total assets and current liabilities divided by current assets jointly).

We have already used total assets of the lessee in the regressions. The other variables we employ are dictated largely by data availability. To include a firm in the regressions using financial ratios, we require that its financial statement be 'reliable'. Firms are omitted if their financial statements are incomplete or if data on the lease application are inconsistent with data on the firm's financial statements. Because of this requirement, the usable sample declines to 82 observations.

The sign of the coefficient of the profitability variable is predicted to be negative; the sign of the coefficient of the leverage variable is predicted to be positive; and the sign of the coefficient of the liquidity variable is predicted to be negative. The results of these regressions are reported in the sixth row in the two panels of table 3.

Several aspects of the results merit comment. First, in each instance, the coefficients of the treasury bond yield, discounted beta, the inverse of the asset's purchase price, and the inverse of the book value of the lessee's assets continue to be positive and significantly different from zero. These results support our hypotheses because they are little changed even though the sample has declined by more than 75 percent. Second, there is some evidence of a relationship between lease yields and the financial condition of the lessee firm. The coefficient of the liquidity ratio is negative as predicted and significant at the 0.01 level with t-statistics of -4.34 and -3.42. However, the other financial variables do not enter as statistically significant (except in one case), and the signs of their coefficients are the opposite of those predicted. Overall, though, we view the results as being remarkably supportive of the predictions of Miller and Upton and McConnell and Schallheim and of our ancillary hypotheses.

5.2. Regressions estimated with an alternative proxy for systematic residual-value risk

One troublesome aspect of our empirical analysis is the measurement of the leased asset's residual-value risk using data from firms that manufacture the leased asset. An alternative procedure is to identify a portfolio of firms whose primary line of business involves the use of the leased asset. For example, it seems reasonable to argue that the market value of American Airlines is highly correlated with the market value of aircraft.

The major disadvantage in the use of asset-user firms to estimate asset betas is that it is more difficult to identify single-asset-user firms than to identify single-asset-manufacturer firms. Nevertheless, for seven of the categories of leased assets, we have identified firms whose values are likely to be tied closely to one of the categories. The seven categories are aircraft, construction equipment, marine equipment, medical equipment, motel and hotel furnishings, railroad rolling stock, and trucks and trailers. These seven categories encompass 130 leases.

For each category, a portfolio of representative asset-user firms is identified. For each of the 130 eligible leases, an unlevered beta is estimated following the same procedure used to estimate betas with asset-manufacturer firms.[8] The yield regressions are then reestimated. The results are reported in table 4. As before, the table contains two panels that report parallel sets of regressions: panel A employs before-tax yields; panel B employs after-tax yields. In addition, within each panel, two parallel sets of regressions (labeled USER and MNFR) are reported. Those labeled USER employ the asset-user betas; those labeled MNFR use asset-manufacturer betas. In each regression, the sample contains 130 leases.

The regressions are estimated with three sets of explanatory variables: (1) the treasury bond yield and discounted beta, (2) the treasury bond yield and undiscounted beta, and (3) the treasury bond yield, discounted beta, and the inverse of the purchase price of the leased asset.[9,10] First, in both panels, the coefficients, t-statistics and R^2's are similar between the pairs of USER and MNFR regressions. Second, in each case the coefficients of the treasury bond yield, discounted beta, and the inverse of the asset cost are postive and significant at the 0.01 level. Third, the coefficients, t-statistics and R^2's in table 4 are similar to those for the corresponding regressions estimated with the full sample in table 3. In sum, then, the regressions estimated with asset-user betas are consistent with our hypotheses.

5.3. A further look at the data

The descriptive statistics in table 2 indicate that the average before-tax lease yield of 18.63 percent is substantially above the yields of Aaa corporate bonds, which ranged from 7.15 percent to 15.49 percent over the period covered by this study. A natural question that arises is: Why would corporations raise capital by means of leasing arrangements when borrowing appears to be a much less expensive form of financing? One hypothesis is that only the largest corporate borrowers are able to issue publicly traded debt. If so, our argu-

---

[8] Two tests were conducted to determine the degree of correspondence between asset-manufacturer and asset-user firms' betas. The first is a matched sample t-test. In this test, unlevered betas were computed over four non-overlapping time intervals for each asset-manufacturer and asset-user firm in the sample. The average unlevered beta was computed for each category of leased assets and the difference between the average unlevered betas estimated with the portfolios of asset-user and asset-producer firms was computed. A t-test indicates that the average difference in betas of 0.023 is not significant ($t = 0.048$). In the second test, a simple correlation was estimated between unlevered asset-user firms' betas and asset-manufacturer firms' betas. For $N = 26$, the simple correlation coefficient is 0.27 with $F = 1.89$. A list of the asset-user firms is available from the authors upon request.

[9] As in table 3, in the after-tax regressions the treasury bond yield is an after-tax yield and this after-tax yield is used to compute discounted beta.

[10] Regressions are not estimated with the lessee's asset value and the various financial ratios because the already reduced sample becomes so small and so heavily concentrated in a few industries that the results become meaningless.

Table 4

Regressions of lease yields on various independent variables for a sample of 130 leases originated over the period 1973–1982; t-statistics in parentheses.[a]

	Intercept	T-bond	D-beta	U-beta	1/Cost	R^2	F	N
A. Regression coefficients with the before-tax lease yield as the dependent variable								
1. USER[b]	−10.68	1.63	24.62			0.36	36.1	130
	(−3.33)	(8.16)	(5.86)					
MNFR[b]	−13.93	1.57	37.61			0.48	58.4	130
	(−5.00)	(9.21)	(8.40)					
2. USER	0.05	1.15		6.00		0.20	16.1	130
	(0.01)	(5.67)		(1.43)				
MNFR	0.71	1.05		6.93		0.21	16.6	130
	(0.23)	(5.26)		(1.69)				
3. USER	−6.84	1.40	14.58		509.62	0.53	48.2	130
	(−2.44)	(8.01)	(3.75)		(6.83)			
MNFR	−10.07	1.41	25.73		425.52	0.59	60.5	130
	(−3.92)	(9.15)	(5.75)		(5.85)			
B. Regression coefficients with the after-tax lease yield as the dependent variable								
1. USER	−2.71	1.63	11.21			0.34	32.4	130
	(−1.40)	(7.89)	(4.72)					
MNFR	−3.35	1.46	15.56			0.39	40.0	130
	(−1.92)	(7.89)	(5.85)					
2. USER	1.95	1.29		4.05		0.24	19.9	130
	(0.94)	(6.29)		(1.71)				
MNFR	3.23	1.19		3.11		0.23	19.2	130
	(1.89)	(5.82)		(1.33)				
3. USER	−0.64	1.41	5.83		354.91	0.60	63.8	130
	(−0.42)	(8.72)	(3.01)		(9.18)			
MNFR	−1.17	1.33	8.60		338.19	0.62	68.1	130
	(−0.83)	(9.07)	(3.82)		(8.76)			

[a]Independent variables are:

T-bond: Yield of the treasury bond with a maturity date closest to the maturity date of the lease, as of the initiation of the lease,

D-beta: leased asset's estimated beta discounted at the corresponding treasury bond yield,

U-beta: leased asset's undiscounted beta,

1/Cost: inverse of the purchase price of the leased asset.

[b]*USER* indicates regressions estimated with user-firm betas and MNFR those estimated with manufacturer-firm betas.

ments suggest that the appropriate benchmarks are the yields on the largest leases issued by the largest lessees. Evidence on this point is presented in table 5.

Table 5 is a cross-tabulation of the lease yields less Aaa corporate bond yields taken from the *Federal Reserve Bulletin*. The entries in the table are averages of individual lease yields less the Aaa corporate bond yields during

Table 5

Cross-tabulations of average yield spreads for a sample of 258 leases originated over the period 1973–1982; cells contain the average of the individual lease yields less the yield of the Aaa corporate bond index as of the origination date of the lease (in each panel, the rows give the asset purchase price quartile and the columns give the book value of the lessee's assets quartile).

		Quartile of book value of lessee's assets[a]				Purchase price marginal[b]
		1	2	3	4	
A. Before-tax lease yield less the Aaa corporate bond yield (% per year)						
Quartile of purchase price of leased asset[c]	1	12.28 (33)	11.62 (22)	10.36 (6)	6.18 (4)	11.50 (65)
	2	11.61 (21)	10.06 (24)	8.96 (13)	10.19 (6)	10.36 (64)
	3	10.55 (9)	9.04 (16)	3.98 (19)	0.97 (21)	5.16 (65)
	4	−3.76 (1)	0.10 (3)	−1.08 (25)	−1.27 (35)	−1.17 (64)
Book value marginal		11.57 (64)	9.88 (65)	3.61 (63)	0.94 (66)	
B. After-tax lease yield less the after-tax Aaa corporate bond yield (% per year)						
Quartile of purchase price of leased asset[c]	1	10.87 (33)	9.74 (22)	10.71 (6)	6.20 (4)	10.19 (65)
	2	9.61 (21)	8.64 (24)	9.24 (13)	7.38 (6)	8.96 (64)
	3	9.00 (9)	7.90 (16)	4.41 (19)	3.10 (21)	5.48 (65)
	4	2.33 (1)	3.40 (3)	2.70 (25)	2.80 (35)	2.78 (64)
Book value marginal		10.06 (64)	8.59 (65)	5.33 (63)	3.52 (66)	

[a] Numbers in parentheses are the number of observations in each cell.

[b] Purchase price marginals are calculated as the average of the yield spreads for each purchase price quartile, where the first quartile includes the 25 percent of the leases with the lowest asset purchase prices, the second quartile includes the 25 percent of the leases with the next lowest asset purchase prices, and so on.

[c] Book value marginals are calculated as the average of the yield spreads for each lessee size quartile, where the first quartile includes the 25 percent of the leases with the smallest book value of lessee's assets, the second quartile includes the 25 percent of the leases with the next lowest book value of lessee's assets, and so on.

the origination month of the lease. Row categories are the purchase prices of the leased asset by quartile. Column categories are the book values of the lessee's assets by quartile. Panels A and B contain average spreads for the before-tax and after-tax yields, respectively. In computing the yield spreads in panel B, the Aaa bond yield was multiplied by one minus the maximum statutory corporate tax rate applicable at the origination of the corresponding lease.

In each panel, the largest yield spread is contained in the upper left-hand corner, which corresponds to the smallest assets leased by the smallest lessees. In both panels, the yield spread contained in the lower right-hand corner is the second smallest one in the panel. This cell corresponds to the largest assets leased by the largest lessees. (The smallest spread in each panel is contained in the lower left-hand corner, but this cell contains only one observation.) In addition, in each panel, the row marginals decline monotonically as the book value of the lessees' assets increases and the column marginals decline monotonically as the purchase price of the leased assets increases. In short, these results indicate that the 'cost' of leasing approaches the 'cost' of issuing debt for large corporations that lease large assets. If small corporations that lease small assets also face significant fixed costs in borrowing to finance their assets, then leasing is no more costly than borrowing, once the 'cost' of each is adjusted for transaction and information costs.

5.4. Lease yields and the role of taxes

One concern in the leasing literature has been whether the value associated with the tax shields generated by leasing arrangements accrues to the lessor or the lessee firm.[11] We have some indirect evidence on this point. For each of the leases in the sample, we determine whether the investment tax credit is retained by the lessor or passed through to the lessee.[12] If the leasing market is perfectly competitive, the value of the tax shield should accrue to the lessee, and after-tax (and after-*ITC*) yields should be indistinguishable regardless of whether the *ITC* is retained by the lessor or passed through to the lessee. That is, in those cases in which the *ITC* is retained by the lessor, the lease payments should be commensurately lower than when it is passed through to the lessee, but the after-tax (and after-*ITC*) lease yields should be indistinguishable.

To examine this issue, we estimate a regression that includes the treasury bond yield, discounted beta (estimated with the portfolio of asset-manufacturing firms), the inverse of the purchase price of the leased asset, the inverse of the lessee's book value, and the lessee's current ratio as independent variables. In addition, a dummy variable that takes on the value of 1.0 when the *ITC* is

---

[11] For discussions of the role of taxes in leasing, see, for example, Brealey and Young (1980), Lewellen, Long and McConnell (1976), Miller and Upton (1976), Myers, Dill and Bautista (1976), Schall (1974), and Smith and Wakeman (1985).

[12] For 122 of the contracts (i.e., 33.6% of the sample), the *ITC* was passed through to the lessee. In 185 contracts (i.e., 51% of the sample), the *ITC* was retained by the lessor. In the remaining cases, the *ITC* was not available for either party, usually because the asset was not a new piece of equipment. Of the leases in which the *ITC* was available, it was retained by the lessor 60.3% of the time. Strickney, Weil and Wolfson (1983) analyze the division of tax benefits associated with the purchase by General Electric Credit Corporation of over $1.5 billion in tax shields related to safe-harbor leasing contracts in 1981.

Table 6

Regressions of after-tax yields, with and without the *ITC*, on five independent variables plus an *ITC* dummy variable for a sample of 82 leases originated over the period 1973–1982; *t*-statistics in parentheses.[a]

Intercept	T-bond	D-beta	1/Cost	1/BV	Liquid	ITC	R^2	F	N
			1. Regression with after-tax lease yield as the dependent variable						
0.89	1.14	5.75	130.65	253.77	−0.05	0.91	0.58	17.6	82
(0.42)	(5.46)	(2.62)	(5.43)	(3.71)	(−3.06)	(1.42)			
		2. Regression with after-tax, but before ITC, lease yield as the dependent variable							
1.46	1.14	4.93	135.06	229.71	−0.06	−2.25	0.66	24.4	82
(0.74)	(5.86)	(2.42)	(6.03)	(3.61)	(−3.59)	(−3.78)			

[a]Independent variables are:

T-bond: yield of the treasury bond with a maturity date closest to the maturity date of the lease, as of the initiation of the lease,
D-beta: Leased asset's estimated beta discounted at the corresponding treasury bond yield,
1/Cost: inverse of the purchase price of the leased asset,
1/BV: inverse of the book value of the lessee's assets,
Liquid: lessee's current assets divided by current liabilities,
ITC: a zero-one dummy variable with the value of one if the lessor retains the investment tax credit.

retained by the lessor and a value of zero when the *ITC* is passed through to the lessee is included. The dependent variable in this regression is the after-tax lease yield. The results are presented in the first row of table 6. Consistent with a perfectly competitive leasing market, the coefficient of the dummy variable is not significant at the 0.05 level. It is, however, significant at the 0.10 level ($t = 1.42$), and the magnitude of the coefficient indicates that the average difference in the yields of the two groups is almost one percent (after adjusting for other factors).

As a further consideration of this issue, after-tax lease yields are recomputed assuming that the *ITC* is always passed through to the lessee. If lease terms are not adjusted to reflect the retention of the *ITC* by the lessor, these yields would be indistinguishable regardless of which party receives the credit. The second row of table 6 reports the results when the regression is re-estimated with the same variables as before, except that the dependent variable is the after-tax yield computed ignoring the *ITC*. In this case, the coefficient of the dummy variable is significantly negative ($t = -3.78$). This result indicates that the terms of lease contracts are adjusted according to which party receives the *ITC*. Because of the marginal significance of the coefficient of the dummy variable in the first regression, however, there remains some ambiguity as to whether the full value of the tax shield is passed through to the lessee firm, as would be predicted in a perfectly competitive market.

6. Summary and conclusion

Miller and Upton (1976) and McConnell and Schallheim (1983) present theoretical models of financial lease valuation in which the lease yield is a function of the risk-free rate of interest and the discounted value of the leased asset's residual-value covariance risk. To test this hypothesis, we compiled a sample of 363 financial leases originated over the period 1973 through 1982. Before- and after-tax lease yields are regressed against the yield of the treasury bond of the same maturity as the lease and a proxy for the discounted value of the leased asset's residual-value covariance risk. The coefficients of both variables are positive and statistically different from zero at conventional levels of significance. These results are consistent with the predictions of Miller and Upton and McConnell and Schallheim.

Additionally, we hypothesize that lease yields are a function of the transaction costs associated with negotiating and writing the lease, the quality and quantity of information about the lessee firm, and the default risk associated with the lessee firm. We further conjecture that: (1) the transaction costs associated with negotiating and writing the lease decline proportionately as the dollar value of the leased asset increases so that the lease yield is an inverse function of the cost of the leased asset; (2) the availability of reliable information about the lessee firm increases as the 'size' of the lessee increases so that lease yields are an inverse function of the book value of the lessee firm's assets; and (3) lease yields are a positive function of the default potential of the lessee firm. Three financial ratios are used as proxies for lessee default potential: (1) a profitability ratio, (2) a liquidity ratio, and (3) a leverage ratio. Additional regressions indicate that, in addition to the yield of the treasury bond of the same maturity as the lease and a proxy for the discounted residual-value covariance risk of the leased asset, lease yields are positively related to the inverse of the purchase price of the leased asset and the inverse of the book value of the lessee's assets and negatively related to the lessee's current ratio. We interpret these results as being consistent with our hypotheses. The failure of the other two financial ratios to enter significantly into the yield regression may be due to the inadequacy of the data or to the inability of these ratios to capture the default potential of lessee firms. These results do suggest that a further inquiry should investigate the predictability of lessee default.

References

Akerlof, George, 1970, The market for lemons: Qualitative uncertainty and the market mechanism, Quarterly Journal of Economics 89, 488–500.

Brealey, Richard A. and Charles M. Young, 1980, Debt, taxes and leasing: A note, Journal of Finance 35, 1245–1250.

Crawford, Peggy J., Charles Harper and John J. McConnell, 1981, Further evidence on the terms of financial leases, Financial Management 10, 7–14.

Geske, Robert, 1977, The valuation of corporate liabilities as compound options, Journal of Financial and Quantitative Analysis 12, 541–542.

Hamada, Robert, 1969, Portfolio analysis, market equilibrium, and corporation finance, Journal of Finance 24, 13–31.

Lewellen, W.G., Michael S. Long and John J. McConnell, 1976, Asset leasing in competitive capital markets, Journal of Finance 31, 787–798.

McConnell, John J. and James S. Schallheim, 1983, Valuation of asset leasing contracts, Journal of Financial Economics 12, 237–261.

Miller, Merton H. and Charles Upton, 1976, Leasing, buying and the cost of capital services, Journal of Finance 31, 761–786.

Myers, S.C., D.A. Dill and A.J. Bautista, 1976, Valuation of financial lease contracts, Journal of Finance 31, 799–819.

Ohlson, James, 1980, Financial ratios and the probabilistic prediction of bankruptcy, Journal of Accounting Research 18, 109–131.

Rubinstein, Mark, 1976, The value of uncertain income streams and the pricing of options, Bell Journal of Economics 7, 407–425.

Schall, Lawrence D., 1974, The lease-or-buy and asset acquisition decision, Journal of Finance 29, 1203–1214.

Smith, Clifford W. and L. MacDonald Wakeman, 1985, Determinants of corporate leasing policy, Journal of Finance 40, 895–908.

Sorenson, Ivar and Ramon Johnson, 1977, Equipment financial leasing practices and costs: An empirical study, Financial Management 6, 33–40.

Stickney, Clyde P., Roman L. Weil and Mark A. Wolfson, 1983, Income taxes and tax-transfer leases, Accounting Review 58, 439–459.

FIVE

PRICING OF DEBT CLAIMS

APPLICATIONS OF OPTION PRICING ANALYSIS

CLIFFORD W. SMITH, JR.
The University of Rochester

1. Introduction

Since the publication of the Black–Scholes (1973) paper in which the pricing models for simple put and call options were originally derived, there has been much work employing the continuous time, option pricing analysis which they developed. In this paper these developments, representing a fundamental advancement in the theory of finance, are summarized and presented so that a unified picture of the state of the art in this area can be more easily acquired.

The rest of the paper is divided into three sections. Section 2 analyzes the simplest contingent claims — European puts and calls. Section 3 examines the pricing of corporate liabilities — the equity and debt of a levered firm, plus more unusual instruments like common stock purchase warrants, subordinated debt, and convertible debt. Finally, section 4 describes the pricing of other contingent claims, such as underwriting contracts, collateralized loans, insurance contracts, and leases.[1]

2. The pricing of European put and call options

2.1 European call option pricing

A European call is an option to buy a share of stock at the maturity date of the contract for a stated amount, the exercise price. Since these assets are contracts between two agents external to the firm, two propositions follow. First, the aggregate quantity of the contracts is always zero; the long positions in this asset

---

[1]This paper is especially written to augment the discussion of option pricing in Smith (1976). The major thrust of that paper is in the investments area. This paper concentrates more on the corporate finance applications of the option pricing model.

James L. Bicksler, Editor, Handbook of Financial Economics
© *North-Holland Publishing Company – 1979*

are exactly equal to the short positions. Secondly, the behavior of the underlying stock price is unaffected by the existence of the option market.[2]

Black and Scholes (1973) demonstrate that a riskless hedge can be created using the proper proportions of call options and shares of underlying stock. Since the hedge is instantaneously riskless, if perfect substitutes yield the same rate of return, then the rate of return to the hedge will equal the riskless rate. From this equilibrium condition the call price can be obtained.

To derive the call price, make the following assumptions: (1) there are no penalties for short sales; (2) transactions costs and taxes are zero; (3) the market operates continuously; (4) the riskless rate is known and constant; (5) the stock price follows a continuous Itô process; (6) the stock pays no dividends; and (7) the option can only be exercised at the terminal date of the contract.

In general, the value of the hedge, V_H, can be expressed as

$$V_H = Q_s S + Q_c c, \tag{1}$$

where V_H is the value of the hedge portfolio, S is the price of a share of the stock, c is the price of a call option to purchase one share of the stock, Q_s is the quantity of stock in the hedge, and Q_c is the quantity of call options in the hedge.

The change in the value of the hedge, dV_H, is the derivative of (1):

$$dV_H = Q_s dS + Q_c dc. \tag{2}$$

(Since at a point in time the quantities of options and stock are given, the change in the value of the hedge results from the change in the prices of the assets.)

Since the stock price is assumed to follow a continuous Itô process and the call price is assumed to be a function of the stock price and time, Itô's lemma can be employed to express the change in the call price. Itô's lemma provides an expression for the differential of functions of variables which follow Itô processes.[3] The change in the call price, dc, can be expressed as

$$dc = \frac{\partial c}{\partial S} dS + \left(\frac{\partial c}{\partial t} + \frac{1}{2} \frac{\partial^2 c}{\partial S^2} \sigma^2 S^2 \right) dt, \tag{3}$$

where $c = c(S, t)$, t is time, and σ^2 is the instantaneous variance rate on the stock price. Note that the only stochastic term on the right-hand side of (3) is the first,

---

[2]This statement is perhaps too strong. If the agents who write option contracts are very different from those people who buy options then there may be "second order of magnitude" effects associated with wealth transfers between these two groups. (Preliminary results of a study of the individuals who transact on the American Options Exchange finds no significant demographic heterogeneity.) Additionally, effects may arise from increased "market completeness and lowered transactions costs" — however, these social benefits are likely to be too small to measure empirically.

[3]A discussion of Itô processes and a derivation of Itô's lemma is provided in the Appendix to this paper.

$(\partial c/\partial S)\mathrm{d}S$; the rest are deterministic. Substituting (3) into (2) yields

$$\mathrm{d}V_H = Q_s\mathrm{d}S + Q_c\left[\frac{\partial c}{\partial S}\mathrm{d}S + \left(\frac{\partial c}{\partial t} + \frac{1}{2}\frac{\partial^2 c}{\partial S^2}\sigma^2 S^2\right)\mathrm{d}t\right].$$ (4)

For arbitrary quantities of stock and options, the change in the value of the hedge, $\mathrm{d}V_H$, is stochastic; however, if the quantities of stock and call are chosen so that Q_s/Q_c equals $-(\partial c/\partial S)$ then the first two terms on the right-hand side of (4) sum to zero. Since these are the only stochastic terms, the change in the value of the hedge becomes riskless. With the appropriate long position in the stock and short position in the call, then an increase in the price of the stock will be offset by the decrease in the value of the short position in the call, and vice versa. Note that the above restriction is placed on the ratio Q_s/Q_c; it makes no difference which asset is short. If the quantities of the stock and option in the hedge portfolio are continuously adjusted in the appropriate manner as asset prices change over time, then the return to the portfolio becomes riskless.

Setting $Q_c = -1$ and $Q_s = (\partial c/\partial S)$ in (4) yields

$$\mathrm{d}V_H = -\left(\frac{\partial c}{\partial t} + \frac{1}{2}\frac{\partial^2 c}{\partial S^2}S^2\sigma^2\right)\mathrm{d}t.$$ (5)

If in equilibrium two perfect substitutes earn the same rate of return, then since this hedge is riskless, its return must equal the riskless rate:[4]

$$\frac{\mathrm{d}V_H}{V_H} \overset{e}{=} r\mathrm{d}t.$$ (6)

Substituting (1) and (5) into (6) defines a differential equation for the value of the option:

$$\frac{\partial c}{\partial t} = rc - rS\frac{\partial c}{\partial S} - \frac{1}{2}\frac{\partial^2 c}{\partial S^2}S^2\sigma^2.$$ (7)

The required boundary condition for the solution of this differential equation is that at the terminal date of the option contract, t^*, the option price must equal the maximum of either the difference between the stock price and the exercise price, $S^* - X$, or zero:[5]

$$c^* = \max\left[S^* - X, 0\right].$$ (8)

[4]The equality sign $\overset{e}{=}$ should be read "equal in equilibrium". This notation is employed to highlight the economic interpretation of this equation which is very different from that of functional relations, $=$, or definitions, $\equiv$.

[5]In general, for the solution of a partial differential equation (a differential equation which is a function of more than one variable) one boundary equation is required for each dimension. Eq. (8) is the boundary condition in the time dimension. In the stock price dimension, the boundary condition is that the call price is zero if the stock price is zero. However, because it is explicitly assumed that the call price is log normally distributed, the stock price cannot be zero, the boundary condition will never be binding, and therefore can be ignored.

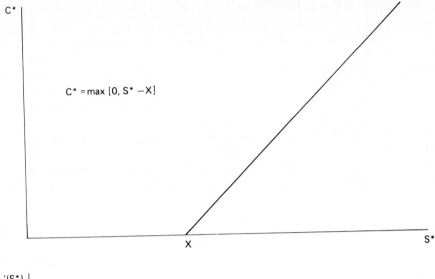

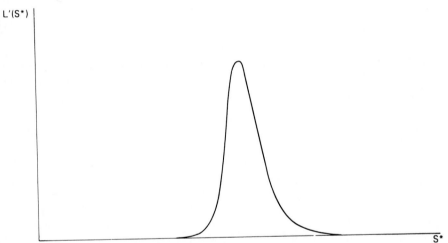

Figure 4.1. Dollar payoff to call as a function of stock price, $C^* = \max[0, S^* - X]$, and log normal density function of stock prices at $t^*, L'(S^*)$.

Before deriving the solution to (7) subject to (8), notice that whatever the form of the solution, it must be a function only of the stock price, S, the exercise price, X, the variance rate, σ^2, time, t^* and t, and the riskless rate, r, because these are the only variables in the problem.

The solution to the differential equation can be found by transforming (7) into the heat exchange equation from physics, for which the solution is known. A more intuitive solution technique[6] relies on the fact that, in describing the

[6]See Friedman (1975, esp. p. 148), for a mathematical proof of the solution technique.

equilibrium return to the hedge, the sole assumption involving preferences of the economic agents in the market is that two assets which are perfect substitutes must earn the same rate of return: no assumptions involving risk preference have been employed. This suggests that if a solution to the problem can be found assuming a particular preference structure, then it must also be the solution to the differential equation for any other preference structure which permits a solution. Therefore, in solving the equation choose the preference structure which simplifies the mathematics.

The simplest preference structure would be one in which all agents are risk neutral. In a risk neutral world the rate of return on all assets would be equal. Therefore, the current call price would be the expected terminal call price $E[c^*]$, discounted to the present:

$$c = e^{-rT}E[c^*], \tag{9}$$

where T is $t^* - t$. The assumption that the distribution of stock prices at any future date will be distributed log normally implies that (9) can be expressed as

$$c = e^{-rT} \int_X^\infty (S^* - X)L'(S^*)\,dS^*, \tag{10}$$

where $L'(S^*)$ is the log normal density function. The payoff function for the call and the density function for the stock are represented in fig. 4.1. A useful theorem for solving this and similar problems is

Theorem.[7] If $L'(S^*)$ is a log normal density function with

$$Q = \begin{cases} 0, & \text{if } S^* > \phi X, \\ \lambda S^* - \gamma X, & \text{if } \phi X \geqslant S^* > \psi X, \\ 0, & \text{if } S^* < \psi X. \end{cases}$$

Then

$$
\begin{aligned}
E[Q] &\equiv \int_{\psi X}^{\phi X} (\lambda S^* - \gamma X)L(S^*)\,dS^* \\
&= e^{\rho T}\lambda S\left[N\left\{ \frac{\ln(S/\psi X) + (\rho + \sigma^2/2)T}{\sigma\sqrt{T}} \right\} - N\left\{ \frac{\ln(S/\phi X) + (\rho + \sigma^2/2)T}{\sigma\sqrt{T}} \right\} \right] \\
&\quad - \gamma X\left[N\left\{ \frac{\ln(S/\psi X) + (\rho - \sigma^2/2)T}{\sigma\sqrt{T}} \right\} - N\left\{ \frac{\ln(S/\phi X) + (\rho - \sigma^2/2)T}{\sigma\sqrt{T}} \right\} \right],
\end{aligned}
$$

where ψ, ϕ, λ, and γ are arbitrary parameters and ρ is the average expected rate of growth in S ($E[S^*/S] = e^{\rho T}$) and $N\{\cdot\}$ is the cumulative standard normal.

[7]The proof of this theorem follows the proof of a less general result in Sprenkle (1964).

Now (10) can be solved by applying theorem 1 with $\lambda = \gamma = e^{-rT}$, $\psi = 1$, $\phi = \infty$ and noting that for a risk neutral world, $\rho \overset{e}{=} r$. Therefore, the solution to the European call pricing problem is

$$c = SN\left\{\frac{\ln(S/X) + (r + \sigma^2/2)T}{\sigma\sqrt{T}}\right\} - e^{-rT}XN\left\{\frac{\ln(S/X) + (r - \sigma^2/2)T}{\sigma\sqrt{T}}\right\}.$$

(11)

Fig. 4.2 illustrates the relationship between the call price and the stock price, given the exercise price, the time to maturity, and the riskless rate.

The solution can be written in general form as

$$c = c(S, X, T, \sigma^2, r),$$

(12)

where

$$\frac{\partial c}{\partial S} > 0; \qquad \frac{\partial c}{\partial \sigma^2} > 0; \qquad \frac{\partial c}{\partial X} < 0; \qquad \frac{\partial c}{\partial r} > 0; \qquad \frac{\partial c}{\partial T} > 0.$$

These partial effects have intuitive interpretations: as the stock price increases, the expected payoff of the option increases. With a higher exercise price, the expected payoff decreases. With a longer time to maturity or with a higher interest rate, the present value of the exercise payment is lower, thus increasing the value of the option. Finally, with a longer time to maturity or with a larger variance rate on the underlying stock price, the probability of a large price change in the security during the life of the option is greater. Since the call price

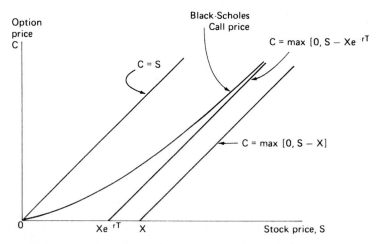

Figure 4.2. Diagram of Black–Scholes call option price for different stock prices, with a given interest rate, variance rate, and time to maturity. The Black–Scholes call option price lies below the maximum possible value, $C = S$ (except where $S = 0$), and above the minimum value, $C = \max[0, S - X\exp(-rT)]$. Note that the curve relating the Black–Scholes call price with the stock price asymptotically approaches $C = \max[0, S - X\exp(-rT)]$ line.

cannot be negative, a larger range of possible stock prices increases the maximum value of the option without lowering the minimum value.

Quite restrictive assumptions have been employed in this section; however, there has been much work by Merton (1973, 1976), Ingersoll (1976), and Cox and Ross (1976) on the effect of the relaxation of the assumptions. The model seems quite robust with respect to relaxing the basic assumptions. For a survey of this literature see Smith (1976).

2.2. European put option pricing

A European put is an option to sell a share of stock at the maturity date of the contract for a stated amount, the exercise price. Therefore, at the expiration date of the option it will be worth either the difference between the exercise price and the stock price or zero, whichever is greater. Merton (1973) has demonstrated that when borrowing and lending rates are equal, then the price of a European put, $p(S,T;X)$ is equal to the value of a portfolio of a European call with the same terms as the put, $c(S,T;X)$, riskless bonds with a face value equal to the exercise price of the options, $XB(T)$, and a short position in the stock, S.

To demonstrate this equivalence, consider two portfolios where Portfolio I contains one European call, one share of stock sold short, and X pure discount bonds maturing at the expiration date of the options with a current value of $B(T)$ and a face value of one dollar; and Portfolio II contains one European put with the same terms as the call (see table 4.1).

With no restriction on short sales, with borrowing and lending rates equal, and with no transaction costs, this position can be reversed. Therefore, if the prices of the put and call do not stand in this relationship, one to another, arbitrage opportunities exist. Thus, the European put option must be priced so that

$$p(S,T;X) = c(S,T;X) - S + XB(T). \tag{13}$$

Table 4.1. Demonstration that a portfolio containing a European call, one share of stock sold short, and discount bonds with a face value of X will yield the same terminal values as a European put.*

Portfolio	Current value	Stock price at $T=0$	
		$S^* < X$	$X < S^*$
I	$c(S,T;X) - S + XB(T)$	$0 - S^* + X$	$S^* - X - S^* + X$
II	$p(S,T;X)$	$X - S^*$	0
Relationship between the terminal values of portfolios I and II		$V_I^* = V_{II}^*$	$V_I^* = V_{II}^*$

*Terminal values of portfolios I and II for different relationships between the stock price and exercise price at the expiration date ($T=0$) of the options.

Black and Scholes (1973) employ (13) with their solution to the European call pricing problem (11) to derive the European put pricing solution:[8]

$$p = SN\left\{\frac{\ln(S/X)+(r+\sigma^2/2)T}{\sigma\sqrt{T}}\right\}$$

$$- Xe^{-rT}N\left\{\frac{\ln(S/X)+(r-\sigma^2/2)T}{\sigma\sqrt{T}}\right\} - S + Xe^{-rT}, \tag{14}$$

$$= - SN\left\{\frac{-\ln(S/X)-(r+\sigma^2/2)T}{\sigma\sqrt{T}}\right\}$$

$$+ Xe^{-rT}N\left\{\frac{-\ln(S/X)-(r-\sigma^2/2)T}{\sigma\sqrt{T}}\right\}. \tag{15}$$

This solution can be written in general form as

$$p = p(S, X, T, \sigma^2, r), \tag{16}$$

where

$$\frac{\partial p}{\partial S} = \frac{\partial c}{\partial S} - 1 < 0,$$

$$\frac{\partial p}{\partial X} = \frac{\partial c}{\partial X} + e^{-rT} > 0,$$

$$\frac{\partial p}{\partial T} = \frac{\partial c}{\partial T} - rXe^{-rT} \gtreqless 0,$$

$$\frac{\partial p}{\partial \sigma^2} = \frac{\partial c}{\partial \sigma^2} > 0,$$

$$\frac{\partial p}{\partial r} = \frac{\partial c}{\partial r} - TXe^{-rT} < 0.$$

These partial effects also have intuitive interpretations. An increase in the stock price increases the probability that the stock price will be above the exercise price, and therefore worthless. An increase in the exercise price increases the likelihood that the stock price will be below the exercise price and therefore valuable. There are two effects, either capable of dominating, from a change in the time to maturity. A longer time to maturity delays the receipt of the proceeds from the expiration of the option; this effect dominates where the ratio of stock price to exercise price is low. A longer time to maturity increases the

---

[8]With the Black–Scholes assumptions, $B(T) = e^{-rT}$. Note that this solution can also be derived using the above technique where:

$$P = \exp(-rT)\int_0^X (X - S^*)L'(S^*)\,dS^*.$$

Applying the above theorem yields (15).

dispersion of the distribution of stock prices at the expiration date, this effect dominates where the ratio of stock price to exercise price is high. An increase in the variance rate also increases the dispersion of the distribution of stock prices at the expiration date increasing the probability that the stock price will be significantly below the exercise price. Of course, the probability that the stock price will be significantly above the exercise price also increases but the put price cannot be below zero. Finally, an increase in the interest rate reduces the present value of the proceeds of the exercise of the option.

3. The pricing of corporate liabilities

3.1. Pricing the debt and equity of a firm

Black and Scholes suggest that the option pricing model can be used to price the debt and equity of a levered firm. Assume that: (1) The firm issues pure discount bonds which prohibit any dividend payments until after the bonds are paid off. The bonds mature at t^*, T time periods from now, at which time the bondholders are paid (if possible), and the residual is paid to the stockholders. (2) The total value of the firm is unaffected by capital structure.[9] (3) There are homogeneous expectations about the dynamic behavior of the value of the firm's assets; the distribution at the end of any finite time interval is lognormal with a constant variance rate of return. (4) There is a known constant riskless rate, r. Then the Black–Scholes call pricing model provides the correct valuation of the equity.

In essence, issuing bonds is equivalent to the stockholders selling the assets of the firm to the bondholders for the proceeds of the issue plus a call option to repurchase the assets of the firm from the bondholders with an exercise price equal to the face value of the bonds. Fig. 4.3 illustrates the payoff function to the equity and the debt. Thus, under the above assumptions, the equity of the firm is like a call option. Applying the Black–Scholes call option solution yields

$$E = VN\left\{\frac{\ln(V/X)+(r+\sigma^2/2)T}{\sigma\sqrt{T}}\right\} - e^{-rT}XN\left\{\frac{\ln(V/X)+(r-\sigma^2/2)T}{\sigma\sqrt{T}}\right\},$$

(17)

[9]Long (1974) emphasizes the point that to apply stochastic calculus it must be assumed that the process describing the total value of the firm can be fully specified without reference to the value of the contingent claims. Thus, this analysis applies to a Modigliani–Miller (1958) world with no taxes or transactions costs of bankruptcy. Jensen and Meckling (1976) suggest that the existence of any agency cost (costs borne by one class of owners of the firm which are imposed by managers or another class of owners — e.g. costs of restrictive covenants within bond contracts, auditing costs, and costs of monitoring managers' activities) would cause the total value of the firm to be a function of the debt equity ratio, and thus would invalidate the specific conclusions of the analysis. However, there is no suggestion that the general form solutions would change.

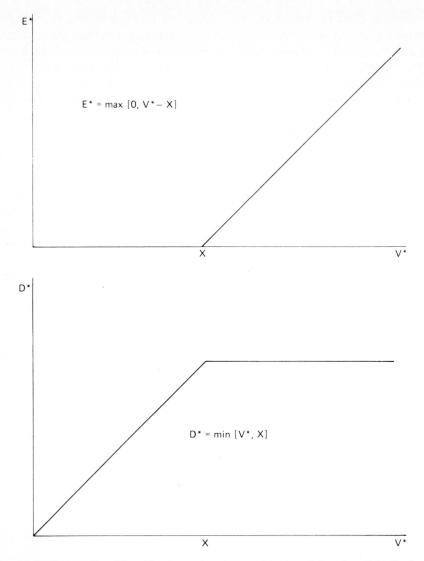

Figure 4.3. Dollar payoff to debt with a face value of X as a function of the value of the firm's assets at the maturity of the debt, $D^* = \min[V^*, X]$; and dollar payoffs to equity as a function of the value of the assets of the firm, $E^* = \max[0, V^* - X]$.

where E is the value of the equity of the firm, V is the value of the assets of the firm, X is the face value of the debt of the firm, σ^2 is the variance rate on V, and T is the maturity date of the debt. The value of the debt, D, is then

$$D = V - E$$

$$= VN\left\{\frac{-\ln(V/X) - (r + \sigma^2/2)T}{\sigma\sqrt{T}}\right\} + e^{-rT}XN\left\{\frac{\ln(V/X) + (r - \sigma^2/2)T}{\sigma\sqrt{T}}\right\}.$$

(18)

In general form, the value of the debt can be expressed as:

$$D = D(V, X, T, \sigma^2, r),$$

(19)

where $\partial D/\partial V$, $\partial D/\partial X > 0$ and $\partial D/\partial T$, $\partial D/\partial \sigma^2$, $\partial D/\partial r < 0$. These partial effects indicated are in the expected direction and have intuitive interpretations: an increase in the value of the firm directly increases the value of the equity and increases the coverage on the debt, thereby lowering the probability of default and increasing the value of the debt. An increase in the promised repayment amount increases the bondholders' claim on the firm's assets thus increasing the value of the debt and, since the stockholders are residual claimants, reduces the current value of the equity. An increase in the time to repayment of the debt or in the riskless rate lowers the present value of the debt and increases the market value of the equity, and finally, an increase in the time to maturity or in the variance rate increases the dispersion of possible values of the value of the firm at the maturity date of the bonds. Since the bondholders have a maximum payment which they can receive, X, an increase in the dispersion of possible outcomes increases the probability that the value of the firm's assets will be below the promised repayment, thereby increasing the probability of default, lowering the value of the debt, increasing the value of the equity.

3.1.1. The option pricing model and the capital asset pricing model

The pricing of the equity (and debt) is consistent with the continuous time capital asset pricing model, which implies that the equilibrium rate of return to an asset at every point in time is

$$\bar{r}_j \stackrel{e}{=} r + \beta_j(\bar{r}_m - r),$$

(20)

where $\bar{r}_j$ is the instantaneous expected return to asset j, $\bar{r}_m$ is the instantaneous expected return to the market portfolio, and $\beta_j[\equiv \text{cov}(\bar{r}_j, \bar{r}_m)/\sigma^2(\bar{r}_m)]$ measures the systematic risk of security j.

If the systematic risk of the firm, β_v, is constant over time, the instantaneous risk of the equity, β_E, will not be stable. By Itô's lemma, the change in the value of the equity, E, is given by

$$dE = \frac{\partial E}{\partial V} dV + \left(\frac{\partial E}{\partial t} + \frac{1}{2} \frac{\partial^2 E}{\partial V^2} \sigma^2 V^2 \right) dt,$$ (21)

and the instantaneous return to the stockholders can be expressed as

$$r_E \equiv \frac{dE}{E} = \frac{\partial E}{\partial V} \frac{V}{E} \frac{dV}{V} + \left(\frac{\partial E}{\partial t} + \frac{1}{2} \frac{\partial^2 E}{\partial V^2} \sigma^2 V^2 \right) \frac{dt}{E}$$

$$\equiv \frac{\partial E}{\partial V} \frac{V}{E} r_v + \left(\frac{\partial E}{\partial t} + \frac{1}{2} \frac{\partial^2 E}{\partial V^2} \sigma^2 V^2 \right) \frac{dt}{E}.$$ (22)

Substituting into the definition of the systematic risk of the equity, β_E, yields

$$\beta_E \equiv \frac{\text{cov}(\tilde{r}_E, \tilde{r}_m)}{\sigma^2(r_m)} \equiv \frac{\partial E}{\partial V} \frac{V}{E} \frac{\text{cov}(\tilde{r}_v, \tilde{r}_m)}{\sigma^2(r_m)} \equiv \frac{\partial E}{\partial V} \frac{V}{E} \beta_v.$$ (23)

Thus, the beta of the equity can be expressed as the elasticity of the value of the equity with respect to the value of the firm, $\varepsilon(E, V)$, times the beta of the firm, β_v:

$$\beta_E \equiv \varepsilon(E, V)\beta_v,$$ (24)

where

$$\varepsilon(E, V) \equiv \frac{\partial E}{\partial V} \frac{V}{E}.$$

Since the elasticity of the value of the stock with respect to the value of the firm is greater than one,[10] the absolute value of the systematic risk of the stock is greater than the absolute value of the systematic risk of the firm; and the algebraic sign will be the same.

3.1.2. Bond covenants

Black and Scholes (1973), Jensen and Meckling (1976), Black and Cox (1976), Myers (1977), and Smith and Warner (1978) analyze the nature of the restrictive

[10]

$$\varepsilon(E, V) = \frac{\partial E}{\partial V} \frac{V}{E} = N\left\{ \frac{\ln(V/X) + (r + \sigma^2/2)T}{\sigma\sqrt{T}} \right\} \frac{V}{E}$$

$$= \frac{VN\left\{ \frac{\ln(V/X) + (r + \sigma^2/2)T}{\sigma\sqrt{T}} \right\}}{VN\left\{ \frac{\ln(V/X) + (r + \sigma^2/2)T}{\sigma\sqrt{T}} \right\} - Xe^{-rT}N\left\{ \frac{\ln(V/X) + (r - \sigma^2/2)T}{\sigma\sqrt{T}} \right\}} > 1.$$

Since the denominator differs from the numerator by the subtraction of a positive magnitude, the elasticity is greater than 1.

covenants which arise in corporate bonds. Since increases in dividend payments lower the ex-dividend value of the firm, reducing the bondholders' claim, bond contracts typically restrict the dividend payments which the firm can make.

If the firm obtains very risky projects (the variance rate is increased) the value of the equity rises, the value of the debt falls. There are three ways for the bondholders to protect themselves. (1) The caveat emptor solution would involve the bondholders' offering a price for the bonds low enough (insisting on a promised interest rate high enough) to compensate the bondholder for the risk associated with the most unfavorable action by the stockholders. If the stockholders do not acquire assets at least as risky as those presumed by the bondholders, then the bondholders will be overcompensated for the risk which they bear. Thus, if this solution is employed, low risk assets will not be acquired by firms with bonds in their capital structure. (2) The stockholders can write a restrictive covenant into the bond issue restricting the kinds of risky assets the firm can acquire. (3) The stockholders can collateralize the bonds (issue secured debt). This minimizes the uncertainty about the nature of the risk of that portion of the firm's assets, since these assets cannot be disposed without the permission of the bondholders.

It should be noted that in the Modigliani–Miller world employed in this option pricing analysis, the firm's owners have neither an incentive nor a disincentive to offer debt instruments which contain covenants. It is true that if the firm can issue claims which contain protective covenants, it will realize a higher price for those claims than it would for unprotected claims (which might sell for a zero price). However, the other claims which the firm issues will sell for a correspondingly lower price — any gain which a covenant provides to the protected claimholders will be a "loss" to other claimholders. Thus, for a given set of production investment decisions it is still the case that no particular set of financial contracts can alter the value of the firm. In this sense, covenants are "irrelevant". For the irrelevance propositions to be violated this analysis must be extended beyond the perfect markets assumptions. See Jensen–Meckling and Smith–Warner for analyses which include costly negotiation and enforcement of contracts.

The analysis has general applicability for a number of important issues in corporate finance and managerial economics. (1) Changes in capital structure and payout policy have implications for the value of the stockholders' and bondholders' claims. (2) The discount due to default risk in corporate bonds can be measured by subtracting the value of the bonds given by (18) from the value of a riskless bond with the same maturity and face value. (3) Coupon bonds are like compound options, or options on options. (4) Since unanticipated changes in the arguments in (17) and (18) affect the market values of the stockholders' and bondholders' claims, this analytical apparatus is useful in analyzing changes in corporate policy. Several papers have explicitly examined these issues.

3.1.3. Risk structure of interest rates

Merton (1974) suggests that since discussions of bond pricing frequently employ yields rather than bond prices, it is convenient to transform (18) into an excess return. Let the yield to maturity of a risky corporate bond with T periods to maturity (provided it does not default), $\hat{r}(T)$, be defined as

$$e^{-\hat{r}(T)T} \equiv D/X. \tag{25}$$

Then the risk premium on risky corporate debt can be measured by

$$\hat{r}(T) - r \equiv (-\ln(D/X)/T) - r. \tag{26}$$

This implicitly defines a risk structure of interest rates. Because of the relationship between the value of the debt and the other variables in the model (i.e. eq. (19)) the risk structure can also be expressed as a function of these variables:

$$\hat{r} = \hat{r}(V, X, T, \sigma^2, r) \tag{27}$$

where

$$\frac{\partial \hat{r}}{\partial V} < 0; \qquad \frac{\partial \hat{r}}{\partial X}; \qquad \frac{\partial \hat{r}}{\partial \sigma^2}; \qquad \frac{\partial \hat{r}}{\partial r} > 0 \quad \text{and} \quad \frac{\partial \hat{r}}{\partial T} \gtreqless 0.$$

The interpretation of the effect on the promised interest rate of the value of the assets, the variance rate, and the riskless rate are straightforward; those values which increase the value of the bonds reduce the promised interest rate. There is a less than proportional increase in the value of the bonds from an increase in the promised repayment because of the increased probability of default; thus, the promised interest rate rises. There are two effects on the promised interest rate of an increase in the time to maturity, either of which can dominate: (1) given the current value of the debt and promised repayment, an increase in the life of the loan lowers the promised interest rate; or (2) an increase in the time to repayment reduces the value of the debt, increasing the promised interest rate.

3.1.4. Coupon bonds

Thus far, only the simplest bond contracts have been considered, contracts which call for only one payment of principal plus interest at the maturity date of the contract. With required interest payments the stockholders' equity is like an option on an option on...an option on the assets of the firm. By paying the last coupon, the stockholders buy the option to purchase the firm by paying the face value of the debt. At the time of the next to last interest payment, the stockholders have an option on an option on an option. Although complicated (see Geske (1977)) the closed form solution to this case involves the same arguments as (17) and (18). Furthermore, it should be clear that a bond with a sinking fund provision will be strictly more valuable than one which is not.

Galai and Masulis (1976) employ comparative static analysis to examine the effect on changes in corporate investment policy. Given their assumptions they show that: (1) acquisitions which increase the variance rate of the firm will increase the value of the equity and decrease the value of the debt; (2) conglomerate mergers which reduce σ^2 increase the value of the debt and decrease the value of the equity; (3) only increases in the scale of the firm which are financed by proportional increases in the debt and equity cause no redistribution of ownership; and (4) spinoffs where assets are distributed only to stockholders reduce the value of the debt.

3.2. Convertible bond pricing

Ingersoll (1977) and Mikkelson (1978) analyze the pricing of a convertible discount bond, B. In addition to the standard assumptions, they assume that the convertible bond and the stock are the only liabilities issued by the company. The convertible bond contract specifies that at the bondholders' option, at the maturity date the bondholders can either receive the face value of the bonds, X, or new shares equal to α, fraction of the firm. Thus, the value of the convertible bonds at the maturity date, B^*, will be

$$B^* = \min\left[V^*, \max\left[X, \alpha V^*\right]\right]. \tag{28}$$

Fig. 4.4 illustrates the payoff function to equity and convertible bonds.

With the above assumptions, Merton has shown that any contingent claim must satisfy the following equation:

$$\frac{\partial f}{\partial t} = \frac{1}{2}\frac{\partial^2 f}{\partial V^2}\sigma^2 V^2 + rV\frac{\partial f}{\partial V} - rf, \tag{29}$$

where $f(V, t)$ is the value of the contingent claim as a function of V and t. Thus, the convertible bond price is the solution to (29) where $B(V, t) \equiv f(V, t)$ subject to (28). Again applying the above solution technique yields the following integral:

$$B = e^{-rT}\left[\int_0^X V^* L'(V^*)\,dV^* + \int_X^{X/\alpha} XL'(V^*)\,dV^* + \int_{X/\alpha}^\infty \alpha V^* L'(V^*)\,dV^*\right]. \tag{30}$$

These integrals can be rewritten as

$$B = e^{-rT}\left[\int_0^X V^* L'(V^*)\,dV^* + \int_X^\infty XL'(V^*)\,dV^* + \int_{X/\alpha}^\infty (\alpha V^* - X)L'(V^*)\,dV^*\right]. \tag{31}$$

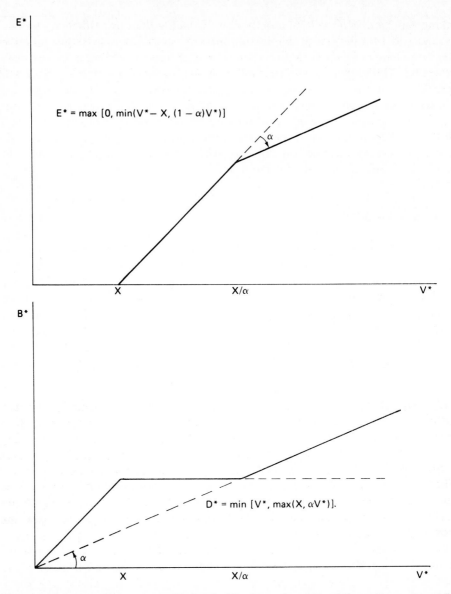

Figure 4.4. Dollar payoffs to a convertible bond with a face value of X and the option to convert the debt into a fraction α of the equity of the firm, as a function of the value of the assets of the firm's assets at the maturity of the convertible bonds, $B^* = \min[V^*, \max(X, \alpha V^*)]$; and dollar payoffs to equity as a function of the value of the assets of the firm, $E^* = \max[0, \min(V^* - X, (1-\alpha)V^*)]$.

The first two terms are the value of a nonconvertible discount bond,[11] $D(V,X,T,\sigma^2,r)$. The third term is just a call option on the α fraction of the firm with exercise price equal to the face value of the bond issue, X.[12] Thus, the convertible bond, B, is equivalent to a nonconvertible bond, D, plus a call option:

$$B(V,X,T,\alpha,\sigma^2,r) = D(V,X,T,\sigma^2,r) + c(\alpha V,X,T,\sigma^2,r), \tag{32}$$

where

$$\frac{\partial B}{\partial V} \equiv \frac{\partial D}{\partial V} + \alpha \frac{\partial C}{\partial \alpha V} > 0,$$

$$\frac{\partial B}{\partial \alpha} \equiv V \frac{\partial C}{\partial (\alpha V)} > 0,$$

$$\frac{\partial B}{\partial X} \equiv \frac{\partial D}{\partial X} + \frac{\partial C}{\partial X} > 0,$$

$$\frac{\partial B}{\partial T} \equiv \frac{\partial D}{\partial T} + \frac{\partial C}{\partial T} \gtreqless 0,$$

$$\frac{\partial B}{\partial \sigma^2} \equiv \frac{\partial D}{\partial \sigma^2} + \frac{\partial C}{\partial \sigma^2} \gtreqless 0,$$

$$\frac{\partial B}{\partial r} \equiv \frac{\partial D}{\partial r} + \frac{\partial C}{\partial r} < 0.$$

If the value of the firm's assets, V, increases, both the "bond" and "call" portion of the convertible debt become more valuable. If the fraction of the firm received through conversion, α, increases, then the "call" portion of the bond becomes more valuable without reducing the "bond" portion. If the face value of the debt increases (from X to X'), the payoff to the bondholders increases. When the value of the firm's assets is between the old face value and the new minimum conversion value (when V^* is between X and X'/α) other payoffs are unaffected. If either the time to maturity or the variance rate increases, the "bond" portion becomes less valuable while the "call" portion becomes more valuable. Either effect can dominate. If the interest rate increases, the present value of the promised repayment is reduced. Since in this bond there is no required dollar outlay at conversion, this is the only effect that must be considered.

For an analysis of callable convertible bonds and convertible preferred stock, see Ingersoll (1977).

[11]This can be seen by using the above theorem with $\psi=1, \phi=1, \lambda=\exp(-rT), \gamma=0$ for the first integral and $\psi=1, \phi=\infty, \lambda=0, \gamma=-\exp(-rT)$ for the second. This yields (18).
[12]Again employ the above theorem with $\psi=1/\alpha, \phi=0, \lambda=\alpha\exp(-rT), \gamma=\exp(-rT)$.

3.3. The pricing of subordinated debt

Black and Cox (1976) analyze the pricing of subordinated debt. They assume that, instead of one debt issue, there are two, one senior and one junior. The issues contain restrictions against dividend payments until after both the bond issues are paid off. Both bonds are discount bonds and both mature at t^*. If the value of the firm at t^* is greater than the face value of the senior debt, X_s, then the senior bondholders receive their promised repayment; if not, the senior bondholders receive the assets of the firm and the junior bondholders and stockholders receive nothing. If the value of the firm is greater than the sum of the face value of the senior debt plus the face value of the junior debt, X_j, then the junior bondholders receive their promised payment, and the stockholders receive the residual. If the value of the firm at t^* is between X_s and $X_s + X_j$, the junior bondholders receive the difference between the value of the firm and the X_s. Thus, the boundary conditions for the equity and respective debt issues are

$$E^* = \max\left[0, V^* - (X_s + X_j)\right], \tag{33}$$

$$D_s^* = \min\left[V^*, X_s\right], \tag{34}$$

$$D_j^* = \max\left[\min(V^* - X_s, X_j), 0\right]. \tag{35}$$

Fig. 4.5 illustrates the payoff function to the equity and junior and senior bonds.

Again, (28) can be applied to define the appropriate differential equation with $E(V, t) \equiv f(V, t)$, $D_s(V, t) \equiv f(V, t)$, or $D_j(V, t) \equiv f(V, t)$, subject to (33), (34) or (35), respectively. These equations can again be solved using the above technique. In a risk neutral world, the value of the equity, senior debt, and junior debt can be expressed as

$$E = e^{-rT} \int_{X_s + X_j}^{\infty} \left(V^* - (X_s + X_j)\right) L'(V^*) \, dV^*, \tag{36}$$

$$D_s = e^{-rt} \left[\int_0^{X_s} V^* L'(V^*) \, dV^* + \int_{X_s}^{\infty} X_s L'(V^*) \, dV^* \right], \tag{37}$$

$$D_j = e^{-rT} \left[\int_{X_s}^{X_s + X_j} (V^* - X_s) L'(V^*) \, dV^* + \int_{X_s + X_j}^{\infty} X_j L'(V^*) c V^* \right]. \tag{38}$$

Inspection demonstrates that the pricing of the senior debt is unchanged. The value of the equity is unchanged with $X \equiv X_s + X_j$. Eq. (38) can be solved to

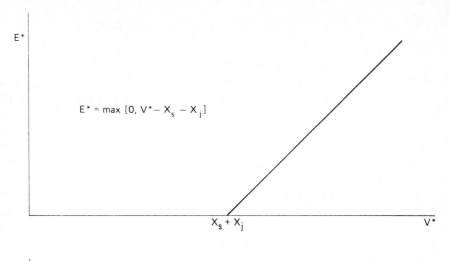

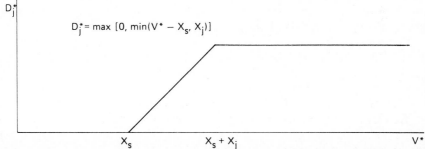

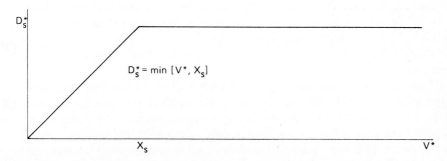

Figure 4.5. Dollar payoffs to a senior debt issue with a face value of X_s as a function of the value of the firm's assets at the maturity date of the bonds, $D_s = \min[V^*, X_s]$; dollar payoffs to a junior debt issue with a face value of X_j as a function of the value of the firm's assets, $D_j = \max[0, \min(V^* - X_s, X_j)]$; and dollar payoffs to the equity as a function of the value of the assets of the firm, $E^* = \max[0, V^* - X_s - X_j]$.

yield the closed-form solution for the value of the junior debt:

$$
\begin{aligned}
D_j = V \Bigg[& N \left\{ \frac{\ln(V/X_s) + (r + \sigma^2/2)T}{\sigma\sqrt{T}} \right\} \\
& - N \left\{ \frac{\ln(V/(X_s + X_j)) + (r + \sigma^2/2)T}{\sigma\sqrt{T}} \right\} \Bigg] \\
- X_s e^{-rT} \Bigg[& N \left\{ \frac{\ln(V/X_s) + (r - \sigma^2/2)T}{\sigma\sqrt{T}} \right\} \\
& - N \left\{ \frac{\ln(V/(X_s + X_j)) + (r - \sigma^2/2)T}{\sigma\sqrt{T}} \right\} \Bigg] \\
+ (X_s + X_j) e^{-rT} N & \left\{ \frac{\ln(V/(X_s + X_j)) + (r - \sigma^2/2)T}{\sigma\sqrt{T}} \right\}.
\end{aligned}
\tag{39}
$$

In general form this can be expressed as

$$
D_j = D_j(V, X_s, X_j, T, \sigma^2, r),
\tag{40}
$$

where

$$
\frac{\partial D_j}{\partial V}, \frac{\partial D_j}{\partial X_j}, > 0; \qquad \frac{\partial D_j}{\partial X_s}, < 0 \quad \text{and} \quad \frac{\partial D_j}{\partial T}, \frac{\partial D_j}{\partial \sigma^2}, \frac{\partial D_j}{\partial r} \gtrless 0.
$$

The ambiguity of the response of the value of the junior debt with respect to the time to maturity of the bonds, the variance rate, and the riskless rate arises because of the dual debt/equity behavior of the instrument. If the value of the firm is "close to" the face value of the senior debt, the junior debt is virtually equivalent to an equity claim. Conversely, if the value of the firm is "close to" the sum of the face values of the junior and senior debt, then it behaves like a debt issue.

Absolute priority. Note that throughout the analysis of the firm's liabilities, the assumptions involving the distribution of the firm's assets among the claimants in the event of bankruptcy has been very clearcut. Here, if the value of the firm is below the face value of the senior debt, the senior debtholders get all the firm's assets and the junior debtholders and equity holders receive nothing. Warner (1977) has examined the law as it is applied to these issues and found that this is not strictly true. In bankruptcy, reorganization is often accompanied by issuance of new claims. The courts have consistently refused to consider the actual market value of the new claims as compared to the old and instead consider the claims satisfied if the face value of the new claim is not less than the face value of the old claim. This suggests that the above closed form solutions will overstate the value of the more senior debt and understate the value of the equity. The value of the junior debt may be over- or understated.

3.4. Pricing of warrants and rights

Smith (1977) employs the Black–Scholes (1973) option pricing framework to derive the equilibrium value for a warrant or rights issue under the standard assumptions plus:

(1) The only liabilities issued by the firm are its common stock and the warrants.
(2) The total proceeds if the warrants are exercised is X (the exercise price per share times the total number of shares sold through the rights issue). The warrants expire after T time periods. If the warrants are exercised, the shares sold through the offering will be a fraction, α, of the total number of shares outstanding ($\alpha \equiv Q_W / Q_S + Q_W$), where Q_W is the number of shares sold through the warrant issue and Q_S is the existing number of shares). Any assets acquired with the proceeds of the warrant issue are acquired at competitive prices.[13]

Given these assumptions, the value of the warrants at the expiration date, W^*, will be either zero, in which case the warrants will not be exercised or, if the warrants are valuable and are exercised, their value is their claim on the total assets of the firm, $\alpha(V^* + X)$ (where V^* is the value of the firm's current assets and X is the proceeds of the exercise of the rights) minus the payment the warrant holders must make, X:

$$W^* = \max[0, \alpha(V^* + X) - X], \tag{41}$$

where W^* is the value of the warrant issue at the expiration date of the issue, t^*, V^* is the value of the firm's assets at the expiration date of the issue, X is the proceeds to the firm of the exercise of the warrants, and α is the fraction of new shares issued through the warrant issue to the total shares of the firm (both old and new) presuming the warrants are exercised.

Given the above assumptions, (29) can again be applied with $W(V,t) \equiv f(V,t)$ to define the differential equation

$$\frac{\partial W}{\partial t} = \frac{1}{2} \frac{\partial^2 W}{\partial V^2} \sigma^2 V^2 + rV \frac{\partial W}{\partial V} - rW, \tag{42}$$

subject to the boundary condition in (41).

---

[13]This last assumption is necessary to avoid the problem of the dependence of the dynamic behavior of the stock price on the probability of the rights being exercised. This problem is similar to that described by Long (1974).

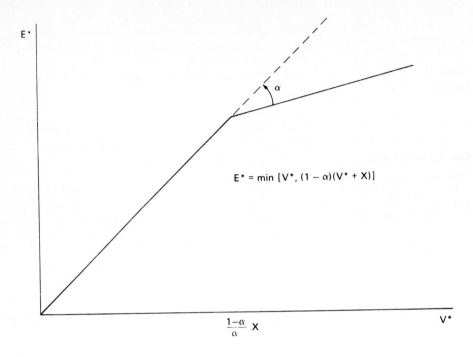

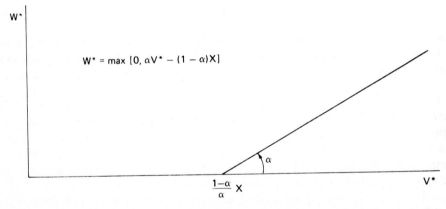

Figure 4.6. Dollar payoffs to a warrant (or rights) issue with exercise price X, representing a claim to a fraction α of the firm's equity, $W^* = \max[0, \alpha V^* - (1 - \alpha)X]$; and dollar payoffs to equity as a function of the value of the assets of the firm, $E^* = \min[V^*, (1 - \alpha)(V^* + X)]$.

To solve the equation, again assume that the market is composed of risk-neutral investors. In that case, the equilibrium rate of return on all assets will be equal; specifically, the expected rate of return on the firm, and the warrants will equal the riskless rate. Then the current warrants price must be the discounted terminal price:

$$W = e^{-rT} \int_{[(1-\alpha)/\alpha]X}^{\infty} [\alpha V^* - (1-\alpha)X] L'(V^*) dV^*, \tag{43}$$

where $L'(V^*)$ is the log normal density function. Fig. 4.6 illustrates the payoff function to the equity and warrant holders.

Eq. (43) can be solved employing the above theorem with $\psi = (1-\alpha)/\alpha$, $\phi = \infty$, $\lambda = \gamma e^{-rT}$, and $\gamma = (1-\alpha)e^{-rT}$ to yield:

$$W = \alpha V N \left\{ \frac{\ln(\alpha V/(1-\alpha)X) + (r+\sigma^2/2)T}{\sigma\sqrt{T}} \right\}$$

$$- e^{-rT}(1-\alpha)XN \left\{ \frac{\ln(\alpha V/(1-\alpha)X) + (r-\sigma^2/2)T}{\sigma\sqrt{T}} \right\}$$

$$\equiv c(\alpha V, T, (1-\alpha)X, \sigma^2, r) = W(V, T, X, \alpha, \sigma^2, r), \tag{44}$$

where

$$\frac{\partial W}{\partial V}, \frac{\partial W}{\partial T}, \frac{\partial W}{\partial \alpha}, \frac{\partial W}{\partial \sigma^2}, \frac{\partial W}{\partial r} > 0 \quad \text{and} \quad \frac{\partial W}{\partial X} < 0.$$

The indicated partial effects have intuitive interpretations. Increasing the value of the firm, decreasing the exercise price (holding the proportion of the firm's shares offered through the warrant issue constant), or increasing the proportion of the firm's shares offered through the warrant issue (holding the total proceeds of the issue constant) increase the expected payoff to the warrants and thus increase the current market value of the warrants. An increase in the time to expiration or the riskless rate lowers the present value of the exercise payment, and thus increases the value of the warrants. Finally, an increase in the time to expiration or the variance rate gives a higher probability of a large increase in the value of the firm and increases the value of the warrants.

4. The pricing of other contingent claims

4.1. The pricing of underwriting contracts

Smith (1977) analyzes the appropriate compensation to an underwriter for the risk he bears in underwriting the sale of additional equity of an all equity firm. In addition to the standard assumptions, make the following assumptions about the underwriting contract:

> Underwriters submit a bid, $\hat{B}$, today which specifies that on the offer date, T time periods from now, the underwriter will pay $\hat{B}$ dollars and receive shares of stock representing fraction α of the total shares of the firm. He can sell the securities at the offer price and receive Ω, or (if the share price is below the offer price) at the market price, $\alpha(V^* + \hat{B})$. If his bid is accepted, he will be notified immediately.

Again, (29) can be employed where $f(V,t)$ is the function representing the value of the underwriting contract (i.e. $U = U(V,t)$). To be well posed, the appropriate boundary condition must be specified. At the offer date the underwriter will pay the firm $\hat{B}$ dollars. The shares which the underwriter receives represent a claim to a fraction γ of the total assets of the firm, $V^* + \hat{B}$. If the offer price is greater than the value of the shares, $\gamma(V^* + \hat{B})$, then the underwriter will sell the shares at the offer price and receive Ω. If, at the offer date the offer price is less than the value of the shares, the underwriter receives the value of the shares. Therefore, the boundary condition is that at the offer date the underwriting contract is worth the minimum of the market value of the shares minus the bid, $\hat{B}$, or the proceeds of the sale at the offer price minus the bid:

$$U^* = \min\left[\alpha(V^* + \hat{B}) - \hat{B}, \Omega - \hat{B} \right]. \tag{45}$$

Again, the above solution technique can be employed to solve (29) subject to (45). In a risk-neutral world, the expected value of the underwriting contract can be expressed as[14]

$$U = \int_0^{\Omega/\alpha - \hat{B}} \left[\alpha(V^* + \hat{B}) - \hat{B} \right] L'(V^*) dV^* + \int_{\Omega/\alpha - \hat{B}}^{\infty} \left[\Omega - \hat{B} \right] L'(V^*) dV^*. \tag{46}$$

Note that this can be rewritten as

$$U = \int_0^{\infty} \left[\alpha(V^* + \hat{B}) - \hat{B} \right] L'(V^*) dV^* - \int_{\Omega/\alpha - \hat{B}}^{\infty} \left[V^* - \left(\frac{\Omega}{\alpha} - \hat{B} \right) \right] L'(V^*) dV^* \tag{47}$$

Eq. (47) can be solved for the risk-neutral case to yield[15]

$$U = e^{rT} \alpha V - (1 - \alpha)\hat{B} - e^{rT} \gamma V N \left\{ \frac{\ln(\alpha V/(\Omega - \alpha\hat{B})) + (r + \sigma^2/2)T}{\sigma\sqrt{T}} \right\}$$

$$+ (\Omega - \hat{B}\alpha) N \left\{ \frac{\ln(\alpha V/(\Omega - \alpha\hat{B})) + (r - \sigma^2/2)T}{\sigma\sqrt{T}} \right\}. \tag{48}$$

---

[14]Since the contract calls for the payment only at t^*, to find the current value of the underwriting contract does not require discounting.

[15]Use theorem 1 with $\psi X = 0$, $\phi X = \infty$, $\lambda S^* = \alpha V^*$, $\gamma X = (1 - \alpha)\hat{B}$. And for the second term, let $\psi X = \Omega/\alpha - \hat{B}$, $\phi X = \infty$, $\lambda S^* = \alpha V^*$, $\gamma X = (\Omega/\alpha) - \hat{B}$.

Eq. (48) is equivalent to a long position in the firm, a cash payment, and writing a call on α of the firm with an exercise price equal to $(\Omega - \alpha\hat{B})$:

$$U = e^{rT}\alpha V - (1-\alpha)B - e^{rT}c(\alpha V, T; \Omega - \alpha\hat{B}),$$

$$= e^{rT}\alpha V - (1-\alpha)B - e^{rT}\alpha c\left(V, T; \frac{\Omega}{\alpha} - \hat{B}\right). \tag{49}$$

If the process of preparing and submitting a bid is costless, then in a competitive equilibrium, the value of the underwriting contract must be zero.[16] Therefore, the bid which would represent a normal compensation for the risk he bears is implicitly defined by the equation[17]

$$\hat{B} - e^{rT}\frac{\alpha}{1-\alpha}\left[V - c\left(V, T; \frac{\Omega}{\alpha} - \hat{B}\right)\right] = 0. \tag{50}$$

The firm generally receives less than the market value of the stock[18] because, given the underwriting contract, if the equilibrium stock price at the offer date is above the offer price then the initial purchaser of the issue receives "rents"; he obtains the shares for less than the market value of the shares. Therefore, if the offer price in the underwriting agreement represents a binding constraint to the underwriter, then in a perfect market underwriting is a more expensive method of raising additional capital than are pre-emptive rights. Therefore, under these conditions underwriting would not be employed.

The above analysis implicitly assumes that the terms of the underwriting contract represent a binding constraint to the underwriter: if the security price is above the offer price, then the offer price presents a constraint to the underwriter and a pure profit opportunity to the potential investor. However, in a market without transactions costs, this should not be the case. If the security price is above the offer price there will be excess demand for the issue. To the extent that the underwriter can, through the rationing process, extract those profits, they will accrue to the underwriter rather than to the initial purchaser. Furthermore, if the underwriter can *systematically* extract those profits, then competitive underwriter bidding would insure that the profits were in fact garnered by the firm. In that case the offer price presents no effective constraint and the competitive bid becomes simply

$$\hat{B} = e^{rT}\left(\frac{\alpha}{1-\alpha}\right)V. \tag{51}$$

Therefore, if through tie-in sales or other means the offer price in an underwriting agreement can be circumvented, then underwriting is no more expensive a

---

[16] If this were not the case, arbitrage profits could be earned by acquiring an underwriting contract and establishing the above hedge.

[17] This equation implicitly defines the bid because $\hat{B}$ appears twice in the equation. The explicit solution for equilibrium bid can be found by standard numerical analysis techniques.

[18] A sufficient condition for the bid to be less than the market value of the shares is that $(1-\alpha)$ be less than e^{rT}. Since T is generally a matter of days, this condition should be met.

method of raising additional capital than a rights offering. However, indirect evidence suggests underwriters are unable to systematically extract these profits.[19]

4.2. The pricing of collateralized loans

The same analysis used to value the debt of a levered firm can also be employed to value collateralized loans. To derive an explicit pricing equation for the equity and debt, make the following assumptions:

(1) There are homogeneous expectations about the dynamic behavior of the value of the collateral. The distribution at the end of any finite time interval is log normal. The variance rate of return is constant.

(2) The collateral provides a continuous flow of service to the borrower. The net value of the flow of services, S, is a constant fraction, s, of the market value of the assets: $s = S/V$.

(3) The dynamic behavior of the value of the assets is independent of the value of the probability of bankruptcy.

(4) There are no costs to voluntary liquidation or bankruptcy. Bankruptcy is defined as the state in which the borrower's assets are less than the promised repayment amount of a maturing loan.

(5) Capital markets and the market for the collateral are perfect. There are no transactions costs or taxes. All participants have free access to all available information. Participants are price takers.

(6) There is a known constant riskless rate, r.

This loan contract is equivalent to the sale of the collateral to the lender by the borrower for a package containing: (1) the proceeds of the loan, D, (2) a lease which allows the borrower to use the assets over the life of the loan, plus (3) a call option to repurchase the assets at the maturity date of the loan, t^*, with an exercise price equal to the promised repayment amount of the loan, X. Thus, the value of the borrower's equity is like a call option plus a lease, and those techniques which have been developed to price options can also be employed to value loans.

Given these assumptions, Merton (1974) has shown that this contingent claim must satisfy the partial differential equation:

$$\frac{\partial D}{\partial t} = rD + (sV + rV)\frac{\partial D}{\partial V} - \tfrac{1}{2}\sigma^2 V^2 \frac{\partial^2 D}{\partial V^2}, \tag{52}$$

where sV is that portion of the flow accruing to this particular contingent claim, and σ^2 is the variance rate on the value of the assets.[19]

---

[19]For example, the underwriter's compensation for debt issues is significantly lower than for a comparable equity issue. Since the debt is less risky, the implicit option would be less valuable.

Employing the above solution technique, the value of the debt can be expressed as

$$D = e^{-rT} \left[\int_0^X V^* L'(V^*) \, dV^* + \int_X^\infty X L'(V^*) \, dV^* \right]. \tag{53}$$

Employing the above theorem, the closed-form solution to this integral, assuming that the total return on the collateral, $\rho + s$, equals the riskless rate, r, can be expressed as

$$D = Ve^{-sT} N \left\{ \frac{-\ln(V/X) - (r - s + \sigma^2/2) T}{\sigma \sqrt{T}} \right\}$$

$$+ Xe^{-rT} N \left\{ \frac{\ln(V/X) + (r - s - \sigma^2/2) T}{\sigma \sqrt{T}} \right\}, \tag{54}$$

$$= D(V, X, T, \sigma^2, s, r), \tag{55}$$

where

$$\frac{\partial D}{\partial V}, \frac{\partial D}{\partial X} > 0 \quad \text{and} \quad \frac{\partial D}{\partial T}, \frac{\partial D}{\partial \sigma^2}, \frac{\partial D}{\partial s}, \frac{\partial D}{\partial r} < 0.$$

The partial effects are the same as those for the corporate bonds with the addition of $\partial D/\partial s > 0$. If the net service flow (for example, for a mortgage loan, s would be the value of the rental services minus the maintenance, insurance and tax expenditures) increases, the expected price appreciation, ρ, falls. Thus, the expected value of the loan at the expiration of the loan will be less, and default is more likely. This decreases the value of the debt.

4.3. The pricing of leases

As was suggested above, the value of the borrower's equity in the collateral is equivalent to a call option to purchase the collateral with the exercise price equal to the promised repayment on the loan, plus a lease. Therefore, the value of the lease equals the value of the collateral minus the value of the debt minus the value of the call:

$$L = V - D - C$$

$$= V - \left[e^{-rT} \int_0^X V^* L'(V^*) \, dV^* + e^{-rT} \int_X XL'(V^*) \, dV^* \right]$$

$$- \left[e^{-rT} \int_X^\infty (V^* - X) L'(V^*) \, dV^* \right]$$

$$= V - \left[e^{-rT} \int_X^\infty V^* L'(V^*) \, dV^* \right]. \tag{56}$$

Notice that this equation has an intuitive interpretation: the value of the lease equals the value of the asset minus a claim on the value of the asset T periods from now. Eq. (56) can be solved to yield

$$L = V[1 - e^{-sT}]. \tag{57}$$

This explicitly points out that, given our assumptions, the value of the lease is independent of any financing decisions.

4.4. The pricing of insurance

Mayers and Smith (1977) and Merton (1977) examine the pricing of insurance contracts and loan guarantees. They assume

(1) The insurance contract calls for the payment of a premium, P, at the current date, t. If at the expiration date of the contract, t^*, the market value of the insured asset, V^*, is less than its insured value, X, then the insurance contract will pay the holder of the policy the difference, $X - V^*$. If the market value of the insured asset is greater than its insured value, then there is no payment.

Thus, at the expiration date the value of the insurance contract, P^*, will be the maximum of either the difference between the insured value and the market value of the asset, or zero:

$$P^* = \max[X - V^*], 0]. \tag{58}$$

This contract is equivalent to a European put option on the asset with an exercise price set at the insured value of the asset. Thus, with the following additional assumptions, the Black–Scholes put pricing solution also yields the general equilibrium price for the above insurance contract:

(2) There are homogeneous expectations about the dynamics of the value of the insured asset, V. The distribution of the value at the end of any finite time integral is log normal. The variance rate, σ^2, is constant.
(3) There is a known constant instantaneously riskless rate, r, which is the same for borrowers and lenders.
(4) Capital markets are perfect: there are no transactions costs or taxes and all traders have free and costless access to all available information. Borrowing and perfect short sales are allowed. Traders are price takers in the capital markets.
(5) Trading takes place continuously, price changes are continuous and assets are infinitely divisible.
(6) The insured asset generates no pecuniary or nonpecuniary flows.

The Black–Scholes European put pricing solution and thus the insurance pricing solution can be expressed as

$$P = - VN\left\{ \frac{-\ln(V/X)-(r+\sigma^2/2)T}{\sigma\sqrt{T}} \right\}$$
$$+ Xe^{-rT}N\left\{ \frac{-\ln(V/X)-(r-\sigma^2/2)T}{\sigma\sqrt{T}} \right\}, \tag{59}$$

where P is the insurance premium, V is the current market value of the insured asset, X is the insured value of the asset, T is the time to the expiration of the contract $(\equiv t^* - t)$, r is the riskless rate of interest, σ^2 is the variance rate on V, and $N\{\cdot\}$ is the cumulative standard normal density function.

If the insured value of the property can be obtained on demand any time while the policy is in force, not just at the expiration date, then the policy is equivalent to an American put. Although the closed form solution to the American put is not known, the general form solution can be expressed as

$$P = P(V, X, T, \sigma^2, r), \tag{60}$$

where

$$\frac{\partial P}{\partial V}, \frac{\partial P}{\partial r} < 0; \qquad \frac{\partial P}{\partial X}, \frac{\partial P}{\partial T}, \frac{\partial P}{\partial \sigma^2} > 0.$$

These partial derivatives have intuitive interpretations: if the value of the insured asset, V, rises, the asset is less likely to have a value below the insured value. Thus, the insurance policy has a smaller expected payout and the required premium is less. If the insured value of the asset, X, is increased, the expected payout is higher and the required premium is higher. If the expiration date of the policy, T, is increased, the required premium increases, for it is more likely that the policy will be employed.[20] If the variance rate, σ^2, increases, there is a higher probability of a large negative change in the value of the asset and a large payout; thus the required premium rises. If the riskless interest rate, r, rises, the present value of any payoffs falls, thus the required premium falls.

The assumptions employed in deriving (59) are fairly restrictive; however, in the special case of mortgage insurance they are generally met. Assume that a loan is secured by a house and that the loan is to be repaid in one lump sum. The insurance premium is paid by the borrower at the origination of the loan and the policy agrees to pay the difference between the promised repayment and the market value of the house if the borrower defaults. If there were no default costs for the borrower, he would default if the market value of the house were less than the promised repayment at the expiration of the loan contract. Thus,

[20]For the simpler contract which was only exercisable at the expiration date (and for European puts) this sign is ambiguous. This is the only partial effect that differs in sign between the two cases.

for the lender a mortgage insurance policy is equivalent to a policy insuring that the value of the house, V^*, will be no less than the promised repayment amount of the loan (see fig. 4.7).

This approach to the analysis of insurance contracts points out that the traditional economic analysis of the supply of insurance is but a special case. It has been established that when events are independent competitively supplied insurance is priced at the "actuarily fair" price, i.e. the price is set equal to the discounted (at the riskless rate) expected payout. The analysis presented above suggests that this is only a special case. The option pricing equations of Black and Scholes (1973) are consistent with the continuous time capital asset pricing model. Specifically, the put is priced according to its marginal risk. Furthermore, the marginal risk of a put is related to the marginal risk of the underlying asset:

$$\beta_p = \varepsilon(P, V)\beta_V, \tag{61}$$

where β_p is the beta of the put, $\varepsilon(P, V)$ is the partial elasticity of the value of the put with respect to the value of the underlying asset, $(\partial P / \partial V)(V / P)$, and β_V is the beta of the underlying asset. Thus, since the elasticity is algebraically less than minus one, the beta of the insurance policy will be zero, and therefore the equilibrium rate of return on the insurance contract will equal the riskless rate, *only if* the marginal risk of the underlying asset is zero. This may be the case for life insurance, but probably not for mortgage or fire insurance. Any systematic risk is not insurable risk; the insuror must be compensated for bearing that risk.

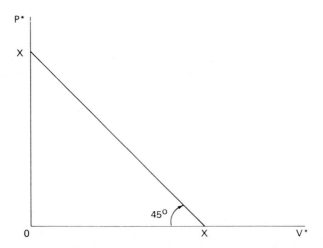

Figure 4.7. Dollar payoffs to a mortgage insurance policy where the promised repayment amount of the loan and the insured value of the loan is X, $P^* = \max[X - V^*, 0]$.

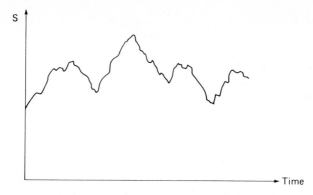

Figure 4.8. sample path of S where S follows an Itô process.

Appendix: An introduction to stochastic calculus

Itô's lemma is a differentiation rule by which functions of certain random variables can be differentiated — specifically, random variables whose movement can be described as an Itô process. An Itô process is a continuous Markov process in continuous time.[21] The sample path of such a process will be continuous (can be drawn without picking the pen up from the paper). Fig. 4.8 illustrates the sample path of a random variable, S, which follows an Itô process through time.

All Itô processes can be prepresented as[22]

$$dS = \mu(S,t)\,dt + \sigma(S,t)\,dZ, \tag{A.1}$$

where dZ is introduced as the Itô differential of a standard Gauss–Wiener process. In many recent finance articles, the return to financial assets is expressed as a differential equation like (A.1). For the understanding of the equation and its implications, it is necessary to understand the meaning of the differential dZ and observe its peculiarities.

If, for example, $q(t)$ is an ordinary (nonrandom) variable, then for any real number $k, k > 1$:[23]

$$(dq(t))^k = 0. \tag{A.2}$$

[21] A Markov process depends at most on the most recent observation.
[22] This can be generated so that S, μ, and σ, are N vectors and $dZ(t)$ is an N vector of standard normal random variables. In that case $Z(t)$ is a multidimensional Wiener process.
[23] This is not strictly true. More precisely what is meant is that if differentials of magnitude $dq(t)$ are the magnitudes of interest, then $(dq(t))^k$ for $k > 1$ will be of a smaller order of magnitude and may be ignored. For the purposes of this exposition, the above, somewhat imprecise, terminology will be employed.

However, it will be shown that a similar statement about dZ is not true. In fact, if $Y = F(t, Z)$ is a function of t and Z, then

$$dY = \left(\frac{\partial F}{\partial t} + \frac{1}{2} \frac{\partial^2 F}{\partial Z(t)^2} \right) dt + \frac{\partial F}{\partial Z(t)} dZ(t). \tag{A.3}$$

While if $y = G(t, q)$ is a function of t and a nonrandom variable, q, the differential is

$$dy = \frac{\partial G}{\partial t} dt + \frac{\partial G}{\partial q(t)} dq(t). \tag{A.4}$$

Eq. (A.4) is a well-known result from ordinary calculus, while (A.3) is a special case of Itô's lemma from stochastic calculus.

Unfortunately, references on stochastic calculus are often written in a form inaccessible to the nonspecialist interested in the application of these concepts. This note represents an attempt to reintroduce these concepts in a simplified and intuitive way.

First, recall two computationally useful results from statistics.

Result 1. Let X be a normal random variable with probability distribution function

$$f(x) = \frac{1}{\sqrt{(2\pi)}\sigma} \exp\left[-(x - x_0)^2 / 2\sigma^2 \right]. \tag{A.5}$$

Then for any positive integer n,[24]

$$E\left[(X - x_0)^n \right] = \begin{cases} (n-1)!!\,\sigma^n, & \text{if } n \text{ is even,} \\ 0, & \text{if } n \text{ is odd.} \end{cases} \tag{A.6}$$

Result 2. Let X be a random variable with distribution function $f_1(x)$ and let $M_n = E(X^n)$, for any positive integer n, let Y be a random variable with conditional distribution function[25]

$$f_2(y|x) = f_2(y|X = x) = \frac{1}{\sqrt{(2\pi)}\sigma} \exp\left[-(y - x)^2 / 2\sigma^2 \right]. \tag{A.7}$$

For any integer $k \geqslant 0$ the following are true:

Result 2a. $E(YX^k) = M_{k+1}$ \hfill (A.8)

---

[24]The double factorial notation means multiply all the odd numbers: $R!! = R(R-2)(R-4)\cdots 3 \cdot 1$, where R is odd.
[25]Note that the conditional mean of Y is x: $E(y|x) = x$.

Proof. $E(YX^k) = \iint_{xy} [yf_2(y|x)\,dy]x^k f_1(x)\,dx$

$$= \int_x E[y|x]x^k f_1(x)\,dx$$

$$= \int_x xx^k f_1(x)\,dx$$

$$= M_{k+1}.$$

Result 2b. $E[Y^2X^k] = \sigma^2 M_k + M_{k+2}.$

(A.9)

Proof. $E[Y^2X^k] = \iint_{xy} [y^2 f_2(y|x)\,dy]x^k f_1(x)\,dx$

$$= \int_x E[y^2|x]x^k f_1(x)\,dx$$

$$= \int_x (\sigma^2 + x^2)x^k f_1(x)\,dx$$

$$= M_k \sigma^2 + M_{k+2}.$$

Note: $\sigma^2 = E[((y|x) - x)^2]$

$$= E[(y^2|x) - 2x(y|x) + x^2]$$

$$= E[y^2|x] - 2xE[y|x] + x^2$$

$$= E[y^2|x] - 2xx + x^2$$

$$= E[y^2|x] - x^2.$$

Therefore: $E[y^2|x] = \sigma^2 + x^2.$

Result 2c. $E[Y^3X^k] = 3\sigma^2 M_{k+1} + M_{k+3}.$

(A.10)

Proof. $E[Y^3X^k] = \iint_{xy} [y^3 f_2(y|x)\,dy]xf_1(x)\,dx$

$$= \int_x E[y^3|x]x^k f_1(x)\,dx$$

$$= \int_x (3\sigma^2 x + x^3)x^k f_1(x)\,dx$$

$$= 3\sigma^2 M_{k+1} + M_{k+3}.$$

Note: $\sigma^3 = E[(y|x) - x)^3]$

$\qquad = E[(y^3|x) - 3(y^2|x)x + 3(y|x)x^2 - x^3]$

$\qquad = E[y^3|x] - 3xE[y^2|x] + 3x^2E[y|x] - x^3$

$\qquad = E[y^3|x] - 3x(\sigma^2 + x^2) + 3x^3 - x^3$

$\qquad = E[y^3|x] - 3x\sigma^2 - x^3.$

Therefore: $E[y^3|x] = 3x\sigma^2 + x^3 + \sigma^3$

But from (A.6), $\sigma^3 = 0$. Then, $E[y^3|x] = 3x\sigma^2 + x^3$.

Result 2d. $E[Y^4X^k] = \sigma^4 M_k + 6\sigma^2 M_{k+2} + M_{k+4}.$ $\qquad$ (A.11)

Proof. $E[Y^4X^k] = \int_x \int_y [y^4 f_2(y|x) dy] x^k f_1(x) dx$

$\qquad\qquad = \int_x E[y^4|x] x^k f_1(x) dz$

$\qquad\qquad = \int_x (3\sigma^4 + 6x^2\sigma^2 + x^4) x^k f_1(x) dx$

$\qquad\qquad = 3\sigma^4 M_k + 6\sigma^2 M_{k+2} + M_{k+4}.$

Note: $3\sigma^4 = E[((y|x) - x)^4]$

$\qquad = E[(y^4|x) - 4(y^3|x)x + 6(y^2|x)x^2 - 4(y|x)x^3 + x^4]$

$\qquad = E[y^4|x] - 4xE[y^3|x] + 6x^2E[y^2|x] - 4x^3E[y|x] + x^4$

$\qquad = E[y^4|x] - 4x(3x\sigma^2 + x^3) + 6x^2(\sigma^2 + x^2) - 4x^3x + x^4$

$\qquad = E[y^4|x] - 6x^2\sigma^2 - x^4.$

Therefore: $E[y^4|x] = 3\sigma^4 + 6x^2\sigma^2 + x^4$.

In the simplest terms, a standard Gauss–Wiener process can be defined as a stochastic process $Z(t)$, such that for any t and t_0, where $t > t_0$, the conditional distribution function of $Z(t)$, given $Z(t_0)$, is given by[26]

$$f(z|z_0) = f_{Z(t)}(z|Z(t_0) = z_0) \qquad (A.12)$$

$$= \frac{1}{\sqrt{(2\pi)(t - t_0)}} \exp\left[-(z - z_0)^2/2(t - t_0)\right]. \qquad (A.13)$$

For such a process, the Itô differential, $dZ(t)$ is defined as

$$dZ(t) = \lim_{h \to 0} (Z(t + h) - Z(t)), \qquad h > 0, \qquad (A.14)$$

[26]Note that the variance of Z is $(t - t_0)$.

or in terms of the differential dt as

$$dZ(t) = Z(t+dt) - Z(t), \qquad dt > 0. \tag{A.15}$$

Proposition 1. Let $dZ(t)$ be as defined in (15), then

$$E[dZ(t)] = 0 \tag{A.16}$$

and

$$E[dZ(t)^2] = dt. \tag{A.17}$$

Proof. (A.16) follows from (A.13) and (A.6). To show (A.17) observe that

$$E[dZ(t)^2] = E[(Z(t+dt) - Z(t))^2]$$
$$= E[Z(t+dt)^2] - 2E[Z(t+dt)Z(t)] + E[Z(t)^2]. \tag{A.18}$$

If $M_0 = 1$ and $M_k = E[Z(t)^k]$, for k a positive integer then from (A.9): $E[Y^2 X^k]$ $= \sigma^2 M_k + M_{k+2}$. Let $Y = Z(t+dt)$ and $X^0 = 1$. Then

$$E[Z(t+dt)^2] = dt + M_2. \tag{A.19}$$

From (A.8): $E[YX^k] = M_2$. Let $Y = Z(t+dt)$ and $X^k = Z(t)^l$. Then:

$$E[Z(t+dt)Z(t)] = M_2. \tag{A.20}$$

Finally, from (5):

$$E[Z(t)^2] = M_2. \tag{A.21}$$

Substituting (A.19)–(A.21) into (A.18) yields:

$$E[dZ^2] = (dt + M_2) - 2M_2 + M_2$$
$$= dt.$$

Thus (A.17) is proved.

Proposition 2. Let $dZ(t)$ be as defined above, then $dZ(t)^2$ is nonrandom and in fact

$$dZ(t)^2 = dt. \tag{A.22}$$

Proof. To prove proposition 2, it will first be shown that the variance of $dZ(t)^2 = 0$. If the variance is zero then $dZ(t)^2$ is nonrandom and the expected value, $E[dZ(t)^2]$, is $dZ(t)^2$. But first, a useful intermediate result will be proved:

$$E[dZ(t)^4] = 0. \tag{A.23}$$

To show this, substitute from (A.15):

$$E[dZ(t)^4] = E[(Z(t+dt) - Z(t))^4]$$
$$= [Z(t+dt)^4] - 4E[Z(t+dt)^3 Z(t)] + 6E[Z(t+dt)^2 Z(t)^2]$$
$$- 4E[Z(t+dt)Z(t)^3] + E[Z(t)^4]. \tag{A.24}$$

From (A.11): $E(Y^4 X^k) = 3\sigma^4 M_k + 6\sigma^2 M_{k+2} + M_{k+4}$. Let $Y = Z(t+dt)$ and $X^k = Z(t)^0$. Then:

$$E[Z(t+dt)^4] = 3dt^2 + 6M_2 dt + M_4. \tag{A.25}$$

From (A.10): $E(Y^3 X^k) = 3\sigma^2 M_{k+1} + M_{k+3}$. Let $Y = Z(t+dt)$ and $X^k = Z(t)^1$. Then:

$$E[Z(t+dt)^3 Z(t)] = 3M_2 dt + M_4. \tag{A.26}$$

From (A.9): $E(Y^2 X^k) = \sigma^2 M_k + M_{k+2}$. Let $Y = Z(t+dt)$ and $X^k = Z(t)^2$. Then:

$$E[Z(t+dt)^2 Z(t)^2] = M_2 dt + M_4. \tag{A.27}$$

From (A.8): $E(Y X^k) = M_{k+1}$. Let $Y = Z(t+dt)$ and $X^k = Z(t)^3$. Then:

$$E[Z(t+dt)Z(t)^3] = M_4. \tag{A.28}$$

Finally, from (A.5):

$$E[Z(t)^4] = M_4. \tag{A.29}$$

Substituting (A.25)–(A.29) into (A.24) and noting from (A.2), $dt^2 = 0$, yields (A.23):

$$E[dZ(t)^4] = (3dt^2 + 6M_2 dt + M_4) - 4(3M_2 dt + M_4)$$
$$+ 6(M_2 dt + M_4) - 4M_4 + M_4$$
$$= 0. \tag{A.30}$$

Now, to see that $dZ(t)^2$ is nonrandom, notice that the variance of $dZ(t)^2$ is zero.

$$\text{var}[dZ(t)^2] = E[(dZ(t)^2 - E[dZ(t)^2])^2]$$
$$= E[dZ(t)^4] - 2E[dZ(t)^2]^2 + E[dZ(t)^2]^2.$$

From (A.23): $E[dZ(t)^4] = 0$; from (A.17): $E[dZ(t)^2] = dt$; and from (A.2): $dt^2 = 0$. Substituting into the above expression yields $\text{var}[dZ(t)^2] = 0$. Consequently, $dZ(t)^2$ is a nonrandom variable, and for nonrandom variables the value of the variable equals the expected value of the variable. From (A.17): $E[dZ(t)^2] = dt$; therefore, since $\text{var}[dZ(t)^2] = 0$, $dZ(t)^2 = E[dZ(t)^2] = dt$. This proves proposition 2.

Proposition 3. For any integer $k \geqslant 3$:

$$E\left[dZ(t)^k\right] = 0. \tag{A.31}$$

Proof. From (A.6), for all odd powers, $E[dZ(t)^k] = 0$. Therefore, it must be shown that $E[dZ(t)^k] = 0$ for $k \geqslant 4$ where k is even. For $k \geqslant 4$ and k even:

$$E\left[dZ(t)^k\right] = E\left[\left(dZ(t)^2\right)^{k/2}\right].$$

From (A.22):

$$E\left[dZ(t)^k\right] = E\left[dt^{k/2}\right].$$

If $k > 4$, then $(k/2) \geqslant 2$, thus, from (A.2):

$$E\left[dZ(t)^k\right] = 0.$$

This proves proposition 3.

Proposition 4. The stochastic process $dZ(t)$ is stationary, since for all t, $dZ(t)$ have the same statistics.

Proposition 5. For $dZ(t)$ as defined in (A.15):

$$dZ(t)dt = 0. \tag{A.32}$$

Proof. It will be first shown that the variance of $(dZ(t))(dt)$ is zero, implying that $(dZ(t))(dt)$ is nonstochastic. Then for a nonstochastic variable, the value equals the expected value:

$$\begin{aligned}
\mathrm{var}\left[dZ(t)dt\right] &= E\left[\left(dZ(t)dt - E[dZ(t)dt]\right)^2\right] \\
&= E\left[dZ(t)^2dt^2\right] - 2E\left[dZ(t)dt\right]^2 + E\left[dZ(t)dt\right]^2 \\
&= dt^2E\left[dZ(t)^2\right] - dt^2E\left[dZ(t)\right]^2.
\end{aligned}$$

From (A.2): $dt^2 = 0$; consequently

$$\mathrm{var}\left[dZ(t)dt\right] = 0.$$

The expected value of $(dZ(t))(dt)$ is

$$E\left[dZ(t)dt\right] = dtE\left[dZ(t)\right].$$

From (A.16): $E[dZ(t)] = 0$. Therefore

$$E\left[dZ(t)dt\right] = 0.$$

Since the variance of $(dZ(t))(dt)$ is zero, $dZ(t)dt$ equals its expected value:

$$dZ(t)dt = E\left[dZ(t)dt\right] = 0.$$

Thus, proposition 5 is proved.

Proposition 6. Let $t > s$. Then $dZ(t)$ and $dZ(s)$ are uncorrelated, i.e.

$$E[dZ(t)dZ(s)] = 0. \tag{A.33}$$

Proof. Let h be a real number, $0 < h < t - s$. Let $M_k = E[Z(s)^k]$ and $M_k' = E[Z(s+h)^k]$. Then, from (A.8), we have:

$$E[Z(t)Z(s)] = M_2, \tag{A.34}$$

$$E[Z(t+h)Z(s)] = M_2, \tag{A.35}$$

$$E[Z(t)Z(s+h)] = M_2', \tag{A.36}$$

$$E[Z(t+h)Z(s+h)] = M_2'. \tag{A.37}$$

Then expanding $E[dZ(t)dZ(s)]$ and substituting (A.34)–(A.37) yields

$$
\begin{aligned}
E[dZ(t)dZ(s)] &= E[(Z(t+h) - Z(t))(Z(s+h) - Z(s))] \\
&= E[Z(t+h)Z(s+h)] - E[Z(t+h)Z(s)] \\
&\quad - E[Z(t)Z(s+h)] + E[Z(t)Z(s)] \\
&= M_2' - M_2 - M_2' + M_2 \\
&= 0.
\end{aligned}
\tag{A.38}
$$

This proves (A.33).

Let $X(t)$ and $X_2(t)$ be two Gauss–Wiener processes. Unless $dX_1(t)$ and $dX_2(t)$ are uncorrelated, $E[dX_1(t)dX_2(t)]$ will be nonzero. In that case its value can be computed. However, before that result is derived the following useful intermediate result will be proved.

Proposition 7. If $Z_1(t)$ and $Z_2(t)$ are standard Gauss–Wiener processes and the differentials $dZ_1(t)$ and $dZ_2(t)$ are defined as in (A.15), then $[dZ_1(t)dZ_2(t)]$ is nonrandom, and can be expressed as

$$dZ_1(t)dZ_2(t) = \rho_t dt, \tag{A.39}$$

where ρ_t is the correlation coefficient between $dZ_1(t)$ and $dZ_2(t)$.

Proof. The expected value of $dZ_1(t)dZ_2(t)$ is

$$
\begin{aligned}
E[dZ_1(t)dZ_2(t)] &= E[dZ_1(t)]E[dZ_2(t)] + \text{cov}[dZ_1(t), dZ_2(t)] \\
&= 0 + \text{cov}[dZ_1(t), dZ_2(t)].
\end{aligned}
$$

The covariance between $dZ_1(t)$ and $dZ_2(t)$ can be written

$$
\begin{aligned}
\text{cov}[dZ_1(t), dZ_2(t)] &= \rho_t \sqrt{\{\text{var}[dZ_1(t)]\}} \sqrt{\{\text{var}[dZ_2(t)]\}} \\
&= \rho_t \sqrt{(dt)} \sqrt{(dt)} \\
&= \rho_t dt.
\end{aligned}
\tag{A.40}
$$

Therefore:

$$E[\,dZ_1(t)\,dZ_2(t)\,]=\rho_t\,dt.$$

The variance of $dZ_1(t)\,dZ_2(t)$ is zero:

$$\begin{aligned}
\operatorname{var}[\,dZ_1(t)\,dZ_2(t)\,] &= E\Big[\big(dZ_1(t)\,dZ_2(t)-E[\,dZ_1(t)\,dZ_2(t)\,]\big)^2\Big]\\
&= E\big[\,dZ_1(t)^2 dZ_2(t)^2\,\big]-E[\,dZ_1(t)\,dZ_2(t)\,]^2\\
&= dt^2-\rho_t^2\,dt^2\\
&= 0.
\end{aligned}$$

Since the variance is zero, then $dZ_1(t)\,dZ_2(t)$ is nonstochastic and its value equals its expected value. Therefore

$$dZ_1(t)\,dZ_2(t)=\rho\,dt,\qquad\qquad\qquad\qquad (A.41)$$

thus proving (A.39).

There is no reason to believe that ρ_t is independent of t. If for all $t,\rho_t=\rho$, then $dZ_1(t)$ and $dZ_2(t)$ are jointly stationary.

Another observation which should be noted is that regardless of whether $dZ_1(t)\,dZ_2(t)$ is zero or not, for $t\neq s, dZ_1(s)\,dZ_2(t)$ could be either zero or nonzero. In typical finance applications, t usually represents time and $dZ_1(t)$ and $dZ_2(t)$ are the returns for two assets in period t. Typical finance applications assume that $dZ_1(s)$ and $dZ_2(t)$ for $t\neq s$ are uncorrelated. It should be stressed that this does not follow from the definition of $dZ_1(t)$ and $dZ_2(t)$, nor does it follow from our knowledge of $E[dZ_1(t)\,dZ_2(t)]$. If the economics of a problem suggests that $dZ_1(s)\,dZ_2(t)=0$ for $t\neq s$, then it should be explicitly stated. If it is not zero, then[27]

$$dZ_1(s)\,dZ_2(t)=\rho_{st}\,dt.\qquad\qquad\qquad\qquad (A.42)$$

In general, ρ is a function of s and t. If it is only a function of $t-s$ (or $s-t$) or it is constant, then it should be so stated.

Proposition 8. If $X(t)$ is a nonstandard Gauss–Wiener process such that

$$dX(t)=\mu(X,t)\,dt+\sigma(X,t)\,dZ(t),\qquad\qquad\qquad (A.43)$$

where $Z(t)$ is a standard Gauss–Wiener process, then the expected value of $dX(t)$ is

$$E[\,dX(t)\,]=\mu(X,t)\,dt,\qquad\qquad\qquad\qquad (A.44)$$

and the variance of $dX(t)$ is

$$\operatorname{var}[\,dX(t)\,]=\sigma^2(X,t)\,dt.\qquad\qquad\qquad\qquad (A.45)$$

---

[27]For example, let $Z_1(s)=Z_2(t)$ (i.e. let Z_1 be Z_2 lagged by $s-t$). Then $dZ_1(s)\,dZ_2(t)=dt$ because by construction $\rho_{st}=1$.

Proof. From (A.16), $E[dZ(t)]=0$. Thus, (A.44) follows immediately. The variance of $dX(t)$ can be expressed as

$$\text{var}[dX(t)] = E\left[\left(\mu(X,t)dt + \sigma(X,t)dZ(t)\right.\right.$$
$$\left.\left. - E[\mu(X,t)dt + \sigma(X,t)dZ(t)]\right)^2\right]$$
$$= E\left[\left(\mu(X,t)dt + \sigma(X,t)dZ(t) - \mu(X,t)dt\right)^2\right]$$
$$= E[\sigma(X,t)dZ(t)]^2$$
$$= \sigma^2(X,t)dt.$$

Thus, (A.45) is proved.

Proposition 9. If $X_1(t)$ and $X_2(t)$ are nonstandard Gauss–Wiener processes such that

$$dX_j(t) = \mu_j(X_1,X_2,t)dt + \sigma_j(X_1,X_2,t)dZ_j,$$

then

$$dX_1(t)dX_2(t) = \rho_t\sigma_1\sigma_2 dt. \qquad (A.46)$$

Proof. The expected value of $dX_1(t)dX_2(t)$ is

$$E[dX_1(t)dX_2(t)] = E[dX_1(t)]E[dX_2(t)] + \text{cov}[dX_1(t),dX_2(t)]$$
$$= \mu_1\mu_2 dt^2 + \text{cov}[dX_1(t),dX_2(t)]$$
$$= \text{cov}[dX_1(t),dX_2(t)].$$

The covariance between $dX_1(t)$ and $dX_2(t)$ can be written as

$$\text{cov}[dX_1(t),dX_2(t)] = \rho_t\sqrt{\{\text{var}[dX_1(t)]\}}\sqrt{\{\text{var}[dX_2(t)]\}}$$
$$= \rho_t\sqrt{(\sigma_1^2 dt)}\sqrt{(\sigma_2^2 dt)}$$
$$= \rho_t\sigma_1\sigma_2 dt.$$

Therefore

$$E[dX_1(t)dX_2(t)] = \rho_t\sigma_1\sigma_2 dt.$$

The variance of $dX_1(t)dX_2(t)$ is zero:

$$\text{var}[dX_1(t)dX_2(t)] = E\left[\left(dX_1(t)dX_2(t) - E[dX_1(t)dX_2(t)]\right)^2\right]$$
$$= E[dX_1(t)^2 dX_2(t)^2] - E[dX_1(t)dX_2(t)]^2$$
$$= \mu_1 dt\mu_2 dt - (\rho_t\sigma_1\sigma_2 dt)^2$$
$$= 0.$$

Therefore, since the variance of $dX_1(t)dX_2(t)$ is zero $dX_1(t)dX_2(t)$ equals the expected value of $dX_1(t)dX_2(t)$. This proves (A.46).

Itô's lemma. Let F be a twice differentiable nonrandom function of t and two stochastic processes $X_1(t)$ and $X_2(t)$ where

$$dX_j(t) = \mu_j(X_1, X_2, t)\,dt + \sigma_j(X_1, X_2, t)\,dZ_j.$$

And if (A.46) holds, then

$$dF[t, X_1(t), X_2(t)] = \left(\frac{\partial F}{\partial t} + \frac{1}{2}\frac{\partial^2 F}{\partial X_1^2}\sigma_1^2 + \frac{\partial^2 F}{\partial X_1 \partial X_2}\rho_t\sigma_1\sigma_2 + \frac{1}{2}\frac{\partial^2 F}{\partial X_2^2}\sigma_2 \right) dt$$

$$+ \frac{\partial F}{\partial X_1}dX_1(t) + \frac{\partial F}{\partial X_2}dX_2(t). \tag{A.47}$$

Proof. If $X_1(t)$ and $X_2(t)$ were nonrandom functions, then from ordinary calculus we know that

$$dF = \frac{\partial F}{\partial t}dt + \frac{\partial F}{\partial X_1}dX_1 + \frac{\partial F}{\partial X_2}dX_2 + \frac{1}{2}\frac{\partial^2 F}{\partial t^2}dt^2 + \frac{1}{2}\frac{\partial^2 F}{\partial X_1^2}dX_1^2$$

$$+ \frac{1}{2}\frac{\partial^2 F}{\partial X_2^2}dX_2^2 + \frac{\partial^2 F}{\partial t \partial X_1}dt\,dX_1 + \frac{\partial^2 F}{\partial t \partial X_2}dt\,dX_2 + \frac{\partial^2 F}{\partial X_1 \partial X_2}dX_1\,dX_2. \tag{A.48}$$

Of course, from (A.2) it follows that all but the first three terms of (A.48) are zero. However, for $X_1(t)$ and $X_2(t)$ stochastic processes, eqs. (A.22), (A.32), and (A.42) must be used for terms containing dX_j^2, $dX_j dt$, and $dX_1 dX_2$:

$$dF = \frac{\partial F}{\partial t}dt + \frac{\partial F}{\partial X_1}dX_1 + \frac{\partial F}{\partial X_2}dX_2 + 0 + \frac{1}{2}\frac{\partial^2 F}{\partial X_1^2}\sigma^2 dt$$

$$+ \frac{1}{2}\frac{\partial^2 F}{\partial X_2^2}\sigma_2^2 dt + 0 + 0 + \frac{\partial^2 F}{\partial X_1 \partial X_2}\rho_t\sigma_1\sigma_2 dt.$$

Rearrangement of terms yields (A.47). The case of more or less than two stochastic processes can be treated similarly.

Example: the Black–Scholes option pricing model. Assume that the returns to the stock are represented by

$$dS/S = \mu\,dt + \sigma\,dZ. \tag{A.49}$$

Then

$$dS = \mu S\,dt + \sigma S\,dZ. \tag{A.50}$$

From (A.44) the expected value of dS is

$$E[dS] = \mu S\,dt. \tag{A.51}$$

From (A.45) the variance of dS is

$$\text{var}[dS] = \sigma^2 S^2\,dt. \tag{A.52}$$

Let the value of a call option written on the stock be a function of the stock price and time

$$C = C(S, t). \tag{A.53}$$

Then (A.47) can be used to express the change in the call price[28]

$$dC = \left(\frac{\partial C}{\partial t} + \frac{1}{2} \frac{\partial^2 F}{\partial S^2} S^2 \sigma^2 \right) dt + \frac{\partial F}{\partial S} dS. \tag{A.54}$$

References

Black, F. and J. C. Cox (1976) "Valuing Corporate Securities: Some Effects of Bond Indenture Provisions", *Journal of Finance* 31, 351–367.

Black, F. and M. Scholes (1973) "The Pricing of Options and Corporate Liabilities", *Journal of Political Economy* 81, 637–659.

Cox, J. C. and I. A. Ross (1976) "The Valuation of Options for Alternative Stochastic Processes", *Journal of Financial Economics* 3, 145–166.

Friedman, A. (1975) *Stochastic Differential Equations and Applications* (Academic Press, New York).

Galai, D. and R. W. Masulis (1976) "The Option Pricing Model and the Risk Factor of the Stock", *Journal of Financial Economics* 3, 53–81.

Geske, R. (1977) "The Valuation of Corporate Liabilities as Compound Options", *Journal of Financial and Quantitative Analysis* 12, 541–552.

Jensen, M. C. and W. H. Meckling (1976) "Theory of the Firm: Managerial Behavior, Agency Costs and Capital Structure, *Journal of Financial Economics* 3, 305–360.

Ingersoll, J. (1976) "A Theoretical and Empirical Investigation of the Dual Purpose Funds: An Application of Contingent Claims Analysis", *Journal of Financial Economics* 3, 83–123.

Ingersoll, J. E. (1977) "A Contingent-Claims Valuation of Convertible Securities", *Journal of Financial Economics* 4, 289–322.

Long, J. B. (1974) "Discussion", *Journal of Finance* 29, 485–488.

Mayers, D. and C. W. Smith (1977) "Toward a Theory of Financial Contracts: The Insurance Policy", unpublished, University of Rochester.

Merton, R. C. (1973) "Theory of Rational Option Pricing", *Bell Journal of Economics and Management Science* 4, 141–183.

Merton, R. C. (1974) "On the Pricing of Corporate Debt: The Risk Structure of Interest Rates", *Journal of Finance* 29, 449–470.

Merton, R. C. (1976) "Option Pricing When Underlying Stock Returns Are Discontinuous", *Journal of Financial Economics* 3, 125–144.

[28]Note that (A.54) is the same expression that is derived if $C(S + \Delta S; t + \Delta t)$ is expanded using a Taylor series with the series truncated after the $(dS)^2$ term:

$$C(S + \Delta S, t + \Delta t) = C(S, t) + \frac{\partial C}{\partial t} \Delta t + \frac{\partial C}{\partial S} \Delta S + \frac{1}{2} \frac{\partial^2 C}{\partial S^2} (\Delta S)^2 \dots$$

Therefore

$$\Delta C = C(S + \Delta S, t + \Delta t) - C(S, t)$$

$$= \frac{\partial C}{\partial t} \Delta t + \frac{\partial C}{\partial S} \Delta S + \frac{1}{2} \frac{\partial^2 C}{\partial S^2} (\Delta S)^2 + \dots.$$

Utilizing the above multiplication rules to express $(\Delta S)^2$ as $\sigma^2 S^2 \Delta t$ yields (A.54). This suggests that for short time intervals when examining functions of random variables which follow an Itô process, that quadratic approximations are exact.

Merton, R. C. (1977) "An Analytic Derivation of the Cost of Deposit Insurance and Loan Guarantees: An Application of Modern Option Pricing Theory", *Journal of Banking and Finance* 1, 3–12.

Mikkleson, W. (1978) "An Examination of the Agency Cost of Debt Rationale for Convertible Bonds and Warrants", unpublished, University of Rochester.

Modigliani, F. and M. A. Miller (1958) "The Cost of Capital, Corporation Finance, and the Theory of Investment", *American Economic Review* 48, 261–297.

Myers, S. C. (1977) "Determinants of Corporate Borrowing", *Journal of Financial Economics* 5, 147–175.

Smith, C. W. (1976) "Option Pricing: A Review", *Journal of Financial Economics* 3, 3–51.

Smith, C. W. (1977) "Alternative Methods for Raising Capital: Rights Versus Underwritten Offerings", *Journal of Financial Economics* 5, 273–307.

Smith, C. W. and J. B. Warner (1978) "On Financial Contracts and Optimal Capital Structure: An Analysis of Bond Covenants", unpublished, University of Rochester.

Sprenkle, C. M. (1964) "Warrant Prices as Indicators of Expectations and Preferences", in: P. Cootner, ed., *The Random Character of Stock Market Prices* (MIT Press, Cambridge, Mass.) pp. 412–474.

Warner, J. B. (1977) "Bankruptcy, Absolute Priority, and the Pricing of Risky Debt Claims", *Journal of Financial Economics* 4, 239–276.

THE VALUATION OF FLOATING-RATE INSTRUMENTS*

Theory and Evidence

Krishna RAMASWAMY

University of Pennsylvania, Philadelphia, PA 19104, USA

Suresh M. SUNDARESAN

Columbia University, New York, NY 10027, USA

Received June 1985, final version received February 1986

A framework for valuing floating-rate notes is developed to examine the effects of (1) lags in the coupon formula, (2) special contractual features and (3) default risk. Evidence from a sample of floaters indicates they sold at significant discounts. While lags in the coupon formulas and other contractual features make these notes more variable, they do not account for the magnitude of the discounts. We conclude that the fixed default premium in the coupon formula of a typical note is inadequate to compensate for time-varying default premiums demanded by investors, who treat other corporate short-term paper as close substitutes.

1. Introduction

The recent experience of rapid and sizable changes in the inflation rate in the 70's has given rise to new debt securities which have coupon yields that vary over time and reflect, by means of a predetermined formula, the prevailing short-term or intermediate-term interest rate. Since 1974, when the first of these 'variable-rate' or 'floating-rate' instruments was issued, this market has grown rapidly. In 1984, the total new issue volume was $39.7 billion, of which U.S. issuers accounted for $10.4 billion.[1] In the mortgage market, adjustable-rate mortgages are now fairly common. Indeed, a similar concept is in force in some regulatory jurisdictions, where the allowed return on utilities' common stock is based on a formula that incorporates current market conditions.

*We are grateful to Clifford Ball, Douglas Breeden, Robert Litzenberger, Craig MacKinlay, Jay Ritter, Myron Scholes, Clifford Smith and the referee for their comments, and to In Joon Kim and Charles Wolf for their comments and assistance.

[1] See Hanna and Parente (1985).

These floating-rate instruments' value is more stable than that of fixed-rate investments. An investor considering a strategy of rolling over short-term instruments (e.g., Treasury Bills) will find a floater attractive, since it substitutes a one-time transactions cost for the repeated transactions cost of the roll-over strategy. An investor considering an investment in fixed-rate notes will demand compensation for any additional risk from the fluctuations in the value of the fixed-rate note compared to an equal investment in variable-rate notes. From the view point of a potential corporate issuer, if the corporation maintains a relatively stable amount of short-term debt which is rolled over at regular intervals, then the issuance of a floating-rate note tied to short-term rates avoids the transactions costs of repeatedly rolling over short debt. This is one reason why banks and financing companies have issued floating-rate notes.[2]

The value of a floating-rate note depends crucially on the specification of its coupon payment rule. Almost all the floaters in the U.S. employ a coupon rule that is 'set off' from a Treasury instrument. That is, the coupon is usually defined as the average of previously issued 6-month (or 3-month, suitably adjusted) Treasury Bill yields, plus a premium or markup to reflect the credit risk of the issuer. The value of a floating-rate note also depends on indenture provisions and on other contractual features, such as callability, convertibility, and on any maximum or minimum restrictions on the payable coupon.

We employ a continuous time valuation model to study the effects of (1) lags in the coupon rule, (2) special contractual features, and (3) the issuer's credit risk. The price history of a sample of U.S. floating-rate notes reveals that while the dynamic properties of these notes follow the corresponding instruments from which these floaters are set off, they have sold at statistically significant discounts subsequent to their issue dates. The results of numerical analysis of the valuation model indicate that neither the lag structure nor the principal contractual features explain the range of observed prices: the level of the default premium expected by investors relative to the fixed markup comes closest to doing so.

Our study complements and extends the work of Cox, Ingersoll and Ross (1980), who placed special emphasis on coupon formulas that can be designed to eliminate basis risk. In the context of a set of examples, they analyzed the behavior of consol floating-rate notes that have call, conversion, and other features. Our study differs from theirs in that (i) we examine formulas which make the coupon rate an average of past rates, as is the case in practice; (ii) we incorporate some of the commonly encountered design features of finitely-lived

---

[2] Chance (1983) also observes that floating-rate notes would have lower transactions costs than a series of short-term loans. Santomero (1983) has studied issues related to the comparison of fixed- and floating-rate instruments.

floating-rate notes; and (iii) we examine the effect of default risk on these floaters.

The plan of the paper is as follows. In section 2, we describe the salient features of corporate issues of floating-rate notes, and present evidence on their price behavior. In section 3, we develop a continuous time valuation model for these notes to examine the lag structure and other contractual features, and report the results of numerical solutions for these cases. In section 4 we study the valuation of corporate floaters subject to default, ignoring the effects of the lag structure and other contractual features. Section 5 contains some concluding comments.

2. Floating-rate notes: Description and price behavior

The specification of the coupon formula is substantially the same across most U.S. floaters, although there is considerable variation in the *type of base rate* [3- or 6-month Treasury Bill yields or LIBOR (London InterBank Offered Rate) rates] and in the nature and magnitude of the markup over the base rate that reflects the issuer's credit risk. The next (usually semi-annual) coupon payable is calculated from the quoted yields of the base-rate instrument from two or three dates immediately prior to the previous coupon payment date, plus the markup. For example, the Citicorp floater maturing in May 2004 pays coupons on the 1st of May and November. The coupon rate on May 1 is the simple average of 6-month bond equivalent yields on Treasury Bills in the auctions conducted during October 8 through October 21 of the previous year (the coupon rate on November 1 is the simple average of 6-month bond equivalent yields on Treasury Bills in the auctions conducted April 7 through April 20 of the same year) plus a predetermined markup. In most cases the markup declines over time: in the Citicorp example, the markup is 105 basis points for the first five years of the floater's life, 100 basis points for the next five years, and 75 basis points thereafter. Almost all issues employ markups that are predetermined but a few define a 'variable' markup as a ratio of the spread between the rate on short-term private-issuer obligations and Treasury Bill rates. For example, the Citicorp floater maturing May 1, 2010 defines the markup as 110% of the differential between 3-month CDs and 3-month Treasury Bills (this ratio declined to 102.5% of the differential after May 1982).

For the majority of floaters, the coupon payment dates and the dates of coupon reset (when the formula is applied to determine the next coupon) are 6 months apart: there are a few floaters whose coupons are paid semi-annually, but whose reset intervals are monthly, and others whose base-rate instrument is an intermediate-term or long-term Treasury index.

The other contractual features of floaters can be quite complex and are generally issue-specific. We list below the most commonly encountered contractual features:

(A) *Floor rate and ceiling features*:   The coupon is found from an average of observable past yields of the base-rate instrument plus a markup, but the coupon is subject to a minimum and a maximum rate (the 'collars').

(B) *Put features*:   The holder has the right to redeem his investment (usually at par) at coupon payment dates, on or after some prespecified date. Notice of redemption typically must be given at least 30 days prior to the coupon payment date.

(C) *Drop–lock features*:   These instruments cease to 'float' when the base rate 'drops' to a prespecified minimum value, whereupon they automatically become fixed-rate notes (the 'lock') with a prespecified coupon and maturity.

(D) *Call features*:   They permit the issuer to redeem the issue on or after a prespecified data at a prespecified set of prices.

(E) *Conversion features*:   They permit the holder to exchange his investment for a fixed-rate note with a prespecified coupon and maturity.

The majority of floating-rate issues to date incorporate put features, floor and ceiling features. In addition, the floating-rate issues are subject to covenants which define default and the rights of the holders of the floating-rate issues on default. The covenants associated with these notes are similar to those discussed by Smith and Warner (1979). An interesting and unique contractual provision defines the manner in which the coupon will be reset, if at the time of reset, publications of the base rate (for example, Treasury Bill yields from *Federal Reserve Bulletins*) are unavailable: this provision defines alternate base rates or a flat rate of interest if no timely information is publicly available.

All the corporate issues are subject to the normal tax laws: coupon income is taxed at the ordinary rate and gains and losses are subject to capital gain rules. There is an influx of municipal issues of floaters, where the coupon is exempt from federal income tax. There has also been a surge of adjustable-rate preferred stock issues, which are floaters in the sense defined above, except that the 'dividend' that is paid is subject to the exclusion rule for intercompany dividends.

Table 1 summarizes the features of six issues that are representative of the sample of floating-rate issues for which we have obtained weekly price data. The Gulf Oil issue is the only one in our sample which has the drop–lock feature, and it is also the only issue whose averaging formula uses the 30-year Treasury yield as the base rate. None of the issues has a ceiling coupon rate, but all of them have a minimum (floor) rate. Three of the issues shown have

Table 1

Description of selected floating-rate notes.

Coupon formula	Issue and year of maturity size rating[a]					
	Citicorp, 1998 $200 M Aaa	Chemical, 2004 $100 M Aaa	Beneficial, 1987 $200 M Aa	Continental, 1987 $200 M Aaa	Girard, 1987 $50 M A	Gulf Oil, 2009 $250 M Aaa
(1) Base	6-month Treasury Bill	6-month Treasury Bill	6-month Treasury Bill	6-month Treasury Bill	6-month Treasury Bill	30-year Treasury bond index
(2) Procedure[b,c]	$+120$ bp, min $7\frac{1}{2}\%$ 1979–83 $+100$ bp, min 7% 1983–88 $+75$ bp, min $6\frac{1}{2}\%$ 1988–1998	$+100$ bp, min $7\frac{1}{2}\%$ 1979–84 $+100$ bp, min 7% 1984–89 $+75$ bp, min $6\frac{1}{2}\%$ 1989–2004	$+50$ bp min 6%	$+50$ bp min 6%	$+65$ bp min $6\frac{1}{2}\%$	$+35$ bp Drop–lock: if yields drop to 8%, issue becomes $8\frac{3}{8}s$ due 2009
Other features[d]	No conversion Callable after 1988 Sinking fund Retires 90% Begins 1989	No conversion Callable after 1989 Sinking fund Retires 97.3% Begins 1985	Convertible to $8\frac{5}{8}s$ due 2004 before 8/1/86 Callable after 1986 Debentures callable after 1991 No sinking fund	Convertible to $8\frac{1}{2}s$ due 2004 before 5/1/86 Callable after 1986 Debentures callable after 1985 Sinking fund (debentures) Retires 91% Begins 1991	Convertible to $9s$ due 1999 before 5/15/86 Callable after 1986 Debentures callable after 1989 Sinking fund (debentures) Retires 91% Begins 1989	Immediately callable when variable Non-callable for 10 years when fixed Sinking fund (debentures) Retires 79.8% Begins 1990

[a] *Moody*'s rating at issue.
[b] bp indicates basis points.
[c] Coupon is reset every 6 months for all these issues.
[d] Sinking funds retire proportion indicated in equal installments over the period.

conversion features, and all but one have sinking funds which apply either to the floater or the debentures into which the convert. None of the issues in our sample has a put feature. The put feature will be employed by the holders if the floater sold below par on coupon payment dates, and the market prices of floaters with put features reflect this.

2.1. Price behavior of floaters

Consider a hypothetical floating-rate note issued by the Treasury: it pays coupons semi-annually, its coupon reset date and coupon payment dates coincide and are exactly 26 weeks apart, and it uses the yield on the newly issued 26-week T-Bill auctioned during the coupon payment week as the base rate. Because of its default-free status, no markup is provided. Cox, Ingersoll and Ross (1980) show, in a fairly general context, that the market price of this floater must be $100 (the face amount) on the ex-coupon dates, and that the dynamic properties of the floater will be identical to that of a Treasury Bill that matures on the next coupon payment date. That these two properties apply to this 'perfectly-indexed' floater is easy to see: the payoff to this floater is identical to the payoff generated by investing $100 in 26-week bills on the coupon payment date, and reinvesting $100 from the proceeds after 26 weeks in new issues of 26-week bills, ignoring transactions costs. The price of the floater will deviate from $100 between coupon payment dates reflecting the basis risk that remains.

In a completely analogous way, we can show that these properties extend to corporate floaters. Consider a corporate floater whose coupon payment dates and coupon reset dates coincide, whose coupon is computed on the reset date as the yield on the corporation's newly issued commercial paper with maturity equal to the time until the next coupon, and whose seniority and other indenture provisions are identical to the floater's. Then, again ignoring transactions costs, investors will receive the same payoff from a rolling investment strategy in commercial paper. It follows that the corporate floater should sell at par on the coupon payment dates, and its dynamic properties should correspond closely[3] to those of the corporation's commercial paper issue maturing on the next coupon payment date.

To see whether these implications are confirmed in the market, we obtained weekly closing prices (offered prices) on a sample of 18 floaters from their issue dates (the earliest being June 1978) to June 1983. This sample was chosen to include only those floaters which had no put features attached, because the put feature would bias the ex-coupon day prices upwards; and except for the Gulf Oil issue, the floaters all employed the 6-month Treasury Bill as the base

---

[3] The comparison between these strategies will not be justified for floaters issued by banks, if there are any *de facto* Federal guarantees on the CDs issued by these institutions.

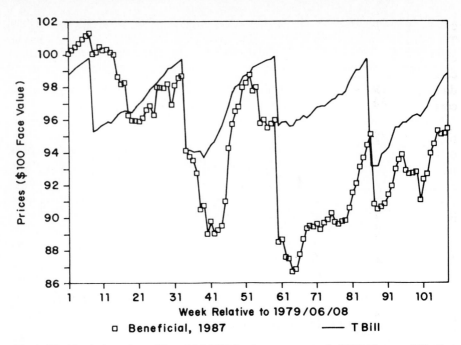

Fig. 1. Weekly closing prices of Beneficial 1987 floating-rate note and of U.S. Treasury Bill. *Note*: The Beneficial prices include the accrued coupon since the previous coupon payment date. The Treasury Bill is chosen to have a maturity date closest to Beneficial's coupon dates; it had a 6-month maturity at issue and it is plotted assuming a $100 face value.

instrument. From this data we selected, for every issue and associated coupon date (except the Gulf Oil issue), the nearest Friday subsequent to the coupon payment date. There were a total of 86 Friday quotes nearest to the coupon date: the average price (*cum* accrued coupon, for the days since the coupon) was $93.55, the standard deviation of this mean was $0.395. These prices ranged from $86.83 to $100.56, and there was no tendency for the longer-maturity floaters to sell at greater discounts. The mean value of the ex-coupon price was thus significantly below the hypothesized value of $100.

To check whether the dynamic properties of these floaters are consistent with those of short-term obligations of the same corporation, we need data on prices of these obligations of fixed maturity. Lacking these data, we are unable to provide this comparison: we show in fig. 1 a plot of the prices of the Beneficial floater maturing in 1987 together with the prices of the 6-month Treasury Bill maturing on the Thursday closest to the next coupon payment date. Note that the Treasury Bill's price per $100 face value is plotted, and the Beneficial issue's price includes the coupon accrued since the immediately previous ex-date which, in turn, includes a default premium. Therefore, the curve corresponding to the floater price should lie everywhere above the Treasury Bill price curve, if the stated default premium were adequate. It is clear that while the initial prices (at issue and through the first coupon) were consistent with these implications, the subsequent prices went to considerable discounts – and the graph indicates that these two instruments were positively correlated. This pattern is also borne out for the other floaters in our sample.

Theoretical considerations lead one to suspect that the potential explanations for these discounts lie in the lag structure of the coupon formulas, in other contractual features, in inadequate default premiums in the coupon formula relative to time-varying default premium demanded in the market. We examine these explanations separately in the next two sections because the simultaneous study of these effects is complicated, and because floating-rate issues have widely varying features.

3. A continuous time valuation model for floating-rate notes

The value of a floating-rate note depends on the dynamics of the term structure of interest rates, on the coupon payment formula, its contractual provisions and on the creditworthiness of the issuer. In this section we ignore credit risk and model the movements in the term structure in order to examine contractual provisions and the coupon payment formula.

A typical coupon payment formula defines the coupon rate as an average of past LIBOR rates or Treasury Bill rates. This feature causes the value of the floater to depend on the *path* of the interest rates to which the coupons are linked. The way in which the coupon is computed has important implications for the intertemporal price behavior of the floater. To see this, let $\{t = 0, 1, 2, \ldots\}$ be dates at weekly intervals and let y_t be the yield on newly issued Treasury Bills maturing at $t + 26$. Consider a hypothetical default-free floater which pays semi-annual coupons x_s at date s given by the coupon payment formula

$$x_s = y_{s-26}, \quad s = 26, 52, 78, \ldots,$$

$$= 0, \quad \text{otherwise.} \tag{1}$$

This coupon payment scheme corresponds to the 'perfectly-indexed' floater discussed in section 2, and such a floater will always sell at par at each ex-coupon date. By contrast, a typical floater has a semi-annual coupon x_s which is an average of past yields,

$$x_s = (y_{s-27} + y_{s-28} + y_{s-29})/3, \quad s = 26, 52, 78, \ldots,$$

$$= 0 \quad \text{otherwise.} \tag{2}$$

In this case the coupon at date s is reset during the interval $[s - 29, s - 27]$ thereby making the valuation problem path-dependent, at least during that interval. If yields on newly issued Treasury Bills were a random walk, then in the absence of liquidity premiums the average ex-coupon value of a typical floater [with a coupon formula as in (2)] would also be equal to the face value. If, on the other hand, these yields displayed a secular trend or a mean reversion, then the typical floater would sell at a predictable discount or premium on the ex-coupon dates.

In a discrete time setting, the valuation of a floater with a coupon formula as in (2) may be carried out in two steps: first, we can value a hypothetical 'elementary' default-free floater whose current coupon rate is the T-Bill yield that prevailed (say) k weeks ago.[4] The second step is to recognize that the value of a floater whose coupon is the simple (linear) average of rates that prevailed at several values of k, is simply the weighted average of the values of 'elementary' floaters, using the same weights as are used in the averaging formula. This procedure is feasible but computationally cumbersome even for small lags and short-maturity floaters: this is because the path of rates (or sufficient information) must be carried along at each stage of the valuation problem. Given our desire to examine the special contractual features of floaters we posed the valuation problem in a continuous time setting where the lag structure as well as these features can be studied with relative ease.

The following assumptions are employed:

(A.1) Trading takes place continuously in frictionless markets; there are no taxes.

(A.2) The term structure is fully specified by the instantaneously riskless rate $r(t)$. Its dynamics are given by

$$dr = \kappa(\mu - r)\,dt + \sigma\sqrt{r}\,dz, \qquad (3)$$

where $\mu, \kappa, \sigma^2 > 0$ and where $\{z(t),\ t > 0\}$ represents a standard Wiener process.

(A.3) The floater is assumed to pay a coupon continuously at the rate $x(t)$, given by

$$x(t) = \beta\int_{\infty}^{0} e^{-\beta s} r(t - s)\,ds, \qquad \beta > 0. \qquad (4)$$

---

[4] In a discrete time setting elementary floaters may be valued by assuming that the short-term interest rate follows a two-state branching process and that bonds are priced according to the local expectations hypothesis [see Cox, Ingersoll and Ross (1981)]. Equivalently, one could apply the arguments of Cox, Ross and Rubinstein (1979) in conjunction with the local expectations hypothesis. We have evaluated floaters using this procedure: the path-dependent nature of the problem increases the computational complexity, and this limits its usefulness considerably.

(A.4) All bonds are priced according to the Local Expectations Hypothesis (LEH). That is, the floater price $F(r(t), x(t), \tau)$ satisfies, at each instant t,

$$E_t[dF] + x(t)\,dt = Fr(t)\,dt, \tag{5}$$

where $\tau \equiv T - t$ denotes the time to maturity of the floater and $E_t[\cdot]$ is the expectations operator.

Market assumptions are embodied in (A.1).[5] The term structure assumptions made in (A.2) and (A.4) help to keep the problem tractable: specifying the term structure in terms of the short rate may not be unrealistic because most floaters have their coupon formulas based on short rates. The specification used for the evolution of the interest rate implies that the current rate $r(t)$ is pulled towards its long-run mean value μ with a speed of adjustment κ, and the instantaneous variance of the change in the rate is proportional to its level. The properties of this process are provided in Cox, Ingersoll and Ross (1985). While alternative specifications of the stochastic process for r can be accommodated quite easily, our choice of the autoregressive square-root diffusion in (3) was motivated by the fact that solutions for discount bond prices were available, which simplified the computations considerably. The choice of the formula for the coupon rate in (A.3) was, however, quite deliberate. More general coupon payment formulas, perhaps dependent on a finite history of rates, lead to descriptions of the state of the system that become unmanageably large. The exponential average formula in relation (4) permits the transition of the continuous coupon rate to be written

$$dx = \beta(r - x)\,dt. \tag{6}$$

Therefore, the levels of $r(t)$ and $x(t)$ at time t [together with the knowledge of their evolution in eqs. (3) and (6)] completely describe the system. Note that a large value for β implies that greater weight is placed on recent rates of interest in determining the current coupon, and indicates that the coupon rate will never be far from the current interest rate. The local expectations hypothesis assumed in (A.4) helps to avoid incorporating preferences into the valuation explicitly: a discussion of this hypothesis is provided by Cox, Ingersoll and Ross (1981).

These assumptions permit the derivation of a valuation equation for the floating-rate note. By taking a suitable short position in a discount bond and a long position in the floater and continuously rebalancing this portfolio, one can construct a locally riskless position. In order to preclude arbitrage this

---

[5] If the coupon formula is close to 'perfect indexation' and investors view these floaters as a substitute for a short-term paper, then the effects of differential taxation of capital gains and of coupon income on the value of the floater are likely to be minor.

portfolio must earn the risk-free rate at each instant. Using this condition and the local expectation hypothesis, it can be shown that the floater price $F(r, x, \tau)$ must satisfy[6]

$$\tfrac{1}{2}\sigma^2 r F_{rr} + \kappa(\mu - r)F_r + \beta(r - x)F_x + x - rF = F_\tau, \qquad (7)$$

where the subscripts denote partial derivatives. The terminal condition which all floaters must satisfy is given by

$$F(r, x, 0) = 1. \qquad (8)$$

The other boundary conditions to the valuation equation will depend on the particular contractual features of the floating-rate note.

There are no known analytical solutions to the valuation equation, even for floaters without the complicated features. We have employed the numerical method of alternating directions [see Brennan and Schwartz (1980)] to solve the equation for a chosen set of contract features.[7] In the rest of this section we present the results of these valuations which apply to floaters which have no default risk. The parameters for the interest rate process are $\kappa = 2$, $\sigma^2 = 0.006$, and unless otherwise noted, $\mu = 9\%$. These represent estimates for the period covering our sample of floaters, consistent with the procedures described in Cox, Ingersoll and Ross (1979) and derived from Treasury Bill prices. The parameter values of β, in the coupon payment formula, are 0.7 and 7; at these values, the difference between the current coupon rate and the current interest rate is expected to be halved in approximately 360 days and 36 days, respectively.[8]

3.1. Straight floaters

The term 'straight' floater is used to mean a floating-rate note that has no contractual feature beyond the coupon rate formula in (4). Fig. 2 provides a

---

[6]This equation can be derived in one of two equivalent ways: either by applying the Local Expectations Hypothesis directly to the floater's value or by usual hedging and continuous rebalancing arguments in conjunction with the LEH.

[7]For the lower boundary conditions with respect to r and x (at $r = 0$ and $x = 0\%$), and for the upper boundary condition with respect to x (at $x = 30\%$), we have employed the partial differential equation (7): for the interest rate process (3), zero is an accessible boundary, provided $\sigma^2 > 2\kappa\mu$. The value of the floater for a given x as r increases should decline to zero. We have employed $F_{rr} = 0$ at the upper bound for r, which was 40%. In all these cases we employed 200 mesh points in the r direction and 150 mesh points in the x direction. We evaluated floaters for maturities up to 10 years by this method, using 100 mesh points along the time axis.

[8]Because we are passing from a realistic setting with coupons found from average bill yields 27, 28, and 29 weeks 'ago' to one in which the continuous coupon is an exponentially weighted average of past rates, no 'best' choice of β suggests itself. Rather, we were guided by a desire to vary β and hence accommodate varying rates of convergence of x to r. We have also tried a β value of 70, which effectively makes the floater 'perfectly indexed'.

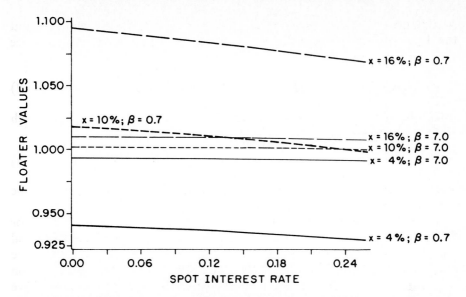

Fig. 2. Straight floater values versus interest rates. *Note*: x is the specified coupon rate on the floater and it reverts to the current interest rate with a speed of adjustment, β. The interest rate r evolves as a diffusion $dr = \kappa(\mu - r)\,dt + \sigma\sqrt{r}\,dz$, where $\kappa = 2$, $\mu = 0.09$ and $\sigma^2 = 0.006$. The floater has 5 years to maturity.

plot of floating-rate values versus interest-rate values for values of $\beta = 0.7$ and 7; for each value of β, plots are provided for coupon rates (x) of 4%, 10%, and 16%.[9] Note that floater values are declining functions of the interest rate r and increasing functions of the coupon rate x. Floaters sell at a premium for coupon values of $x = 10\%$ and $x = 16\%$: this behavior, especially at high interest rates, follows because the coupon averaging scheme places less weight on the current interest rate with $\beta = 0.7$, and because interest rates are reverting to 9%. As β increases to 7, the straight floater values are bunched together, regardless of the substantial differences in the coupon values. The range of floater values with $\beta = 7$ is 0.993 to 1.010, in contrast to the range of floater values (0.925 to 1.10) with a β value of 0.7. This is consistent with one's intuition: as β increases the floater tends to become a perfectly indexed instrument, with future coupons tending to the prevailing interest rate. As a result one would expect the floater to sell close to its face value.

[9] The floater values were increasing and nearly linear in the coupon rates (x) for a given value of the interest rate r. We have chosen to show the graphs for $x = 4$, 10 and 16% to avoid clutter and to indicate the ranges at which sizable discounts and premiums occur.

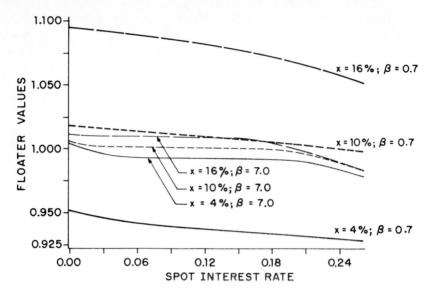

Fig. 3. Floater values (with ceiling and floor coupon rate) versus interest rates. *Note:* x is the specified coupon rate on the floater and it reverts to the current interest rate with a speed of adjustment, β; it is subject to a ceiling and floor rate of 15% and 5%, respectively. The interest rate r evolves as a diffusion $dr = \kappa(\mu - r)dt + \sigma\sqrt{r}\,dz$, where $\kappa = 2$, $\mu = 0.09$ and $\sigma^2 = 0.006$. The floater has 5 years to maturity.

3.2. Floaters with ceiling and floor coupons

Consider the imposition of a floor and a ceiling on the coupon rate. Let x^f represent the floor rate and x^c represent the ceiling rate. The state of the system is still $\{r(t), x(t)\}$ but the coupon payments are bounded by the floor and ceiling rates. In the region where the state variable $x(t) > x^c$, the coupon will be x^c, although the difference $x(t) - x^c$ will surely affect the value of the floater. In other words, if the past rates are such that the ceiling constraint will be binding in the foreseeable future, the floater will at a discount relative to a floater whose coupon 'floats' without a ceiling. Similar comments apply for the floor rate.

The floater values are obtained by solving the valuation equation (7) subject to the terminal condition (8) and relevant boundary conditions.[10] Fig. 3 displays the results for floaters with 5 years to maturity and coupons which are subject to a ceiling rate of 15% and a floor rate of 5%.

---

[10] The boundary conditions remain as noted earlier. In the partial differential equation, however, the term representing the payout to the security is the floor or the ceiling rate whenever that is in force.

At the high β value of 7, the unconstrained coupon rate is very close to the current interest rate and the floater is relatively inelastic to interest rates, except in regions where the interest rate stays above the ceiling coupon or below the floor coupon rate – for in this case the floater behaves like a fixed-rate note in that its sensitivity to interest rates is high. At the lower β value of 0.7, the unconstrained coupon value can deviate considerably from the current interest rate; and the floater again displays a higher sensitivity to interest rates, especially below 5% and above 15%. A comparison of figs. 2 and 3 confirms that the imposition of floor and ceiling coupons increases the sensitivity of floater values to interest rates.

3.3. Floaters with 'drop–lock' feature

Floating-rate notes with a 'drop–lock' feature cease to float when the rate of interest reaches a prespecified minimum. We assume that the issue ceases to 'float' when the rate of interest falls to a prespecified floor of r^f and becomes a fixed-rate instrument for its remaining life, and that the fixed coupon rate is simply r^f. The drop–lock feature imposes a lower boundary condition on the partial differential equation, given by

$$\lim_{r \downarrow r^f} F(r, x, \tau) = \int_{s=t}^{T} r^f P(r^f, T - s)\, ds + P(r^f, T - t),$$

where $P(r, \tau)$ is the value of a default-free discount bond paying \$1 in τ periods. For the assumed stochastic process (5), the discount bond pricing function $P(r, \tau)$ has been derived by Cox, Ingersoll and Ross (1985). This permits a straightforward numerical solution to (7) subject to the terminal condition (8) and relevant boundary conditions to obtain values of a floater with a drop–lock feature. In figs. 4 and 5 results are shown for a floater whose 'lock' becomes effective at $r = r^f = 8\%$. In fig. 4 we have used a long-run mean rate of 10% and in fig. 5 we have used a long-run mean rate of 6%. When the interest rate is below 8%, the floater behaves like a fixed-rate note with a continuous coupon of 8% and sells at a discount (fig. 4), reflecting the fact that the interest rate is expected to revert to 10%. As the interest rate moves up from 8%, floater prices increase dramatically, regardless of their current coupon levels. This can be attributed to two effects: first, the interest rate is pulled towards its long-run mean, reflecting higher future coupons for floaters whose current coupons are 8%. Second, as the rate increases, the probability of 'drop–lock' decreases, and as a result future cash flows are expected to be higher.

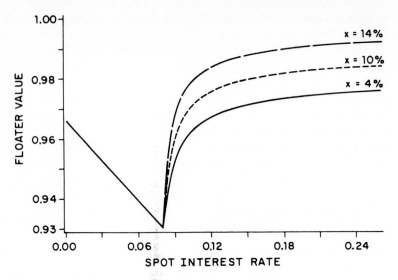

Fig. 4. Floater values (with drop–lock feature) versus interest rates (long-run mean interest rate = 10%). *Note*: When the interest rate reaches 8% (drop), the issue becomes a fixed-rate note (the lock) at 8% coupon until maturity. x is the specific coupon rate on the floater and it reverts to the current interest rate with a speed of adjustment, β. The interest rate r evolves as a diffusion $dr = \kappa(\mu - r)dt + \sigma\sqrt{r}\,dz$, where $\kappa = 2$, $\mu = 0.10$ and $\sigma^2 = 0.006$. The floater has 5 years to maturity.

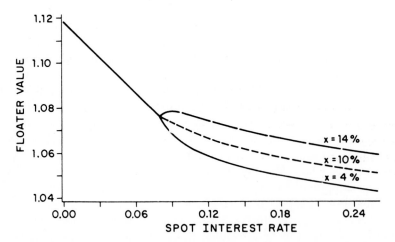

Fig. 5. Floater values (with drop–lock feature) versus interest rates (long-run mean interest rate = 6%). *Note*: When the interest rate reaches 8%, the issue becomes a fixed-rate note at 8% coupon until maturity. x is the specified coupon rate on the floater and it reverts to the current interest rate with a speed of adjustment, β. The interest rate r evolves as a diffusion $dr = \kappa(\mu - r)dt + \sigma\sqrt{r}\,dz$, where $\kappa = 2$, $\mu = 0.06$ and $\sigma^2 = 0.006$. The floater has 5 years to maturity.

The results in fig. 5 are quite different, however. The differences come about because of the location of the 'drop–lock' rate of 8% relative to the long-run mean rate of 6%. This implies that the interest rates will be pulled towards 6%: consequently, the floaters sell at a premium for the entire range of interest rates. In the range of interest rates from 0 to 8%, the floater becomes a fixed-rate note paying a continuous coupon of 8% and sells at a premium: beyond 8%, there are two effects, as discussed earlier, except that they tend to counterbalance each other in this case. In other words, increases in interest rates increase the future coupon flows, but the tendency is for the interest rate to revert to 6% which is below the 'drop–lock' rate of 8%.

We have examined the effects of put features within this framework. If the investor has the right to put the floater to the issuer (at par) at any time, then the floater will always sell at a premium, and the premium will increase as the current interest rate falls below the coupon rate. For the parameter values chosen above, a floater with 5 years to maturity and a coupon rate of 10% will be put to the issuer only if the interest rate rises above 25%. The put feature will clearly not contribute to *discounts* at the ex-coupon dates even in a discrete time setting, because the investors will exercise the put feature in that case.[11]

The results reported in this section confirm that floaters will tend to sell at discounts or premiums when the current coupon rate is below or above the current interest rate, and that these deviations from par will shrink if the coupon formula places greater weight on more recent rates.[12] Distant lags in the coupon formula, and the contractual features examined here tend to increase the range of price fluctuations that are predicted: however, there will be no systematic bias towards the prediction of discounts, unless the current coupon rate is well below the current interest rate. Indeed, for the straight floaters examined, the discounts predicted would approach those reported in section 2 only at a coupon rate of 4% and at an interest rate in excess of 10%, with $\beta = 0.7$. Because the deviations of coupon rates from market rates is never that large and because even moderate premiums are not observed, it seems unlikely that lags or contractual features will serve to explain the reported prices.

[11] For high values of β, the coupon rate is fairly close to the current short-term rate and therefore the floater tends to sell close to par. Under this setting, the put feature will not have much value. On the other hand, if the coupon averaging rule causes the coupon rate to deviate significantly from the current short-term rate, then the put feature will be of value to the investor.

[12] We computed the floater values for alternate values of σ^2 and found that they were quite insensitive to this parameter. Considerations of computational expense limited the number of evaluations we could conduct – we varied the β values, and the effects were as reported above.

4. Pricing of corporate floating-rate notes

Corporate floating-rate notes are subject to default risk, and rational investors will take this risk into account when valuing these notes. A corporate floater should sell at a discount relative to a government floater if they both have identical coupon payments. The magnitude of this price discount will depend on the probability of default, on the contractual provisions that define payoffs contingent upon default, and on the premium demanded in the market for similar instruments. Since the coupons to a corporate floater contain a markup to reflect the credit risk, the floater's price should be closer to par and any deviations will depend on the relationship between the markup stated in the floater and the premium demanded in the market.

Ideally, default risk should be modelled simultaneously with the coupon averaging formula. Such an approach, however, renders the valuation problem virtually intractable because floater values will depend on three state variables: the interest rate, the coupon rate and a variable which proxies for credit risk. In order to keep the problem computationally manageable, we assume that the continuous coupon rate on the floater will be the *current* interest rate plus a fixed premium π. This permits us to describe the state of the system with two state variables – the interest rate and a variable that captures default risk. Furthermore, it allows us to abstract from the effects of coupon averaging (examined in section 3) and enables us to focus on the impact of default risk on the floater value.

The traditional approach to modelling default risk, pioneered by Merton (1974) and extended by Black and Cox (1976) assumes that the market value of the issuing firm follows an exogenously specified stochastic process and that the term structure is deterministic (and flat). The payoffs to the creditors, both over time and contingent on bankruptcy are then specified in detail. The latter depends on the economic events in bankruptcy and the way in which the reorganization boundary is specified. In the context of corporate zero-coupon debt, the lower reorganization boundary is usually defined such that whenever the value of the issuing firm falls to a prespecified level, the bondholders take over the firm. The empirical application of this approach to corporate fixed-rate debt has yielded disappointing results; Jones, Mason and Rosenfeld (1984) found that the observed spreads between corporate fixed-rate debt and government debt are too large to be explained with reasonable parameter values. The application of this method to floating-rate notes requires an important modification: the coupon stream associated with a floating-rate note will become known if a deterministic term structure is assumed. This makes the valuation of floating-rate debt trivial and indistinguishable from the valuation of fixed-rate debt. Hence, it becomes essential to model uncertainty in the term structure. We applied the traditional approach to the floater valuation problem, retaining the assumptions on the term structure spelled out in section 3 and assuming that the value of the firm follows a lognormal diffusion. We find that, regardless of the choice of the reorganization boundary, this approach is simply unable to account for the magnitude of the discounts that are reported in section 2.[13]

These findings lead us to consider an alternative approach which employs an instrumental variable to account for default risk. This variable is the default premium that is expected by investors on newly issued short-term obligations, which are close substitutes. Short-term obligations represent the natural instrument in this context because coupons are readjusted to short-term rates repeatedly; for floaters whose coupons are adjusted at longer intervals and tied to intermediate-term rates, the intermediate-term default premium is appropriate. This choice of the instrument has important implications. First, it delinks the value of the issuing firm and the risk premium demanded by investors on its debt obligation, and as a result it avoids specifying the economic events that occur upon bankruptcy – although it should be clear that the default premium and the value of the firm should be inversely related. Second, because the premium will differ across firms with differing credit risk, this choice focuses attention on floaters issued by firms in the same risk 'class'. As a result, issues related to business risk and leverage are not treated explicitly. Finally, because this default premium is time-varying and because we are modeling floaters with fixed markups in their coupons, this choice of an explanatory variable is not self-referential – rather it rests on the assumption that these floaters and newly issued short-term obligations are close substitutes.

In this framework, the floater value depends on two variables in addition to τ: (a) the current rate of interest $r(t)$ which evolves according to eq. (3), and (b) the instrumental variable, $p(t)$, which is the expected market premium on newly issued short-term obligations. The floater is assumed to pay a coupon continuously at the rate $r(t) + \pi$, where π is set at the time of issuance. We assume that the floater is valued at each t to provide the investor with the instantaneous cum-coupon return $r(t) + p(t)$, which is the return promised on newly issued short-term obligations of similar risk. This assumes a pricing condition which is similar to the Local Expectations Hypothesis, modified to reflect credit risk:

$$E_t[dF] + (r(t) + \pi) dt = F\{r(t) + p(t)\} dt, \qquad (9)$$

---

[13] We employed a fixed lower reorganization boundary as well as a time-varying boundary equal to the discounted face value. In both cases, the floater values were quite insensitive to interest rate levels.

where $F(r, p, \tau; \pi)$ is the price of a floater with a time to maturity τ, paying a continuous coupon at a rate $r(t) + \pi$. It is noteworthy that for extremely general processes on r and p the floater will sell at par, provided that the coupon rate is time-varying and set at $r(t) + p(t)$ for all t. Therefore, the price behavior of the floater will depend, in part, on the location of $p(t)$ relative to the fixed premium π. Our specification in (9) only defines the expected return over an infinitesimal holding period. For any finite holding period, the default premiums will be maturity-specific and therefore will differ from p. In order to complete the description of the pricing problem we need to specify the dynamics for $p(t)$. We rely here on the empirical findings of Fama (1986). In his analysis of default premiums in money market instruments, Fama reports that these are related to the stage of the business cycle. This regularity is captured in our choice of the mean-reverting stochastic process for $p(t)$:

$$\mathrm{d}p = \kappa_p(\mu_p - p)\,\mathrm{d}t + \sigma_p\sqrt{p}\;\mathrm{d}z_p. \tag{10}$$

In (10) $\{z_p(t), t > 0\}$ is a standard Wiener process which may be correlated with the process $\{z(t), t > 0\}$; μ_p is the long-run mean of the premium, $p\sigma_p^2$ is the variance of the changes in the premium; and κ_p is the speed of adjustment. One implication of (10) is that the volatility of the changes in the default premiums is higher at higher levels of default premiums. Using (3), (9) and (10), one can derive the valuation equation that the floater's value must satisfy:

$$\tfrac{1}{2}F_{rr}\sigma^2 r + \tfrac{1}{2}F_{pp}\sigma_p^2 p + F_{pr}\sigma_{rp}\sqrt{r}\,\sqrt{p} + F_r\kappa(\mu - r)$$

$$+ F_p\kappa_p(\mu_p - p) + (r + \pi) - F(r + p) = F_\tau. \tag{11}$$

Note that when the continuous coupon flow rate is set at $(r + p)$, the floater always sells at par, and this serves as a natural benchmark to evaluate coupon rules[14] of the form $(r + \pi)$. We expect the floater to sell at a discount when $p(t) > \pi$; this discount structure could persist for a long time if the speed of adjustment factor κ_p is small and $p(t) > \pi$. In an analogous manner if $\mu_p > \pi$, then we expect the floater to sell almost always at a discount, especially for large values of κ_p.

The valuation equation (11) has a terminal condition given by

$$F(r, p, 0; \pi) = 1.$$

---

[14] This method can also accommodate coupon formulas in which the stated default premium declines over time in a prespecified way.

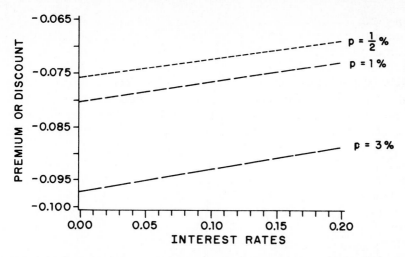

Fig. 6. Discounts for corporate floaters versus interest rates. *Note*: p is the default premium demanded of newly issued short-term corporate paper. It evolves as a diffusion $dp = \kappa_p (\mu_p - p) dt + \sigma_p \sqrt{p}\, dz_p$, where $\kappa_p = 1$, $\mu_p = 0.025$, $\sigma_p^2 = 0.002$. The interest rate r evolves a diffusion $dr = \kappa(\mu - r) dt + \sigma\sqrt{r}\, dz$, where $\kappa = 2$, $\mu = 0.10$, $\sigma^2 = 0.006$, and $\text{cov}\{dz_p, dz\} = 0$. The floater has 10 years to maturity, with a continuously indexed-coupon rate $r + \pi$. $\pi = 0.01$ is the fixed default premium.

We provide below the results which are obtained by solving eq. (11) using the numerical method of alternating directions.[15] We maintain the parameter values of the interest rate process, and for the process on the market premium we assume $\kappa_p = 1$ and $\sigma_p^2 = 0.002$. The low value of κ_p was chosen so that the default premium p will exhibit a random walk pattern documented by Fama (1986). We use different values for the long-run mean market premium μ_p, ranging from 0.0075 to 0.025. The stated premium π was held fixed at 0.01. We compute the prices of floaters with maturities of 5 and 10 years. Fig. 6 contains the results corresponding to $\mu_p = 0.025$ for floaters maturing in 10 years: even when $p(t) = \pi = 1\%$, this floater sells at a discount of about 8% relative to its par value. This result is due to the fact that in the long run, the stated premium is inadequate compensation for the risk borne by investors.[16] As $p(t)$ increases, the discount become larger at all levels of interest rates. Holding $p(t)$ fixed, as the interest rates increase, the discounts decrease: at high rates of interest, the required premium is relatively a minor component of

[15] Brennan and Schwartz (1980) discuss this procedure. The numerical solution of the valuation equation requires additional boundary conditions. At $r = 0$ and $p = 0$, the valuation equation itself served as the lower boundary. $F_{rr} = 0$ and $F_{pp} = 0$ served as upper boundary conditions for r and p, respectively. The upper boundary for p was chosen to be 10%, and the covariance σ_{rp} was set to zero.

[16] Puglisi and Cohen (1981) have made a similar observation.

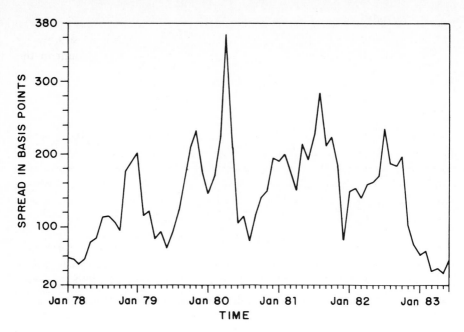

Fig. 7. Spread of CD yields over Treasury Bills (6-month maturity).

the total return from a floater where the coupon is indexed to the interest rate. We examined these issues for a floater maturing in 5 years. The results were quite similar and the discounts ranged from 4% to about 6.5%. We further investigated these issues for different values of σ_p^2. The results were fairly robust, indicating that for the specification used here, the volatility of the changes in default premiums did not significantly affect the valuation of floaters. It should be clear that, as in the case examined here, if the markup in the formula is fixed, then a put feature appended to the contractual terms will have considerable value.

To see whether an increase in the required default premium could have explained the floater discounts reported in section 2, we plot the spread between Certificates of Deposit of 6-month maturity and 6-month Treasury Bills from January 1978 to June 1983 (fig. 7). We have chosen to plot the spread for this instrument because it is most appropriate to short-term issues of financial corporations: the data are from Salomon Brothers' *Analytical Record of Yields and Yield Spreads*. The spread shows a marked increase over this period, and the level of the spread in June 1979 is consistent with the 50 basis point markup provided in the Beneficial floater at that time. The subsequent discounts exhibited by the floaters in our sample are broadly consistent with the increase in the spread over this period: it is possible to interpret these data as indicating an upward shift in the long-run mean premium μ_p. Further empirical work needs to be conducted to estimate the parameters of the process on interest rates and the default premium in this context.

5. Conclusion

We have developed models for the valuation of floating-rate notes, incorporating into the theoretical framework coupon averaging formulae, and several contractual features that are observed in issues of corporate floaters. The solutions presented for plausible parameter values indicate that ignoring default risk, these features taken singly cause these floaters to fluctuate in value more than one would find desirable, given the motivation for their issuance. For a plausible set of parameters it appears that the floater will sell at a discount whenever the stated default premium in the coupon formula is less than the long-run mean of the default premium expected by the market. We conclude that the observed discounts can be rationalized only if the stated premiums are much less than the premiums demanded by the investors.

References

Black, Fischer and John C. Cox, 1976, Valuing corporate securities: Some effects of bond indenture provisions, Journal of Finance 31, 351–368.

Brennan, Michael J. and Eduardo S. Schwartz, 1980, Savings bonds: Theory and empirical evidence, Monograph series in finance and economics (New York University, New York).

Chance, Don M., 1983, Floating rate notes and immunization, Journal of Financial and Quantitative Analysis 18, 365–380.

Cox, John C., Jonathan E. Ingersoll, Jr. and Stephen A. Ross, 1979, Duration and the measurement of basis risk, Journal of Business 52, 51–61.

Cox, John C., Jonathan E. Ingersoll, Jr. and Stephen A. Ross, 1980, An analysis of variable rate loan contracts, Journal of Finance 35, 389–403.

Cox, John C., Jonathan E. Ingersoll, Jr. and Stephen A. Ross, 1981, A reexamination of traditional hypotheses of the term structure of interest rates, Journal of Finance 36, 769–799.

Cox, John C., Jonathan E. Ingersoll, Jr. and Stephen A. Ross, 1985, A theory of the term structure of interest rates, Econometrica 53, 385–407.

Cox, John C., Stephen A. Ross and Mark Rubinstein, 1979, Options pricing: A simplified approach, Journal of Financial Economics 7, 229–263.

Fama, Eugene F., 1986, Term premiums and default premiums in money markets, Journal of Financial Economics 17, 175–196.

Hanna, Jeffrey and Gioia M. Parente, 1985, Floating-rate financing quarterly – January 1985, Bond market research (Salomon Brothers, New York).

Jones, E. Philip, Scott P. Mason and Eric Rosenfeld, 1984, Contingent claims analysis of corporate capital structures: An empirical investigation, Journal of Finance 39, 611–625.

Merton, Robert C., 1974, On the pricing of corporate debt: The risk structure of interest rates, Journal of Finance 29, 449–470.

Puglisi, Donald J. and Deborah L. Cohen, 1981, Floating rate notes: Alternative to short-term investments, Federal Home Loan Bank Board Journal, 1–7.

Santomero, Anthony M., 1983, Fixed versus variable rate loans, Journal of Finance 38, 1363–1380.

Smith, Clifford W., Jr. and Jerold B. Warner, 1979, On financial contracting: An analysis of bond covenants, Journal of Financial Economics 7, 117–161.

The Real Function
of Bond Rating Agencies

L. Macdonald Wakeman*

I've just heard Moody's is going to downgrade our bonds. What do we do?

Nothing.

Nothing? But the price will drop like a stone when the rating change is announced.

No it won't. The market already knows we've been doing badly. Our bond and stock prices have been dropping for the last year. The rating change just reflects the bond's higher risk.

But if a rating change doesn't affect the bond's price, whey did we bother to pay for the rating in the first place?

Because having a rating lowered our interest costs when we issued the bonds. The important point is not what rating you have, but whether or not you have a rating.

Wait, you're saying that our rating doesn't matter . . . and yet it does matter?

Let me try to explain:

DO BOND RATINGS PROVIDE NEW INFORMATION?

The belief that bond rating services largely determine the interest rate that a debt issuer must pay is widely held among corporate officers, city managers, and state officials. One company official estimated that the 1978 downgrading of Pacific Telephone's debt by Moody's Investors Service raised its interest cost by approximately $35 million; New York City officials stated in 1972 that the city would have saved $40 million in interest costs if its rating had been raised earlier; and Governor DuPont, after vainly lobbying to prevent the downgrading of his state's bonds in 1977, noted that Delaware would pay a penalty for the lower rating. Financial analysts searching for under- and over-rated issues bolster this belief. So do articles in publications such as *Barrons, The Financial Times, Fortune,* and *The Wall Street Journal* implying that rating agencies determine the debt market's assessment of a bond's risk.

Concern about this concentration of market power has led academics, busi-

---

*Assistant Professor of Finance at the Graduate School of Management, University of Rochester; previously taught at M.I.T. and Boston University. Dr. Wakeman's research, published both in the U.S. and overseas, has been concerned with such topics as bond market efficiency, optimal tax depreciation, forward exchange markets, and the relationship between inflation and interest rates. He has served as Economic Advisor to the Commission of the European Communities and as a consultant to local government authorities and financial institutions.

410

nessmen, and politicians to suggest that the bond rating industry be reformed, federally regulated, or even nationalized.

But the major assumption underlying these proposals has no basis in fact. Contrary to the popular notion, the bond market does not react to rating changes. Bonds with lower ratings do indeed pay higher interest costs, but to blame the rating is to confuse cause with effect. A bond rating does not actively determine, but simply mirrors, the market's assessment of a bond's risk. Hence, a rating change does not *affect,* but merely *reflects,* the market's altered estimation of a bond's value.

To clarify this point, let's examine the response of the capital markets when a rating change is announced. The most current and carefully done research is unanimous on this point. Neither the company's bond nor its common stock shows any unusual behavior—whether on the day of, or during the week and month surrounding, the announcement of the rating change. Our conclusion: rating change announcements provide no new information to the capital markets.

What our research shows instead is that bond rating changes convey information that has long been reflected in bond prices. Companies experiencing changes in their bond ratings *do* see significant changes in the prices of their securities; however, these changes occur, on average, more than a year before the rating change. The evidence is emphatic on this point. The rating agencies downgrade a bond only after the company has done poorly, and after the risk levels of both the company's bonds and common stock have increased. Upgradings come only after it has become clear that the company's performance has enhanced the bond's value.

Nor is there any special effect when bonds are upgraded into, or downgraded below, the "investment grades" (Moody's "Baa" and above). Although the Comptroller of the Currency's ruling in 1936 prohibited federally chartered banks from holding non-investment grade bonds, no "segmentation" in the pricing of bonds resulted then or now. There are no major discontinuities in pricing that would suggest the market makes a sharp distinction between "investment grade" and less than "investment grade" bonds. Furthermore, an analysis of the performance of bonds downgraded from Baa or upgraded from Ba in the 1970's has shown the same reaction to the bond rating change announcement—none.

This evidence raises some interesting questions: what events cause the rating services to change a bond's rating? And what methods do they use to detect changes in the risk levels of bonds? Three distinct pieces of evidence suggest that the rating services respond to changes reflected in nothing more current than companies' published accounting reports. First, and most obviously, Moody's gives accounting-based explanations (e.g., changes in coverage and leverage ratios) for more than two-thirds of the bond rating changes not resulting from specific events such as mergers or new financing. Second, the monthly distribution of Moody's rating changes is not uniform; instead a significantly larger number of rating changes occur in the months of May and June, shortly after the publication of most companies' annual reports.

The third piece of evidence is provided by studies attempting to "explain" and thus predict ratings and rating changes. Such studies construct models simulating the bond rating process which correctly classify up to 80% of the bonds in their samples using data derived only from published accounting statements.

Armed with such a model, an investor could pursue a strategy of buying under-rated issues at "bargain" prices. To test this hypothesis, the studies attempt to use their models to "beat the market" by capitalizing on rating "errors." Their findings show that an investment strategy based on such a systematic attempt to identify and profit from incorrectly rated bonds does not enable an investor to outperform the market. The exercise is pointless because the model's predicted rating is itself based on publicly available information. The "bargain" never existed because the bond prices had already incorporated all relevant information, including published accounting statements, about the companies.

A RATIONALE FOR THE EXISTENCE OF BOND RATING AGENCIES

But if a rating change does not convey new information to the capital markets, what services do the rating agencies provide? Initially they provided investors with data on companies—and, more particularly, with measures of bond risk—at low cost.

Why do investors demand this data? Because collecting the information required to make portfolio choices is costly. With many investors demanding such information, efficient producers of information can expect to gain by reducing investors' duplication of effort. This point was most directly expressed, and the opportunity seized, by the founder of Moody's Investors Service, who said, "Somebody, sooner or later, will bring out an industrial statistical manual, and when it comes, it will be a gold mine."

Once having compiled such a manual, John Moody had a comparative advantage in producing measures of the relative risks of holding bonds. In 1909 he published the first bond ratings, providing measures which were convenient, comprehensible, and inexpensive.

What information do such measures provide? Though bond ratings do not provide timely information, our studies consistently demonstrate that there is a close relationship between a bond's rating and its level of risk. A bond rating thus incorporates into a single, easily communicated code all the major ingredients of the bond's risk. Although likely to lag behind significant changes in a company's prospects—changes which would warrant a rating change—current bond ratings do contain information about the relative risk of a company's securities.

Over the past 60 years, the rating agencies have acquired a reputation for accurately evaluating and reporting the risks of new bond issues. Having achieved a large measure of credibility and authority, these ratings have been used by some investors to check the performance of trustees and fund managers. For instance, by the 1930's, bond ratings were being used both to circumscribe the discretionary powers of fiduciary trustees (many trust agreements limited investments in debt instruments to bonds with higher ratings), and to monitor their performance (agreements often required trustees to sell bonds that had been downgraded to an unsatisfactory rating). At the same time, courts recognized the rating agencies as "disinterested authorities" and accepted the use of ratings by executives and trustees as evidence of "sound discretion" on their part. More recently, ratings have become recognized inputs to the regulatory process for banks and insurance companies.

The crucial question, then, is this: if the information provided by bond ratings is not "new," then what is the value of this credibility established by the rating agencies? And who benefits most from the information and assurance provided by published ratings?

The fact that Moody's and Standard & Poor's both have long lists of subscribers indicates that there is a demand by investors for such information. However, the additional fact that bond ratings do not appear to influence investors' pricing of bonds—at least, after the initial issue—suggests that investors are not the main beneficiaries of rating services. They have access to other, more timely sources of information which enable them to price securities without much reliance on current ratings.

If the demand is allegedly coming from investors, why do the issuing companies bear the cost of having their bonds rated? The answer lies partly in an explanation of how the bond market prices securities.

Like all lenders, potential buyers of new bonds recognize that managers (as the representatives of shareholder interests) might have an incentive to take actions—after the bonds are issued—which would reduce the value of those bonds by transferring wealth to the shareholders. (In modern finance literature, this conflict of interest between bondholders, shareholders, and managers is called the "agency" problem.) In the extreme case, management could simply pay out the proceeds of the debt offering (in the absence of any covenants) to shareholders and liquidate the assets of the company. In less obvious ways, management could reduce the value of the bonds by making significant changes in the investment or financing policies of the company. They could, for instance, acquire riskier companies or undertake riskier projects, thus increasing the risk and lowering the value of the outstanding bonds. On the financing side, they could take on even larger amounts of debt, further leveraging the company's assets. Both of these management actions would reduce the value of the bondholders' claim by making the bonds more risky. Because a bond is a fixed-income claim, the bondholder does not share in the increased upside potential associated with a highly leveraged financial policy or a higher-risk investment strategy.

The possibility of such action is recognized by potential bondholders when pricing a bond issue. Unless offered protection from such management behavior, typically in the form of loan covenants, they will expect the worst to happen and require higher returns for holding the bonds. Rather than accept lower prices, management and shareholders will find it in their own interest to have restrictive covenants written (provided they are not too restrictive) which, by offering bondholders protection from such management incentives, will increase the issue price of the bond.

The same argument holds for providing bondholders and shareholders with information about the company. An old and sensible maxim says that investors pay a discount for uncertainty, never a premium. By furnishing investors with detailed financial statements, and by paying a reputable auditor to validate them, management is effectively raising the price it receives for new securities.

The rating agencies, then, by analyzing the company's statements at the time of issue and by offering an independent judgment of the new bond's risk, provide an initial low-cost assessment of the credit standing of the issuing company. Furthermore, the rating services have a comparative advantage in monitoring the changing position of the bond vis-a-vis the company over time. Provided with these services, which in turn offer investors both information and greater assurance about future management actions, companies continue to pay rating agencies to have their bonds rated, and to have their performance monitored. The use of Moody's or S & P's is thus a cost-effective strategy which increases the net proceeds of the debt issue to the issuing company.

Let's summarize our argument about the role of the rating agencies: they attest to the relative quality of the bond issue and to the accuracy of the accompanying information about the issuing company; and they further monitor that bond's risk over the life of the bond. In so doing, the rating agencies enable the bonds to be sold to the public at a higher price than would be otherwise possible. This higher price reflects both economies of scale in the collection of information and the reduction of "agency costs"* incurred when issuing new debt. That the bond rating agencies continue to prosper is strong evidence that the cost to companies of having their bonds rated is more than covered by the increased proceeds from the sale of the bonds.

Another piece of evidence supporting our argument is that private placements are rarely certified by bond rating agencies. In a private placement, the single bondholder (or small group of bondholders) normally has excellent knowledge of the issuer and can monitor the bond's performance inexpensively. There is also no problem of duplication of effort in enforcing covenants. Under these circumstances, there will be little demand for the services of a bond rating agency. Our theory thus implies that the crucial determinant of whether a company should seek a bond rating is not the size of the issue, but rather the number of potential bondholders. The larger the number of potential bondholders, the more valuable to the issuing company will be the information and assurance provided investors by the bond rating agencies.

---

*In the finance literature, the "agency costs" of issuing debt are identified as follows: (1) the direct, measurable costs of writing, monitoring, and enforcing covenants, (2) the cost of the opportunities foregone by imposing such covenants, and (3) the costs (in the form of lower proceeds than otherwise from the issue of the bonds) caused by remaining investor uncertainty about managements' future actions.

THE BOTTOM LINE ON BOND RATINGS

What, then, are the implications of our theory and evidence for corporate financial policy?

1 It is in a company's interest to pay for a public issue of new debt to be rated because the greater certainty and assurance provided investors increases the net proceeds to the company at the time of issue.

2 In deciding whether to have its bonds rated, management should regard the number of bondholders as a major variable. The greater the number of potential bondholders, the greater the benefits of having a bond rating.

3 Attempts by investors to predict either ratings or rating changes, even if successful, are pointless because they do not allow an investor to earn above normal profits.

4 Because the markets do not view bond rating changes as conveying timely information, no effort should be made to induce a rating service either to upgrade a bond or to refrain from downgrading a bond. The resources expended would be better devoted to improving the company's performance.

SELECTED REFERENCES

Altman, Edward I., 1977, "Statistical Replication of Bond Quality Ratings: A Worthwhile or Futile Exercise?," *Working Paper* (New York University, NY).

Jensen, Michael C. and William H. Meckling, 1976, "Theory of the Firm: Managerial Behavior, Agency Costs and Ownership Structure," *Journal of Financial Economics 3*, 305–360.

Kaplan, Robert S. and Gabriel Urwitz, 1977, "Statistical Methods of Bond Ratings: A Methodological Inquiry," *Working Paper*, (Carnegie-Mellon University, Pittsburgh, PA).

Melicher, Ronald W. and David F. Rush, 1974, "Systematic Risk, Financial Data, and Bond Rating Relationships in a Regulated Industry Environment," *Journal of Finance 29*, 537–544.

Pinches, George E. and J. Clay Singleton, 1978, "The Adjustment of Stock Prices to Bond Rating Changes," *Journal of Finance 33*, 29–44.

Rozeff, Michael S., 1976, "The Relationship of Bond Betas to Bond Returns and Agency Ratings with a Test of the Capital Asset Pricing Model," *Working Paper*, (University of Iowa, Iowa City, IA).

Sherwood, Hugh C., 1976, "How Corporate and Municipal Debt is Rated," (John Wiley & Sons, NY).

Urwitz, Gabriel, 1975, "Evidence on the Information Content of Market Determined Risk Measures of Corporate Bonds," *Working Paper*, (Carnegie-Mellon University, Pittsburgh, PA).

Wakeman, L. Macdonald, 1980, "Bond Market Inefficiency: The Evidence Reexamined," *Working Paper*, (The University of Rochester, Rochester, NY).

Wakeman, L. Macdonald, 1981, "The Function of Bond Rating Agencies: Theory and Evidence," *Working Paper*, (The University of Rochester, Rochester, NY).

Weinstein, Mark, 1977, "The Effect of a Rating Change Announcement on Bond Prices," *Journal of Financial Economics 5*, 329–350.

SIX

CORPORATE FINANCIAL STRATEGY

CORPORATE FINANCING AND INVESTMENT DECISIONS WHEN FIRMS HAVE INFORMATION THAT INVESTORS DO NOT HAVE*

Stewart C. MYERS

MIT/NBER, Cambridge, MA 02139, USA

Nicholas S. MAJLUF

Universidad Catolica de Chile, Santiago, Chile

Received August 1982, final version received February 1984

This paper considers a firm that must issue common stock to raise cash to undertake a valuable investment opportunity. Management is assumed to know more about the firm's value than potential investors. Investors interpret the firm's actions rationally. An equilibrium model of the issue–invest decision is developed under these assumptions. The model shows that firms may refuse to issue stock, and therefore may pass up valuable investment opportunities. The model suggests explanations for several aspects of corporate financing behavior, including the tendency to rely on internal sources of funds, and to prefer debt to equity if external financing is required. Extensions and applications of the model are discussed.

1. Introduction

Consider a firm that has assets in place and also a valuable real investment opportunity. However, it has to issue common shares to raise part or all of the cash required to undertake the investment project. If it does not launch the project promptly, the opportunity will evaporate. There are no taxes, transaction costs or other capital market imperfections.

Finance theory would advise this firm to evaluate the investment opportunity as if it already had plenty of cash on hand. In an efficient capital market, securities can always be sold at a fair price; the net present value of selling securities is always zero, because the cash raised exactly balances the present value of the liability created. Thus, the decision rule is: take every positive-NPV project, regardless of whether internal or external funds are used to pay for it.

*This paper draws on Majluf (1978) and an earlier (1978) joint working paper, but it has undergone several major revisions and expansions. We thank Fischer Black, George Constantinides, Roger Gordon, Rene Stulz and the referee, Harry DeAngelo, for valuable comments. The Office of Naval Research sponsored the initial work on this paper.

Journal of Financial Economics 13 (1984) 187–221. © North-Holland Publishing Company.

What if the firm's managers know more about the value of its assets and opportunities than outside investors do? As we will show, nothing fundamental is changed so long as managers invest in every project *they* know to have positive NPV. If they do this, the shares investors buy will be correctly priced *on average*, although a particular issue will be over or underpriced. The manager's inside information creates a side bet between old and new stockholders, but the equilibrium issue price is unaffected.

However, if managers have inside information there must be some cases in which that information is so favorable that management, if it acts in the interest of the *old* stockholders, will refuse to issue shares even if it means passing up a good investment opportunity. That is, the cost to old shareholders of issuing shares at a bargain price may outweigh the project's NPV. *This* possibility makes the problem interesting: investors, aware of their relative ignorance, will reason that a decision *not* to issue shares signals 'good news'. The news conveyed by an issue is bad or at least less good. This affects the price investors are willing to pay for the issue, which in turn affects the issue–invest decision.

If the firm finally decides *not* to issue and therefore *not* to invest – and we will show formally how this can happen – real capital investment is misallocated and firm value reduced. Of course, we would also expect management to try to rearrange the firm's capital structure to avoid being caught in this 'financing trap' the next time the firm has a positive-NPV investment. Thus, our analysis of how asymmetric information affects firms' issue–invest decisions may lead us to explain some corporate financing choices as attempts by firms to avoid the problems we have just introduced.

The first problem is to figure out the equilibrium share price conditional on the issue–invest decision, assuming rational investors, and also a rational firm which bases the issue–invest decision on the price it faces. This paper addresses that problem, and solves it under reasonable simplifying assumptions.

The assumptions are set out and discussed in section 2. This section also contains a numerical example. A general formulation and solution is given in section 3.

However, section 3's results raise deeper issues. Our solution assumes that management acts in the interests of 'old' (existing) stockholders. It also assumes those stockholders are *passive*, and do not adjust their portfolios in response to the firm's issue–invest decision, except possibly to buy a predetermined fraction of any new issue.

This assumption makes financing matter. A firm with ample financial slack – e.g., large holdings of cash or marketable securities, or the ability to issue default-risk-free debt – would take all positive-NPV opportunities. The same firm without slack would pass some up. Also, with this assumption about management's objective, our model predicts firms will prefer debt to equity if they need external funds.

If old shareholders are assumed to be *active*, and to rebalance their portfolios in response to what they learn from the firm's actions, then financing does *not* matter: financial slack has no impact on investment decisions. Even with ample slack, the firm will pass up some positive-NPV investments.

We can choose from three statements about management's objective under asymmetric information:

(1) Management acts in the interests of *all* shareholders, and ignores any conflict of interest between old and new shareholders.
(2) Management acts in old shareholders' interest, *and* assumes they are *passive*.
(3) Management acts in old shareholders' interest, but assumes they rationally *rebalance* their portfolios as they learn from the firm's actions.

We have so far found no compelling theoretical justification for favoring any one of these statements over the other two. A theory, or at least a story, could be developed to support any one of the three statements. We will suggest some of these stories as we go along. However, we do not claim to have a theory of managerial behavior fully supporting our model. We treat the three statements as possible *assumptions* about managerial behavior. Since we cannot judge the assumptions' realism, we turn instead to their positive implications.

The three statements yield substantially different empirical predictions. Statement 2 leads at this stage of the empirical race, because it explains why stock prices fall, on average, when firms announce an equity issue. Moreover, it explains why debt issues have less price impact than stock issues. We briefly review this evidence in section 4.

A model based on (a) asymmetric information and (b) management acting in the interests of passive, old stockholders may explain several aspects of corporate behavior, including the tendency to rely on internal sources of funds and to prefer debt to equity if external financing is required. Some of the model's implications are discussed in sections 5 and 6 of the paper. We defer the customary introductory review of the literature until the end of section 2, after our assumptions have been more fully explained.

2. Assumptions and example

We assume the firm (i.e., its managers) has information that investors do not have, and that both managers and investors realize this. We take this information asymmetry as given – a fact of life. We side-step the question of how much information managers should release, except to note the underlying assumption that transmitting information is costly. Our problem disappears if managers can costlessly convey their special information to the market.

The firm has one existing asset and one opportunity requiring investment I. The investment can be financed by issuing stock, drawing down the firm's cash balance or selling marketable securities. The sum of cash on hand and marketable securities will be referred to as *financial slack* (S).

Financial slack should also include the amount of default-risk-free debt the firm can issue. (Discussion of risky debt is deferred to section 3.) However, it's simpler for our purposes to let the firm use risk-free borrowing to reduce the required investment I. We thus interpret I as required *equity* investment.

The investment opportunity evaporates if the firm does not go ahead at time $t = 0$. (We could just as well say that delay of investment reduces the project's net present value.) If $S < I$, going ahead requires a stock issue of $E = I - S$. Also, the project is 'all or nothing' – the firm can't take part of it.

We assume capital markets are perfect and efficient with respect to publicly available information. There are no transaction costs in issuing stock. We also assume that market value of the firm's shares equals their expected future value conditional on whatever information the market has. The future values could be discounted for the time value of money without changing anything essential.[1] Discounting for risk is not considered, because the only uncertainty important in this problem stems from managers' special information. Investors at time $t = 0$ do not know whether the firm's stock price will go up or down when that special information is revealed at $t = 1$. However, the risk is assumed to be diversifiable.[2]

We can now give a detailed statement of who knows what when.

2.1. A three-date model

(1)   There are three dates, $t = -1$, 0 and $+1$. At $t = -1$, the market has the same information the management does. At $t = 0$, management receives additional information about the value of the firm's asset-in-place and investment opportunity, and updates their values accordingly. The market does not receive this information until $t = +1$.

(2)   The value of the asset-in-place at $t = -1$ is the expected future value $\bar{A} = E(\tilde{A})$; the distribution of $\tilde{A}$ represents the asset's possible (updated) values at $t = 0$. Management's updated estimate at $t = 0$ is a, the realization of $\tilde{A}$.[3]

(3)   The net present value (NPV) at $t = -1$ of the investment opportunity is $\bar{B} = E(\tilde{B})$. The distribution of $\tilde{B}$ represents the asset's possible updated

---

[1]We could interpret our time subscript not as calendar time, but just the state of information available to the firm and market.

[2] That is, managers may have inside information about the firm, but not about the market or the economy.

[3]An analogy may help make this clear. Think of a share of IBM stock on January 1 ($t = -1$). A could be the unknown distribution of the February 1 price, a the actual price on February 1 ($t = 0$). However, a fur trapper snowed in on the upper MacGregor River might not learn the February 1 price until March 1 ($t = +1$).

NPVs at $t = 0$. Management's updated estimate at $t = 0$ is b, the realization of $\tilde{B}$.

(4) Negative values for a and b are ruled out. This makes sense for the asset-in-place because of limited liability. It makes sense for the investment opportunity because the opportunity is discarded if it turns out to have a negative NPV at $t = 0$. In other words, the distribution of $\tilde{B}$ is truncated at zero.

(5) Management acts in the interest of the 'old' shareholders, those owning shares at the start of $t = 0$. That is, they maximize $V_0^{old} = V(a, b, E)$, the 'intrinsic' value of the old shares conditional on the issue–invest decision and knowledge of the realizations a and b. However, the market value of these shares will not generally equal V^{old}, since investors know only the distribution of $\tilde{A}$ and $\tilde{B}$ and whether shares are issued. Let P' be the market value at $t = 0$ of old stockholders' shares if stock is issued, and P the market value at $t = 0$ if stock is not issued.

Old stockholders are assumed passive. They 'sit tight' if stock is issued; thus the issue goes to a different group of investors. If the firm has ample slack, and thus does not need to issue shares in order to invest, old shareholders also sit tight if the investment is made. Thus, acting in old stockholders' interest amounts to maximizing the true or intrinsic value of the *existing shares*. (Here 'true' or 'intrinsic' value means what the shares would sell for, conditional on the firms' issue–invest decision, if investors knew everything that managers know.)

We realize this passive-stockholder assumption may be controversial. We will discuss it further in section 4 below.

(6) Slack, S, is fixed and known by both managers and the market. The information available to management and the market is summarized below:

	$t = -1$ (symmetric information)	$t = 0$ (information advantage to managers)	$t = +1$ (symmetric information)
Information available to:			
Managers	Distributions of $\tilde{A}$ and $\tilde{B}$; S	a, b; S	a, b; remaining S, if any
Market	Distributions of $\tilde{A}$ and $\tilde{B}$; S	Distributions of $\tilde{A}$ and $\tilde{B}$; S; also E, either $E = 0$ or $E = I - S$	a, b; remaining S, if any

2.2. Example

The following example should give a better understanding of the problem just posed and the steps required to solve it. Also, the example shows why a firm may pass up a positive-NPV opportunity in a rational expectations equilibrium.

There are two equally probable states of nature. The true state is revealed to management at $t = 0$ and to investors at $t = +1$. Asset values are:

	State 1	State 2
Asset-in-place	$a = 150$	$a = 50$
Investment opportunity (NPV)	$b = 20$	$b = 10$

The firm has no cash or marketable securities ($S = 0$). The investment opportunity requires $I = 100$, so the firm must issue stock to raise $E = 100$ if it goes ahead.

Consider a trial solution in which the firm issues stock and undertakes the project regardless of whether the favorable or unfavorable state occurs. In that case, $P' = 115$ because $\bar{A} + \bar{B} = 115$.

In state 1, the true value of the firm, including 100 raised from the stock issue, is 270. That is $V \equiv V^{\text{old}} + V^{\text{new}} = 270$. The *market* value at $t = 0$ is $P' + E$ (the old shares' market value is P', the new shares' is E). Thus,

$$V^{\text{old}} = \frac{P'}{P' + E} \cdot V = \frac{115}{215} \cdot 270 = 144.42,$$

$$V^{\text{new}} = \frac{E}{P' + E} \cdot V = \frac{100}{215} \cdot 270 = 125.58.$$

In state 2,

$$V = V^{\text{old}} + V^{\text{new}} = 160,$$

$$V^{\text{old}} = \frac{115}{215} \cdot 160 = 85.58,$$

$$V^{\text{new}} = \frac{100}{215} \cdot 160 = 74.42.$$

Note that both old and new shares are correctly priced to investors, who regard the two states as equally probable.

$$P' = 1/2(144.42 + 85.58) = 115,$$

$$E = 1/2(125.58 + 74.42) = 100.$$

Because the firm issues stock in both states, the decision to issue tells investors nothing about the true state.

But this trial solution is not the equilibrium solution. Look at the payoffs to old stockholders:

Payoff	Issue & invest ($E = 100$)	Do nothing ($E = 0$)
V^{old} in state 1	144.42	150
V^{old} in state 2	85.58	50

With these payoffs, the optimal strategy is to issue and invest only in state 2, because in state 1, the market value of the old stockholders' shares is lower when shares are issued. However, if the firm follows this strategy, issuing stock signals state 2 and P' drops to 60. The equilibrium payoffs are:

Payoff	Issue & invest ($E = 100$)	Do nothing ($E = 0$)
V^{old} in state 1	—	150
V^{old} in state 2	60	—

Thus the firm passes up a good investment project (NPV = $+20$) in state 1. Its *market* values at $t = 0$ will be $P' = 60$ (state 2) and $P = 150$ (state 1). The *average* payoff to old stockholders is $1/2(150 + 60) = 105$. There is a loss of 10 in ex ante firm value – i.e., at $t = -1$, $V = 105$ vs. a potential value of 115.

In general, whether the firm decides to issue and invest depends on the relative values of a and b in the two states. For example, suppose we had started with the following table:

	State 1	State 2
Asset-in-place	$a = 150$	$a = 50$
Investment opportunity (NPV)	$b = 100$	$b = 10$

If you work through this case, you will find that the trial solution, in which the firm is assumed to issue and invest in both states, is also the equilibrium solution. The investment opportunity is so valuable in state 1 that the firm cannot afford to pass it up, even though new shares must be sold for less than they are really worth. Since shares are issued in both states, the decision to issue conveys no information, and $P' = \bar{A} + \bar{B} = 155$.

But now let us go back to the original project values, which force the firm not to issue or invest in state 1. In this case we can show that the firm is better off with cash in the bank. If $S = 100$, the payoffs, net of the additional cash investment, are:

Payoff	Invest	Do nothing
V^{old} in state 1	170	150
V^{old} in state 2	60	50

The firm invests in both states[4] and the ex ante value of the firm's real assets is 115, 10 higher than before, because the firm avoids a 50 percent chance of being forced to pass up investment with an NPV of 20. You could say that putting 100 in the bank at $t = -1$ has an ex ante NPV of 10.

2.3. Discussion

The conventional rationale for holding financial slack – cash, liquid assets, or unused borrowing power – is that the firm doesn't want to have to issue stock on short notice in order to pursue a valuable investment opportunity. Managers point to the red tape, delays and underwriting costs encountered in

---

[4] These payoffs appear to be create incentive to leave the cash in the bank, and issue stock in state 2. However, that action would immediately reveal the true state, forcing P' down to 60. If the firm does not have to issue stock to undertake the project, smart investors will assume the worst if it does issue, and the firm will find the issue unattractive.

stock issues. They also typically say: 'We don't want to be forced to issue stock when our firm is undervalued by the market.'

A financial economist might respond by asking: 'Managers may have superior information, but why should that be a *dis*advantage? If we admit that the firm is sometimes undervalued, then sometimes it must be overvalued. Why can't firms take advantage of the market by issuing securities only when the firm is overpriced?'

Our examples suggest answers for these questions: slack has value because without it the firm is sometimes unwilling to issue stock and therefore passes up a good investment opportunity. Slack does not allow the firm to take advantage of investors by issuing only when stock is overvalued: if investors know the firm does not *have to* issue to invest, then an attempt to issue sends a strong pessimistic signal.

Slack is clearly unnecessary if the firm has a 'private line' to existing stockholders. However, private communication to old stockholders would be difficult and also illegal. Slack is also unnecessary if the firm can compel its old stockholders to buy *and hold* the new issue; in this case, the conflict between old and new stockholders does not exist.

Our examples suggest that slack allows the firm to avoid external financing, and thereby to avoid entangling its investment decisions in possible conflicts of interest between old and new shareholders.[5] Slack therefore allows the firm to avoid the consequences of managers' inside information. Unfortunately, this conclusion is not as neat as it appears at first, for it rests on assuming that old stockholders are passive, and do not rebalance their portfolios when they learn whether the firm invests. If they do rebalance, conflicts of interest between old and new shareholders occur even if the firm has ample slack. We return to this point in section 4.

2.4. Information costs

The value of slack disappears if the firm can costlessly convey its special knowledge to all investors, new as well as old. One way to justify our contrary assumption is to think of cases in which values depend on proprietary information which, if released to the market, would be released to competitors also, consequently reducing either the value of its asset-in-place, the NPV of its investment opportunity, or both.

The firm cannot convey that information by saying: 'We have great prospects, but we can't tell you the details.' In our model, the firm always has the incentive to do this, so such statements carry no information. The firm has to supply *verifiable detail* sufficient to indicate the true state of nature. The costs

---

[5]Rights issues resolve the conflict of interest only if old stockholders can be compelled to exercise their rights and hold the newly issued shares.

of supplying, absorbing and verifying this information may be significant. Yet making it public will in most cases tell the firm's competitors all they want to know.[6]

There can also be information asymmetries when there is no need to guard proprietary information. Educating investors takes time and money. After all, the managers' information advantage goes beyond having more facts than investors do. Managers also know better what those facts mean for the firm. They have an insider's view of their organization and what it can and cannot do. This organizational knowledge is part of managers' human capital; they acquire it as they work, by conscious effort as well as by trial and error. An outside investor who tried to match an equally intelligent manager on this dimension would probably fail. By this argument, the separation of ownership from professional management naturally creates asymmetric information.

2.5. Related work

Our problem is similar to the one addressed by Akerlof (1970), who showed how markets can break down when potential buyers cannot verify the quality of the product they are offered. Faced with the risk of buying a lemon, the buyer will demand a discount, which in turn discourages the potential sellers who do *not* have lemons. However, in our paper, the seller is not offering a single good, but a *partial* claim on two, the asset-in-place and the new project. Moreover, the seller gives up one of them (the new project) if the partial claim is not sold. Without this more complex structure, we would have little to say, beyond noting that securities can be lemons too.

Akerlof's paper was one of the first investigations of the economics of unevenly distributed information. The assumption of asymmetric information underlies extensive recent work on agency costs, signalling, adverse selection, etc. A detailed review of all that is not needed here. However, several articles are directly relevant to our problem:

(1) Campbell (1979) assumes that firms have proprietary information that would be costly to convey to the market. He describes the resulting financing difficulties and possible remedies. His main point is to provide a new rationale

---

[6] What is it that competitors want to know? There are two possibilities:
(a) They want to know the *value* of the firm's assets and opportunities – in our example, the true state, $s = 1$ or 2. (In the example, the firm cannot help revealing the true state if it has to issue to invest.)
(b) They want to know technology, product design, management strategy, etc. – that is, *how* the value is generated. In this case, knowing the true state would not help competitors at all.

We assume that the investment opportunity's NPV is independent of whether stock has to be issued to finance it. Thus we are implicitly assuming (b), not (a). But if (a) is important, then slack may have still another payoff: If the firm does not have to issue to invest, it can more easily conceal the true value of its assets and growth opportunities. Its ex ante investment opportunity set, described by the distribution of $\tilde{B}$, may be more favorable with slack than without it.

Issuing stock can fully reveal the true state s only in simple two-state examples. But these comments also apply – if suitably watered down – to the more general cases in section 3.

for debt financing through financial intermediaries. It may, for example, be possible to reveal proprietary information to a bank without revealing it to competitors; the bank could then finance a new project on terms which are fair to old stockholders. This line of analysis is further explored in Campbell and Kracaw (1980).

However, Campbell does not consider what happens if a firm with proprietary information does attempt a public issue. He presents no formal equilibrium model of security pricing and of the financing and investment decisions of the firm.

(2) Leland and Pyle (1977) consider an entrepreneur seeking additional equity financing for a single venture. The entrepreneur knows the project's expected return but outside investors do not. However, the outside investors observe the fraction of the entrepreneur's personal wealth committed to the project, and set their valuation accordingly. The greater the entrepreneur's willingness to take a personal stake in the project, the more investors are willing to pay for their share of it.[7]

This suggests a possible extension to our model. If managers *also* are (old) stockholders, then managers' inside information may be conveyed by the amount of the new issue they are willing to buy for their personal portfolios.

(3) Bhattacharya and Ritter (1983) pose a problem similar to ours, but end up pursuing a different issue. We fix the extent of managers' inside information and examine the equilibrium issue–invest decision. They ask how much information the firm *should* reveal, assuming that each revelation provides information to competitors as well as investors, and therefore reduces the value of the firm. They show that the firm may be able to convey its true value to investors without revealing everything its competitors would like to know. However, their search for signalling equilibria carries them a long way from this paper's analysis.

(4) Rendleman (1980) also sets a problem similar to ours. His investors may over- or undervalue the firm's assets or investment opportunities or misassess its risk. He focuses on the choice between debt and equity financing, but does not derive a full equilibrium model. For example, he shows that undervalued firms will typically prefer debt, but does not model the market's response to the firm's choice of debt over equity. In general management's choice of financing must convey information about the firm's intrinsic value and actual risk. In our model however, the firm *never* issues equity when it has the option to issue debt, regardless of whether the firm is over- or undervalued. We prove this later in the paper.

(5) Giammarino and Neave (1982) present a model in which the firm and investors have different perceptions of the risk – e.g., variance – of the return

---

[7]Downs and Heinkel (1982) present empirical evidence supporting the Leland–Pyle analysis.

on an investment opportunity, but agree on the mean return. They concentrate on the choice among financing instruments, and develop a rationale for convertibles. Our model is in most respects more general, since we allow different information about any aspect of the distributions of asset values. However, we do not consider convertibles as such. We have further comments on these authors' results in section 4.

(6) Miller and Rock (1982) present a model of dividend policy under asymmetric information. If the amount of investment and external financing is held fixed, the cash dividend paid by the firm reveals its operating cash flow. Thus, a larger-than-expected dividend reveals larger-than-expected cash flow, and stock price increases. A larger-than-expected external financing reveals lower-than-expected cash flow, which is bad news for investors. Thus Miller and Rock's model predicts that announcements of new security issues will, on average, depress stock price. So does our model, as we will show in section 3. However, ours also yields more specific hypotheses about what kinds of securities firms choose to issue and how that choice affects the magnitude of the stock price change. These issues, and the relevant empirical evidence, are discussed further in section 4.

(7) There are other theoretical papers exploring how managers' inside information is signalled to investors. They include Bhattacharya's work on dividend policy (1979), Grossman and Hart's (1981) work on takeover bids, and Ross's (1977, 1978) papers on 'financial incentive signalling', in which a manager's employment contract leads him to convey information about the firm's prospects through a choice of its capital structure. There are also tempting analogies between our paper and the literature on credit rationing. See, for example, Jaffee and Russell (1976) and Stiglitz and Weiss (1981).

3. The formal model

In this section, we give a formal statement and solution of the model introduced in section 2. We assume $0 \leq S < I$ so that some or all of the project must be financed by a stock issue. By varying slack S, we vary the size of the required issue, $E = I - S$.

If the firm, knowing the true values a and b, does not issue, it forfeits the investment opportunity, so $V^{\mathrm{old}} = S + a$. The slack remains in cash or liquid assets. If it does issue and invest, $E = I - S$ and

$$V^{\mathrm{old}} = \frac{P'}{P' + E}(E + S + a + b).$$

Old stockholders are better off (or will be at $t = +1$) if the firm issues only when

$$S + a \le \frac{P'}{P' + E}(E + S + a + b),$$

or when

$$\frac{E}{P' + E}(S + a) \le \frac{P'}{P' + E}(E + b),$$

[(share of existing assets and slack going to new stockholders) ≤ (share of increment to firm value obtained by old stockholders)]. The condition can also be written

$$(E/P')(S + a) \le E + b. \tag{1}$$

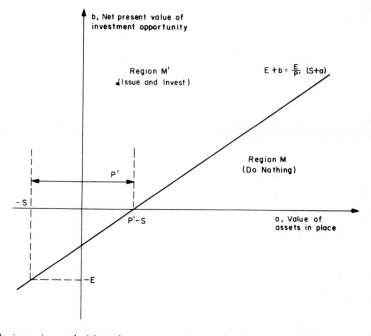

Fig. 1. The issue–invest decision when managers know more than investors about the value of the firm's assets-in-place (a) and the net present value of its investment opportunities (b). The firm issues stock only if (a, b) falls in region M'. E is the amount of new equity required to finance the investment, P' the equilibrium value of the firm conditional on issue, and S is the amount of financial slack (financing available from internal sources).

Thus the line

$$(E/P')(S+a) = E + b \tag{1'}$$

divides the joint probability distribution of $\tilde{A}$ and $\tilde{B}$ into two regions, as shown in fig. 1. If the actual outcome (a, b) falls in region M', the firm issues and invests. If the outcome falls in region M, the firm does nothing: it is willing to give up the NPV of its investment opportunity rather than sell shares for less than the shares are really worth. (Fig. 2 displays the numerical example presented above in the format of fig. 1.)

Remember that the joint probability distribution of a and b is restricted to the Northeast quadrant of fig. 1. Region M' is at the top left of this quadrant. The firm is most likely to issue when b, the realization of project NPV, is high and a, the realization of value of the asset-in-place, is low. The higher b is, the more old stockholders gain from issuing and investing. The lower a is, the more attractive the issue price P'.

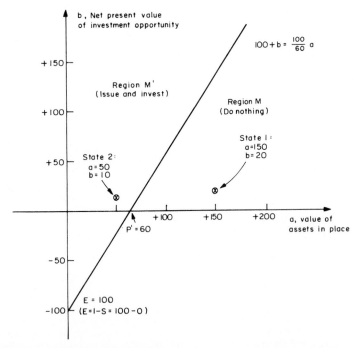

Fig. 2. Solution for example from section 2. In this case, the firm issues and invests in state 2, when assets-in-place are worth 50 and the net present value of the investment opportunity is 10 – i.e., where $(a, b) = (50, 10)$. It does not issue or invest in state 1, where $(a, b) = (150, 20)$. The states are assumed equally probable. Firm value conditional on issue is $P' = 60$.

Of course P' itself depends on the probability densities of $(\tilde{A}, \tilde{B})$ in the regions M and M', and the boundaries of M and M' depend on P'. Thus P', M and M' are simultaneously determined. The stock issue will be fairly priced to investors if

$$P' = S + \overline{A}(M') + \overline{B}(M'), \tag{2}$$

where $\overline{A}(M') \equiv \mathrm{E}(\tilde{A}|E = I - S)$ and $\overline{B}(M') \equiv \mathrm{E}(\tilde{B}|E = I - S)$. These expectations reflect only the information available to investors: the distribution of $\tilde{A}$ and $\tilde{B}$ and the decision to issue, which tells investors that the true values a and b satisfy eq. (1).

3.1. Properties of equilibrium

These equilibrium conditions imply that the firm may pass up good opportunities rather than selling stock to raise funds. This occurs with probability $F(M)$. The ex ante loss in value is $L \equiv F(M)\overline{B}(M)$. There is no loss when the firm has sufficient slack to finance the investment – that is, $L = 0$ when $S \geq I$. If on the other hand, $S < I$, as we will assume in the following discussion, the ex ante loss increases as E, the size of the required equity issue, increases. Since $E = I - S$, the loss also increases with the required investment I and decreases with slack available S.[8]

3.1.1. Special cases

'Corner solutions', in which the firm always issues stock or never issues stock, are rarely encountered in this model given reasonable joint probability distributions for $\tilde{A}$ and $\tilde{B}$. This occurs because both $\tilde{A}$ and $\tilde{B}$ are random and have positive means, and because the investment decision cannot be postponed. The following special cases do give corner solutions, however. First, if a is known by investors as well as managers, then stock is always issued when $b \geq 0$, and thus $L = 0$. To show this, first substitute a for $\overline{A}(M')$ in eq. (2),

$$P' = S + a + \overline{B}(M').$$

Since $\overline{B}(M') \geq 0$, $P' \geq S + a$. The firm will issue stock if

$$\mathrm{E}\left(\frac{S + a}{P'}\right) \leq E + b.$$

---

[8]A formal proof is given in Majluf (1978, pp. 286–290, see also pp. 142–143).

This condition must be satisfied, because $(S + a)/P' \leq 1$ and $b \geq 0$. The firm will issue whenever the investment opportunity has zero or positive NPV ($b \geq 0$). The market value of the old stockholders' stake in the firm, conditional on issue, is therefore $P' = S + a + \overline{B}$.

In our model, asymmetric information restricted to investment opportunities never prevents a stock issue. The terms of sale may be favorable to the firm (if $b < \overline{B}$) or unfavorable (if $b > \overline{B}$), but even in the latter case the firm is better off issuing than losing the project entirely.

This suggests that some firms would be better off splitting assets in place away from growth opportunities. For example, if the asset-in-place can be sold for a, without affecting b, then the problems addressed in this paper evaporate.[9] If the investment opportunity has zero or positive NPV ($b \geq 0$), then the firm sells the asset-in-place. If the proceeds cover the investment required ($a \geq I$), it goes ahead. However, it also goes ahead if $a < I$, because selling the asset-in-place reveals its true value. As we have just shown, asymmetric information restricted to investment opportunities never prevents a stock issue.[10]

On the other hand, the firm might simply spin off its asset-in-place as a separately-financed company. In our model, stockholders are better off *ex ante* holding two firms rather than one, providing that the spinoff does not reduce the values of the distributions $\tilde{A}$ and/or $\tilde{B}$.

Now consider the case in which the firm has no investment opportunities ($\tilde{B} = 0$ in all states of the world). Here things break down totally:[11] stock is never issued, except possibly when a is at a definite lower bound. Let $a_{\min}$ denote the lower bound: assume that both investors and the firm know that a cannot be less than $a_{\min}$. (Note we have reintroduced asymmetric information about a.) Then P' cannot be less than $a_{\min} + S$, because everyone would then know the firm's shares were underpriced. But $P' > a_{\min} + S$ can also be ruled out, for it leads to a contradiction. To see why, substitute $P' = a_{\min} + S + e$ in eq. (1). With $e > 0$, the firm issues only if $a \leq a_{\min} + e$. Therefore, $\overline{A}(M') < a_{\min} + e$ and $P' > S + \overline{A}(M')$, which violates eq. (2).

So the only possibility for P' when $b = 0$ is $P' = a_{\min} + S$. In that case, the firm only issues when $a = a_{\min}$. It never issues when $a > a_{\min}$, because then

$$ \mathrm{E}\left(\frac{S + a}{P'} \right) > E, $$

which violates eq. (1).

---

[9] What if only part of the asset-in-place can be sold? If it can be sold at intrinsic value, the firm treats the proceeds as additional slack and looks again at its issue–invest decision.

[10] What if the asset-in-place can only be sold at a discount? What if the potential buyer does not know its true value? What if sale of the asset-in-place reduces b? These questions are worth exploring.

[11] This is the case of market breakdown analyzed by Akerlof (1970).

If b is positive and investors know its value, the firm will issue and invest in at least some states where $a > a_{min}$. It may issue in *all* states – that is, if b is large enough, it may issue even if a is far out on the right-hand tail of its distribution.

One insight of this model is that you need asymmetric information about *both* assets in place and investment opportunities to get interesting solutions. For example, without asymmetric information about assets-in-place, stock is always issued when the firm has a positive-NPV opportunity; asymmetric information does not affect real investment decisions.

3.1.2. The impact of stock issues on stock price

In our model, the decision to issue stock always reduces stock price, unless the issue is a foregone conclusion. That is equivalent to saying that $P' < P$ if the probability of issue is less than 1.0. (Note that this rules out the 'corner solution' in which investors know what managers know about the value of assets in place.) If the firm is *sure* to issue, then the issue conveys no information, and $P' = P$.

The proof is simple. Note that $P = \overline{A}(M) + S$, the expected value of assets in place and slack conditional on *not* issuing, or in other words, conditional on the realizations a and b falling in region M in fig. 1. Assume M is not empty – there is some probability of no issue. Then a glance at fig. 1 shows that all realizations of a which fall in M exceed $P' - S$, and $\overline{A}(M)$ must exceed $P' - S$. Since $P - S = \overline{A}(M)$, $P - S > P' - S$ and $P > P'$.

Or look at it this way: the *reason* a firm decides *not* to issue is that $a > P'(1 + b/E) - S$. [This follows from reversing and rearranging eq. (1).] Since $b/E \geq 0$, the decision not to issue signals $a > P' - S$ or $a + S > P'$. In other words, it signals that the true values of slack and assets in place exceed P', the price of the 'old' shares if new shares are issued. Since $P = \overline{A}(M) + S$, P must exceed P', and price must fall when the issue–invest decision is revealed.

Note that both P and P' incorporate all information available to investors. They are rationally-formed, unbiased estimates of the firm's intrinsic value. They reflect knowledge of the firm's decision *rule* as well as its decision. P exceeds P' because investors rationally interpret the decision not to issue as good news about the true value of the firm.[12]

---

[12]Issue costs do not appear to change the structure of our model in any fundamental way. However, we comment on them here because including them may qualify our proof that stock price falls when the firm issues shares.

Suppose the firm incurs issue costs of T dollars. This increases the amount it has to issue to finance the project from E to $E + T$. That is, it must issue a gross amount $E + T$ in order to net E.

3.1.3. Comment

Why should stock issues always convey bad news? Might not investors view some issues as confirming the existence of a positive-NPV opportunity? That ought to be good news, not bad.

We will now explain why our model rules out this optimistic response. To do so requires a bit of backtracking, however.

We have assumed that $\tilde{B}$, the NPV of the firm's investment opportunity at $t = 0$, is non-negative. Negative-NPV investments ($\tilde{B} < 0$) would never be undertaken. Even if the firm encountered a negative-NPV investment and raised sufficient money to undertake it, it would never go ahead. It would put the money in the bank instead, or into some other *zero*-NPV investment. (It can buy other firms' shares, for example.) Thus, the distribution of $\tilde{B}$ is truncated at $\tilde{B} = 0$.

There may, however, be a high probability that the realization b will be exactly zero. What does the firm do when this happens (when $b = 0$)? Answer: it follows the rule stated above, issuing if

$$(E/P')(S + a) \le E + b,$$

[eq. (1)] or, with $b = 0$, if $P' \ge S + a$ or $a \le P' - S$. In fig. 1, the points (a, b) for which $b = 0$ and $a < P' - S$ lie on the horizontal axis to the left of the line separating regions M and M'. In other words, M' *includes* (its share of) the horizontal axis.

The higher issue costs are, the smaller the fraction of the post-issue shares held by old stockholders. The firm issues and invests if:

$$V_{\text{issue}}^{\text{old}} = \frac{P'}{P' + E + T}(E + S + a + b) \ge S + a = V_{\text{no issue}}^{\text{old}},$$

or if

$$\frac{E + T}{P'}(S + a) \le E + b.$$

The market value P' of the old stockholders' shares conditional on issue is $\bar{A}(M')\bar{B}(M') + S - T$. The region M' is now defined by the inequality given just above.

Issue costs appear to lead to two main differences in the equilibrium properties of the model. First, the firm may issue and invest when its investment opportunity's NPV is positive, but less than T ($0 \le b < T$). This creates a different sort of real resource cost. In this region, the project actually has *negative* NPV once issue costs are allocated to it ($b - T < 0$). Nevertheless, the investment may be rational if managers know the value of assets-in-place is sufficiently low. If this outcome is possible, the ex ante market value of the firm will be marked down accordingly.

Second, we can no longer say for sure that $P' < P$, and that the decision to issue shares drives down the price. The proof given in the text follows from the observation that $\bar{A}(M) > P' + S$. With issue costs, the corresponding statement is $\bar{A}(M) > P'(E/(E + T)) - S$. It is conceivable that $\bar{A}(M)$ would fall between $P'(E/(E + T)) - S$ and $P' - S$. The conditions under which this might happen are worth investigating further. For present purposes, however, we have to assume that transaction costs are a second-order effect.

Since the firm issues whenever (a, b) falls in region M', *even when it has only zero-NPV opportunities*, the decision to issue does not signal 'positive-NPV investment' but only 'region M'.' We have already shown that the rational investor reaction to region M' is 'bad news'.

This does not imply that the firm will always issue when it has no positive-NPV opportunity ($b = 0$). It issues only when the value of its assets-in-place is low enough to make the issue attractive – i.e., when $a \le P' - S$. Moreover, the higher the probability that $b = 0$, other things equal,[13] the lower P', and the lower the probability of issue. In the limit, when $b > 0$ is ruled out entirely, the firm will never issue, except possibly when the realization of a falls at a definite lower bound. (This is one of the corner solutions discussed above.)

The intuition that stock issues confirm the existence of positive-NPV projects must therefore be rejected if our model is right. That intuition might be borne out if managers could commit to refrain from issuing when $b = 0$, but this is not a credible policy if managers act in the old shareholders' interests.

3.2. Numerical solutions

The analysis presented so far establishes that the firm may rationally forego a valuable investment opportunity if common stock must be issued to finance it. We would also like to have some indication of the probability of this event and the magnitude of the ex ante loss in firm value. For that we have to turn to numerical methods.

The key to a numerical solution is of course P': once we know it, we can use eq. (1') to separate regions M' and M. Unfortunately, we cannot guarantee a unique P' – it depends on the joint probability distribution of a and b.[14] Nor can we give a more specific analytical expression for P', although calculating P' by numerical methods is not difficult. The method we have used is:

(1) Start by setting $P' = S + \bar{A} + \bar{B}$. This assumes the firm always issues stock if $b > 0$.

(2) Then determine the regions M and M', assuming the firm faces this trial value for P' and acts in the old stockholders' interest.

(3) Calculate a new trial value of $P' = S + \bar{A}(M') + \bar{B}(M')$ based on the regions M and M' from step 2.

(4) Continue until P' converges.

This procedure gives the highest equilibrium P'. In our numerical experiments this value has always been a unique solution for joint lognormal distributions

---

[13] 'Other things' includes the expectation of $\tilde{B}$ given that it is positive.

[14] Majluf (1978, pp. 279–285) shows that at least one equilibrium P' exists if there is a positive probability that the firm will issue stock.

Table 1

Expected ex ante losses in firm value when the value of assets-in-place ($\tilde{A}$) and the net present value of investment opportunities ($\tilde{B}$) are lognormally distributed. $\tilde{A}$ and $\tilde{B}$ are assumed independently distributed, with expectations $\overline{A} = 100$ and $\overline{B} = 1$ or 10, and standard deviations $\sigma_A = 10$ or 100 and $\sigma_B = 10$. The probability distributions reflect information available to investors before the firm reveals whether it will issue and invest. The investment required is $I = 10$ or 100. Financial slack, S, is varied between 0 and 100 percent of I. The losses are expressed as a percent of $\overline{B}$. The probability that the firm *will* issue is given in parentheses.[a]

		$I = 10$		$I = 100$	
		---	---	---	---
S	$\overline{B}/I$	$\sigma_A = 10$	$\sigma_A = 100$	$\sigma_A = 10$	$\sigma_A = 100$
0	0.01	99.8	100 −	98.5	99.9
		(0.1)	(0 +)	(1.2)	(0.1)
	0.10	17.8	97.8	2.8	68.8
		(68.4)	(1.6)	(94.1)	(28.0)
50	0.01	94.1	100 −	68.7	97.1
		(3.2)	(0 +)	(21.7)	(2.1)
	0.10	5.1	84.4	0.4	39.4
		(87.0)	(11.2)	(98.6)	(51.7)
90	0.01	19.9	97.0	5.7	65.0
		(65.2)	(1.9)	(85.8)	(25.9)
	0.10	0.1	18.7	0 +	5.1
		(99.5)	(70.5)	(100 −)	(89.6)
100	0.01	0	0	0	0
		(0)	(0)	(0)	(0)
	0.10	0	0	0	0
		(0)	(0)	(0)	(0)

[a]*Source*: Majluf (1978, tables 4 and 6).

of $\overline{A}$ and $\overline{B}$, and also for joint normal distributions truncated to exclude negative $\tilde{A}$'s and $\tilde{B}$'s.

Table 1 illustrates the results obtained in extensive numerical experiments.[15] It shows L, loss in market value at $t = -1$, as a percent of $\overline{B}$, the average NPV of the investment opportunity. It also shows $F(M')$, the probability the firm will issue stock and invest. $\tilde{A}$ and $\tilde{B}$ are assumed joint lognormally distributed and slack is varied from zero to the required investment I. Note that:

(a)   Increasing slack reduces $L/\overline{B}$ and increases $F(M')$.
(b)   Increasing project NPV ($\overline{B}/I$) reduces $L/\overline{B}$.
(c)   Reducing the standard deviation of assets in place σ_A reduces the loss in value. (We showed above that $L = 0$ when $\sigma_A = 0$.)

We also experimented with the standard deviation of B and the correlation of $\tilde{A}$ and $\tilde{B}$, but found no uniform effects.

[15]Reported in Majluf (1978, pp. 165–183).

3.3. Debt financing

So far, we have assumed that the firm can raise external funds only by issuing stock. Now we will adapt the model to include the choice between debt and equity issues.

If the firm can issue default-risk-free debt, our problem disappears: the firm never passes up a positive-NPV investment. If it can only issue risky debt, our problem is only alleviated: the firm sometimes passes up positive-NPV investments, but the average opportunity loss is less with debt than with equity financing. The general rule seems to be: better to issue safe securities than risky ones.

This requires more careful discussion. Assume the money needed for the investment opportunity $(I - S)$ can be financed by debt, D, or equity, E. Assume for the moment that these are two distinct policies announced at $t = -1$ and adhered to in $t = 0$. That is, the firm must choose debt or equity before managers know the true values a and b.

The firm issues and invests if V^{old}, the intrinsic value of the old stockholders' equity, is higher with the issue than without it. If it does issue, V^{old} equals total firm value less the value of the newly issued securities.

Suppose equity is issued. Then $V^{old} = a + b + I - E_1$, where E_1 is the newly issued shares' market value at $t = +1$, when investors learn a and b. The issue price of these shares is just $E = I - S$ at $t = 0$. Thus $V^{old} = S + a + b - (E_1 - E) = S + a + b - \Delta E$; ΔE is the new shareholders' capital gain or loss when the truth comes out at $t = +1$, conditional on the firm's issue of shares at $t = 0$.

The firm will issue and invest only if

$$S + a \leq S + a + b - \Delta E, \tag{3}$$

or if $b \geq \Delta E$. The investment's NPV must equal or exceed the capital gain on newly issued shares. (Note: ΔE may be positive or negative. At equilibrium investors *expect* it to be zero. The firm knows the true value.)

If debt is issued, we follow exactly the same argument, with D and D_1 substituted for E and E_1, and reach the same conclusion: the firm will issue and invest only if b equals or exceeds $\Delta D \equiv D_1 - D$. Of course if the debt is default-risk-free, $\Delta D = 0,$[16] and the firm always issues and invests when $b \geq 0$. Thus, the ability to issue risk-free debt is as good as financial slack. If the debt is not default-risk-free, ΔD may be positive or negative. Option pricing theory

---

[16] That is, the change in the debt value at $t = 1$ is independent of the firm-specific information revealed to investors at that time. Other things, such as a general shift in interest rates, may change debt value, but that is irrelevant here.

tells us that ΔD will have the same sign as ΔE, but that its absolute value will always be less.[17] We so assume for the moment.

Now compare the issue–invest decisions for debt vs. equity financing. Since $b \geq 0$, the firm will always invest when ΔD and ΔE are zero or negative. Suppose ΔD and ΔE are positive (good news in store for investors at $t = +1$). If the firm is willing to issue equity and invest, it is also willing to issue debt ($\Delta D < \Delta E$, so $b \geq \Delta E$ implies $b > \Delta D$). However, debt is issued in some states where equity is not ($\Delta D \leq b < \Delta E$). Thus, the ex ante value of the firm is higher under the debt-financing policy, because the loss in market value (L) due to underinvestment is less.

Now suppose the choice of debt or equity is not preannounced, but chosen at $t = 0$, after the firm knows the values a and b. This seems a more complicated problem, for the choice could give an additional signal to investors. It's tempting to say the overvalued firm would issue equity and the undervalued firm debt.[18]

In our model, however, *the firm never issues equity. If it issues and invests, it always issues debt*, regardless of whether the firm is over- or undervalued. A proof follows.

The payoff to old stockholders (V^{old}) if neither debt or equity is issued is $a + S$. The additional payoffs to issuing and investing are $b - \Delta E$ with equity financing and $b - \Delta D$ with debt financing. An equity issue therefore signals that $b - \Delta E > b - \Delta D$, that is $\Delta E < \Delta D$.

Remember that ΔE and ΔD are the gains realized by new stock or bondholders at $t = +1$ when the firm's true value is revealed. They depend on a, b, S and the decision to issue and invest. If there is an equilibrium in which equity is issued, there is a price P'_E at which investors can rationally expect $\Delta E = 0$. For debt, the equilibrium firm value is P'_D and investors expect $\Delta D = 0$. Given a, b and S, ΔE and ΔD have the same sign, but $|\Delta E| > |\Delta D|$.

However, there is no equilibrium price P'_E at which the firm can issue stock. It prefers stock to debt only if P'_E is high enough that $\Delta E < \Delta D$. This occurs only if $\Delta E < 0$, implying a sure capital loss for new stockholders. Therefore, there can be no price P'_E at which (1) the firm is willing to issue stock rather than debt and (2) investors are willing to buy.

To put it another way: suppose the firm announced at $t = -1$ that it would issue debt if it issued any security. It could not change its mind and issue equity at $t = 0$, because investors would assume this meant $\Delta E < 0$ and refuse

---

[17]See, for example, Galai and Masulis (1976). The option pricing framework of course rests on more restrictive assumptions than those used so far in this paper. We return to these assumptions below.

[18]This is Rendleman's conclusion (1980). As noted above, he does not work out a full equilibrium solution.

to buy. On the other hand, a firm which announced a policy of equity financing at $t = -1$ would be forced to change its mind, and to issue debt at $t = 0$ if it issued at all. Equity would be issued at $t = 0$ only if debt were ruled out at $t = -1$; yet we showed above that precommitting to equity financing is always inferior to precommitting to debt.

Thus, our model may explain why many firms seem to prefer internal financing to financing by security issues and, when they do issue, why they seem to prefer bonds to stock. This has been interpreted as managerial capitalism – an attempt by managers to avoid the discipline of capital markets and to cut the ties that bind managers' to stockholders' interests. In our model, this behavior *is* in the stockholders' interest.

3.4. Equity issues in asymmetric information models

The chief difficulty with this analysis of the debt–equity choice is that we end up leaving no room at all for stock issues. We could of course recreate a role for them by introducing agency or bankruptcy costs of debt, as discussed in, for example, Jensen and Meckling (1976), Myers (1977), and Smith and Warner (1979). But it is also possible to rationalize equity issues in models based on information asymmetries alone.

Our proof that debt dominates equity uses the standard option-pricing assumption that percentage changes in value are lognormally distributed with a constant variance rate known by everyone. However, suppose there is a large information asymmetry about the (future) variance rate. If investors underestimate the variance rate, the firm will be tempted to issue debt, but if they overestimate it, the firm will be tempted to issue equity, other things equal. Thus, a decision to issue equity may not signal a sure capital loss for new stockholders, but simply that the firm is safer than prospective bondholders think. Thus equity issues are not completely ruled out in equilibrium.

Giammarino and Neave (1982) set up a model in which the managers and investors share the same information about *everything except risk*. In this case, equity issues dominate debt issues, because the only time managers want to issue debt is when they know the firm is riskier than investors think. Investors, realizing this, refuse to buy. Only equity, or perhaps a convertible security, is issued in equilibrium.

Firms actually seem to favor debt over equity issues, not the reverse. We believe asymmetric information about firm value is a stronger determinant of financing behavior than asymmetric information about risk, and we will so assume in subsequent comments, although future empirical research could of course prove us wrong. On the theoretical side, an obvious next step is to analyze the debt–equity choice in a version of our model which explicitly allows information asymmetry on the two dimensions of firm value and firm variance.[19]

4. Assumptions about management's objectives

We have shown that ample financial slack allows the firm to avoid external financing and to disentangle investment decisions from conflicts of interest between old stockholders and new investors. However, this result depends on management's acting in the interest of *passive* stockholders. We will now consider how rational stockholders react to the firm's investment decision. We show that, in frictionless capital markets, their reaction does not depend on whether the investment is financed with internal or external funds.[20]

4.1. The irrelevance of financing

Take the simplest case, in which the firm can only issue stock. When the firm has inadequate slack ($S < I$), we showed that the firm may pass up valuable investment opportunities. This loss would be avoided if old stockholders could be compelled to buy *and hold* the new issue – in other words, to accept the new asset in their own portfolios. In general, this will not be their optimal portfolio strategy, however, so new shareholders enter, creating the conflict.

Now suppose the firm has ample slack ($S = I$). Old stockholders arrive at $t = 0$ with shares representing a portfolio of three items: an asset in place, a growth opportunity and cash. If the growth opportunity is taken, the cash vanishes, and the portfolio changes to two assets in place. The old stockholders 'buy' all of the new asset via the firm's internal financing. However, there is nothing to force them to hold it. The same portfolio motives that would prevent them from buying all of a new issue should prompt them to sell part of their shares if the firm uses its cash to buy a risky real asset.

There is no deadweight loss so long as the firm buys this asset whenever it has positive NPV ($b > 0$). However, suppose managers start to worry about the price old shareholders trade at when they rebalance their portfolios after an internally-financed investment is made. Table 2 sets out equilibrium conditions for this case. The left-hand block (case I) shows old shareholders' payoffs if the firm has no slack. We assume old shareholders *could* buy all of the new issue. Therefore, we earmark $C = I$ dollars of cash and other securities and take it as potentially available for investment. However, their optimal portfolio calls for

---

[19] Note that the general version of our model, as described in eqs. (1) and (2), allows asymmetric information about any feature of the joint distribution ($\tilde{A}, \tilde{B}$). But addressing the choice among financing instruments requires more specific assumptions.

[20] We thank George Constantinides for suggesting this possibility.

investing αI in the new issue. The resulting equilibrium conditions are slight generalizations of those given in section 3 above (we previously took $\alpha = 0$).

In the right-hand block (case II), the firm holds the same amount of cash *on behalf of* old shareholders. If the firm invests this cash, they recoup part of it by selling shares to raise $(1 - \alpha)I$. Their fractional ownership thus ends up as $(P'' - (1 - \alpha)I)/P''$. Note that P'', the market price of the firm conditional on investment, includes the investment I. It's convenient to substitute $P''_{net} \equiv P'' - I$.

At equilibrium, $P''_{net} = \bar{A}(M'') + \bar{B}(M'')$, where M'' indicates the states in which investment by the firm is in the old shareholders' interest given the price P''_{net} facing them when they sell.

The equilibrium conditions for the two cases shown in table 2 are identical. The firm's investment decision is independent of whether cash starts out in the shareholders' bank accounts or the firm's. The firm passes up good investment opportunities in the same states, so the ex ante loss L is the same for the two cases.[21] So are the market prices conditional on the decision to invest: $P' = P''_{net}$.

The choice between debt and equity financing should not matter either. Suppose the starting position is case I in table 2. The firm borrows $C = I$ dollars from its stockholders. That transforms case I into II, if the debt is default-risk-free. The final equilibrium investment decision and stock price are unaffected.

If the debt carries default risk, old shareholders are exposed to the firm's business risk through their new debt securities as well as their stock. Therefore, when the firm invests, they will raise $(1 - \alpha)I$ by selling a mixture of debt and equity securities – the same fraction of their holdings of each. However, the same final equilibrium is reached again.

If the risky debt is sold to outsiders, old shareholders would buy part of the debt issue, and sell some of their shares. However, as long as capital markets

---

[21] If old shareholders are willing to hold all of any new investment – i.e., if $\alpha = 1$ in table 2's expressions – the firm always invests if $b > 0$. This is, of course, the ex ante optimal policy; the problem is enforcing it. Old shareholders could enforce it by purchasing 100 percent of any new issue (case I) or by not selling any of their shares (case II).

However, note that the incentive for old shareholders to buy all of a new issue is strongest if they act in concert. Management looks at the overall α. An investor who holds, say, one percent of the firm's stock, and who acts alone, buying one percent of the new issue, will reap only one percent of his action's rewards. If arranging a group action is costly, then individual investors' incentives will not make $\alpha = 1$ overall.

In case II, $\alpha = 1$ if old shareholders do *not* trade when the firm invests. Financial slack helps by making sure that old shareholders buy all of the new project, at least temporarily. Trading costs then limit the extent of selling. If their portfolios are 'sticky', the conflict of interest between old and new shareholders is reduced. However, any investor who sells out will not face the full cost of his actions, since management's decision depends on old stockholders' overall participation in the new project.

Table 2

Equilibrium conditions for the issue–invest decision with and without financial slack.

	(I) Firm has no slack $(S = 0)$, and must issue the amount I in order to invest. Shareholders have cash $C = I$ and invest αI in new issue. Managers know a, the value of assets-in-place, and b, the net present value of the investment opportunity, but investors do not.	(II) Firm has $S = I$. However, if it invests, shareholders sell a portion of their holdings to recover $(1 - \alpha)I$ in cash. Managers and investors have the same information as in case I.
Value to old shareholders (V^{old})		
No issue:	$C + a = I + a$	$S + a = I + a$
Issue:	$(1 - \alpha)I + \dfrac{P' + \alpha I}{P' + I}(I + a + b)$	$(1 - \alpha)I + \dfrac{P'' - (1 - \alpha)I}{P''}(I + a + b)$ or $(1 - \alpha)I + \dfrac{P''_{\text{net}} + \alpha I}{P''_{\text{net}} + I}(I + a + b)$
Issue if:	$I + a < (1 - \alpha)I + \dfrac{P' + \alpha I}{P' + I}(I + a + b)$	$I + a < (1 - \alpha)I + \dfrac{P''_{\text{net}} + \alpha I}{P''_{\text{net}} + I}(I + a + b)$
At equilibrium:[a]	$P' = \bar{A}(M') + \bar{B}(M')$	$P''_{\text{net}} = \bar{A}(M'') + \bar{B}(M'')$

[a] The equilibrium values of the firm (P' in case I and P''_{net} in case II) are identical. Thus, the investment decision can be independent of whether financing comes from internal funds or a stock issue. Here we assume that investors rebalance their portfolios when the firm reveals its investment decision.

are frictionless, and all traders understand what is going on, the final result is the same.

We thus obtain an (MM) proposition of financial irrelevance, where all the action comes from the firm's decision to invest. If this tack is taken, our model's empirical implications change. We could not explain firms' demands for slack, their apparent preference for internal financing, or for debt over equity issues. A fall in stock price on announcement of a stock issue would be explained as an information effect. That is, the issue would not matter in itself, but only as a signal of the decision to invest.

However, before we turn to the empirical evidence, we will devote a few more words to the competing descriptions of management objectives and shareholder responses when managers know more than shareholders do.

4.2. Ex ante optimal policies

Old shareholders are better off ex ante, and on average ex post, if management takes all positive-NPV projects. Perhaps compensation packages have features that prompt managers to follow this rule. Social conventions or corporate cultures that encourage managers to maximize 'long-run value' may have the same effect. Also, following the rule may be in managers' self-interest: a manager who does *not* allow conflicts between old and new shareholders' interests to block positive-NPV projects could demand a higher salary ex ante than one who does.

However, management must take *some* responsibility for financing. Consider the extreme instruction: 'Take all positive-NPV projects and issue securities at *any* price.'

The 'wrong' price for a security issue does not affect firm value. It just transfers value from some securityholders to others. Nevertheless, the instruction is not credible. Public stockholders would not support it, because it would leave them unprotected against sweet deals given to insiders or their friends.[22]

Of course this sort of sweet deal is illegal. An outside investor hurt by one of them could sue, and probably win if the mispricing were obvious and the motive clear. The law requires a manager to worry about the terms of financing; we think it encourages the manager to look at financing from the viewpoint of the *passive* investor.

Consider the altered instructions: 'Take all positive-NPV projects, and issue securities at a fair price conditional on market information only.' In other words, managers should use their special information about investments, but ignore it when it comes to financing.[23] However, these instructions are still not fully credible, not only because of the mental discipline required, but also because managers' *personal* interests are likely to be more closely aligned with *old* stockholders' interests than with new stockholders'.

Consider a manager who is also a stockholder. If he always buys *and holds* a pro rata share of any new issue, and maximizes the intrinsic value of his holdings, then his interests will be aligned with all securityholders', and he will maximize the intrinsic value of the firm.

However, most managers would not want to buy a pro rata share of every new issue, even if the issue is fairly priced from their point of view. The reasons why can be traced to the same portfolio considerations which prevent old stockholders from buying all of every new issue – loss of diversification and, in extreme cases, limits to personal wealth. If the manager does not buy all of

---

[22] Existing securityholders could protect against this ripoff by taking a pro rata share of each new issue. But this would be cumbersome at best. It would also invite a different kind of ripoff, in which outside securityholders buy an overpriced issue while insiders and their friends sell or sell short.

[23] This suggests the idea that managers could avoid conflicts between old and new shareholders by *concealing* the firm's investment decision. Take case II in table 2, where the firm has ample slack. Suppose its investment decision is not revealed until $t = +1$. Then the firm's actions prompt no trading at $t = 0$, and good investment opportunities are not bypassed. In case I, on the other hand, the investment decision cannot be concealed because a stock issue necessarily comes first.

every new issue then his interests as a shareholder are those of an (informed) old shareholder.

There is still another complication: a manager–shareholder who has inside information will be tempted to trade on it. If the outside market is (semi-strong form) efficient, the manager will want to sell half the time and buy the other half. In particular, he will want to abstain from half of new issues, and buy more than a pro rata share of the others. He will also want to buy or sell if the firm does not issue. The potential trading profit will depend on the issue–invest decision, although apparently not in any tractable way. We doubt the managers' interests will be aligned with any outside investor's if the managers are given free rein to trade on personal account.

4.3. Empirical evidence

It is easy to see why managers should take all positive-NPV projects, but hard to build a completely convincing theory explaining why they would always do so. We think it more likely that managers having superior information act in old stockholders' interest. We also think that existing empirical evidence supports our view.

If management acts in old shareholders' interests, our model predicts that the decision to issue and invest causes stock price to fall. If management took all *and only* positive-NPV projects, even when issuing and investing reduces the intrinsic value of the 'old' shares, the same decision would either increase stock price or leave it unchanged. The decision to invest would reveal the existence of an attractive project (i.e., $b > 0$). This is good news, unless investors knew for sure that the firm would have that investment opportunity. It cannot be bad news in any case.

Recent papers by Korwar (1982), Asquith and Mullins (1983) and Dann and Mikkelson (1984) show significant negative average price impacts when a new stock issue is announced. 'Information effects' are an obvious explanation. However, as far as we know, ours is the only complete model explaining how such an information effect could occur in a rational expectations equilibrium.

Of course our model predicts that stock prices will *always* fall when investors learn of a new stock issue. But the model holds everything but the issue–investment decision constant. In particular, it ignores the flow to investors of other information about the firm's prospects. This flow creates a random error in any measurement of how a stock price changes in response to a specific event.

If our interpretation of these results is accepted, we can set aside, at least for the present discussion, models assuming managers simply 'accept all positive-NPV projects'.

If managers act in old shareholders' interests, do they assume those shareholders are passive or active? Do they just maximize the existing shares' value, or do they work out how rational shareholders' portfolio choices depend on their decisions?

These questions can also be answered empirically. If managers assume active shareholders, then only the investment decision matters. Good investments are foregone even when the firm has plenty of cash to pay for them. However, if managers assume passive stockholders, then financing matters and firms will adapt their financing policy to mitigate the loss in value from foregone investment opportunities. For example, managers will try to build up financial slack on order to avoid situations in which a security issue is required to finance a valuable investment opportunity. If information asymmetries relate primarily to firm value, rather than risk, managers will favor debt over equity financing if external capital is required.

In our framework, the 'passive investor' assumption gives a variety of interesting hypotheses about corporate financing. That is why we use the assumption for most of this paper's formal analysis.

We noted that Dann and Mikkelson (1984) found a significant negative average price impact when *stock* issues are announced. They also looked at a sample of debt issues, and found *no* significant price impact. Our model may be able to explain this difference.[24]

The 'passive investor' assumption implies that stock price falls when stock is issued. However, stock price should *not* fall if default-risk-free debt is issued, because the ability to issue risk-free debt is equivalent to having ample financial slack, and having ample slack insures that the firm will take all positive-NPV projects. Thus, in our model the only information conveyed by the decision to issue risk-free debt and invest is that the firm has a positive-NPV project. This causes a *positive* price change unless the project's existence was known beforehand.

Under the 'active investor' assumption, the decision to invest would be bad news, and the choice of debt over equity financing would not make the news any better. Choosing this assumption would give us no way to explain Dann and Mikkelson's results.

Of course, the debt issues examined by Dann and Mikkelson were not literally default-risk-free. But if the probability of default on these issues was small, their negative 'information effect' should likewise be small.[25]

5. Extensions and implications

Having explained our model formally, and having discussed its assumptions and some of its empirical implications, we can now turn to a few extensions,

---

[24] Miller and Rock's model would predict the same negative stock price impact regardless of the type of security issued.

[25] You would expect that the riskier the instrument issued, the greater the issues' impact on the market value of the firm. However, we have not been able to prove that this positive relationship is always monotonic.

qualifications, and further observations.[26] We specifically address two questions:

(1) What happens when the information asymmetry is temporary and what happens when it is permanent but the firm has no immediate need for funds, except to build up slack?
(2) What does our model say about mergers?

Discussing these questions leads us to other issues, for example, the implications of managers' superior information for dividend policy.

5.1. An easy way out

There is of course an easy way out of the problems described in this paper – an easy way to avoid any loss of market value: just issue stock at $t = -1$, when managers and the market are assumed to share the same information. That is one lesson of our model. If managers know more than the market does, firms should avoid situations in which valuable investment projects have to be financed by stock issues. Having slack solves the problem, and one way to get slack is to issue stock when there is no asymmetric information.

That is not an easy way out, however, if the information asymmetry is permanent. Suppose managers are always one period ahead of the market. At $t = -1$, for example, managers would know $\bar{A}$ and $\bar{B}$, but investors would not. Investors at $t = -1$ would see $\tilde{A}$ and $\tilde{B}$ as random variables. At $t = 0$, they would find out the means $\bar{A}$ and $\bar{B}$ (and the underlying distributions of $\tilde{A}$ and $\tilde{B}$) but by that time managers would know the realizations a and b.

Assume the firm has insufficient slack to undertake the project, and also, to keep things simple, that the amount of slack is fixed unless equity is issued to increase it and the investment required to undertake the project is known. Consider the decision to issue $E = I - S$ dollars of stock at $t = -1$. If the firm does *not* issue, its true value at $t = -1$ is

$$V_{old}(\text{no issue}) = \bar{A} + \bar{B} + S - L,$$

where L is the ex ante loss in firm value attributable to insufficient slack. That is, L reflects the probability the firm will choose to pass up a positive-NPV investment at $t = 0$, and the loss in value if it does. Of course, investors do not know how big L is, because they do not know the distributions of $\tilde{A}$ and $\tilde{B}$. However, they do know that L goes to zero if the firm issues stock at $t = -1$

---

[26] 'Our model' includes the assumption that managers act in old stockholders' interests, and that those stockholders are passive in the sense discussed above.

in order to raise the additional cash $E = I - S$ needed to assure investment at $t = 0$.

This brings us back to the same problem we started with in section 2. We have an 'asset-in-place' worth $\bar{A} + \bar{B} + S - L$ and an 'investment opportunity' worth L. Managers know these values but investors have only probability distributions. Thus, the firm's decision to issue and the price investors are willing to pay are governed by eqs. (1) and (2). Managers may or may not issue stock at $t = -1$: it depends on the price they can issue it for. If investors are too pessimistic, relative to what managers know, managers may accept the ex ante loss L and take a chance that the firm will be able to issue and invest at $t = 0$ if the NPV of its investment opportunity turns out positive.

We will not here pursue analysis of the optimal issue strategy in this dynamic setting. However, we have shown that the problems addressed in this paper do not go away when the firm has no immediate real investment opportunity. Given asymmetric information, a firm with valuable future real investment opportunities is better off with slack than without it. Moreover, it should build up slack through retention rather than stock issues. This is consistent with actual retention policies of most public firms, which limit dividends so that they will rarely have to go to the market for fresh equity.

Thus we add one item in favor of the list of possible arguments for dividend payouts low enough to avoid reliance on external equity financing. On the other hand, dividends would alleviate the problems posed in this paper if they help signal the true value of $\tilde{A}$, thus reducing σ_A. However, this is not necessarily an argument for high average payout; it merely supports payout policies with a high correlation of changes in dividends and changes in the value of assets in place. This could explain why dividend payments respond to changes in earnings, not market value, if book earnings primarily reflect the performance of assets-in-place.

At this point, we revert to our original three-date model, in which asymmetric information is important only at $t = 0$.

5.2. Mergers

Our model's main message is this: given asymmetric information, a firm with insufficient financial slack may not undertake all valuable investment opportunities. Thus, a firm that has too little slack increases its value by acquiring more.

One way to do this is by merger. In our model, a merger always creates value when one firm's surplus slack fully covers the other's deficiency.[27] Of course

---

[27]If the merged firms' total slack does not fully cover their investment requirements, the merger may or may not increase value. See Majluf (1978, pp. 239–256).

this gain is only one of dozens of possible merger motives. But we have nothing to say here about other benefits or costs, so we will assume them away here.

It turns out that the same conditions that create a potential gain from transferring surplus slack between merger partners will also complicate the merger negotiations, and in some cases rule out any possibility of their successful completion. Consider a firm with an existing business, a good investment opportunity, but insufficient slack to pay for it. It seeks a merger with a cash-rich firm. The would-be buyer only knows the distributions of $\tilde{A}$ and $\tilde{B}$, not the true values a and b.

Let Q' be the proposed merger price. That is, if the merger offer is accepted, the shareholders of the cash-poor firm receive Q' in cash or shares.[28] If the offer is turned down, that firm's shareholders forego the investment and are left with $S + a$. Thus, given a and b, the offer will be accepted if $Q' \geq S + a$. However, the cash-rich firm will only offer $Q' = S + \bar{A}(N') + \bar{B}(N')$, where $\bar{A}(N')$ and $\bar{B}(N)$ are the expectations of $\tilde{A}$ and $\tilde{B}$ conditional on observing that the cash-poor firm is willing to go through with the deal.

Under these assumptions, the merger would never occur. The cash-poor firm can always do better by issuing stock directly to investors, because P' always exceeds Q'.[29]

In our model, the decision to sell shares always carries negative information, regardless of whether the shares are sold to investors generally or to a specific acquiring firm. The buyers or buyers discount the shares so that cost equals expected payoff. If the firm issues $E = I - S$, old shareholders retain a stake, but if their firm is sold they are completely disengaged from it. The decision to sell all of the firm via merger, rather than issue the fraction $E/(P' + E)$, drives down market price below P', because the firm has chosen to sell more stock than absolutely necessary to cover the investment I. [We assume that (1) the acquiring firm's slack exceeds the selling firm's deficiency $(I - S)$, (2) the acquiring firm has other assets, and (3) everyone knows what these assets are worth.]

---

[28]We assume for simplicity that the true value of any shares used to finance the merger is independent of a and b. A more elaborate analysis is needed if they are not independent. A further complication is introduced if (1) the merger is financed by shares and (2) the buying firm's management has superior information about what those shares are worth.

[29]A proof follows. Define $a*(N')$ as the breakeven value of a, the value at which the cash-poor firm is just indifferent to being acquired at the equilibrium price Q'. Note that $Q' = a*(N') + S$. Refer again to the requirement for the firm to issue stock (1'), $E/P'(S + a) \leq E + b$. If P' were equal to Q', the firm would issue and invest at $a*(N')$ for any $b > 0$. That is, if $P' = Q' = S + a*(N')$,

$$\frac{E}{P'}(S + a) = \frac{E}{S + a*(N')}(S + a*(N')) = E < E + b.$$

Thus $a*(M')$, the breakeven value of a at which the firm is just willing to issue stock, exceeds $a*(N')$ for any $b > 0$. Thus,

$$\bar{A}(M') + \bar{B}(M') > \bar{A}(N') + \bar{B}(N') \quad \text{and} \quad P' > Q'.$$

Negotiated mergers thus seem to be ruled out (in this simple case) regardless of financing, because the cash-poor firm can always do better by issuing stock. How can mergers be explained under the premises of this paper?

There are two possible explanations. First, there may be partial or total disclosure of internal information during negotiation.[30] Second, the merger may go through if the buyer rather than the seller takes the initiative. In our model, firms with plenty of slack should seek out acquisition targets which have good investment opportunities and limited slack, and about which investors have limited information. Such firms sell at a discount from their average potential value $\overline{A} + \overline{B} + S$.[31] A tender offer made directly to the slack-poor firm's shareholders, at a price above $\overline{A} + \overline{B} + S - L$, but below $\overline{A} + \overline{B} + S$, makes both the bidder and the target's shareholders better off *ex ante*, although neither buyer nor sellers know the true value $a + b + S$. A cash tender offer conveys no bad news about $a + b + S$, so long as the target's management are not accomplices. Perhaps this explains why most mergers are initiated by buyers. A firm that actively seeks to be bought out may end up a wallflower. The more actively management seeks to sell, the less an outsider will assume their firm is worth.

6. Conclusion

We have presented a model of the issue–invest decision when the firm's managers have superior information. We can sum up by reviewing some of the model's most interesting properties:

(1) It is generally better to issue safe securities than risky ones. Firms should go to bond markets for external capital, but raise equity by retention if possible. That is, external financing using debt is better than financing by equity.

(2) Firms whose investment opportunities outstrip operating cash flows, and which have used up their ability to issue low-risk debt, may forego good investments rather than issue risky securities to finance them. This is done in the existing stockholders' interest. However, stockholders are better off *ex ante* – i.e., on average – when the firm carries sufficient financial slack to undertake good investment opportunities as they arise.

The ex ante loss in value increases with the size of the required equity issue. Thus, increasing the required investment or reducing slack available for this investment also increases the ex ante loss. In addition, numerical simulations

---

[30] The cash-poor firm would prefer to negotiate with a firm that is not a competitor. A competitor might back out of the negotiations and take advantage of information acquired in them. This hazard is less in a 'conglomerate' merger.

[31] We assume the target firm has not yet declared its issue–invest decision.

indicate the loss decreases when the market's uncertainty about the value of assets in place is reduced, or when the investment opportunity's expected NPV is increased.

(3)   Firms can build up financial slack by restricting dividends when investment requirements are modest. The cash saved is held as marketable securities or reserve borrowing power.

The other way to build slack is by issuing stock in periods when managers' information advantage is small; firms with insufficient slack to cover possible future investment opportunities would issue in periods where managers have no information advantage. However, we have not derived a generally optimal dynamic issue strategy.

(4)   The firm should not pay a dividend if it has to recoup the cash by selling stock or some other risky security. Of course dividends could help convey managers' superior information to the market. Our model suggests a policy under which changes in dividends are highly correlated with managers' estimate of the value of assets in place.[32]

(5)   When managers have superior information, and stock is issued to finance investment, stock price will fall, other things equal. This action is nevertheless in the (existing) stockholders' interest. If the firm issues safe (default-risk-free) debt to finance investment, stock price will not fall.

(6)   A merger of a slack-rich and slack-poor firm increases the firm's combined value. However, *negotiating* such mergers will be hopeless unless the slack-poor firms' managers can convey their special information to the prospective buyers. If this information cannot be conveyed (and verified), slack-poor firms will be bought out by tender offers made directly to their shareholders.

Of course, the six items stated just above depend on the specific assumptions of our model and may not follow in other contexts. We have only explored one of many possible stories about corporate finance. A full description of corporate financing and investment behavior will no doubt require telling several stories at once.

References

Akerlof, G.A., 1970, The market for 'lemons': Quality and the market mechanism, Quarterly Journal of Economics 84, 488–500.

Asquith, P. and D.W. Mullins, 1983, Equity issues and stock price dilution, Working paper, May (Harvard Business School, Cambridge, MA).

Bhattacharya, S., 1979, Imperfect information, dividend policy and the 'bird in the hand fallacy', Bell Journal of Economics 10, 259–270.

Bhattacharya, S. and J.R. Ritter, 1983, Innovation and communication: Signalling with partial disclosure, Review of Economic Studies 50, 331–346.

---

[32] However, there is no mechanism in our model to insure that such a policy would be faithfully followed.

Campbell, T.S., 1979, Optimal investment financing decisions and the value of confidentiality, Journal of Financial and Quantitative Analysis 14, 913–924.

Campbell, T.S. and W.A. Kracaw, 1980, Information production, market signalling, and the theory of financial intermediation, Journal of Finance 35, 863–882.

Dann, L.Y. and W.H. Mikkelson, 1984, Convertible debt issuance, capital structure change and financing-related information: Some new evidence, Journal of Financial Economics, this issue.

Downes, D.H. and R. Heinkel, 1982, Signalling and the valuation of unseasoned new issues, Journal of Finance 37, 1–10.

Galai, D. and R. Masulis, 1976, The option pricing model and the risk factor of stock, Journal of Financial Economics 3, 53–82.

Giammarino, R.M. and E.H. Neave, 1982, The failure of financial contracts and the relevance of financial policy, Working paper No. 82-3 (Queen's University, Kingston, Ont.).

Grossman, S.J., 1981, An introduction to the theory of rational expectations under asymmetric information, Review of Economic Studies 48, 541–559.

Grossman, S.J. and O.D. Hart, 1981, The allocational role of takeover bids in situations of asymmetric information, Journal of Finance 36, 253–270.

Hess, A.C. and P.A. Frost, 1982, Tests for price effects of new issues of seasoned securities, Journal of Finance 36, 11–25.

Jensen, M.C. and W. Meckling, 1976, Theory of the firm: Managerial behavior, agency costs and capital structure, Journal of Financial Economics 3, 305–360.

Korwar, A.N., 1981, The effect of new issues of equity: An empirical examination, Working paper (University of California, Los Angeles, CA).

Leland, H. and D. Pyle, 1977, Information asymmetries, financial structure and financial intermediaries, Journal of Finance 32, 371–387.

Majluf, N.S., 1978, Study on mergers: A rationale for conglomerate mergers, Unpublished Ph.D. dissertation (MIT, Cambridge, MA).

Miller, M.H. and K. Rock, 1982, Dividend policy under asymmetric information, Working paper, Nov. (Graduate School of Business, University of Chicago, Chicago, IL).

Myers, S.C., 1977, Determinants of corporate borrowing, Journal of Financial Economics 5, 147–175.

Myers, S.C. and N.S. Majluf, 1978, Stock issues and investment policy when firms have information investors do not have, Working paper (Sloan School of Management, MIT, Cambridge, MA).

Rendleman, R.J., 1980, Information asymmetries and optimal project financing, Working paper (Graduate School of Business, Duke University, Durham, NC).

Ross, S.A., 1978, Some notes on financial-incentive signalling models, activity choice and risk preferences, Journal of Finance 33, 777–792.

Ross, S.A., 1977, The determination of financial structure: The incentive-signalling approach, Bell Journal of Economics 8, 23–40.

Smith, C.W., and J.B. Warner, 1979, On financial contracting: An analysis of bond covenants, Journal of Financial Economics 7, 117–161.

Stiglitz, J.E., and A. Weiss, 1981, Credit rationing in markets with imperfect information, Part I, American Economic Review 71, 393–410.

INVESTMENT BANKING AND THE CAPITAL ACQUISITION PROCESS

Clifford W. SMITH, Jr.*

University of Rochester, Rochester, NY 14627, USA

Received March 1985, final version received August 1985

This paper reviews the theory and evidence on the process by which corporations raise debt and equity capital and the associated effects on security prices. Findings from related transactions are used to test hypotheses about the stock price patterns accompanying announcements of security offerings. Various contractual alternatives employed in security issues are examined; for example, rights or underwritten offers, negotiated or competitive bid, best efforts or firm commitment contracts, and shelf or traditional registration. Finally, incentives for underpricing new issues are analyzed.

1. Introduction

Corporations raise external capital by selling a range of different securities which they market in a variety of different ways. The *Dealers' Digest* (1985) reports that $355.3 billion in public securities sales have been underwritten between 1980 and 1984. Of that total value, 24 percent is common stock, 5 percent is preferred stock, 2 percent is convertible preferred stock, 63 percent is debt, and 6 percent is convertible debt. Contracts negotiated between the issuing firm and underwriter comprise 95 percent of the offers, while in 5 percent the underwriter is selected through a competitive bid. Shelf registration accounts for 27 percent of the issues, while 73 percent are registered employing traditional procedures.

Capital markets play an important role in the theory of corporate financial economics; for example, capital market prices provide vital signals for corporate investment decisions. Yet we do not have a detailed understanding of the various contractual arrangements in the process of raising capital, or of the influence of this process on corporate financial and investment policy.

*I would like to thank Armen Alchian and the participants at the MERC Conference on Investment Banking and the Capital Acquisition Process, especially H. DeAngelo, M. Jensen, D. Mayers, R. Masulis, W. Schwert, R. Stulz and J. Warner for their comments. This research was supported by the Managerial Economics Research Center, Graduate School of Management, University of Rochester.

Journal of Financial Economics 15 (1986) 3–29. © North-Holland Publishing Company.

Section 2 examines the theory and evidence related to announcements of security offerings by public corporations. Average stock price reactions to public security issues are either negative or not significantly different from zero. Several hypotheses have been offered to explain these price reactions. The hypotheses also have implications for price reactions in related events, such as dividend changes and security repurchases. It is therefore possible to evaluate their relative merit by drawing on existing evidence about price reactions to these related announcements.

Section 3 examines the marketing of corporate securities. Securities can be sold through either a rights or an underwritten offering. Underwriters' services can be obtained through either a negotiated or a competitive bid contract. Finally, the securities can be registered with the Securities and Exchange Commission (SEC) through either the new shelf or traditional registration procedures. Data on the costs, pricing, and frequency of use of these marketing methods for different securities provide a clearer understanding of the incentives important in choosing among them.

Section 4 examines the special case of initial public equity offerings. They are typically sold through either firm commitment or best effort contracts. Underwriters, on average, price initial public offerings significantly lower than their after-market price. The hypotheses which explain these choices are examined.

Section 5 presents brief concluding remarks, and suggests issues for further study.

2. On the corporation's choice of security to offer

A public corporation seeking external capital must first decide what type of claim to sell. In choosing the type of security to issue, it is important to understand the market reaction to the announcement. Table 1 summarizes two-day common stock price reactions adjusted for general market price changes (abnormal returns) to announcements of public issues of common stock, preferred stock, convertible preferred stock, straight debt and convertible debt by industrial and utility firms. Four generalizations about relative magnitudes are suggested in table 1: (1) the average abnormal returns are non-positive; (2) abnormal returns associated with announcements of common stock sales are negative and larger in absolute value than those observed with preferred stock or debt; (3) abnormal returns associated with announcements of convertible securities are negative and larger in absolute value than those for corresponding non-convertible securities; and (4) abnormal returns associated with sales of securities by industrials are negative and larger in absolute value than those for utilities.

There are several hypotheses for this pattern of relative stock price effects: (1) *Optimal Capital Structure* – firms have an optimal capital structure and

Table 1

Average two-day abnormal common stock returns and average sample size (in parentheses) from studies of announcements of security offerings. Returns are weighted averages by sample size of the returns reported by the respective studies (unless noted otherwise, returns are significantly different from zero).

| | Type of issuer | |
Type of security offering	Industrial	Utility
Common stock	-3.14^a (155)	-0.75^b (403)
Preferred stock	$-0.19^{c,*}$ (28)	$+0.08^{d,*}$ (249)
Convertible preferred stock	-1.44^d (53)	-1.38^d (8)
Straight bonds	$-0.26^{c,*}$ (248)	$-0.13^{f,*}$ (140)
Convertible bonds	-2.07^c (73)	n.a.^{g}

[a] Source: Asquith and Mullins (1986), Kolodny and Suhler (1985), Masulis and Korwar (1986), Mikkelson and Partch (1986), Schipper and Smith (1986).
[b] Source: Asquith and Mullins (1986), Masulis and Korwar (1986), Pettway and Radcliffe (1985).
[c] Source: Linn and Pinegar (1985), Mikkelson and Partch (1986).
[d] Source: Linn and Pinegar (1985).
[e] Source: Dann and Mikkelson (1984), Eckbo (1986), Mikkelson and Partch (1986).
[f] Source: Eckbo (1986).
[g] Not available (virtually none are issued by utilities).
*Interpreted by the authors as not statistically significantly different from zero.

these price reactions reflect the change in the value of the firm associated with the adjustment of the firm's liability structure; (2) *Implied Cash Flow Change* – the stock price changes provide information about future expected net operating cash flows; (3) *Unanticipated Announcements* – stock price changes reflect only the unanticipated component of the announcement, hence the more predictable an event, the smaller the associated stock price change; (4) *Information Asymmetry* – corporate managers have more information than the marginal purchaser of securities, hence corporate managers are more likely to issue securities when they are overpriced in the market; (5) *Ownership Changes* – transactions that change the distribution of control rights in the firm affect the value of the firm's shares. These hypotheses are examined to identify the extent to which each helps explain the price effects in table 1. The hypotheses are not mutually exclusive. However, each hypothesis also has implications for price reactions to related announcements. Augmenting the observations in table 1 with empirical evidence from the analysis of other events helps identify relative orders of importance.

2.1. Optimal capital structure and relative price effects

With fixed investment policy and no contracting costs or taxes, the value of the firm is independent of the structure of its liabilities [Modigliani and Miller (1958)]. This capital structure irrelevance hypothesis implies that the function relating leverage and the value of the firm is a horizontal line. Alternatively, if taxes or contracting costs are important, or if investment policy and capital structure are interdependent, then the market value of the firm depends on the structure of its liabilities. In the case of the capital structure relevance hypothesis, the function relating firm value and leverage is concave.[1] But neither hypothesis by itself provides a satisfactory explanation of the estimates in table 1. Maximizing behavior by firms implies that in voluntary transactions such as security sales, the firm should structure the transaction to yield the highest possible value of the firm. Thus, if a transaction moves a company along a given leverage-value function, the irrelevance hypothesis implies there should be no abnormal returns associated with announcements of security sales, while the capital structure relevance hypothesis implies the abnormal returns should be non-negative. Therefore, the negative returns in table 1 are inconsistent with both predictions.

Reductions in firm value associated with apparently voluntary security sales present a puzzle. It is possible that security sales are optimal responses to an adverse change in the firm's prospects, and the negative price reaction is due to the revelation of the adverse change. Even if a security sale might itself increase the value of the firm, it could lead potential securityholders to believe the firm has received bad news. Of course, if the announcement of the transaction is also associated with a shift in the leverage-value function, then the theory has no implication for the magnitudes observed in table 1. Without a theory capable of differentiating between movement along a given leverage-value function and a shift in the function, it is difficult to test hypotheses about optimal capital structure by looking at the stock price reactions to announcements of security sales. Therefore, at the current stage of development, studies of financing decisions provide relatively weak tests of optimal capital structure theories.

2.2. Implied changes in expected net operating cash flow and relative price effects

The firm's cash-flow identity states that sources must equal uses of funds. Therefore, an announcement of a new security sale must be matched either by an increase in new investment expenditure, a reduction in some liability (such

---

[1]Various analyses emphasize different characteristics of claims such as corporate taxes [Modigliani and Miller (1962), Brennan and Schwartz (1978)], personal taxes [DeAngelo and Masulis (1980)], transactions costs of bankruptcy [Kraus and Litzenberger (1973)] and agency costs [Jensen and Meckling (1976), Myers (1977), Smith and Warner (1979)].

as debt retirement or share repurchase), an increased dividend or a reduction in expected net operating cash flow. In the Miller and Rock (1985) analysis of dividends, they hypothesize that investors draw inferences about implied changes in expected net operating cash flows from corporate dividend announcements. They suggest that larger-than-expected dividend payments are associated with larger-than-expected internally generated cash flows from operations, and thus the dividend increase represents good news for investors. The evidence in table 1 is generally consistent with this hypothesis if the hypothesis is modified to consider security sales, so that unexpected security sales are associated with smaller-than-expected cash flows from operations, and thus security sales represent bad news for investors.

This argument can be generalized to consider other announcements which do not explicitly link sources and uses of funds. In general, to predict the implied change in cash flow, everything except net operating cash flow and the announcement policy variable is held fixed. Thus, announcements of security repurchases, increases in investment expenditures or higher dividend payments are associated with implied increases in expected cash flow; and security offerings, reductions in investment expenditures or lower dividend payments are associated with implied reductions in expected cash flow. If there is an implied increase in the corporation's expected net operating cash flow, the value of the firm should rise and there should be a corresponding increase in the value of the firm's equity.

Table 2 summarizes the evidence from studies of announcements of sales of new securities, stock repurchases, dividend changes and changes in investment policy grouped by their effect on implied changes in expected cash flows. The evidence of generally positive abnormal returns in the upper panel of table 2 associated with implied increases in cash flows, and generally negative abnormal returns in the lower panel associated with implied decreases in cash flows, is consistent with the hypothesis that security market participants draw inferences about changes in operating cash flow from announcements that do not explicitly associate sources with uses of funds.

The hypothesis that investors infer changes in net operating cash flows from investment, financing, and dividend policy announcements predicts non-positive price reactions to announcements of security sales. However, this hypothesis does not predict differential reactions to debt versus equity sales, convertible versus non-convertible issues or sales by industrial versus utility firms.

2.3. Unanticipated announcements and relative price effects

Because stock price changes reflect only the unanticipated component of the announcement, the magnitude of the stock price change at the announcement will vary inversely with the degree of predictability of the announcement if

Table 2

Average two-day common stock abnormal returns and average sample size from studies of changes in financing, dividend, and investment policy, grouped by implied changes in expected corporate cash flows. Returns are weighted averages by sample size of the returns reported by the respective studies (unless otherwise noted, returns are significantly different from zero).

Type of announcement	Average sample size	Two-day announcement period return
Implied increase in expected corporate cash flow		
Common stock repurchases		
intra-firm tender offer[a]	148	16.2%
open market repurchase[b]	182	3.6
targeted small holding[c]	15	1.6
Calls of non-convertible bonds[d]	133	−0.1*
Dividend increases		
dividend initiation[e]	160	3.7
dividend increase[f]	280	0.9
specially designated dividend[g]	164	2.1
Investment increases[h]	510	1.0
Implied decrease in expected corporate cash flow		
Security sales		
common stock[i]	262	−1.6
preferred stock[j]	102	0.1*
convertible preferred[k]	30	−1.4
straight debt[l]	221	−0.2*
convertible debt[l]	80	−2.1
Dividend decreases[f]	48	−3.6
Investment decreases[h]	111	−1.1

[a] Source: Dann (1981), Masulis (1980), Vermaelen (1981), Rosenfeld (1982).
[b] Source: Dann (1980), Vermaelen (1981).
[c] Source: Bradley and Wakeman (1983).
[d] Source: Vu (1986).
[e] Source: Asquith and Mullins (1983).
[f] Source: Charest (1978), Aharony and Swary (1980).
[g] Source: Brickley (1983).
[h] Source: McConnell and Muscarella (1985).
[i] Source: Asquith and Mullins (1986), Masulis and Korwar (1986), Mikkelson and Partch (1986), Schipper and Smith (1986), Pettway and Radcliff (1985).
[j] Source: Linn and Pinegar (1985), Mikkelson and Partch (1986).
[k] Source: Linn and Pinegar (1985).
[l] Source: Dann and Mikkelson (1984), Eckbo (1986), Mikkelson and Partch (1986).
*Interpreted by the authors as not significantly different from zero.

other effects are held constant. The evidence in tables 1 and 2 appears consistent with this hypothesis.

Predictability of debt versus equity offers.   Expected growth in assets or expected debt repayment (either from maturing issues or sinking-fund provisions) require the firm to issue additional debt to maintain its capital structure.[2] Given a target capital structure and unchanged cash flows, debt repayment must be matched with new debt issuance. The more predictable are principal repayments, the more predictable are new debt issues. Similarly, the predictability of earnings (and thus internally generated equity) will determine the predictability of the new externally obtained equity funds. In general, a new debt issue is likely to be more predictable than a new equity issue because principal repayments are more predictable than earnings.

Another reason for the greater predictability of public debt offerings is related to the cost structures of public versus private debt. Flotation costs for publicly placed debt have a larger fixed component and more pronounced economies of scale than bank debt. Thus, a firm will tend to use bank lines of credit until an efficient public issue size is reached, then the firm will issue public debt and retire the bank debt. If potential security holders can observe the amount of bank borrowing and the pattern of public debt issuance, then predictable announcements of public bond issues should have smaller price reactions [see Marsh (1982) for evidence on the use of short-term debt to predict public debt issues].

Predictability of industrial versus utility offers.   Table 1 shows significant differences between the price reactions of industrials and utilities to new equity sales. Utilities appear to employ external capital markets more extensively than do industrials. If the higher frequency of use by utilities is associated with greater predictability of security issuance, then utilities should show a smaller observed stock price reaction to announcements of new security sales. But that raises the question of why the reliance on external capital markets differs between industrials and utilities.

A policy of paying larger dividends increases the frequency with which the corporation must go to the capital markets to raise new equity [Rozeff (1982) and Easterbrook (1984)]. If, when new funds are raised, the capital market provides effective monitoring of the firm's activities, then such a policy disciplines the firm more frequently and lowers agency costs. Firms with high investment rates and high demands for new capital frequently use capital markets anyway; for them the additional benefits of increased monitoring from

---

[2] Note that the economies of scale documented in the schedule of flotation costs generally make it optimal to make discrete rather than continuous leverage adjustments. For simplicity we ignore those flotation cost issues at present.

higher dividends would be small. But utilities historically have both high demands for new capital and high dividend payout rates. I hypothesize that if the dividend rate is lowered and the frequency of selling new equity in capital markets is reduced, utility stockholders are likely to be damaged in the rate regulation process. By paying high dividends, the regulated firm subjects both its regulatory body as well as itself to capital market discipline more frequently. Stockholders are less likely to receive lower-than-normal levels of compensation due to lower allowed product prices when the regulatory authority is more frequently and effectively monitored by capital markets. Therefore, high dividends are a method of assuring a regulated firm's stockholders that they will receive a normal rate of return on the invested capital. This policy of high dividends also implies that the external security issuance by utilities is more predictable than for non-utilities. The smaller abnormal stock price changes for utilities than industrials is consistent with this hypothesis.[3]

Hypotheses about the predictability of announcements help explain the observed difference in announcement returns of common stock versus debt issues and industrials' versus utilities' offerings.[4] However, these hypotheses apparently do not explain differences in announcement returns between common and preferred stock or between convertible and non-convertible issues.

2.4. Information asymmetry and relative price effects

Suppose that a potential purchaser of securities has less information than corporate managers, and corporate managers are more likely to issue securities when the market price of the firm's traded securities is higher than management's assessment of their value. This implies that the stock price effects of security issues will be greater the more the asymmetry in information between insiders and other security market participants [see Myers and Majluf (1984) and Myers (1984)]. Since debt and preferred stock are more senior claims, their values are less sensitive to changes in firm value than is common stock, and thus the information asymmetry problem is less severe. Similarly, convertible debt and convertible preferred stock are more sensitive to changes in firm value than non-convertible debt and preferred, but less so than common stock. Finally, in the rate regulation process, managers of utilities generally petition their respective regulatory authorities for permission for new security sales.

---

[3]Citizens Utilities is an apparent counter example to this hypothesis. Because of its special tax status, it is allowed no new equity issues, and perhaps for that reason has a very low payout ratio. It also has an AAA debt rating and the highest rate of return to stockholders among all utilities, and it appears to have the best record in rate regulation proceedings. See also Long (1978).

[4]Also, the evidence in table 2 of increases in dividends is consistent with this hypothesis. Dividend initiations are expected to have a larger unanticipated component than the ordinary dividend increases.

This petitioning process could reduce the price reaction of utilities' announcements relative to industrials for any of three reasons: (1) it could reduce the differential information between manager and outsiders; (2) it could limit managers' discretion as to what security to sell; and (3) it could reduce managers' ability to time security offerings to take advantage of any differential information.

Thus, while the information asymmetry hypothesis does not predict the direction of announcement returns for debt or preferred issues, it offers a potential explanation of greater price changes associated with common stock than preferred or debt, for convertible than non-convertible issues, and for industrials than utilities.

While the evidence across classes of securities is consistent with the information asymmetry hypothesis, some data within security classes is apparently inconsistent. When Eckbo (1986) and Mikkelson and Partch (1986) disaggregate their bond data by rating class, neither study finds higher rated, less risky (and thus less sensitive to firm value) bonds to be associated with smaller abnormal returns. Eckbo also finds more negative abnormal returns to mortgage bonds than non-mortgage bonds.[5]

The information asymmetry hypothesis can be distinguished from hypotheses about implied cash flow changes by examining evidence from events that explicitly associate sources and uses of funds. Just as the information asymmetry hypothesis implies no obvious predictions about dividend or investment accouncements, the analysis of implied changes in net operating cash flows makes no prediction about the market reaction to announcements of exchange offers. The evidence in table 3 from exchange offers, conversion-forcing calls of convertible securities, and security sales where the proceeds are used for debt retirement suggests that: (1) the sign of the abnormal return and the sign of the leverage change are the same, and (2) the larger the change in leverage, the greater is the absolute value of the abnormal price reaction. Thus, debt-for-common offers have larger stock price reactions than preferred-for-common offers, and common-for-debt offers have larger negative price reactions than common-for-preferred offers.

Combining the information asymmetry hypothesis and the hypothesis on implied changes in net operating cash flows provides additional insight into the difference between reported announcement effects of debt and equity. For example, in the upper panel of table 2, announcements of calls of non-convertible debt are associated with implied increases in expected net operating cash flow but yield an insignificant negative return. However, this event is also on average associated with a reduction in leverage. When Vu (1986) disaggregates his sample of calls of bonds by change in leverage, he finds that for the 72

---

[5]As Stulz and Johnson (1985) argue, secured debt should be less sensitive to firm value than non-secured debt.

Table 3

Summary of two-day announcement effects associated with exchange offers, security sales with designated uses of funds, and calls of convertible securities. With sources and uses of funds associated, these transactions represent virtually pure financial structure changes.

Type of transaction	Security issued	Security retired	Average sample size	Two-day announcement period return
Leverage-increasing transactions				
Stock repurchase[a]	Debt	Common	45	21.9%
Exchange offer[b]	Debt	Common	52	14.0
Exchange offer[b]	Preferred	Common	9	8.3
Exchange offer[b]	Debt	Preferred	24	2.2
Exchange offer[c]	Income bonds	Preferred	24	2.2
Transactions with no change in leverage				
Exchange offer[d]	Debt	Debt	36	0.6*
Security sale[f]	Debt	Debt	83	0.2*
Leverage-reducing transactions				
Conversion-forcing call[e]	Common	Convertible preferred	57	−0.4*
Conversion-forcing call[e]	Common	Convertible bond	113	−2.1
Security sale[f]	Convertible debt	Debt	15	−2.4
Exchange offer[b]	Common	Preferred	30	−2.6
Exchange offer[b]	Preferred	Debt	9	−7.7
Security sale[f]	Common	Debt	12	−4.2
Exchange offer[b]	Common	Debt	20	−9.9

[a] Source: Masulis (1980).

[b] Source: Masulis (1983). Note: These returns include announcement days of both the original offer and for about 40 percent of the sample, a second announcement of specific terms of the exchange.

[c] Source: McConnell and Schlarbaum (1981).

[d] Source: Dietrich (1984).

[e] Source: Mikkelson (1981).

[f] Source: Eckbo (1986), Mikkelson and Partch (1986).

*Not statistically different from zero.

firms that decrease leverage, there are significant stock price announcement returns of −1.1 percent; for the 30 firms with no change in leverage, +0.3 percent; and for the 31 firms that increase leverage, +0.9 percent.

2.5. Changes in ownership and relative price effects

In some transactions, part of the observed price reaction reflects important changes in the ownership and control of the firm. Table 4 summarizes the results from studies of transactions with potentially important control implications. The upper panel summarizes results of transactions where the organi-

Table 4

Summary of cumulative abnormal common stock returns and average sample size from studies of announcements of transactions which change corporate control or ownership structure. Returns are weighted averages by sample size of the returns reported by the respective studies (unless otherwise noted, results are significantly different from zero).

Type of announcement	Average sample size	Cumulative abnormal returns
Organizational restructuring		
Merger: Target[a]	113	20.0%
Bidder[a]	119	0.7*
Spin-off[b]	76	3.4
Sell-off: Seller[c]	279	0.7
Buyer[d]	118	0.7
Equity carve-out[e]	76	0.7*
Joint venture[f]	136	0.7
Going private[g]	81	30.0
Voluntary liquidation[h]	75	33.4
Life insurance company mutualization[i]	30	56.0
Savings & Loan Association charter conversion[j]	78	5.6
Proxy fight[k]	56	1.1
Ownership restructuring		
Tender offer: Target[l]	183	30.0
Bidder[l]	183	0.8*
Large block acquisition[m]	165	2.6
Secondary distribution: Registered[n]	146	−2.9
Non-registered[n]	321	−0.8
Targeted share repurchase[o]	68	−4.8

[a]Source: Dodd (1980), Asquith (1983), Eckbo (1983), Jensen and Ruback (1983).
[b]Source: Hite and Owers (1983), Miles and Rosenfeld (1983), Schipper and Smith (1983), Rosenfeld (1984).
[c]Source: Alexander, Benson and Kampmeyer (1984), Rosenfeld (1984), Hite and Owers (1985), Jain (1985), Klein (1985), Vetsuypens (1985).
[d]Source: Rosenfeld (1984), Hite and Owers (1985), Jain (1985), Klein (1985).
[e]Source: Schipper and Smith (1986).
[f]Source: McConnell and Nantell (1985).
[g]Source: DeAngelo, DeAngelo and Rice (1984).
[h]Source: Kim and Schatzberg (1985).
[i]Source: Mayers and Smith (1985).
[j]Source: Masulis (1985).
[k]Source: Dodd and Warner (1983).
[l]Source: Bradley, Desai and Kim (1985), Jensen and Ruback (1983).
[m]Source: Holderness and Sheehan (1985), Mikkelson and Ruback (1985).
[n]Source: Mikkelson and Partch (1985).
[o]Source: Dann and DeAngelo (1983), Bradley and Wakeman (1983).
*Interpreted by authors as not significantly different from zero.

zation is restructured. The evidence suggests that organizational restructuring on average benefits stockholders. In the lower panel, value effects associated with a change in the distribution of ownership are examined. The evidence suggests that announcements of transactions that increase ownership concentration raise share prices, while those that reduce concentration lower share prices.

Organizational restructuring is sometimes accompanied by a security offering. For example, Schipper and Smith (1986) examine firms that sell common stock of a previously wholly owned subsidiary. In contrast to the negative returns from the sale of corporate common stock reported in table 1, these 'equity carve-outs' are associated with significant positive returns of 1.8 percent for the five days around the announcement.[6] There are important control implications of the public sale of a minority interest in a subsidiary. For example, management of the subsidiary can have a market-based compensation package that more accurately reflects subsidiary performance [see Smith and Watts (1982, 1984)]. Schipper and Smith document that 94 percent of the carve-outs adopted incentive compensation plans based on the subsidiary's stock. The evidence from equity carve-outs is also consistent with the information asymmetry hypothesis. If management expects that the subsidiary is undervalued, then by segregating the subsidiary's cash flows and selling separate equity claims, the firm can more effectively capture that gain.

Some security sales involve potentially important ownership structure changes. For example, Masulis and Korwar (1986) isolate 56 offerings (not in table 4) for which, in addition to the primary equity issue, there is also a registered secondary offering by the firm's management. The two-day announcement period return for the offers is −4.5 percent, compared to −3.1 percent for the average industrial equity offering.

3. Security offerings by public corporations

After a firm decides on the security to issue, it must choose among a number of methods to market it. The firm can offer the securities on a pro rata basis to its own stockholders through a rights offering; it can hire an underwriter to offer the securities for sale to the public; or it can place the securities privately. If the firm uses an underwriter,[7] it can negotiate the offering terms with the underwriter, or it can structure the offering internally, then put it out for

---

[6] These positive returns are observed in spite of potentially large costs associated with these transactions. For example, the required information disclosures about the subsidiary are increased and the nature of the transactions that can take place between the parent and the subsidiary (to avoid potential conflict of interests between the parent's and subsidiary's outside stockholders) are restricted.

[7] Without exception, the analysis summarized here assumes effective competition within the investment banking industry. In fact, there are no effective barriers to entry in the industry. Effective competition provides strong incentives to supply efficient combinations of contractual provisions including services, fees, and underpricing.

competitive bid. The underwriting contract can be a firm commitment or a best efforts offering. Finally, the issue can be registered with the Securities and Exchange Commission under its traditional registration procedures, or, if the firm qualifies, it can file a shelf registration in which the firm registers all securities it intends to sell over the next two years.

3.1. Rights versus underwritten offerings

The two most frequently employed methods by which public corporations market new securities are rights offerings and firm commitment underwritten offerings. In an underwritten offering, initial negotiation focuses on the amount of capital, the type of security, and the terms of the offering. If the firm and underwriter agree to proceed, the underwriter begins to assess the prospects. The investigation includes an audit by a public accounting firm and a legal opinion from a law firm. The issuing firm, the investment banker, the auditing firm and the law firm all typically participate in filing the required registration statements with the Securities and Exchange Commission (as well as with the appropriate state securities commissions). The offering can only proceed when the registration statement becomes effective. Although oral sales efforts are permitted, any indications of interest are not legally enforceable commitments of customers. No written sales literature other than a 'red herring' prospectus and 'tombstone advertisements' are permitted between the filing and offer date. The 'Rules of Fair Practice' of the National Association of Security Dealers require that once the underwriters file the offer price with the SEC, the securities cannot be sold above this price, although they can be offered at a lower price if the syndicate 'breaks'.

In a rights offering, each stockholder receives options to buy newly issued securities. One right is issued for each share held. The contract states the number of rights required to purchase one unit of the newly issued security, the exercise price, and the expiration date. Rights offerings must be registered with the SEC. Rights typically trade on the exchange on which the stock is listed.

Smith (1977) documents that the out-of-pocket expenses of an equity issue underwritten by an investment banker are from three to thirty times higher than the costs of a non-underwritten rights offering. Yet over 80 percent of the equity offerings he examines employ underwriters.[8] Eckbo (1986) finds five percent of bond issues between 1964 and 1981 are sold through rights offers.

A number of authors have argued that investment bankers are effective in monitoring the firm's activities.[9] The monitoring is potentially valuable be-

---

[8]Hansen and Pinkerton (1982) document that firms which employ rights offerings have high ownership concentrations. Although they claim to resolve the paradox about the use of rights offerings, they ignore all costs except direct costs reported to the SEC and, as Smith and Dhatt (1984) indicate, overstate the significance of their statistical tests.

[9]See Rozeff (1982), Easterbrook (1984), Booth and Smith (1986), Heinkel and Schwartz (1985), and Schneller (1985).

cause of the differential information between managers and outside stockholders. Thus, in addition to a marketing function, the investment banker performs a monitoring function analogous to that of bond rating agencies [Wakeman (1981), Fama and Jensen (1985)], of independent auditing firms [Jensen and Meckling (1976), Watts (1977), DeAngelo (1981)],[10] of outside members of a firm's board of directors [Fama (1980)], and of insurance companies [Mayers and Smith (1982)]. In each case, it is argued that while the activity is expensive, it is justified because periodic exposure of the firm's decision makers to effective monitoring raises the price external securityholders are willing to pay for the firm.[11]

3.2. Negotiated versus competitive bid contracts

Rule 50 of the Public Utilities Holding Company Act of 1935 requires registered public utility holding companies to sell securities through competitive bid, unless the firm obtains an exemption from the SEC. The Commission generally grants exemptions only if the firm cannot secure competitive bids or if it judges the market conditions to be 'unsettled'. Utilities not organized as holding companies are not affected by the Act.

Bhagat and Frost (1986) compare the issue costs for public utility firms that sell common stock using competitive bid and negotiated underwritten contracts. They measure total issue costs as the sum of underwriter's commissions, issuer-borne expenses and underpricing. They examine a sample of 552 offerings between 1973 and 1980 in which 73 are competitive bid and 479 are negotiated. Of the 479 negotiated offerings, 28 are negotiated after obtaining an exemption from the Securities and Exchange Commission. Bhagat and Frost estimate that the total issue costs are higher for firms which use negotiated offerings by 1.2 percent of the proceeds. Moreover, they find each

---

[10] The monitoring hypothesis for both investment bankers and independent auditing firms is also suggested by the evidence in Burton and Roberts (1967) and Carpenter and Strawser (1971) that a significant fraction of changes in auditing firms is associated with new securities offerings.

[11] The major observation that seems inconsistent with the monitoring explanation of the investment banker's function is the evidence that Smith (1977) and Bhagat (1983) provide. They examine firms that eliminate the preemptive right from the corporate charter. If investment bankers provide a valuable monitoring function, the benefit should be forecast and impounded when firms change policies. Thus, examination of returns around the elimination of the preemptive right (which requires firms to offer new shares first on a pro rata basis to existing shareholders) should pick up the present value of the incremental benefit from increased use of underwriters. But Bhagat finds a significant negative stock return at the proxy mailing date. Neither Bhagat nor Smith find significant returns at the annual meeting date when the vote is taken. There are two important qualifications of the evidence from preemptive right elimination. First, given the evidence in table 1 that the average response to new equity issues is negative, the negative effect observed by Bhagat could measure the higher probability of a stock offering. It is likely that firms only incur the expense to eliminate the preemptive right if they anticipate making an offering. Second, neither Smith nor Bhagat distinguish between firms who had used rights alone and firms that normally had their rights offerings underwritten. Neither the difference in monitoring nor out-of-pocket expenses are as great when comparing underwritten issues with underwritten rights offerings.

component of cost (commissions, issuer-borne expenses and underpricing) higher in negotiated offerings.

The Bhagat and Frost evidence is consistent with that of Logue and Jarrow (1978), Ederington (1976) and Dyl and Joehnk (1976). Logue and Jarrow find that for a sample of 122 utility common stock issues between 1963 and 1974, the average underwriting commissions are 1.2 percent higher for negotiated offerings than competitive bid. Ederington examines 1081 issues of public utility and industrial bond offerings between 1964 and 1971. He finds that the offering yields on negotiated issues are approximately seven to eight basis points higher than the yields on equivalent competitive bid issues offered at the same time. And although underwriter spreads are on average less for competitive bid than negotiated issues, there are periods where negotiated bids are less expensive. Dyl and Joehnk examine a sample of 312 competitive bids and 71 negotiated new issues of debt by public utilities between 1972 and 1974. They find that the average underwriters' commission as a fraction of proceeds is higher by 0.13 percent and the yield on the debt is higher by 36 basis points for negotiated than for competitive bid offers. These differences are evident across bond rating classes. Moreover, the results occur despite the fact that the average negotiated offer was approximately $10 million larger than the average competitive bid; with economies of scale in the investment banking industry, larger issues are expected to receive lower percentage fees.

Thus, the evidence suggests that competitive bid offerings involve lower total flotation costs than negotiated offerings. Yet it appears that the major users of competitive bids are regulated firms which are required to do so. Firms not facing a regulatory constraint overwhelmingly choose negotiated offers.

Bhagat and Frost suggest that this behavior can be explained by differences in incentives between managers and shareholders and the costs of controlling the firm's managers. They conjecture that managers might benefit from: (1) side payments from investment bankers – especially those investment bankers who are members of the corporate board of directors, (2) increased compensation if managerial compensation is tied to accounting profits,[12] and (3) less variation in cost (a benefit if the managers are risk-averse) since they offer evidence that the variance of issuing costs is higher for competitive bid offerings.

An alternative explanation follows from the hypothesis that there is information asymmetry between managers and outside securityholders that produces a derived demand for monitoring. In a competitive bid offering, the issuing firm specifies the details of the offering – the type of security, the issue date and (if it is a bond) the covenants. Thus, differential information available to managers can be used in setting the terms of the offering without constraints from

---

[12] Since future consulting services could be bundled into the underwriter's fee, and since costs of selling securities do not go through the income statement but are charged directly to the capital account, accounting earnings are higher though cash flows are lower.

negotiation with investment bankers. And because the firm retains this additional flexibility, potential securityholders reduce the price they are willing to pay for the issue. Moreover, if it is difficult to control the use of information received by investment bankers not awarded the contract, then companies with potentially sensitive information are likely to find competitive bids costly. If the effective monitoring provided through a competitively bid offering is less than that provided through a negotiated underwritten issue, then firms would have incentives to employ negotiated offerings, even though the flotation costs are higher.

The monitoring hypothesis has implications for the cross-sectional distribution of competitive bid versus negotiated offerings. Firms with smaller information asymmetry between outside securityholders and managers will more likely use competitive bids. Thus, if the rate regulation process reduces the differential information, regulated utilities not subject to Rule 50 should use competitive bids more frequently than unregulated firms. Similarly, since competitive bids allow the issuing firm's management to specify the date of the offering, if the informational asymmetry problem is severe, competitive bids will be expensive. Thus, firms with less discretion in the timing of security offerings should more frequently employ competitive bids. Finally, with more senior claims, the informational asymmetry problem is less severe because the value of the claim is less sensitive to firm value. Thus straight debt, secured debt and non-convertible preferred stock should be sold through competitive bids more frequently than common stock, convertible preferred stock or convertible bonds.

However, Bhagat (1985) finds evidence which is consistent with this monitoring hypothesis. He examines the price reaction of firms affected by the suspension of Rule 50, which requires public utilities holding companies to seek competitive bids. He finds that at the announcement, share prices fall, and on reinstatement of the rule, share prices rise. Since the SEC suspends the rule when market conditions are 'unsettled', Bhagat's test may pick up adverse changes in underlying market conditions. However, that would require that the Commission either moves very fast or has valuable information about the state of the market otherwise unavailable to securityholders. Neither of these conditions seem plausible.

3.3. Shelf versus traditional registration

In March 1982, the SEC authorized Rule 415 on an experimental basis. It permitted certain firms to employ shelf registration for public security issues. Rule 415 was made permanent in November 1983. The procedure is called shelf registration because it allows companies to register securities, 'put them on the shelf', and then issue the securities whenever they choose. It permits firms with more than $150 million of stock held by investors unaffiliated with the company to specify and register the total dollar amount of securities they expect to sell publicly over the next two years. After the securities are registered, the firm can then offer and sell them for up to two years on a continuous basis. Rule 415 also allows the firm to modify a debt instrument and sell it without first filing an amendment to the registration statement. Thus, shelf registration allows qualifying firms additional flexibility both in structuring debt issues and in timing for all security issues.

The shelf registration procedure has been employed more frequently with debt than equity offerings. However, if the problem of differential information between managers and potential securityholders is severe, fewer equity issues should be registered through shelf procedures. With the additional timing flexibility given management, there is an increased opportunity to exploit inside information. Potential securityholders anticipating this problem would lower the amount they are willing to pay. Hence, stock price reactions to announcements of new equity offerings registered under Rule 415 should have more negative stock price reactions than if they were registered under traditional registration procedures.

Shelf registration procedures also should affect the structure of flotation costs. For example, shelf registration should lower fixed costs of public debt issues. This could lead qualified firms to change their practices with respect to debt offerings. Rather than use a line of credit at a bank until a large public issue can be made, firms could use the shelf registration process to place several smaller issues rather than having one large issue. Liquidity advantages with respect to secondary markets could be retained by having multiple issues with the same coupon rate, coupon dates, maturity dates and covenants.

Kidwell, Marr and Thompson (1984) and Rogowski and Sorensen (1985) examine the implications of allowing firms to choose between shelf and traditional registration procedures in issuing bonds. Both use regression techniques for a cross-section of issues to examine the alternative costs. They conclude that shelf registration lowers the interest rate by between 20 to 40 basis points.

4. Initial public equity offerings

Privately owned corporations face two major alternatives: to remain private or to become a public corporation. A public corporation incurs a number of obligations not imposed on private firms.[13] For example, the SEC requires

---

[13] See DeAngelo, DeAngelo and Rice (1984). Fairly strict limits control the maximum number of equityholders a firm may have and still remain private. This limitation implies that the larger the firm, the greater the underdiversification cost imposed on the equityholders. The equity claims are also less liquid since some otherwise feasible transfers are restricted by regulation and would jeopardize the firm's private status. Note that since this constraint is on the ownership distribution of the firm, it generates a potential conflict among the stockholders of a private corporation. For example, if there can be no more than 20 equityholders to maintain private corporation status, but currently there are 15, a stockholder selling his shares to more than one person who is not currently a stockholder consumes degrees of freedom of the remaining equityholders.

Table 5

Summary of estimated underpricing of new securities at issuance by type of offering. Underpricing is measured by the average percentage change from offer prices to after-market price.

Type of offering	Study	Sample period	Sample size	Estimated underpricing
Initial public equity offering	Ibbotson (1974)	1960–1969	120	11.4%
Initial public equity offering	Ibbotson and Jaffe (1975)	1960–1970	2650	16.8
Initial public equity offering	Ritter (1984)	1960–1982	5162	18.8
		1977–1982	1028	26.5
		1980–1981	325	48.4
Initial public equity offering	Ritter (1985)	1977–1982		
firm commitment			664	14.8
best efforts			364	47.8
Initial public equity offering	Chalk and Peavy (1985)	1974–1982	440	13.8
firm commitment			415	10.6
best efforts			82	52.0
Equity carve-outs	Schipper and Smith (1986)	1963–1983	36	0.19
Seasoned new equity offering	Smith (1977)	1971–1975	328	0.6
Seasoned new utility equity offering	Bhagat and Frost (1986)	1973–1980	552	−0.30
negotiated			479	−0.25
competitive bid			73	−0.65
Primary debt issue	Weinstein (1978)	1962–1974	412	0.05

periodic filings which can be costly in three dimensions: (1) the out-of-pocket production costs, (2) the value of management's time, and (3) the reduction in firm value from disclosing valuable information otherwise unavailable to the firm's competitors.

Private firms that choose to go public typically obtain the services of an underwriter and have an initial public equity offering. Initial public equity offerings are an interesting special case of security offerings. They differ from offerings previously discussed in two important ways: (1) The uncertainty about the market clearing price of the offering is significantly greater than for public corporations with claims currently trading. (2) Because the firm has no traded shares, examination of stock price reactions to announcements (as in section 2) are impossible. The first difference affects the way these securities are marketed; the second limits the ways researchers can study the offerings.

4.1. Underpricing

Examination of the return behavior of initial public equity offerings from offer price to after-market indicates that the average issue is offered at a significant discount from the price expected in the after-market; however, after-market returns appear to be normal [Ibbotson (1975), Ibbotson and Jaffe (1975), Ritter (1984, 1985) and Chalk and Peavy (1985)]. Table 5 summarizes the results from studies of offer prices for initial public equity offerings as well as new issues of seasoned equity and bonds. For initial public equity offerings, the average underpricing appears to exceed 15 percent.

Hypotheses have been offered to explain underpricing of new issues [Baron (1982), Ritter (1985), Chalk and Peavy (1985), Rock (1986) and Beatty and Ritter (1986)]. Baron focuses on the asymmetry in information between the issuing firm and the investment banker. The other authors focus on the asymmetry of information between informed and uninformed potential securityholders.

The Rock and the Ritter analyses of underpricing assume that markets are efficient in a very specific sense – that the marginal investment in information yields a normal expected return. Potential securityholders can be divided into three groups: (1) marginal investors who are indifferent about investing in information, (2) inframarginal investors who are better informed and thus earn abnormal returns, and (3) inframarginal investors who rationally choose (either because of the size of their portfolio or the opportunity cost of their time) not to invest in information.

In an offering, there is uncertainty about the market-clearing price. If the offer prices are set at their expected market-clearing price, uninformed investors systematically earn below normal returns; if an issue is underpriced, informed investors also submit bids and the issue is rationed; and if the issue is overpriced, informed investors are less likely to submit bids and the issue is more likely to be undersubscribed. Hence, uninformed investors systematically receive more of overpriced issues and less of underpriced issues. Uninformed investors anticipate this adverse selection and bid only if the offer price is below their expected after-market price by enough to compensate for their expected losses on overpriced issues. This implies that the average underpricing is greater for issues with greater price uncertainty.

Baron (1982) analyzes an optimal contract for advising and marketing services between a firm and its investment banker. He hypothesizes that the investment banker is better informed about the market demand for the firm's securities than is the firm. Since the firm must compensate the investment banker for providing advice in setting the offer price for the issue and for marketing the securities, the optimal offer price is a decreasing function of the uncertainty about the market demand for the issue, while the value of delegation to the underwriter is an increasing function of the uncertainty.

Thus, while the alternative hypotheses focus on different information problems – (1) between informed and uninformed potential securityholders and (2) between the issuing firm and its investment banker – the two yield similar implications about which firms employ which contract for a given issue.

Beatty and Ritter (1986) attempt to test the underpricing hypotheses using data from initial public offerings. They argue that there is an equilibrium amount of underpricing. If an investment banker underprices too much, given the characteristics of the issue, the investment banker loses future offerings. If the investment banker underprices too little, he loses investors. Beatty and Ritter estimate an underpricing function and examine the average deviation of 49 investment bankers who handled four or more initial public offerings during the period 1977–1981. They compare subsequent performance of the 24 underwriters whose average deviation from their estimated normal underpricing is greatest with that of the remaining 25 underwriters whose average deviation is least. For the 24 with the greatest deviation, their market share goes from 46.6 to 24.5 percent and five of the 24 cease operations during 1981–1982. For the 25 with the smallest deviation, their market share goes from 27.2 to 21.0 percent and one of the 25 ceases operation.

Schipper and Smith find that for their sample of initial public offerings, which result from equity carve-outs, the average underpricing is only 0.19 percent. It seems plausible that potential asymmetric information problems are less severe for this subset of initial offerings than the average; thus, less underpricing is expected. Yet it is surprising that the measured underpricing is so similar to that of seasoned new issues.[14]

As table 5 shows, security issues by public corporations are also underpriced. Smith finds seasoned new equity issues underpriced by 0.6 percent, Bhagat and Frost find seasoned equity issues by utilities overpriced by 0.3 percent, and Weinstein finds new bonds underpriced by 0.05 percent. Parsons and Raviv (1985) extend Rock's analysis of underpricing initial public equity offerings to consider seasoned new equity offerings. In a seasoned offering, potential security holders have the option of buying after the announcement but before the offering, at the offering or in the after-market. Again, the asymmetry in information among investors implies that the offer price will be set systematically below both the security price between the announcement and the offer date as well as below the expected after-market price.[15] This hypothesis implies that underpricing should be greater with competitive bid than negotiated offerings, and with shelf than traditional registration procedures. (Unfortunately, this implication for shelf issues is somewhat more difficult to test because of the proximity of the announcement and issue dates.)

Smith and Chalk and Peavy indicate that the average measured underpricing could overstate the cost imposed on issuers if the underwriter can extract gains

---

[14] This underpricing evidence combined with the clustering of event dates provides potential corroboration of the Ibbotson and Jaffee (1975) and Ritter (1984) hypotheses about the non-stationary time series behavior of underpricing.

[15] Note that the Bhagat and Frost evidence is potentially consistent with the Parsons and Raviv hypothesis if one recognizes the difference in transactions costs in the two transactions. The transaction generating the closing price will as frequently be initiated by a buy order as a sell order; on average, the closing price represents the midpoint of the bid–ask spread. Moreover, the transaction generating the closing price involves brokerage fees. There are no purchaser-borne fees in a primary distribution. Phillips and Smith (1980) estimate the bid–ask spread at 0.6 percent and the brokerage fees for individuals at 0.4 percent. Thus, the purchaser's expenditure is the closing price plus half the bid–ask spread plus the brokerage fee. These adjustments exceed Bhagat and Frost's measured overpricing.

by rationing ex post underpriced issues. Then, competition among underwriters transfers the expected gains back to the issuer through the quoted offer fees.

4.2. Best efforts versus firm commitment contracts

Two alternative forms of underwriting contracts are typically employed in initial public equity offerings. The first is a firm commitment underwriting agreement under which the underwriter agrees to purchase the whole issue from the firm at a particular price for resale to the public. The second is a best efforts underwriting agreement under which the underwriter acts only as a marketing agent for the firm.[16] The underwriter does not agree to purchase the issue at a predetermined price, but sells the security and takes a predetermined spread, with the firm taking the residual. The agreement generally specifies a minimum amount that must be sold within a given period of time; if this amount is not reached, the offering is cancelled. Ritter (1985) reports that 35 percent of initial public equity offerings from 1977–1982 are sold with best efforts contracts, although they represent only 13 percent of the gross proceeds.

The information problem between informed and uninformed potential security holders, as well as the information and contracting problems between the issuing firm and its investment banker, influence the choice between firm commitment and best efforts contracts. Ritter (1985) contrasts the preceding argument for underpricing firm commitments with the incentives in a best efforts contract. He argues that in a best efforts contract, if the issue is overpriced and the issue sales fall short of the minimum specified in the underwriting contract, the offer is cancelled and the losses to uninformed investors are reduced. Structuring the contract in this manner reduces the problem faced by uninformed potential securityholders, and thus reduces the discount necessary to induce them to bid.

Ritter argues that the relative attractiveness of the two contracts varies with changes in the amount of uncertainty associated with the issue. The prohibition against raising prices for an oversubscribed issue imposed by the Rules of Fair Practice of the National Association of Security Dealers is analogous to the firm giving a call option to potential stockholders [see Smith (1979)]. Thus, in a firm commitment offering, the expected proceeds to the firm are reduced if the uncertainty about after-market prices is higher. In a best efforts contract, the firm again gives the call because of the rule against raising the price, but the firm also gives an option to potential shareholders to put the shares back to the firm if the issue is undersubscribed. Thus, with more uncertainty about after-market prices, best efforts contracts become relatively more attractive.

---

[16]Booth and Smith (1986) report that in non-initial offerings from 1977–1982, best efforts contracts are used in two percent of the equity offerings, two percent of convertible issues, no preferred stock issues, and eight percent of debt issues.

Mandelker and Raviv (1977), Baron (1979, 1982) and Baron and Holmstrom (1980) hypothesize that there is uncertainty among the capital market participants about the market-clearing price for the securities. Furthermore, their models focus on the conflict of interest between the issuing firm and its underwriter. They derive optimal contracts, either best efforts or firm commitment, based on the uncertainty associated with the issue and the degree of risk aversion of the issuer and investment banker. Mandelker and Raviv assume symmetric information when the contract is negotiated between the firm and the investment banker. Baron (1979) also assumes symmetric information between the investment banker and the issuing firm but considers the potential conflict of interest because of the issuer's inability to observe the investment banker's marketing effort. Baron and Holmstrom assume symmetric information at the time of contracting but allow the investment banker to acquire information during the pre-selling period before the offering. Baron (1982) allows the investment banker to have better information about the market at the time the contract is negotiated. In their analyses a firm commitment offering is more likely to be optimal: (1) the more risk-averse the issuer, (2) the less risk-averse the investment banker, (3) the less the uncertainty about the market clearing security price, (4) the less the asymmetry in information between the issuer and the investment banker, and (5) the more observable the investment banker's effort.

Therefore, both lines of analysis predict that best efforts contracts are more likely the greater the uncertainty of the after-market issue price. Ritter tests this hypothesis using the after-market standard deviation of returns as a proxy for ex ante uncertainty. He estimates the after-market standard deviation using the first 20 quoted bid prices after the offering. He finds that the average standard deviation for 285 best efforts offerings is 7.6 percent, and is statistically significantly above the 4.2 percent standard deviation of 641 firm commitment offerings. This is consistent with the hypothesis that issues with greater uncertainty are more likely to employ best efforts than firm commitment contracts.

5. Unresolved issues

The growth of knowledge about the process of raising capital has been substantial. I believe that this area will continue to receive a great deal of attention, particularly because a number of interesting questions have been suggested by this examination of the capital acquisition process: (1) Do stock price reactions to announcements of new security sales differ between rights and underwritten offers? (2) Marsh (1979) reports that in 1975, 99 percent of the new equity in England was raised through rights offers. Why is there the dramatic difference in use of rights between the United States and the United Kingdom? (3) Researchers typically have contrasted underwritten offers with non-underwritten rights offers, yet in a significant fraction of rights offers, underwriters are retained on a standby basis. Under what circumstances are rights offerings with standby underwriting contracts optimal? (4) Standby underwriting contracts typically are either single-fee agreements or two-fee agreements which specify both a 'standby fee' and a 'take-up fee' based on the number of rights handled. What determines the optimal fee structure? (5) Underwriters typically trade in the secondary market during and immediately after a security offering. Why is this 'stabilization' activity beneficial? (6) Underwritten equity offers frequently include a 'green shoe' option which gives the underwriter the right to buy additional shares from the firm at the offer price. For which offers is that provision optimal? (7) If we restrict ourselves to companies not constrained by Rule 50 of the Public Utilities Holding Company Act, how does frequency of use of competitive bids vary with the type of security? With the size of the offering? With the industry of the issuing firm? And with the ownership concentration of the firm? (8) Are convertible bonds and convertible preferred stock underpriced at issue? (9) Are there differences in underpricing between issues registered under Rule 415 versus traditional procedures?

References

Ahrony, Joseph and Itzhak Swary, 1980, Quarterly dividend and earnings announcements and stockholder's returns: An empricial analysis, Journal of Finance 35, 1–12.

Alexander, Gordon J., P. George Benson and Joan M. Kampmeyer, 1984, Investigating the valuation effects of announcements of voluntary corporate selloffs, Journal of Finance 39, 503–517.

Asquith, Paul, 1983, Merger bids, uncertainty, and stockholder returns, Journal of Financial Economics 11, 51–83.

Asquith, Paul and David Mullins, 1983, The impact of initiating dividend payments on shareholder wealth, Journal of Business 56, 77–96.

Asquith, Paul and David Mullins, 1986, Equity issues and offering dilution, Journal of Financial Economics, this issue.

Baron, David P., 1979, The incentive problem and the design of investment banking contracts, Journal of Banking and Finance 3, 157–175.

Baron, David P., 1982, A model of the demand for investment banking advising and distribution services for new issues, Journal of Finance 37, 955–976.

Baron, David P. and Bengt Holmstrom, 1980, The investment banking contract for new issues under asymmetric information: Delegation and the incentive problem, Journal of Finance 35, 1115–1138.

Beatty, Randolph P. and Jay R. Ritter, 1986, Investment banking, reputation, and the underpricing of initial public offerings, Journal of Financial Economics, this issue.

Bhagat, Sanjai, 1983, The effect of pre-emptive right amendments on shareholder wealth, Journal of Financial Economics 12, 289–310.

Bhagat, Sanjai, 1985, The effect of management's choice between negotiated and competitive equity offerings on shareholder wealth, Journal of Financial and Quantitative Analysis, forthcoming.

Bhagat, Sanjai and Peter A. Frost, 1986, Issuing costs to existing shareholders in competitive and negotiated underwritten public utility equity offerings, Journal of Financial Economics, this issue.

Booth, James R. and Richard L. Smith, III, 1986, Capital raising, underwriting and the certification hypothesis, Journal of Financial Economics, this issue.

Bradley, Michael, Anand Desai and E. Han Kim, 1983, The rationale behind interfirm tender offers: Information or synergy?, Journal of Financial Economics 11, 183–206.

Bradley, Michael and L. M. Wakeman, 1983, The wealth effects of targeted share repurchases, Journal of Financial Economics 11, 301–328.

Brennan, Michael and Eduardo Schwartz, 1978, Corporate income taxes, valuation, and the problem of optimal capital structure, Journal of Business 51, 103–114.

Brickley, James, 1983, Shareholder wealth, information signaling and the specially designated dividend: An empirical study, Journal of Financial Economics 12, 187–209.

Burton, John C. and William Roberts, 1967, A study of auditor changes, Journal of Accountancy, 31–36.

Carpenter, Charles G. and Robert H. Strawser, 1971, Displacement of auditors when clients go public, Journal of Accountancy, 55–58.

Chalk, Andrew J. and John W. Peavy, III, 1985, Understanding the pricing of initial public offerings, Unpublished manuscript (Southern Methodist University, Dallas, TX).

Charest, Guy, 1978, Dividend information, stock returns, and market efficiency – II, Journal of Financial Economics 6, 297–330.

Dann, Larry, 1980, The effect of common stock repurchase on stockholder returns, Unpublished dissertation (University of California, Los Angeles, CA).

Dann, Larry, 1981, Common stock repurchases: An analysis of returns to bondholders and stockholders, Journal of Financial Economics 9, 113–138.

Dann, Larry and Harry DeAngelo, 1983, Standstill agreements, privately negotiated stock repurchases and the market for corporate control, Journal of Financial Economics 11, 275–300.

Dann, Larry Y., David Mayers and Robert J. Raab, Jr., 1977, Trading rules, large blocks and the speed of price adjustment, Journal of Financial Economics 4, 3–22.

Dann, Larry Y. and Wayne H. Mikkelson, 1984, Convertible debt issuance, capital structure change and financing-related information: Some new evidence, Journal of Financial Economics 13, 157–186.

Dealers' Digest Inc., 1985, Five year directory of corporate financing 1980–1984, Anthony V. Ricotta, ed. (Mason Slaine, New York).

DeAngelo, Harry, Linda DeAngelo and Edward M. Rice, 1984, Going private: Minority freezeouts and shareholder wealth, Journal of Law and Economics 27, 367–401.

DeAngelo, Harry and Ronald Masulis, 1980, Optimal capital structure under corporate and personal taxation, Journal of Financial Economics 8, 3–29.

DeAngelo, Linda, 1981, Auditor independence, 'low balling', and disclosure regulation, Journal of Accounting and Economics 3, 113–127.

Dietrich, J. Richard, 1984, Effects of early bond refundings: An empirical investigation of security returns, Journal of Accounting and Economics 6, 67–96.

Dodd, Peter, 1980, Merger proposals, management discretion and stockholder wealth, Journal of Financial Economics 8, 105–138.

Dodd, Peter and Richard S. Ruback, 1977, Tender offers and stockholder returns: An empirical analysis, Journal of Financial Economics 5, 351–374.

Dodd, Peter and Jerold B. Warner, 1983, On corporate governance: A study of proxy contests, Journal of Financial Economics 11, 401–438.

Dyl, Edward A. and Michael D. Joehnk, 1976, Competitive versus negotiated underwriting of public utility debt, Bell Journal of Economics 7, 680–689.

Easterbrook, Frank H., 1983, Two agency-cost explanations of dividends, American Economic Review 74, 650–659.

Eckbo, B. Espen, 1983, Horizontal mergers, collusion, and stockholder wealth, Journal of Financial Economics 11, 241–273.

Eckbo, B. Espen, 1986, Valuation effects of corporate debt offerings, Journal of Financial Economics, this issue.

Ederington, Louis H., 1976, Negotiated versus competitive underwritings of corporate bonds, Journal of Finance 31, 17–28.

Fama, Eugene F., 1978, The effect of a firm's investment and financing decisions, American Economic Review 68, 272–284.

Fama, Eugene F., 1980, Agency problems and the theory of the firm, Journal of Political Economy 88, 288–307.

Fama, Eugene F. and Michael C. Jensen, 1985, Residual claims and investment decisions, Journal of Financial Economics 14, 101–119.

Gilson, Ronald J. and Reinier H. Kraakman, 1984, The mechanisms of market efficiency, Virginia Law Review 70, 549–644.

Hansen, Robert S. and John M. Pinkerton, 1982, Direct equity financing: A resolution of a paradox, Journal of Finance 37, 651–665.

Heinkel, Robert and Eduardo S. Schwartz, 1984, Rights versus underwritten offerings: An asymmetric information approach, Unpublished manuscript (University of British Columbia, Vancouver).

Hite, Gailen L. and James E. Owers, 1983, Security price reactions around corporate spin-off announcements, Journal of Financial Economics 12, 409–436.

Hite, Gailen L. and James E. Owers, 1985, Sale divestitures: Implications for buyers and sellers, Unpublished manuscript (Southern Methodist University, Dallas, TX).

Holderness, Clifford G. and Dennis P. Sheehan, 1985, Raiders or saviors? The evidence on six controversial investors, Journal of Financial Economics 14, 555–579.

Ibbotson, Roger, 1975, Price performance of common stock new issues, Journal of Financial Economics 2, 235–272.

Ibbotson, Roger G. and Jeffrey F. Jaffe, 1975, 'Hot issue' markets, Journal of Finance 30, 1027–1042.

Jain, Prem C., 1985, The effect of voluntary sell-off announcements on shareholder wealth, Journal of Finance 40, 209–224.

Jensen, Michael C. and William H. Meckling, 1976, Theory of the firm: Managerial behavior agency costs and ownership structure, Journal of Financial Economics 3, 305–360.

Jensen, Michael C. and Richard S. Ruback, 1983, The market for corporate control: The scientific evidence, Journal of Financial Economics 11, 5–50.

Kidwell, David S., M. Wayne Marr and G. Rodney Thompson, 1984, SEC Rule 415: The ultimate competitive bid, Journal of Financial and Quantitative Analysis 19, 183–195.

Kim, E. Han and John D. Schatzberg, 1985, Voluntary liquidation and stockholder returns, Unpublished manuscript (University of Michigan, Ann Arbor, MI).

Klein, April, 1984, The effects of voluntary corporate divestitures on shareholders' wealth, Unpublished manuscript (University of Chicago, Chicago, IL).

Kolodny, Richard and Diane Rizzuto Suhler, 1985, Changes in capital structure, new equity issues, and scale effects, Journal of Financial Research 8, 127–136.

Kraus, Alan and Robert Litzenberger, 1973, A state preference model of optimal financial leverage, Journal of Finance 28, 911–922.

Linn, Scott and J. Michael Pinegar, 1985, The effect of issuing preferred stock on common stockholder wealth, Unpublished manuscript (University of Iowa, Iowa City, IA).

Logue, Dennis E. and Robert A. Jarrow, 1978, Negotiation vs. competitive bidding in the sale of securities by public utilities, Financial Management 7, 31–39.

Mandelker, Gershon and Artur Raviv, 1977, Investment banking: An economic analysis of optimal underwriting contracts, Journal of Finance 32, 683–694.

Marsh, Paul, 1979, Equity rights issues and the efficiency of the UK stock market, Journal of Finance 34, 839–862.

Marsh, Paul, 1982, The choice between equity and debt: An empirical study, Journal of Finance 37, 121–144.

Masulis, Ronald M., 1980, Stock repurchase by tender offer: An analysis of the causes of common stock price changes, Journal of Finance 35, 305–319.

Masulis, Ronald, 1983, The impact of capital structure change on firm value: Some estimates, Journal of Finance 38, 107–126.

Masulis, Ronald, 1985, Changes in ownership structure: Conversions of mutual savings and loans to stock charter, Unpublished manuscript (University of California, Los Angeles, CA).

Masulis, Ronald W. and Ashok Korwar, 1986, Seasoned equity offerings: An empirical investigation, Journal of Financial Economics, this issue.

Mayers, David and Clifford Smith, 1982, On the corporate demand for insurance, Journal of Business 55, 281–296.

Mayers, David and Clifford Smith, 1985, Ownership structure and control: The mutualization of stock life insurance companies, Journal of Financial Economics, forthcoming.

McConnell, John and Chris J. Muscarella, 1985, Corporate capital expenditure decisions and the market value of the firm, Journal of Financial Economics 14, 399–422.

McConnell, John and Timothy Nantell, 1985, Corporate combinations and common stock returns: The case of joint ventures, Journal of Finance 40, 519–536.

McConnell, John and Gary Schlarbaum, 1981, Evidence on the impact of exchange offers on security prices: The case of income bonds, Journal of Business 54, 65–85.

Mikkelson, Wayne, 1981, Convertible calls and security returns, Journal of Financial Economics 9, 237–264.

Mikkelson, Wayne H. and M. Megan Partch, 1985, Stock price effects and costs of secondary distributions, Journal of Financial Economics 14, 165–194.

Mikkelson, Wayne H. and M. Megan Partch, 1986, Valuation effects of security offerings and the issuance process, Journal of Financial Economics, this issue.

Mikkelson, Wayne H. and Richard S. Ruback, 1985, Corporate investments in common stock, Journal of Financial Economics, forthcoming.

Miles, J. and J. Rosenfeld, 1983, A empirical analysis of the effects of spin-off announcements on shareholder wealth, Journal of Finance 38, 1597–1606.

Miller, Merton, 1977, Debt and taxes, Journal of Finance 32, 261–276.

Miller, Merton and Kevin Rock, 1985, Dividend policy under asymmetric information, Journal of Finance, forthcoming.

Modigliani, Franco and Merton Miller, 1958, The cost of capital, corporation finance and the theory of investment, American Economic Review 48, 261–297.

Modigliani, Franco and Merton Miller, 1963, Corporate income taxes and the cost of capital: A correction, American Economic Review 53, 433–443.

Myers, Stewart, 1977, Determinants of corporate borrowing, Journal of Financial Economics 5, 147–175.

Myers, Stewart, 1984, The capital structure puzzle, Journal of Finance 39, 575–592.

Myers, Stewart C. and Nicholas S. Majluf, 1984, Corporate financing and investment decisions when firms have information that investors do not have, Journal of Financial Economics 13, 187–221.

Parsons, John and Artur Raviv, 1985, Underpricing of seasoned issues, Journal of Financial Economics 14, 377–397.

Pettway, Richard H. and Robert C. Radcliffe, 1985, Impacts of new equity sales upon electric utility share prices, Financial Management 14, 16–25.

Phillips, Susan M. and Clifford W. Smith, Jr., 1980, Trading costs for listed options: The implications for market efficiency, Journal of Financial Economics 8, 179–201.

Ritter, Jay R., 1984, The 'hot issue' market of 1980, Journal of Business 57, 215–240.

Ritter, Jay R., 1985, The choice between firm commitment and best effort contracts, Unpublished manuscript (University of Pennsylvania, Philadelphia, PA).

Rock, Kevin, 1985, Why new issues are underpriced, Journal of Financial Economics, this issue.

Rogowski, Robert J. and Eric H. Sorensen, 1985, Deregulation in investment banking: Shelf registrations, structure, and performance, Financial Management 14, 5–15.

Rosenfeld, Ahron, 1982, Repurchase offers: Information adjusted premiums and shareholders' response, MERC monograph series MT-82-01 (University of Rochester, Rochester, NY).

Rosenfeld, James D., 1984, Additional evidence on the relation between divestiture announcements and shareholder wealth, Journal of Finance 39, 1437–1448.

Rozeff, Michael S., 1982, Growth, beta and agency costs as determinants of dividend payout ratios, Journal of Financial Research 5, 249–259.

Schneller, Meir I., 1984, Dividend policy and the stockholders–management conflict, Unpublished manuscript (University of Pennsylvania, Philadelphia, PA).

Schipper, Katherine and Abbie Smith, 1983, Effects of recontracting on shareholder wealth: The case of voluntary spin-offs, Journal of Financial Economics 12, 437–467.

Schipper, Katherine and Abbie Smith, 1986, A comparison of equity carve-outs and seasoned equity offerings: Share price effects and corporate restructuring, Journal of Financial Economics, this issue.

Scholes, Myron, 1972, Market for securities: Substitution versus price pressure and the effects of information on share prices, Journal of Business 45, 179–211

Smith, Clifford, 1977, Alternative methods for raising capital: Rights versus underwritten offerings, Journal of Financial Economics 5, 273–307.

Smith, Clifford, 1979, Applications of option pricing analysis, in: J. L. Bicksler, ed., Handbook of financial economics (North-Holland, Amsterdam) 80–121.

Smith, Clifford and Jerold Warner, 1979, On financial contracting: An analysis of bond covenants, Journal of Financial Economics 7, 117–161.

Smith, Clifford and Ross Watts, 1982, Incentive and tax effects of U.S. executive compensation plans, Australian Journal of Management 7, 139–157.

Smith, Clifford and Ross Watts, 1984, The structure of executive compensation contracts and the control of management, Unpublished manuscript (University of Rochester, Rochester, NY).

Smith, Richard L. and Manjeet Dhatt, 1984, Direct equity financing: A resolution of a paradox: A comment, Journal of Finance 39, 1615–1618.

Stulz, Rene M. and Herb Johnson, 1985, An analysis of secured debt, Journal of Financial Economics 14, 501–521.

Vermaelen, Theo, 1981, Common stock repurchases and market signalling, Journal of Financial Economics 9, 139–183.

Vetsuypens, Michel, 1985, Agency costs, asset substitution, and voluntary corporate divestitures: A test of bondholder wealth expropriation, Unpublished manuscript (University of Rochester, Rochester, NY).

Vu, Joseph D., 1986, An examination of corporate call behavior on nonconvertible bonds, Journal of Financial Economics, forthcoming.

Wakeman, Lee M., 1981, The real function of bond rating agencies, Chase Financial Quarterly 1, 18–26.

Watts, Ross L., 1977, Corporate financial statements, a product of the market and political processes, Australian Journal of Management 2, 53–75.

Weinstein, Mark, 1978, The seasoning process of new corporate bond issues, Journal of Finance 33, 1343–1354.

SOME EVIDENCE ON THE UNIQUENESS OF BANK LOANS*

Christopher JAMES

University of Oregon, Eugene, OR 97403, USA

Received April 1986, final version received June 1987

This paper presents evidence that banks provide some special service with their lending activity that is not available from other lenders. I find evidence that bank borrowers, not CD holders, bear the cost of reserve requirements on CDs. In addition, I find a positive stock price response to the announcement of new bank credit agreements that is larger than the stock price response associated with announcements of private placements or public straight debt offerings. Finally, I find significantly negative returns for announcements of private placements and straight debt issues used to repay bank loans.

1. Introduction

Although the economic rationale for commercial banks and other financial intermediaries is not well understood, recent theories of financial intermediation have focused on the role of banks in information production and transmittal [see, for example, Leland and Pyle (1977), Campbell and Kracaw (1980), and Diamond (1984)]. Banks and other intermediaries, the argument goes, have a cost advantage over other outsiders in producing and transferring information, either because of something intrinsic in the intermediation process, as Leland and Pyle and Diamond suggest, or because information production and the provision of transaction and other intermediary services are complementary activities. An implication of this view is that bank loans are different from publicly placed debt because banks know more about a company's prospects than other investors do.

The emphasis on information transmission contrasts sharply with an alternate hypothesis about the role of banks in the economy. The alternative holds that their special function is to provide transaction services through the issuance of demand deposits. On the asset side, banks are assumed to be simply passive portfolio managers [see Fama (1980)].

*A portion of this study was completed while I was visiting the University of Michigan. Thanks to James Brickley, Larry Dann, Mark Flannery, Ronald Lease, Wayne Mikkelson, Greg Niehaus, Megan Partch, Peggy Wier, seminar participants at the University of Oregon, University of Rochester, and New York University, an anonymous referee, and especially René Stulz (the editor) for helpful comments.

Journal of Financial Economics 19 (1987) 217–235. © North-Holland Publishing Company.

This paper provides evidence on whether commercial banks provide any special service with their lending activity that is not available from other lenders (i.e., on whether bank loans are unique). This evidence comes first from an examination of the incidence of the reserve requirement tax, and second from an analysis of the stock price response to announcements of bank loans, private placements of debt, and public straight debt issues.

My first examination extends research by Fama (1985), who studies the incidence of reserve requirements on bank certificates of deposit (CDs). He argues that because close substitutes for bank CDs, such as commercial paper or bankers' acceptances, exist and because CDs provide no special transaction services, reserve requirements on CDs must be borne by bank borrowers. In support of this conjecture, Fama finds no significant differences between the average yields on CDs and on high-grade commercial paper or bankers' acceptances. Fama concludes that because bank borrowers bear the cost of reserve requirements there must be something special about bank loans that distinguishes them from other types of privately placed and publicly placed debt.

A problem with Fama's conclusion is that the reserve requirement tax could be at least partially offset by a subsidy from the Federal Deposit Insurance Corporation (FDIC) in the form of deposit insurance supplied at less than actuarially fair prices. A more powerful test of the incidence of the reserve tax, provided here, examines the behavior of CD rates around changes in reserve requirements, when no offsetting changes in deposit insurance prices occur. My results support Fama's conclusion that the reserve tax is borne by bank borrowers.

A second source of evidence on the uniqueness of bank loans comes from a comparison of stock price responses to the announcements of bank loan agreements and other types of debt offerings. In analyzing the function of commercial banks, Kane and Malkiel (1965) and more recently Fama (1985) and Bernanke (1984), argue that bank loans are a form of inside debt, because banks have information about the borrower that is not available to other securities holders. As inside debt, bank loans are a way of avoiding the underinvestment problem associated with information asymmetries. Specifically, in the context of the Myers and Majluf model (1984), loans by banks (as inside debt) are similar to financial slack (internally generated funds). One testable implication of the bank-debt-as-inside-debt hypothesis is that because bank loans avoid the information asymmetries associated with public debt offerings, a non-negative stock price response will be associated with their announcement. For similar reasons, if private placements acquired by insurance companies are also inside debt, a non-negative stock price response is expected.

I examine the stock price response to publicly announced bank credit agreements, private placements, and publicly placed straight debt issues.

Abnormal performance is positive and statistically significant for bank loan announcements and nonpositive for publicly placed straight debt issues. These results are similar to those reported by Mikkelson and Partch (1986). Surprisingly, a negative and statistically significant stock price response is observed for debt placed privately with insurance companies. Most notably, I find a negative stock price response for private placements and straight debt issues used to repay bank loans. These results suggest that bank loans are unique, but they are not fully consistent with the inside-debt argument, as I discuss below.

The remainder of the paper is organized into five sections. In section 2, I analyze the incidence of the reserve requirement tax. In section 3, I describe my sample of bank credit agreements and debt offerings. The stock price effects associated with these borrowing arrangements are examined in section 4. In section 5, several explanations for the observed stock price behavior are explored. A brief conclusion is provided in section 6.

2. Incidence of the reserve requirement

The current reserve requirement on short-term CDs with original maturity of less than 180 days is 3%. In the absence of any special service provided to bank borrowers *or* any special service to CD holders, a reserve requirement tax would result in the elimination of CD financing. In a competitive deposit market other depositors (non-CD holders) will not bear the tax, because if a bank attempted to shift the tax to them, other banks not issuing CDs would bid them away. Bank stockholders cannot be expected to pay the tax because non-bank lenders (who are not subject to the reserve tax) would have a higher risk-adjusted return.

Fama (1985) argues that CD holders do not bear the reserve requirement tax and that therefore bank loans are special. This conclusion is based on his finding no significant difference between the yield on CDs and the yields on commercial paper and bankers' acceptances. Fama's evidence is not fully convincing, for two reasons. First, the reserve tax could be borne not by borrowers but by the FDIC through the provision of deposit insurance at less than actuarially fair prices. Second, CDs are insured only to $100,000, whereas the typical denomination is $1 million, so their rates may contain a defaul* premium. If the default risk on CDs is greater than for commercial paper, observed yields on the two securities may be identical even though CD owners pay the reserve tax.

An alternative method of examining the incidence of the reserve tax is to examine the behavior of CD yields in relation to the yields on other money market instruments around changes in reserve requirements. Without any contemporaneous change in insurance costs, an increase in reserve require-

Table 1

Average annual yields to maturity on high-grade certificates of deposit, commercial paper, and Treasury bills and yield spreads (January 1977 to December 1984, sample size = 471).[a]

	Panel A: *Average annual yields (weekly data)*	
Instrument	3% reserve requirement period Jan. 1977–Nov. 1978 July 1980–Dec. 1984	5% reserve requirement period Nov. 1978–July 1980
90-day CDs	10.67	11.89
30-day CDs	10.52	11.59
90-day commercial paper	10.59	11.83
30-day commercial paper	10.40	11.51
90-day Treasury bills	9.74	10.66
30-day Treasury bills	9.11	10.01

Panel B: *Average annual yield spread (in percent) between CDs and other money market instruments (standard errors in parentheses)*

Spread[b]	3% reserve requirement period Jan. 1977–Nov. 1978 July 1980–Dec. 1984	5% reserve requirement period Nov. 1978–July 1980	Entire sample period
$SPCDTB_{90}$	0.931 (0.04)	1.211 (0.07)	0.992 (0.03)
$SPCDTB_{30}$	1.412 (0.05)	1.581 (0.09)	1.455 (0.04)
$SPCDCP_{90}$	0.073 (0.01)	0.038 (0.02)	0.065 (0.01)
$SPCDCP_{30}$	0.117 (0.01)	0.078 (0.02)	0.110 (0.01)

[a] Yields are based on weekly (Friday close) price quotes from the traders at Bank of America for high-grade CDs and for dealer-placed commercial paper rated A1–P1. All data were obtained from Data Resources Inc. DRI-FACS file.

[b] $SPCDTB_{90}$ = average annual yield spread between 90-day CDs and 90-day Treasury bills,
$SPCDTB_{30}$ = average annual yield spread between 30-day CDs and 30-day Treasury bills,
$SPCDCP_{90}$ = average annual yield spread between 90-day CDs and 90-day commercial paper,
$SPCDCP_{30}$ = average annual yield spread between 30-day CDs and 30-day commercial paper.

ments should reduce the yield on CDs in relation to other yields if depositors pay the reserve tax.

Changes in the reserve requirements applied to CDs during the 1978–1980 period provide an opportunity to examine the incidence of the reserve tax. Effective November 2, 1978, and continuing through July 24, 1980, the Federal Reserve imposed a supplemental reserve requirement of 2% on all CDs in excess of $100,000. In addition, during this period, marginal reserve requirements of from 5% to 10% were imposed on CDs in excess of a base amount.[1]

[1] See table A7 of the *Federal Reserve Bulletin* for a list of reserve requirements.

The effect of these changes was to raise the reserve requirement on all large CDs from 3% to 5% and as high as 15% for CDs issued in excess of the base amount.

To examine the effect of these changes and the incidence of the reserve tax, I obtained weekly secondary market price quotes and computed yields for thirty- and ninety-day high-grade CDs, commercial paper, and Treasury bills. These data were obtained from Data Resources, Inc. (DRI), for the period January 1, 1977 to January 1, 1985.

Table 1 presents the average annual yield on CDs, commercial paper, and Treasury bills during the period in which a 3% reserve requirement was effective and the period in which a minimum 5% reserve requirement was imposed. Table 1 also contains the average spreads between CDs and other money market instruments for the 1977–1984 period. I find no statistically significant difference in the average spread between CDs and commercial paper or Treasury bills during the two periods. Assuming a competitive banking industry, the evidence presented in table 1 supports Fama's conclusion that bank borrowers and not CD holders bear the reserve tax.

3. Description of the sample and methodology

3.1. Random sample of firms

I am not aware of any source that provides information by company on new bank loan agreements. To obtain a sample of these financing events, I selected 300 companies at random from the population of firms contained in the 1983 Center for Research on Security Prices (CRSP) daily return file that were listed on the first trading day in 1974. I included companies in the sample if they were listed in the *Moody's Industrial, Transportation*, or *Utilities* manuals. (Excluded from the sample were financial companies.) I then searched the *Wall Street Journal Index* for information on each firm over the ten-year period 1974–1983 to identify all public straight debt offerings for cash, private placements of debt, and bank borrowing agreements that did not coincide with other financing, dividend, or earnings announcements.

The bank loan agreements in the sample consist of new credit agreements and the expansion of existing agreements. They include both extensions of lines of credit (commitments to lend) and term loans. The typical agreement, however, involves a line of credit where, at the firm's option, borrowing can be converted into a term loan.

Privately placed debt agreements consist of debt sold for cash to a restricted number of institutional investors. Most (approximately 70%) of the agreements involve an insurance company as the lender.

The total sample consists of 207 financing announcements. There are eighty announcements of bank loan agreements, thirty-seven announcements of

Table 2

Distribution by year of announcements of bank credit agreements, privately placed debt, and publicly placed straight debt for a random sample of 300 NYSE- and AMEX-traded non-financial firms (1974–1983).

Year of announcement	Bank loan agreements	Privately placed debt	Public straight debt
1974	9	4	5
1975	11	7	13
1976	7	7	8
1977	8	7	4
1978	1	8	6
1979	8	1	9
1980	11	1	10
1981	9	1	9
1982	10	1	16
1983	6	0	10
Total	80	37	90

private placements, and ninety announcements of public straight debt offerings. Table 2 presents the distribution of announcements by type of event by year for the period 1974–1983. Although there is no discernible time pattern for the number of bank loan or straight debt announcements, the number of private placement announcements decreases substantially after 1978.[2]

3.2. Descriptive statistics

Table 3 contains summary statistics for the debt offerings in my sample. Row 1 contains the amount of each type of offering. As table 3 indicates, public debt offerings are larger on average than private offerings. For bank loan agreements and private placements, the loan amounts reported may overstate the amount actually borrowed by the firm. In many cases these are commitments to lend, and the entries in row 1 of table 3 are based on the amount of the commitment.[3]

[2] The number and dollar volume of privately placed debt is reported in the *Investment Dealer's Digest*. The dollar value (in millions) and number of privately placed bond issues during the period are:

	1974	1975	1976	1977	1978
Dollar value	$8,214	11,856	17,811	21,797	18,511
Number of issues	696	685	717	1,017	900

	1979	1980	1981	1982	1983
Dollar value	15,270	10,750	10,860	10,397	10,360
Number of issues	786	640	556	531	525

[3] Private placements have many of the same features as bank loan agreements. The borrower is typically given an option to borrow up to some prespecified amount over a period of one to five years. See Zinbarg (1975).

Table 3

Descriptive statistics for commercial bank loans, privately placed debt, and publicly placed straight debt for a random sample of 300 NYSE- and AMEX-traded non-financial firms (1974–1983).[a]

	Type of borrowing					
	Commercial bank loans (sample size = 80)		Privately placed debt (sample size = 37)		Public straight debt (sample size = 90)	
Descriptive measure	Mean (Range)	Median	Mean (Range)	Median	Mean (Range)	Median
Debt amount (millions of dollars)	72.0 (4–800)	35.0	32.3 (5–120)	25.0	106.2 (10–1,000)	75.0
Firm size (millions of dollars)[b]	675 (28.6–10,311)	212	630 (20.2–6,365)	147	2,506 (47–59,540)	1,310
Debt amount/market value of common stock	0.72 (0.04–2.6)	0.46	0.52 (0.04–2.6)	0.25	0.26 (0.02–1.5)	0.15
Maturity of debt (years)[c]	5.6 (0.6–12)	6.0	15.34 (3–25)	15.0	17.96 (1–40)	20.0
Number of firms	52		34		43	
Number of firms with publicly traded debt outstanding[d]	25		16		30	

[a] Statistics given in the first row are the mean followed by the median. The range is provided in the second row.

[b] Firm size is for December 31 of the year immediately preceding the security offering or borrowing. Firm size equals the book value of all liabilities and preferred stock plus the market value of common stock outstanding. The market value of common stock is the product of the number of shares outstanding and the closing price per share at year-end preceding the announcement. Closing prices are from the Security Owners Stock Guide. The book value of liabilities and the number of shares outstanding are from Moody's manuals.

[c] Maturity of the loan or debt offering is from the Wall Street Journal article. No information on maturity was provided for twenty-four bank loans, two private placements, and nine straight debt offerings. For bank loans that are convertible to term loans, the maturity of the term loan is used.

[d] Firms are classified as having publicly traded debt if the Moody's manual report the firm had rated debt outstanding at year-end preceding the financing announcement.

Firms using private placements and bank loans are on average smaller than firms using public offerings of straight debt. The average firm size in both the bank loan sample and the private placement sample is about 25% of the average firm size in the straight debt sample. This finding is consistent with Brealey and Myers's (1985) view that private placements and bank loans typically involve small and medium-sized companies.

Row 4 of table 3 presents the average maturity of each type of borrowing. Bank loans are of considerably shorter maturity than either privately placed debt or straight debt. Indeed, the longest-term bank loan is twelve years, less than the median maturity of either privately placed or publicly placed debt.

3.3. Methodology

The market model is used to obtain estimates of abnormal stock returns around the announcement of the financing events. The announcement is defined as the date of the first report of the borrowing agreement or debt offering in the *Wall Street Journal*. The market model was estimated on daily returns for the period that begins 120 trading days before and ends 120 trading days following the announcement (event) date, excluding 41 trading days centered around the event date. The abnormal stock return or prediction error for firm j over day t is defined as

$$PE_{jt} = R_{jt} - \left(\hat{\alpha}_j + \hat{\beta}_j R_{mt} \right),$$

where R_{jt} is the rate of return of security j over period t, R_{mt} is the rate of return on the CRSP equal-weighted market index over period t, and $\hat{\alpha}_j$ and $\hat{\beta}_j$, are ordinary least squares estimates of firm j's market model parameters.

The daily prediction errors are averaged over all firms within a particular group to produce a daily portfolio average prediction error:

$$APE_t = 1/N \sum_{j=1}^{N} PE_{jt},$$

where N is the number of firms in the sample. I calculate a two-day announcement period abnormal return by summing the prediction errors for day -1 and day 0. This procedure incorporates the possibility that the announcement may have been made during trading hours the previous day and reported with a one-day lag.

Tests of statistical significance of the average prediction errors are based on standardized prediction errors. The two-day standardized prediction error for firm j is defined as

$$SPE_j = \sum_{t=-1}^{0} PE_{jt}/S_j,$$

where

$$S_j = \left[2V_j^2 \left[1 + \frac{1}{M} + \frac{(R_{mt} - R_m)^2}{\sum_{i=1}^{M} (R_{mi} - R_m)^2} \right] \right]^{1/2},$$

and V_j^2 is the residual variance of the market model regression for firm j, M is the number of days in the estimation period (199), and R_m is the mean market return over the estimation period.

Table 4

Average two-day percentage prediction errors (APE) on the announcement of commercial bank loans, privately placed debt, and publicly placed straight debt offerings for a random sample of 300 NYSE- and AMEX-traded non-financial firms (1974–1983).

Type of event	APE	Z-value[a]	Proportion negative[b] (sample size)
Bank loan agreement	1.93%	3.96	0.34[d] (80)
Private placement	−0.91%	−1.87	0.56 (37)
Public straight debt	−0.11%	−0.40	0.56 (90)
Bank loan agreement borrowing indicated[c]	1.71%	3.20	0.35[d] (71)
Bank loan agreement no borrowing indicated[d]	3.68%	1.71	0.23[e] (9)

[a] The null hypothesis is that the average standardized prediction error equals zero. $Z = \sqrt{N}(ASPE_t)$, where $ASPE_t$ is the average standardized prediction error and N is the number of firms in the sample.

[b] The null hypothesis is that the proportion of negative prediction errors equals 0.5. The test statistic is a Wilcoxon signed ranks statistic.

[c] Loan agreements in which the *Wall Street Journal* article describing the agreement indicates borrowing has occurred or is expected to occur under the loan agreement.

[d] Sign test statistic is significant at 0.05 level.

[e] Sign test statistic is significant at 0.01 level.

The average standardized prediction error is

$$ASPE_t = \frac{1}{N} \sum_{j=1}^{N} SPE_{jt}.$$

Assuming the individual prediction errors are cross-sectionally independent, the following Z-statistic can be computed:

$$Z = \sqrt{N}(ASPE_t),$$

which is asymptotically distributed unit normal under the hypothesis that the average standardized prediction error equals zero.

4. Stock price response to borrowing arrangements

Table 4 reports the average stock price response to the announcement of bank loan agreements, private placements, and public straight debt offerings. The average prediction error for bank loan agreements is positive and statistically significant at the 0.01 level. In addition, 66% of the prediction errors are positive.[4] There is no statistically significant difference between announcements of bank loan agreements in which immediate borrowing is indicated and announcements in which no immediate borrowing is indicated.

The positive stock price response to bank loan agreements contrasts with the non-positive response to public offerings of securities reported by other researchers.[5] As table 4 indicates, I also find a non-positive stock price response associated with the announcement of a public offering of straight debt. The average two-day prediction error associated with straight debt offerings is -0.11 percent, not statistically different from zero at the 0.10 level.

If the positive response to bank loan agreements is the result of some benefit from the intermediation process, but a benefit not unique to commercial banks, one would expect to observe a similar response to debt placed privately with insurance companies. As table 4 indicates, however, the average two-day prediction error associated with the announcement of privately placed debt is -0.91 percent, which is significantly different from zero at the 10% level (p-value of 0.063). Moreover, the difference between the average prediction error of bank loan agreements and of privately placed debt agreements is statistically significant at the 0.01 level.

5. Interpretation of the average stock price response

The difference in abnormal performance among announcements of bank loans, private placements, and straight debt offerings may arise because these debt offerings (or the borrowers using them) differ systematically in some important feature, such as the maturity of the issue or the purpose of the borrowing, that is unrelated to the identity of the lender. Alternatively, bank loans may differ from other types of borrowing because banks provide some special service with their lending activity. A testable implication of the second explanation is that the share price response to the announcement of bank loans will differ from the share price response to announcements of private placements or public debt offerings with characteristics similar to commercial bank loans.

In this section I examine the share price response associated with announcements of bank loans, private placements, and straight debt offerings grouped by stated purpose of the borrowing, the maturity of the offering, the default risk of the borrower, and the size of the borrower.

---

[4] Mikkelson and Partch (1986) also report a positive and statistically significant response to the announcement of bank credit agreements. They, however, focus on public securities offerings and do not explore differences in the stock price response associated with bank loan agreements and private placements.

[5] See Dann and Mikkelson (1984), Mikkelson and Partch (1986), Eckbo (1986), Asquith and Mullins (1986), and Masulis and Korwar (1986).

Table 5

Average two-day prediction errors (APE) on the announcement of commercial bank loans, privately placed debt, and publicly placed straight debt offerings grouped by stated purpose of the borrowing for a random sample of 300 NYSE- and AMEX-traded non-financial firms (1974–1983).

	Type of borrowing								
	Bank loan agreements[a] (sample size = 80)			Private placements (sample size = 37)			Public straight debt (sample size = 90)		
	APE (Z-value)[b]	Sample size	Average maturity[c]	APE (Z-value)	Sample size	Average maturity	APE (Z-value)	Sample size	Average maturity
Repay debt	1.14% (1.64)	17	6.5	0.51% (0.69)	5	14.2	-0.35% (-0.43)	32	17.4
Capital expenditure	1.20% (1.05)	24	5.9	-0.23% (0.02)	5	16.6	0.55% (1.63)	34	18.9
General corporate purposes	4.67% (2.54)	8	4.6	0.26% (0.31)	9	17.1	0.07% (0.24)	9	17.1
Repay bank loans	3.10% (2.35)	11	5.8	-2.07%[d] (-3.18)	18	14.4	-1.63%[e] (-1.74)	12	18.4
No purpose given	1.74% (1.79)	20	4.7	—	—	—	0.69% (0.73)	3	14.0

[a] Stated purpose is the primary purpose given in the *Wall Street Journal* article describing the borrowing. In cases in which multiple purposes are given, the first purpose listed is used to classify the event.

[b] The null hypothesis is that the average standardized prediction error equals zero. $Z = \sqrt{N}(ASPE_t)$, where $ASPE_t$ is the average standardized prediction error and N is the number of firms in the sample.

[c] Maturity of the loan or debt offering is from the *Wall Street Journal* article describing the offering. Maturity is in years.

[d] The return is significantly different, at the 0.01 significance level, from the average prediction error for the sample of other private placements for which the stated purpose is other than repaying bank loans.

[e] This return is significantly different, at the 0.05 level, from the average prediction error for the sample of other straight debt issues for which the stated purpose is other than repaying bank loans.

5.1. Analysis of borrowing agreements by stated purpose

One explanation for the positive abnormal performance associated with bank loan agreements is based on the asymmetric information model of Myers and Majluf (1984). Bank loans may serve as a form of inside debt if banks have inside information about the value of the firm's growth prospects and bank loan rates reflect this information. Myers's and Majluf's model pertains to new financing, however, and offers no prediction about borrowing for other purposes. Examining the stock price response to bank loans grouped by stated purpose provides one test of the inside-debt hypothesis.

All borrowing announcements are placed into one of five purpose categories: (1) refinance debt, (2) capital expenditures, (3) general corporate purposes, (4) repayment of bank loans, and (5) no purpose given. The classification by purpose is based on information contained in the *Wall Street Journal* article describing the announcement. Where several purposes are stated, borrowing is classified by the first purpose listed or, where indicated, the primary purpose of the borrowing.

The average two-day prediction errors for bank loans, private placements, and straight debt offerings grouped by purpose are presented in table 5. Table 5 also includes the average maturity of each type of borrowing. The average prediction errors for bank loans are positive for all stated purposes, although general corporate purposes and the repayment or refinancing of bank debt are the only two categories in which the average prediction errors are statistically different from zero at the 0.01 level. There are, however, no significant differences (at the 0.10 level) between the mean returns for bank loans classified by purpose.

In only one category, the repayment of bank loans, is the average prediction error for private placements significantly different from zero. The average prediction error for this category is negative and appears to be the major component of the negative average prediction error associated with private placements reported in table 4. Moreover, the average prediction error for private placements used to repay bank loans is statistically different (at the 0.01 significance level) from that of private placements used for other purposes.

In the sample of straight debt offerings, only the repayment of bank loans category has an average prediction error significantly different from zero at the 0.10 level. The average two-day prediction error is -1.63 percent (p-value $=$ 0.08).

Two findings in this section are of particular interest. First, there is no significant difference between the share price response to bank loans used to refinance debt (either existing bank loans or other debt offerings) and bank loans used for capital expenditures. The same conclusion is reached if the capital expenditures and general corporate purpose categories are combined. Therefore, the positive average abnormal returns associated with the announcement of new bank loans cannot be attributed solely to avoidance of information asymmetries associated with *new* investments. The second finding is the statistically significant decrease in share price for privately placed debt and straight debt used to refinance bank loans. This result is curious; why do managers use private placements to refinance bank loans, given the adverse share price reaction? One possible explanation is the difference in maturity between bank loans, private placements, and public debt offerings. This issue is explored in the next section.

5.2. Analysis of borrowing arrangements by maturity of the offers

The difference in average abnormal performance among borrowing arrangements may be attributed to differences in the average maturity of the issue. As table 3 indicates, bank loans have a shorter average maturity than do private placements and straight debt offerings in the sample.

Maturity of the debt issue may be important in explaining the differences in abnormal performance for several reasons. First, as suggested by Merton (1974) and Ho and Singer (1982), short-term debt may be less risky than long-term debt. In particular, Ho and Singer demonstrate that holding the market value of debt constant, an increase in the time to maturity of the debt will increase the elasticity of the value of the bond with respect to the value of the firm.[6] Myers and Majluf (1984) predict that the stock price response to the announcement of a new security issue depends on the sensitivity of the value of new securities to changes in firm value. This implies that the absolute value of the stock price response to the announcement of a debt offering should increase with the time to maturity of the offering.

Flannery (1986) provides a second reason for the importance of maturity. He argues that a firm's choice of maturity can provide a signal about management's assessment of earnings prospects. Flannery shows that, with transactions costs associated with new debt issues, managers who believe their firm is undervalued by outsiders can signal the true value of the firm by issuing short-term debt (i.e., debt repayable before cash flows are realized). When the undervalued firm's true prospects are revealed, refunding occurs at a lower default risk premium. Overvalued firms, on the other hand, find a short-term debt strategy more expensive because any initial cost savings from issuing short-term debt are more than offset by higher transaction costs of refinancing and higher subsequent refinancing costs (in terms of a higher default risk premium).

---

[6]With a discount bond, to maintain a constant market value of debt as its maturity increases the promised terminal payment to debt holders must also increase. In addition, note that the elasticity of risky debt equals the weighted average of the elasticity of equity for the unlevered firm and the elasticity of riskless debt (which is zero). An increase in the maturity of debt makes the expected payoff characteristics of debt more similar to those of equity (by raising the terminal payment) and therefore increases the elasticity of debt.

Easterbrook (1984) and Fama (1985) provide a third reason why maturity might matter. Both authors focus on the agency costs of monitoring managers. Easterbrook argues that the costs of monitoring are lower if the firm is frequently in the market for new capital.[7] The issuance of new securities triggers a review of the firm's earnings prospects by intermediaries (investment bankers and commercial banks). These intermediaries send reliable signals to existing as well as new claimants on the firm about the firm's ability to meet fixed-pay-off contracts. The intermediaries send reliable signals by bonding performance, directly through their own investment or indirectly through the value of their reputation. Fama (1985, p. 36) argues that bank loans avoid duplication of information costs:

> Bank loans usually stand last or close to last in the line of priority among contracts that promise fixed pay-offs. Bank loans are short-term and the renewal process triggers periodic evaluation of the organization's ability to meet low-priority fixed pay-off contracts. Positive renewal signals from bank loans mean that other agents with higher fixed pay-off claims need not undertake similar costly evaluations of their claims.

A firm's decision to commit to periodic evaluations can therefore provide a positive signal of management's assessment of the firm's earnings prospects.

The hypothesis that the positive share price response associated with bank loan announcements is due *solely* to the shorter maturity of bank loans I call the *maturity hypothesis*. If the difference in abnormal performance is due solely to the shorter maturity of bank loans, one would expect to observe a positive share price response for public straight debt offerings and private placements with maturities similar to those of bank loans.

The maturity hypothesis is not necessarily inconsistent with the hypothesis that banks provide some special service to borrowers. For example, Black (1975), Fama (1985), and Kane and Malkiel (1965) argue that banks have a cost advantage in making loans to depositors. The inside information provided by a continuing deposit history is particularly valuable, they argue, in making and monitoring repeating short-term loans. This argument explains why banks may have lower costs to originate short-term repeating loans but does not explain why firms use private placements or publicly placed long-term debt to refinance bank loans. If a continuing relationship between the bank and its loan customers results in lower costs of refinancing, banks also should have a comparative advantage in making long-term loans to these customers. There-

---

[7] Rozeff (1982) presents a similar argument in his analysis of the determinants of dividend payout ratios. He argues that dividend payments are a device that reduces the agency cost of equity by requiring the firm to acquire external funds more frequently. The suppliers of new funds require the firm to supply new information about the firm's earnings prospects. The agency cost savings from higher dividend payments are offset by higher transactions costs associated with new financing. These two opposing influences produce an optimum dividend payout ratio.

fore, although a change in a firm's earnings prospects may result in a shift in its maturity preference, it is not clear why this action also results in a change in the intermediary used (e.g., from banks to insurance companies). One explanation is that banks are constrained from making long-term loans.[8] This constraint could arise from regulatory pressure or a preference by banks for matching the maturity of their assets with the maturity of their liabilities.[9]

To test the maturity hypothesis, I divided the straight debt and private placement announcements into two groups, one consisting of offerings with a maturity of less than ten years and a second consisting of offerings with a maturity of ten years or more. I then analyzed the stock price response to borrowing announcements in the two groups.

My results are reported in table 6. Although the average prediction errors are larger for short-term offerings than for longer-term borrowing, the difference in average returns is not statistically significant. As an additional test of the maturity hypothesis I estimated the relation between the two-day prediction error and the maturity of the offering for each type of borrowing arrangement, using weighted least squares. The weights used in the regression analysis are the reciprocal of the standard error of each firm's abnormal returns. My results reveal no statistically significant relation between the share price response to the announcement of the offering and the maturity of the offering. These results, together with those reported in table 6, are inconsistent with the maturity hypothesis.

5.3. Other explanations

The other potential explanations for the differences in abnormal performance among borrowing arrangements are: differences in the risk of the debt issued, differences in the size of borrowing firms, and differences in the size of debt offering in relation to the size of borrowing firm. Smith and Warner (1977) argue that private placements contain more detailed restrictive covenants and are more likely to be used by riskier firms than is publicly placed debt. Differences in default risk may explain the differences in abnormal returns that I find. Alternatively, abnormal performance may be related to firm size. The announced ability to borrow may be good news for small firms (which borrow primarily from banks), but not much news at all for large firms (which

---

[8] The presence of a supply constraint is suggested by the lack of activity in the long-term commercial loan market. In my sample, only one bank loan has a maturity of more than ten years. The Federal Reserve Board's *Survey of the Terms of Bank Lending* indicates banks specialize in short-term loans. The survey for August 1985 indicates only 12% of commercial loans made have maturities of more than one year. These loans have an average maturity of four years.

[9] Although no federal regulations limit the maturity of commercial loans, a factor used in bank examinations to determine asset quality and capital requirements is the maturity mismatch of a bank's assets and liabilities. See Spong (1985).

Table 6

Average two-day percentage prediction errors (APE) on the announcement of private placements and straight debt offerings classified by maturity for a random sample of 300 NYSE- and AMEX-traded non-financial firms (1974–1983).

Type of event	APE	Z-value[a]	Sample size	Average maturity[b]
Straight debt, maturity less than 10 years	0.766%	1.625[c]	25	5.4 years
Straight debt, maturity greater than 10 years	−0.441%	−0.537	57	21 years
Private placements, maturity less than 10 years	−0.232%	−0.193	5	5.6 years
Private placements, maturity greater than 10 years	−1.011%	−2.002	32	17 years

[a] The null hypothesis is that the average standardized prediction error equals zero. $Z = \sqrt{N}(ASPE_t)$, where $ASPE_t$ is the average standardized prediction error and N is the number of firms in the sample.

[b] Maturity of the loan or debt offering is from the *Wall Street Journal* article describing the offering.

[c] Significantly different (at the 0.10 level) from the APE for straight debt issues with maturity greater than ten years at the 0.10 level.

use publicly placed debt) that have other ways of disseminating information. Bank borrowing may therefore be simply a proxy for firm size. Finally, the relative size of the offering may be an important determinant of the stock price response if it serves as a proxy for changes in leverage.

As a proxy for the default risk of the borrower, I obtained for each firm the rating of its most recently issued debt prior to each announcement in my sample. Debt ratings are from the *Moody's* manual. Panel A in table 7 provides the proportion of firms with debt outstanding in three rating categories: AA or better, A, and BAA and below. The proportion of firms in each rating category, as well as the proportion of firms with rated debt is similar for the private placement and bank loan samples. A higher proportion of the straight debt offerings is in the AA or better and A rated categories. If the rating of outstanding debt provides a proxy for default risk, firms announcing new bank loans and private placements have a higher default risk than those announcing straight debt offerings.

Myers and Majluf (1984) predict that abnormal performance is related to the sensitivity of the value of the securities issued to changes in the firm value. Default risk can affect the sensitivity. Panel B of table 7 provides two-day average prediction errors for each type of borrowing grouped by rating. For each type of borrowing arrangement, the abnormal returns are larger the higher the debt rating. This result is consistent with the prediction of Myers's and Majluf's model. The results in table 7 are *not* consistent, however, with the hypothesis that differences in default risk explain the difference in stock price

Table 7

Debt ratings for a random sample of 300 NYSE- and AMEX-traded non-financial firms announcing bank loan agreements, private placements, and straight debt offerings (1974–1983), and average two-day percentage prediction errors for firms grouped by rating of outstanding debt.

Panel A: Debt rating[a]

Type of event	Proportion of firms rated AA or better[b]	Proportion of firms rated A	Proportion of firms rated BAA or below	Proportion of firms with rated debt
Bank loan agreements	0.12 (5)	0.10 (4)	0.78 (25)	0.48 (34)
Private placements	0.12 (2)	0.20 (3)	0.68 (11)	0.47 (16)
Public straight debt offerings	0.31 (20)	0.41 (27)	0.28 (18)	0.69 (65)

Panel B: Average two-day prediction errors by debt rating[c]

	Rated A or better	Rated BAA or below	Not rated
Bank loan agreements	3.89% (2.82)	1.77% (1.92)	1.76% (2.184)
Private placements	1.18% (1.68)	0.30% (0.211)	−2.03% (−2.90)
Public straight debt offerings	0.40% (1.72)	−0.32% (−1.42)	−1.08% (−1.45)

[a] Rating refers to the bond rating of the most recently issued debt prior to announcement. Ratings were obtained from *Moody's* manuals.
[b] Sample size is in parentheses.
[c] Z-value in parentheses; the null hypothesis is that the average standardized prediction error equals zero. $Z = \sqrt{N}(ASPE_t)$, where $ASPE_t$ is the average standardized prediction error and N is the number of firms in the sample.

response to different types of borrowing agreements. The proportion of firms in each rating category is similar for bank loans and private placements, but the abnormal return associated with bank loans is positive (on average and in each rating category), whereas the abnormal return for private placements is negative.

As table 3 indicates, firms in the bank loan sample are smaller than firms in the straight debt sample. To determine whether differences in firm size can explain differences in abnormal performance I estimate the following cross-sectional equation:

$$STRET_i = \alpha_1 + \alpha_2 STMVCS_i + \alpha_3 Issue\ I + \alpha_4 Issue\ II + \varepsilon_i, \qquad (1)$$

where $STRET_i$ is the two-day standardized prediction error for firm i;

$STMVCS_i$ is the market value of common stock divided by the standard error of the two-day prediction errors for firm i; *Issue I* equals 1 if issue is a private placement, zero otherwise; *Issue II* equals 1 if issue is a straight debt offering, zero otherwise; and ε_i is the error term.

The results are presented below (*t*-statistics in parentheses):

$$STRET_i = 0.305 + 1.17E^{-9}STMVCS_i - 0.554 \; Issue \; I - 0.306 \; Issue \; II,$$
$$\quad\;\; (1.75) \quad (1.61) \qquad\qquad\quad (-1.97) \qquad\quad (-1.83)$$

$$R^2 = 0.05.$$

The results indicate no statistically significant relation between the stock price response to the borrowing announcement and the size of the firm after controlling for issue type. These results indicate that differences in abnormal returns among borrowing agreements are not the result of differences in firm size.

I obtain similar results when firm size is measured as the sum of the market value of common stock and the book value of all other liabilities. In addition, I find no statistically significant relation between abnormal returns and firm size within each type of borrowing arrangement. Finally, I obtain similar results when the relative size of the offer, defined as the ratio of the amount of the offering to the market value of the firm's outstanding common stock, is substituted for the size variable in eq. (1).

6. Summary and conclusions

Significant positive abnormal returns accrue to stockholders of firms announcing new bank loan agreements, whereas negative abnormal returns accrue to stockholders of firms announcing private placements. In addition, negative and statistically significant abnormal returns are associated with the announcement of private placements and straight debt issues used to retire bank debt.

One possible explanation for the difference in abnormal performance is that bank loans differ in some important feature such as maturity. Alternatively, bank loans may differ from other types of borrowing because of some special service provided by banks with their lending activity. An analysis of differences in the maturity, borrower default risk, borrower size, and purpose of the borrowing indicates that differences in abnormal performance are not due *solely* to differences in characteristics of the loan or characteristics of the borrowers. This result, together with the evidence concerning the incidence of reserve requirements, suggests that banks provide some special service not available from other lenders. Further research is needed to identify that unique service or unique attribute of bank loans, and to explain its relation to the market value of the firm.

References

Asquith, Paul and David Mullins, 1986, Equity issues and offering dilution, Journal of Financial Economics 15, 61–90.

Bernanke, Ben, 1983, Non-monetary effects of the financial crisis in the propagation of the great depression, American Economic Review 73, 257–276.

Black, Fisher, 1975, Bank fund management in an efficient market, Journal of Financial Economics 2, 323–339.

Brealey, Richard and Stewart Myers, 1984, Principles of corporate finance (McGraw Hill, New York).

Campbell, Tim and William Kracaw, 1980, Information production, market signaling, and the theory of intermediation, Journal of Finance 35, 863–882.

Dann, Larry and Wayne Mikkelson, 1984, Convertible debt issuance, capital structure change and financing-related information: Some new evidence, Journal of Financial Economics 13, 157–186.

Diamond, Douglas, 1984, Financial intermediation and delegated monitoring, Review of Economic Studies 51, 393–414.

Easterbrook, Frank, 1984, Two agency-cost explanations of dividends, American Economic Review 74, 650–660.

Eckbo, Espen, 1986, Valuation effects of corporate debt offerings, Journal of Financial Economics 15, 119–152.

Fama, Eugene, 1980, Banking and the theory of finance, Journal of Monetary Economics 10, 10–19.

Fama, Eugene, 1985, What's different about banks?, Journal of Monetary Economics 15, 29–36.

Flannery, Mark J., 1986, Asymmetric information and risky debt maturity choice, Journal of Finance 41, 19–38.

Ho, Thomas, S.Y. and Ronald Singer, 1982, Bond indenture provisions and the risk of corporate debt, Journal of Financial Economics 10, 375–406.

Kane, Edward and Burton Malkiel, 1965, Bank portfolio allocation, deposit variability and the availability doctrine, Quarterly Journal of Economics 79, 113–134.

Leland, Haynes and David Pyle, 1977, Information asymmetries, financial structure and financial intermediaries, Journal of Finance 32, 371–387.

Masulis, Ronald and Ashok Korwar, 1986, Seasoned equity offerings: An empirical investigation, Journal of Financial Economics 15, 91–118.

Merton, Robert, 1974, On the pricing of corporate debt: The risk structure of interest rates, Journal of Finance 29, 449–465.

Mikkelson, Wayne and Megan Partch, 1986, Valuation effects of securities offerings and the issuance process, Journal of Financial Economics 15, 31–60.

Myers, Stewart and Nicholas Majluf, 1984, Corporate financing and investment decisions when firms have information that investors do not have, Journal of Financial Economics 13, 157–187.

Rozeff, Michael S., 1982, Growth, beta and agency costs as determinants of dividend payout ratios, Journal of Financial Research 5, 249–259.

Smith, Clifford and Jerold Warner, 1979, On financial contracting: An analysis of bond covenants, Journal of Financial Economics 7, 111–161.

Spong, Kenneth, 1985, Banking regulation: Its purposes, implementation and effects (Federal Reserve Bank of Kansas City, KS).

Zinbarg, Edward, 1975, The private placement loan agreement, Financial Analyst Journal 31, 33–52.

INVESTMENT BANKING, REPUTATION, AND THE UNDERPRICING OF INITIAL PUBLIC OFFERINGS*

Randolph P. BEATTY

University of Pennsylvania, Philadelphia, PA 19104, USA

Jay R. RITTER

University of Michigan, Ann Arbor, MI 48109, USA

Received August 1984, final version received June 1985

This paper develops and tests two propositions. We demonstrate that there is a monotone relation between the (expected) underpricing of an initial public offering and the uncertainty of investors regarding its value. We also argue that the resulting underpricing equilibrium is enforced by investment bankers, who have reputation capital at stake. An investment banker who 'cheats' on this underpricing equilibrium will lose either potential investors (if it doesn't underprice enough) or issuers (if it underprices too much), and thus forfeit the value of its reputation capital. Empirical evidence supports our propositions.

1. Introduction

Ibbotson (1975) and Ritter (1984), among others, provide convincing evidence that initial public offerings are, on average, underpriced. In this paper, we argue that there is an equilibrium relation between the expected underpricing of an initial public offering and the ex ante uncertainty about its value. We also argue that this underpricing equilibrium is enforced by the investment banking industry. Furthermore, we present empirical evidence supporting our propositions.

Our results are crucially dependent upon the fact that, while many initial public offerings shoot up in price, many other issues decline in price once they start trading. Consequently, even though on average initial public offerings are underpriced, an investor submitting a purchase order cannot be certain about an offering's value once it starts publicly trading. We call this uncertainty

*We wish to acknowledge useful discussions with Sanjai Bhagat, Harry DeAngelo, John Finnerty, Robert Heinkel, Kevin Rock and Robert Verrecchia, and with seminar participants at the University of Pennsylvania, Columbia, Berkeley, UCLA and the University of Rochester MERC Conference on Investment Banking and the Capital Acquisition Process. Detailed comments were also received from the editors of this journal, John Long and Cliff Smith. An earlier version of this paper was presented at the June 1984 Western Finance Association meetings. The data on initial public offerings have been generously made available by Howard and Co.

Journal of Financial Economics 15 (1986) 213–232. © North-Holland Publishing Company.

about the value per share 'ex ante uncertainty'. We argue that the greater is the ex ante uncertainty, the greater is the (expected) underpricing.

We also consider how this underpricing equilibrium is enforced. We argue that an issuing firm, which will go public only once, cannot make a credible commitment by itself that the offering price is below the expected market price once it starts trading.[1] Instead, an issuing firm *must* hire an investment banker to take the firm public.[2] An investment banker is in a position to enforce the underpricing equilibrium because it will be involved in many initial public offerings over time. We argue that any investment banker who 'cheats' on the underpricing equilibrium by persistently underpricing either by too little or by too much, will be penalized by the marketplace.

The structure of this paper is as follows. In section 2, we develop the relation between ex ante uncertainty and expected initial return. In section 3, we address the issue of how this underpricing equilibrium is maintained. Section 4 describes the data used in our empirical tests. In section 5, we present the empirical evidence and interpret our results. Section 6 consists of a summary and concluding remarks. We also include an appendix providing a formal model in which our underpricing result is demonstrated.

2. The relation between ex ante uncertainty and expected initial return

Numerous studies have found that, on average, initial public offerings are underpriced. Ritter (1984), for instance, reports that for the approximately 5000 firms that went public during 1960–82 in the U.S., the average initial public offering was trading at a price 18.8 percent higher than its offering price shortly after public trading started.[3] The magnitude of this underpricing is

---

[1] The reason that a single issuing firm cannot, for example, post a bond to guarantee that there is a positive expected initial return, is that it is never observable. All that is observable is the realized initial return, which has two components – an expected initial return plus an 'error' term.

[2] There are other reasons for hiring an investment banker aside from our argument. Investment bankers have a comparative advantage at distributing securities, for example. Furthermore, given the public good nature of information, potential investors may demand that the issuing firm hire reputable certifiers of information, i.e., a public accounting firm and an investment banker, so that individual investors do not have to incur costs that are simultaneously being incurred by other potential investors. We do not address these other reasons.

[3] The 18.8 percent average price appreciation was computed using two slightly different methodologies. For 1960–76, the return period over which this was measured is from the offering date to the end of the calendar month of offering, and this return is computed by subtracting the return on the market from the raw return over the period, which varies from 1 to 31 days in length. The data from 1960–70 are from Ibbotson and Jaffe (1975). For 1977–82, the return period is from the offering date to the first recorded closing bid price, which is usually on the same day as the offering. These 1977–82 returns are not adjusted for market movements. For the 1960–76 period, there are many missing observations (approximately 8 percent of all initial public offerings, usually smaller offerings, are omitted). For 1977–82, there are no omissions. The differences in return calculations, and the difference in the missing observation rates, reflect the improved quality of price data from the over-the-counter market over time. For further discussion of the 18.8 percent figure, see Ritter (1984), pp. 216–218.

substantially greater than that found for equity issues of firms that are already public, as documented by Smith (1977).

This persistent underpricing does not imply that an investor can expect to realize excess returns, however, due to institutional features of the market. The most salient feature of the initial public offering market is that, once the issuing firm and its managing underwriter (we use the terms underwriter and investment banker interchangeably) set an offering price, any excess demand for the issue creates a situation of quantity rationing, rather than further adjustment of the offering price. The majority of initial public offerings are subject to this quantity rationing. If this rationing was random across issues, it would merely mean that, for a given investor, the investment on which these high average initial returns was being earned was smaller than desired. The extent of rationing, however, is not random across issues.[4]

While on average initial public offerings have positive initial returns, a large fraction of them have price declines. The offerings that shoot up in price are much more commonly oversubscribed than those that decline in price. Consequently, an investor submitting purchase orders for all issues will find that one is allocated shares in the offerings that go up less frequently than in the offerings that decline in price. This creates a situation where the average initial return conditional upon receiving shares is lower than the average initial return conditional upon submitting a purchase order. In other words, an investor faces a 'winner's curse': if one is allocated the requested number of shares, one can expect that the initial return will be less than average.

If, on average, initial public offerings are underpriced, somebody must be realizing excess returns, even if a representative investor isn't. Since only some offerings go up in price, a potential investor has an incentive to incur costs doing security analysis to discern which issues are likely to appreciate in price. In equilibrium, the investors incurring these costs will earn sufficient profits to cover their costs. But this is what creates the winner's curse problem for the investors who are attempting to free ride. It is these free riders who are what we term representative investors. [In the appendix, following Rock (1982, 1986), we term investors who choose to incur information acquisition costs informed investors, and those who don't, uninformed investors. The uninformed investors are the free riders, the representative investors.]

Faced with this winner's curse problem, a representative investor will only submit purchase orders if, on average, initial public offerings are underpriced. The magnitude of the difference between the conditional returns, and thus the degree of underpricing, is directly related to the ex ante uncertainty about the value of an issue. This is because, as the ex ante uncertainty increases, the

---

[4] The extent of the rationing can be severe. The personal records of a major investor in initial public offerings which we were allowed to confidentially inspect disclosed that he was allocated less than 5 percent of the requested shares in many offerings.

winner's curse problem intensifies. Roughly speaking, there is more to lose as ex ante uncertainty increases. Consequently, in order to be willing to submit a purchase order for shares in an offering with greater ex ante uncertainty, a representative investor will demand that more money be 'left on the table', in an expected value sense, via underpricing. This argument leads to our first proposition:

Proposition 1. The greater is the ex ante uncertainty about the value of an issue, the greater is the expected underpricing.

In the appendix, we formally prove Proposition 1 using Rock's (1982, 1986) model of the underpricing of initial public offerings.

It should be emphasized that the ex ante uncertainty which leads to the underpricing does not correspond to the CAPM concept of systematic risk. A representative investor who diversifies by submitting purchase orders for many initial public offerings in the face of the winner's curse problem merely guarantees that the realized average initial return will be less than the unconditional average initial return on the issues for which purchase orders were submitted.

3. What mechanism enforces the underpricing equilibrium?

In the previous section, we argued that the expected underpricing of an initial public offering increased as ex ante uncertainty increased. While this is an intuitively appealing result, a question concerning how this equilibrium is enforced naturally arises. Why doesn't an issuing firm 'cheat' and set too high an offering price? How is it that, on average, a representative investor is compensated for the winner's curse risk that one faces?

If investors were not able to somehow be assured that an issuing firm was leaving money on the table, in an expected value sense, the initial public offering market might indeed by subject to a 'lemons' problem [see Akerlof (1970)]. This is because each issuing firm, which will go public only once, has no incentive to leave money on the table. However, if there is an intermediary with an incentive to appropriately price issues, then it is possible to overcome this potential problem. In the market for initial public offerings, this intermediary is the managing underwriter for an issue. This role for investment bankers is possible because an investment banking firm underwrites many offerings over time. Because of the repeat business with potential purchasers, an investment banker can develop a reputation and earn a return on this reputation.[5]

---

[5] See Allen (1984), Klein and Leffler (1981) or Rogerson (1983) for models where there is quality variation. A closely related model is Telser's (1980) theory of self-enforcing agreements. In the context of Telser's model, the two parties voluntarily contracting are a representative investor and an investment banker. Gilson and Kraakman (1984, pp. 613–621) discuss the importance of investment bankers' reputations.

For an investment banker to find that it is in its interest to enforce the underpricing equilibrium when setting an offering price, there are three necessary conditions. The first condition is that the investment banker is uncertain what the market price of the stock once it starts trading will be, for otherwise the underwriter could perfectly price each and every issue, and there would be no winner's curse problem facing investors.[6] The second condition is that the investment banker has non-salvagable reputation capital at stake, on which it can earn a return. The third condition is that the ability to earn a return on this non-salvagable reputation capital drops if the underwriter 'cheats' by underpricing too much or too little.

The first necessary condition is specific to the underpricing equilibrium in the market for initial public offerings. The other two necessary conditions are the standard conditions in the recent literature on reputation and product quality. They can be summarized by the statement that the net present value of future quasirents that a reputable investment banker can expect to earn exceeds the short-run gain from opportunistic behavior. This willingness to not behave opportunistically is what is meant, we feel, by having a good reputation. An investment banker will find that it is not in its interest to behave opportunistically if it has a stock of reputation capital ('goodwill') built up, on which it is earning a return in the form of, for example, having lower distribution costs, or being able to charge higher underwriting fees.[7]

This argument produces our second proposition. If the underpricing equilibrium is enforced by investment bankers with reputation capital at stake, any investment banking firm that cheats must lose customers, for otherwise there would be no incentive not to cheat. If, on average, an investment banker does not underprice its offerings enough, the average initial return will be too low, and investors subject to the winner's curse problem will cease doing business with this underwriter. On the other hand, if an investment banker underprices its offerings too much, so that the average initial return is too high, potential issuers will cease using this underwriter. Whether or not an underwriter will lose its entire business or not depends upon the 'quality' of information – i.e., whether or not potential clients can discern whether mispricing is systematic or due to random events in a small sample. [See Rogerson (1983) for an elucidation of this point.] Since underwriters that underprice either too much or too little should lose business, we have a testable implication:

Proposition 2.   Underwriters whose offerings have average initial returns that are not commensurate with their ex ante uncertainty lose subsequent market share.

---

[6] While underwriters may have a relatively good idea of the state of demand for an issue by the time they set an offering price, they aren't able to forecast demand perfectly. It is not unusual to see an underwriter misestimate the aftermarket price by 20 percent or more.

[7] A reputable investment banker can get a higher offering price for an issue, so that a proportional fee schedule will result in a higher total commission for the underwriter. Firm-specific capital discourages opportunistic behavior.

4. Data

In section 2, we derived a proposition relating the degree of expected underpricing of an initial public offering to the ex ante uncertainty of the issue. In section 3, we argued that underwriters who do not enforce this underpricing equilibrium should lose market share. This section provides a description of the proxies that we use for ex ante uncertainty, and defines market share. We also describe the sample with which we test our propositions.

Proposition 1 relates the distribution of initial returns to ex ante uncertainty.[8] The proxies that we use to test this proposition are (i) the log of one plus the number of uses of proceeds listed in the prospectus, and (ii) the inverse of the gross proceeds.

The content of the Uses of Proceeds section in a prospectus can range from no mention of specific uses to detailed cost allocations for the firm's expected production–investment decisions. We have compiled the number of specific uses for which a dollar amount is quantified in each prospectus, a number which varies from 0 (for several secondary offerings where the issuing firm receives none of the proceeds) to 32 among the firms going public.

The number of uses of proceeds listed is a proxy for ex ante uncertainty largely as a result of Securities and Exchange Commission (SEC) regulation. Firms appear to be reluctant to give highly detailed specifications of what they will do with their net proceeds for two reasons: increased exposure to legal liability, and disclosure of proprietary information to competitors. The SEC, however, requires more speculative issues to provide relatively detailed enumerations of the uses of proceeds, while not requiring more established issuers to be very explicit.[9] As a result of this regulation, issues for which there is

---

[8] Initial returns are defined as $(v_t - OP)/OP$, where OP is the offering price and v_t is the closing bid price on the first day of public trading. In some cases, the closing bid price on the first day of trading is not available. In these situations, the first recorded closing bid price has been used. The closing bid prices were taken from the *Daily Stock Price Record* for the firms listed on NASDAQ. For the 9.9 percent of firms not listed on the NASDAQ, the following data sources (in order of priority) were employed:

(1) *Going Public: The IPO Reporter*;
(2) *National Stock Summary*;
(3) lead underwriter;
(4) issuing firm's officer for stockholder relations.

These prices are generally within a few days of the offering date, so that market movements can be presumed to have had only a minor influence. None of our initial return calculations adjust for market movements. The average initial return was 14.1 percent for the second subperiod, while the average daily market return was less than 0.1 percent, as measured by the dividend-inclusive S&P 500 index. Consequently, adjustments for market movements in the initial return calculations would result in only minor changes.

[9] The SEC's Regulation S-K governs the required disclosures in the non-financial portions of the prospectus. The differential requirements are a result of de facto case precedents, rather than explicit regulations. As Schneider, Manko and Kant (1983, pp. 10–11) state: 'In the course of administration over the years, the Commission has given specific content to the general disclosure requirements. It often requires disclosures on a number of points within the scope of the [registration] form but not explicitly covered by the form itself.'

greater ex ante uncertainty tend to have a greater number of the uses of proceeds listed.

Our second proxy for ex ante uncertainty is the inverse of the gross proceeds raised in an offering. This captures the empirical regularity that smaller offerings are more speculative, on average, than larger offerings.[10] With the range of gross proceeds being $100,000 to $109,854,000, expressed in terms of 1982 purchasing power, the reciprocal has a range of 0.0000000091 to 0.00001.

To test our propositions, we use a data set of all firms that conducted SEC-registered initial public offerings of common stock during 1977–82, a total of 1028 firms.[11] We split this sample into two approximately equal-sized subperiods for our tests. The first subperiod includes the 483 firms that went public between 1977 and the first quarter of 1981. The second subperiod includes the 545 firms that went public between the second quarter of 1981 and 1982. These subperiods have different lengths because the rate at which firms went public was much lower during the first 3 years of the sample than during the last 3 years.

We divide the sample into two subperiods for two reasons. The first reason is that Proposition 2 predicts changing market shares, so dividing the sample into subperiods is required in order to test this proposition. The second reason is that there was a pronounced 'industry effect' for natural resource issues from January 1980 to March 1981, as documented by Ritter (1984). Rather than resorting to ad hoc industry effect dummy variables, to test Proposition 1 we restrict ourselves to the 1981.II–1982 subperiod during which the relation between risk and initial return does not appear to be subject to industry effects.

In our tests of Proposition 2, we analyze whether there is a relation between mispricing by investment bankers and subsequent change in market share. For these tests, we define an investment banker's market share in a subperiod as the fraction of initial public offerings that the underwriter managed or co-managed, where co-managed offerings are counted in net terms, i.e., two offerings co-managed with another underwriter give the same market share as

---

[10] See Ritter (1985, table 6).

[11] Initial Public Offerings registered under Regulation A (common stock offerings below $1,500,000) are not included in this count. The primary data source is Howard and Co.'s *Going Public: The IPO Reporter*. In addition to the 1028 initial public offerings in the 1977–82 period, *Going Public* lists 47 other offerings that we exclude due to one of four special features. These features are discussed in Ritter (1984, pp. 216–217, footnote 2). Of relevance to this paper is that of the 47 excluded, 36 were removed due to not using an underwriter. Firms not using an underwriter fall into two categories: bank stocks and very small offerings. Both categories tend to be sold locally, and many fail to develop an active public market. Of the non-bank, non-underwritten offerings, the average gross proceeds is only $1.5 million, as contrasted with an average of $6.6 million for the 1028 firms in our sample (neither of these figures has been adjusted for price level changes). We view these non-underwritten offerings as equivalent in many respects to private placements. (In particular, frequently no active public market develops.) Consequently, we exclude these firms on the grounds that they represent something substantially different from going public. We do not view a non-underwritten offering as a viable alternative to the use of an investment banker for most firms going public. Of course, this is consistent with our theory in section 3.

Table 1

Standardized average residuals, average initial returns, and market shares for underwriters of four or more initial public offerings during first subperiod, 1977–1981.I.[a]

Rank	Underwriter	Standardized average residual	Percentage average initial return in subperiod 1	Percentage market shares		
				Subperiod 1	Subperiod 2	% change
1	Laidlaw, Adams & Peck	-7.147	-7.2	0.93	0.46	-50.8
2	*J. Daniel Bell & Co.	3.433	101.8	3.11	0.73	-76.4
3	B.J. Leonard & Co.	3.382	64.1	1.66	0.18	-88.9
4	Blinder, Robinson & Co.	3.301	90.5	6.21	1.65	-73.4
5	Hambrecht & Quist	2.877	19.1	3.73	2.42	-35.2
6	E.J. Pittock & Co.	2.870	75.3	2.48	0.92	-63.1
7	*OTC Net	2.581	135.4	2.48	1.83	-26.1
8	First Financial Securities	2.142	110.1	1.45	0.55	-62.0
9	*Culverwell & Co.	2.122	137.5	0.83	0.18	-77.8
10	Neideger/Tucker/Bruner	2.091	88.0	1.24	0.55	-55.7
11	Blyth, Eastman, Paine, Webber	2.079	27.5	1.31	0.46	-65.0
12	Alex. Brown & Sons	1.993	14.2	1.24	1.59	28.0
13	Engler & Budd	1.968	75.2	2.17	0.73	-66.2
14	Johnson-Bowles	1.870	104.2	0.72	0.18	-74.7
15	*American Western Securities	1.869	74.5	2.48	0.37	-85.2
16	Robertson, Colman, Stephens, & Woodman	1.816	14.5	1.14	1.07	-6.0
17	M. H. Meyerson & Co.	1.793	117.5	0.62	0.64	3.4
18	Rotan Mosle	1.677	20.6	1.76	1.01	-42.7
19	*John Muir & Co.	-1.610	5.6	4.76	2.20	-53.8
20	Fitzgerald, DeArman & Roberts	1.536	129.5	1.04	1.38	32.9
21	N. Donald & Co.	1.523	54.7	1.35	0.55	-59.1
22	D. H. Blair & Co.	1.433	26.4	1.86	3.58	92.0
23	First Colorado Investments & Securities	1.259	197.5	0.93	0.37	-60.6
24	Wall Street West	1.204	67.5	1.04	0.92	-11.4

25	Schneider, Bernet & Hickman	1.094	20.8	0.62	0.73	18.2
26	Bache, Halsey, Stuart, Shields	1.066	12.0	0.52	0.73	41.8
27	Bateman, Eichler, Hill, Richards	−1.055	3.5	1.14	1.01	−11.4
28	Lehman Brothers Kuhn Loeb	0.994	11.4	0.83	0.09	−88.9
29	Security Traders	0.986	31.3	0.83	0.18	−77.8
30	Shearson/American Express	0.983	11.4	1.62	1.41	−13.3
31	Montgomery Securities	0.982	17.0	0.55	1.22	121.6
32	Mountain-Pacific Investment Co.	0.895	40.8	0.83	0.18	−77.8
33	Goldman, Sachs & Co.	0.889	13.1	0.58	0.37	−37.4
34	Dean Witter Reynolds	0.811	13.1	0.55	0.61	10.8
35	Smith, Barney, Harris, Upham & Co.	−0.728	2.1	0.83	0.46	−44.6
36	Hanifen, Imhoff	0.530	24.3	2.38	0.55	−76.9
37	E. F. Hutton & Co.	−0.413	3.5	1.17	1.59	35.5
38	Jay W. Kaufman & Co.	0.464	27.5	0.83	0.64	−22.4
39	Sherwood Securities	0.448	22.2	0.52	0.73	41.8
40	L. F. Rothschild, Unterberg, Towbin	0.334	7.1	2.42	2.60	7.6
41	Kidder, Peabody & Co.	0.327	6.3	1.14	0.64	−43.6
42	Merrill Lynch White Weld	0.304	6.2	0.83	1.16	40.3
43	Rauscher, Pierce, Refsnes	−0.284	5.2	0.45	0.55	22.7
44	Securities Clearing of Colorado	0.278	21.3	1.04	1.01	−2.5
45	*M. S. Wien & Co.	0.256	16.6	1.66	0.37	−77.8
46	Alstead, Strangis & Dempsey	0.211	17.1	1.14	0.73	−35.5
47	Bond, Richman & Co.	0.167	17.7	0.93	0.18	−80.3
48	Rooney, Pace	−0.141	11.2	2.90	2.84	−1.9
49	Moseley, Hallgarten, Estabrook & Weeden	−0.051	7.5	0.93	0.37	−60.6

[a] The first subperiod is 1977–1982.I; the second subperiod is 1981.II–1982. Percentage market shares are calculated as the net number of offerings managed or co-managed divided by the total number of initial public offerings in a subperiod. The underwriters with asterisks ceased operations during the second subperiod. The standardized average residual is defined as $\bar{r}_i \div (\sigma_i \div \sqrt{N_i})$, where $\bar{r}_i$ is the investment banker's mean residual from the table 2 equation for predicting initial returns, and $(\sigma_i \div \sqrt{N_i})$ is the standard deviation of this mean.

one solely-managed offering. Approximately one quarter of all offerings are co-managed, and three quarters are solely managed. (We have also duplicated our tests using a definition of market share where offerings are weighted by the gross proceeds involved. The qualitative results are similar to those that we report in the next section.) In table 1, we provide data on the average initial returns and market shares for 49 major underwriters of initial public offerings.

5. Empirical evidence and interpretation of the results

To test whether there is a positive relation between initial return and ex ante uncertainty, as predicted by Proposition 1, we regress initial returns on two proxies for ex ante uncertainty, using the 545 firms in the second subperiod. We use weighted least squares (WLS) because of the heteroscedasticity that is present in an ordinary least squares regression. This heteroscedasticity should be present, since higher ex ante uncertainty should be reflected in a greater dispersion of initial returns. To get efficient parameter estimates in our empirical work, however, homoscedastic disturbance terms are desired.[12] Consequently, we weight our regression by a factor which is proportional to the precision of the disturbance terms. In particular, we multiply both left-hand and right-hand side variables by log[1000 + sales], where sales is the annual revenues of the issuing firm in the 12 months prior to going public, expressed in terms of 1982 purchasing power. Since we are multiplying by this weight, issuing firms with no operating histories are given less weight in the regressions than more established firms for which the ex ante uncertainty is likely to be less. With the range of sales being 0 to $867,806,000, the range of the weighting factor is from 6.91 to 20.58.

In table 2, we report the results of a WLS regression using initial returns as the dependent variable. As explanatory variables, we use the log of one plus the number of uses of proceeds, and the reciprocal of the gross proceeds expressed in terms of 1982 purchasing power.[13] The positive coefficients on

---

[12] Our results are nearly identical using ordinary least squares rather than weighted least squares. Furthermore, the WLS results are robust to a variety of weighting factors.

[13] The regression results that we report in table 2 have been selected from a series of unreported regressions undertaken in preliminary work. This selection process makes interpretation of the *t*-statistics difficult. During our preliminary work, we ran a regression including, as explanatory variables, log(1 + number of uses of proceeds), the reciprocal of gross proceeds, log(1 + age), log(1 + sales) and log(1 + number of risk factors). The *F*-statistic on this regression is 13.83, which is significant at the 0.001 α-level with (5,539) degrees of freedom. The existence of multicollinearity in the independent variables of this all-inclusive regression led to the selection of our parsimonious model. In addition, we considered the daily aftermarket standard deviation as a proxy for ex ante uncertainty. The reason that we don't use the daily aftermarket standard deviation in our reported tests, in spite of its obvious appeal as a proxy for ex ante uncertainty, is that it is unavailable for the 9.9 percent of the firms that weren't listed on NASDAQ. These omitted firms are primarily 'penny stocks'. Excluding these firms makes it difficult to come up with an absolute standardized average residual for the underwriters who specialized in penny stocks. Consequently, it is difficult to test our hypothesis regarding changing market shares.

Table 2

Weighted least squares regression results with initial return as the
dependent variable.[a]

Constant	Log(1 + number of uses of proceeds)	Reciprocal of gross proceeds	R^2
− 0.0268	0.0691	83,578	0.07
(0.0360)	(0.0209)	(18,561)	

[a] Standard errors in parentheses. The sample is comprised of
all 545 underwritten S.E.C.-registered initial public offerings
from April 1981 to December 1982. The weighting factor is log
[1000 + sales], where sales is the most recent 12-month revenues
for the issuing firm expressed in terms of 1982 purchasing power.
The means of the variables are: 13.25 for the weighting factor,
1.74 for the log of one plus the number of uses of proceeds and
0.000000423 for the reciprocal of gross proceeds. Gross proceeds
is measured in dollars of 1982 purchasing power. The average
initial return is 0.141, or 14.1 percent.

these variables indicate that investors interpret these measures as positively
correlated with ex ante uncertainty. The coefficient of 83,578 on the inverse of
gross proceeds indicates that smaller offerings, ceteris paribus, have substantially higher average initial returns.

We interpret the results in table 2 as showing that, as Proposition 1 states,
there is a positive relation between ex ante uncertainty and expected underpricing.[14]

It is worth noting that the R^2 is quite low at 0.07. This is as it should be. If
the R^2 was high, it would imply that the *actual* initial return on an offering is
predictable. The theory states that there is a positive relation between ex ante
uncertainty and *expected* initial return. The reason for this positive relation is
that it is difficult for investors to predict the actual initial return on a high-risk
issue, giving rise to the winner's curse problem, even though the average initial
return in a large sample can be predicted with reasonable accuracy. Consequently, the low R^2 is consistent with Proposition 1.

To test Proposition 2, we have computed the market shares of all underwriters of four or more initial public offerings during the first subperiod.[15]
These underwriters are listed in table 1. In fig. 1, we graph the average initial

[14] We are, of course, testing a joint hypothesis. The joint hypothesis is that there is a positive
relation between ex ante uncertainty and average initial returns, *and* that we have adequate
proxies for ex ante uncertainty.

[15] We restrict our analysis to underwriters of 4 or more offerings because, given the variation in
initial returns, it is difficult to view the fringe underwriters of 3 or fewer offerings as having much
of a track record to analyze. The qualitative conclusions do not change if the cutoff is at 3 or 5
instead of 4.

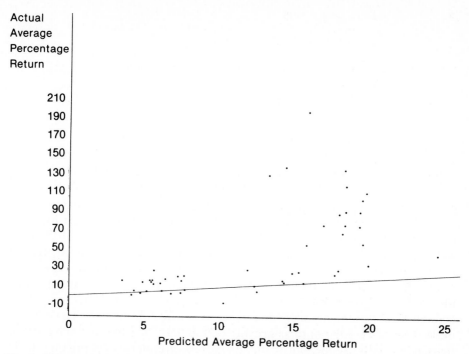

Fig. 1. Relation between the actual average percentage initial return (vertical axis) and the predicted average percentage initial return (horizontal axis) for the 49 underwriters of 4 or more issues during 1977–1981.I. Predicted average initial returns are based upon regression results reported in table 2. The line drawn has a slope of one and an intercept of zero.

return and average predicted initial return during the first subperiod for each of the 49 investment bankers that meet this criterion. The predicted initial returns are computed using the table 2 regression, which was estimated over the second subperiod. Note that the predicted average initial returns show a rather wide range, which is due to the tendency of underwriters to specialize in offerings of a given 'quality class'.[16] Also plotted is a line with a slope of one along which all 49 points would lie if every investment banking firm enforced the underpricing equilibrium with no error.

To analyze the relation between market share changes and mispricing, we define the 'absolute standardized average residual' as follows:

For each firm j taken public by underwriter i, we first compute a predicted initial return $E(p_{ij})$ based upon the regression coefficients reported in table 2. We subtract this predicted initial return from the actual initial return, p_{ij}, to

---

[16] The specialization of underwriters by quality of offering is a very strong tendency. Titman and Trueman (1985) present a model predicting this. Ritter (1985) finds that underwriters also tend to specialize by contract, where the choices are between firm commitment and best efforts contracts.

get the residual for each issue:

$$r_{ij} = p_{ij} - E(p_{ij}).$$

For each underwriter, we then compute the average residual

$$\bar{r}_i = \frac{1}{N_i} \sum_{j=1}^{N_i} r_{ij},$$

where N_i is the number of offerings taken public by underwriter i.

To discern whether or not, in a statistically significant sense, an underwriter is mispricing its issues, we divide $\bar{r}_i$ by $\sigma_i / \sqrt{N_i}$, the standard deviation of the mean initial return, to get our standardized average residual. Dividing by $\sigma_i / \sqrt{N_i}$, where σ_i is the standard deviation of the residuals of underwriter i, controls for the fact that, as an underwriter's track record becomes longer, a potential issuer or investor is able to discern whether or not it is 'off the line', with reference to fig. 1, more clearly. The absolute standardized average residual is the absolute value of the standardized average residual.

In table 1, we have ranked underwriters in terms of their absolute standardized average residuals. The 24 underwriters with the largest absolute standardized average residuals we refer to as pricing 'off the line'. The other 25 underwriters are referred to as pricing 'on the line'. In table 3a, we report the market shares by subperiod for the categories of underwriters pricing off the line and on the line. For the 24 underwriters off the line, their market share fell from 46.6 percent in the first subperiod to 24.5 percent in the second subperiod, a 47 percent decrease. The 25 firms pricing on the line saw their market share fall by only 23 percent. (Both of these groups had their market shares eroded by increased competition during the second subperiod, primarily from 'major bracket' investment banking firms that previously had not had a major presence in the initial public offering market.)

Also reported in table 3a is the fact that 5 out of the 24 underwriters pricing off the line in the first subperiod ceased operations during the second subperiod. (They went out of business – they didn't merge.) This contrasts with only 1 out of 25 among those underwriters pricing on the line. A formal statistical test of the proposition that the probability of ceasing operations is independent of the categorization of an underwriter involves the hypergeometric distribution, which assumes 'sampling without replacement'.[17] For 6 out of

---

[17]The hypergeometric distribution, which is described in most introductory mathematical statistics and probability textbooks, gives

$$\text{prob}(x) = \binom{K}{x}\binom{M-K}{n-x} \Big/ \binom{M}{n},$$

where x is the number of underwriters ceasing operations in a sample of size n (24), M is the number of underwriters (49), and K is the number of underwriters ceasing operations in the population (6). Given these parameters, the probability that $x \geq 5$ is 0.0856.

Table 3a

Change in market share by underwriter category.[a]

Underwriter performance 1977–1981.I	Market share		Fraction ceasing operations during 1981.II–1982
	1977–1981.I	1981.II–1982	
24 underwriters 'off the line'	46.6%	24.5%	5/24
25 underwriters 'on the line'	27.2%	21.0%	1/25
All other underwriters	26.2%	54.5%	11/197

[a]Market share computed by allocating a fraction of one-half or one-third to each co-manager of an initial public offering if 2 or 3 underwriters co-managed an offering. Market share computations are based upon all 1028 firms going public during 1977–82 using an underwriter. Each of the 49 underwriters evaluated managed or co-managed at least 4 initial public offerings during the 1977–1981.I subperiod. They are listed in table 1. The 26.2% of offerings done by other underwriters (126.67 out of 483 offerings) in the first subperiod used 104 different underwriters. For the 54.5% of offerings done by other underwriters (297 out of 545 offerings) in the second subperiod, 161 different underwriters were used. For the 1977–82 period as a whole, 246 underwriters managed or co-managed at least one offering.

Table 3b

Ordinary least squares regression results with percentage change in market share as dependent variable.[a]

Constant	Absolute standardized average residual	R^2	N
−12.85 (10.54)	−10.83 (5.59)	0.07	49

[a]Standard errors in parentheses. The mean of the dependent variable is −28.4 percent, with a standard derivation of 49.3. Market shares calculated by dividing the net number of initial public offerings of underwriter i by the total number of offerings in each subperiod. Co-managed offerings counted as one-half or one-third. The mean of the explanatory variable is 1.42, with a standard deviation of 1.26. The absolute standardized average residual is defined as $|\bar{r}_i \div (\sigma_i \div \sqrt{N_i})|$, where $\bar{r}_i$ is the investment banker's mean residual from the table 2 equation for predicting initial returns, and $(\sigma_i \div \sqrt{N_i})$ is the standard deviation of this mean.

49 underwriters ceasing operations, the probability that, in a random sample of 24 underwriters, 5 or more went out of business in the second subperiod is 9 percent.

In table 3b instead of categorizing underwriters as to whether or not they are off the line, we regress the percentage change in market share on absolute standardized average residuals for the 49 underwriters of interest. The slope coefficient of -10.83 in this regression implies that as the value of the explanatory variable changes from one standard deviation below the mean to one standard deviation above, the expected market share drops by 27.3 percent, an economically meaningful change. With a t-statistic of 1.94 on the slope coefficient, the one-tailed p-value is 3 percent.

While these tests of Proposition 2 are not independent, we interpret all of these results as providing support for the proposition that the market does penalize underwriters who cheat on the underpricing equilibrium by underpricing too much or too little.

6. Summary and conclusions

In this paper we have argued that there is a positive relation between the ex ante uncertainty about an initial public offering's value and its expected initial return. Using two proxies for this uncertainty, we have provided empirical evidence in support of this proposition. An implication of this finding is that, if the level of ex ante uncertainty is endogenous, an issuing firm has an incentive to reduce this uncertainty by voluntarily disclosing information.

We have also argued that the mechanism by which this underpricing equilibrium is enforced is via the investment banking industry. In order for investment bankers to find it in their interest to maintain the underpricing equilibrium, three conditions are necessary. These are that (i) the underwriters are not perfect forecasters of the aftermarket price, (ii) each underwriter must have non-salvagable reputation capital at stake on which it is earning a return, and (iii) any underwriter who cheats by, on average, pricing 'off the line' must lose clients. We find that investment bankers pricing off the line in one subperiod do in fact lose market share in the subsequent subperiod, although the relation is a noisy one. We interpret these empirical findings as supporting our argument that investment bankers enforce the underpricing equilibrium.

Appendix: Underpricing in an asymmetric information model

This appendix provides a formal model of the underpricing of initial public offerings. It uses the asymmetric information model introduced by Rock (1982, 1986). In this model, an issuing firm is uncertain about its value per share. It must set an offering price, OP, however, and then solicit purchase orders from the public at this price. If the issue is oversubscribed, the shares are allocated in proportion to the excess demand. Investors are also uncertain about the value of a share, but for a cost c, an investor can become informed about the price per share, v, that will prevail once the stock starts trading. Investors who do not incur this cost are termed uninformed investors, and their knowledge about v is limited to knowing its probability density function, denoted by $f(v)$. Issuing firms and their investment bankers are assumed to be among the uninformed. (This last assumption's purpose is to make the issuing parties uncertain about the true value per share. Otherwise, there would be no need to underprice.)

Informed investors, each of whom has investable wealth of $W - c$, will submit purchase orders only if the offering is underpriced ($v > OP$). This behavior by informed investors creates an adverse selection problem for uninformed investors. For underpriced issues ($v > OP$), both informed and uninformed investors will submit purchase orders, and uninformed investors will be allocated only some of the shares that trade at a premium in the aftermarket. For overpriced issues ($v < OP$), however, only uninformed investors submit purchase orders, so the uninformed are allocated 100 percent of all the issues that trade at a discount in the aftermarket. Consequently, if an uninformed investor is allocated shares in an initial public offering, there is a greater than usual chance that the issue will start trading at a discount in the aftermarket. In other words, for an uninformed investor, the expected return conditional upon being allocated shares is less than the expected return conditional upon submitting a purchase order. But an uninformed investor will participate in the market only if the expected return conditional upon being allocated shares is non-negative. This can only happen if, on average, issuers underprice their shares. The owners of a firm going public, who typically have a large proportion of their wealth invested in the firm, would be willing to pay this price if they are sufficiently risk-averse.

With the number of investors who choose to become informed endogenous [as in Rock (1982, ch. II)], the equilibrium conditions converge to two equations. These two conditions are (i) zero expected profits for informed investors and (ii) zero expected profits for uninformed investors. The first condition can be expressed as

$$N \cdot c = \alpha \int_{OP}^{\infty} n(v - OP) f(v) \, dv, \tag{1}$$

where N is the number of informed investors, c is the cost per investor of becoming informed, α is the fraction of shares allocated to informed investors when an offering is underpriced, OP is the offering price, n is the number of shares, and v is the after-market price. The left-hand side is the aggregate cost of becoming informed. The right-hand side is the proportion of each underpriced issue that will be allocated to informed investors, multiplied by the gross profits on underpriced issues. The product of these gives the gross profits earned by informed investors.

The second equilibrium condition, zero expected profits for the uninformed, occurs when the aggregate losses on overpriced issues (the uninformed get all of the losing issues) equal the uninformed's share of the gross profits on underpriced issues:

$$\int_0^{OP} n(OP - v) f(v) \, dv = (1 - \alpha) \int_{OP}^{\infty} n(v - OP) f(v) \, dv. \tag{2}$$

Eqs. (1) and (2) hold for any probability density function for the aftermarket price. Between them, they imply that, due to the winner's curse problem facing uninformed investors, all of the profits accruing to investors due to underpricing will be received by informed investors. Investors seeking these profits, however, will incur sufficient costs so that the aggregate costs of becoming informed equal the amount of money 'left on the table':

$$N \cdot c = \int_0^{\infty} n(v - OP) f(v) \, dv = n[\mathrm{E}(v) - OP]. \tag{3}$$

In eq. (3), the number of investors who choose to become informed, N, determines the required amount of underpricing, $\mathrm{E}(v) - OP$. The decision to become informed is analogous to the decision to buy a call option giving the right to buy shares if $v > OP$. Just as with standard option pricing analysis, this option is worth more, ceteris paribus, the greater is the dispersion of v, which for new issues corresponds to greater ex ante uncertainty. Since the price of the option is the fixed cost c, the greater is the ex ante uncertainty, the greater is the number of investors who choose to become informed. This is why there is a positive relation between ex ante uncertainty and the degree of underpricing of initial public offerings.

We now formally demonstrate, under fairly restrictive conditions, our underpricing result. As the above argument indicates, however, we believe the result is much more general. In this demonstration, let the fraction of underpriced issues allocated to informed investors, α, be given by

$$\alpha = \frac{N(W - c)}{N(W - c) + OP \cdot n}, \tag{4}$$

where $(W - c)$ is the investment per informed investor (no borrowing or short-selling is allowed). This expression assumes that aggregate uninformed demand is sufficient to fully subscribe an issue. Consequently, for underpriced issues, aggregate informed demand is given by $N(W - c)$ and aggregate uninformed demand is equal to $OP \cdot n$, resulting in eq. (4).

While eqs. (1), (2), and (3) hold for any probability density function for the aftermarket price, $f(v)$, comparative static results do not necessarily hold for any arbitrary probability density function (p.d.f.). Our results hold for p.d.f.'s of the increasing failure rate class, an example of which is the uniform distribution, which we use to generate comparative static results. Consequently, let $f(v) = 1/(b - a)$, on $[a, b]$, $b > a \geq 0$, where a replaces 0 and b replaces ∞ in the limits of integration in eqs. (1) and (2).

Performing the integration in eq. (1) using a uniform distribution, and solving for N/n, the number of informed investors per share, results in

$$\frac{N}{n} = \left(\frac{1}{b-a}\right)\left(\frac{1}{2c}\right)(OP - b)^2 - \frac{OP}{W - c}. \tag{1'}$$

Performing the integrations in eq. (2) results in

$$\frac{N}{n} = \frac{OP}{W - c}\left(\frac{OP - b}{OP - a}\right)^2 - \frac{OP}{W - c}. \tag{2'}$$

Eqs. (1') and (2') hold for parameter values of W, a, b, c and n such that the number of informed investors, N, is strictly positive. If this is not the case, there is no adverse selection against the uninformed. If there is no adverse selection, a pooling equilibrium would exist in which there is no underpricing.

In the two-equation system given by (1') and (2'), the endogenous variables are N, the number of informed investors, and OP, the optimal offering price. [In Rock (1982, ch. II) the number of informed investors, N, is endogenous. This is not the case with the analysis in Rock (1986).] Equating eqs. (1') and (2') results in a quadratic equation for the issuing firm's optimal offering price:

$$OP^2 - 2[a + (b - a)C]OP + a^2 = 0, \tag{5}$$

where $C \equiv c/(W - c)$. C is the cost of becoming informed as a fraction of the investable wealth of the informed. The quadratic equation (5) has roots of

$$OP_{1,2} = a + (b - a)C \pm \sqrt{2aC(b - a) + C^2(b - a)^2}. \tag{6}$$

Of the two roots, the $-\sqrt{\cdot}$ root is not economically meaningful, in that the offering price would be less than a, the lower limit of the p.d.f. for the aftermarket price. This would mean that there is no possibility of a loss for any investor submitting a purchase order. Thus, the (unique) offering price is given by the $+\sqrt{\cdot}$ root.

Before analyzing the effect of a decrease in the dispersion of possible aftermarket prices on the optimal OP, it will be useful to rewrite expression

(6), noting that

$$a = \frac{b+a}{2} - \frac{b-a}{2} \quad \text{where} \quad \frac{b+a}{2} = E(v).$$

The equilibrium offering price is

$$OP = E(v) + (C - \tfrac{1}{2})(b-a)$$

$$+ \sqrt{2E(v)C(b-a) - C(b-a)^2 + C^2(b-a)^2}. \qquad (7)$$

Note that C must be less than one-half, since OP is bounded by a below and $E(v)$ above.

We can now prove our fundamental underpricing proposition:

Proposition 1.   The greater is the ex ante uncertainty about the value of an issue, the greater is the expected underpricing.

Proof.   Holding $E(v)$ constant, we want to demonstrate that

$$\frac{\partial OP}{\partial(b-a)} < 0.$$

Differentiating eq. (7), we have

$$\frac{\partial OP}{\partial(b-a)} = C - \tfrac{1}{2} + \frac{CE(v) - C(b-a) + C^2(b-a)}{\sqrt{2E(v)C(b-a) - C(b-a)^2 + C^2(b-a)^2}}. \qquad (8)$$

Since $a < OP < E(v)$, from eq. (7) we know that

$$0 > (C - \tfrac{1}{2})(b-a) + \sqrt{2E(v)C(b-a) - C(b-a)^2 + C^2(b-a)^2},$$

which can be rewritten as

$$0 > (C - \tfrac{1}{2})(b-a) + \frac{2E(v)C(b-a) - C(b-a)^2 + C^2(b-a)^2}{\sqrt{2E(v)C(b-a) - C(b-a)^2 + C^2(b-a)^2}}.$$

Cancelling the common $(b-a)$ term in the numerator, we have

$$0 > (C - \tfrac{1}{2}) + \frac{2E(v)C - C(b-a) + C^2(b-a)}{\sqrt{2E(v)C(b-a) - C(b-a)^2 + C^2(b-a)^2}}. \qquad (9)$$

The right-hand side of eq. (9) is identical to eq. (8), except for the $2E(v)C$ term. Since eq. (9) is negative, eq. (8) must be negative, since $2E(v)C > E(v)C$. This completes the proof.

This model is based upon the institutional characteristics of firm commitment offerings. Firm commitment offerings were used to raise 87% of the gross proceeds of initial public offerings in the U.S. during the 1977–82 period that we use in our empirical tests.

References

Akerlof, G.A., 1970, The market for 'lemons': Quality uncertainty and the market mechanism, Quarterly Journal of Economics 84, 488–500.

Allen, F., 1984, Reputation and product quality, Rand Journal of Economics 15, 311–327.

Gilson, R.J. and R. Kraakman, 1984, The mechanisms of market efficiency, Virginia Law Review 70, 549–644.

Going Public: The IPO Reporter, 1977–82, Published weekly (Howard & Co., Philadelphia, PA).

Ibbotson, R.G., 1975, Price performance of common stock new issues, Journal of Financial Economics 3, 235–272.

Ibbotson, R.G. and J.J. Jaffe, 1975, 'Hot issue' markets, Journal of Finance 30, 1027–1042.

Klein, B. and K.B. Leffler, 1981, The role of market forces in assuring contractual performance, Journal of Political Economy 89, 615–641.

National Stock Summary, 1977–82 (National Quotation Bureau, New York).

Ritter, J.R., 1984, The 'hot issue' market of 1980, Journal of Business 57, 215–240.

Ritter, J.R., 1985, The choice between firm commitment and best efforts contracts, Unpublished working paper (University of Michigan, Ann Arbor, MI).

Rock, K., 1982, Why new issues are underpriced, Unpublished Ph.D. dissertation (University of Chicago, Chicago, IL).

Rock, K., 1986, Why new issues are underpriced, Journal of Financial Economics, this issue.

Rogerson, W.P., 1983, Reputation and product quality, Bell Journal of Economics 2, 508–516.

Schneider, C.W., J. Manko and R. Kant, 1983. Going public: Practice, procedure, and consequences (Packard Press, Philadelphia, PA).

Smith, C.W., 1977, Alternative methods for raising capital: Rights versus underwritten agreements, Journal of Financial Economics 5, 273–307.

Standard and Poor's, 1977–82, Daily stock price record for over-the-counter stocks (Standard and Poor's Corporation, New York).

Telser, L.G., 1980, A theory of self-enforcing agreements, Journal of Business 53, 27–44.

Titman, S. and B. Trueman, 1985, Information quality and the valuation of new issues, Unpublished working paper (University of California, Los Angeles, CA).

AN EMPIRICAL INVESTIGATION OF CALLS OF NON-CONVERTIBLE BONDS*

Joseph D. VU

University of Illinois, Chicago, IL 60680, USA

Received July 1984, final version received July 1985

This paper examines call behavior of corporate issuers of non-convertible bonds. Evidence from a sample of 102 calls indicates that the market value of the called bonds is usually below the call price at the time of the announcement. The stock price reactions to call announcements are positively related to the direction of the change in leverage. When the call relaxes restrictive covenants, the firm on average pays a larger premium to call debt. The premium is a minimum estimate of the potential opportunity costs of restrictive covenants.

1. Introduction

This study examines call behavior of corporate issuers of non-convertible bonds and the impact of calls on the market price of securities. Investigation of the security price changes on the announcement date provides insight into the motivations for financial managers to call bonds.

If managers' incentive is to maximize the current market value of a firm's common stock, the call policy should minimize the market value of a straight (non-convertible) bond. Therefore, in a perfect financial market a bond should be called if the market value of the bond exceeds the call price.

Rational investors take the call feature into account when they buy or sell straight bonds. If investors know that the firm will call the bond as soon as its price exceeds the call price, no investor is willing to pay more than the call price for the bond. As a result, the market price of the bond may reach the call price, but will not rise above it. This gives the following perfect market rule for calling straight bonds: Call the bond when, and only when, the market

*This paper is based in part on my Ph.D. dissertation at the University of Chicago. I would like to thank my committee – George Constantinides, Robert Hamada, Robert Holthausen, Richard Leftwich, Merton Miller, and especially my chairman, Eugene Fama – for their help and encouragement. I have also benefited from the suggestions of Jonathan Ingersoll, Donald Keim, Wayne Mikkelson (the referee for the Journal of Financial Economics), Harry Roberts, and the participants in the finance workshop at the University of Chicago. This research is partially supported by the Kemper Foundation and by the Loyola University of Chicago.

Journal of Financial Economics 16 (1986) 235–265. © North-Holland Publishing Company.

price reaches the effective call price (i.e., the stated call price plus accrued interest).[1]

One of the objectives of the study is to investigate if firms follow the perfect market rule in calling non-convertible bonds. If call policies deviate from the perfect market rule, then we want to know what factors explain the observed policies. To this end, the stock price behavior on the call announcement date is observed. With regard to the explanation for changes in stock price, four hypotheses are developed:

(1) Bond Refunding Hypothesis

This hypothesis states that the main reason for calling a bond is to reduce interest costs. Bond refunding can be viewed as an investment decision which requires a cash outlay followed by interest savings in future years. If the present value of the interest savings exceeds the cash outlay, the refunding is profitable to the firm.

(2) Leverage Hypothesis

(a) Potential tax effect: The leverage hypothesis claims that the main motive for calls is to change the capital structure of a firm. If there is a tax-subsidy connected with the deductibility of interest payments, the stock price reaction to call announcements should be in the same direction of the change in leverage.

(b) Information effect: The change in financial leverage associated with a call may convey information to investors about the future performance of the firm. Any change in stock price observed on the call announcement date may reflect the information content of the call.

(3) Wealth Transfer Hypothesis

Calling a bond when its market value is below the call price will benefit bondholders at the expense of stockholders. Thus, at the time the call is announced, the wealth transfer hypothesis predicts a decrease in stock price and an increase in the price of the called bond.

(4) Restrictive Covenant Hypothesis

This hypothesis claims that the main reason for calling a bond is to eliminate a restrictive covenant not contained in the indentures of other debt issues of the firm.

Because these hypotheses are not mutually exclusive, it is difficult to separate any one from the others. It could be that each works well for only a subset of the sample, and none can completely explain the observed call behavior.

---

[1] The perfect market rule for calling straight bonds is identical to the optimal call policy for convertible bonds, discussed by Brennan and Schwartz (1977) and Ingersoll (1977). The argument assumes that both investors and the firm act rationally, and that the bond is correctly priced in a perfect capital market.

The paper is organized in the following format. Section 2 describes the data. In section 3, the observed call behavior of a sample of NYSE and AMEX firms is investigated and compared with the perfect market rule. The main finding is that the market value of the called bonds is usually below the call price at the time of the announcement, but some firms call their non-convertible bonds long after the market value of the bond first exceeds the call price. Section 4 describes four hypotheses developed as possible explanations of the call behavior. Section 5 presents the empirical evidence on each hypothesis. The data suggest that there are several motives for calls and no single predominant one. Finally, section 6 gives the conclusions and summary.

2. Description of data

The empirical analysis of the paper is limited to cases in which an entire bond issue was called for redemption. Partial redemptions and open market repurchases are not investigated because their exact call or repurchase dates were usually not available. Moreover, most partial redemptions are used to satisfy sinking fund provisions, which have different economic consequences from a call that eliminates the entire bond.

Data on all non-convertible bond issues[2] of industrial, public utility, and transportation firms called for redemption during the period from October 1962 to April 1978 were collected from *Moody's Industrial Manual*, *Public Utility Manual*, and *Transportation Manual*, *Moody's Bond Survey*, and the *Standard & Poor's Corporation Bond Guide*. These publications report the redemption date and the outstanding face value of the called bonds, the size and the issue date of new bonds in the case of refunding (generally about one month before the redemption date), and the date new bonds are filed with the Securities and Exchange Commission. The call announcement date was found in the *Standard & Poor's Corporation Called Bond Record*, *The Wall Street Journal*, and *The Wall Street Journal Index*. The announcement date was double-checked with press releases and the notice of call given by the company whenever this information was available. In selecting the sample, two criteria were applied:

(1) The bond call had an identifiable announcement date with no other firm-specific event reported in the three days surrounding the announcement date.
(2) Daily stock price data were available on the Center for Research in Security Prices (CRSP) excess returns tapes at the University of Chicago.

Restricting the sample to common stock issues included in the CRSP daily excess returns file means that only firms listed on the New York or American

---

[2]AT&T bonds are excluded because most of the redemptions are done by AT&T's subsidiaries whose common stocks are not traded.

Stock Exchange were studied. Such a sample allows the investigation of the effect of calls on common stock returns around the announcement date. For the period from October 1962 through April 1978, there are 348 bond calls, most of which were made by firms with stock traded over-the-counter.

Using the two criteria described above, the sample size is reduced to 133 calls.

3. Observed call behavior of NYSE and AMEX firms

In a perfect capital market, the optimal policy is to call a non-convertible bond when its market value just reaches the call price.[3] Table 1 presents the observed call behavior of non-convertible-issuing firms from October 1962 to April 1978. To be included in table 1, the called bonds must have a market price available around the announcement date. Since some called bonds are privately placed and some are traded infrequently, the overall sample of 133 call events is reduced to 102. Column (1) lists the 102 called bonds chronologically according to the call announcement date in column (7).

Column (8) of table 1 shows the earliest month in which the market price of the bonds is equal to the effective call price. Had the firms followed the optimal timing of calls in a perfect financial market, they would have called the bonds at the time indicated in column (8). If the market price of the bond remains below the effective call price from the time of issue until the actual call announcement, a 'none' appears in column (8). The 'NA' notation is used when the bond had a call protection period in which the bond was non-callable or non-refundable.

Column (8) of table 1 shows that there is a disparity between the observed and the theoretically optimal timing of calls for 41 firms in the sample. These firms called their non-convertible bonds long after the market value of the bonds first exceeded the call price. Starting from the call announcement date, we go back to preceding months to identify the earliest month in which the bond price is equal to the call price. That month corresponds to the optimal timing of calls in a perfect financial market.

Column (9) of table 1 shows the percentage by which the bond price exceeds the call price immediately before the announcement date. Although the bond price may exceed the call price in the past, at the time of the call announcement, 75% of the bonds in the sample have a bond price below the call price. The percentage discount of market value to call price range from 6.1% to -50.6%. with a mean -4.7%, and a median of -1.1%. Fifteen percent of the firms have discounts in excess of ten percent. These large discounts tend to cluster in the period 1967–69 and 1971–75. Most of the firms with large

---

[3] See Brennan and Schwartz (1977), Ingersoll (1977), and Constantinides and Grundy (1983) for a detailed description of the optimal call policy.

percentage discounts are small companies measured by the market value of stock. Moreover, they usually do not issue new debt, causing their financial leverage to decrease.

Column (10) of table 1 shows the dollar amount of discount of market value to call price, which has a range from $1,110,000 to $-$5,420,200. The mean of the distribution is $-$315,000, indicating that on average, the firms pay bondholders $315,000 for the privilege of calling bonds before maturity. The median dollar discount is $-$154,000.

To see how stockholders are affected potentially by the payment to bondholders, column (11) of table 1 shows the dollar amount of discount of market value to call price as a percentage of the common stock market value immediately before the call announcement date. The results indicate that the potential effect on stockholders' wealth is small, with a mean of only -0.3% and a smallest value of -4.4%.

Column (12) of table 1 shows the ratio of the maximum value of the tax subsidy to the total market value of the stock. This ratio measures the largest potential tax effect on stock price, and is computed as $(B' - B + \Delta d)\,\tau/S$. B' is the face value of the new bond in refunding cases, B is the market value of the called bond, τ is the statutory marginal tax rate of the firm, and Δd is the change in short-term debt associated with the bond call. Δd is a positive number when a firm refinances a bond using bank loans or short-term credits. The results indicate that the maximum potential tax effect is substantial for some individual firms, but small on average.

To see if some firms delay calling their bonds, additional data are collected and reported in table 2 for 41 firms that did not call when the bond price first reached the call price. These firms are identified by comparing columns (7) and (8) in table 1. For each firm, the monthly bond prices are collected from the earliest month in which the bond price is equal to the call price until twelve months later. These bond prices are taken from the *Moody's Bond Record* and the *Standard and Poor's Bond Guide*. About half of the bond prices represent a sales price; the remaining are the average of the bid and ask prices. In thirteen cases, the bonds are called within a year from the time the bond price first equals or exceeds the call price. Consequently, for these bonds, the time series of bond prices is less than twelve months.

Column (4) and table 2 shows the number of months in which the market value of the bond is greater than or equal to the call price. During the twelve-month period, market prices of 85% of the bonds exceed the call price for at least four months.

Column (5) of table 2 shows the number of *consecutive* months in which the bond price is greater than or equal to the call price. This is a more rigid test because it eliminates the effect of any temporary jump in bond price. During the twelve-month period, market prices of 63% of the bonds exceed the call price for at least four consecutive months.

Table 1

Sample of 102 called bonds whose market values are available around the announcement date, 1962–1978.

Non-convertible bond (1)	Maturity	Coupon rate (%) (2)	Call price (3)	Amount retired (in millions) (4)	Amount retired ÷ amount issued (5)	Bond refunding (6)	Call announcement date (7)	Earliest month in which market price ≥ call price[a] (8)	Percentage excess of market value over call price immediately before announcement date (9)	Dollar amount of excess of market value over call price immediately before announcement date (in thousands) (10)	Dollar amount of excess of market value over call price ÷ market value of stock (%) (11)	Maximum value of tax subsidy ÷ market value of stock (%) (17)
1. Consolidated Edison	1989	5.25	106.07	75.0	100.0	Yes	10-03-62	July 1960[b]	0.2	-135	0.011	-0.205
2. Union Oil of California	1975	6.50	104.25	6.5	100.0	No	10-11-62	None	-4.1	-276	-0.058	-0.707
3. Allegheny Power System	1989	5.13	106.33	14.0	100.0	Yes	11-09-62	May 1962	0.0	5	0.001	-0.107
4. Coca Cola	1974	4.00	100.00	3.4	62.4	No	11-27-62	None	-0.6	-22	-0.002	-0.155
5. Columbia Gas System	1984	5.38	104.75	23.5	94.0	Yes	01-14-63	March 1960	1.2	294	-0.035	0.006
6. Central & South West	1990	5.00	103.37	12.0	100.0	Yes	01-25-63	Feb. 1961	-1.0	-99	-0.010	-0.123
7. Middle South Utilities	1989	5.63	107.35	15.0	100.0	Yes	01-25-63	None	-3.1	-503	-0.084	-0.052
8. Eastern Gas & Fuel Associates	1965	3.50	100.55	32.9	63.0	No	02-05-63	Oct. 1945[b]	-4.9	-1638	-1.087	-11.013
9. Texas Utilities	1989	5.25	106.76	20.0	100.0	Yes	02-06-23	Sept. 1961	-0.7	-154	-0.012	0.150
10. Long Island Lighting	1989	5.25	106.77	25.0	100.0	Yes	03-18-63	Sept. 1961	0.0	-5	-0.001	1.379
11. Utah Power & Light	1987	5.25	106.24	15.0	100.0	Yes	03-22-63	Dec. 1957[b]	0.4	59	0.031	-0.267
12. American Natural Gas	1982	6.25	107.50	28.1	94.0	Yes	03-29-63	June 1958[b]	-1.2	-353	-0.058	0.012
13. Central & South West	1989	5.13	105.29	16.0	100.0	Yes	04-05-63	Sept. 1961	0.2	40	0.004	0.718
14. Wisconsin Electric Power	1989	5.38	106.53	3.0	100.0	Yes	04-17-63	None	-2.1	-68	-0.018	0.086
15. Textron	1970	5.00	100.00	6.9	57.0	No	04-23-63	None	0.3	12	0.011	-2.323
16. Tampa Electric	1990	5.00	107.00	24.8	99.2	Yes	05-03-63	None	-3.3	-868	-0.352	-0.142
17. Dayton Power & Light	1987	5.00	104.60	50.0	100.0	Yes	05-07-63	Jan. 1958[b]	-0.5	-265	-0.101	-0.421
18. Consolidated Edison	1989	5.13	105.31	75.0	100.0	Yes	05-10-63	Aug. 1960[b]	1.4	1100	0.074	-0.182
19. Pacific Lighting	1983	5.13	105.40	31.5	90.0	Yes	07-03-63	May 1963	0.6	193	0.042	0.739
20. American Natural Gas	1977	6.25	106.26	24.0	80.0	Yes	07-24-63	April 1959	-0.2	-62	-0.010	0.392
21. Community Public Service	1987	5.38	105.86	7.9	98.8	Yes	07-31-63	None	-1.4	-113	-0.210	1.169
22. Homestake Mining	1969	5.88	104.50	0.7	10.0	No	07-31-63	None	-3.8	-138	-0.133	-0.356
23. Texas Eastern Transmission	1978	5.63	103.85	31.0	88.6	No	08-02-63	NA	-1.1	-366	-0.103	-4.669
24. General Public Utilities	1990	5.38	107.20	9.1	91.0	Yes	09-06-63	Sept. 1962	-0.2	-19	-0.002	-0.046
25. Wheeling Steel	1970	3.25	101.50	9.8	22.3	Yes	10-01-63	June 1945	-1.8	-178	-0.268	-0.226
26. Wisconsin Public Service	1989	5.25	105.84	7.9	98.8	Yes	10-04-63	May 1963	-0.1	-6	-0.004	-0.155
27. Puget Sound Water & Light	1989	5.50	106.05	40.0	100.0	Yes	11-27-63	Sept. 1961	-1.0	-432	-0.346	-0.833
28. Lehigh Valley Industries	1974	5.00	102.50	0.8	5.3	No	11-27-63	None	-3.3	-27	-0.470	-7.057
29. Ashland Oil & Refining	1965	3.00	100.25	1.3	26.0	No	01-28-64	None	-2.4	-30	-0.012	-0.252
30. Standard Thomson	1967	5.00	102.00	0.5	28.6	No	03-17-64	None	-2.0	-08	-0.284	-8.865
31. Washington Water Power	1964	3.50	100.00	19.1	86.8	Yes	03-31-64	Aug. 1941[b]	-0.6	-118	-0.082	-0.352
32. Pacific Lighting	1984	5.38	105.33	28.2	94.0	Yes	09-02-64	NA	-0.1	-93	-0.019	1.085

No. Company	Year	Coupon	Price	%	%	Conv.	Date	Call protection				
33. Southern Company	1989	5.75	101.34	5.6	31.1	No	01-04-65	July 1962	3.6	205	0.013	-0.182
34. Washington Water Power	1990	5.38	105.38	15.0	100.0	Yes	01-29-65	NA	-0.9	-141	-0.089	0.108
35. Pacific Petroleums	1973	5.50	102.25	20.1	67.0	No	04-01-65	None	-0.7	-150	-0.065	-4.224
36. Bristol-Myers	1968	3.00	100.25	4.6	30.7	No	11-16-65	Jan. 1949[b]	-7.6	-359	-0.029	-0.168
37. Gulf & Western	1975	5.50	104.00	1.0	57.1	No	03-10-66	None	-7.2	-75	-0.036	-0.226
38. Swift	1973	2.88	100.00	1.1	2.2	No	03-28-66	Oct. 1949[b]	-7.9	-91	-0.027	-0.143
39. Tenneco	1976	6.00	104.00	1.6	69.6	No	05-23-66	None	-5.1	-98	-0.009	-0.069
40. Ling Temco Vought	1978	4.13	101.75	11.6	77.3	No	06-09-67	None	-11.8	-1392	-0.475	-1.708
41. Foremost & McKesson	1973	3.50	101.00	19.3	64.3	No	07-20-67	Jan. 1954[b]	-13.0	-2572	-1.237	-3.957
42. Essex Chemical	1975	6.00	103.00	1.4	22.2	No	10-31-67	None	-13.5	-207	1.311	-3.797
43. Glen Gery Shale Brick	1971	5.50	101.00	3.3	82.5	Yes	12-21-67	None	-6.9	-228	-2.066	19.164
44. OKC	1976	5.75	103.25	6.2	93.9	Yes	01-14-68	None	-12.3	-383	-2.054	12.352
45. Canadian Breweries	1969	4.00	100.25	0.8	16.0	No	03-19-68	None	-4.2	-32	-0.018	-0.232
46. Fedders	1979	5.50	104.00	2.3	60.5	No	07-08-68	None	-18.3	-428	-0.246	-0.594
47. American Tobacco	1969	3.00	100.00	7.7	7.7	No	10-15-68	Dec. 1945[b]	-2.5	-192	-0.021	-0.430
48. Chicago & Eastern Ill. Railroad	1985	3.75	102.00	5.9	62.1	No	06-09-69	None	-8.7	-538	-1.218	-6.561
49. National Distillers & Chemical	1974	3.38	100.50	5.1	12.8	No	06-26-69	Sept. 1949[b]	-19.2	-978	-0.353	-0.790
50. Central Maine Power	1970	3.50	100.00	17.4	96.1	Yes	08-20-70	June 1941[b]	-0.8	-131	-0.128	1.406
51. National General	1974	5.50	100.00	1.1	5.5	No	10-19-70	June 1941[b]	-4.0	-43	-0.053	-0.642
52. Pacific Lighting	1971	3.00	100.00	5.7	49.6	No	12-01-70	None	-0.8	-43	-0.011	-0.710
53. City Investing	1975	3.88	100.00	10.5	42.0	No	09-27-71	None	-23.4	2454	-0.617	-0.950
54. Colonial Stores	1977	4.90	101.66	2.1	42.0	No	11-09-71	None	-19.4	-405	-0.379	-0.775
55. Cooper Tire & Rubber	1974	5.25	100.00	0.5	14.3	No	02-25-72	None	-7.6	-41	-0.133	-0.775
56. Trans Union Corp.	1973	4.25	100.00	1.2	6.0	Yes	03-15-72	July 1953[b]	-2.2	-27	-0.006	-0.128
57. Iowa Electric Light & Power	1992	6.38	103.13	10.0	100.0	No	03-23-72	NA	-18.9	-2013	-2.517	1.413
58. Winn Dixie Stores	1976	3.75	100.00	4.2	21.0	No	09-20-72	None	-11.2	-473	0.075	-0.287
59. Philip Morris	1979	4.88	106.63	9.7	24.3	No	10-31-72	NA	-12.2	-1188	-0.044	0.151
60. Pioneer Natural Gas	1977	5.50	100.38	3.3	26.4	No	02-07-73	None	-7.2	-193	-0.127	-0.986
61. American Brands	1976	3.25	100.75	2.2	4.4	No	07-10-74	March 1954	-5.0	-271	-0.031	-0.115
62. Fansteel	1977	4.75	101.44	0.2	6.6	No	08-27-74	None	-9.6	-15	-0.093	-0.541
63. N.Y. State Electric & Gas	1992	4.50	100.25	8.4	56.0	Yes	09-10-74	None	-50.6	-5422	-3.492	-1.320
64. Raybestos Manhattan	1975	10.88	100.00	25.0	100.0	No	01-14-75	June 1974	0.0	8	0.031	4.955
65. Savannah Electric & Power	1985	5.25	103.13	2.0	67.7	No	03-10-75	None	-46.5	-970	-4.382	-2.439
66. Laclede Gas	1975	9.00	100.00	10.0	100.0	No	04-29-75	NA	0.0	00	0.000	-6.823
67. Melville Shoe	1980	4.88	102.80	4.2	35.0	No	05-01-75	None	-19.7	-954	-0.229	-0.391
68. Moly Corp.	1976	5.50	100.00	1.9	15.2	No	07-07-75	None	-7.0	-225	-0.439	-1.656
69. Skelly Oil	1976	8.15	100.00	25.0	100.0	No	09-22-75	NA	0.1	625	0.082	-1.585
70. Union Oil of California	1976	8.25	100.63	125.0	100.0	No	10-31-75	NA	0.5	33	0.043	-4.088
71. May Department Stores	1977	5.00	100.00	3.8	15.1	No	01-28-76	None	-5.6	-211	-0.031	-0.254
72. General Telephone & Electronics	1976	8.75	100.00	50.0	100.0	No	02-27-76	Aug. 1975[b]	2.0	985	0.029	-0.716
73. Litton Industries	1976	8.75	100.00	60.0	100.0	No	07-02-76	NA	0.8	450	0.095	-6.058
74. Columbus & Southern Ohio Elec.	1996	8.00	100.00	25.0	100.0	Yes	08-25-76	Dec. 1975[b]	0.8	188	0.055	0.350
75. Rockwell International	1977	7.30	100.00	48.6	97.2	No	08-27-76	NA	-0.1	-58	-0.006	-2.553
76. Philips Industries	1977	10.00	100.00	15.0	100.0	No	09-14-76	April 1976	0.5	75	0.174	-16.783
77. Diamond Shamrock	1978	3.38	100.00	6.8	45.3	No	10-29-76	March 1954	-5.5	-371	-0.021	-0.177
78. Northwest Industries	2000	10.00	105.00	6.1	98.0	No	11-19-76	None	-3.8	-185	-0.029	-0.465

Table 1 (continued)

Non-convertible bond (1)	Maturity	Coupon rate (%) (2)	Call price (3)	Amount retired (in millions) (4)	Amount retired ÷ amount issued (5)	Bond refunding (6)	Call announcement date (7)	Earliest month in which market price ≥ call price[a] (8)	Percentage excess of market value over call price immediately before announcement date (9)	Dollar amount of excess of market value over call price immediately before announcement date (in thousands) (10)	Dollar amount of excess of market value over call price ÷ market value of stock (%) (11)	Maximum value of tax subsidy ÷ market value of stock (%) (12)
79. Southern Natural Resources	1978	4.50	100.00	3.8	12.7	No	11-23-76	None	-5.7	-219	-0.044	-0.349
80. Tenneco	1977	5.13	109.00	12.2	24.4	No	11-30-76	None	-1.5	-252	-0.009	-0.202
81. General Public Utilities	1980	10.25	103.43	58.0	100.0	No	12-03-76	Jan. 1976[b]	1.3	771	0.076	-2.879
82. United Technologies	2000	9.00	108.08	50.0	100.0	No	12-21-76	NA	-5.6	-3040	-0.311	-2.504
83. Cities Service	1978	7.00	100.00	50.0	100.0	No	12-23-76	NA	-0.4	-185	-0.012	-1.556
84. Wisconsin Electric Power	2000	9.25	100.97	9.9	99.0	No	01-20-77	NA	6.1	610	0.109	-0.911
85. King's Department Stores	1990	10.00	103.00	4.9	82.2	No	02-07-77	None	0.0	00	0.000	-.2614
86. Wisconsin Public Service	2000	9.25	107.34	45.0	100.0	Yes	02-08-77	Dec. 1976[a]	0.0	18	0.008	-0.713
87. Wisconsin Gas	1990	10.75	107.92	12.0	80.0	Yes	02-09-77	Nov. 1976[b]	-1.4	-184	-0.227	-0.496
88. Swift	1990	7.38	100.00	50.0	100.0	No	03-01-77	NA	-0.3	-125	-0.036	-6.986
89. South Carolina Electric & Gas	2000	9.88	107.04	30.0	100.0	Yes	03-16-77	Nov. 1976[b]	0.4	138	0.037	-0.289
90. General Telephone & Electronics	2000	9.75	108.12	70.0	100.0	No	04-12-77	Dec. 1976[b]	-1.3	-959	-0.024	0.083
91. Seagram	1978	7.50	110.50	50.0	100.0	No	05-10-77	NA	0.0	00	0.000	-3.294
92. Boeing	1978	5.00	100.00	2.2	5.5	No	07-01-77	None	-4.9	-107	-0.009	-0.081
93. Tenneco	1978	3.50	100.00	1.7	6.8	No	07-01-77	None	-5.0	-84	-0.003	-0.026
94. Mid-Continent Telephone	2000	10.50	110.00	16.7	83.5	No	07-15-77	June 1972[b]	-3.3	-608	-0.355	-4.986
95. Central Telephone & Utilities	1995	9.25	106.94	28.2	94.0	Yes	07-22-77	NA	-2.9	-884	-0.151	0.245
96. Sierra Pacific Power	2000	9.75	107.40	15.0	100.0	Yes	08-19-77	NA	-4.7	-753	-0.671	0.856
97. Cincinnati Gas & Electric	2000	9.63	108.25	10.0	100.0	No	08-30-77	Oct.1976[b]	0.9	100	0.021	-1.105
98. Piedmont Natural Gas	1995	10.25	107.58	10.4	94.5	Yes	08-30-77	NA	-1.1	-128	-0.327	4.834
99. American Natural Resources	1995	10.00	107.09	26.9	89.7	Yes	11-22-77	Dec. 1976	0.3	78	0.008	0.005
100. International Tel. & Tel.	1981	6.50	100.50	7.4	49.1	No	11-23-77	None	-12.9	-958	-0.029	-0.095
101. Talley Industries	1978	11.63	106.25	4.2	100.0	No	12-09-77	None	-4.7	-212	-0.450	-4.330
102. Standard Oil of Indiana	1983	6.75	101.00	9.6	38.4	No	04-27-78	NA	-3.0	-288	-0.004	-0.061
									Mean: -4.7	Mean: -315	Mean: -0.270	Mean: -0.930

[a] NA: Not applicable because of a call protection period.
[b] Market price of bond exceeds call price by at least 1%.

527

Table 2

Comparison of 41 monthly bond prices and call prices starting from the earliest month in which bond prices are equal to call prices, 1962–1977.

Non-convertible bond	Call announcement date	Length of time series	Number of months in which bond price ≥ call price	Number of consecutive months in which bond price ≥ call price	Number of consecutive months in which bond price exceeds call price by at least 1 or 2%
(1)	(2)	(3)	(4)	(5)	(6)
1. Consolidated Edison	10-03-62	12	6	3	2
2. Allegheny Power System	11-09-62	6	6	6	0
3. Columbia Gas System	01-14-63	12	6	2	2
4. Central & South West	01-25-63	12	12	12	0
5. Eastern Gas & Fuel Associates	02-05-63	12	12	12	4
6. Texas Utilities	02-06-63	12	7	7	0
7. Utah Power & Light	03-22-63	12	5	3	3
8. American Natural Gas	03-29-63	12	5	2	0
9. Central & South West	04-05-63	12	12	12	0
10. Dayton Power & Light	05-07-63	12	10	6	2
11. Consolidated Edison	05-10-63	12	3	1	0
12. Pacific Lighting	07-03-63	2	2	2	0
13. American Natural Gas	07-24-63	12	6	3	0
14. General Public Utilities	09-06-63	11	8	8	0
15. Wheeling Steel	10-01-63	12	8	5	3
16. Wisconsin Public Service	10-04-63	5	5	2	0
17. Puget Sound Water & Light	11-27-63	12	12	12	0
18. Washington Water Power	03-31-64	12	12	12	11
19. Southern Company	01-04-65	12	12	10	5
20. Bristol Myers	11-16-65	12	12	12	0
21. Swift	03-28-66	12	12	12	1

Table 2 (continued)

Non-convertible bond (1)	Call announcement date (2)	Length of time series (3)	Number of months in which bond price ≥ call price (4)	Number of consecutive months in which bond price ≥ call price (5)	Number of consecutive months in which bond price exceeds call price by at least 1 or 2% (6)
22. Foremost & McKesson	07-20-67	12	12	12	4
23. American Tobacco	10-15-68	12	12	12	4
24. National Distillers & Chemical	06-26-69	12	12	12	6
25. Central Maine Power	08-20-70	12	12	12	5
26. Pacific Lighting	12-01-70	12	12	5	3
27. Trans Union	03-15-72	12	12	12	4
28. American Brands	07-10-74	12	3	2	0
29. Raybestos Manhattan	01-14-75	7	4	3	0
30. General Telephone & Electronics	02-27-76	6	6	6	1
31. Columbus & Southern Ohio Electric	08-25-76	8	8	8	0
32. Philips Industries	09-14-76	5	3	3	0
33. Diamond Shamrock	10-29-76	12	10	3	0
34. General Public Utilities	12-03-76	11	7	3	1
35. Wisconsin Public Service	02-08-77	2	2	2	1
36. Wisconsin Gas	02-09-77	4	4	4	1
37. South Carolina Electric & Gas	03-16-77	4	4	4	3
38. General Telephone & Electronics	04-12-77	4	2	1	1
39. Mid-Continent Telephone	07-15-77	12	9	8	0
40. Cincinnati Gas & Electric	08-30-77	12	6	4	2
41. American Natural Resources	11-22-77	12	12	12	2

Firms may be reluctant to call bonds when the market value is just equal to the call price because most firms must give thirty days' notice to bondholders. During this period, the market price of the bond can fall below the call price. Moreover, there are transaction costs in calling a bond, especially if the called bond is refinanced by a new bond issue. In order to take into consideration the notice period and transaction costs, column (6) of table 2 shows the number of consecutive months in which the bond price exceeds the call price by at least 1% and 2%, respectively. Twenty-two percent of the bonds have market values that exceed the call price by 1% or more for at least four consecutive months. When the 2% filter is used, only one bond out of 41 has market values that exceed the call price for at least four consecutive months.

Column (9) of table 1 shows evidence that most firms call non-convertible bonds when the market value is below the call price. To document more about this phenomenon, a time series of the average percentage and dollar discounts of market value to call price is computed for a thirteen-month period up to and including the month of the call announcement. Because many of the called bonds do not have price quotations available for all thirteen months due to limited public interest and, in some cases, the relation between the market value of the bond and the call price cannot be established because of the call protection period, the sample size is reduced to 88 bonds.

Table 3 shows the average percentage and dollar discounts of market value to call price for a thirteen-month period up to and including the month of the

Table 3

The average percentage and dollar amount of the discount of market value to call price from preceding 12 months until the call announcement month for 88 non-convertible bonds, 1962–1978 (*t*-statistics are in parentheses).[a]

Month	$(P-C)/C$ (%)		$(P-C)n$ (in thousands of dollars)	
−12	−7.13	(−9.08)	−725.0	(−6.17)
−11	−7.03	(−8.46)	−683.0	(−5.80)
−10	−6.85	(−8.71)	−651.1	(−5.74)
−9	−6.53	(−8.21)	−593.9	(−5.84)
−8	−6.45	(−7.86)	−572.2	(−5.95)
−7	−6.40	(−7.82)	−571.9	(−5.91)
−6	−6.23	(−7.47)	−554.0	(−5.29)
−5	−5.91	(−6.72)	−489.7	(−4.83)
−4	−5.89	(−6.61)	−465.4	(−4.89)
−3	−5.58	(−6.33)	−442.1	(−4.19)
−2	−5.47	(−5.91)	−381.4	(−3.95)
−1	−5.34	(−5.72)	−383.6	(−4.30)
−0	−0.76	(−1.52)	−66.1	(−1.19)

[a]P = market value of the called bond, C = call price, n = number of called bonds outstanding.

call announcement. For both the percentage and dollar amount, the average discount of market value to call price falls steadily during the twelve-month preceding the call announcement. The *t*-statistics are all greater than two standard errors from zero. This finding indicates that firms tend to call non-convertible bonds when the market value is below the call price. The steady decline in the average discount may reflect rising market interest rates before call announcement or possible leakage of information about the call. Bond prices adjust quickly to the call announcement. The discount disappears after the call announcement date. In month 0, the average percentage discount is only -0.76%, which is 1.5 standard errors from zero.

4. Hypotheses regarding call policies

In this section, four hypotheses are developed as possible explanations of different motives for calls. The predicted effects of calls on stock price are also presented.

4.1. Bond refunding hypothesis

According to this hypothesis, the main reason for calling a bond is to reduce interest costs. When market interest rates decline sufficiently in the period following a bond issue, a company can save interest costs by calling the old bond and floating a new bond at a lower coupon rate. Bond refunding can be viewed as an investment decision which requires a cash outlay followed by interest savings in future years. The cost of refunding are (1) the call premium on the old bond and (2) the flotation costs of the new bond. If the present value of the interest savings exceeds the cash outlay, the refunding is profitable to the firm.

The analysis in this paper uses a simpler, but cruder, method of analyzing refunding: compare the coupon interest on the new bond with the adjusted interest rate of the old bond (coupon interest expense/call price of the old bond). The refunding operation is classified as having a positive net present value if the coupon interest rate on the new bond is lower. A profitable refunding implies a positive stock price reaction to a call announcement.

4.2. Leverage hypothesis

The leverage hypothesis claims that the main motive for calls is to change the capital structure of a firm.

4.2.1. Potential tax effects

A cash-rich firm can reduce its debt–equity ratio by calling its bonds and financing the retirement with internal funds. Elimination of the tax-subsidy associated with the deductibility of interest payments implies a decrease in stock price. However, Miller (1977) demonstrates that the existence of a corporate income tax, together with different personal income tax rates across individuals and securities (debt and equity), can imply that there is no optimal leverage from the point of view of an individual firm. As such, Miller's theory asserts that the stock price is unaffected when a firm calls its outstanding debt and finances the call with internal funds.

When the new bond has approximately the same value as the old debt, there is no change in the capital structure. Both the tax-subsidy model and Miller's theory predict that the firm's stock price will remain unchanged. If the stock price rises at all, it is probably due to other effects, such as information conveyed by the bond refunding or the profitability of the refunding.

When the market value of the new debt exceeds the market value of the old debt, the financial leverage of the firm increases. The stock price will increase if the additional tax deductions provided by interest payments are not offset by other costs or tax effects. On the other hand, Miller's theory suggests that the price of the stock remains the same.

4.2.2. Information conveyed by a call

The change in financial leverage associated with the call may convey information to investors about the future performance of the firm. The conveyance of information may be just a by-product of the call and not the purpose of the call.

Ross (1977) suggests that higher financial leverage can be used by managers to convey favorable inside information about the future of the firm. Leland and Pyle (1977) focus on owners instead of managers. Although their model does not use debt as a direct signal, financial leverage is positively correlated with the firm's value. Vermaelen (1981) argues that the information hypothesis explains to a large extent the abnormal returns observed after a repurchase tender offer.

4.3. Wealth transfer hypothesis

Section 3 provides evidence that most firms call non-convertible bonds when the market value is below the call price. According to the wealth transfer hypothesis, bondholders benefit at the expense of stockholders due to the premium paid for the bonds. Thus, at the time the call is announced, the wealth transfer hypothesis implies that the stock price will drop, and the price of the called bond will increase.

4.4. Restrictive covenant hypothesis

Firms may call outstanding debt when the market value is below the call price in order to eliminate restrictive indenture provisions. The elimination of such indenture provisions may be part of the preliminary moves in preparation for a merger or a sale of assets. A test of this hypothesis is to compare the restrictive covenants of the called bond with those of the bonds that are not called. In the case of refunding, the indenture provisions of the called bonds are also compared with those of the newly-issued bond. This hypothesis implies that retirement of the called bonds relaxes a restriction not contained in the indentures of other debt issues of the firm.

5. Empirical analysis and results

5.1. Evidence on the bond refunding hypothesis

The bond refunding hypothesis is tested by comparing the coupon interest rate of the new bond with the adjusted interest rate of the old bond (coupon interest charges/call price). This is a cruder test than a formal net present value anlaysis because it ignores the time value concept as well as the flotation costs of the new bond. A call is grouped in the refunding sample if the *Moody's Manual* or *The Wall Street Journal* states explicitly that the firm floated a new debt issue to replace the called bond. From the overall sample of 133 calls, 38 calls are classified as refunding.

Table 4 compares the new bond's coupon rate and the adjusted interest rate of the old bond for 38 refundings. It is predicted that the new coupon rate should be lower than the adjusted coupon rate of the old bond. The results are, on average, consistent with the prediction because the mean of the new coupon rate is 5.85%, which is lower than the mean of the adjusted old rate of 6.07%. Although the difference between means of 0.22% is not statistically significant, the result is driven by one outlier: the refunding of Central Maine Power.[4] If this refunding is excluded, the mean of the new coupon rate becomes 5.76%, which is significantly lower than the mean of the adjusted old rate of 6.14% ($t = 3.53$). The examination of individual refunding cases reveals that 19% of bond refundings do not result in an interest saving for the firm because the new coupon rate exceeds the adjusted old coupon rate.

To measure the effect of refunding on the average discount of market value to call price, a sample of 88 calls is examined. This sample, described in section 3, consists of bonds that have market values for twelve months that precede and the month of the call announcement. This sample is divided into two subsamples: the refunding subsample (34 events) and the non-refunding sub-

---

[4] The most extreme observation was the refunding operation of Central Maine Power (firm no.27 in table 4) where the new coupon rate exceeded the adjusted old coupon rate by 5.80%. However, Central Maine Power is not a good example of pure refunding because the old bond has only two months to maturity with an outstanding amount of $17.4 million while the new bond had a twenty-five year maturity, and the $35 million issue was much larger. The prospectus of the new bond indicates that the purpose of the new issue was to retire the old bond, the balance to be used to repay short-term debt and for construction.

Table 4

Comparison of the new bond coupon rate and the adjusted interest rate of the old bond for 38 called non-convertible bonds, 1962–1977.

Non-convertible bond (1)	Call announcement date (2)	New bond coupon rate (%) (3)	Adjusted interest rate of old bond (coupon interest/ call price) (%) (4)	Adjusted interest rate of old bond − new bond coupon rate (%) (5) = (4) − (3)
1. Consolidated Edisoni	10-03-62	4.38	4.95	0.57
2. Allegheny Power System	11-09-62	4.38	4.82	0.44
3. Columbia Gas System	01-14-63	4.38	5.14	0.76
4. Central & South West	01-25-63	4.13	4.84	0.71
5. Middle South Utilities	01-25-63	4.38	5.24	0.86
6. Texas Utilities	02-06-63	4.25	4.92	0.67
7. Long Island Lighting	03-18-63	4.40	4.92	0.52
8. Utah Power & Light	03-22-63	4.50	4.94	0.44
9. American Natural Gas	03-29-63	4.50	5.81	1.31
10. Central & South West	04-05-63	4.38	4.87	0.49
11. Wisconsin Electric Power	04-17-63	4.50	5.05	0.55
12. Tampa Electric	05-03-63	4.25	4.67	0.42
13. Dayton Power & Light	05-07-63	4.45	4.78	0.33
14. Consolidated Edison	05-10-63	4.40	4.87	0.47
15. Pacific Lighting	07-03-63	4.38	4.87	0.49
16. American Natural Gas	07-24-63	4.88	5.88	1.00
17. Community Public Service	07-31-63	4.50	5.08	0.58
18. General Public Utilities	09-06-63	4.63	5.02	0.39
19. Wheeling Steel	10-01-63	5.45	3.20	−2.25
20. Wisconsin Public Service	10-04-63	4.38	4.96	0.58
21. Puget Sound Water & Light	11-27-63	4.58	5.19	0.61
22. Washington Water Power	03-31-64	4.58	3.50	−1.08
23. Pacific Lighting	09-02-64	4.58	5.11	0.53
24. Washington Water Power	01-29-65	4.58	5.11	0.53
25. Glen Gery Shale Brick	12-21-67	6.50	5.45	−1.05
26. OKC	01-14-68	5.75	5.57	−0.18

Table 4 (continued)

Non-convertible bond (1)	Call announcement date (2)	New bond coupon rate (%) (3)	Adjusted interest rate of old bond (coupon interest/ call price) (%) (4)	Adjusted interest rate of old bond − new bond coupon rate (%) (5) = (4) − (3)
27. Central Maine Power	08-20-70	9.30	3.50	− 5.80
28. Iowa Electric Light & Power	03-23-72	7.63	5.98	− 1.65
29. Raybestos Manhattan	01-14-75	8.88	10.88	2.00
30. Columbus & Southern Ohio Electric	08-25-76	8.88	8.00	− 0.88
31. Wisconsin Public Service	02-08-77	8.20	8.62	0.42
32. Wisconsin Gas	02-09-77	8.38	9.96	1.58
33. South Carolina Electric & Gas	03-16-77	8.38	9.23	0.85
34. General Telephone & Electronics	04-12-77	8.50	9.02	0.52
35. Central Telephone & Utilities	07-22-77	8.25	8.65	0.40
36. Sierra Pacific Power	08-19-77	8.63	9.08	0.45
37. Piedmont Natural Gas	08-30-77	8.63	9.53	0.90
38. American Natural Resources	11-22-77	8.63	9.34	0.71
		Mean: 5.85	Mean: 6.07	Mean: 0.22

The distribution of the difference between the adjusted interest rate of the old bond and the new bond coupon rate

Adjusted interest rate of the old bond−new bond coupon rate (%)	Number of bonds	Percentage of bonds in the sample
2% or more	1	3
1.5 to 1.99	1	3
1.0 to 1.49	2	5
0.5 to 0.99	16	42
0.0 to 0.49	11	29
− 0.01 to − 0.49	1	3
− 0.5 to − 0.99	1	3
− 1.0 to − 1.49	2	5
− 1.5 to − 1.99	1	3
− 2.0 or more	2	5
	38	100

Table 5

The relation between bond refunding and the average percentage and dollar amount of the discount of market value to call price for 88 called non-convertible bonds, 1962–1977 (t-statistics are in parentheses).[a]

Month	Bond refunding (34 events)		Non-refunding (54 events)	
	$(P-C)/C$ (%)	$(P-C)n$ (in thousands of dollars)	$(P-C)/C$ (%)	$(P-C)n$ (in thousands of dollars)
−12	−3.06 (−3.42)	−536.6 (−3.15)	−9.70 (−9.57)	−843.7 (−5.35)
−11	−3.04 (−3.35)	−545.1 (−2.79)	−9.54 (−8.89)	−769.8 (−5.22)
−10	−2.98 (−3.35)	−538.1 (−3.12)	−9.28 (−9.00)	−722.3 (−4.82)
−9	−2.55 (−3.38)	−433.7 (−3.42)	−9.03 (−8.35)	−694.7 (−4.81)
−8	−2.59 (−3.17)	−403.2 (−3.47)	−8.85 (−7.87)	−678.8 (−4.93)
−7	−2.41 (−3.06)	−376.6 (−3.33)	−8.91 (−7.93)	−694.9 (−5.00)
−6	−2.48 (−3.09)	−328.5 (−2.95)	−8.58 (−7.38)	−696.1 (−4.54)
−5	−2.25 (−2.94)	−310.3 (−3.06)	−8.23 (−6.54)	−602.6 (−3.99)
−4	−2.11 (−2.77)	−220.9 (−2.70)	−8.26 (−6.48)	−619.4 (−4.33)
−3	−1.77 (−2.31)	−128.1 (−1.21)	−7.94 (−6.33)	−639.8 (−4.17)
−2	−1.75 (−2.28)	−88.8 (−0.80)	−7.69 (−5.72)	−565.6 (−4.16)
−1	−1.84 (−2.57)	−201.0 (−2.36)	−7.49 (−5.41)	−498.5 (−3.74)
	Mean: −2.40	Mean: −342.6	Mean: −8.62	Mean: −668.9

[a] P = the market value of the called bond, C = the call price, n = the number of called bonds outstanding.

sample (54 events). Ninety-one percent of firms in the refunding subsample are public utilities. Refunding calls are concentrated heavily in 1963 and 1977, years of declining interest rates. Because firms usually refund when the coupon rate is higher than market interest rates, causing the bond price to be above the par value, it is predicted that the average percentage and dollar discounts of market value to call price are smaller for the refunding subsample than those of the non-refunding subsample.

Table 5 shows the relation between bond refunding and the average percentage and dollar discounts of market value to call price for twelve months that precede the call announcement date. The result is consistent with the prediction, showing a discount of -1.84% for the refunding subsample in the month preceding the call announcement date, while discount is -7.49% for the non-refunding subsample. The mean differences between these subsamples in month -1 for the percentage and dollar discounts are 3.10 and 1.69 standard errors from zero, respectively. Similar to the results of the overall sample, the percentage and dollar discounts of both the refunding and non-refunding subsamples fall steadily from month -12 to month -1. The examination of the percentage discount of market value to the call price of each individual firm reveals that even in the refunding subsample, 71% of the firms have bond prices below the call price immediately before the call announcement.

The results are more striking for the non-refunding subsample. Not only is the average percentage discount larger, almost all firms have bond prices below the call price in month -12, and 87% of the firms still have a large percentage discount in month -1. The evidence indicates that a substantial majority of non-refunding calls pay bondholders more than market value in redeeming the bond before maturity.

Although the results are, in general, consistent with the bond refunding hypothesis, a reduction in interest payments is not the only motive for calls. Even in the case of refunding, many firms explicitly state other purposes for issuing the new bond in the prospectus.

5.2. Evidence on the leverage hypothesis

5.2.1. Empirical methods

To measure the price effects of calls, common stock excess returns are analyzed around the announcement date. The returns are obtained from the CRSP Daily Excess Return tape. The excess returns are computed as follows: betas of common stocks are computed according to the methodology described in Scholes and Williams (1977). Stocks are ranked according to their betas. On the basis of this ranking, stocks are grouped in ten equal portfolios for the next year. The excess return is the actual stock return minus the return on the portfolio that contains the stock.

Using the methodology of Fama, Fisher, Jensen and Roll (1969) to analyze the effect of call announcement on security prices, the average daily excess return on a portfolio of stocks of calling firms is computed for sixty trading days before the announcement date (day 0) until sixty days after. This period corresponds roughly to a six-month observation period. The average daily portfolio excess return is defined as

$$XRET_t = \frac{1}{n} \sum_{i=1}^{n} e_{i,t},$$

where n is the number of stocks in the portfolio and $e_{i,t}$ is the excess return on stock i at time t. The cumulative average daily excess return from sixty trading days before the announcement date to date T is computed as

$$CUMRET_{-60}^{T} = \sum_{t=-60}^{T} XRET_t.$$

To test whether the daily average common stock excess return on event date t, $XRET_t$, is significantly different from zero, the following t-statistic is computed:

$$t = XRET_t / \hat{\sigma}(XRET_t),$$

where $\hat{\sigma}(XRET_t)$ is the sample standard deviation of portfolio returns around the event date (sixty days before the announcement until sixty days after the announcement, excluding the event date).

To test whether the cumulative common stock excess return from t to $t + n$, $CUMRET_t^{t+n}$, is significantly different from zero, the following t-statistic is computed:

$$t = \hat{\sigma}(CUMRET_t^{t+n}) / CUMRET_t^{t+n},$$

where $\hat{\sigma}(CUMRET_t^{t+n}) = \sqrt{n}\,[\hat{\sigma}(XRET_t)]$, and $\hat{\sigma}(XRET_t)$ is the sample standard deviation of the daily average common stock excess returns during the period t to $t + n$. This approach assumes that the daily portfolio excess returns are independent and identically distributed.

5.2.2. Grouping of call events

In order to test the leverage hypothesis, the overall sample of 133 call events is broken down to three subsamples according to the change in financial leverage. If the firm called back a bond without issuing any new bond or the size of the new bond is sufficiently smaller than the book value of the outstanding old bond (more than 10%), then this redemption case is grouped into the decrease-in-leverage subsample. There are 72 call events in this group. Although 10% is chosen arbitrarily, its choice does not affect the result significantly because most of the 72 decrease-in-leverage calls are cases where the companies called back their bonds without floating any new bonds or using bank debt.

If a firm refunds the old bond by issuing a new bond or using a bank debt whose size is sufficiently larger (more than 10%) than that of the old bond, this refunding case is grouped into the increase-in-leverage subsample. There are 31 events in this group. In order to belong to the increase-in-leverage subsample, the firm must state explicitly that it is refunding or using short-term debt to replace the called bond. In the absence of any explicit statement, the call event is grouped in the decrease-in-leverage subsample.

If a firm floats a new bond whose size is approximately equal to that of the called bond (10% or less difference in size), this refunding case is grouped into the unchanged-leverage subsample. There are thirty events in this group.

5.2.3. Empirical results

The daily average common stock excess returns of firms calling non-convertible bonds are computed for each day in the period that begins sixty days before the announcement date (day 0) and ends sixty days after the announcement date. Day 0 is the date of the earliest report of the call announcement in *The Wall Street Journal* or the *Standard & Poor's Corporation Called Bond Record*. Column (1) of table 6 presents days relative to the call announcement date. Columns (2) and (3) show the average common stock excess returns (*XRET*) and the cumulative average common stock excess returns (*CUMRET*). The *t*-values of *XRET* are shown in column (4). Column (5) presents the percentage number of common stocks with positive excess returns.

The average excess return on the announcement date is not significantly different from zero for the overall sample. When the sample is broken down into the subsamples according to the change in financial leverage, however, the average returns are all significant on the announcement date. For the decrease-in-leverage subsample, the day 0 average excess return, and is −0.98%, the largest single daily average excess return, and is −4.18 standard errors from zero. Except day 0, none of the average excess returns within ten days around the announcement date is different from zero at the 5% level. Column (5) of table 6 shows that only 18% of the stocks in the decrease-in-leverage subsample have positive excess returns on the announcement date. This result indicates that the average negative excess return on day 0 cannot be attributed to a few large negative returns.

Table 6

Average excess returns, cumulative average excess returns, T-values of average excess returns, and the percentage number of stocks with positive excess returns for various samples of called non-convertible bonds, 1962–1978.[a]

	Overall sample (133)				Decrease-in-leverage sample (72)			
Day	XRET (%)	CUMRET (%)	t	Percentage of stocks with positive XRET	XRET (%)	CUMRET (%)	t	Percentage of stocks with positive XRET
(1)	(2)	(3)	(4)	(5)	(2)	(3)	(4)	(5)
-60	-0.177	-0.177	-1.37	0.49	-0.070	-0.070	-0.28	0.44
-50	0.177	-0.352	1.37	0.47	0.437	0.954	1.74	0.57
-40	-0.063	-0.475	-0.49	0.44	-0.009	0.396	-0.04	0.47
-30	-0.124	-1.023	-0.96	0.50	-0.162	-0.001	-0.64	0.51
-20	-0.080	-1.017	-0.63	0.50	-0.223	-0.601	-0.89	0.49
-10	0.070	-0.838	0.54	0.46	0.110	0.893	0.44	0.38
-5	0.049	-0.642	0.38	0.53	-0.061	1.216	-0.24	0.50
-4	0.093	-0.734	-0.72	0.53	-0.080	1.136	-0.32	0.56
-3	0.110	-0.624	0.85	0.58	0.101	1.237	0.40	0.60
-2	0.114	-0.510	0.88	0.50	0.199	1.436	0.79	0.50
-1	-0.001	-0.511	-0.01	0.50	-0.040	1.395	-0.16	0.50
0	-0.150	-0.661	-1.16	0.47	-0.982	0.413	-4.18	0.18
1	0.087	-0.574	0.67	0.49	-0.109	0.522	-0.43	0.47
2	0.082	-0.492	0.63	0.45	0.036	0.558	0.14	0.43
3	-0.169	-0.661	-1.31	0.44	-0.285	0.273	-1.13	0.42
4	-0.278	-0.940	-2.15	0.41	-0.381	-0.108	-1.52	0.39
5	0.092	-0.848	0.71	0.44	0.186	0.077	0.74	0.43
10	-0.083	-0.989	-0.64	0.45	-0.217	-0.213	-0.87	0.46
20	0.024	-1.037	0.19	0.47	0.124	0.593	0.49	0.53
30	0.001	-0.895	0.01	0.45	-0.050	0.906	-0.20	0.42
40	0.032	-0.614	0.25	0.46	0.209	1.770	0.83	0.50
50	0.247	-0.760	1.91	0.53	0.050	1.413	0.20	0.47
60	0.094	-0.505	0.72	0.53	0.255	2.247	1.01	0.58

Table 6 (continued)

	Increase-in-leverage sample (31)				Unchanged leverage sample (30)			
Day	XRET (%)	CUMRET (%)	t	Percentage of stocks with positive XRET	XRET (%)	CUMRET (%)	t	Percentage of stocks with positive XRET
(1)	(2)	(3)	(4)	(5)	(2)	(3)	(4)	(5)
-60	-0.018	-0.018	-0.05	0.58	-0.412	-0.412	-1.69	0.50
-50	-0.402	-1.464	-1.16	0.35	0.071	-1.625	0.29	0.37
-40	0.151	-1.953	0.44	0.39	-0.492	-0.386	-2.02	0.40
-30	-0.057	-3.554	-0.16	0.45	-0.123	-0.397	-0.50	0.53
-20	-0.150	-4.231	-0.43	0.45	-0.043	-1.347	-0.18	0.57
-10	0.020	-3.633	0.06	0.52	0.077	-1.720	0.32	0.60
-5	0.549	-3.383	1.59	0.55	-0.279	-1.929	-1.14	0.57
-4	-0.328	-3.711	-0.95	0.39	-0.019	-1.947	-0.08	0.63
-3	0.005	-3.706	0.01	0.52	-0.059	-2.006	-0.24	0.60
-2	0.220	-3.485	0.64	0.52	-0.091	-2.097	-0.37	0.47
-1	0.249	-3.236	0.72	0.55	0.014	-2.083	0.06	0.43
0	0.876	-2.360	2.61	0.84	0.543	-1.540	2.27	0.77
1	0.036	-2.324	0.10	0.61	-0.193	-1.733	-0.79	0.40
2	0.078	-2.245	0.23	0.42	0.220	-1.513	0.90	0.53
3	-0.248	-2.493	-0.71	0.39	-0.107	-1.620	-0.44	0.57
4	-0.305	-2.799	-0.88	0.45	-0.160	-1.780	-0.66	0.40
5	-0.109	-2.908	-0.32	0.51	0.052	-1.728	0.21	0.40
10	-0.180	-2.823	-0.52	0.29	-0.025	-1.514	-0.10	0.60
20	0.152	-3.370	0.44	0.42	-0.183	-3.330	-0.75	0.40
30	0.261	-2.430	0.75	0.52	0.038	-4.572	0.16	0.47
40	-0.034	-2.337	-0.10	0.35	-0.220	-4.239	-0.90	0.47
50	0.721	-2.256	2.09	0.52	0.289	-4.230	1.18	0.67
60	-0.272	-1.892	-0.79	0.48	-0.138	-4.778	-0.57	0.47

[a] Day 0 is the date of the earliest report of the call announcement in *The Wall Street Journal* or the *Standard & Poor's Corporation Called Bond Record*.

For the increase-in-leverage subsample, the day 0 average excess return is 0.88%, which is 2.61 standard errors from zero, and 84% of the returns are positive. Except day 0, none of the average excess returns within twenty days surrounding the announcement date is significantly different from zero.

Although the leverage hypothesis does not predict any change in stock price on the call announcement date of the unchanged-leverage subsample, table 6 shows that the day 0 average excess return is 0.54%. This is also more than two standard errors from zero.

The results in this section indicate that the day 0 average excess returns are consistent with the predictions of the leverage hypothesis.[5] This evidence is similar to the results of the study of exchange offers by Masulis (1980). He reports positive stock price changes for leverage-increasing events. However, unlike the dramatic two-day return associated with announcements of tender offers and exchange offers, the average stock price effects of calls are less than one percent.

Although the results provide weak evidence supporting the leverage hypothesis, it is doubtful that changing the capital structure is the main motive for calls.[6] The observed price change can represent a combination of two or more of the effects predicted by different hypotheses. Furthermore, if firms want to change the capital structure, there are better and more efficient ways than calling bonds and paying a premium to bondholders. For example, firms can easily issue more debt such as bank loans to increase financial leverage or to pay off accounts payable to reduce financial leverage.

The stock price effects may reflect information conveyed by leverage-changing calls. That is, the leverage changes associated with calls may convey an unanticipated change in the earning prospects of firms. The observed price effects suggest that leverage increases release favorable information, while leverage decreases release unfavorable information.

---

[5]An alternative method of testing the leverage hypothesis is to use cross-sectional regression analysis to measure the effects of leverage on the stock return on the call announcement date. The model is

$$XRET_{day\ 0} = \alpha + \beta(LEV) + \varepsilon,$$

where LEV is the maximum tax effect of leverage relative to the market value of the stock [shown in column (12) of table 1].

The results are obtained from the ordinary least squares regression of 102 bonds call (t-statistics are in parentheses),

$$XRET_{day\ 0} = \begin{array}{cc} -0.211 & + \quad 0.080(LEV), \\ (-1.49) & (2.13) \end{array} \qquad R^2 = 0.04.$$

The coefficient of the leverage variable is positive and significant at the 5% level. This evidence reinforces the results in table 6.

[6]Vu (1983) reports the results of a questionnaire sent to all the firms in the sample of 102 calls, asking for reasons of the call. Only one out of 52 responding firms states explicitly that it wants to reduce its debt–equity ratio before the end of the year.

5.3. Evidence on the wealth transfer hypothesis

Column (10) of table 1 measures the dollar amount of the discount of the bond market value to the call price for each firm in the sample. The ratio of the dollar discount to the market value of the stock represents the wealth transfer effect on the stock price. Column (11) of table 1 shows that the wealth transfer is small.[7] The mean is -0.3%, and the smallest value is -4.4%.

5.4. Evidence on the restrictive covenant hypothesis

This section examines the indentures of called bonds and compares them with those of the noncalled bonds and newly issued bonds. Evidence is provided that when call relaxes restrictive covenants, the firm on average pays a larger premium to call debt.

If the predominant motive for calls is to eliminate unfavorable restrictive covenants, then the indentures of the called bonds should be different from those of the non-called bonds and newly issued bonds. The indenture provisions of a called bond are classified as more restrictive if they have at least one covenant that is not required in other outstanding bonds, or a covenant of the called bond imposes a more severe constraint. For example, the $5\frac{7}{8}$ Homestake Mining bond that was called on 7-31-1963 has a covenant forcing the company to maintain net working capital at the greater of $5,000,000 or consolidated funded debt. The non-called bond does not have any working capital requirement. This comparison alone would make the called bond of Homestake Mining more restrictive. In addition, the called bond prohibits the creation of prior or equal funded debt unless four conditions are satisfied. The non-called bond has less restrictive terms because it only prohibits the creation of senior funded debt unless the same four conditions are met.[8] This provision alone would also classify the called bond of Homestake as being more restrictive.

The indentures of the 102 called bonds with market value data are examined in the Moody's industrial, public utility, and transportation manuals. These manuals contain a short description of the standard indenture provisions for the publicly-traded bonds of the firms. These descriptions are compared with the more complete indenture provisions in the bond prospectus provided by 36 firms in the sample. The prospectus gives a thorough description of all the covenants of the called bond.

---

[7] The wealth transfer hypothesis is also tested by grouping the 102 common stocks into three subsamples, according to the relation between the market value of the called bond and the call price. The average excess returns on day 0 of all three subsamples are not significantly different from zero.

[8] The $5\frac{7}{8}$ coupon bond was called because of its restriction on the creation of additional debt. When the treasurer of Homestake Mining was asked about the motive for the call, he replied: 'The company was positioning itself to raise substantial amounts of new funds for expansion of mining activities and the indenture (of the called bond) restricted new borrowings.'

Of the sample of 102 calls, 47 are by public utilities, 54 by industrial firms, one call is by a transportation firm.

5.4.1 Public utility sample

Investigation of the indenture provisions of all outstanding debt of the public utility sample reveals that: 100% of the bonds contain restrictions on the issuance of additional debt; 79% have restrictions on dividend payment; 81% require a sinking fund; 71% constrain the disposition of assets; and 69% require maintenance of assets.[9]

For the public utility sample of 47 events, only five called bonds[10] (11%) have more restrictive covenants than those of the remaining bonds which are not called, or of the newly-issued bond in the case of refunding. The majority of the called bonds (80%) by public utilities have indenture provisions which are identical to or even less restrictive than those of the non-called bonds or of the newly-issued bond. This qualitative evidence suggests that the restrictive covenant hypothesis may be valid for a small subset of calls by public utility firms but not for the majority of calls.

5.4.2. Industrial and transportation sample

Unlike the public utility sample, only 7% of the firms in the sample of 55 refund the bonds. Moreover, 36% of the called bonds represent the only long-term debt in the capital structure. Investigation of the indenture provisions of all outstanding debt reveals that: 81% of the bonds contain restrictions on the issuance of additional debt; 79% have restrictions on dividend payment; 95% include sinking fund provisions; 52% restrict lien or mortgage on property owned; 41% constrain the disposition of assets; 10% require maintenance of assets; and 12% restrict merger activities.

There must be at least one remaining bond in the capital structure after the call announcement to compare the restrictive covenants of the called bonds with those of the remaining bonds that are not called or of the newly-issued debt. This sample has 36 observations (65% of the industrial and transportation sample). Unlike the public utility sample, 50% of the called bonds in this sample have more restrictive indenture provisions than those of the non-called bonds or of the newly-issued debt. For these eighteen bonds, table 7 compares

---

[9]Smith and Warner (1979) examine bond covenants of a random sample of 87 public issues of debt which were registered with the Securities and Exchange Commission between January 1974 and December 1975. They reported that 90.8% of the bonds contain restrictions on the issuance of additional debt; 23.0% have restrictions on dividend payment; 39.1% restrict merger activities; and 35.6% constrain the firm's disposition of assets.

[10]These five bonds are: Washington Water Power (call announcement date: 3-31-64, refunding), Central Maine Power (8-20-70, refunding), Iowa Electric Light & Power (3-23-72, refunding), Southern National Resources (11-23-76, no refunding) and General Public Utilities (12-3-76, no refunding, and the only bond in the capital structure of the parent company).

Table 7

Restrictive covenants of called bonds, remaining bonds or newly-issued bonds, and the discounts of the bond price to call price for 18 called non-convertible bonds, 1963–1976.

Non-convertible bonds (1)	Call announcement date (2)	Restrictive covenants of the called bonds (3)	Restrictive covenants of the remaining bonds or newly-issued debts (4)	Percentage discount of bond price to call price (%) (5)	Dollar amount of discount of bond price to call price (in thousands) (6)
1. Homestake Mining	07-31-63	Sinking fund Working capital requirements Creation of additional debt	Smaller amount of sinking fund None Less restrictive terms	−3.8	−138
2. Wheeling Steel	10-01-63	Sinking fund Creation of additional debt Dividend restrictions Restrict lien on property	Smaller amount of sinking fund None None None	−1.8	−178
3. Bacific Petroleums	04-01-65	Sinking fund Creation of addition debt Restrict mortgage on property Dividend restrictions	Smaller amount of sinking fund None None Dividend restrictions	−0.7	−150
4. Bristol-Myers	11-16-65	Sinking fund Creation of addition debt Dividend restrictions	Smaller amount of sinking fund Less restrictive terms Less restrictive terms	−7.6	−359
5. Tenneco	05-23-66	Sinking fund Working capital requirement Creation of additional debt Dividend restrictions	None None None More restrictive terms	−5.1	−98
6. Essex Chemical	10-31-67	Sinking fund Working capital requirement Restrict mortgage on property Creation of additional debt	Smaller amount of sinking fund None None Less restrictive terms	−13.5	−207

	Date	Covenants			
7. Glen Gery Shale Brick	12-21-67	Sinking fund Restrict mortgage on property Creation of additional debt None Dividend restrictions	None None None Working capital requirement Less restrictive terms	-6.9	-228
8. OKC	01-14-68	Creation of additional debt Sinking fund Dividend restrictions Restrict mortgage on property	None Same terms None None	-12.3	-383
9. American Tobacco	10-15-68	Sinking fund Creation of additional debt Restrict mortgage on property	Smaller amount of sinking fund Less restrictive terms Same terms	-2.5	-192
10. Chicago & Eastern Illinois Railroad	06-09-69	Sinking fund Creation of additional debt None	Smaller amount of sinking fund None Dividend restrictions	-8.7	-538
11. National Distillers & Chemical	06-26-69	Sinking fund Creation of additional debt Dividend restrictions Restrict mortgage on property	Larger amount of sinking fund Same terms Less restrictive terms Less restrictive terms	-19.2	-978
12. National General	10-19-70	Sinking fund Dividend restrictions	Larger amount of sinking fund None	-4.0	-43
13. City Investing	09-27-71	Sinking fund Restrict selling property Creation of additional debt Dividend restrictions	None None None None	-23.4	-2450
14. Melville Shoe	05-01-75	Sinking fund Restrict mortgage on property Creation of additional debt Dividend restrictions	Larger amount of sinking fund None None Similar terms	-19.7	-954

Table 7 (continued)

Non-convertible bonds (1)	Call announcement date (2)	Restrictive covenants of the called bonds (3)	Restrictive covenants of the remaining bonds or newly-issued debts (4)	Percentage discount of bond price to call price (%) (5)	Dollar amount of discount of bond price to call price (in thousands) (6)
15. May Department Stores	01-28-76	Sinking fund Creation of additional debt Dividend restrictions None	Smaller amount of sinking fund Similar terms Similar terms Restrict mortgage on property	−5.6	−211
16. Litton Industries	07-02-76	None Restrict mortgage Creation of additional debt Restrict sale and leaseback Dividend restrictions	Sinking fund None None None Less restrictive terms	0.8	450
17. Diamond Shamrock	10-29-76	Sinking fund Restrict mortgage on property Restrict consolidation & sales of assets None None	Larger amount of sinking fund Similar terms None Dividend restrictions Creation of additional debt	−5.5	−371
18. United Technologies	12-21-76	Sinking fund Restrict lien on property Restrict sale and leaseback Creation of additional debt Dividend restrictions	Similar terms None None None Less restrictive terms	−5.6	−3040
				Mean: −8.1	Mean: −559

restrictive covenants with those of the non-called bonds or of the newly-issued debt. Columns (5) and (6) of table 7 show the percentage and dollar discounts of the bond price to the call price at the time of the call announcement. The discounts represent a minimum estimate of the benefits of removing the restrictive covenants. The mean of the dollar discount is −$559,000.[11] Furthermore, for seventeen out of eighteen firms in this sample, the dollar discount is negative, which implies that these firms pay bondholders a premium in order to eliminate the restrictive covenants.[12] For comparison, the average dollar discount of the overall sample of 102 bond calls shown in table 1, is −$315,000. A part of the average $559,000 premium that firms pay bondholders is tax-deductible: the difference between the call price and the face value of the bond. The tax-deductible amount is small because for eleven out of eighteen firms in this sample, the call price exceeds the face value by 1% or less.

5.4.3. Summary of the evidence on the restrictive covenant hypothesis

The evidence for the public utility sample provides stronger support for the leverage and bond refunding hypotheses than for the restrictive covenant hypothesis, because the majority of the called bonds' indenture provisions are not more restrictive than those of the non-called bonds or of the newly-issued debt. Moreover, most public utility refundings increase the maturity and size of the corporate debt.

The industrial and transportation sample provides stronger evidence in support of the restrictive covenant hypothesis. For a sample of called bonds which have more restrictive provisions than those of the non-called bonds or newly-issued debt, seventeen out of eighteen firms pay bondholders more than the market value of the bond.. The average premium of $559,000 is a low estimate of the potential opportunity costs of restrictive covenants discussed by Smith and Warner (1979),[13] if relaxation of restrictive covenants is the sole motive of the calls.

6. Conclusions and summary

This paper examines call behavior for corporate non-convertible bonds and the impact of calls on the market price of securities. Similar to Ingersoll's (1977) study of convertible bonds, the study finds that some firms wait long

---

[11] The average percentage and dollar discounts of bond price to the call price for five 'restrictive' bonds in the public utility sample are −4.9% and −$342,000.

[12] Fourteen out of eighteen firms in the sample belong to the decrease-in-leverage subsample. Therefore, the observed dollar discount may include a corporate tax effect.

[13] Although Smith and Warner (1979) did not present any precise dollar magnitude of the direct and opportunity costs of complying with the restrictive covenants, these authors claim that such costs are economically important. They wrote: 'Our analysis indicates that observed bond covenants involve expected costs which are large enough to help account for variation in debt contracts across firms. This is consistent with the costly contracting hypothesis.'

after the market value of bonds first exceeds the call price before calling their straight bonds. The decision to delay the timing of calls does not necessarily imply that the firm is acting suboptimally because transaction costs and market imperfections may prevent the firm from calling exactly at the optimal time.

When firms finally call their bonds, the market value of the called bonds is usually below the call price. Although the percentage discounts of market value to call price are large, the dollar discounts are small when measured relative to the market value of common stock.

Empirical evidence on the bond refunding hypothesis shows that most refundings are profitable, but that few industrial firms call their debt to refund.

When the overall sample of the called bonds is divided into three subsamples according to the change in leverage, evidence is provided that the stock price reactions to call announcements depend on the direction of change in leverage. This finding is similar to the results of Masulis's (1980) study of exchange offers.

Although bondholders benefit when firms call bonds whose market value is below the call price, no evidence is found that stockholders are expropriated. In fact, stockholders may benefit if the call results in eliminating burdensome restrictive covenants, thus allowing the firm to undertake profitable but risky investment projects. An examination of bond indenture agreements reveals that when the call relaxes restrictive covenants, the firm on average pays a larger premium to call debt. The premium is a minimum estimate of the potential opportunity costs of restrictive covenants discussed by Smith and Warner (1979).

After examining evidence on various hypotheses, it is concluded that none provides a complete explanation of the observed call behavior. The data suggest that there are several motives for calls and no single predominant one.

References

Brennan, M. and E. Schwartz, 1977, Convertible bonds: Valuation and optimal strategies for call and conversion, Journal of Finance 32, 1699–1715.

Constantinides, G. and B. Grundy, 1983, Are convertibles called late?, Unpublished manuscript (University of Chicago, Chicago, IL).

Ingersoll, J., 1977, An examination of corporate call policies on convertible securities, Journal of Finance 32, 463–478.

Fama, E., L. Fisher, M. Jensen and R. Roll, 1969, The adjustment of stock prices to new information, International Economic Review 10, 1–21.

Leland, H. and D. Pyle, 1977, Information asymmetrics, financial structure, and financial inter-mediation, Journal of Finance 32, 371–388.

Masulis, R., 1980, The effects of capital structure change on security prices: A study of exchange offers, Journal of Financial Economics 8, 139–177.

Miller, M.H., 1977, Debt and taxes, Journal of Finance 32, 261–275.

Modigliani, F. and M.H. Miller, 1963, Corporate income taxes and the cost of capital: A correction, American Economic Review 53, 433–443.

Ross, S., 1977, The determination of financial structure: The incentive-signalling approach, Bell Journal of Economics 8, 23–40.

Scholes, M. and J. Williams, 1977, Estimating betas from non-synchronous data, Journal of Financial Economics 5, 309–327.

Smith, C. and J. Warner, 1979, On financial contracting: An analysis of bond covenants, Journal of Financial Economics 7, 117–161.

Vermaelen, T., 1981, Common stock repurchases and market signalling: An empirical study, Journal of Financial Economics 9, 139–183.

Vu., J., 1983, An examination of corporate non-convertible bond calls and their impact on security prices, Unpublished Ph.D. dissertation (University of Chicago, Chicago, IL).

THE EFFECTS OF CAPITAL STRUCTURE CHANGE ON SECURITY PRICES

A Study of Exchange Offers

Ronald W. MASULIS*

University of California, Los Angeles, CA 90024, USA

Received March 1979, final version received February 1980

This study considers the impact of capital structure change announcements on security prices. Statistically significant price adjustments in firms' common stock, preferred stock and debt related to these announcements are documented and alternative causes for these price changes are examined. The evidence is consistent with both corporate tax and wealth redistribution effects. There is also evidence that firms make decisions which do not maximize stockholder wealth. In addition, a new approach to testing the significance of public announcements on security returns is presented.

1. Introduction

Corporate finance theory has not yet determined the consequences of fragmenting a firm's probability distribution of future market value into classes of securities. Modigliani–Miller (1958) demonstrate that when production–investment decisions are held fixed, the value of a firm is invariant to the composition of its capital structure given a perfect capital market (frictionless and perfectly competitive) and no taxes.[1] Fama–Miller (1972, pp. 167–170) further demonstrate that under the added condition of complete protective covenants or 'me-first rules' the values of a firm's individual securities are invariant to capital structure changes. However, the

*This is based on my Ph.D. dissertation written at the University of Chicago. I would like to thank my committee — Nicholas Gonedes, Albert Madansky, Merton Miller, Harry Roberts, Myron Scholes, and especially my chairman, Robert Hamada — for their help and encouragement. I have also benefitted from the suggestions of Walter Blum, Stephen Brown, Paul Cootner, Harry DeAngelo, Lawrence Fisher, George Foster, Michael Jensen, Roger Ibbotson, John Long, David Mayers, Wayne Mikkelson, Clifford Smith, G. William Schwert, the referee, Richard Ruback, and the participants in the finance workshops at Chicago, Rochester, UCLA and elsewhere. This study was partially supported by the Center for Research in Security Prices at the University of Chicago. The author takes full responsibility for remaining errors.

[1]In this proof, Modigliani–Miller assumed that the firm's debt was riskless. However, this was later shown to be only a simplifying assumption; see Fama–Miller for risky debt with perfect me-first rules and Fama (1978) for risky debt without perfect me-first rules.

Journal of Financial Economics 8 (1980) 139–178. © North-Holland Publishing Company

firm value and security value invariance propositions can fail under corporate and personal taxation (or bankruptcy costs) and under incomplete protective covenants, respectively, In short, various currently held theories make very different predictions as to the relationships between capital structure and the valuation of the firm and its individual securities.

Classic microeconomic theory presumes that firms act solely to maximize securityholders' wealth or firm net present value. But Jensen–Meckling's (1976) careful exploration of the agency relationships of corporate organization suggests that incentive conflicts can motivate maximization of stockholder wealth or management wealth at the expense of firm value maximization. In a similar vein, Bulow–Shoven (1978) analyze situations where management is induced to maximize wealth of debtholders. Thus, the existence of incentive conflicts provides a variety of motivations for capital structure changes.

This study tests the predictions of many of the currently held theories by analyzing the effects which particular capital structure changes have on the market prices of the firms' securities. Other studies have not controlled for asset structure changes which occur at the time of capital structure changes.[2] This study avoids this problem by analyzing two instances where corporate financial decisions result in close approximations to pure capital structure changes: intrafirm exchange offers and recapitalizations. These two events are unique in that they do not entail any firm cash inflows or outflows (with the exception of expenses) while they cause major changes in the firm's capital structure. These changes are effected through a private exchange between the firm and one or more classes of its securityholders.

Section 2 reviews the current theories of optimal capital structure and sets forth the predicted price adjustments for major security classes according to the type of exchange offer announced. Section 3 describes the exchange offer process and the related data sample. Section 4 introduces a new methodology for testing the significance of exchange offer announcements on the portfolio rates of return of the firms' common stock, preferred stock, and debt. Section 5 presents portfolio daily returns surrounding tender offer

---

[2]For instance, a new issue of debt involves a cash inflow while a repurchase of equity causes a cash outflow. These simultaneous cash flows result in equal changes in the value of the firm's assets and, in general, change the distributional properties of the firm's asset structure at the exact moment of the capital structure change. Consequently most recent studies of capital structure changes are contaminated by simultaneous asset structure changes. Boness–Chen–Jatusipitak (1974) studied the impact of issuing additional debt by 33 utility companies on common stock weekly residual rates of return; Kim–McConnell–Greenwood (1977) studied the impact of formation of 24 captive financing subsidiaries on the common stock and long term debt monthly residual rates of return; and Masulis (1980) studied the impact of the announcement of 199 stock tender offers on common stock daily rates of return. An earlier study by Scholes (1972) analyzed the impact of announcements of 696 rights issues for common stock on common stock monthly rates of return. It is significant that in each of these studies the common stock's announcement return was directly related to the direction of the leverage change.

announcements for major security classes. The security returns comprising these portfolios are futher segregated by type of exchange offer to isolate their potential economic causes. Section 6 summarizes the findings and implications of this study.

2. Review of corporate finance theory

Major theories of capital structure hypothesize two valuation effects arising from capital structure change: a corporate tax effect and an expected cost of bankruptcy effect. Changes in a firm's after tax value predicted by these theories imply like directional changes in the values of the firm's individual risky securities.[3]

2.1. Corporate and personal income taxes

In a world with corporate taxation, tax deductible interest payments subsidize the issuance of debt [Modigliani–Miller (1963)]. Increasing outstanding debt increases a firm's tax shield; this in turn increases a firm's value by the amount of the tax shield capitalized over its life multiplied by the corporate tax rate. With the introduction of differential personal taxation across investors, where debt interest income is taxed at a higher rate than capital gains income derived from stock, the earlier Modigliani–Miller conclusion is no longer definitive. In this case, corporate tax deductions are at least partially offset by additional personal tax liabilities of the acquiring debtholders. Miller (1976) shows that for equilibrium to exist in a perfect capital market with corporate and differential personal income tax rates, debt policy can have no effect on firm market value. In this case, a given firm should be indifferent to the level of outstanding debt since there is no optimal level of debt for the firm (though there is an optimal aggregate level of debt).

With the introduction of investment tax shields or leverage related cost, DeAngelo–Masulis (1979) demonstrate that the existence of a personal tax bias against debt income diminishes but does not eliminate the net corporate tax benefit of debt.[4] Moreover, a unique optimal capital structure will often exist in this tax environment, where at the margin, the corporate tax advantage of debt exactly offsets the personal tax disadvantage of holding debt. Given the conflicting predictions of these competing theories, resolution of this controversy requires empirical evidence.

---

[3]For a description of the assumed relationship between the firm value and the values of risky debt and equity, see Black–Scholes (1973) and Merton (1974), and for the relationship between firm value and the value of preferred stock, see Merton (1974).

[4]A somewhat different argument is made by Kraus–Litzenberger (1973), Brennan–Schwartz (1978) and Kim (1977) who link the usefulness of the debt tax shield to the probability of solvency. Their models also imply that the present value of the debt tax shield increases at a decreasing rate since the probability of bankruptcy is rising with the increase in debt.

2.2. Expected costs of bankruptcy and reorganization

Baxter (1967), Robichek–Myers (1966), Kraus–Litzenberger (1973) and Scott (1976) argue that the expected cost of involuntary bankruptcy and reorganization (Chapters X and XI proceedings) has a significant impact on the value of a levered firm. These costs include lawyers' and accountants' fees, court costs, and the cost of managerial time consumed in bankruptcy and reorganization proceedings.[5] Furthermore as the probability of incurring these costs of bankruptcy rises, the value of the firm decreases. Consequently, a firm altering its leverage (defined as the face value of debt divided by the market value of the firm) should experience a like change in the probability of bankruptcy, causing an opposite change in its value. This change in firm value must cause an equal change in the sum of the market values of the firm's risky securities, with the impact being shared among all these securities.

Firms in financial distress often prefer a voluntary recapitalization or merger rather than involuntary bankruptcy and reorganization (bankruptcy proceedings under Chapters X and XI). For example, if a financially distressed firm successfully recapitalizes through an exchange offer, thereby avoiding bankruptcy, Gould's (1973) analysis suggests that the expenses of the exchange offer are the only costs of 'bankruptcy and reorganization' borne by the firm. Similarly, Haugen–Senbet (1978) show that costs of a debtholder takeover and voluntary firm recapitalization represent an alternative upper bound on bankruptcy costs (debtholders purchasing the firm's stock). These studies imply that the costs of anticipated present and future exchange offers make up a large proportion of the 'expected costs of bankruptcy and reorganization'.

Combining corporate taxes and bankruptcy costs, the models of Robichek–Myers and Kraus–Litzenberger yield predictions of an optimal capital structure where increases in leverage beyond the optimum lead to expected marginal bankruptcy costs which exceed the marginal tax benefits of debt, while decreases in leverage below the optimum lead to a loss of marginal tax benefits of debt which exceeds the savings in expected marginal bankruptcy costs. Consequently, if managers maximize firms' net present values, these tax–bankruptcy cost models will predict net positive tax effects when firms *increase* leverage and net positive expected cost of bankruptcy savings when firms *decrease* leverage.

The second theory of capital structure change associated with leverage costs arises from the agency costs associated with the separation of management and ownership in the firm. These agency costs increase as managers

---

[5]Warner's (1976) estimates of the direct costs of bankruptcy for a limited sample of railroads indicate that their magnitude is small relative to firm value. Also there are the previously mentioned leverage related costs which Jensen–Meckling define as agency costs.

own less of the firm's equity since the optimal monitoring of managerial decisions and the level of perquisite consumption by management rises. The introduction of debt decreases these stockholder–manager agency costs by increasing the managers' proportional ownership in the firm's equity. However, as the leverage rises, a second agency cost arises — that between stockholders and bondholders — and for sufficiently large leverage this cost will exceed the stockholder–manager agency costs savings. The resulting agency cost function is convex, yielding an optimal capital structure at the point where total agency costs are minimized (see Jensen–Meckling). This model's qualitative predictions of firm valuation effects from leverage change do not appear easily distinguishable from those of the corporate tax-bankruptcy cost models of Robichek–Myers and Kraus–Litzenberger. However, the Jensen–Meckling model also allows for wealth redistributions among classes of securityholders, an effect explained below.

2.3. Wealth redistributions and incomplete protective covenants

Unlike the previous two hypotheses, which predict changes of the same sign in both firm value and security prices, the wealth redistribution hypothesis predicts offsetting changes in the values of individual classes of securities and no change in firm value. Protective covenants or me-first rules are defined as incomplete if management can change the firm's asset or capital structure to redistribute wealth among classes of securityholders (Fama–Miller).[6] As Jensen–Meckling clearly show, securities with incomplete protective covenants can exist because the costs of monitoring and enforcing complete protective covenants exceed the value of the protection obtained from having them (in terms of higher security prices).[7] In other words, given that securities with incomplete protective covenants are less costly to supply due to lower monitoring and enforcement costs, and given that investors assess these securities to be less valuable due to the probability of future losses, we should observe these securities to have lower market prices than otherwise equivalent securities.[8] Consequently, while holders of outstanding securities with incomplete protective covenants (particularly preferred stock and debt) are subject to potentially adverse redistributions of wealth, they receive implicit market determined compensation for being subject to these potential losses through the security's lower purchase price.

---

[6]See Fama–Miller and Fama (1978) for further discussion of protective covenants. Smith–Warner (1979) describe alternative forms that those protective covenants can take on.

[7]See Galai–Masulis (1976), case study 2 in particular, and also Litzenberger–Sosin (1977) for examples.

[8]Even without the existence of transaction costs of supplying protective covenants, securities with incomplete protective covenants sell at a lower price due to demand side considerations alone as Black–Cox (1976) demonstrate for some special cases with incomplete protective covenants.

Capital structure changes can induce redistributions of wealth when there are explicit or implicit limitations in securities' protective covenants. Protective covenants are explicitly incomplete if one or more classes of senior securities fails to strictly preclude increases in the amount of securities of equal or senior standing.[9] Protective covenants are implicitly limited if the courts choose not to adhere strictly to the 'absolute priority rule'[10] in the adjudication of bankruptcy cases. This rule states that in any plan of reorganization, 'beginning with the topmost class of claims against the debtor, each class in descending rank must receive full and complete compensation for the rights surrendered before the next class below may properly participate',[11] thus suggesting that even complete protective covenants can be rendered ineffective in a bankruptcy proceeding.[12]

It follows from the preceding analysis that particular capital structure changes result in different wealth redistributions. The exchange of additional debt for existing common stock, which is not fully anticipated, causes outstanding debtholders to bear an adverse redistribution of wealth because of implicitly and possibly explicitly incomplete protective covenants. At the same time the preferred stockholders are made worse off by the conversion of junior claims (common stock) into senior claims (debt). The common stockholders, who are the residual claimants of the firm, gain, since a portion of their junior claims are converted into senior claims of greater market value.

Under an exchange of preferred stock for existing common stock, outstanding preferred stockholders experience an adverse redistribution of wealth analogous to that experienced by outstanding debtholders in the previous case, while the impact on common stockholders is qualitatively identical to the previous case. Furthermore, there is no direct impact on the debtholders from explicitly incomplete covenants.[13]

Under an exchange of debt for existing preferred stock, preferred stockholders who are able to convert at least a portion of their lower priority preferred stock claims for higher priority debt claims at their pre-

---

[9]The existence of transaction costs of changing the asset or capital structure offers a certain degree of 'natural protection' to securityholders with incomplete protective covenants, since in both cases there are transaction costs borne by the firm in the process of redistributing wealth among classes of securityholders, Technological limitations on the number of profitable investment projects also offer some measure of natural protection.

[10]For a further discussion of this legal definition, see Blum (1958) and Blum and Kaplan (1974).

[11]See *Collier on Bankruptcy* (1972, 6A id. 11.06 pp. 613–617).

[12]However the degree of compensation to more senior claimants will generally .exceed the degree of compensation paid to junior claimants for their respective claims on the insolvent firms.

[13]However, debtholders can experience a small negative effect from implicitly incomplete covenants since the level of priority of junior claims has increased. Specifically, the issuance of preferred stock for common stock increases the probability that in a bankruptcy/reorganization the junior securityholders will receive a larger share of the firm's assets.

announcement prices are made better off at the expense of the outstanding debtholders. Due to explicit and/or implicit limitations in protective covenants, the debtholders now bear greater risk of default but receive the same interest payments from the firm. Preferred stockholders who do *not* or cannot convert their preferred stock to debt are hurt because claims of equal standing are elevated to senior standing, thereby increasing the preferred stock's risk of loss.[14]

If corporate tax and/or bankruptcy cost effects exist, a change in capital structure can cause a change in the firm's investment decisions that change the firm's rate of return variance inducing a secondary redistribution effect. When the firm's variance is decreased the senior non-convertible debt and preferred stock increase in value while the common stock, warrants and conversion feature of debt and preferred stock decrease in value (and vice versa for a decrease in variance). This secondary redistribution of wealth can reinforce or reduce the primary redistribution of wealth discussed previously. Given the far-ranging implications of this redistribution of wealth hypothesis for the effects of corporate financing decisions on the values of firm securities, it is important to determine its empirical validity and level of significance.

2.4. Summary of theoretical predictions

Table 1 summarizes the predicted effects of capital structure change given by the three hypotheses: interest deductibility under corporate taxation, expected costs of bankruptcy and reorganization and wealth redistributions under incomplete protective covenants. Observed security price changes can reflect the impacts of all three hypotheses. There are three categories of capital structure change shown: exchanges of debt for outstanding common stock, exchanges of preferred stock for outstanding common stock and exchanges of debt for outstanding preferred stock. The qualitative predictions of the three hypotheses are given for the change in market values of each major class of firm securities. It is assumed in each case that the senior security is being issued to retire the junior security.[15] It is important to note that when firm debt is increased the predictions of the corporate tax hypothesis are opposite from those of the expected cost of bankruptcy hypothesis. On the other hand, while these two hypotheses individually make

---

[14]Under implicit covenant limitations common stockholders can be hurt to a small extent, because in an involuntary reorganization common stockholders can still receive some payment from the firm but the size of this payment is diminished as the preferred stock is converted into higher priority debt claims.

[15]The debt and preferred stock on table 1 are assumed to be nonconvertible securities. If this were not the case, the security would experience not only the effects of otherwise similar nonconvertible securities but also the effects experienced by the common stock into which the security is convertible.

Table 1

Predicted corporate tax, bankruptcy cost and redistribution effects on the values of outstanding security classes classified by type of exchange offer increasing firm leverage.[a]

Change in market value of existing security classes	Capital structure changes classified by type and effects								
	Debt for common			Preferred for common			Debt for preferred		
	Corporate tax	Bankruptcy cost	Redistribution	Corporate tax	Bankruptcy cost	Redistribution	Corporate tax	Bankruptcy cost	Redistribution
Common stock	Positive	Negative	Positive	None	None	Positive	Positive	Negative	None or negative
Preferred stock	Positive	Negative	Negative	None	None	Negative	Positive	Negative	Positive
Risky debt	Positive	Negative	Negative	None	None	None or negative	Positive	Negative	Negative

[a]If the direction of the exchange is reversed, security valuation effects presented in the body of the table will be reversed. Note that the predicted change in a security's value is the sum of these three individual effects.

[b]This holds only for preferred stock issues involved in the offer.

uniform qualitative predictions for the values of each of the firm's major classes of securities, this is not the case for the predictions of the redistribution of wealth hypothesis. The differential predictions described in table 1 are important for the interpretation of the empirical results.

2.5. Predictions of other theories

Although there is no limit to the number of theories which predict effects due to capital structure changes, at least two other recently developed theories have interested financial theorists. The first theory posits that managers, motivated to communicate insider information concerning firm value to the public, undertake costly capital structure changes that act as validated signals of this information [Ross (1977) and Leland–Pyle (1977)]. It is suggested that firms signal an increase in firm asset value by increasing leverage in Ross, and by decreasing leverage in Leland–Pyle. However, neither of these models specifies the new information that management is releasing concerning firm asset value, making separation of this signalling effect from other hypothesized effects of capital structure change difficult. As a consequence, the signalling hypothesis will not be formally tested.

Other types of information effects are also possible. For instance, the agency cost model predicts that a firm's capital structure affects management incentives to make particular firm related decisions. Consequently, the likelihood of future capital structure and asset structure decisions will be altered in predictable directions given a current change in capital structure. This is an information effect quite separate from the effect predicted by the Ross model which also could affect security price adjustments. Other information effects are also conceivable.

A second alternative hypothesis explaining the observed security price effects of exchange offer announcements is the offer premium hypothesis. An exchange offer premium is defined as the difference between the preannouncement market price of the security being retired minus the postannouncement market value of the securities being offered in exchange. The hypothesis presumes that the price of the security being purchased by means of an exchange offer must rise by the amount of the exchange offer premium to ensure a continuance of secondary market trading. This requires that some securityholders must be indifferent to tendering to the firm or selling in the secondary market. It is implicitly assumed under this hypothesis that there is an upward sloping supply curve for the security being tendered, possibly due to heterogeneous capital gains liabilities. It follows that while some securityholders will prefer to tender, others will not. As a result, there will be an intra-security class redistribution of wealth to those securityholders tendering from those securityholders not tendering. Furthermore, at the end of the offer period, the security's price should fall by more than the exchange offer premium to reflect both the wealth loss experienced by the remaining securityholders and the end of the opportunity to tender the security to the firm at a price premium (relative to the pre-announcement price).

3. Description of exchange offers and sample properties

3.1. Exchange offers and recapitalizations

An example of a typical exchange offer is CIT Financial Corporation's January 1968 offer to exchange $100 face value of 6.75 percent non-convertible debentures for each share of outstanding $5 par non-convertible preferred stock tendered. CIT Financial's preferred stockholders' acceptance of this offer resulted in the issuance of $46 million in debentures and the retirement of 462,500 shares of preferred stock.

Generally speaking, an exchange offer gives one or more security classes the right to exchange part or all of their present holdings for a different class of firm securities. Although generally open for one month, the offer is often extended for an additional number of weeks just prior to the initial expiration date. The terms of exchange offered to the tendering securityholders typically involve a package of new securities of greater market value (in terms of pre-exchange offer announcement prices) than those being tendered, with the difference in these securities' values considered an exchange offer premium. Most exchange offers state a maximum number of securities which can be exchanged and a maximum duration for the offer. Indenture restrictions on the firm generally limit the magnitude of any repurchases of common stock through new issues of preferred stock or debt. In addition, many offers are contingent upon acceptance by a minimum number of securityholders. The exchange offer process generally lasts four to five months during which the firm issues a number of announcements regarding the proposed exchange. On average, initial announcement dates precede the beginning of the exchange offer by nine weeks, and the average life of the offer is about seven weeks.[16]

In contrast to the voluntary securityholder participation and relatively long time period an exchange offer is open, recapitalizations generally require the participation of all securityholders of the affected class and occur at a single point in time.[17] The management of the corporation generally proposes a plan of recapitalization which, if approved by the board of

---

[16]A few firms announced exchange offers with unusually long intervals between the initiation of the offer and its termination date. While this implies a longer delay before the capital structure change is to occur, and hence a possible impact on the size of the security price changes, no further analysis is made due to the small number of events involved.

[17]For a more extensive discussion of recapitalizations, see Guthmann–Dougall (1962).

directors is then submitted to those securityholders who will be directly affected by the changes. The plan of recapitalization, which requires the approval of a majority of each affected security class, generally requires that all holders of the class of securities being retired accept the exchange of securities. From this point on, the term exchange offer will include recapitalizations.[18]

3.2. Tax consequences of exchange offers[19]

An increase in a firm's outstanding debt resulting from an exchange offer produces two complementary effects on corporate income tax liabilities: an original issue discount[20] (or premium) on the new debt issue and tax deductible debt interest payments. An original issue discount, which is treated as an expense of the corporation, is the difference between the face value of the debt and its issue price. If an original issue discount is less than $\frac{1}{4}$ of 1 percent of the redemption price at maturity multiplied by the number of complete years to maturity (5% for a twenty year bond), the issue discount is considered zero. Since 1969, original issue discounts must be allocated equally over the life of the debt instrument. The effect of an original issue discount is to increase a firm's corporate tax deductions derived from the flotation of a given amount of a new debt when it is issued at a significant price discount. Just the opposite effect occurs under an original issue premium. Similarly, when a firm redeems debt at a price below (above) the issue price, the difference is treated as ordinary income (or loss).

With respect to personal income taxation, the most important feature of the tax code is that the corporate income tax deductions derived from interest payments, original issue discounts, and redemption premiums are personal income tax liabilities of the debtholders. Thus, any change in the corporation's taxable income has an equal, though opposite, effect on the taxable income of investors acquiring or tendering this debt. This does not mean that the taxes paid to the government are invariant under this voluntary transfer of tax liabilities, because the marginal income tax rates of the corporation and these securityholders can differ.

Stockholders can also incur a capital gains tax liability by tendering their stock for debt just as if they had sold their stock for cash.[21] Thus, these offers often occur when the stocks are selling at historically low prices, a

---

[18]Recapitalizations comprise a relatively small portion of our sample (23 events out of a total sample of 163 events).

[19]See Bittker–Eustice (1971) for a more thorough discussion of the tax questions covered here.

[20]See Section 368(a) (1) of the Internal Revenue Code.

[21]If, after tendering shares, the investor holds 80 percent or more of the firm's shares and voting control which he initially held, this repurchase may be treated as a cash dividend under Section 302 of the Internal Revenue Code.

point at which most stockholders incur little or no capital gains liability on the exchange of their stock for debt.

3.3. Expenses incurred in the exchange offer process

Firms making exchange offers incur significant expenses in this process, including compensation paid to broker–dealers, accounting and legal fees for registering the securities under Federal and State security laws, and stock transfer taxes. Estimates of the cost of direct administrative and legal services, assuming the offer is fully subscribed, range between 0.1 percent and 10 percent of the market value of the common stock prior to the initial offer announcement. These cost estimates average about 2 percent of the stock's value. Consequently, even if the change in capital structure has no tax, bankruptcy cost, or other effects on firm value, these transaction costs alone would result in a small negative effect.

3.4. Incomplete protective covenants

Debt and preferred stock issues with incomplete covenant protection against the effects of exchange offers must exist if redistributions of wealth unrelated to the abrogation of the 'absolute priority rule' are to exist. For 20 percent of the firms in the sample, indentures of outstanding debt issues do not preclude or require compensation for the issuance of new debt of either equal or senior standing.[22] In analyzing the effects of exchange offers on debt issues, special attention is given to the evidence of redistributions of wealth experienced by the holders of debt issues with such incomplete protective covenants.

3.5. Sources of exchange offer announcements and sample design

Initially all proposed exchange offers and recapitalizations made in the 14-year period between mid-1962 and mid-1976 were collected. Public announcement dates of the proposed capital structure changes were obtained primarily from the Wall Street Journal Index, firm prospectuses, and questionnaires which were sent to all presently existing companies listed in the sample.[23]

Exchange offers are classified primarily by the direction of their effect upon firm leverage. Approximately two-thirds of the sample involves increases in leverage. Of this group, the largest percentage is represented by exchanges of debt for common stock, while for decreases in leverage, exchanges of common for preferred stock are most numerous.

---

[22]This evidence is obtained from exchange offer prospectuses.

[23]About 85 percent of these firms responded positively to the questionnaire and, in most cases, provided copies of relevant press releases and other related material.

The following sample selection criteria were imposed in order to limit the observable price effects solely to the announcement of exchange offers and to confine the sample to those events having reliable data sources:

(1) Only offers with a determinate initial announcement date and by companies having common stock listed on the NYSE or the ASE at the time of the proposal were included.

(2) Only offers which alter the level of debt or preferred stock outstanding were considered (offers must involve more than one major class of firm securities, i.e., common, preferred, or debt).[24]

(3) Cash and other asset distributions associated with the exchange offer were limited to a maximum of 25 percent of the value of the affected securities being tendered in the offer.

(4) Firms with announcements of other major asset structure or capital structure changes which were made within one week prior to or following the initial offer announcement were excluded.[25]

Of the 188 offers initially found to meet the first two criteria, 163 remained after the entire screening process.[26] Even after passing this screening process, the offer must still be considered an *approximation* to a pure capital structure change because claims to fractional shares of new securities were paid in cash, some offers involve 'small' cash distributions and there are transaction costs of making the offer.[27]

While it is difficult to be certain that a specific public announcement conveys only one particular type of information, our sample design minimizes the probability that new information regarding firm asset values and risk characteristics is being released in close proximity to the exchange offer

---

[24]If debt, common and preferred stock are all involved in the exchange offer, it is required that the change in debt and preferred stock outstanding be in the same direction while the change in common stock outstanding be in the opposite direction. Exchanges whose sole effects are to increase debt coupon rates and weaken indenture covenants, increase debt maturity, or increase debt coupon rates while decreasing debt face value, are among those events excluded from this analysis.

[25]Thus, announcements of new issues, redemptions or repurchases of securities, mergers, acquisitions, spinoffs, major new investments, large new contracts and large changes in net income which exceed 25 percent of the value of the securities tendered in the offer, as well as announcements of changes in dividend policy, late payment of debt interest, impending bankruptcy, major discoveries, and new patents which were made within one week of the initial offer announcement disqualified those events from the sample.

[26]There are 19 and 6 events eliminated by criteria (3) and (4), respectively. Of the 19 events eliminated by criterion (4), almost all were the result of other announcements made on the date of the initial exchange offer announcement. In addition, one should note that of the 163 events in our sample, 29 indefinitely postponed or cancelled their offers.

[27]Exchanges having a cash or asset component in the offer less than 25 percent of the newly issued securities' value represented 23 events in the final sample.

announcement. However, the relationship between security price changes and capital structure change can still be confounded if capital structure change announcements *consistently* communicate particular insider information concerning firm value to the market or have a significant impact on the market assessment of future changes in the firm's asset or capital structure.[28] However, no systematic patterns of later (or earlier) capital or asset structure changes were observed in the years that the offers occurred. A more extensive analysis of the properties of the final exchange offer sample is available in Masulis (1978).

3.6. Security daily rates of return

Rates of return for NYSE and ASE listed common stocks for the three months surrounding the announcement date were obtained from the Center for Research in Security Prices Daily Rate of Return Tape covering the period mid-1962 through mid-1976. The market rate of return is approximated by the rate of return on the Standard and Poors 500 Stock Index, which weights the stocks comprising the index by their relative market values.

Daily rates of return for preferred stock are calculated for the ten trading days before and after the initial exchange offer announcement data using the closing prices listed in Standard and Poor's *NYSE Daily Stock Record* and *ASE Daily Stock Record*. Bid–ask averages are used when traded prices are unavailable, and cash dividends are added to the rates of return on their ex-dividend dates.

Bond rates of return are also calculated for ten trading days around the initial exchange offer announcement. Daily *sale* prices were obtained from the *Wall Street Journal*; if unavailable, bid–ask averages were not used due to limitations in data availability and reliability. Rates of return are adjusted for daily interest accruals and coupon payment dates. Interest coupon rates and payment dates were obtained from Standard and Poor's monthly *Bond Guide*.

While our overall sample is limited to firms with common stock listed on the NYSE or ASE at the time of the exchange offer announcement, the outstanding preferred stock or debt issues of the sample firms are not subject to this criterion. Not surprisingly, only a subset of the firms in the exchange offer sample have preferred stock and/or debt issues listed and actively traded on one of the two major stock exchanges.

---

[28]Criterion (4) could in principle induce some selection bias in the results, in that exchange offers may be associated with the signalling of insider information concerning firm value and risk would be partially filtered out by our sample criteria.

4. Methodology

4.1. Portfolio formation in event time

For this analysis, portfolios are formed in event time; so that each portfolio daily rate of return represents an average of security returns for a common event date. The event date is defined as the number of trading days before or after the announcement date under scrutiny, where day 0 is the date of the actual announcement.[29]

Security returns are not calculated for days when security prices are unavailable, and as a result these securities are not included in the portfolio returns for these days. If a trading halt in the security occurs on the day after the announcement date. the next trade price is substituted for the day 1 closing price, so that the announcement effect will not be obscured.

4.2. Preferred stock and debt portfolio rates of return

The returns of the actively traded issues of preferred stock or debt listed on the NYSE or ASE require further adjustment. To eliminate any bias in portfolio returns due to over-representation of firms with multiple issues of a given security class, security returns are weighted. The weights used are the reciprocals of the number of security issues per exchange offer represented in a given portfolio, so that each exchange offer has equal weight in a given portfolio of securities.

Separate portfolios of convertible and non-convertible debt and preferred stock are formed in much of the analysis not only because differential price effects are predicted for various types of capital structure changes (their convertibility into common stock implies that these securities should share in the same effects observed for the common stock), but also because the convertible securities' rate of return variance and systematic risk, on average, are considerably higher than those of the non-convertible securities. This latter characteristic would tend to obscure effects of exchange offers on the non-convertible issues.

4.3. Measurement of information effects on security prices

To assess the average magnitude and statistical significance of security price changes or rates of return which accompany specific corporate announcements, security specific announcement effects must be separated from unrelated market pricing effects. Assume that the stochastic process generat-

---

[29]Earlier studies using this approach include Fama–Fisher–Jensen–Roll (1969), Jaffe (1974), Ibbotson (1975), and Ellert (1976).

ing security rates of return is

$$\tilde{r}_{it} = \mu_{it} + \tilde{\varepsilon}_{it},$$

where $E(\tilde{\varepsilon}_{it}) = 0$ and $\mathrm{cov}(\tilde{\varepsilon}_{it}, \tilde{\varepsilon}_{it-1}) = 0$ for all i and all t.

The serially uncorrelated stochastic disturbance term, $\tilde{\varepsilon}_{it}$ represents both marketwide influences and security specific effects. The non-stochastic term μ_{it} is a market determined function of the assumed asset pricing model and security specific attributes (e.g. distributional properties of security returns). This general formulation of security returns process is clearly consistent with the well known variants of the Capital Asset Pricing Model.[30]

A security's expected return can also be written as a function of the conditional expectations of its disturbance term,

$$E(\tilde{r}_{it}) = \mu_{it} + E(\tilde{\varepsilon}_{it} \mid \theta_{it} = 0)P(\theta_{it} = 0) + E(\tilde{\varepsilon}_{it} \mid \theta_{it} = 1)P(\theta_{it} = 1),$$

where $\theta_{it} = 0$ means that no capital structure change is announced by firm i at time t, while $\theta_{it} = 1$ means that a specific capital structure change is announced by firm i at time t, and $P(\theta_{it} = X)$ is the probability that $\theta_{it} = X$.

As shown in table 1, the sign of $E(\tilde{\varepsilon}_{it} \mid \theta_{it} = 1)$ is a function of the security class and the type of capital structure change announced. Consequently, if such an announcement is known to have occurred in a given period, the security's conditional expected return will differ from μ_{it} in a predictable direction.

In order to assess the impact of new information on security prices, it is necessary to separate ε_{it} from the announcement period returns by subtracting out an estimate of μ_{it}. The conventional approach to estimating μ_{it} is to first estimate a variant of the market model which specifies a statistical relationship between contemporaneous security and market returns (the most widely used formulation being $\tilde{r}_{it} = \alpha_i + \beta_i \tilde{r}_{mt} + \hat{\varepsilon}_{it}^*$). The market's announcement period return is then substituted into the estimates relationship to yield $\hat{\mu}_{it} = \hat{\alpha}_i + \hat{\beta}_i r_{mt}$.[31] An alternative approach for estimating μ_{it}, termed the Comparison Period Returns approach, is utilized in this study. In this alternative approach, a security's mean return μ_{it} is estimated from a time series of the security's returns over a representative period (not including the announcement period) which is defined as the comparison period. This yields an unbiased estimate of μ_{it} given that the security's return process is stationary over the period of observation. Once $\hat{\mu}_{it}$ is determined, the announcement period disturbance term ε_{it} can, in turn, be estimated. Since μ_{it} is not known for certain in either approach, estimation error will

---

[30]For a further discussion of this point, see Ross (1976).

[31]This approach assumes that the correct specification of the market model is being estimated and that this relationship is stationary over the observation period. Note that μ_{it} includes the stochastic market-related disturbance term, so that $\tilde{\varepsilon}_{it}^*$ is a security-specific disturbance term; while in the Comparison Period Approach $\tilde{\varepsilon}_{it}$ includes a market-related disturbance term.

exist in $\hat{\varepsilon}_{it}$ and furthermore, the disturbance term can be affected by other factors in addition to the announcement under study (such as deviations from the mean return on the market). However, since the first of these two influences on $\hat{\varepsilon}_{it}$ is independent across securities, its impact can be minimized by forming a 'portfolio' in event time of these individual securities experiencing a common announcement effect. Furthermore, when the sample of announcement dates is strictly non-contemporaneous in calendar time, the latter influence on $\hat{\varepsilon}_{it}$ will be independent across securities in event time, regardless of whether the impact of the market return has been subtracted out or not.

4.4. Testing procedure: The comparison period returns approach

Under the Comparison Period Returns approach, it is useful to view the portfolio's *announcement period* expected return as equal to the average of the individual securities' expected disturbance terms conditional on a common announcement $E(\tilde{\varepsilon}_{it}|\,\theta_{it}=1)$ plus the portfolio's *comparison period* expected return. Consequently, a test of whether or not the announcement period disturbance term is zero can be formulated by simply testing whether the announcement period mean return is significantly different from the comparison period mean return. In the alternative market model approach, one tests whether or not the announcement period return minus $\hat{\mu}_{it}$ is significantly different from zero.

Given that security returns are independent across non-contemporaneous calendar time and that the second and third moments are finite, portfolio daily returns and time series averages of portfolio daily returns approach normal distributions for large samples under the Central Limit Theorem.[32] A related random variable which will also be studied is the portfolio's percentage of security daily returns that are positive for a given event day. To obtain the distribution of this random variable, classify the independent security returns in the portfolio as one if positive or zero if non-positive. This yields a set of binary variables which are Bernoulli distributed. Summing (or averaging) these binary variables yields a binomially distributed random variable which also approaches a normal distribution in large samples under the Central Limit Theorem.

Assuming that portfolio daily returns and percent of security returns positive are normally distributed and stationary, significance tests of leverage change announcement effects on security prices can be constructed. Under these assumptions, a conventional t test for the the equality of announcement

---

[32]Further, there is a condition on the smallness of the absolute third moment which must also hold; see Dhrymes (1970, pp. 104–105). One could alternatively standardize the individual security returns by their respective standard deviations estimated over the time period prior to the comparison period to increase the rate of convergence of the distribution to a normal distribution.

period and comparison period means is used to test the null hypothesis of no leverage effect against the alternative hypothesis of a positive or negative leverage effect depending on the particular hypothesis under consideration.[33] In this approach, the standard error is computed from the time series of portfolio daily returns from the announcement and comparison periods.

Applying the Comparison Period Returns approach in this study, it is assumed that the appropriate length of the comparison period is 60 trading days before and after the initial announcement date for common stock and 10 trading days before and after the initial announcement date for preferred stock and debt. To evaluate the reasonableness of this procedure, Masulis (1978) compared the pre- and post-announcement subperiods of the overall comparison period. On the whole, the data indicates that the two subperiods exhibit very similar mean returns, and that aggregating these subperiods has little effect on the comparison period returns' mean and standard deviation, relative to the magnitude of the announcement effect.[34] There are a number of advantages to the Comparison Period Returns- approach used in this study.[35] First, the difficulties associated with using the alrernative Market Model approaches, namely the problem of determining the appropriate

---

[33]See Mood–Graybill–Boes (1974, p. 435). This is a standard difference of means test statistic which is t distributed with parameter $T_1 + T_2 - 2$,

$$t \equiv \frac{(\bar{r}_1 - \bar{r}_{t0})}{\sqrt{\{(T_1 - 1)s_1^2 + (T_2 - 1)s_2^2\}/\{T_1 + T_2 - 2\}}\sqrt{\{1/T_1 + 1/T_2\}}},$$

where T_1 = number of portfolio daily returns in the comparison period, T_2 = number of portfolio daily returns in the announcement period, $\bar{r}_1$ = portfolio's comparison period mean daily return, s_1 = standard deviation of the comparison period mean return, $\bar{r}_{t0}$ = portfolio's announcement period mean daily return, and s_2 = standard deviation of the announcement period mean daily return.

The test procedure used here is similar in spirit to tests using a matched pair comparison, though the pairs are of unequal size. Note that this t test assumes that the true standard deviations for the two periods are equal.

[34]A t test for the difference between the two means could not reject the null hypothesis of equal means at a 5 percent significance level. Implicit in the use of pre- and post-announcement returns is the presumption that the security's unconditional expected return μ_{it} is unaffected by the announcement being studied, and therefore that the security's post-announcement comparison subperiod mean return is likewise unaffected. In the case of exchange offers, it is presumed that any leverage induced changes in security risk and expected return occur beyond the end of the comparison period. Specifically a change in leverage will cause a like change in the risk and expected return of the firm's common stock at the time of the capital structure change under Proposition II of Modigliani–Miller (1958). Note that an announced future change in leverage has no impact on the stockholder's risk bearing in the interim period prior to the actual period of the leverage change. Consequently there should be no change in the stock's expected return in the interim period. For the exchange offer sample being studied, the initial offer announcement, on average, precedes the actual capital structure change by four months, which is considerably beyond the end of the chosen comparison period. If this were not the case, the comparison period should be restricted to the period preceding the initial announcement date. One exception to this argument is the secondary leverage change caused by a change in firm market value, which is assumed to be empirically insignificant.

[35]However, the announcement effects were tested for significance using various standard market model approaches where similar findings were obtained, as described in Masulis (1978).

market index and the associated estimation error and specification error involved in correctly determining a security return's specific contemporaneous relationship with the market return are avoided.[36] Comparing these two approaches using simulations based on monthly returns drawn from non-contemporaneous calendar time, Brown–Warner (1980) conclude that the Comparison Period Returns approach is at least as powerful and often more powerful than market adjusted approaches such as the one-factor market model.[37]

4.5. Format of the tables

A series of tables follows in which the portfolio's announcement period mean daily returns are compared with the portfolio's mean daily return for a pre- and post-announcement period which is termed the comparison period. In each table, column 1 indicates the number of trading days before or after the exchange offer announcement date (where day 0 is the announcement date), column 2 contains the portfolio daily returns, and column 3 shows the percentages of securities with strictly positive daily returns. Near the bottom of each table are the mean and standard deviation of the comparison period portfolio daily returns, along with the mean and standard deviation of the comparison period mean percentage of security daily returns strictly positive. These statistics are calculated excluding the two-day announcement period (day 0 and day 1).

5. Empirical results

In the results to follow initial announcement effects for increases and decreases in leverage on common stock returns are presented. The sample of common stocks is segmented by type of exchange offer into returns predicted to exhibit tax and offsetting bankruptcy effects, only redistribution effects and all three effects. The sample of preferred stocks is likewise segmented by type of exchange offer into returns predicted to exhibit tax and offsetting bankruptcy and redistribution effects, only redistribution effects, and tax, redistribution and offsetting bankruptcy effects. In analyzing debt, convertible issues are separated from non-convertible issues, and their respective returns segmented into exchange offers predicted to cause tax and offsetting bankruptcy and redistribution effects or no effect on debt prices. Lastly, debt returns of issues having obviously incomplete protective covenants, which are predicted to exhibit larger redistribution effects, are separated from the returns of other debt issues.

---

[36]See the discussion by Roll (1977), Gonedes (1973) and others.

[37]This conclusion should be even stronger in the case of daily returns as used in this study since the significance of the market model as indicated by its R^2 is much lower for daily data than for monthly data.

5.1. Initial announcement effects on common stock

A basic question this study seeks to answer is whether or not an alteration in a firm's capital structure has any measurable impact on its securities' prices. A partial answer to this question is contained in table 2, where the

Table 2

Common stock rates of return for initial announcements of offers increasing and decreasing leverage.

Increasing leverage announcements N = 106			Decreasing leverage announcements N = 57		
Event day	Portfolio daily returns (%)	% of stock returns > 0	Event day	Portfolio daily returns (%)	% of stock returns > 0
− 30	0.27	38.0	− 30	1.16	39.0
− 29	− 0.40	36.0	− 29	− 0.48	27.0
− 28	− 0.34	25.0	− 28	− 0.92	30.0
− 27	− 0.04	31.0	− 27	1.26	41.0
− 26	0.38	41.0	− 26	− 0.49	30.0
− 25	0.05	39.0	− 25	0.28	29.0
− 24	− 0.19	26.0	− 24	1.22	45.0
− 23	0.16	33.0	− 23	0.16	44.0
− 22	− 0.30	32.0	− 22	0.60	40.0
− 21	0.20	34.0	− 21	0.87	40.0
− 20	0.15	35.0	− 20	0.01	30.0
− 19	0.04	33.0	− 19	0.15	40.0
− 18	0.02	38.0	− 18	− 0.43	44.0
− 17	0.08	39.0	− 17	− 0.08	33.0
− 16	− 0.02	38.0	− 16	− 0.01	32.0
− 15	0.69	35.0	− 15	− 0.20	39.0
− 14	− 0.18	35.0	− 14	0.24	33.0
− 13	− 0.18	32.0	− 13	0.74	47.0
− 12	0.51	43.0	− 12	0.12	23.0
− 11	0.35	42.0	− 11	− 0.23	32.0
− 10	− 0.38	42.0	− 10	− 0.54	28.0
− 9	− 0.34	31.0	− 9	1.02	44.0
− 8	0.03	43.0	− 8	0.17	39.0
− 7	0.53	41.0	− 7	− 0.13	33.0
− 6	0.40	36.0	− 6	1.43	33.0
− 5	0.29	42.0	− 5	− 0.43	30.0
− 4	0.16	31.0	− 4	− 0.09	30.0
− 3	0.62	43.0	− 3	0.60	46.0
− 2	0.15	40.0	− 2	1.20	36.0
− 1	0.50	38.0	− 1	0.74	49.0
0	4.51	69.0	0	− 2.98	11.0
1	3.12	58.0	1	− 2.39	25.0
2	0.00	37.0	2	0.06	30.0
3	− 0.71	27.0	3	− 0.60	33.0
4	0.21	40.0	4	0.26	28.0
5	− 0.09	34.0	5	0.46	32.0
6	− 0.54	26.0	6	0.30	21.0

Table 2 (continued)

Increasing leverage announcements $N = 106$			Decreasing leverage announcements $N = 57$		
Event day	Portfolio daily returns (%)	% of stock returns > 0	Event day	Portfolio daily returns (%)	% of stock returns > 0
7	0.15	30.0	7	0.31	35.0
8	−0.26	27.0	8	0.39	39.0
9	−0.06	39.0	9	−0.14	37.0
10	0.19	37.0	10	−0.47	29.0
11	−0.08	29.0	11	0.41	33.0
12	0.46	37.0	12	−0.68	28.0
13	−0.33	34.0	13	−1.03	26.0
14	−0.87	20.0	14	0.95	37.0
15	−0.05	38.0	15	−0.21	35.0
16	0.00	38.0	16	−0.21	30.0
17	0.56	39.0	17	−0.28	26.0
18	0.41	36.0	18	0.90	39.0
19	0.09	40.0	19	1.00	34.0
20	0.05	38.0	20	0.88	37.0
21	0.53	45.0	21	0.74	30.0
22	0.20	36.0	22	−1.00	21.0
23	−0.01	36.0	23	−1.11	28.0
24	−0.52	25.0	24	0.89	40.0
25	0.10	26.0	25	0.08	23.0
26	0.48	42.0	26	0.57	33.0
27	−0.23	32.0	27	−0.96	30.0
28	0.35	41.0	28	0.92	33.0
29	0.35	37.0	29	−0.45	32.0
30	0.17	35.0	30	0.60	30.0

Comparison period
Portfolio mean daily return = 0.07
Standard deviation = 0.35
Mean percent of stock daily
  returns > 0 = 35.0
Standard deviation = 5.10

Comparison period
Portfolio mean daily return = 0.12
Standard deviation = 0.66
Mean percent of stock daily
  returns > 0 = 33.0
Standard deviation = 6.38

effects on common stock of the initial exchange offer proposals to increase and decrease leverage are presented along with stock returns for half the 120-day comparison period. The observed announcement date price adjustments in the common stock are dramatic. For leverage increases, the common stock portfolio two-day announcement period return is 7.6 percent.[38] Moreover,

[38]It is virtually impossible to determine whether an announcement is made before or after the close of the stock market; if the latter is the case, the effect should not be seen in the rate of returns until day 1. Furthermore, if the news media is the source of the initial public announcement, it is presumed that the announcement actually occurred on the previous *trading* day. This means that weekend announcements appearing in print on Monday will be incorrectly attributed to the previous Friday.

given that more than 79 percent of these 106 common stocks have positive returns for the two-day announcement period,[39] we can conclude that these results are not due to a few large outliers. Testing for significant differences between the portfolio's announcement period mean daily return and mean percentage of daily returns strictly positive from their respective comparison period means yields t statistics of 14.6 and 7.8, respectively, which are statistically significant at the 5 percent level.

For the portfolio of leverage decreases, the two-day announcement period return is -5.4 percent, while over 84 percent of these 57 common stocks have negative returns for the announcement period. Testing for significant differences between the portfolio's announcement period mean daily return and mean percentage of daily returns strictly positive from their respective comparison period means yield t statistics of 6.1 and 5.1, respectively, which are also statistically significant. Thus, the stock price change appears to have the same qualitative relationship to announced leverage changes regardless of the direction of the change and in both cases represents highly significant deviations from the comparison period means. The lack of any discernible lagged effects after day 1 is consistent with the stock market prices efficiently processing new information in exchange offer announcements. Looking at portfolio daily returns, there is little evidence of significant pre-announcement information leaks. However, in testing for insider information leaks in certain subsamples of exchange offers, Masulis (1978) found evidence suggesting insider information leaks for 10 percent of the offers.

Increases and decreases in leverage are jointly studied in most of the following analysis. Returns associated with announcements of negative changes in firm leverage are 'normalized' by multiplying these securities' rates of return by a minus one before they are averaged with returns of securities associated with announcements of positive changes in leverage. Thus, all the 'normalized' announcement period returns should exhibit the effects of increasing leverage. The theoretical presumption is that the effects of capital structure change are unidirectional once standardized for the direction of the firm's leverage change. Not all theories are consistent with this presumption. Specifically, some theories of optimal capital structure predict that the sign of the *combined* tax and bankruptcy cost effects is positive in all cases given that the firms are maximizing net present value. Consequently the *combined* effects of taxes and bankruptcy costs are not undirectional once standardized for the direction of leverage change. However the previous evidence is

---

[39]This is compared to a mean of 42 percent of these stocks having a two-day positive return for the twenty-day comparison period surrounding the announcement period. The low percent of stocks having a strictly positive two-day return reflects the significant probability that a realized return can equal zero due to either non-trading of the security, or a price change that is less than $1/8.

inconsistent with this asymmetric effect. Note that the entire time series is 'normalized', not just the two-day announcement period. In a portfolio context this is analogous to short selling securities of firms announcing decreases in leverage.

5.1.1. Separation of corporate tax and redistribution effects

In an attempt to isolate the causes of the large exchange offer announcement effects, offers are separated by type of capital structure change. Based on the earlier discussion summarized in table 1 (row 1), common stock experiences positive corporate tax and redistribution effects and a negative bankruptcy cost effect in debt-for-common exchange offers. In debt-for-preferred offers, common stock experiences a positive corporate tax effect and a negative bankruptcy cost effect. In preferred-for-common offers, common stock experiences a positive redistribution effect. These predictions suggest that the average effect of debt-for-common offer announcements should be equal to the sum of the average effects of debt-for-preferred and preferred-for-common offer announcements. Furthermore, a comparison of the latter two types of exchange offers yields separate estimates of the corporate tax and bankruptcy cost effects and the redistribution effect, assuming no other effects such as those discussed at the end of section 2 are present.

In table 3, only the portfolio of common stock returns for 20 trading days around the announcement date are presented; the remainder of the comparison period results can be found in Masulis (1978). Table 3 shows an announcement period return of 9.79 percent for debt-for-common exchange offer portfolio. The t statistic of the difference between announcement and comparison period mean daily returns is 12.5. The announcement period return for preferred-for-common exchange offer portfolio of 3.34 percent is still large, but considerably below that for debt-for-common offer portfolio. The associated t statistic for the difference in announcement and comparison period mean daily returns is 4.5. Finally, in the case of debt-for-preferred exchange offers, the portfolio's announcement period return is 4.63; these returns are again less than that found for the debt-for-common offer portfolio. The t statistic for the difference in announcement and comparison period mean daily returns is 5.8. In each case, the portfolio announcement period mean daily return and mean percentage of positive common stock daily returns are significantly different from their respective comparison period means (the t statistics for the difference between the announcement period and comparison period mean percentages of positive daily returns for the three samples are 8.2, 4.5 and 5.8, respectively).

These results (especially the statistically significant announcement effects for columns two and three) indicate the presence of a redistribution effect

Table 3

Common stock rates of return for initial offer announcements.[a]

Debt-for-common exchange offers N = 85			Preferred-for-common exchange offers N = 43			Debt-for-preferred exchange offers N = 43		
Event day	Portfolio daily returns (%)	% of stock returns > 0	Event day	Portfolio daily returns (%)	% of stock returns > 0	Event day	Portfolio daily returns (%)	% of stock returns > 0
−10	−0.22	39.0	−10	0.19	47.0	−10	0.22	53.0
−9	−0.74	27.0	−9	−0.72	28.0	−9	0.14	35.0
−8	0.14	41.0	−8	−0.75	37.0	−8	0.01	42.0
−7	0.49	39.0	−7	0.60	44.0	−7	0.41	35.0
−6	0.19	42.0	−6	0.02	44.0	−6	−1.02	35.0
−5	0.45	38.0	−5	0.52	47.0	−5	−0.23	44.0
−4	−0.04	25.0	−4	0.50	47.0	−4	0.26	35.0
−3	0.23	32.0	−3	−0.90	28.0	−3	1.00	47.0
−2	−0.57	37.0	−2	−0.04	37.0	−2	−0.32	38.0
−1	0.85	43.0	−1	−0.66	35.0	−1	−0.50	24.0
0	6.01	73.0	0	2.13	67.0	0	1.96	69.0
1	3.78	61.0	1	1.21	51.0	1	2.67	56.0
2	−0.06	34.0	2	0.57	51.0	2	−0.65	37.0
3	−0.32	27.0	3	−0.59	35.0	3	0.20	37.0
4	−0.47	25.0	4	0.63	44.0	4	0.26	49.0
5	0.18	39.0	5	−0.94	26.0	5	−0.18	40.0
6	−1.02	24.0	6	−0.22	33.0	6	0.46	42.0
7	−0.20	33.0	7	−0.06	37.0	7	0.25	35.0
8	−0.45	25.0	8	−0.22	33.0	8	−0.43	26.0
9	0.22	36.0	9	−0.58	40.0	9	0.22	40.0
10	0.29	32.0	10	0.09	51.0	10	0.42	38.0

Comparison period
Portfolio mean daily return = −0.04
Standard deviation = 0.54
Mean percent of stock daily returns > 0 = 33.0
Standard deviation = 6.79

Comparison period
Portfolio mean daily return = 0.02
Standard deviation = 0.51
Mean percent of stock daily returns > 0 = 40.0
Standard deviation = 7.14

Comparison period
Portfolio mean daily return = 0.06
Standard deviation = 0.55
Mean percent of stock daily returns > 0 = 37.0
Standard deviation = 7.09

[a]To highlight the announcement effect ±10 trading days of the sample of ±60 days are presented. The data eliminated showed no large positive or negative values nor any unusual patterns. The entire table is presented in Masulis (1978).

and a somewhat greater corporate tax effect.[40] However, a comparison of the debt-for-common exchange offer announcement returns with the sum of the debt-for-preferred and preferred-for-common announcement returns points out the limitations of this standard procedure for analyzing average announcement effects. Given that the *magnitudes* of the proposed capital structure changes across offers are not homogeneous, it comes as no surprise that the announcement effect of debt-for-common exchange offer portfolio does not equal the sum of the announcement effects of the other two exchange offer portfolios. In a separate paper, Masulis (1979) develops a cross-sectional model which relates individual announcement rates of return to the size of each announced capital structure change to obtain a more accurate measure of the magnitudes of the corporate tax and redistribution effects. The estimated model has statistically significant tax effect and redistribution effect coefficients which support the findings of this study.

The positive impact of debt-for-preferred exchange offers on common stock returns indicates that the tax effect is on average larger than the expected cost of bankruptcy effect. This is also consistent with the prediction of a zero or small negative redistribution effect. However, by separating debt-for-preferred offers by direction of leverage change, the predictions of the Robicheck–Myers and Kraus–Litzenberger models, which are conditional on the firm's maximizing net present value, can be tested. While the samples are small, as seen in table 4, the results for 20 trading days around the initial offer announcement support a net corporate tax effect in both subsamples. The portfolio's announcement period mean daily returns in both cases exceed their respective comparison period mean returns and have *t* statistics of 2.32 for increasing leverage announcements and 5.20 for decreasing leverage announcements. The results for the decreasing leverage subsample appear to indicate that firms do not always maximize stockholder wealth and/or that the expected cost of bankruptcy is generally not large enough to offset the tax benefits of debt. This is a puzzling result which could be explained in a number of ways. First management may not always choose to maximize net firm value which is the same conclusion Smith (1977) makes for a different capital structure related decision. This conclusion is potentially consistent with the prediction of the Jensen–Meckling analysis of management's incentives to avoid bankruptcy so as to maximize the value of their labor contracts with the firm even at the expense of not maximizing stockholder wealth. Alternatively this negative portfolio announcement period return could be the result of a negative signalling effect caused by the leverage

---

[40]Note that the positive tax effect experienced by the portfolio of common stocks does not necessarily imply a linear relationship between a change in debt outstanding and the change in common stock value as in the prediction of the Modigliani–Miller (1963) tax model. This result is also consistent with a concave relationship such as that predicted by the Brennan–Schwartz (1978) model.

Table 4

Common stock rates of return for initial offer announcements.

Offers to exchange debt for outstanding preferred stock N = 34			Offers to exchange preferred stock for outstanding debt N = 9		
Event day	Portfolio daily returns (%)	% of stock returns > 0	Event day	Portfolio daily returns (%)	% of stock returns > 0
−10	0.13	56.0	−10	−0.59	33.0
−9	0.13	35.0	−9	−0.19	22.0
−8	−0.28	47.0	−8	−1.10	22.0
−7	0.38	41.0	−7	−0.51	22.0
−6	−0.01	29.0	−6	4.85	33.0
−5	0.39	47.0	−5	2.56	22.0
−4	0.84	41.0	−4	1.91	44.0
−3	1.35	50.0	−3	0.31	22.0
−2	−0.14	41.0	−2	1.09	38.0
−1	−0.40	24.0	−1	0.92	38.0
0	1.50	65.0	0	−3.91	0.0
1	0.63	50.0	1	−10.38	0.0
2	−0.17	38.0	2	2.46	33.0
3	−0.43	29.0	3	−2.55	22.0
4	0.76	53.0	4	1.64	44.0
5	−0.26	38.0	5	−0.14	22.0
6	0.42	44.0	6	−0.61	22.0
7	0.58	32.0	7	1.00	44.0
8	−0.65	26.0	8	−0.41	11.0
9	−0.25	41.0	9	−1.97	11.0
10	0.20	41.0	10	−1.20	33.0

Comparison period
 Portfolio mean daily return = 0.12
 Standard deviation = 0.57
 Mean percent of stock
  daily returns > 0 = 38.0
 Standard deviation = 8.50

Comparison period
 Portfolio mean daily return = 0.18
 Standard deviation = 1.84
 Mean percent of stock
  daily returns > 0 = 29.0
 Standard deviation = 15.57

decrease, or some other negative information effect. Given the small sample involved, a definitive answer to this question does not seem possible at this time.

5.1.2. *Effects of offer cancellation and termination announcements*

Masulis (1978)[41] explored two important related announcements, offer cancellations and offer expirations or terminations, and found that for the 20 cancellation announcements, the announcement period return (trading days

[41]A number of additional exchange offer related announcements are studied in Masulis (1978), however, these announcement effects were small in magnitude and generally not statistically significant with the exception of the announcement of the offer terms or alteration of terms.

−1, 0, and 1) for the portfolio of common stock was −6.86 percent.[42] This announcement period mean daily return is statistically significantly different from the comparison period mean (the t statistic was 3.84). Furthermore, the cancellation announcement period return was approximately the same magnitude but opposite the direction of the initial exchange offer announcement period return.

Termination announcements are also predicted to cause negative effects of similar magnitude to the cancellation effects if, as some researchers have suggested, announcement period price changes are primarily due to exchange offer premiums. (An exchange offer premium is defined as the difference between the post-announcement market value of the securities being offered in exchange and the pre-announcement market price of the security being retired.) Without an exchange offer premium effect, an offer termination should have only small negative impact relative to the effects of initial announcement. This small price change reflects a relatively small adjustment in market expectations of an otherwise larger capital structure change were the offer to be extended (and only in the cases where the announced termination date is prior to the previously stated final expiration date). The termination period return for a portfolio of 124 non-cancelled offers (a subset of offers where exact termination dates were available) was found to be −0.89 percent which is much smaller than the initial exchange offer announcement period portfolio return. This finding is evidence inconsistent with the exchange offer premium hypothesis described in section 2.

5.2. Offer announcement effects on preferred stock

While a significant positive relationship between common stock price changes and proposed changes in firm leverage has been observed, the question remains as to whether capital structure change announcements have any effect on the prices of the actively traded preferred stock or debt. In an attempt to answer this question, preferred stock daily returns are separated by type of announced capital structure change to allow for the different predicted effects shown in table 1 (row 2).

To make the following results easier to interpret, plots are included of the portfolio's daily returns, standardized by subtracting μ, the 19-day trading comparison period mean of these daily returns and dividing the remainder by five times the standard deviation of these daily returns, σ. Values greater than five standard deviations from the mean are plotted at the five standard deviation points. At the bottom of the plot is a scale measuring the number of standard deviations from the comparison period mean return that a given portfolio daily return lies.

---

[42]Since the data on the cancellation announcements was less accurate, trading day −1 was also included in the announcement period.

Convertible Preferred Stock Issues

STANDARDIZED PORTFOLIO DAILY RETURNS

THERE ARE 26 SECURITIES IN THIS SAMPLE OF 14 EVENTS

EVENT DAY	PORTFOLIO RET (%)	% STOCK RET>0
-10	-0.20	38.
-9	0.22	35.
-8	-0.40	27.
-7	0.04	42.
-6	-0.14	23.
-5	0.17	42.
-4	0.27	35.
-3	0.09	38.
-2	-0.50	27.
-1	-0.34	27.
0	0.79	54.
1	0.79	54.
2	-0.28	31.
3	0.00	31.
4	0.57	42.
5	-0.23	23.
6	-0.37	23.
7	0.20	50.
8	0.26	38.
9	-0.26	35.
10	0.08	38.

$\mu-5\sigma$ $\mu-4\sigma$ $\mu-3\sigma$ $\mu-2\sigma$ $\mu-1\sigma$ μ $\mu+1\sigma$ $\mu+2\sigma$ $\mu+3\sigma$ $\mu+4\sigma$ $\mu+5\sigma$

MEAN PORTFOLIO DAILY RETURN= -0.04   STANDARD DEVIATION= 0.29   MEAN PERCENTAGE OF POSITIVE STOCK RETURNS= 34.   STANDARD DEVIATION= 7.7?

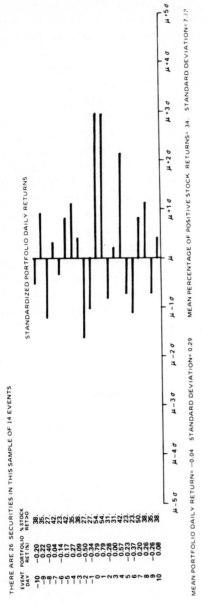

Nonconvertible Preferred Stock Issues

STANDARDIZED PORTFOLIO DAILY RETURNS

THERE ARE 11 SECURITIES IN THIS SAMPLE OF 9 EVENTS

EVENT DAY	PORTFOLIO RET (%)	% STOCK RET>0
-10	-0.55	27.
-9	-0.75	27.
-8	0.45	36.
-7	-0.08	45.
-6	0.86	55.
-5	0.48	55.
-4	-0.42	18.
-3	-0.33	64.
-2	0.44	9.
-1	-0.61	55.
0	1.01	27.
1	0.74	45.
2	0.02	73.
3	0.13	36.
4	-0.02	36.
5	-0.18	36.
6	-0.18	27.
7	-0.18	36.
8	-0.47	9.
9	-0.41	27.
10	-0.47	9.

$\mu-5\sigma$ $\mu-4\sigma$ $\mu-3\sigma$ $\mu-2\sigma$ $\mu-1\sigma$ μ $\mu+1\sigma$ $\mu+2\sigma$ $\mu+3\sigma$ $\mu+4\sigma$ $\mu+5\sigma$

MEAN PORTFOLIO DAILY RETURN= -0.02   STANDARD DEVIATION= 0.46   MEAN PERCENTAGE OF POSITIVE STOCK RETURNS= 35.   STANDARD DEVIATION= 17.90

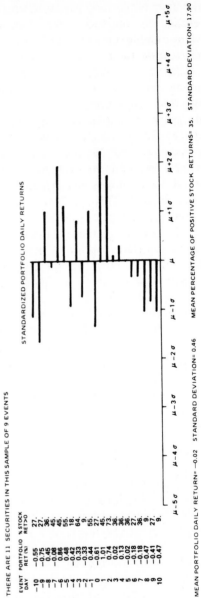

Fig. 1. Preferred stock rates of return for announcements of debt for common exchange offers.

The predicted effect of a debt-for-common capital structure change on preferred stock valuation is ambiguous, since the positive corporate tax effect can be offset by negative bankruptcy cost and redistribution effects. Fig. 1 presents the weighted average returns ('normalized' for the direction of the leverage change) for this subsample of 27 issues of convertible preferred stock representing 14 separate exchange offers. The two-day announcement period return for this portfolio of preferred stocks is 1.58 percent which is in the same direction as that observed for common stock. The t statistic of 3.96 indicates a statistically significant difference between the announcement period and the 19-day comparison period mean daily returns, implying that the corporate tax effect exceeds the bankruptcy cost and redistribution effects for these preferred stock issues. This result appears to be due to the convertibility of these issues, since the two-day announcement period return of 0.20 percent for the portfolio of non-convertible preferred stock shown in the lower half of fig. 1 is much smaller. The t statistic for the difference between this portfolio's announcement period mean daily return and comparison period mean is 0.57, which is not statistically significant.

Although no corporate tax or bankruptcy cost effects are predicted in the case of preferred-for-common exchange offers, a negative redistribution effect (assuming common stock is retired and preferred stock is issued) is predicted. Consistent with this prediction, the upper half of fig. 2 shows a striking negative two-day announcement period return of -5.6 percent where the t statistic of 5.8 indicates that the announcement period mean daily return is statistically different from the comparison period mean at a 5 percent significance level. It should be noted that this effect is due primarily to the non-convertible preferred stock issues in the portfolio.[43]

The 23 preferred stock issues associated with the 18 debt-for-preferred exchange offers are predicted to experience both positive redistribution and corporate tax effects and a negative bankruptcy cost effect.[44] The lower half of fig. 2 shows a large positive portfolio return of 3.4 percent for the two-day announcement period with an associated t statistic of 6.2, indicating that the announcement period mean daily return is significantly different from the comparison period mean daily return. This result, representative of both convertible and non-convertible preferred stock issues, is consistent with the predictions of both corporate tax and redistribution effects.

5.3. Offer announcement effects on debt

Referring back to table 1 (row 3) for debt-for-common and debt-for-preferred exchange offers (which increase leverage), risky debt issues are

---

[43]Convertible and non-convertible preferred stock issues are separately analyzed by type of exchange offer. However, for brevity, these results are only summarized.

[44]In cases where preferred stock is being retired, only issues of preferred stock involved in the offer are included in the portfolios; as is assumed in table 1.

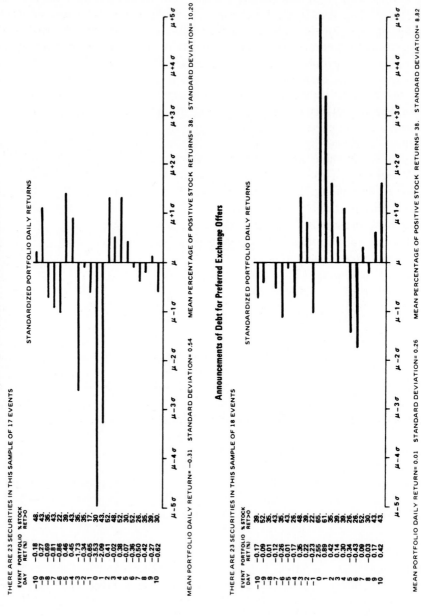

Fig. 2. Preferred stock rates of return for announcements of exchange offers involving changes in preferred stock.

predicted to experience a positive corporate tax effect and negative bankruptcy cost and redistribution effects.[45] Throughout the following analysis, the impact of exchange offer announcements is separately assessed for the outstanding convertible and non-convertible debt issues. Also considered are the effects of leverage change on securities with one form of incomplete protective covenants: namely, outstanding debt issues which do not preclude new issues of debt of equal or senior standing.

5.3.1. Convertible and non-convertible debt

After separating debt issues into convertible and non-convertible securities, it becomes clear that the effects of capital structure change are strikingly different for these two groups. Fig. 3 presents the portfolio daily returns over a 21-day trading period centered around the exchange offer announcement date for the two types of securities. While the portfolio of 47 convertible debt issues (representing 32 exchange offers) experiences a 0.2 percent gain in price, the portfolio of 49 non-convertible debt issues (representing 26 exchange offers) experiences a loss of 0.3 percent for the two-day announcement period. The t statistics for the difference between these two announcement period mean daily returns from the comparison period means are 1.45 and 3.1, respectively, with only the latter return being statistically significant at a 5 percent level. These results indicate that changes in convertible debt prices are positively related to changes in the underlying common stock prices, a finding which can be due to both their convertibility and anti-dilution clauses. The latter feature generally requires that favorable adjustments be made in the exercise price of the convertible securities when common stock is repurchased or non-cash rights are offered to the common stockholders increasing the value of the warrants and convertibles beyond that due to the rise in stock price.[46] In contrast, the non-convertible debt issues are predicted to experience negative bankruptcy cost and redistribution effects which appear to exceed the predicted positive tax effect.

5.3.2. Debt issues with incomplete protective covenants

If a redistribution effect does cause part of the price change in debt issues, separating debt issues according to whether or not they have incomplete

---

[45]Given that no effect is predicted for preferred-for-common exchange offers, the debt issues associated with these offers are excluded. Separate tests of this prediction were not made due to the very small sample size involved.

[46]For a more in-depth discussion and survey of standard anti-dilution clauses, see Kaplan (1965). It is also possible that the positive tax effect exceeds the negative bankruptcy cost and redistribution effects for this subsample.

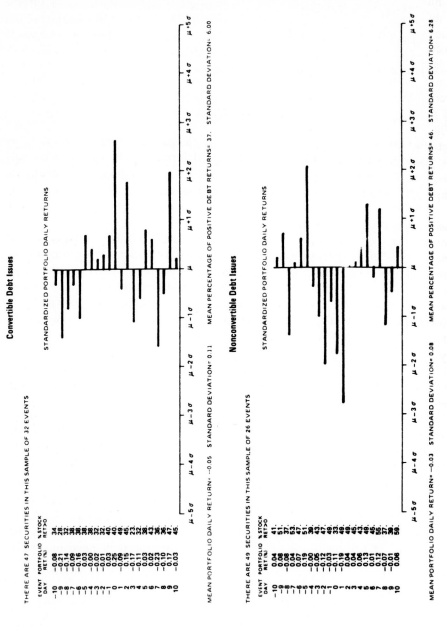

Fig. 3. Debt rates of return for announcements of exchange offers separated by convertibility.

protective covenants ,should confirm this prediction.[47] Partitioning the debt into those issues which prohibit the issuance of additional debt of equal (or senior) standing without debtholder approval (termed 'covenant protected debt') and those which do not (termed 'unprotected debt'), yields the results shown in fig. 4. For the portfolio of 52 convertible and non-convertible securities with this covenant protection, the announcement period return is a positive 0.18 percent. The *t* statistic of 1.28 indicates that the announcement period mean daily return is not statistically different from the comparison period mean. In contrast, the announcement period return for the portfolio of 44 securities without this covenant protection shows a loss of 0.77 percent. The *t* statistic of 3.0 indicates that the announcement period mean daily return is statistically different from the comparison period mean. Moreover, as the redistribution hypothesis predicts, the debt issues with incomplete protective covenants are, on average, adversely affected by the announced capital structure changes.

To explore this issue in more depth, the portfolio of outstanding debt issues having obviously incomplete protective covenants is separated into convertible and non-convertible issues. The upper half of fig. 5 presents the exchange offer announcement's impact on the 26 convertible debt issues represented in the previous figure. The portfolio announcement period return is −0.45 percent. The associated *t* statistic for the difference between the announcement period and comparison period mean daily returns of 0.93 is not statistically significant. Importantly, convertible debt issues with incomplete protective covenants do not share in the sizeable price gain experienced by the common stock and the convertible debt issues as a whole.

The lower half of fig. 5 presents the announcement effect for the corresponding portfolio of 18 non-convertible debt issues. The announcement period return is −0.84 percent, with a *t* statistic of 2.7, which indicates a significant difference in the announcement period mean daily return from the comparison period mean daily return. Interestingly, the magnitude of the adverse announcement effect for the portfolio of non-convertible debt issues with incomplete protective covenants is almost three times the magnitude of the announcement effect for the portfolio of all non-convertible debt issues. This is consistent with the prediction of the redistribution hypothesis. Note that similar results for debt and preferred stock are obtained when we replicated these analyses without adjusting the announcement returns for nontrading. However, as expected, the magnitude of the effects is lowered. Furthermore, announcements of increases and decreases in leverage were separately examined and were found to be consistent with the normalization procedure.

---

[47]This may not be strictly true since we are not controlling for the magnitudes of the leverage changes in the different subsamples.

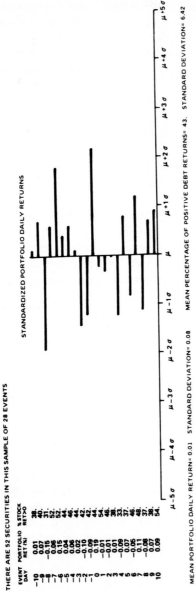

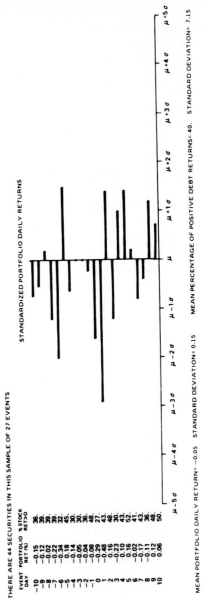

Fig. 4. Debt rates of return for announcements of exchange offers separated by covenant protection.

Convertible Debt Issues with Incomplete Protective Covenants

THERE ARE 26 SECURITIES IN THIS SAMPLE OF 19 EVENTS

STANDARDIZED PORTFOLIO DAILY RETURNS

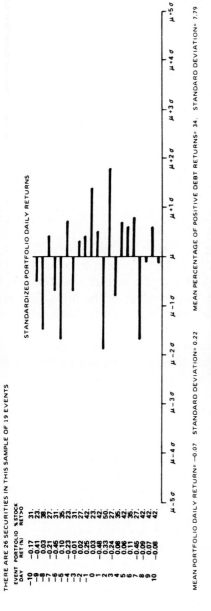

EVENT DAY	PORTFOLIO RET (%)	% STOCK RET>0
-10	-0.17	31.
-9	-0.41	23.
-8	0.03	38.
-7	-0.21	27.
-6	-0.45	31.
-5	0.10	35.
-4	-0.23	23.
-3	-0.01	31.
-2	0.02	27.
-1	0.25	42.
0	0.03	23.
1	-0.48	42.
2	0.33	50.
3	-0.24	27.
4	0.08	35.
5	0.06	42.
6	0.11	35.
7	-0.45	27.
8	-0.09	42.
9	0.07	42.
10	-0.08	42.

MEAN PORTFOLIO DAILY RETURN= -0.07   STANDARD DEVIATION= 0.22   MEAN PERCENTAGE OF POSITIVE DEBT RETURNS= 34.   STANDARD DEVIATION= 7.79

Nonconvertible Debt Issues with Incomplete Protective Covenants

THERE ARE 18 SECURITIES IN THIS SAMPLE OF 11 EVENTS

STANDARDIZED PORTFOLIO DAILY RETURNS

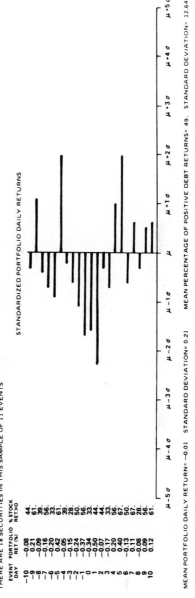

EVENT DAY	PORTFOLIO RET (%)	% STOCK RET>0
-10	-0.08	44.
-9	0.21	61.
-8	0.09	39.
-7	-0.16	56.
-6	-0.20	33.
-5	0.42	61.
-4	-0.05	39.
-3	-0.15	28.
-2	-0.24	50.
-1	-0.37	56.
0	-0.34	33.
1	-0.50	44.
2	-0.07	44.
3	0.20	33.
4	-0.13	56.
5	0.40	67.
6	0.11	50.
7	-0.08	67.
8	0.09	28.
9	0.12	56.
10		61.

MEAN PORTFOLIO DAILY RETURN= -0.01   STANDARD DEVIATION= 0.21   MEAN PERCENTAGE OF POSITIVE DEBT RETURNS= 49.   STANDARD DEVIATION= 12.64

Fig. 5. Unprotected debt rates of return for announcements of exchange offers separated by convertibility.

5.4. Relationship to other empirical studies

5.4.1. Implications for capital market efficiency

This study shares some commonality of approach with the empirical studies of capital market efficiency. In the process of testing the significance of capital structure change announcements on security valuation, one is implicitly testing the efficiency of the capital market in processing this particular type of information. In this study, we observe that the initial exchange offer announcement has a pronounced effect on daily security rates of return, especially in the case of common stock. At the same time, there is very little evidence of any lagged price adjustments in the vicinity of the initial exchange offer announcement period. These results, based on daily data for common stock, preferred stock and debt, support the efficient market hypothesis.

5.4.2. Implications for previous merger studies

Some important implications for merger studies can be derived from our results. First of all, it does not necessarily follow that a change in common stock value which occurs on the announcement of a merger is a reflection of a similar change in firm value. Changes in the values of the firm's debt and preferred stock (which can potentially be offsetting) must be analyzed before this inference can be made.

Second, in a merger (as well as an acquisition or divestiture) the associated change in capital structure of the surviving firm can easily cause effects of the same order of magnitude as those induced by the exchange offers studied here. Consequently, it does not necessarily follow that a change in firm value or in security prices resulting from a merger announcement is due to the economic effects of a change in firm asset structure. The observed effects may be due in great part to the associated capital structure changes[48] (e.g., corporate tax effects and redistribution effects), which most empirical studies of mergers have ignored.[49] Moreover, by failing to note price changes in the firm's securities other than its common stock, most of these studies have tended to associate changes in the value of the firm's common stock with changes in the value of the firm itself.[50] The previous results shed some light on the empirical significance of this omission.

---

[48]Refer to Galai–Masulis for a further analysis of these combined effects.

[49]One notable exception is the recent study by Kim–McConnell (1977).

[50]For example, see the studies done by Ellert (1976), Mandelker (1974), Hogarty (1970), and Reid (1968).

6. Conclusions

Analyzing a sample of relatively pure capital structure change announcements, evidence is found of statistically significant effects on the portfolio returns of the firm's common stock, preferred stock, and debt. This evidence indicates both a corporate debt tax shield effect and a wealth redistribution effect across security classes; no direct evidence of an expected cost of bankruptcy effect is found. A new methodology is utilized to test the effects of new information on security prices and differs significantly from previous studies. The Comparison Period Returns method is a straightforward testing procedure for assessing the significance of capital structure change announcements which is independent of the particular asset pricing model specified.

A comparison between the qualitative predictions of the hypotheses given in table 1 and the average price adjustments observed for major security classes at the time of capital structure change announcements support the following findings:

(1) Capital structure changes predicted to cause either a corporate debt tax shield effect or a wealth redistribution effect are associated with security price changes consistent with these predictions.

(2) Security price changes are relatively larger in cases where the corporate tax and redistribution effects are predicted to reinforce each other, and smaller in cases where the corporate tax and redistribution effects are predicted to run counter to each other.

(3) Offsetting price changes in individual firms' major security classes are observed, as predicted by the wealth redistribution hypothesis for the various capital structure changes studied.

(4) As predicted by the wealth redistribution hypothesis, relatively large price adjustments are observed for debt issues which do not restrict the issuance of new debt of equal or senior standing.

(5) On average, stockholders are adversely affected by a decrease in leverage, which suggests that firms do not always follow a policy of maximizing stockholder wealth. These decisions may or may not be consistent with maximizing the firm's net present value.

(6) No evidence of a bankruptcy cost effect is found for the firms decreasing leverage in case where wealth redistribution effects are not present. This surprising result appears to be inconsistent with the predictions of the corporate tax–bankruptcy cost models of optimal leverage.

In summary, the qualitative predictions of the corporate tax and wealth redistribution effects resulting from a capital structure change are observed, as detailed in table 1, for all three major classes of firm securities. No evidence of an expected cost of bankruptcy effect is observed. Nevertheless, it is always possible that a portion of the observed price adjustment is due to other effects not considered here such as the signalling hypothesis. This is a question left for future research.

References

Baxter, N., 1967, Leverage, risk of ruin and the cost of capital, Journal of Finance 22, Sept., 395–403.

Bittker, B. and J. Eustice, 1971, Federal income taxation of corporations and shareholders, Abridged ed. (Warren, Gorham and Lamont, Boston).

Black, F. and J. Cox, 1976, Valuating corporate securities: Some effects of bond indenture provisions, Journal of Finance 31, May, 351–368.

Black, F. and M. Scholes, 1973, The pricing of options and corporate liabilities, Journal of Political Economy 81, May/June, 637–654.

Blum, W., 1958, Full priority and full compensation in corporate reorganizations: A reappraisal, University of Chicago Law Review 25, Spring, 417–444.

Blum, W. and S. Kaplan, 1974, The absolute priority doctrine in corporate reorganizations, University of Chicago Law Review 41, 273–313.

Boness, A., A. Chen and S. Jatusipitak, 1974, Investigations of nonstationary prices, Journal of Business 47, 518–537.

Brennan, M. and E. Schwartz, 1978, Corporate Income Taxes, Valuation and the Problem of Optimal Capital Structure, Journal of Business, Jan., 103–114.

Brown, S. and J. Warner, 1980, Measuring security price performance, Journal of Financial Economics, forthcoming.

Bulow, J. and J. Shoven, 1978, The bankruptcy decision, Bell Journal of Economics, Autumn, 437–456.

Collier, W., 1940, Collier on bankruptcy, 14th ed. (M. Bender and Co., Albany, NY).

DeAngelo, H. and R.W. Masulis, 1980, Optimal capital structure under corporate and personal taxation, Journal of Financial Economics 8, March 3–30.

Dhrymes, P., 1970, Econometrics (Harper and Row, New York).

Ellert, J., 1976, Mergers, antitrust law enforcement and stockholder returns, Journal of Finance 31, May, 715–732.

Fama, E., 1978, The effects of a firm's investment and financing decisions on the welfare of its securityholders, American Economic Review, June, 272–284.

Fama, E. and M.H. Miller, 1972, The theory of finance (Holt, Reinhart and Winston, New York).

Fama, E., L. Fisher, M. Jensen and R. Roll, 1969, The adjustment of stock prices to new information, International Economic Review 10, Feb., 1–21.

Galai, D. and R. Masulis, 1976, The option pricing model and the risk factor of stocks, Journal of Financial Economics 3, Jan./March, 53–81.

Gonedes, N., 1973, Evidence on the information content of accounting numbers: Accounting-based and market-based estimates of systematic risk, Journal of Financial and Quantitative Analysis 13, June, 407–443.

Gould, J.P., 1973, Economics of legal conflict, Journal of Legal Studies, June, 279–300.

Guthmann, H.G. and H.E. Dougall, 1962, Corporate financial policy, 4th ed. (Prentice-Hall, Englewood Cliffs, NJ).

Haugen, R. and L. Senbet, 1978, The insignificance of bankruptcy costs to the theory of optimal capital structure, Journal of Finance 33, May, 383–394.

Hogarty, T., 1970, The profitability of corporate mergers, Journal of Business 43, June, 317–327.

Ibbotson, R., 1975, Price performance of common stock new issues, Journal of Financial Economics 2, Sept., 235–266.

Jaffe, J., 1974, The effect of regulation changes on insider trading, Bell Journal of Economics and Management Science, Spring, 92–121.

Jensen, M. and W. Meckling, 1976, Theory of the firm: Managerial behavior, agency costs and ownership structure, Journal of Financial Economics 3, Oct., 305–360.

Kaplan, R. and R. Roll, 1972, Investor evaluation of accounting information: Some empirical evidence, Journal of Business, April, 225–257.

Kaplan, S., 1965, Piercing the corporate boilerplate: Anti-dilution clauses in convertible securities, University of Chicago Law Review 33, Autumn, 1–30.

Kim, H., 1978, A mean variance theory of optimal capital structure and corporate debt capacity, Journal of Finance 33, March, 45–63.

Kim, H. and J. McConnell, 1977, Corporate merger and the co-insurance of corporate debt, Journal of Finance 32, May, 349–366.

Kim, H., J. McConnell J. and P. Greenwood, 1977, Capital structure rearrangements and me first rules in an efficient capital market, Journal of Finance 32, June, 789–810.

Kraus, A. and R. Litzenberger, 1973, A state preference model of optimal financial leverage, Journal of Finance 28, Sept., 911–921.

Leland, H. and D. Pyle, 1977, Informational asymmetrics, financial structure and financial intermediation, Journal of Finance 32, May, 371–387.

Mandelker, G., 1974, Risk and return: Merging fims, Journal of Financial Economics 1, Dec., 303–336.

Masulis, R., 1978, The effects of capital structure change on security prices, Unpublished Ph.D. dissertation (University of Chicago, Chicago, IL).

Masulis, R., 1979, A model of stock price adjustments to capital structure changes, Working paper, May (Graduate School of Management, University of California, Los Angeles, CA).

Masulis, R., 1980, Stock repurchase by tender offer: An analysis of the causes of common stock price changes, Journal of Finance, May.

Merton, R., 1974, On the pricing of corporate debt, the risk structure of interest rates, Journal of Finance, May, 449–470.

Miller, M., 1977, Debt and taxes: Presidential address of annual meeting of American Finance Association, Journal of Finance 32, May, 261–275.

Miller, M. and F. Modigliani, 1966, Some estimates of the cost of capital to the electric utility industry, 1954–57, American Economic Review 56, June, 333–391.

Modigliani, F. and M. Miller, 1958, The cost of capital, corporate finance and the theory of investment, American Economic Review 48, June, 261–297.

Modigliani, F. and M. Miller, 1963, Corporate income taxes and the cost of capital: A correction, American Economic Review 53, June, 433–443.

Mood, A., F. Graybill and D. Boes, 1974, Introduction to the theory of statistics, 3rd ed. (McGraw-Hill, New York).

Reid, S., 1968, Mergers, managers and the economy (McGraw-Hill, New Yotk).

Robicheck, A. and S. Myers, 1966, Problems in the theory of optimal capital structure, Journal of Financial and Quantitative Analysis 1, 1–35.

Roll, R., 1977, A critique of the asset pricing theory's tests; Part I on: Past and potential testability of the theory, Journal of Financial Economics, March, 129–176.

Ross, S., 1976, The arbitrage theory of capital asset pricing, Journal of Economic Theory 13, 341–360.

Ross, S., 1977, The determination of financial structure: The incentive-signalling approach, Bell Journal of Economics, Spring, 23–40.

Scholes, M., 1972, The market for securities: Substitution versus price pressure and the effects of information on share prices, Journal of Business 45, April, 179–211.

Scott, J., 1976, A theory of optimal capital structure, Bell Journal of Economics and Management Science, Spring 33–54.

Smith, C., 1977, Alternative methods for raising capital: Rights versus underwritten offerings, Journal of Financial Economics, Dec., 273–308.

Smith, C. and J. Warner, 1979, On financial contracts and optimal capital structure: An analysis of bond covenants, Journal of Financial Economics, June, 117–161.

Warner, J., 1977, Bankruptcy costs: Some evidence, Journal of Finance, May, 337–347.

SEVEN

THE MARKET FOR CORPORATE CONTROL

THE MARKET FOR CORPORATE CONTROL

The Scientific Evidence*

Michael C. JENSEN

University of Rochester, Rochester, NY 14627, USA

Richard S. RUBACK

Massachusetts Institute of Technology, Cambridge, MA 02139, USA

Received March 1983, final version received April 1983

This paper reviews much of the scientific literature on the market for corporate control. The evidence indicates that corporate takeovers generate positive gains, that target firm shareholders benefit, and that bidding firm shareholders do not lose. The gains created by corporate takeovers do not appear to come from the creation of market power. With the exception of actions that exclude potential bidders, it is difficult to find managerial actions related to corporate control that harm shareholders. Finally, we argue the market for corporate control is best viewed as an arena in which managerial teams compete for the rights to manage corporate resources.

1. The analytical perspective

1.1. Definition

Corporate control is frequently used to describe many phenomena ranging from the general forces that influence the use of corporate resources (such as legal and regulatory systems and competition in product and input markets) to the control of a majority of seats on a corporation's board of directors. We define corporate control as the rights to determine the management of corporate resources — that is, the rights to hire, fire and set the compensation of top-level managers [Fama and Jensen (1983a, b)]. When a

*The authors are, respectively, Professor and Director, Managerial Economics Research Center, Graduate School of Management, University of Rochester, and Assistant Professor, Sloan School of Management, Massachusetts Institute of Technology. We have benefited from the comments of Paul Asquith, Fischer Black, Michelle Bonnice, Michael Bradley, Andrew Christie, Frank Easterbrook, Richard Leftwich, Paul Malatesta, Terry Marsh, Robert Merton, Wayne Mikkelson, Walter Oi, Charles Plosser, Katherine Schipper, G. William Schwert, Clifford Smith, René Stulz, Jerold Warner, Martin Zimmerman, and especially Harry DeAngelo, Linda DeAngelo and John Long. This research is sponsored by the Managerial Economics Research Center of the University of Rochester, Graduate School of Management.

Journal of Financial Economics 11 (1983) 5–50. North-Holland Publishing Company

bidding firm acquires a target firm, the control rights to the target firm are transferred to the board of directors of the acquiring firm. While corporate boards always retain the top-level control rights, they normally delegate the rights to manage corporate resources to internal managers. In this way the top management of the acquiring firm acquires the rights to manage the resources of the target firm.

1.2. Managerial competition

We view the market for corporate control, often referred to as the takeover market, as a market in which alternative managerial teams compete for the rights to manage corporate resources. Hence, the takeover market is an important component of the managerial labor market; it complements the internal and external managerial labor markets discussed by Fama (1980). Viewing the market for corporate control as the arena in which management teams compete is a subtle but substantial shift from the traditional view, in which financiers and activist stockholders are the parties who (alone or in coalition with others) buy control of a company and hire and fire management to achieve better resource utilization. The managerial competition model instead views competing management teams as the primary activist entities, with stockholders (including institutions) playing a relatively passive, but fundamentally important, judicial role. Arbitrageurs and takeover specialists facilitate these transactions by acting as intermediaries to value offers by competing management teams, including incumbent managers. Therefore, stockholders in this system have relatively little use for detailed knowledge about the firm or the plans of competing management teams beyond that normally used for the market's price setting function. Stockholders have no loyalty to incumbent managers; they simply choose the highest dollar value offer from those presented to them in a well-functioning market for corporate control, including sale at the market price to anonymous arbitrageurs and takeover specialists. In this perspective, competition among managerial teams for the rights to manage resources limits divergence from shareholder wealth maximization by managers and provides the mechanism through which economies of scale or other synergies available from combining or reorganizing control and management of corporate resources are realized.

Takeovers can occur through merger, tender offer, or proxy contest, and sometimes elements of all three are involved. In mergers or tender offers the bidding firm offers to buy the common stock of the target at a price in excess of the target's previous market value. Mergers are negotiated directly with target manager's and approved by the target's board of directors before going to a vote of target shareholders for approval. Tender offers are offers to buy shares made directly to target shareholders who decide individually whether to tender their shares for sale to the bidding firm. Proxy contests occur when an insurgent group, often led by a dissatisfied former manager or large stockholder, attempts to gain controlling seats on the board of directors.

1.3. Overview of the issues and evidence

Manne's (1965) seminal article initiated an interest in how the market for control influences large corporations, and knowledge about many facets of the market for corporate control has recently increased considerably. This body of scientific knowledge about the corporate takeover market provides answers to the following questions:

1. How large are the gains to shareholders of bidding and target firms?
2. Does opposition to takeover bids by the managers of target firms reduce shareholder wealth?
3. Do takeovers create market power in product markets?
4. Does antitrust opposition to takeovers impose costs on merging firms?
5. Is shareholder wealth affected by proxy contests?
6. Are corporate voting rights valuable?

A brief overview of the evidence provides a useful guide to the more detailed discussion that follows. Numerous studies estimate the effects of mergers and tender offers on the stock prices of the participating firms. Tables 1 and 2 present a summary of stock price changes (measured net of marketwide price movements) for successful and unsuccessful takeovers in these studies. The returns in the tables represent our synthesis of the evidence. Discussion of the details of the studies and the issues that lie behind the estimates in the tables is contained in section 2, 'The Wealth Effects of Takeover Activities'.

Table 1

Abnormal percentage stock price changes associated with successful corporate takeovers.[a]

Takeover technique	Target (%)	Bidders (%)
Tender offers	30	4
Mergers	20	0
Proxy contests	8	n.a.[b]

[a]Abnormal price changes are price changes adjusted to eliminate the effects of marketwide price changes.
[b]Not applicable.

Table 2

Abnormal percentage stock price changes associated
with unsuccessful corporate takeover bids.[a]

Takeover technique	Targets (%)	Bidders (%)
Tender offers	−3	−1
Mergers	−3	−5
Proxy contests	8	n.a.[b]

[a]Abnormal price changes are price changes adjusted
to eliminate the effects of marketwide price changes.
[b]Not applicable.

Table 1 shows that target firms in successful takeovers experience statistically significant abnormal stock price changes of 20% in mergers and 30% in tender offers. Bidding firms realize statistically significant abnormal gains of 4% in tender offers and zero in mergers. Table 2 shows that both bidders and targets suffer small negative abnormal stock price changes in unsuccessful merger and tender offer takeovers, although only the −5% return for unsuccessful bidders in mergers is significantly different from zero. Stockholders in companies that experience proxy contests earn statistically significant average abnormal returns of about 8%. Somewhat surprisingly, these returns are not substantially lower when the insurgent group loses the contest.

The contrast between the large stock price increases for successful target firms and the insignificant stock price changes for unsuccessful targets indicates that the benefits of mergers and tender offers are realized only when control of the target firm's assets is transferred to a bidding firm. This suggests that stockholders of potential target firms are harmed when target managers oppose takeover bids or take other actions that reduce the probability of a successful acquisition. Moreover, since target managers replaced after takeovers lose power, prestige and the value of organization-specific human capital, they have incentives to oppose a takeover bid even though shareholders might benefit substantially from acquisition. However, management opposition to a takeover bid will benefit stockholders if it leads to a higher takeover price or otherwise increased stock prices. Thus, the effect of management opposition on shareholder wealth is an empirical matter.

The evidence indicates that the effect of unsuccessful takeover attempts varies across takeover techniques, and the reasons for these differences are not currently known. In unsuccessful mergers the target's stock price falls to about its pre-offer level. In unsuccessful tender offers the target's stock price remains substantially above its pre-offer level, unless a subsequent bid does not occur in the two years following the initial offer. If such a subsequent bid does not occur, the target's stock price reverts to its pre-offer level. Finally, in proxy contests the 8% increase in equity values does not depend on the outcome of the contest.

The abnormal stock price changes summarized in tables 1 and 2 indicate that transfer of the target-firm control rights produces gains. The evidence reviewed in section 3, 'Antitrust and the Source of Merger Gains', indicates that the merger gains do not come from the creation of product market power. This is an important finding since the evidence also indicates antitrust opposition to takeovers imposes costs on merging firms by restricting transfers of corporate control. The takeover gains apparently come from the realization of increased efficiencies or synergies, but the evidence is not sufficient to identify their exact sources.

Section 4 contains a discussion of conflicts of interest between management and stockholders as well as estimates of the effects on stock prices of various managerial actions and proxy contests, and estimates of the value of corporate voting rights. Evidence presented in section 4 indicates that some actions that reduce the probability of takeovers, such as corporate charter changes, do not reduce shareholder wealth. In contrast, managerial actions that eliminate potential bidders, such as targeted large-block repurchases or standstill agreements, apparently are costly to shareholders. Section 5 discusses unsettled issues and suggests directions for future research.

2. The wealth effects of takeover activities

Numerous studies estimate the effects of takeovers on stock prices of bidder and target firms around the time of announcement of takeover attempts. Such 'event studies' use estimates of the abnormal stock price changes around the offer announcement date as a measure of the economic effects of the takeover. Abnormal returns are measured by the difference between actual and expected stock returns. The expected stock return is measured conditional on the realized return on a market index to take account of the influence of marketwide events on the returns of individual securities.[1]

Early event studies of takeovers, including Mandelker (1974), Ellert (1976), and Langetieg (1978), use the effective date of merger (the date of final

[1]Fama, Fisher, Jensen and Roll (1969) first used this methodology in their study of the price effects of stock splits. Brown and Warner (1980, 1983) provide a detailed discussion of the techniques and various methodological issues regarding their use and interpretation. For simplicity we avoid discussing the details of the abnormal return estimation technique used in each of the studies summarized here. The techniques used in the papers to calculate the abnormal returns are generally similar and, more importantly, the results appear robust with respect to the various estimation techniques used although Malatesta (1983) raises some interesting questions regarding the effects of the use of constrained estimation techniques. The methodologically oriented reader is referred to the original studies for details on these matters.

approval by target shareholders) as the **event** date. The expected price effects will occur on or before the first public announcement of a takeover. Therefore, because the announcement date occurs at random times prior to the effective date, using the latter as the event date makes it difficult to identify changes in security prices that are due to the takeover event itself. [See Dodd and Ruback (1977).] Because of this difficulty, we focus on studies that, following Dodd and Ruback, analyze abnormal returns around the time of the first public announcement of a takeover.

Table 3 summarizes the estimated abnormal returns for successful and unsuccessful bidding and target firms around announcements of tender offers and mergers. Panel A of table 3 reports the results of the tender offer studies. The results of the merger studies are contained in panels B.1 through B.3 of table 3, which provide measures of abnormal price changes for different time periods around the merger offer announcement. The table identifies the author(s) and year of publication of each study, the time period of the sample, the timing of the event period over which the abnormal returns are estimated, the sample size and *t*-statistic. In some cases the abnormal returns are obtained from studies whose primary purpose is to examine other issues,[2] for example, the antitrust implications of mergers. In some of these cases the numbers of interest for table 3 are not directly presented and we have calculated the relevant abnormal returns and *t*-statistics from data in the articles. In several cases authors have provided estimates not published in the study. Italicized *t*-values are calculated by us using the methods described in footnote a to table 3. Unavailable data are denoted by 'n.a.'.

2.1 Target-firm stockholder returns

Successful target returns. The thirteen studies summarized in table 3 indicate that targets of successful takeover attempts realize substantial and statistically significant increases in their stock prices. The estimates of positive abnormal returns to targets of *successful tender offers*[3] in the month or two surrounding the offer shown in table 3, panel A, are uniformly positive ranging from 16.9% to 34.1%, and the weighted average abnormal return across the seven studies is 29.1%.[4]

For targets of *successful mergers*, the estimated abnormal returns immediately around the merger announcement in panel B.1 of table 3 range

---

[2]Eckbo (1983), Malatesta (1983), Wier (1983), Ruback (1983a), Bradley (1980), Bradley, Desai and Kim (1982, 1983), and Jarrell and Bradley (1980).

[3]Various definitions of a successful offer are used by the authors. Generally an offer is considered successful if the bidder acquires a substantial fraction of the number of shares initially sought.

[4]The weighted average abnormal return uses sample sizes as weights and ignores the issues associated with overlapping samples. Available data do not allow the calculation of *t*-values for any of the weighted averages.

Table 3

Abnormal returns associated with mergers and tender offers; sample size and t-statistic[a] are given in parentheses.

Study	Sample period	Event period	Bidding firms		Target firms	
			Successful (%)	Unsuccessful (%)	Successful (%)	Unsuccessful (%)
Panel A. Tender offers: Announcement effects						
Dodd and Ruback (1977)	1958–1978	Offer announcement month	+2.83 (124, 2.16)	+0.58 (48, 1.19)	+20.58 (133, 25.81)	+18.96 (36, 12.41)
		The month of and month following offer announcement	+3.12 (124, 2.24)	−1.71 (48, −0.76)	+21.15 (133, 15.75)	+16.31 (36, 6.32)
Kummer and Hoffmeister (1978)	1956–1974	Offer announcement month	+5.20 (17, 1.96)	n.a.	+16.85 (50, 10.88)	+21.09 (38, 11.87)
Bradley[b] (1980)	1962–1977	Twenty days before through twenty days after the offer announcement	+4.36 (88, 2.67)	−2.96 (46, −1.31)	+32.18 (161, 26.68)	+47.26 (97, 30.42)
Jarrell and Bradley (1980)	1962–1977	Forty days before through twenty days after the offer announcement	+6.66 (88, 3.35)	n.a.	+34.06[c] (147, 25.48)	n.a.
Bradley, Desai and Kim (1983)	1963–1980	Ten days before through ten days after the offer announcement	n.a.	−0.27 (94, 0.24)	n.a.	+35.55[d] (112, 36.61)
Bradley, Desai and Kim (1982)	1962–1980	Ten days before through ten days after the offer announcement	+2.35 (161, 3.02)	n.a.	+31.80 (162, 36.52)	n.a.
Ruback (1983a)	1962–1981	Five days before through the offer announcement	n.a.	−0.38 (48, −0.63)	n.a.	n.a.
Weighted average abnormal return[e,h]			+3.81 (478, n.a.)	−1.11 (236, n.a.)	+29.09 (653, n.a.)	+35.17 (283, n.a.)

Table 3 (continued)

Study	Sample period	Event period	Bidding firms		Target firms	
			Successful (%)	Unsuccessful (%)	Successful (%)	Unsuccessful (%)
Panel B.1. Mergers: Two-day announcement effects						
Dodd (1980)	1970–1977	The day before and day of the offer announcement	−1.09 (60, −2.98)	−1.24 (66, −2.63)	+13.41 (71, 23.80)	+12.73 (80, 19.08)
Asquith (1983)	1962–1976	The day before and day of the offer announcement	+0.20 (196, 0.78)	+0.50 (89, 1.92)	+6.20 (211, 23.07)	+7.00 (91, 12.83)
Eckbo (1983)	1963–1978	The day before through the day after the offer announcement	+0.07[f] (102, −0.12)	+1.20[g] (57, 2.98)	+6.24[f] (57, 9.97)	+10.20[g] (29, 15.22)
Weighted average abnormal return[h]			−0.05 (358, n.a.)	+0.15 (212, n.a.)	+7.72 (339, n.a.)	+9.76 (200, n.a.)
Panel B.2. Mergers: One-month announcement effects						
Dodd (1980)	1970–1977	Twenty days before through the first public announcement	+0.80 (60, 0.67)	+3.13 (66, 2.05)	+21.78 (71, 11.93)	+22.45 (80, 10.38)
Asquith (1983)	1962–1976	Nineteen days before through the first public announcement day	+0.20 (196, 0.25)	+1.20 (87, 1.49)	+13.30 (211, 15.65)	+11.70 (91, 6.71)
Eckbo (1983)	1963–1978	Twenty days before through ten days after the public announcement	+1.58[f] (102, 1.48)	+4.85[g] (57, 3.43)	+14.08[f] (57, 6.97)	+25.03[g] (29, 12.61)
Asquith,[i] Bruner and Mullins (1983)	1963–1979	Twenty days before the announcement day through the announcement day	+3.48 (170, 5.30)	+0.70 (41, 0.41)	+20.5 (35, 9.54)	+10.0 (19, 3.45)
Malatesta (1983)	1969–1974	Public announcement month	+0.90 (256, 1.53)	n.a.	+16.8 (83, 17.57)	n.a.
Weighted average abnormal return[h]			+1.37 (784, n.a.)	+2.45 (251, n.a.)	+15.90 (457, n.a.)	+17.24 (219, n.a.)

Panel B.3. Mergers: Total abnormal returns from offer announcement through outcome

Study	Window				
Dodd (1980)	Ten days before offer announcement through ten days after outcome date	−7.22 (60, −2.50)	−5.50 (66, −2.05)	+33.96 (71, 7.66)	+3.68 (80, 0.96)
Asquith (1983)	The day before offer announcement through outcome date	−0.10 (196, −0.05)	−5.90 (89, −3.15)	+15.50 (211, 6.01)	−7.50 (91, −1.54)
Wier[j] (1983)	Ten days before offer announcement through ten days after cancellation date	n.a.	+3.99 (16, 0.89)	n.a.	−9.02 (17, −1.82)
Weighted average abnormal return[h]		−1.77 (256, n.a.)	−4.82 (171, n.a.)	+20.15 (282, n.a.)	−2.88 (188, n.a.)

[a] Not available = n.a.

The non-italicized t-statistics were obtained directly from the cited study or calculated using standard errors reported in the study. In the absence of this information, we have approximated the t-statistics. The italicized t-statistics in panel A are calculated as: $t = \bar{X}\sqrt{N}/S\sqrt{T}$, where $\bar{X}$ is the reported abnormal return, N is the number of observations in the sample, T is the number of days over which the abnormal returns are cumulated, and S is the per day per observation standard deviation. $S = 2.39\%$ and is calculated as the average of the implied per day observation standard deviation in all of the studies. The italicized t-statistics in panel B.w were calculated as: $t = \bar{X}\sqrt{N}/S\sqrt{\bar{T}}$, where $\bar{T}$ is the average number of days in the average cumulative return, and the standard deviation is from the original study.

[b] These data are plotted in Bradley (1980). Bradley provided the numerical values in private correspondence.

[c] The abnormal return for successful targets is measured over the period forty days before through five days after the offer announcement.

[d] The abnormal return for unsuccessful targets in the announcement month.

[e] The weighted average excludes the announcement month results of Dodd and Ruback (1977) and includes their results for the month of and month following the announcement.

[f] Includes mergers which were not challenged by antitrust authorities.

[g] Sample consists of mergers that were challenged by antitrust authorities. Eckbo (1983) reports that most of these acquisitions were not completed.

[h] The abnormal returns are weighted by samples in calculating the weighted average. Overlapping sample problems are ignored.

[i] Asquith, Bruner and Mullins (1983) provided the data for successful and unsuccessful target firms in private correspondence.

[j] Sample includes only mergers that are cancelled after antitrust complaints under Section 7 of the Clayton Act.

from 6.2% to 13.4%, and the weighted average abnormal return is 7.7%.[5] Abnormal returns measured over holding periods of approximately one month surrounding the merger announcement are presented in panel B.2. The weighted average one-month return is 15.9% which is about twice the magnitude of the two-day abnormal returns. This comparison suggests that almost half of the abnormal returns associated with the merger announcements occur prior to their public announcement.[6]

Panel B.3 presents abnormal returns from the first public announcement through the outcome day that incorporate all effects of changing information regarding the offer that occur after the initial announcement. These returns are the most complete measures of the profitability of the mergers to target shareholders in table 3,[7] but they underestimate the gains to target shareholders because they do not include the premium on shares purchased by the bidder prior to the completion of the merger.[8] Dodd (1980) and Asquith (1983) report these total abnormal returns for successful targets as 34% and 15.5% respectively, and the weighted average of the two estimates is 20.2%.

Unsuccessful target returns. The weighted average abnormal returns to stockholders of target firms involved in *unsuccessful tender offers* shown in table 3, panel A, is 35.2%. The comparable one-month abnormal return for targets of *unsuccessful mergers* in panel B.2 is 17.2%. As panels A, B.1 reveal, these weighted average abnormal returns for targets of unsuccessful takeover attempts are approximately equal to those for targets of successful takeovers. Hence, on average the market appears to reflect approximately equal expected gains for both successful and unsuccessful takeovers at the time of the first public announcement. However, one-month announcement abnormal returns are an insufficient measure of stock price changes associated with unsuccessful takeover attempts because they do not include

---

[5]The *Wall Street Journal* publication date is conventionally used as the announcement date even though the actual announcement of the offers often occurs on the day prior to the publication day.

[6]Keown and Pinkerton (1981) also find that roughly half of the price adjustment occurs prior to the public announcement date. They incorrectly conclude that 'impending merger announcements are poorly held secrets' and that the pre-announcement price adjustments reflect insider trading and the leakage of inside information. They provide no tests of the plausible alternative hypothesis that the price adjustments prior to the 'announcement day' are unbiased responses to public information that increases the probability of a takeover. For many purposes the relatively crude characterization of an event as the *Wall Street Journal* announcement date or the company's formal announcement date is satisfactory. However, for many events there is literally no single 'event day', only a series of occurrences that increase or decrease the probability of an outcome such as a takeover. Inferences about insider trading or leakage require careful consideration of these issues.

[7]Interestingly the target stock price changes appear to capture all of the target value changes associated with the merger. See Kim and McConnell (1977) and Asquith and Kim (1982) who find no merger announcement effects on publicly-traded bond prices.

[8]See Ruback (1982) for calculation of gains to target shareholders that appropriately includes the proceeds to the tendering shareholders on repurchased shares.

the stock price response to the information that the offer failed. The correct measure of the wealth effects, therefore, is the cumulative return from the offer through the termination announcement. The weighted average return to *unsuccessful merger* targets from the initial announcement through the outcome date presented in panel B.3 is -2.9%. Thus, all of the announcement gains are lost over the time that the merger failure becomes known.

In contrast to the behavior of stock prices of targets of unsuccessful mergers, stock prices of targets of *unsuccessful tender offers* remain substantially above their pre-offer level even after the failure of the offer. Unfortunately, the tender offer studies do not present data on the cumulative abnormal return for unsuccessful tender offers from the initial announcement through the outcome date. Nevertheless, some information can be extracted from the abnormal returns following the initial announcement. Dodd and Ruback (1977) find an abnormal return of -2.65% for targets of unsuccessful tender offers in the month following the initial announcement, but the cumulative abnormal return over the entire year following the announcement is only -3.25% $(t=0.90)$.

Bradley, Desai and Kim (1983) analyze the post-failure price behavior of a sample of 112 targets of *unsuccessful tender offers* that they segment into two categories: 86 targets that received subsequent takeover offers and 26 targets that did not receive such offers.[9] Returns in the announcement month for the two subsamples are 29.1% and 23.9% respectively, and both are statistically significant. From the announcement month of the initial unsuccessful offer through the following two years, the average abnormal return for the targets that *received* subsequent offers is 57.19% $(t=10.39)$. In contrast, the average abnormal return over the same two-year period for targets that *did not receive* subsequent offers is an insignificant -3.53% $(t=-0.36)$, and recall this return includes the announcement effects. Thus, the positive abnormal returns associated with unsuccessful tender offers appear to be due to the anticipation of subsequent offers; target shareholders realize additional positive abnormal returns when a subsequent offer is made, but lose the initial announcement gains if no subsequent offer occurs.[10]

Summary: The returns to targets.   In summary, the evidence indicates that targets of *successful tender offers* and *mergers* earn significantly positive abnormal returns on announcement of the offers and through completion of the offers. Targets of *unsuccessful tender offers* earn significantly positive

---

[9]These data seem to indicate that the probability of becoming a takeover target rises substantially after an initial unsuccessful offer occurs.

[10]This evidence casts doubt on the earlier conjectures by Dodd and Ruback (1977) that unsuccessful tender offers lead to target shareholder gains through the disciplining of existing inefficient managers. It is also inconsistent with the argument made by DeAngelo, DeAngelo and Rice (1982) that part of the target price change in takeover offers represents the value of implicit information about target profitability that is revealed by the offer announcement.

abnormal returns on the offer announcement and through the realization of failure. However, those targets of unsuccessful tender offers that do not receive additional offers in the next two years lose all previous announcement gains, and those targets that do receive new offers earn even higher returns. Finally, targets of *unsuccessful mergers* appear to lose all positive returns earned in the offer announcement period by the time failure of the offer becomes known.

2.2 Bidding-firm stockholder returns

Successful bidders. The abnormal returns for bidders in *successful tender offers* summarized in panel A of table 3 are all significantly positive and range from 2.4% to 6.7%, with a weighted average return of 3.8%. Thus, bidders in successful tender offers realize significant percentage increases in equity value, although this increase is substantially lower than the 29.1% return to targets of successful tender offers.

The evidence on bidder returns in *mergers* is mixed and therefore more difficult to interpret than that for bidders in tender offers. On the whole it suggests that returns to bidders in mergers are approximately zero. The two-day abnormal returns associated with the announcement of a merger proposal summarized in panel B.1 of table 3 differ considerably across studies. Dodd (1980) finds a significant abnormal return of -1.09% for 60 successful bidders on the day before and the day of the first public announcement of the merger — indicating that merger bids are, on average, negative net present value investments for bidders. However, over the same two-day period, Asquith (1983) and Eckbo (1983) report slightly positive, but statistically insignificant, abnormal returns — suggesting that merger bids are zero net present value investments. In contrast to the mixed findings for the immediate announcement effects, all five estimates of the one-month announcement effects in panel B.2 of table 3 are positive, but only the estimate of 3.48% by Asquith, Bruner and Mullins (1983) is significantly different from zero. The weighted averages are 1.37% for the one-month announcement effects and -0.05% for the two-day announcement effects.

Panel B.3 of table 3 contains the results of two studies that report the total abnormal return for successful bidding firms from the initial announcement day through the outcome announcement day. If the initial announcement is unanticipated, and there are no other information effects, this cumulative abnormal return includes the effects of all revisions in expectations and offer prices and therefore is a complete measure of the equity value changes for successful bidders. The weighted average of the two estimates is -1.77%, and the individual estimates are -7.22% for 60 successful bidders and -0.1% for 196 successful bidders.

The estimated abnormal returns to successful bidding firms in all six studies summarized in panels B.1 through B.3 of table 3 suggest that mergers are zero net present value investments for bidders[11] — except for the Dodd (1980) estimates in panels B.1 and B.3. It is difficult to understand the reason for the substantial difference between Dodd's estimates and the others. His sample period and methodology are similar to those of the other studies, although his sample is restricted to acquisition proposals for NYSE firms that 'are initially announced in the form of a merger' and is therefore somewhat more restrictive than others. His sample 'does not include merger proposals that were preceded by a tender offer and does not include "defensive mergers" where a target firm finds a merger partner in response to a tender offer by a third firm' [Dodd (1980, p. 107)]. Lacking obvious clues to explain the difference in Dodd's estimates, we're left with the conjecture that his results are sample specific even though there is no apparent reason why this should be induced by his sample selection criteria.[12]

Malatesta (1983) provides estimates of total abnormal *dollar* returns to the equity holders of successful bidding firms in the period 1969–1974 that are consistent with Dodd's results. He reports an average loss of about $28 million ($t = -1.85$) in the period four months before through the month of announcement of the merger outcome (indicated by announcement of board/management approval) of the merger.

Unsuccessful bidders. Inferences about the profitability of takeover bids can also be made from the behavior of bidding-firm stock prices around the time of termination announcements for unsuccessful acquisition attempts. Positive abnormal returns to a bidding firm in response to the announcement that a takeover attempt is unsuccessful (for reasons other than bidder cancellation) are inconsistent with the hypothesis that takeovers are positive net present value investments. Dodd reports insignificant average abnormal returns of 0.9% for 19 bidders on the day before and day of announcement of merger termination initiated by targets. If mergers are positive return projects, these target-termination announcement returns should be negative. Dodd also reports positive termination announcement returns of 1.38% for 47 bidders in his bidder-termination subsample. These positive returns are consistent with the hypothesis that bidders maximize shareholder wealth and cancel mergers after finding out they overvalued the target on the initial offer.

Ruback (1983a) uses data on unsuccessful bidders to test directly for value-maximizing behavior of bidders. He argues that wealth-maximizing bidders

[11]There are, however, classic examples which seem to contradict the conclusion that merger bids are zero net present value investments. For example, see the detailed examination of the 1981 DuPont–Conoco merger by Ruback (1982) in which DuPont paid $7.54 billion, the largest takeover in U.S. corporate history. The value of DuPont fell by $789 million ($-9.9\%$) over the takeover period, and $641 million of the decline occurred on the day of the announcement of DuPont's first offer.

[12]After discussing the issues with us, Dodd was kind enough to recheck and replicate his results — no data or computer programming errors were found.

will abandon takeover attempts when increments in the offer price would make the takeover a negative net present value investment. For 48 bidders in competitive tender offers (defined by the presence of multiple bidders), he finds the average potential gain to the unsuccessful bidder from matching the successful offer price is $-\$91$ million ($t = -4.34$). The potential gain is calculated as the abnormal bidder equity value change associated with the original announcement of the unsuccessful bid minus the additional cost if the higher successful bid were matched. Furthermore, 41 bidders did not match higher offer prices that would have resulted in a negative net present value acquisition.[13] These results are consistent with value-maximizing behavior by bidding firms.

Problems in measuring bidder returns. There is reason to believe the estimation of returns is more difficult for bidders than for targets. Since stock price changes reflect changes in expectations, a merger announcement will have no effect if its terms are fully anticipated in the market. Furthermore, targets are acquired once at most, whereas bidders can engage in prolonged acquisition programs. Malatesta (1981, 1983) and Schipper and Thompson (1983a) point out that the present value of the expected benefits of a bidder's acquisition program is incorporated into the share price when the acquisition program is announced or becomes apparent to the market. Thus, the gain to bidding firms is correctly measured by the value change associated with the initial information about the acquisition program and the incremental effect of each acquisition. The abnormal returns to bidding firms associated with mergers reported in table 3 measure only the incremental value change of each acquisition and are therefore potentially incomplete measures of merger value to successful bidders.

Bidding firms do not typically announce acquisition programs explicitly; this information is generally revealed as the bidders pursue takeover targets. However, Schipper and Thompson (1983a) find that for some firms the start of a takeover program can be approximately determined. They examine the stock price behavior of 30 firms that announced acquisition programs during the period 1953 through 1968. The information that these firms intended to pursue an acquisition program was revealed either in annual reports or specific announcements to the financial press, or in association with other corporate policy changes. For 13 firms in their sample, Schipper and Thompson are unable to identify a specific month in which the acquisition program was adopted. For these firms, December of the program-adoption year is used as the announcement month. Four of the remaining 17 firms

---

[13]In the remaining 7 observations, the unsuccessful bidders did not match the successful offer price even though the data suggest that the matching would have been a positive net present value investment. The average potential gain for these 7 observations is $23 million ($t = 0.64$). The low t-value suggests that these 'mistakes' are not statistically significant. However, as noted in Ruback (1983a), the measured potential gains are likely to underestimate the actual potential gains when the probability of success is less than one.

had multiple announcements of their programs and the date of the last announcement is used for these firms.

The difficulties in identifying the exact announcement date imply that the capitalized values of the acquisition program are impounded into stock prices prior to the Schipper and Thompson 'announcement month'. Consistent with the hypothesis that mergers are positive net present value investments for bidding firms, they find abnormal returns of 13.5% ($t = 2.26$) for their sample of 30 firms in the 12 months prior to and including the 'event month'. However, the imprecise announcement month, the resultant necessity for measuring abnormal returns over a 12-month interval, and contemporaneous changes in corporate policy make it difficult to determine with confidence the association between positive abnormal returns and initiation of the acquisition program. For example, suppose 'good luck' provided bidder management with additional resources to try new projects such as mergers. As Schipper and Thompson discuss, in this case stock prices would show the pattern evidenced in their study even if the mergers have zero net present value.[14]

Asquith, Bruner and Mullins (1983) also examine the profitability of merger programs. They focus on the abnormal returns associated with the first four bids after the initiation of a merger program, arguing that the earlier bids in a merger program should contain more information about the profitability of the program than later bids. This suggests that the price response associated with the first few bids should be greater than the price response associated with later bids. They analyze the abnormal returns for successive merger bids (up to four) of 156 firms that initiated merger programs in the period 1963–1979 after eight years without a bid. Their results indicate that merger bids (both successful and unsuccessful) are positive net present value investments, as evidenced by significant average bidder gains of 2.8% ($t = 5.20$) in the 20 days prior to and including the first public announcement. However, there is little evidence that the major gain to the acquisition program is capitalized into the bidder's stock price on announcement of the early mergers. The returns, sample size and t-statistics by merger sequence number are:

	Merger sequence number			
	1	2	3	4
Abnormal return	2.4%	3.7%	2.4%	2.8%
(N, t-statistic)	(70, 2.21)	(59, 3.13)	(47, 1.37)	(38, 2.38)

[14]Schipper and Thompson conclude that negative abnormal stock price changes for their acquiring firms around times of restrictive regulatory changes help resolve this ambiguity and

In addition to the problems caused by prior capitalization of the gains from takeover bids, measuring the gains to bidding firms is also difficult because bidders are generally much larger than target firms. Thus, even when the dollar gains from the takeover are split evenly between bidder and target firms, the dollar gains to the bidders translate into smaller percentage gains. Asquith, Bruner and Mullins (1983) report that the abnormal returns of bidding firms depend on the relative size of the target. For 99 mergers in which the target's equity value is 10% or more of the bidder's equity value, the average abnormal return for *bidders* is 4.1% ($t = 4.42$) over the period 20 days before through the day of announcement. For the 115 remaining mergers in which the target's equity value is less than 10% of the bidder's equity value, the average abnormal return for bidders is 1.7% ($t = 2.00$). Furthermore, the precision of the estimated gains is lower for bidders than for targets because the normal variation in equity value for the (larger) bidder is greater, relative to a given dollar gain, than it is for the target. Thus, even if the gains are split equally, the relative sizes of bidding and target firms imply that both the average abnormal return and its t-statistic will be smaller for bidding firms.

Returns to bidders also show evidence of other measurement problems. Several studies show indications of systematic reductions in the stock prices of bidding firms in the year following the event. These post-outcome negative abnormal returns are unsettling because they are inconsistent with market efficiency and suggest that changes in stock price during takeovers overestimate the future efficiency gains from mergers. Table 4 presents the cumulative abnormal returns in the year following takeovers in six different studies. One of the post-announcement abnormal returns in the two tender offer studies in panel A of table 4 is not significantly different from zero. In addition, the post-outcome abnormal returns for the merger studies reported in panel B of table 4 provide evidence of systematic reductions in stock price. Langetieg (1978) and Asquith (1983) report significant negative abnormal returns in the year following the outcome announcement. Malatesta (1983) finds insignificant negative abnormal returns in the year following the merger announcement for his entire sample, although he finds significant negative abnormal returns for bidders in mergers occurring after 1970 and for bidders with smaller equity value.

There are several potential explanations for the negative post-outcome abnormal returns. One hypothesis is that the studies impose ex post selection bias by using information that is not available at the announcement date to

---

make the evidence that the programs were positive net present value projects for acquirers 'more compelling'. However, this conclusion cannot be drawn. Negative returns on the imposition of regulatory changes that impose higher future costs on bidders would also be observed if the original acquisition programs were negative net present value projects as long as the regulatory changes do not cause the bidders to abandon their acquisition programs.

Table 4

Summary of post-outcome abnormal returns for tender offers and mergers; sample size and t-statistic[a] are given in parentheses.

Study	Sample period	Event period	Bidding firms		Target firms	
			Successful (%)	Unsuccessful (%)	Successful (%)	Unsuccessful (%)
Panel A. Tender offers						
Dodd and Ruback (1977)	1958–1978	Month after through 12 months after the offer announcement	-1.32 (124, -0.41)	-1.60 (48, -0.52)	+7.95 (133, 0.85)	-3.25 (36, 0.90)
Bradley, Desai and Kim (1983)	1962–1980	Month after through 12 months after the offer announcement	n.a.	-7.85[b] (94, -2.34)	n.a.	+3.04 (112, 0.90)
Panel B. Mergers						
Mandelker (1974)	1941–1962	Month after through 12 months after the effective date	+0.60 (241, 0.31)	n.a.	n.a.	n.a.
Langetieg (1978)	1929–1969	Month after through 12 months after the effective date	-6.59 (149, -2.96)	n.a.	n.a.	n.a.
Asquith (1983)	1962–1976	Day after through 240 days after the outcome announcement	-7.20 (196, -4.10)	-9.60 (89, -5.41)	n.a.	-8.7 (91, -2.11)
Malatesta (1983)	1969–1974	Month after through 12 months after approval for entire sample	-2.90 (121, -1.05)	n.a.	n.a.	n.a.
		Month after through 12 months after approval for mergers occurring after 1970	-13.7 (75, -2.88)	n.a.	n.a.	n.a.
		Month after through 12 months after approval for firms with equity value under $300 million	-7.70 (59, -1.51)	n.a.	n.a.	n.a.

[a]Not available = n.a.
The t-statistics either come directly from the cited study, or were calculated from implied standard deviations available in the cited study, or come from an earlier draft of the study.

[b]This abnormal return covers the period from the day after through 180 days after the offer.

select samples. Alternatively, the negative drift could be caused by non-stationary parameters or other forms of model misspecification, but Langetieg (1978) finds these factors do not explain the negative post-outcome returns in his sample. Schipper and Thompson (1983a) argue that regulatory changes that reduced the profitability of mergers could explain the negative abnormal returns, but Malatesta (1983) finds significant negative abnormal post-outcome returns of -13.7% $(t=2.88)$ for mergers occurring after the regulatory changes. Explanation of these post-event negative abnormal returns is currently an unsettled issue.

Summary: The returns to bidders. The reported positive returns to *successful bidders* in *tender offers* and the generally negative returns to *unsuccessful bidders* in both *mergers* and *tender offers* are consistent with the hypothesis that mergers are positive net present value projects. The measurement of returns to bidders in mergers is difficult, and perhaps because of this the results are mixed. The evidence suggests, however, that returns to *successful bidding* firms in *mergers* are zero. Additional work on this problem is clearly warranted.

2.3. The total gains from takeovers

The evidence indicates that shareholders of target firms realize large positive abnormal returns in completed takeovers. The evidence on the rewards to bidding firms is mixed, but the weight of the evidence suggests zero returns are earned by successful bidding firms in mergers and that statistically significant but small positive abnormal returns are realized by bidders in successful tender offers. Since targets gain and bidders do not appear to lose, the evidence suggests that takeovers create value. However, because bidding firms tend to be larger than target firms, the sum of the returns to bidding and target returns do not measure the gains to the merging firms. The dollar value of small percentage losses for bidders could exceed the dollar value of large percentage gains to targets.

Malatesta (1983) and Bradley, Desai and Kim (1982) measure the changes in total dollar value associated with completed takeovers. Malatesta examines a matched sample of targets and their bidders in 30 successful mergers and finds a significant average increase of $32.4 million $(t=2.07)$ in their combined equity value in the month before and month of outcome announcement. The acquired firms earned $18.6 million $(t=5.41)$ of the combined increase in equity value, and acquiring firms earned $13.8 million $(t=0.91)$. Bradley, Desai and Kim (1982) report positive but statistically insignificant total dollar gains to bidders and targets in 162 tender offers of $17.2 million $(t=1.26)$. However, the average percentage change in total value of the combined target and bidder firms is a significant 10.5% $(t=6.58)$. This evidence indicates that changes in corporate control increase the combined market value of assets of the bidding and target firms.

3. Antitrust and the source of merger gains

The evidence indicates that, on average, takeovers result in an upward revaluation of the target's equity, and that shareholders of target firms realize a substantial increase in wealth as a result of completed takeovers. Understanding the source of the gains to merging firms is important since acquisition attempts often meet strong opposition, sometimes from target management, sometimes from antitrust authorities. Target managers, for example, often argue that target shareholders are harmed by takeovers; indeed, the common use of the emotion-laden term 'raider' to label the bidding firm suggests that the bidder's gains are coming at the expense of the target firm's shareholders. The evidence summarized above indicates that this argument is false; the bidder's gains (if any) do not appear to be simple wealth transfers from target shareholders.[15] Acquisition attempts are also opposed by target firms, competitors, and antitrust authorities, among others, who argue that mergers are undesirable because they reduce competition and create monopoly power.[16] Such opposition has delayed merger completion, caused merger cancellations, and resulted in court-ordered divestiture of previously completed acquisitions.[17] In addition, the evidence indicating positive net benefits to merging firms, together with the zero or positive abnormal returns to bidding firms, is inconsistent with the hypothesis that takeovers are motivated by non-value-maximizing behavior by the managers of bidding firms.

3.1. The source of takeover gains

Various sources of gains to takeovers have been advanced. Potential reductions in production or distribution costs, often called synergies, could occur through realization of economies of scale, vertical integration, adoption of more efficient production or organizational technology,[18] increased utilization of the bidder's management team, and reduction of agency costs by bringing organization-specific assets under common ownership.[19]

---

[15]See Bradley (1980) for an extended discussion of these issues in the context of tender offers.

[16]Arguments by target management that a takeover should be prohibited on antitrust grounds seems particularly self-interested and inconsistent with maximization of shareholder wealth.

[17]For example, the Justice Department's request for additional information from Mobil during the Conoco takeover prohibited Mobil from buying Conoco common stock and prevented Mobil from actively competing with DuPont and Seagram for control of Conoco, even though Mobil's offer was approximately one billion dollars higher. Ruback (1982) analyzes this takeover in detail.

[18]See Chandler (1962, 1977) and Williamson (1975, 1981) for discussion of advantages of the multidivisional form of organization which seems common to merged firms. Bradley, Desai and Kim (1982) investigate the role of specialized resources in merger gains.

[19]See Klein, Crawford and Alchian (1978) for discussion of the agency costs of outside ownership of organization-specific assets.

Financial motivations for acquisitions include the use of underutilized tax shields, avoidance of bankruptcy costs, increased leverage, and other types of tax advantages.[20] Takeovers could increase market power in product markets. Finally, takeovers could eliminate inefficient target management. Each of these hypotheses predicts that the combined firm generates cash flows with a present value in excess of the sum of the market values of the bidding and target firms. But the abnormal returns do not identify which components of the present value of net cash flows have changed. Studies of the abnormal returns to takeover participants cannot, therefore, distinguish between these alternative sources of gains.

Two important exceptions are the studies by Stillman (1983) and Eckbo (1983), which use the equity price changes of firms that *compete* in product markets with the merged target to reject the hypothesis that takeovers create market power. The market power hypothesis implies that mergers increase product prices thereby benefiting the merging firms and other competing firms in the industry. Higher prices allow competing firms to increase their own product prices and/or output, and therefore the equity values of competing firms should also rise on the offer announcement.

Stillman (1983) examines the abnormal returns for rival firms in 11 horizontal mergers. The small sample size arises from his sample selection criteria. Of all mergers challenged under Section 7 of the Clayton Act, these 11 are the merger complaints in unregulated industries whose rivals were identified in the proceedings and for which constraints on data availability were met. While this screening process creates a small sample, it reduces ambiguity about the applicability of the test and the identity of rivals. He finds no statistically significant abnormal returns for rival firms in nine of the mergers examined. Of the remaining two mergers, one exhibits ambiguous results and the other is consistent with positive abnormal returns for rivals. Stillman's evidence, therefore, is inconsistent with the hypothesis that the gains from mergers are due to the acquisition of market power.

Eckbo (1983) uses the stock price reaction of rivals at the announcement of the antitrust challenge as well as at the announcement of the merger to test the market power hypothesis. Eckbo's final sample consists of 126 challenged horizontal mergers and, using product line classifications rather than records of court and agency proceedings, he identifies an average of 15 rivals for each merger. He also identifies rivals for 65 unchallenged horizontal mergers and 58 vertical mergers.

Eckbo's results indicate that rival firms have positive abnormal returns around the time of the first public announcement of the *merger*. Rivals of unchallenged mergers realized abnormal returns of 1.1% ($t = 1.20$) and rivals of challenged mergers realized abnormal returns of 2.45% ($t = 3.02$) in the

---

[20]See Benston (1980, p. 21).

period 20 days prior to and 10 days following the first public announcement. These results are consistent with the market power hypothesis.

Eckbo uses the stock price reactions of *rivals* at announcement of the *antitrust challenge* to reject the market power hypothesis. The market power hypothesis predicts negative abnormal returns for rival firms at the time the complaint is filed because the complaint reduces the probability of completion of the merger (which, it is assumed, would have generated market power), and the concomitant increase in output prices is then less probable. In the period 20 days before through 10 days after the antitrust challenge, the rivals to 55 challenged mergers realize statistically insignificant average abnormal returns of 1.78% ($t = 1.29$). This finding is inconsistent with the market power hypothesis, which implies the returns of rivals should be significantly negative at the complaint announcement. Furthermore, Eckbo reports that rivals with a positive market reaction to the initial merger announcement do not tend to have negative abnormal returns at the time of complaint. Thus, Eckbo's evidence is inconsistent with the market power hypothesis.

Although the evidence in Eckbo (1983) and Stillman (1983) is inconsistent with the market power hypothesis, identification of the actual source of the gains in takeovers has not yet occurred. There is evidence in Asquith (1980, 1983), Malatesta (1983), Langetieg (1978), Ellert (1976), and Mandelker (1974) that target firms experience negative abnormal returns in the period prior to approximately six months before the acquisition.[21] This below normal performance is consistent with the hypothesis that inefficient target management caused target firms to perform badly, but there is currently no evidence that directly links these negative pre-merger returns to inefficiency. Eckbo's results, moreover, are inconsistent with the target inefficiency hypothesis. His evidence indicates that the gains are more general, extending to rivals in the industry as well as to the specific target firm, and removal of inefficient target management is unlikely to be an industry-wide phenomenon.

It would be surprising to find that all the gains reflected in table 3 are due to a single phenomenon such as elimination of inefficient target management. Some of the gains are also likely to result from other synergies in combining two or more independent organizations, and discovery of the precise nature of these synergies is a complicated task. Ruback (1982), for example, examines the DuPont–Conoco merger to determine the source of the revaluation that occurred; the stockholders of the target, Conoco, realized gains of about \$3.2 billion whereas stockholders of the bidder, DuPont, incurred losses of almost \$800 million. The DuPont–Conoco merger, therefore, 'created' about \$2.4 billion of additional market value. Ruback

---

[21]The declines reported by Asquith (1983), Malatesta (1983), Langetieg (1978) and Ellert (1976) are statistically significant.

explores a variety of different explanations for the revaluations, including synergy, the release of new information, undervalued oil reserves, replacement of inefficient target management, and departures from stockholder wealth maximization by the management of DuPont. None of these hypotheses provide an adequate explanation for the revaluation, although it is impossible to reject the hypothesis that DuPont had some special new information about Conoco's assets. These results suggest it is difficult to identify the source of the gains from takeovers — even in the context of a single takeover.

Information effects of various kinds might also play a role in explaining the behavior of stock prices at times of takeovers. For example, DeAngelo, DeAngelo and Rice (1982) conjecture that information effects associated with bidder management's possession of inside information about its own value might help explain the difference in bidder returns in tender offers and merger proposals. The evidence indicates that bidders in successful tender offers earn small positive returns and that successful merger bidders earn approximately zero returns. Tender offers are frequently cash offers,[22] and mergers are usually stock and other security exchange offers. When bidder management's inside information (unrelated to the acquisition) indicates its stock is undervalued it will prefer a cash offer and vice versa for a stock offer.[23] Therefore, astute market participants will interpret a cash offer as good news and a stock offer as bad news about the bidder's value and incorporate this information into bidder stock prices along with the estimated value of the acquisition. This argument implies that returns to bidders in cash tender offers will be higher than in mergers, if other aspects of the deals are approximately equivalent.

The inside information argument is as yet untested. However, it implies that stock prices fall when new shares are sold and rise when shares are repurchased, and this implication is consistent with the price effects associated with intrafirm capital structure changes found by a growing number of authors. For example, prices generally fall on the exchange of common and preferred stock for bonds [Masulis (1980a)], on the call and conversion of convertible bonds to stock [Mikkelson (1981, 1983)], on the issuance of convertible debt [Dann and Mikkelson (1982)], on the issuance of stock through rights offerings [Smith (1977)], and on the sale of common stock in secondary offering [Scholes (1972)], while prices generally rise on repurchases of common stock [Dann (1981), Vermaelen (1981), Masulis (1980b) and Rosenfeld (1982)]. The only inconsistent evidence is the

---

[22]Bradley (1980), Jarrell and Bradley (1980) and Bradley, Desai and Kim (1983) sample only cash offers; Dodd and Ruback (1977) and Ruback (1983a) sample both cash and security exchange tender offers.

[23]See Myers and Majluf (1981) who argue that sale of shares by a target through merger can reveal negative information about the target's value.

significant negative returns associated with targeted buybacks of large blocks of stock documented by DeAngelo and Rice (1983) and Bradley and Wakeman (1983). However, the targeted buyback evidence seems well explained by other factors, as discussed in section 4.5 below.

3.2. The costs of antitrust actions

The evidence indicates that merger gains do not come from the acquisition of market power, but rather from some source of efficiencies that also appears to be available to rival firms in the industry. Given this evidence it is of interest to examine the effects of antitrust actions on merging firms.

In their studies of antitrust merger actions, Ellert (1976), Wier (1983) and Eckbo (1983) demonstrate that antitrust opposition to takeovers imposes substantial costs on target firm shareholders. Wier examines the abnormal returns for firms involved in mergers which were opposed by antitrust authorities under Section 7 of the Clayton Act. Her sample contains mergers involving 16 bidding firms and 17 target firms that were cancelled after antitrust complaints. The cumulative abnormal return from 30 days before through the proposal announcement is 9.25%. During the period *following* the proposal announcement through the complaint period and the cancellation day, all the previous target firm announcement gains are eliminated; the cumulative abnormal return is -12.43%. Bidding firms in her sample appear to show no abnormal returns at the time of proposal announcement or cancellation.

Wier (1983) also examines the abnormal returns associated with the announcement of antitrust complaints for 111 completed mergers, and her data reveal significant abnormal returns of -2.58% for the day before through the day after the complaint announcement. Ellert (1976) reports an abnormal return of -1.83% ($t = -3.24$) in the complaint month for 205 defendants in antitrust merger cases over the period 1950–1972. Similarly, Eckbo (1983) reports an average abnormal return of -9.27% ($t = -7.61$) for 17 target firms on the day before through the day after the announcement of an antitrust complaint. In addition, Wier finds that the abnormal return for 32 firms that completed their mergers and were later convicted of antitrust violations is -2.27% ($t = -4.11$) from the day before through the day after the conviction announcement. However, she finds no significant abnormal returns on announcement of the outcome for 30 firms whose antitrust suits were dismissed and for 66 firms that settled their antitrust suits. Dismissal or settlement of a suit, unless fully expected, would generally represent good news. As Wier points out, the absence of significant abnormal returns at these announcements is puzzling.

There is also evidence consistent with the hypothesis that Federal Trade Commission antitrust actions benefit rivals of merging firms by restricting competition. Eckbo (1983) finds that rivals of mergers challenged by the Federal Trade Commission earn essentially zero abnormal returns on the day of the merger announcement and significantly positive abnormal returns on the day of the complaint announcement. In contrast, rivals of mergers challenged by the Justice Department earn significantly positive abnormal returns on the merger announcement and essentially zero abnormal returns on the complaint announcement. Eckbo (1983) concludes: 'This evidence strongly contradicts the [market power] hypothesis and gives some support to a "rival producer protection" rationale for the behavior of the FTC towards these mergers.'

In sum, the negative abnormal returns associated with antitrust complaints, Section 7 convictions, and cancellations of mergers induced by antitrust actions indicate that antitrust opposition to takeovers imposes substantial costs on the stockholders of merging firms. This finding is particularly interesting given that the evidence indicates merger gains do not arise from the creation of market power but rather from the acquisition of some form of efficiencies.

3.3. The effects of takeover regulation

In addition to antitrust regulation, the imposition of security regulations governing takeovers appears to have reduced the profitability of takeovers. The effect of changes in tender offer regulations (such as the Williams Amendment and state tender offer laws) on the abnormal returns to bidding and target firms, is examined in Smiley (1975) and Jarrell and Bradley (1980). Smiley finds that the Williams Amendment increased the abnormal returns to target firms by 13%. Jarrell and Bradley find that the target's average abnormal return increased after the Williams Amendment and the bidder's average abnormal return decreased. They find that average abnormal returns for 47 target firms prior to the Williams Amendment were 22% ($t = 12.9$) in the period 40 days before through five days after the first public announcement of the takeover. In comparison, the average abnormal return for 90 targets subject to regulation under the Williams Amendment is 40% ($t = 19.2$) and the returns to 20 targets subject to both the Williams Amendment and state tender offer laws is 35% ($t = 5.1$). For bidders, the average abnormal return in the period 40 days before through 20 days after the first public announcement is 9% ($t = 3.5$) for 28 unregulated offers, 6% ($t = 2.1$) for 51 offers regulated by the Williams Amendment, and 4% ($t = 0.7$) for 9 offers regulated by the Williams Amendment and state tender offer laws. Asquith, Bruner and Mullins (1983) provide similar evidence. For mergers prior to October 1, 1969, they report average abnormal returns to bidders of 4.40% over the period 20 days before through the first public announcement and average abnormal returns of 1.7% to bidders in mergers after October 1, 1969.

The evidence seems to indicate that the regulations increased the returns to the target's shareholders at the expense of the shareholders of bidding firms, but the tests are not sufficient to draw this conclusion from the data. Suppose the regulations have no effect whatsoever except to eliminate the low-value offers. By raising transactions costs and imposing restrictions on takeovers, the regulations could simply truncate the distribution of takeovers that would actually occur. This truncation of less profitable takeovers would reduce the returns to shareholders of firms that do not become targets and have no effect on the returns to those that do become targets, but it would increase the *measured* average abnormal returns for targets of completed takeovers. The effect of such truncation on the abnormal returns to bidding firms is less clear since no well-developed theory exists that determines the division of the net benefits between target and bidding firms.

Schipper and Thompson (1983a) examine the effect of four regulatory changes that occurred in 1968–1970: Accounting Principle Board Opinions 16 and 17, the 1969 Tax Reform Act, the 1968 Williams Amendment, and its 1970 extension. Each of these regulatory changes restricts bidders and thereby reduces the profitability of bidding firms. The abnormal return for bidders engaged in merger programs at the time of four regulatory changes is interesting because, in an efficient market, the effect of the regulatory changes is impounded in the bidder's stock price on announcement of the changes. They find an average abnormal return of -1.3% $(t=4.5)$ during the 15 months in which events related to regulatory change occurred between January 1967 and December 1970. Schipper and Thompson (1983b) use an alternative technique to estimate the effects of the regulatory changes. They report that the Williams Amendment reduced the equity values of acquiring firms by about 6%. The Schipper and Thompson event-type tests are more precise than the comparison of abnormal returns to bidders before and after regulation, and they indicate that the regulatory changes impose costs on bidding firms. Their approach cannot be used to assess the effect of the regulations on target firms because it is difficult, if not impossible, for the market to identify future target firms.[24] If market participants cannot identify targets prior to the bids, appreciable changes in stock price will not be observed for targets of future takeovers at times of regulatory changes.

4. Manager–stockholder conflicts of interest

4.1. Corporate control: The issues

Takeovers serve as an external control mechanism that limits major

[24]Palepue (1983) uses a binary logit model to identify determinants of the probability of acquisition. While he finds several variables that are statistically significant, the overall explanatory power of the model is negligible.

managerial departures from maximization of stockholder wealth.[25] It is unlikely, however, that the threat of takeover ensures complete coherence of managerial actions and maximization of stockholder wealth. Because of the existence of other control mechanisms, the inability of the takeover market to eliminate all departures from maximization of stockholder wealth does not imply that these departures are prevalent in modern corporations.[26] The limitations of the takeover market also do not imply that the departures, when they occur, are costly to shareholders; some of the costs are borne by managers themselves through reductions in their salaries.[27]

Measurement of the costs of manager–stockholder conflict by direct examination of managerial decisions is difficult for reasons that include the difficulty in identifying the benefits to managers that emanate from particular decisions, the difficulty in determining the information base for the decision, errors in the stock market assessment of value, and the difficulty in ex post auditing of decisions. For example, suppose the announcement of a capital investment is associated with a decline in the firm's stock price, suggesting that the investment reduces shareholder wealth. There is no particular reason in this case to suspect that the decision benefits managers.[28] Furthermore, the price decline could be an error due to the market's lack of inside information possessed by managers. Alternatively, even if the investment is value-maximizing, the decline in price could result from an exogenous reduction in profitability that the investment reveals to the market. Finally, even when the investment proves to be a negative net present value

---

[25]The average abnormal returns to target shareholders in tables 1 and 3 are not measures of the extent of managerial departures from stockholder wealth maximization. For example, in addition to the gains from eliminating inefficient managers, they include the gains from efficiency innovations and synergies available to the combined firm.

[26]See Fama and Jensen (1983a, b, c) and Jensen (1983) for discussions of agency costs, control and survival in a theory of organizations that views conflicts of interests in a general fashion.

[27]See Jensen and Meckling (1976, p. 328) and Fama (1980). However, unless the cost of perfectly enforcing managerial contracts is zero, the agency costs of managerial discretion will not be zero. Zero costs of managerial discretion imply zero costs of constructing a managerial performance measurement, evaluation and compensation system that perfectly reflects in the manager's salary all deviations from shareholder wealth maximization. Contrary to Fama's (1980) argument, this implication holds even for the monitoring performed by the managerial labor market. Consider, for example, a case in which the value of a manager's human capital that is specific to his current organization is large relative to the value of his general human capital. (The value of general human capital means the value of human capital in its highest-value use outside the manager's current organization.) In this case, fluctuations in the value of his general human capital, even if they perfectly reflect the manager's deviations from maximization of shareholder wealth, will have no direct effect on his welfare. Therefore, the managerial labor market will not eliminate the agency costs between managers and stockholders in such situations.

[28]For example, the evidence presented by Mikkelson (1981, 1983) and Masulis (1980a) indicates that call and conversion of convertible bonds to common stock and exchange of common and preferred stock for bonds is associated with statistically significant stock price declines. Except for cases in which managerial compensation depends on earnings per share, it is difficult to see how managers benefit from such capital structure changes.

investment, it is difficult, given uncertainty, to distinguish between managerial incompetence, managerial opportunism or mere bad luck.

Some evidence on the costs of managerial departures from maximization of stockholder wealth can be obtained by focusing on changes in the rules that govern manager–stockholder interactions. Corporate charter changes that affect the probability of a future outside takeover are good examples. The evidence summarized in section 2 indicates that shareholders in successful takeover targets realize substantial wealth increases. Managers of potential targets, however, can suffer welfare losses in takeovers — for example, through their displacement as managers and the resulting loss of organization-specific human capital. In such situations, managers have incentives to take actions that reduce the probability of an outside takeover and thereby benefit themselves at the expense of shareholders.

However, the conflict between shareholder interests managerial opposition to takeovers is not clear cut. Corporate charter changes that increase the ability of target managers to control the outcome of a takeover bid can enable managers to extract a higher offer price from the bidder or to solicit higher offers from other bidders. Jarrell and Bradley (1980) and DeAngelo and Rice (1983) argue that uncoordinated wealth-maximizing decisions by individual shareholders can result in takeovers that grant a larger share of the takeover gains to the shareholders in the bidding firm.

Suppose a firm has 100 shares of common stock with a market price of $9.50 per share and a total market value of $950. Economies with total value of $50 can be realized only if the firm is merged with firm A. Firm A makes a two-part takeover bid, offering $12 per share for up to 51 shares and $7 per share for the remaining 49 shares.[29] Note that if the offer is successful, the bidder obtains the target firm for $955 — an amount only $5 over its market value. Shareholders of firm A therefore receive $45 of the $50 total takeover gain. As table 5 illustrates, each shareholder faces the classic 'prisoner's dilemma' problem. Acting independently, each shareholder maximizes his wealth by tendering, although all target shareholders are better off if nobody tenders until they receive a larger fraction of the takeover gains.[30] This problem is reduced by requiring bidders to get

[29]Such two-part offers were used in the Conoco, Marathon and Brunswick takeover attempts, perhaps to reduce minority shareholder blocking power. Dodd and Ruback (1977) present evidence that non-selling target shareholders receive positive abnormal returns of 17.4% ($t = 6.68$) in subsequent 'cleanup' offers of outside minority interests. DeAngelo, DeAngelo and Rice (1982) find abnormal returns of 30.4% to minority shareholders and indications of minority blocking power in going private transactions. (See section 4.7 below.) Others have argued [see Grossman and Hart (1980)] that shareholders face free-rider problems when there is a holdout premium available. They argue that if holdout premiums exist, free-rider problems prevent takeovers from succeeding even when they are profitable for all parties. In such a situation shareholders as a group would be better off if two-part offers are made by potential bidders.

[30]If less than 51% of the shares are tendered and the offer is therefore unsuccessful, the tendering shareholder receives $12 per share as compared to the $9.50 market value if he does not tender. This assumes, for simplicity, that the bidder does not abandon the takeover effort. If

Table 5

Per share dollar payoff to individual shareholder who either tenders his shares or keeps his shares.

	Offer outcome	
	---	---
Individual action	Unsuccessful ($)	Successful ($)
Tender	12.00	9.55
Don't tender	9.50	7.00

simultaneous approval of more target shareholders, and enabling management to act as agent for target shareholders can help accomplish this. If antitakeover amendments increase the bargaining power of target managers to elicit a higher offer price they could benefit target shareholders.[31]

It is worth noting that firm A in the example cannot take advantage of the target shareholder's prisoner's dilemma problems to acquire the target at less than its market value of $950 (perhaps by offering $12 for 51 shares and $5 for the rest for a total of $857). If firm A attempts this action, competition from other firms will drive the total offer to the target's current market value of $950 if there are no gains from merger. Thus as Bradley (1980) argues, competition prevents corporate raiding or corporate piracy.[32]

The remainder of this section discusses several studies that estimate the effects on stock price of managerial actions that can affect the probability that a firm will be a takeover target — including changes in the state of incorporation, adoption of antitakeover charter amendments, managerial opposition to takeovers, going private transactions, standstill agreements, and targeted large block repurchases. The results of the studies are mixed. On the one hand, there is little or no evidence of a decline in stock price that is associated with either changes in the state of incorporation, or adoption of antitakeover charter amendments, and outside selling shareholders gain substantially in going private transactions. On the other hand, there is

---

abandonment occurs the target firm could then become the bidder and use the same strategy to take over firm A. If the offer is successful and 100% of the shares are tendered, the shareholder expects to receive a minimum of $9.55 per share ($12 per share on 51% of his shares and $7 per share on 49% of his shares if he tenders immediately). If he does not tender immediately he will receive only $7 per share. Since, independent of the outcome, immediate tendering has higher value, the optimal non-collusive decision is to tender.

[31]For simplicity we have assumed the $50 gain is independent of the takeover bargaining procedures. Easterbrook and Fischel (1982a) examine the implications of various gain-sharing rules for the creation of gains.

[32]The timing of the offer expiration is obviously important to the bidding process because it could limit competition and is worthy of additional analysis.

evidence that shareholders are harmed by targeted large block repurchases and standstill agreements. Overall, the evidence indicates that negative returns are associated with managerial actions regarding takeovers (1) if the action eliminates a takeover bid or causes a takeover failure, or (2) if the action does not require formal stockholder approval either through voting or tendering decisions.

4.2. Changes in state of incorporation

Corporate charters specify the governance rules for corporations, including rules that establish conditions for mergers (such as the percentage of stockholders that must approve a takeover). Individual states specify constraints on charter rules that differ from state to state. This variation in state law means that changing the state of incorporation affects the contractual arrangement among shareholders effected through the corporate charter, and these changes can affect the probability that a firm will become a takeover target.

Dodd and Leftwich (1980) investigate changes in stockholder returns associated with changes in the state of incorporation for 140 firms during the period 1927–1977. Of these firms, 126 reincorporated in Delaware, a state that provides few constraints on charter rules and therefore provides greater contractual freedom for shareholders and managers. Delaware also provides a set of well-defined legal precedents that facilitate contracting and resolution of disputes. Only six firms left Delaware, and there were only eight changes in states of incorporation that did not involve Delaware.

One explanation for reincorporation in Delaware is that managers use Delaware's minimal restrictions on charter rules to exploit shareholders. An alternative explanation is that the more lenient Delaware code enables managers to take actions to increase shareholder wealth that are not possible (or are more costly) under the more restrictive charters in other states. For example, for a portion of the sample period Delaware required only simple majority stockholder approval for mergers, while many other states required greater than majority approval. Under these conditions, reincorporation in Delaware reduces the costs of merger approval and thereby raises the probability of becoming a bidder or a target in a takeover.

Dodd and Leftwich attempt to isolate the first public announcement of a change in the state of incorporation, but in many instances it is likely that the announcement date they identify is not the first public announcement of the reincorporation. Therefore, the market reaction to the change is likely to be incorporated in stock prices prior to the 'event day' and this prior response reduces the power of their tests. They find abnormal returns to shareholders of firms that changed their state of incorporation of about 30% ($t = 7.90$) over the period 24 months prior to and including the announcement month — abnormal returns that seem too large to be caused solely by changes in the state of incorporation. Dodd and Leftwich use a variety of tests to determine the source of these gains, including examination of 50 firms for which precise *Wall Street Journal* announcement dates are obtainable, analysis of changes in systematic risk, and elimination of the largest positive abnormal return for each firm over the 25-month interval. These additional tests suggest that firms changed their state of incorporation after a period of superior performance and that the change itself is associated with small positive abnormal returns. Importantly, they find no evidence of a decline in stockholder wealth at times when the state of incorporation is changed — an observation inconsistent with the hypothesis that the changes are motivated by managerial exploitation of shareholders.

4.3. Antitakeover amendments

Firms can amend their charters to make the conditions for shareholder approval of mergers more stringent. These antitakeover amendments include super-majority provisions and provisions for the staggered election of board members. By increasing the stringency of takeover conditions, such amendments can reduce the probability of being a takeover target and therefore reduce shareholder wealth. However, as explained above, by increasing the plurality required for takeover approval, the amendments could benefit shareholders by enabling target management to better represent their common interests in the merger negotiations.

DeAngelo and Rice (1983) and Linn and McConnell (1983) examine the effect of the adoption of antitakeover amendments on stock prices of the adopting firms. DeAngelo and Rice examine 100 firms that adopted super-majority, staggered board, fair price, and lock-up provisions over the period 1974–1978. Shareholders of these firms realized statistically insignificant abnormal returns of -0.16% ($t = -0.41$) on the day of and the day after the mailing date of the proxy containing the proposals. Over the period 10 days before through 11 days after the proxy mailing date the cumulative abnormal returns are an insignificant -0.90% ($t = -0.70$). These results suggest the adoption of antitakeover provisions does not reduce stockholder wealth, although DeAngelo and Rice point out that the results might be positively biased if the proposal of the amendment communicates to target shareholders an increased probability of a takeover attempt and its associated gains.

Linn and McConnell (1983) find no significant abnormal returns on the proxy mailing date for a sample of 388 firms that adopted antitakeover amendments ove the period 1960–1980. They argue, however, that it is difficult to identify the precise date on which information about the antitakeover provisions is released. The information could be released on the date the board approves the amendments (which occurs prior to the proxy mailing date) or on the date of stockholder approval (which follows the proxy mailing date). Hence, they examine the abnormal stock returns throughout the amendment process. For 170 firms in which the day of board approval is available, the cumulative abnormal returns from the day of board approval through the day before the proxy mailing date is an insignificant 0.71% ($t = 1.20$). For 307 firms they find significant average abnormal returns of 1.43% ($t = 3.41$) over the period from the proxy mailing date through the day before the stockholders meeting. In the 90-day period beginning with the stockholders meeting, the cumulative abnormal returns are an insignificant 0.86% ($t = 1.65$). These results provide weak evidence in favor of the hypothesis that antitakeover amendments increase stockholder wealth. The results also suggest that the proxy mailing date is not the date when the information is incorporated in stock prices, a finding that is inconsistent with market efficiency.

Linn and McConnell also examine the abnormal returns to 49 firms that removed previously enacted antitakeover amendments. Over the period between board approval and proxy mailing, these firms experienced a statistically significant average abnormal return of -3.63% ($t = -2.33$). This result implies shareholders benefit from the presence of antitakeover amendments, but leaves a puzzle in understanding why they were removed in these 49 cases. In a related test, Linn and McConnell examine the abnormal stock returns of 120 firms incorporated in Delaware when the fraction of shareholders required to approve a merger was reduced by Delaware from two-thirds to a simple majority. The average abnormal return in the month of the change in the Delaware law is -1.66% ($t = -2.15$), and each of these 120 firms subsequently adopted antitakeover amendments. However, these 120 firms were selected because they adopted antitakeover amendments. This selection bias means that these returns are also consistent with the hypothesis that changes in the Delaware law on average had no effect on stockholder wealth.

Consistent with the DeAngelo and Rice results, the Linn and McConnell results imply that on average antitakeover amendments do not decrease stockholder wealth. In addition, the Linn and McConnell evidence is weakly supportive of the hypothesis that on the average such amendments increase shareholder wealth.[33]

4.4. Managerial opposition to takeovers

Target firm managers can make outside takeovers more difficult in ways

[33]H. DeAngelo and E. Rice have suggested to us that when a super-majority provision grants acquisition blocking power to a manager or other stockholder (for example a manager holding 21% of the stock when an 80% super-majority provision is implemented) the stock price effects will be more pronounced. This hypothesis has not as yet been studied.

other than through adoption of antitakeover corporate charter amendments. Since target shareholders benefit from takeovers, explicit managerial actions to prevent a takeover *independent of the price offered* appear to be an instance of managerial pursuit of self-interest at the expense of shareholders. Managerial opposition to a takeover in order to elicit a larger premium can increase the benefits of the takeover for shareholders. Such opposition can take the form of press releases and mailings that present the manager's position, the initiation of certain court actions, and the encouragement of competing bids.[34] However, it is difficult to argue that actions which *eliminate* a potential bidder are in the stockholder's best interests. Actions that can eliminate a takeover bid include cancellation of a merger proposal by target management without referral to shareholders, initiation of antitrust complaints, standstill agreements, or premium repurchases of the target's stock held by the bidder.

Kummer and Hoffmeister (1978) examine the abnormal returns associated with tender offers that are opposed and unopposed by target management. The average abnormal return of target shareholders in the announcement month is 16.45% ($t = 15.16$) for the 44 successful targets in which managers did not oppose the offer, versus 19.80% ($t = 13.62$) for 21 targets in which managers opposed the offer. Thus, managerial resistance is associated with higher premiums for offers that proved successful. However, fifteen of the 21 targets in which managers opposed the offer were not acquired within ten months, and the shareholders of these firms incurred abnormal losses of 11.7% in the ten months following the initial offer. This pattern of abnormal returns is consistent with our earlier interpretation of the stock price behavior of unsuccessful targets and with the results of Bradley, Desai and Kim (1983): Stock prices rise at the announcement of the initial bid and then decline if future takeover bids do not materialize. The Kummer and Hoffmeister results are consistent with the hypothesis that, on average, management opposition benefits target shareholders. The question remains, however, whether the shareholders of the targets of unsuccessful takeover bids could be made better off by less intensive managerial opposition — opposition that would allow their mergers to succeed without reducing the higher premiums in the otherwise successful offers. There appears to be an interesting free-rider problem here; although it might pay targets in general to establish a credible opposition threat, the costs to a particular target's

---

[34]See Easterbrook and Fischel (1981a, b, 1982a, b), Gilson (1981, 1982a, b), Bebchuk (1982a, b) and the references therein for discussion of various antitakeover tactics of target management and arguments regarding whether target management should remain passive in the presence of tender offers or whether they should take actions to help run an auction for the firm by encouraging competing bids. The effects of target management actions on the rewards to investment in takeover activities and therefore on the overall frequency of bids is an important aspect of this issue.

shareholders imply they would not want a manager to let an above market offer fail.

The higher average return to targets with managerial opposition to takeovers is also consistent with the hypothesis that such opposition harms stockholders of target firms by reducing the frequency of takeover offers. For example, the higher returns could arise because only the more highly profitable takeovers are pursued when bidders believe managerial opposition will lower the probability of success and raise the expected costs.[35] If managerial opposition simply raises costs, bids will be lower than they would be otherwise and low profit takeovers would not occur. As explained earlier, this truncation of the distribution of takeovers would raise the measured average profitability of manager-opposed takeovers. Since the target's board and management must approve a merger offer before it can go to a shareholder vote, hostile takeovers must be accomplished by gaining control of the board either through tender offers or other accumulation of shares or proxies. The evidence in tables 1 and 3 indicates that premiums to targets in tender offers are greater than premiums to targets in mergers. This could be due to the truncation phenomenon. Moreover the truncation hypothesis is consistent with the evidence that the gains to *bidders* are also larger in tender offers.

Dodd's (1980) evidence indicates that managerial opposition harms stockholders. He partitions his sample into 26 mergers that appear to be terminated by targets and 54 mergers that are terminated by either bidders or an unidentified party. In the target-terminated subsample, the cumulative abnormal returns from ten days prior to the first public announcement of the offer through ten days after termination is about $+11\%$ for the target firms. In contrast, the abnormal return over the same period for the 'bidder-terminated' subsample is an insignificant 0.2%. The average abnormal target return on the day before and day of termination announcement is a significant -5.57% for the cancellations by the target and a significant -9.75% for the cancellations by the bidder. If targets cancel mergers in anticipation of more profitable future takeover bids that will benefit stockholders, the abnormal returns to targets on announcement of cancellation would be positive rather than negative. The negative returns are consistent with the hypothesis that target managers who cancel such mergers are not acting in the stockholder's interest. In addition, the complete loss of gains to targets where bidders cancel indicates that when bidders back out (perhaps because they find they overestimated the value of the target), the target price returns to its pre-offer level.

---

[35]The costs associated with making an unsuccessful takeover bid sometimes go far beyond the search costs and the administrative, legal and other out of pocket expenses. See Ruback (1983b) for a discussion of the losses incurred by Gulf when they withdrew their bid for Cities Service.

4.5. Targeted large block stock repurchases

Currently available evidence suggests that managerial opposition to a takeover does not reduce shareholder wealth unless the resistance eliminates potential takeover bids. Two papers, Dann and DeAngelo (1983) and Bradley and Wakeman (1983), examine the effect on stockholder returns of privately negotiated or targeted stock repurchases. In a privately negotiated or targeted repurchase, a firm repurchases a block of its common stock from an individual holder, generally at a premium. These premiums can be interpreted as payments to potential bidders to cease takeover activity. The evidence indicates that such repurchases are associated with significantly negative abnormal stock returns for the shareholders of the repurchasing firm, and significantly positive abnormal returns for the sellers. Dann and DeAngelo report an average premium over the market price of 16.4% on 41 negotiated repurchases involving a premium, and for these 41 repurchases they report an average abnormal return on the repurchasing firm's stock of -1.76% $(t = -3.59)$ on the day before and day of announcement. For 17 instances of non-premium targeted large block repurchases in which the price was equal to or below the market price, Dann and DeAngelo report insignificant average abnormal returns of -0.34% $(t = -0.33)$ on the day before and day of announcement. Bradley and Wakeman report abnormal returns of -2.85% $(t = -5.82)$ for 61 firms that repurchased a single block of common stock and abnormal returns of 1.40% $(t = 2.24)$ for 28 selling firms. They also present regression estimates indicating the total value of non-participating shareholders' stock declines dollar for dollar with increases in the premium paid to the seller, and that selling firm shareholders gain commensurately. The combined evidence presented by Dann and DeAngelo, and Bradley and Wakeman indicates that premium targeted large block repurchases reduce the wealth of non-participating stockholders.

The reductions in shareholder wealth associated with targeted repurchases suggest that explicit managerial actions to eliminate takeover bidders are costly to non-participating stockholders. Bradley and Wakeman reinforce this interpretation by examining 21 firms whose targeted repurchases were associated with a takeover cancellation. For these firms the average abnormal return the day prior to through the day after announcement of the repurchase is -5.50% $(t = -7.14)$. Over the same event period, 40 firms that made targeted repurchases unaccompanied by merger cancellations experienced average abnormal returns of -1.39% $(t = -1.97)$. Thus, targeted repurchases are more costly to non-participating stockholders when they are used to thwart takeover attempts.

The evidence on the negative effect of targeted repurchases on shareholder wealth is especially interesting when contrasted with the large positive abnormal returns ranging from 12.4% to 18.9% from the day before to 30 days after the announcement of non-targeted repurchase tender offers documented by Masulis (1980), Dann (1981), Vermaelen (1981) and Rosenfeld (1982).[36] Moreover, Dann and Vermaelen document positive abnormal returns of 4.1% and 3.4% for 121 and 243 open-market repurchases over the same event interval. Bradley and Wakeman report abnormal returns of 1.9% for repurchases from insiders, 1.6% for repurchases of small shareholdings, and 0.6% for 40 targeted repurchases where no merger bid is involved (all over the same 32-day event period). All these estimates of repurchase effects are positive and are in striking contrast to the average abnormal returns of −12.5% over the same 32-day event interval for two targeted share repurchases which involve a merger bid. The evidence provides fairly strong indications that targeted large block repurchases at premiums over market price reduce the wealth of non-participating shareholders.

4.6. Standstill agreements

Dann and DeAngelo (1983) examine the effects of standstill agreements on stock prices. Standstill agreements are voluntary contracts in which a firm agrees to limit its holdings of another firm, and, therefore, not to mount a takeover attempt. The 30 firms in their sample that obtained standstill agreements earned average abnormal returns of −4.52% ($t = −5.72$) on the day before and day of announcement of the agreement. In addition, the 19 firms entering standstill agreements that were unaccompanied by repurchases earned average abnormal returns of −4.04% ($t = −4.49$) in the same event period. Bradley and Wakeman (1983) present regression evidence suggesting that the 'news of the merger termination and the announcement of a standstill agreement have the same informational content'. This evidence also supports the hypothesis that managerial opposition that thwarts takeover bids reduces the wealth of non-participating stockholders.

4.7. Going private transactions

DeAngelo, DeAngelo and Rice (1982) examine the returns to stockholders in 72 'going private' proposals for firms listed on the New York or American Stock Exchanges in the period 1973–1980. In pure going private proposals the public stock ownership is replaced by full equity ownership by an incumbent management group and the stock is delisted. In leveraged buyouts (also included in their sample) management shares the equity with private outside investors. They find abnormal returns for the public stockholders of 30.4% ($t = 12.4$) in the period 40 days before through the announcement of the going private proposal — gains that are virtually identical to the 29.1% weighted average returns in interfirm tender offers shown in table 3, panel A.

---

[36]Sample sizes range from 119 to 199.

They argue that the gains from going private are due to 'savings of registration and other public ownership expenses, and improved incentives for corporate decision makers under private ownership'. There is no evidence that outside stockholders are harmed in these transactions, which are commonly labeled 'minority freezeouts'. Moreover, the fact that stockholder litigation occurred in over 80% of the going private proposals that did not involve third parties provides a hint that these premiums are due to the blocking power typically accorded minority stockholders in going private transactions.

4.8. Direct evidence on stockholder control

The evidence on takeovers and actions that affect the probability of takeovers suggests that takeovers serve to limit managerial departures from maximization of stockholder wealth. Conflicts of interest between owners and managers can, however, be limited in the absence of takeovers through mergers or tender offers. Stockholders elect the board of directors and the board of directors directly monitors managers. Stockholders can change managers by electing a different board of directors, and voting rights and proxy contests are therefore important aspects of the general control process.

In this section we first examine the empirical evidence on internal transfers of control provided in the study by Dodd and Warner (1983) of the abnormal equity returns around the time of 96 proxy fights over the period 1962–1978. We then discuss the Lease, McConnell and Mikkelson (1983) study of the value of voting rights.

Proxy contests. In a proxy fight, dissident shareholders solicit votes to elect directors who differ from management's proposed slate. If the proxy fight results in dissidents obtaining a majority of seats on the board of directors, some change in corporate control occurs. Since both takeovers and proxy fights transfer control over assets, it is likely that the announcement of a proxy fight will be associated with an increase in equity value if the assets are to be put to superior uses. However, in a takeover the bidder offers a premium to target shareholders so that the stock price of the target can rise even if no higher value uses for the target's assets exists — the premium representing in this case a wealth transfer from bidding firm shareholders to target firm shareholders. Thus, examination of changes in equity value associated with proxy fights provides direct evidence on the gains resulting from changes in management and presumably, therefore, from changes in managerial decisions on resource utilization.

Dodd and Warner (1983) study a sample of 96 proxy contests in the period 1962–1978. They report that stockholders of firms realize a significant positive average abnormal return of 1.2% ($t = 2.52$) on the day before and day of the first *Wall Street Journal* announcement of a control contest.

Furthermore, Dodd and Warner argue that information about the forthcoming proxy contest is available prior to the initial *Wall Street Journal* announcement, and that 1.2% is therefore a downward-biased estimate of the abnormal stock price increase due to the contest. Over the period 59 days before through the initial announcement of the contest the abnormal return is 11.9% ($t = 5.09$). The significant positive abnormal return on the announcement day and the period prior to it suggests that proxy contests increase equity values and redirect the assets of the firm to more profitable uses. This implication is strengthened by the positive abnormal returns of 8.2% ($t = 2.78$) over the period 59 days prior to contest announcement through the day of the election outcome announcement in the *Wall Street Journal*.

If the gains to stockholders associated with a proxy fight are due solely to potential changes in management, equity prices should decline when dissidents do not obtain board representation. The results in Dodd and Warner indicate that the acquisition of even partial dissident representation on the board is associated with positive abnormal returns, and complete failure to obtain representation results in negative abnormal returns. In 56 contests in which dissidents obtained seats on the board of directors, the abnormal return on the day before and day of the outcome announcement is 1.1% ($t = 2.38$). Alternatively, in the 40 contests in which the dissidents failed to obtain seats, stock prices fell by 1.4% ($t = -1.67$) on the day before and day of the outcome announcement. However, the holding-period returns throughout the entire control contest indicate that the positive average effect of the contest is realized regardless of the outcome. Over the period sixty days prior to the initial announcement through the outcome announcement, the average abnormal return for contests in which dissidents win seats is virtually identical to that for contests in which dissidents win no seats. (These contest period estimates, of course, have much higher standard errors than the outcome announcement effects.)

Thus, while the relation between the revision in stock prices and announcement of the election outcome supports the importance of board representation, the magnitude of the revision is small relative to the total gains. The combined implication of the Dodd and Warner results is that, independent of the outcome, control contests increase equity values and the increase is larger when the dissidents win seats.

The value of control. We define corporate control as the rights to determine the management of corporate resources, and these rights are vested in the corporation's board of directors. Lease, McConnell and Mikkelson (1983) examine an important aspect of control, the value of rights to vote in elections to select the board of directors and to vote on other matters that require stockholder approval. They identify 30 firms that have two classes of common stock that differ only in their voting rights. Both classes have identical claims to dividends and are treated equally on liquidation. They calculate the ratio of month end prices for the two classes of stock over the time in which the two classes traded in the period 1940–1978. For 18 firms with voting and non-voting common stock and without voting preferred stock, the average premium for the voting stock is 3.79%. Of the 360 month end price ratios in their sample, 336 indicate that the voting stock traded at a premium. For the 9 firms without voting preferred stock that have two classes of voting common stock which differ only in voting rights, the common stock with superior voting rights traded at an average premium of 6.95% and 393 of the 468 month end price ratios indicate a premium for the stock with superior voting rights. Finally, for four firms with voting preferred, the class of common stock with superior voting rights traded at an average discount of 1.17%.

While the discount for stock with superior voting rights in firms that have voting preferred remains an unexplained puzzle, the weight of the Lease, McConnell and Mikkelson evidence indicates that voting rights are valuable. In addition, Dodd and Warner (1983) present evidence that voting rights are valuable. For 42 proxy contests with record dates that follow the initial announcement of the proxy contest, they report that stock prices fall on average by 1.4% ($t = -3.02$) on the day after the record date (the day the stock goes ex-vote).

5. Unsettled issues and directions for future research

Careful examination of the reaction of stock prices to various control-related events has greatly increased our understanding of the market for corporate control. Nevertheless, much remains to be learned, and the measurement of effects on stock prices will continue to play an important role in this research effort. We are, however, reaching the point of rapidly diminishing returns from efforts that focus *solely* on stock price effects. Further progress toward understanding the market for corporate control will be substantially aided by efforts that examine other organizational, technological and legal aspects of the environment in addition to the effects of takeovers on stock prices. Of course, the relationship between these other factors and stock price effects will be of continuing importance to future research. This section is devoted to discussion of a number of unsettled issues and suggests some directions for future research.

5.1. Competition among management teams

In our view the takeover market is an arena in which alternative management teams compete for the rights to manage corporate resources.[37]

---

[37]This phenomenon is made particularly evident by the simultaneous mutual tender offers that have become common recently, the so-called 'Pac Man' defense. See Herzel and Schmidt (1983) for a penetrating discussion of these offers.

In small takeovers management teams can consist of a single proprietor (with staff) or a partnership of managers. Competing management teams are also commonly organized in the corporate form, especially in large takeovers. In these cases the managerial team consists of the top-level internal managers and a board of directors. The board acts as the top-level control device and is the repository of the control rights acquired by the team. The competition among management teams is complex, and it is not yet fully described by theory or evidence. The following discussion, however, suggests an analytical approach and directions for future research.

The contractual setting.   Analysis of the competition among management teams in the market for corporate control must begin with a specification of the analytically important aspects of the institutional and contractual environment.[38] In particular, the nature of the rights of each of the parties in the set of contracts that define the open corporation are important to the functioning of the market for corporate control. The corporation is a legal entity that serves as the nexus for a set of contracts among independent agents. One implication of this view is that the corporation has no owners. Instead, stockholders are agents in the nexus of contracts who specialize in riskbearing. Indeed, unrestricted common stock residual claims are the unique contractual aspect of the open corporate form that distinguishes it from all other forms of organization. Its residual claims are unrestricted in the sense that they are freely alienable and do not require the claimant to have any other role in the organization — in contrast, for example, to the residual claims of closed corporations that are generally restricted to agents with other roles in the organization. This unrestricted alienability enables separation of the riskbearing and management functions and therefore facilitates the realization of the benefits of specialization of these two functions. In this view, control of the agency problems of separation of residual riskbearing from management functions requires separation of the management function (initiation and implementation) from the control function (ratification and monitoring). Observation indicates this always occurs and that boards of directors or trustees are the common institutional device for accomplishing this separation.

The board of directors in the open corporation is elected by vote of the residual claimants who, while retaining the rights to ratify certain major decisions by shareholder vote, delegate most management and control rights to the board. The board in turn delegates most of its management and control rights to the internal managers while retaining the rights to ratify certain major decisions. Most importantly, the board of directors always retains the top-level control rights, that is, the rights to hire, fire and set the compensation of the top-level managers. Board membership consists of

[38]This discussion draws on the analysis in Jensen and Meckling (1976, 1979), Fama (1980), and especially Fama and Jensen (1983a, b).

internal managers and external agents with expertise of value to the organization. Moreover, the complex contractual arrangements that define the open corporation are embedded in a legal system that further defines the contracts and rights of the parties. For example, the legal system imposes fiduciary responsibility on board members and managers and delineates the legal rights and remedies available to shareholders who challenge the actions of board members and managers.

The unrestricted alienability of the common stock residual claims of the open corporation is essential to the existence of the market for control. Unrestricted alienability allows the existence of a stock market that facilitates transfer and valuation of the claims at low cost. Low cost transferability makes it possible for competing outside managers to bypass the current management and board of directors to acquire the rights to manage the corporation's resources. These control rights can be acquired by direct solicitation of stockholders, either through tender offers or proxy solicitation. Outside management teams can also acquire the management rights by merger negotiations with the target's management and board subject to ratification by vote of the stockholders.

The internal control system has its foundation in the corporate charter and is strengthened or weakened by day to day operating practices and procedures and by the quality of the individuals who hold board seats and positions in top management. Competition from alternative management teams in the market for corporate control serves as a source of external control on the internal control system of the corporation. Alternative institutional forms such as professional partnerships, non-profit organizations and mutuals do not receive the benefits of competition from alternative management teams in an external control market.[39] Of course, internal competition in each of these organizations and the external regulatory environment (such as in banking) contributes to the control function. But the corporation alone receives the benefits of the private external control market in addition to the internal control mechanisms.

When a breakdown of the internal control system imposes large costs on shareholders from incompetent, lazy or dishonest managers, takeover bids in the market for corporate control provide a vehicle for replacing the entire internal control system. Competing managers who perceive the opportunity to eliminate the inefficiencies can offer target shareholders a higher-valued alternative than current management while benefiting their own shareholders and themselves. Similar incentives come into play when the acquisition of substantial synergy gains requires displacement of an efficient current management team.

---

[39]Fama and Jensen (1983a, b, c) provide detailed analyses of these alternative organizational forms and their survival properties. Mayers and Smith (1981, 1982) and Smith (1982) provide a discussion of conflict resolution, contracting practices and the differences between mutual and corporate organizational forms in the insurance and banking industries.

Management teams receive the assistance of legal and financial institutions with expertise in both offensive and defensive takeover strategies. Sometimes this assistance is acquired under direct contract (for example, legal services) and on other occasions the assistance is provided by independent agents acting in their own interest. Takeover specialists, sometimes referred to as 'raiders' — who acquire specialized expertise in takeover strategy and in ferreting out and amassing a controlling block of shares — perform an important function in facilitating transfers of control. Such agents may or may not take control of a firm. They can succeed solely by developing expertise in discovering companies where potential takeover gains exist and in amassing blocks of shares sufficient to enable other management teams to acquire the control rights. The takeover specialists' gains come from transferring their shares to these other acquirers at the takeover price. Arbitrageurs perform an important role by specializing in valuing the competing offers and providing a market that allows investors to delegate both the valuation and riskbearing function during the takeover period.

5.2. Directions for future research

Many interesting and important research issues are suggested by the managerial competition view of the market for corporate control. It also suggests new perspectives on a number of unresolved issues that promise significant advances in the development of a theory of organizations.[40]

Examination of the costs and benefits to competing management teams of success or failure in the takeover market will aid in understanding the forces that determine when and why takeovers are initiated, and why target managers oppose or acquiesce to such proposals. Factual knowledge about the career paths and compensation experience of bidder and target management personnel will be valuable in such efforts. For example: How does management turnover frequency in takeover situations compare with that in non-takeover conditions? Do target managers lose their jobs more frequently in unfriendly takeovers than in friendly or 'white knight' acquisitions? What happens to the managers of targets who successfully avoid takeover? When target managers remain with the merged firm, how do they fare in compensation, rank and rapidity of promotion in the merged firm? How do target managers who leave the merged entity fare in the external labor market? What happens to managers of successful and unsuccessful bidding firms, and how does their experience (compensation, promotion, etc.) relate to the stock price effects of the outcomes? What is the relative frequency with which takeovers are motivated by inefficient target management versus the acquisition of other economies or synergies? What

---

[40]See Jensen (1983) for a discussion and overall perspective on organisation theory and methodology and the emerging revolution in the science of organizations.

are the synergies that contribute to takeover gains? How are takeover frequency and terms affected by (1) antitakeover amendments, (2) golden parachutes (that is, contractual employment guarantees and compensation in the event of control changes), and (3) various other managerial actions to oppose takeovers?

The definition of the market for corporate control as the arena in which managers compete for resources to manage raises a variety of questions regarding the form of the competition. Takeover strategies, both offensive and defensive, have received relatively little attention in the academic literature. The managerial competition model provides an interesting framework for the evaluation of alternative strategies. For example, bidders in hostile takeovers typically try to reduce the time that the offer is outstanding by keeping it secret prior to its announcement and by structuring offers (e.g., two-part offers) so that early tendering is beneficial to shareholders. Incumbent managers attempt to lengthen the time that an offer is outstanding. These opposing strategies are consistent with managerial competition; the bidder tries to reduce the incumbent management team's ability to compete, and targets want more time to respond to the bid or to seek out other bidders that offer better opportunities for themselves and their shareholders. This is consistent with the observation that potential targets prepare takeover defenses prior to the occurrence of a hostile bid.

The managerial competition perspective also helps explain the types of defensive strategies used by target firms. For example, suppose the incumbent management team has reliable information that its equity is underpriced. If this information cannot be made public, the managerial competition model predicts that incumbent managers will attempt to find a white knight. The information could be released to the white knight, perhaps through a confidential information center, and both the incumbent management team and the shareholders of the target would benefit. While this analysis is preliminary and speculative, the interactions between the incentives of competing management teams and the strategies they adopt is an interesting area for future research. Knowledge resulting from such research will allow us to understand better the determinants of the offer, such as structure (single or two part, cash or exchange of securities), timing, type of offer (tender, merger, or proxy contest), and tax effects. Understanding takeover strategy also requires more detailed knowledge of the effects of voting rules [see Easterbrook and Fischel (1983)], the determinants of effective control, the effects of institutional ownership, and the effects of specialized takeover agents and arbitrageurs [see Wyser-Pratte (1982)].

Detailed knowledge of the control market should also provide insights regarding the reasons for spinoffs and divestitures, and why joint ventures, which can be thought of as partial mergers, are used in some cases and not in others. Why, for example, are joint ventures often used for new ventures and not for ongoing operations, for example, by divestiture of a corporate division into a joint venture with outside partners? A thorough understanding of spinoffs, divestitures, takeovers and joint ventures should also help us understand the discounts and premiums on closed-end funds and, in particular, why closed-end funds selling at substantial discounts are not either liquidated or turned into open-end funds [see Thompson (1978)].

Finally, a number of more familiar issues require substantial additional research to complete our knowledge. No one as yet has studied the prices paid by white knights in mergers; folklore holds that embattled target managers search out such friendly merger partners to rescue them from an unfriendly takeover. But if the takeover premiums paid by white knights are generally no lower than other offers, shareholders are not harmed. In addition, precise measurement of the returns to bidders in takeovers is still an unsettled issue. Finally, knowledge of the sources of takeover gains still eludes us.

5.3. Conclusions

Many controversial issues regarding the market for corporate control have yet to be settled and many new issues have yet to be studied. It is clear, however, that much is now known about this market. Indeed, it is unlikely that any set of transactions has been studied in such detail. In brief, the evidence seems to indicate that corporate takeovers generate positive gains, that target firm shareholders benefit, and that bidding firm shareholders do not lose. Moreover, the gains created by corporate takeovers do not appear to come from the creation of market power. Finally, it is difficult to find managerial actions related to corporate control that harm stockholders; the exceptions are those actions that eliminate an actual or potential bidder, for example, through the use of targeted large block repurchases or standstill agreements.

While research on the market for corporate control has mushroomed, it is, in our opinion, a growth industry. Much exciting and valuable knowledge remains to be discovered, and there are valuable prospects for beneficial interdisciplinary exchange among lawyers, economists, accountants, and organization theorists. An important result of this research will be a greatly expanded set of knowledge about the functioning of this enormously productive social invention: the corporation.[41]

[41]See also Meckling and Jensen (1982).

References

Asquith, Paul, 1980, A two-event study of merger bids, market uncertainty, and stockholder returns, Ph.D. dissertation (University of Chicago, Chicago, IL).

Asquith, Paul, 1983, Merger bids, uncertainty, and stockholder returns, Journal of Financial Economics 11, this issue.

Asquith, Paul, Robert F. Bruner and David W. Mullins, Jr., 1983, The gains to bidding firms from merger, Journal of Financial Economics 11, this issue.

Asquith, Paul and E. Han Kim, 1982, The impact of merger bids on the participating firms' security holders, Journal of Finance 37, 1209–1228.

Bebchuk, Lucian, 1982a, The case for facilitating competing tender offers: A reply and extension, Stanford Law Review 35, 23ff.

Bebchuk, Lucian, 1982b, The case for facilitating competing tender offers, Harvard Law Review 95, 1028ff.

Benston, George J., 1980, Conglomerate mergers: Causes, consequences, and remedies (American Enterprise Institute for Public Policy Research, Washington, DC).

Bradley, Michael, 1980, Interfirm tender offers and the market for corporate control, Journal of Business 53, 345–376.

Bradley, Michael, Anand Desai and E. Han Kim, 1982, Specialized resources and competition in the market for corporate control, Working paper (University of Michigan, Ann Arbor, MI).

Bradley, Michael, Anand Desai and E. Han Kim, 1983, The rationale behind interfirm tender offers: Information or synergy?, Journal of Financial Economics 11, this issue.

Bradley, Michael and L. MacDonald Wakeman, 1983, The wealth effects of targeted share repurchases, Journal of Financial Economics 11, this issue.

Brown, Stephen J. and Jerold B. Warner, 1980, Measuring security price performance, Journal of Financial Economics 8, 205–258.

Brown, Stephen J. and Jerold B. Warner, 1983, Using daily stock returns in event studies, Unpublished manuscript (University of Rochester, Rochester, NY).

Chandler, Alfred D., Jr., 1962, Strategy and structure (MIT Press, Cambridge, MA).

Chandler, Alfred D., Jr., 1977, The visible hand: The managerial revolution (Belknapp Press, Cambridge, MA).

Dann, Larry Y., 1981, Common stock repurchases: An analysis of returns to bondholders and stockholders, Journal of Financial Economics 9, 113–138.

Dann, Larry Y. and Harry DeAngelo, 1983, Standstill agreements, privately negotiated stock repurchases, and the market for corporate control, Journal of Financial Economics 11, this issue.

Dann, Larry Y. and Wayne H. Mikkelson, 1982, Convertible debt issuance, capital structure change and leverage-related information: Some new evidence, Unpublished manuscript (Amos Tuck School of Business, Hanover, NH).

DeAngelo, Harry, Linda DeAngelo and Edward M. Rice, 1982, Going private: Minority freezeouts and stockholder wealth, Managerial Economics Research Center working paper no. MERC 82-18 (Graduate School of Management, University of Rochester, Rochester, NY).

DeAngelo, Harry and Edward M. Rice, 1983, Antitakeover charter amendments and stockholder wealth, Journal of Financial Economics 11, this issue.

Dodd, Peter, 1980, Merger proposals, management discretion and stockholder wealth, Journal of Financial Economics 8, 105–138.

Dodd, Peter and Richard Leftwich, 1980, The market for corporate charters: 'Unhealthy competition' versus federal regulation, Journal of Business 53, 259–283.

Dodd, Peter and Richard Ruback, 1977, Tender offers and stockholder returns: An empirical analysis, Journal of Financial Economics 5, 351–374.

Dodd, Peter and Jerold B. Warner, 1983, On corporate governance: A study of proxy contests, Journal of Financial Economics 11, this issue.

Easterbrook, Frank H. and Daniel R. Fischel, 1981a, The proper role of a target's management in responding to a tender offer, Harvard Law Review 94, 1161–1203.

Easterbrook, Frank H. and Daniel R. Fischel, 1981b, Takeover bids, defensive tactics, and shareholders' welfare, The Business Lawyer 36, 1733–1750.

Easterbrook, Frank H. and Daniel R. Fischel, 1982a, Corporate control transactions, Yale Law Journal 91, 698–737.

Easterbrook, Frank H. and Daniel R. Fischel, 1982b, Auctions and sunk costs in tender offers, Stanford Law Review 35, 1–21.

Easterbrook, Frank H. and Daniel R. Fischel, 1983, Voting in corporate law, Journal of Law and Economics 26, June, forthcoming.

Eckbo, B. Espen, 1983, Horizontal mergers, collusion, and stockholder wealth, Journal of Financial Economics 11, this issue.

Ellert, J.C., 1975, Antitrust enforcement and the behavior of stock prices, Unpublished dissertation (University of Chicago, Chicago, IL).

Ellert, J.C., 1976, Mergers, antitrust law enforcement and stockholder returns, Journal of Finance 31, 715–732.

Fama, Eugene F., 1980, Agency problems and the theory of the firm, Journal of Political Economy 88, 288–307.

Fama, Eugene F., Larry Fisher, Michael C. Jensen and Richard Roll, 1969, The adjustment of stock prices to new information, International Economic Review 10, 1–21.

Fama, Eugene F. and Michael C. Jensen, 1983a, Separation of ownership and control, Journal of Law and Economics 26, June, forthcoming.

Fama, Eugene F. and Michael C. Jensen, 1983b, Agency problems and residual claims, Journal of Law and Economics 26, June, forthcoming.

Fama, Eugene F. and Michael C. Jensen, 1983c, Organizational forms and investment decisions, Managerial Economics Research Center working paper no. MERC 83-03, April (Graduate School of Management, University of Rochester, Rochester, NY).

Gilson, Ronald J., 1981, A structural approach to corporations: The case against defensive tactics in tender offers, Stanford Law Review 33, 819–891.

Gilson, Ronald J., 1982a, The case against shark repellent amendments: Structural limitations on the enabling concept, Stanford Law Review 34, 775–836.

Gilson, Ronald J., 1982b, Seeking competitive bids versus pure passivity in tender offer defense, Stanford Law Review 35, 51–67.

Grossman, S. and O. Hart, 1980, Takeover bids, the free-rider problem, and the theory of the corporation, Bell Journal of Economics, Spring, 42–64.

Herzel, Leo and John R. Schmidt, 1983, Simultaneous mutual tender offers, Unpublished manuscript, March (Mayer, Brown and Platt, Chicago, IL).

Jarrell, Gregg and Michael Bradley, 1980, The economic effects of federal and state regulations of cash tender offers, Journal of Law and Economics 23, 371–407.

Jensen, Michael C., 1983, Organization theory and methodology, Accounting Review 58, 319–339.

Jensen, Michael C. and William H. Meckling, 1976, Theory of the firm: Managerial behavior, agency costs and ownership structure, Journal of Financial Economics 3, 305–360.

Jensen, Michael C. and William H. Meckling, 1979, Rights and production functions: An application to labor-managed firms and codetermination, Journal of Business 52, 469–506.

Keown, Arthur J. and John M. Pinkerton, 1981, Merger announcements and insider trading activity: An empirical investigation, Journal of Finance 36, 855–869.

Kim, H. and J. McConnell, 1977, Corporate mergers and co-insurance of corporate debt, Journal of Finance 32, 349–363.

Klein, Benjamin, Robert Crawford and Armen A. Alchian, 1978, Vertical integration, appropriable rents, and the competitive contracting process, Journal of Law and Economics 21, 297–326.

Kummer, D. and R. Hoffmeister, 1978, Valuation consequences of cash tender offers, Journal of Finance 33, 505–516.

Langetieg, T., 1978, An application of a three-factor performance index to measure stockholders gains from merger, Journal of Financial Economics 6, 365–384.

Lease, Ronald C., John J. McConnell and Wayne H. Mikkelson, 1983, The market value of control in publicly-traded corporations, Journal of Financial Economics 11, this issue.

Linn, Scott C. and John J. McConnell, 1983, An empirical investigation of the impact of 'antitakeover' amendments on common stock prices, Journal of Financial Economics 11, this issue.

Malatesta, Paul H., 1981, Corporate mergers, Unpublished Ph.D. dissertation (University of Rochester, Rochester, NY).

Malatesta, Paul H., 1983, The wealth effect of merger activity and the objective functions of merging firms, Journal of Financial Economics 11, this issue.

Mandelker, Gershon, 1974, Risk and return: The case of merging firms, Journal of Financial Economics 1, 303–335.

Manne, Henry G., 1965, Mergers and the market for corporate control, Journal of Political Economy 73, 110–120.

Masulis, Ronald W., 1980a, The effects of capital structure change on security prices: A study of exchange offers, Journal of Financial Economics 8, 139–178.

Masulis, Ronald W., 1980b, Stock repurchase by tender offer: An analysis of the causes of common stock price changes, Journal of Finance 35, 305–319.

Mayers, David and Clifford W. Smith, Jr., 1981, Contractual provisions, organizational structure, and conflict control in insurance markets, Journal of Business 54, 407–434.

Mayers, David and Clifford W. Smith, Jr., 1982, Toward a positive theory of insurance, Monograph 1982-1 (Salomon Brothers Center for the Study of Financial Institutions, New York University, New York, NY).

Meckling, William H. and Michael C. Jensen, 1982, Reflections on the corporation as a social invention, in: Controlling the giant corporation: A symposium (Center for Research in Government Policy and Business, Graduate School of Management, University of Rochester, Rochester, NY).

Mikkelson, Wayne H., 1981, Convertible calls and security returns, Journal of Financial Economics 9, 237–264.

Mikkelson, Wayne H., 1983, Capital structure change and decreases in stockholders' wealth, Proceedings of Conference on Corporate Capital Structures in the United States (National Bureau of Economic Research, Cambridge, MA) forthcoming.

Myers, Stewart C. and Nicholas J. Majluf, 1981, Stock issues and investment policy when firms have information that investors do not have, Working paper no. 1258-81 (Massachusetts Institute of Technology, Cambridge, MA).

Palepue, Krishna, 1983, The determinants of acquisition likelihood, Unpublished manuscript (Harvard University, Boston, MA).

Rosenfeld, Ahron, 1982, Repurchase offers: Information adjusted premiums and shareholders' response, Working paper (Krannert Graduate School of Management, Purdue University, West Lafayette, IN).

Ruback, Richard S., 1982, The Conoco takeover and stockholder returns, Sloan Management Review 23, 13–33.

Ruback, Richard S., 1983a, Assessing competition in the market for corporate acquisitions, Journal of Financial Economics 11, this issue.

Ruback, Richard S., 1983b, The Cities Service takeover: A case study, Journal of Finance, May, forthcoming.

Schipper, Katherine and Rex Thompson, 1983a, Evidence on the capitalized value of merger activity for acquiring firms, Journal of Financial Economics 11, this issue.

Schipper, Katherine and Rex Thompson, 1983b, The impact of merger-related regulations on the shareholders of acquiring firms, Journal of Accounting Research 21, forthcoming.

Scholes, Myron, 1972, Market for securities: Substitution versus price pressure and the effects of information on share prices, Journal of Business 45, 179–211.

Smiley, Robert, 1975, The effect of the Williams amendment and other factors on transactions costs in tender offers, Industrial Organization Review 3, 138–145.

Smith, Clifford W., Jr., 1977, Alternative methods for raising capital: Rights versus underwritten offerings, Journal of Financial Economics 5, 273–307.

Smith, Clifford W., Jr., 1982, Pricing mortgage originations, Areuea Journal 10, 313–330.

Stillman, Robert, 1983, Examining antitrust policy toward horizontal mergers, Journal of Financial Economics 11, this issue.

Thompson, Rex, 1978, Closed-end investment companies: The implications of discounts and premiums for efficiency in the capital markets and the market for corporate control, Ph.D. dissertation (University of Rochester, Rochester, NY).

Vermaelen, T., 1981, Common stock repurchases and market signalling: An empirical study, Journal of Financial Economics 9, 139–183.

Wier, Peggy G., 1983, The costs of antimerger lawsuits: Evidence from the stock market, Journal of Financial Economics 11, this issue.

Williamson, Oliver E., 1975, Markets and hierarchies: Analysis and antitrust implications (Free Press, New York, NY).

Williamson, Oliver E., 1981, The modern corporation: Origins, evolution, attributes, Journal of Economic Literature 19, 1537–1568.

Wyser-Pratte, Guy P., 1982, Risk arbitrage II, Monograph 1982-3-4 (Salomon Brothers Center for the Study of Financial Institutions, New York University, New York, NY).

The Market for Corporate Control:
The Empirical Evidence Since 1980

Gregg A. Jarrell, James A. Brickley, and
Jeffry M. Netter

C orporate takeovers have been very big business in the 1980s. The Office of the
Chief Economist (OCE) of the Securities and Exchange Commission estimates
that shareholders of target firms in successful tender offers from 1981 through
1986 received payments in excess of $54 billion over the value of their holdings before
the tender offers. Almost $38 billion of the total was received after 1984. If we include
the increased wealth of target firm shareholders resulting from leveraged buyouts,
mergers, and corporate restructurings (prompted in large part by the threat of
takeovers) these numbers are even larger. W. T. Grimm & Co. collects similar data for
a larger sample of change-of-control transactions, including mergers and leveraged
buyouts. They estimate that from 1981 to 1986 the total dollar value of the premiums
over the pre-announcement price paid for securities involved in change-of-control
transactions was $118.4 billion.[1] Corporate restructurings have created even more

---

[1] These estimates understate the total premiums (dollar value of the percentage increase in the target's stock
price caused by the takeover) paid in change-of-control transactions. OCE's sample is limited to the first
successful tender offer for a firm. Thus, if an "auction" for the firm develops, resulting in an even higher
offer price, they do not capture that additional premium. In addition, no account is made for tender offers
that do not ultimately succeed. Shareholders may sell their shares in the market at the premium induced by
the offer before it is known that the offer fails. The W. T. Grimm data also understates the total profits
earned by stockholders because they calculate the premium based on the market price only five days before
the initial public announcement and do not capture the premium attributable to increases in share prices
that occur more than five days in advance of a public announcement.

■ *Gregg A. Jarrell is Senior Vice-President, Alcar Group Inc., Skokie, Illinois; James A. Brickley
is Associate Professor, William E. Simon Graduate School of Business Administration, University
of Rochester, Rochester, New York; Jeffry M. Netter is Senior Financial Economist, Office of the
Chief Economist, United States Securities and Exchange Commission, Washington, DC.*

Reprinted from Journal of Economic Perspectives, Vol. 2, No. 1, Winter 1988.

wealth. For example, Jensen (1986) estimated that the restructurings of Phillips, Unocal and Arco created total gains to shareholders of $6.6 billion by reducing investment in negative net present value projects.

There are numerous factors behind the high level of takeover activity in the 1980s. For example, antitrust regulators have come to understand that in the increasingly competitive international marketplace U.S. interests are well-served by domestic mergers that could be objectionable in a more closed economy. Today's antitrust regulators almost never object to vertical combinations, and even horizontal mergers between industry leaders—completely taboo before the 1980s—are often allowed today.

Deregulation also has induced merger and acquisition activity by calling forth new skills and strategies, and new management teams to implement them. Many of the mergers, takeovers, and restructurings over the last ten years have occurred in industries that recently were deregulated such as airlines and transportation, financial services, broadcasting, and oil and gas. For example, transportation and broadcasting together accounted for 20 percent of all mergers and acquisition activity from 1981 and 1984 while oil and gas accounted for another 26.3 percent (Jensen, 1986).

Other factors motivating the high level of takeover and restructuring activity in the 1980s include innovations in takeover financing, less potent state antitakeover regulations, the retreat by the Federal courts and regulatory agencies from protecting besieged target firms, and learning about the possible returns to this type of activity. These factors are critical to understanding why firms that were considered "untouchable" not long ago have been the targets of hostile takeovers with increasing frequency. This growing list includes USX, CBS, Phillips, and TWA, to name just a few.

The Council of Economic Advisors (CEA) in the 1985 *Economic Report of the President* provides data on the extent of the takeover activity in the 1980s and the importance of large transactions in explaining this activity. The CEA states that the increase in merger and acquisition activity in the 1980s is due to a large increase in the size of the largest transactions. Their evidence indicates that in the period 1981 to 1984 the average annual reported real value of mergers and acquisitions was 48 percent greater than in any four year period from the late 1960s to the early 1970s. In addition, of the 100 largest acquisition transactions recorded through 1983, 65 occurred after 1982 and only 11 took place prior to 1979.

Returns to Bidders and Targets

Critics of takeovers question whether tender offers, mergers, and leveraged buyouts produce net gains to society. Critics argue any gains to a given party are simply redistributions resulting from losses to someone else (or more colorfully put, a pirating of assets by modern financial buccaneers). Also critics contend that battles for corporate control divert energy from more productive endeavors.[2] In this section, we find that such criticisms are ill founded, and thus conclude that battles for corporate control serve a beneficial function for the economy.

The market for corporate control is the market for the right to control the management of corporate resources. In a takeover, an outside party seeks to obtain control of a firm. There are several types of takeovers, including mergers, hostile and friendly tender offers, and proxy contests. In a merger the bidder negotiates an agreement with target management on the terms of the offer for the target and then submits the proposed agreement to a vote of the shareholders. In a tender offer, a bidder makes an offer directly to shareholders to buy some or all of the stock of the target firm. A "friendly" tender offer refers to offers that are supported by target management. The most controversial type of takeovers are "hostile" tender offers, which are tender offers that are opposed by target managements. In a proxy contest, a dissident group attempts through a vote of shareholders to obtain control of the board of directors. Finally, leveraged buyouts are buyouts of shareholder's equity, heavily financed with debt by a group that frequently includes incumbent management.

Many of the studies reviewed in this paper are event studies that measure the effects of certain unanticipated events (such as a takeover or other control contest) on stock prices, after correcting for overall market influence on security returns. Any finding of abnormal returns, therefore, shows how the stock market views the impact of the event on the firm's common stockholders. (See Brown and Warner, 1985, for a more thorough review of event study methods.)

Returns to Shareholders of Target Companies

Shareholders of target companies clearly benefit from takeovers. Jarrell and Poulsen (1987a) estimate the premiums paid in 663 successful tender offers from 1962 to December 1985. They find that premiums averaged 19 percent in the 1960s, 35 percent in the 1970s, and from 1980 to 1985 the average premium was 30 percent. These figures are consistent with the 13 studies of pre-1980 data contained in Jensen and Ruback (1983) which agree that targets of successful tender offers and mergers before 1980 earned positive returns ranging from 16 percent to 30 percent for tender offers.[3]

Similar results are contained in studies of leveraged buyouts and going private transactions. Lehn and Poulsen (1987) find premiums of 21 percent to shareholders in

---

[2] Many critics of acquisition activity (such as the Business Roundtable) are primarily concerned with alleged abuses arising from hostile takeovers. The other types of acquisition activity are approved by target firms' management who allegedly are the individuals most concerned with the welfare of the target firm and its shareholders.

[3] Jensen and Ruback (1983) review 13 studies published between 1977 and 1983—six on mergers and seven on tender offers. Their survey provides a concise summary of the pre-1980 data. But because of the lengthy review process for academic journals, the most up-to-date sample used in these studies ends in 1981, and most do not go beyond the late 1970s. This paper can be considered an update of Jensen and Ruback with a focus on recent empirical studies that cover takeovers made in the 1980s.

93 leveraged buyouts taking place from 1980 to 1984. DeAngelo, DeAngelo and Rice (1984) find an average 27 percent gain for leveraged buyouts between 1973 and 1980.

OCE (1985a) measures premiums paid by comparing the price per share offered by the bidder to the trading price of the stock one month before the offer, not adjusting for changes in the market index (also see Comment and Jarrell, forthcoming). Using a comprehensive sample of 225 successful tender offers from 1981 through 1984, including over-the-counter targets, OCE finds the average premium to shareholders to be 53.2 percent. OCE has updated these figures for 1985 and 1986 and finds a decrease over the last two years. OCE finds that the average premium is 37 percent in 1985 and 33.6 percent in 1986.[4]

While the evidence reported thus far indicates substantial gains to target shareholders, it probably understates the total gains to these shareholders. In many cases events occur before a formal takeover offer, so studies that concentrate on the stock price reactions to formal offers will understate the total gains to shareholders.

Several recent empirical studies examine the stock market reaction to events that often precede formal steps in the battle for corporate control. Mikkelson and Ruback (1985a) provide information on the stock price reaction to Schedule 13D filings. Schedule 13D must be filed with the SEC by all purchasers of 5 percent of a corporation's common stock, requiring disclosure of, among other things, the investor's identity and intent. Mikkelson and Ruback find significant price reactions around the initial announcement of the filing, and that the returns depend on the intent stated in the 13D. The highest returns, an increase of 7.74 percent, occurred when the filer in the statement of intent indicated some possibility of a control change. However, the abnormal returns were only 3.24 percent if the investor reported the purchase was for investment purposes. Holderness and Sheehan (1985) find a differential stock market effect to 13D filings depending on the identity of the filer. They show the filings of six "corporate raiders" increased target share prices by a significantly greater amount than a sample of other filers (5.9 percent to 3.4 percent).

More direct evidence that significant stock price increases occur prior to formal announcements of corporate events is contained in OCE (1987c) which finds a significant increase in the stock price of target firms in 172 successful tender offers in the period before any announcement of the offer. OCE finds a run-up in stock prices of 38.8 percent of the total control premium by the close of day *before* the offer announcement. The announcement date is, in the parlance of Wall Street, the date the target firm was put "in play" and represents some event having significant implications for corporate control. For example, the in-play date in some cases is the formal offer but in other cases is the eventual bidder's filing of a Schedule 13D with corporate control implications for the target.

---

[4] The OCE (1985a) study also explicitly tests and rejects the popular theory that two-tier tender offers disadvantage target shareholders. Some observers argue that two-tier offers—in which the bidder first makes an offer for control of the firm and then makes a "clean-up" offer for remaining shares at a lower price—coerces shareholders to tender to avoid the clean-up price. OCE finds that two-tier offers have overall premiums that are nearly identical to the average for any-or-all offers and that there is no evidence that two-tier offers "stampede" shareholders into unwise trading decisions.

Table 1

**Cumulative excess returns to successful bidders
for tender offers during 1960 to 1985, by decade**

Trading-day Interval	Cumulative excess returns in percent			
	All	1960s	1970s	1980s
− 10 to + 5	1.14	4.40	1.22	− 1.10
(*t*-stat.)	(2.49)	(4.02)	(2.12)	(− 1.54)
− 10 to + 20	2.04	4.95	2.21	− 0.04
(*t*-stat.)	(3.31)	(3.52)	(2.87)	(− 0.04)
Number of observations	405	106	140	159

Source: Jarrell and Poulsen (1987a)

While some commentators argue that price run-up before the formal announcements of tender offers indicates the presence of illegal insider trading, OCE's evidence
demonstrates that the legal market for information can explain much of the run-up.
OCE shows that a significant portion of the run-up can be explained by three readily
identifiable influences on pre-bid trading: media speculation, the bidder's foothold
acquisition in the target, and whether the bid is friendly or hostile. Systematic
relations between these factors and run-up in target share prices indicate that there is
an active market for information about impending takeover bids and a large portion
of the run-up can be explained by factors other than illegal insider trading. OCE's
results on pre-bid market activity are supported by Comment (1986).

Returns to Shareholders of Acquiring Companies

The 1980s evidence on bidders comes from Jarrell and Poulsen (1987a), with
data on 663 successful tender offers covering 1962 to 1985. Table 1 summarizes the
excess returns to 440 NYSE and AMEX bidders. For the entire sample period bidders
on average realized small, but statistically significant, gains of about 1 to 2 percent in
the immediate period around the public announcement. Most interesting is the
apparent secular decline in the gains to successful bidders in tender offers. Consistent
with the previous studies reviewed by Jensen and Ruback (1983), Table 1 shows
positive excess returns of five percent during the 1960s, and a lower, but still
significantly significant, positive average of 2.2 percent over the 1970s. However, the
159 cases from the 1980s show statistically insignificant losses to bidders.

How the Distribution of Takeover Gains Is Determined

Companies that are targets of takeovers receive the bulk of the value created by
corporate combinations and these gains are not offset by losses to acquirers. As one
might predict, an important factor in determining how these takeover gains are split

seems to be how many bidders are trying to acquire the target company. In fact, the secular decline in the stock returns to bidders probably reflects the increased competition among bidders and the rise of auction-style contests during the 1980s.[5]

Conditions which foster an increase in multiple bidding tend to increase target premiums and reduce bidder returns. For example, Jarrell and Bradley (1980) demonstrate that Federal (Williams Act) and state regulations of tender offers have this effect because they impose disclosure and delay rules that foster multiple-bidder, auction contests and preemptive bidding.[6] In addition to greater regulation, other factors contributing to this increased competition include court rulings protecting defensive tactics, the inventions of several defenses against takeovers, and the increase in sophisticated takeover advisers to implement them.

Interesting support for this theory in the banking industry is provided by James and Wier (1987). Federal and state banking regulations effectively limit the number of eligible acquisition partners, thus affecting the number of potential substitutes for bidders or targets in particular transactions. For 39 proposed banking acquisitions, James and Wier measure a positive relation between the bidder's share of the takeover gains and the number of alternative targets, and a negative relation between the bidder's share and the number of alternative bidders.[7]

The Source of Takeover Gains

Shareholders of target companies definitely gain from mergers and tender offers. But much uneasiness has been expressed at who might be paying for those gains. In their summary several years ago, Jensen and Ruback (1983, p. 47) were forced to conclude that "knowledge of the sources of takeover gains still eludes us."[8] The studies they reviewed did not allow them to judge the many redistributive theories, which suggest that shareholder gains are offset by economic losses to others. Since then, many popular "redistributive theories" have been examined. The evidence has led many financial economists like Jensen (1986, p. 6) to attribute takeovers, leveraged buyouts, and restructurings to "productive entrepreneurial activity that improves the control and management of assets and helps move assets to more productive uses." We now turn to a review of the most important of these redistributive theories.

---

[5] Bradley, Desai, and Kim (1984) show that targets gain more in multiple bidder than single bidder contests.
[6] The Williams Act contains the Federal regulations of tender offers and was enacted in July 1968. Its main components are disclosure requirements, a regulated minimum offer period, and antifraud provisions that give target management standing to sue for injunctive relief.
[7] Other evidence supporting this point includes a recent paper by Guerin-Calvert, McGuckin, and Warren-Boulton (1986) that reexamines the effects of state and Federal regulations of tender offers. They also find the regulations increase the incidence of multiple-bidder auction takeovers among all control contests. Also consistent with this result is the evidence on the French experience presented by Eckbo and Langohr (1986). They show that the imposition of disclosure-only (not delay) rules governing tender offers in France significantly shifted the gains in French takeovers from acquirers to targets.
[8] Jensen and Ruback review the empirical work testing the market power theory of takeovers by Eckbo (1983) and Stillman (1983). This theory is that increased monopoly power in product markets explains takeover gains. Jensen and Ruback conclude the evidence rejects this theory as the source of gains from takeovers. Recent papers by Eckbo and Wier (1985) and by Eckbo (1985) provide empirical support for the conclusion that except in isolated cases, increased market power cannot explain the gains from takeovers.

Short-Term Myopia and Inefficient Takeovers. This theory is based on an allegation that market participants, and particularly institutional investors, are concerned almost exclusively with short-term earnings performance and tend to undervalue corporations engaged in long-term activity. From this viewpoint, any corporation planning for long-term development will become undervalued by the market as its resource commitments to the long-term depress its short-term earnings, and thus will become a prime takeover candidate.

Critics of this theory point out that it is blatantly inconsistent with an efficient capital market. Indeed, if the market systematically undervalues long-run planning and investment, it implies harmful economic consequences that go far beyond the costs of inefficient takeovers. Fortunately, no empirical evidence has been found to support this theory. In fact, a study of 324 high research and development firms and of all 177 takeover targets during 1981–84 by the SEC's Office of the Chief Economist (OCE, 1985b) shows evidence that (1) increased institutional stock holdings are not associated with increased takeovers of firms; (2) increased institutional holdings are not associated with decreases in research and development; (3) firms with high research and development expenditures are not more vulnerable to takeovers; and (4) stock prices respond positively to announcements of increases in research and development expenditures.

Further evidence opposing the myopia theory is provided by Hall (1987) in an NBER study and by McConnell and Muscarella (1985). Hall studies data on acquisition activity among manufacturing firms from 1977 to 1986. She presents evidence that much acquisition activity has been directed towards firms and industries which are less intensive in R & D activity. She also finds that firms involved in mergers show little difference in their pre- and postmerger R & D performance compared with industry peers. McConnell and Muscarella, in a study of 658 capital expenditure announcements, show that stock prices respond positively to announcements of increased capital expenditures, on average, except for exploration and development announcements in the oil industry.

Undervalued Target Theory. Recalcitrant target management and other opponents of takeovers often contend that because targets are "undervalued" by the market, a savvy bidder can offer substantial premiums for target firms while still paying far below the intrinsic value of the corporation. By this theory, it becomes the duty of target managements to defend vigorously against even high premium offers since remaining independent, it is argued, can offer shareholders greater rewards over the long term than are offered by opportunistic bidders seeking short-term gains.

However, the evidence shows the promised long-term gains from remaining independent do not usually materialize. When a target defeats a hostile bid, its post-defeat value reverts to approximately the (market adjusted) level obtaining before the instigation of the hostile bid (Bradley, Desai and Kim, 1983; Easterbrook and Jarrell 1984; Jarrell 1985; Ruback, 1986). Bhagat, Brickley and Lowenstein (1987) used option pricing theory to show that the announcement period returns around cash tender offers are too large to be explained by revaluations due to information about undervaluation.

This evidence indicates that the market does not, on average, learn much of anything that is new or different about target firms' intrinsic values through the tender offer process, despite the tremendous attention lavished on targets, and the huge amounts of information traded among market participants during takeover contests. If undervaluation had indeed been present, then the deluge of new information on the intrinsic value of targets should have caused fundamental price corrections even in the event of takeover defeats. But in the overwhelming majority of cases studied, prices dropped rather than increased for target firms that fought off takeovers.

Do Tax Effects Motivate Mergers and Takeovers? Tax motives have long been suspected as an important cause of merger and acquisition activity. Indeed, the Tax Reform Act of 1986 contains several provisions aimed at reducing the tax benefits available through mergers.[9] Most recent studies, however, assign tax benefits a minor role in explaining merger and takeover activity. Auerbach and Reishus (1987a) study 318 mergers and acquisitions during 1968–83 to estimate the tax benefits available in these transactions from increased use of tax losses and credits. They found that these tax benefits in general were not a significant factor in the majority of large acquisitions. In a fair number of transactions, however (potentially 20 percent of the mergers), tax factors did appear to be significant enough to affect the decision to merge.[10] Lehn and Poulsen (1987) find, in their study of leveraged buyouts from 1980–84, that the premiums paid are directly related to potential tax benefits associated with these transactions, suggesting that in part these leveraged buyouts are motivated by tax considerations.

In summary, acquiring firms' tax losses and credits, and the option to step-up the basis of targets' assets without paying corporate level capital gains, are two tax benefits that appear to have had some impact on merger activity. However, the evidence suggests that much of the takeover activity in the last twenty years was not tax motivated.

Do Bondholders Lose From Takeovers? Some critics of takeovers suggest that the premiums paid by bidders are not a result of any wealth enhancing changes, but instead represent a redistribution from the holders of the target's bonds and preferred equity. For example, the bonds of an acquiring firm can drop in value if the acquiring firm pays cash for a riskier target firm. Given that the combined value of the two firms remains unchanged, the decline in the bond value will be captured as a gain by

---

[9]A review of the effects on the takeover market of the change of the 1986 Tax Reform Act is contained in Steindel (1986). The 1986 Tax Reform Act repeals the General Utilities doctrine, which states that corporations liquidating their businesses are not subject to capital gains tax on the value of their assets. A firm using General Utilities in a liquidation (the purchaser of at least 80 percent of the stock of a corporation may treat the transaction for tax purposes as a liquidation) avoids the tax liability that comes with appreciated assets. Steindel argues that the repeal of the General Utilities doctrine combined with the changes in corporate tax rates reduces the attractiveness of many mergers and acquisitions. Other tax changes with effects on takeover activity include the increase in the personal capital gains tax and new rules on the transfer of net operating loss carryforwards.

[10]However, Auerbach and Reishus (1987b) compare actual mergers over 1968–1983 with a control group of nonmerging firms and conclude that the potential increase in interest deductions and unused tax losses and tax credits of the acquired firms have not driven acquisitions.

some other class of security holder (such as common stockholders).[11] However, the empirical evidence does not support this argument.

Denis and McConnell (1986) examine the returns on various classes of the securities of a sample of 132 mergers in the period 1962 to 1980. Denis and McConnell's results are consistent with earlier studies in that they find gains to mergers and no losses to bondholders. Their results indicate that on average holders of common stock, convertible and nonconvertible preferred stock, and convertible bonds in the acquired firm gain from a merger. Those who hold nonconvertible bonds in the acquired firm and convertible bonds, nonconvertible bonds, and nonconvertible preferred stock in the acquiring firm neither gain nor lose in a merger. Denis and McConnell also find some evidence that the acquiring firms' common shareholders do not lose and may gain from mergers, especially in the days immediately following the announcement. Lehn and Poulsen's (1987) study of 108 leveraged buyouts from 1980 to 1984 finds no support for the redistribution theory. They find no evidence that the shareholder value created by the leveraged buyouts comes at the expense of preferred shareholders or bondholders. In sum, the evidence provides no support for the hypothesis that the supposed gains from acquisitions are actually transfers from the holders of senior securities to the holders of common stock.

Do Labor's Losses Finance Takeovers? Recent takeovers in the airline industry have involved conflict between acquiring-firm management and the (usually) unionized labor of the target firm. These conflicts have contributed to the popular generalization that shareholder premiums from takeovers come largely at the expense of labor. Shleifer and Summers (1987) articulate this view more rigorously focusing on implicit long-term contracts between labor and incumbent (target) management. They argue raiders can sometimes exploit these contracts by buying a controlling share of the equity and financing the premium by using pressure tactics to force significant wage concessions. In theory, this activity can be socially inefficient by ruining the market for these implicit long-run labor contracts and forcing labor and management to use less efficient contracting devices.

This redistributive theory from labor to shareholders has not been tested widely, but a recent NBER study by Brown and Medoff (1987) presents statistical evidence based on Michigan's employment and wages that fails to support it. Although this close look at Michigan is not necessarily indicative of the U.S. experience (for example, it contains few large mergers or hostile tender offers), the results are that wages and employment rise on average for firms that are involved in acquisitions.

Summary of Source of Gains

The various redistribution theories of takeover gains have been the subject of considerable empirical work since the Jensen and Ruback (1983) review. Most convincing is the empirical rejection of the undervaluation theory: target firms cannot be depicted generally as being "undervalued" by the stock market. Also soundly

---

[11] The senior security holders of the target firm can also lose depending on the takeover's effect on the riskiness of their claims.

rejected by the data is the short-term myopia theory. The evidence gives tax-benefits theories at least a minor role in explaining merger and tender offer activity. Finally, evidence is inconsistent with the theories that the stock-price gains to shareholders come from bondholders and labor.

Although some individuals (incumbent management, for example) obviously lose in at least some takeovers, the literature, while not conclusive, offers little or no support for the notion that the redistribution theories explain a major portion of the apparent gains from takeovers. It has been impossible so far to find systematic losses which could offset the enormous gains to target and bidding firm shareholders from mergers, tender offers, and other corporate-control activities. We therefore conclude that evidence is consistent with the notion that these corporate transactions reflect economically beneficial reshufflings of productive assets.

The Effects of Defending Against Hostile Takeovers

Defensive strategies against hostile takeovers have always been controversial since they pose a conflict of interest for target management. After all, takeovers can impose significant welfare losses on managers, who may be displaced and lose their organization-specific human capital. These conflicts may tempt some managers to erect barriers to hostile takeovers, thus insulating themselves from the discipline of the outside market for control at the expense of their shareholders and the efficiency of the economy.

However, providing target management with the power to defend against hostile takeover bids might also help target shareholders during a control contest. Target management can in certain cases defeat bids that are "inadequate." Although this rationale is popular, the evidence discussed earlier shows that in very few cases do these alleged long-term gains of independence actually materialize. The other benefit of resistance comes when resistance by target management helps promote a takeover auction. Litigation and other blocking actions can provide the necessary time for the management of the target firm to "shop" the target and generate competing bids. This auction rationale for resistance is harder to reject statistically. Evidence on occasional shareholder losses after the defeat of a takeover attempt does not in itself disprove the auction theory. This negotiating leverage can be expected to fail in some cases, with the sole bidder becoming discouraged and withdrawing. It is a gamble. The hypothesis is rejected only if the harmful outcome of defeating all bids is sufficiently frequent and costly to offset the benefits of inducing higher takeover prices. One must also consider the social cost of tender offers that never occur because of the presence of defensive devices. Unfortunately, this deterrence effect is very difficult to measure and we present no direct evidence of the extent of these costs.

Evidence on the effects of defensive measures by target management is obtained mainly from two approaches, the event-type study and the outcomes-type study. The event-type study recognizes that an efficient market must judge this cost-benefit tradeoff when it adjusts the market value of a firm in response to the adoption of a charter amendment or some other kind of resistance. Alternatively, the outcomes-type study examines the actual outcomes of control contests over a significant time horizon among firms using a common kind of resistance—say all firms adopting poison pills. That is, an event study measures the stock price reaction to the introduction of defensive devices while outcomes studies follow the use of defensive devices in control contests to determine their effects on the outcomes of the contests.

Many defensive measures must be approved by a vote of the shareholders. Hence, voting has the potential to block management-sponsored proposals that harm shareholders, depending on the costs and benefits to individual shareholders from collecting relevant information and voting. In general, a shareholder with a small amount of shares will not invest heavily in the voting process since a small number of shares will not generally affect the outcome regardless of how they are voted. However, if individual voting and information costs are near zero even the shareholder with few shares can be expected to vote against management on value-decreasing proposals. Alternatively, large outside block holders (like institutional investors) internalize more of the benefits from participation in the voting process and can be expected to take an active interest in voting on antitakeover proposals even when the information gathering and voting costs are positive. Since voting rights can block harmful measures, we distinguish between two broad categories of defensive measures, those receiving approval by voting shareholders and those adopted unilaterally by management.

Defensive Measures Approved by Shareholders

Antitakeover amendments generally operate by imposing new conditions that must be satisfied before changing managerial control of the corporation. They are almost always proposed by management and they usually require majority voting approval by shareholders. Proposed antitakeover amendments are very rarely rejected by voting shareholders; Brickley, Lease, and Smith (forthcoming) find for a sample of 288 management-sponsored antitakeover proposals in 1984 that about 96 percent passed.

Supermajority Amendments. Most state corporation laws set the minimum approval required for mergers and other important control transactions at either one-half or two-thirds of the voting shares. Supermajority amendments require the approval by holders of at least two-thirds and sometimes as much as nine-tenths of the voting power of the outstanding common stock. These provisions can apply either to mergers and other business combinations or to changing the firm's board of directors or to both. Pure supermajority provisions are very rare today, having been replaced by similar provisions that are triggered at the discretion of the board of directors. This allows the board to waive the supermajority provisions allowing friendly mergers to proceed unimpeded.

Five years ago, Jensen and Ruback (1983) found mixed evidence on the effect of supermajority amendments passed before 1980. However, a more recent study by Jarrell and Poulsen (1987b), derived from OCE (1985c), covers 104 supermajority amendments passed since 1980 and reports significant negative stock-price effects of over 3 percent around the introduction of the proposals. They also show that firms passing supermajority amendments have relatively low institutional stockholdings (averaging 19 percent) and high insider holdings (averaging 18 percent), which they interpret as helping to explain how these amendments received voting approval despite their harmful wealth effect. That is, firms proposing these amendments have fewer blockholders with incentives to invest in the voting process. Jarrell and Poulsen further conjecture that the increased shareholder resistance to harmful supermajority amendments helps explain their declining popularity in contrast to the success of the fair price amendment which appear less likely to harm shareholders (as discussed below).

Fair Price Amendments. The fair price amendment is a supermajority provision that applies only to nonuniform, two-tier takeover bids that are opposed by the target's board of directors. Uniform offers that are considered "fair" circumvent the supermajority requirement, even if target management opposes them. Fairness of the offer is determined in several ways. The most common fair price is defined as the highest price paid by the bidder for any of the shares it has acquired in the target firm during a specified period of time. Jarrell and Poulsen (1987b) report that 487 firms adopted fair price charter provisions between 1979 and May 1985, with over 90 percent of these coming in the very recent period of 1983 to May 1985.

The stock price effects reflect the low deterrence value of the fair price amendment. Jarrell and Poulsen (1987b) report an average loss of 0.73 percent around the introduction of these amendments, which is not statistically significant. They also show that firms adopting fair price amendments have roughly normal levels of insider holdings (12 percent) and of institutional holdings (30 percent). They interpret this evidence as supporting the view that shareholder voting retards adoption of harmful amendments, especially when insider holdings are low and institutional holdings are high. Further support for this view is provided by Brickley, Lease, and Smith (forthcoming) who document that "no" votes on antitakeover amendments (especially ones that harm shareholders) increase with institutional and other outside blockholdings, while "no" votes decrease with increases in managerial holdings.

Dual-Class Recapitalizations. These plans restructure the equity of a firm into two classes with different voting rights. Although several methods are used, the common goal is to provide management or family owners with voting power disproportionately greater than provided by their equity holdings under a "one share-one vote" rule.[12]

Evidence before and after 1980 has confirmed that the market generally values shares with voting power more than those without. Lease, McConnell, and Mikkelson (1983) examine 30 firms having dual-class common stock and show that voting stock on average trades at a significant premium, ranging from one to seven percent. A recent paper by OCE (1987a) examines the monthly stock prices of 26 OTC and

---

[12] For over 60 years, the New York Stock Exchange did not allow any member firm to have a dual-class capitalization structure, but it has recently proposed a liberalization to allow dual-class listings in response to competitive pressures from Amex and OTC markets. Amex currently allows dual-class listings with some restrictions, and the OTC market has no restrictions beyond usual state-law requirements.

AMEX firms having dual-class common and shows an average discount of four to five percent for low-vote common, though the discount is reduced when the low-vote stock has rights to preferential dividends.

Of course, the fact that the market values voting power does not demonstrate that dual-class recapitalizations reduce the overall price of stock. DeAngelo and DeAngelo (1985) examine in detail 45 firms that had dual-voting common stock as of 1980. They find that, after restructuring, management and family insiders control a median of 57 percent of the votes and 24 percent of the common stock cash flows. This confirms that dual-class structures often confer substantial voting powers on incumbent management. However, DeAngelo and DeAngelo also suggest that the shareholders of the firms in this sample found it beneficial to contract with incumbent management to limit the competition for management of their firms. They argue that shareholders rationally accept a reduced potential for hostile takeovers in return for other benefits, such as greater incentives for incumbents to make specific long-term investments in human capital.

Two recent studies have addressed the empirical question of whether dual-voting structures are beneficial, as DeAngelo and DeAngelo suggest, or harmful to outside shareholders. Partch (1987) examines the stock-price reaction around the announcement of the proposed dual-class recapitalizations for 44 firms. She reports nonnegative share-price effects. However, for more recent recapitalizations, Jarrell and Poulsen (forthcoming, extending OCE 1987a, 1987d) find negative effects at the announcement of dual-class recapitalizations. For a sample of 89 firms delisting from 1976 through 1987, they report an average abnormal stock price effect of $-.93$ percent.

If dual-class recapitalization proposals are viewed primarily as takeover defenses, their announcement should cause negative stock price reactions, similar to those observed at the announcement of supermajority amendments. However, firms announcing dual-class recapitalizations have some unusual characteristics. Jarrell and Poulsen (forthcoming) find that the average net-of-market return to their 94 dual-class firms over the year preceding the recapitalization is over 37 percent. Jarrell and Poulsen and Partch both find that insider holdings average 44 percent before the recapitalization, and that recapitalization significantly increases insider voting control. These two characteristics suggest that the typical dual-class firm is already controlled by insiders and the recapitalization provides a means to raise needed capital for positive net present value projects without the dilution of control.

Changes in the State of Incorporation.   Changing the state of incorporation can affect the contractual arrangements between management and shareholders. For example, some states such as Ohio, Indiana, and New York have elements in their corporate codes that make takeovers more difficult than in other states. Dodd and Leftwich (1980) find that firms change their state of incorporation after a period of superior performance and that the change itself is associated with small positive excess returns. More recently, Romano (1985) finds a statistically significant price increase around the reincorporation announcement in a sample of firms that reincorporate for various reasons. However, in the subsample of 43 firms who reincorporated as an antitakeover device she found a small statistically insignificant price increase at the announcement of a reincorporation. The evidence is not conclusive but it does indicate that reincorporating in a new state does not on average harm shareholders.

Reduction in Cumulative Voting Rights.   Cumulative voting makes it possible for a group of minority shareholders to elect directors even if the majority of shareholders oppose their election. Dissidents in hostile takeovers and proxy contests will often attempt to elect some board members through the use of cumulative voting. Bhagat and Brickley (1984) examine the stock price reaction to 84 management sponsored charter amendments that either eliminate or reduce the effect of cumulative voting. Since these amendments decrease the power of dissident shareholders to elect directors, they increase management's ability to resist a tender offer. Bhagat and Brickley find statistically significant negative abnormal returns of about one percent at the introduction of these charter amendments.

Defensive Measures That Do Not Require Shareholder Approval

Four general kinds of defensive measures do not require voting approval by shareholders: general litigation, greenmail, poison pills, and the use of state antitakeover laws. With the exception of general litigation, these defensive actions are associated on average with negative stock-price reactions indicating that in most cases they are economically harmful to stockholders of companies whose management enacted them.

Litigation by Target Management.   As described earlier, litigation can be expected to hurt shareholders of some target companies by eliminating takeovers and to help shareholders of other companies by giving their management time and weapons to cut a better deal. Jarrell (1985) examines 89 cases involving litigation against a hostile suitor based on charges of securities fraud, antitrust violations, and violations of state or Federal tender offer regulations. His results show that litigation usually delays the control contest significantly and that litigating targets are frequently the beneficiaries of auctions. The 59 auction-style takeovers produced an additional 17 percent excess return to shareholders over the original bid, while the 21 targets that remained independent lost nearly all of the original average premium of 30 percent. Overall, Jarrell concludes that this evidence cannot reject the theory that on average target litigation is consistent with shareholder wealth maximization.[13]

However, harm can result from certain types of defensive litigation. Netter (1987) finds that litigation based in part on a claim alleging the filing of a false Schedule 13D Item 4 can be detrimental to target shareholders. In an exhaustive sample of all cases where target management filed a suit alleging (among other things) that a bidder filed a false 13D Item 4, he finds that target shareholders are better off if their management loses the case than if they win. If the target firm wins the case its share price declines by a significant amount (an abnormal return of negative 3.37 percent in the two-day window around the decision) while if the bidder wins, the stock price of the target firm increases by a significant amount (positive 3.15 percent abnormal return in the two-day window.

---

[13]Jarrell also notes that while defensive litigation redistributes premiums it also, by reducing incentives to engage in takeovers and through the cost of the litigation itself, can reduce social welfare.

Targeted Block Stock Repurchases (Greenmail). Greenmail occurs when target management ends a hostile takeover threat by repurchasing at a premium the hostile suitor's block of target stock. This controversial practice has been challenged in federal courts, in congressional testimony, and in SEC hearings, and it has brought negative publicity both to payers and to receivers of greenmail. In reviewing earlier studies, Jensen and Ruback (1983) conclude that greenmail repurchases are associated with significantly negative abnormal stock returns for the shareholders of the repurchasing firms (probably because they eliminate potential takeover bids) and significantly positive abnormal stock returns for shareholders of the selling firms. These negative effects of greenmail repurchases contrast sharply with the normally positive stock-price effects associated with nontargeted offers to repurchase a company's own stock.

Since then, three new empirical studies have contributed to a more complex and less conclusive discussion of greenmail transactions. These studies indicate that it is not necessarily in the interests of shareholders to ban greenmail payments. Such a ban has the potential to discourage outside investment in the potential target's stock by investors anticipating greenmail payments and hence reduces the incentives of outsiders to monitor managers.

Mikkelson and Ruback (1985a) examine 39 cases of greenmail (based on 13Ds filed during 1978–80). They find a significant stock-price loss of 2.3 percent upon the announcement of the repurchases. However, they also report an average gain of 1.7 percent over the entire period including the original stock purchase by the hostile suitors. Holderness and Sheehan's (1985) outcome-type study includes 12 cases of greenmail, and they report a pattern of returns consistent with the evidence of Mikkelson and Ruback. Although the greenmail transaction itself harms target shareholders, the net returns to stockholders resulting from the initial purchase and related events is positive. A more comprehensive sample of targeted block stock repurchases is covered by OCE (1984). This study includes 89 cases of large repurchases (blocks greater than 3 percent of the outstanding common stock) from 1979 to 1983. The initial announcement of investor interest induces a positive return averaging 9.7 percent, while the greenmail transaction is associated with a stock price loss of 5.2 percent.

Poison Pills. Since its introduction in late 1982, the "poison pill" has become the most popular and controversial device used to defend against hostile takeover attempts. Poison pill describes a family of shareholder rights agreements that, when triggered by an event such as a tender offer for control or the accumulation of a specified percentage of target shares by an acquirer, provide target shareholders with rights to purchase additional shares or to sell shares to the target at very attractive prices. These rights, when triggered, impose significant economic penalties on a hostile acquirer.

Poison pills are considered very effective deterrents against hostile takeover attempts because of two striking features. First, pills can be cheaply and quickly altered by target management if a hostile acquirer has not pulled the trigger. This feature pressures potential acquirers to negotiate directly with the target's board. Second, if not redeemed, the pill makes hostile acquisitions exorbitantly expensive in most cases. As an obstacle to hostile takeover attempts, the poison pill is unmatched except by dual-voting recapitalizations or direct majority share ownership by incumbent management. The concern over poison pills was heightened by the Delaware Supreme Court's 1985 ruling in *Moran v. Household International*[14] that poison pills do not require majority voting approval by shareholders.

The most comprehensive study of poison pills is Ryngaert (forthcoming), which is an outgrowth of OCE (1986). The Ryngaert study features an exhaustive collection of 380 poison pills adopted from 1982 to December 25, 1986. Over 80 percent of these were adopted after the *Household* decision. Ryngaert divides his sample into discriminatory pills (the most restrictive) and flip-over pills (the least restrictive). He also accounts for whether firms are subject to takeover speculation and whether confounding events occur close to the announcement of the pill that contaminate the data. The stock-price effect over the 283 cases with no confounding events is a statistically significant $-.34$ percent. Focusing on 57 cases subject to takeover speculation, the average loss is 1.51 percent, also statistically significant. These results are supported by the findings of Malatesta and Walkling (forthcoming).

Discriminatory pills have more harmful effects on shareholder wealth than do flip-over pills. Also, the discriminatory pills that threaten the hostile suitor with severe dilution have become increasingly popular. Ryngaert reports that pill-adopting managements own a surprisingly low average of around 3.0 percent of their firms' outstanding stock. This fact, together with high institutional holdings, suggest that many of these firms would have difficulty obtaining shareholder voting approval if it were required.

Ryngaert also examines the stock-price effects of important court decisions emanating from legal battles involving pill defenses during 1983–86. He shows that 15 of 18 pro-target, pro-poison pill decisions have negative effects on the target's stock price, and 6 of 11 pro-acquirer decisions have positive effects on the target stock price. This evidence is inconsistent with the theory that pill defenses improve shareholder wealth by strengthening management's bargaining position in control contests.

Although these losses are not large in percentage terms, these empirical tests suggest that poison pills are harmful to target shareholders.

State Antitakeover Amendments. In addition to the Williams Act at the Federal level, tender offers are regulated by many states. So-called first-generation state antitakeover regulations are antitakeover laws that were passed by the states before the 1982 Supreme Court decision in *Edgar v. Mite*.[15] The Jarrell and Bradley (1980) study of state and Federal regulation of tender offers finds that first generation state regulations significantly increase the premiums paid in tender offers. Smiley (1981) illustrates the deterrent effects of these early state takeover regulations.

However, first generation antitakeover laws were generally extinguished in *Edgar v. Mite* when the Supreme Court ruled the Illinois antitakeover law unconstitutional. Justice White's opinion held the Illinois takeover statute was preempted by the Williams Act and constituted an undue and direct burden on interstate commerce. As

---

[14] *Moran v. Household International*, 490 A.2d 1059 (1985).
[15] *Edgar v. Mite*, 457 U.S. 624, 102 S. Ct. 2629 (1982).

a result over 20 states passed second generation antitakeover laws to attempt to pass constitutional muster under the Supreme Court's reasoning. While some of them have also been ruled unconstitutional, the Supreme Court in 1987 (*CTS v. Dynamics Corp. of America*) ruled the Indiana antitakeover law constitutional.[16] This decision already is leading states to pass third generation antitakeover laws that would be constitutional under the CTS reasoning.

Two recent studies, Ryngaert and Netter (1987, based on OCE, 1987c) and Schumann (1987) provide more direct evidence on the wealth effects of state antitakeover regulations. Ryngaert and Netter examine the stock price effects of the passage of the Ohio antitakeover law on shareholders of firms chartered in Ohio. This act was passed during (and apparently motivated by) Sir James Goldsmith's attempted hostile takeover of Goodyear. They find that the passage of the law was accompanied by a significant stock-price loss of up to 3.24 percent to the shareholders of firms incorporated in Ohio with less than 30 percent inside ownership. This evidence on the impact of state takeover laws is supported by Schumann (1987) who finds a decline of approximately one percent to shareholders of New York firms on the announcement and passage of a New York antitakeover law. While these laws potentially could be beneficial to the individual states (if jobs are kept in the state by preventing takeovers), shareholders are harmed by state antitakeover regulations.

Summing Up Defensive Tactics

Four years ago Jensen and Ruback (1983) reviewed empirical studies of antitakeover charter amendments, shark repellents, changes of incorporation, and greenmail. They conclude (p. 47): "It is difficult to find managerial actions related to corporate control that harm stockholders; the exception are those actions that eliminate an actual or potential bidder, for example, through the use of targeted large block repurchases or standstill agreements."

Since their review, the defensive arsenal available to target management has been strengthened. These defensive tactics have been developed through a fascinating process of sequential innovations, as specific defenses arise to counter improved bidder finances and other tactics. In 1983, the now common fair-price amendment was a novel idea and the poison pill was not yet invented. Financial economists in academia and government have kept close pace with these developments, providing timely analyses of new charter amendments, poison pill defenses, greenmail transactions, and so on. While Jensen and Ruback were correct in predicting this area would be a "growth industry," we cannot reiterate their then-accurate conclusion that harmful defensive tactics are rare.

Conclusion

In the 1980s, the market for corporate control has been increasingly active, and the quantity of output of academic researchers studying corporate control questions

---

[16]*CTS v. Dynamics Corp. of America*, 107 S. Ct. 1637 (1987).

has mirrored the market activity. This review has confirmed the basic conclusions of Jensen and Ruback's (1983) review article and has shed light on some questions Jensen and Ruback were forced to leave unanswered. Financial researchers continue to find larger premiums being paid to target shareholders for later tender offers than for earlier tender offers. Acquirers, however, receive at best modest increases in their stock price, and the winners of bidding contests suffer stock-price declines as often as they do gains. This pro-target division of takeover gains appears to be partially a result of improved defensive tactics that can effectively delay execution of the bid and allow the target to receive improved bids from others or fashion a defensive restructuring and stock buyback. The evidence further suggests that the premiums in takeovers represent real wealth gains and are not simply wealth redistributions.

Prominent in the 1980s are new studies of defensive measures, such as antitakeover charter amendments, targeted block stock repurchases (greenmail), dual-voting recapitalizations, state antitakeover laws, and poison pills. The general finding, although it is far from conclusive, is that defensive measures that require shareholder voting approval are less likely to be harmful to shareholder wealth than are defensive measures not subject to shareholder approval. Fair-price charter amendments and dual-class recapitalizations that require shareholder approval are not shown to be harmful to stock value, while poison pills and greenmail-type repurchases that do not need shareholder approval appear on average to reduce shareholder value. However, some proposals that require a favorable vote from shareholders to implement (e.g., supermajority provisions and the elimination of cumulative voting) on average appear to reduce shareholder wealth. These findings raise serious questions about whether the business judgment rule is operating too broadly as a shield for defensive actions by target managements.

■ *We are especially grateful to Joseph Stiglitz, Timothy Taylor, and Annette Poulsen for their many helpful comments and suggestions. The Securities and Exchange Commission as a matter of policy disclaims responsibility for any private publication or statement by any of its employees. The views expressed here are those of the authors and do not necessarily reflect the views of the Commission or the authors' colleagues on the Staff of the Commission.*

References

Auerbach, Alan J. and David Reishus, "Taxes and the Merger Decision." In Coffee, J. and Louis Lowenstein, eds., *Takeovers and Contests for Corporate Control*, Oxford: Oxford University Press, 1987a.

Auerbach, Alan J. and David Reishus, "The Effects of Taxation on the Merger Decision," NBER Working Paper, 1987b.

Bhagat, Sanjai, and James Brickley, "The Value of Minority Shareholder Voting Rights," *Journal of Law and Economics*, 1984, *27*, 339–365.

Bhagat, Sanjai, James Brickley, and Uri Lowenstein, "The Pricing Effects of Inter-Firm Cash Tender Offers, *Journal of Finance*, 1987, *42*, 965–986.

Bradley, Michael, Amand Desai, and E. Han Kim, "Determinants of the Wealth Effects of Corporate Acquisitions," working paper, The University of Michigan, 1984.

Bradley, Michael, Amand Desai, and E. Han Kim, "The Rationale Behind Interfirm Tender Offers: Information or Synergy?" *Journal of Financial Economics*, 1983, *11*, 183–206.

Brickley, James, Ronald Lease, and Clifford Smith, "Ownership Structure and the Voting on Antitakeover Amendments," *Journal of Financial Economics*, forthcoming.

Brown, Charles and James L. Medoff, "The Impact of Firm Acquisitions on Labor," NBER Working paper, 1987.

Brown, Stephen J. and Jerold B. Warner, "Using Daily Stock Returns: The Case of Event Studies," *Journal of Financial Economics*, 1985, *14*, 3–31.

Comment, Robert, "Price and Volume Before Tender Offers: Market Anticipation Activity or Inside Trading, working paper New York University, 1986.

Comment, Robert and Gregg A. Jarrell, "Two-Tier Tender Offers: The Imprisonment of the Free Riding Shareholder," *Journal of Financial Economics*, forthcoming.

Council of Economic Advisors, "The Market for Corporate Control," *Economic Report of the President*, 1985, 187–216.

DeAngelo, Harry, and Linda DeAngelo, "Managerial Ownership of Voting Rights: A Study of Public Corporations With Dual Classes of Common Stock," *Journal of Financial Economics*, 1985, *14*, 33–69.

DeAngelo, Harry, Linda DeAngelo, and Edward M. Rice, "Going Private: Minority Freezeouts and Stockholder Wealth," *Journal of Law and Economics*, 1984, *27*, 367–402.

Denis, Debra K., and John J. McConnell, "Corporate Mergers and Security Returns," *Journal of Financial Economics*, 1986, *16*, 143–187.

Dodd, Peter, and Richard Leftwich, "The Market for Corporate Charters: 'Unhealthy Competition' Versus Federal Regulation," *Journal of Business*, 1980, *53*, 259–283.

Easterbrook, Frank H., and Gregg A. Jarrell, "Do Targets Gain From Defeating Tender Offers?" *New York University Law Review*, 1984, *59*, 277–299.

Eckbo, B. Espen, "Merger and the Market Concentration Doctrine: Evidence from the Capital Market," *Journal of Business*, 1985, *58*, 325–349.

Eckbo, B. Espen, and Herwig Langohr, "The Effect of Disclosure Regulations and the Medium of Exchange on Takeover Bids," Working paper, 1986.

Guerin-Calvert, Margaret, Robert H. McGuckin, and Frederick R. Warren-Boulton, "State and Federal Regulation in the Market for Corporate Control," U.S. Department of Justice, Economic Analysis Group Discussion Paper 86-4, 1986.

Hall, Bronwyn H., "The Effect of Takeover Activity on Corporate Research and Development," working paper, NBER, 1987.

Holderness, Clifford G. and Dennis P. Sheehan, "Raiders or Saviors? The Evidence on Six Controversial Investors," *Journal of Financial Economics*, 1985, *14*, 555–579.

James, Christopher M., and Peggy Weir, "Determinants of the Division of Gains in Corporate Acquisitions: Evidence from the Banking Industry, working paper, University of Oregon, 1987.

Jarrell, Gregg A., "The Wealth Effects of Litigation by Targets: Do Interests Diverge in a Merge?" *Journal of Law and Economics*, 1985, *28*, 151–177.

Jarrell, Gregg A., and Michael Bradley, "The Economic Effects of Federal and State Regulations of Cash Tender Offers," *Journal of Law and Economics*, 1980, *23*, 371–407.

Jarrell, Gregg A., and Annette B. Poulsen, "Bidder Returns," working paper, 1987a.

Jarrell, Gregg A., and Annette B. Poulsen, "The Effects of Recapitalization with Dual Classes of Common Stock on the Wealth of Shareholders," *Journal of Financial Economics*, forthcoming.

Jarrell, Gregg A., and Annette B. Poulsen, "Shark Repellents and Stock Prices: The Effects of Antitakeover Amendments Since 1980," *Journal of Financial Economics*, 1987b, *19*, 127–168.

Jensen, Michael C., "The Takeover Controversy: Analysis and Evidence," *Midland Corporate Finance Journal*, 1986, 6–32.

Jensen, Michael C., and Richard S. Ruback, "The Market for Corporate Control: The Scientific Evidence," *Journal of Financial Economics*, 1983, *11*, 5–50.

Lease, Ronald C., John J. McConnell, and Wayne H. Mikkelson, "The Market Value of Control in Publicly Traded Corporations," *Journal of Financial Economics*, 1983, *11*, 439–472.

Lehn, Kenneth, and Annette B. Poulsen, "Sources of Value in Leveraged Buyouts." In *Public Policy Towards Corporate Takeovers*. New Brunswick, NJ: Transaction Publishers, 1987.

Malatesta, Paul H., and Ralph A. Walkling, "Poison Pill Securities: Stockholder Wealth, Profitability, and Ownership Structure," *Journal of Financial Economics*, forthcoming.

McConnell, John J. and Chris J. Muscarella, "Capital Expenditure Decisions and Market Value of the Firm," *Journal of Financial Economics*, 1985, *14*, 399–422.

Mikkelson, Wayne H. and Richard S. Ruback, "An Empirical Analysis of the Interfirm Equity Investment Process," *Journal of Financial Economics*, 1985, *14*, 523–553.

Netter, Jeffry M. "Shareholder Wealth Effects of Litigation Based on Allegedly False Schedule 13D Item 4 Disclosure," working paper, 1987.

Office of the Chief Economist, Securities and Exchange Commission, "The Economics of Any-or-All, Partial, and Two-Tier Tender Offers," 1985a.

Office of the Chief Economist, Securities and Exchange Commission, "Update—The Effects of Dual-Class Recapitalizations on Shareholder Wealth: Including Evidence from 1986 and 1987," 1987d.

Office of the Chief Economist, Securities and Exchange Commission, "The Effects of Poison Pills on the Wealth of Target Shareholders," 1986.

Office of the Chief Economist, Securities and Exchange Commission, "The Impact of Targetted Share Repurchases (Greenmail) on Stock Prices," 1984.

Office of the Chief Economist, Securities and Exchange Commission, "Institutional Ownership, Tender Offers and Long Term Investment," 1985b.

Office of the Chief Economist, Securities and Exchange Commission, "Shareholder Wealth Effects of Ohio Legislation Affecting Takeovers," 1987b.

Office of the Chief Economist, Securities and Exchange Commission, "Shark Repellents and Stock Prices: The Effects of Antitakeover Amendments Since 1980," 1985c.

Office of the Chief Economist, Securities and Exchange Commission, "Stock Trading Before the Announcement of Tender Offers: Insider Trading or Market Anticipation?" 1987c.

Office of the Chief Economist, Securities and Exchange Commission, "The Effects of Dual-Class Recapitalizations on the Wealth Of Shareholders," 1987a.

Partch, Megan. "The Creation of A Class of Limited Voting Common Stock and Shareholders" Wealth," *Journal of Financial Economics*, 1987, *18*, 313–339.

Romano, Roberta, "Law as a Product: Some Pieces of the Incorporation Puzzle," *Journal of Law Economics and Organization*, 1985, *1*, 225–267.

Ruback, Richard S., "An Overview of Takeover Defenses," working paper #1836-86, Massachusetts Institute of Technology, 1986.

Ryngaert, Michael, "The Effect of Poison Pill Securities on Shareholder Wealth," *Journal of Financial Economics*, forthcoming.

Ryngaert, Michael, and Nettter Jeffry, "Shareholder Wealth Effects of the Ohio Antitakeover Law," working paper, 1987.

Schumann, Laurence, "State Regulation of Takeovers and Shareholder Wealth: The Effects of New York's 1985 Takeover Statutes," Bureau of Economics Staff Report to the Federal Trade Commission, March 1987.

Shleifer, Andrei and Lawrence Summers, "Hostile Takeovers as Breaches of Trust," working paper, NBER, 1987.

Smiley, Robert, "The Effect of State Securities Statutes on Tender Offer Activity," *Economic Inquiry*, 1981, *19*, 426–435.

Steindel, Charles, "Tax Reform and the Merger and Acquisition Market: The Repeal of General Utilities," *Federal Reserve Bulletin of New York*, Autumn 1986, 31–35.

Agency Costs of Free Cash Flow, Corporate Finance, and Takeovers

By MICHAEL C. JENSEN*

Corporate managers are the agents of shareholders, a relationship fraught with conflicting interests. Agency theory, the analysis of such conflicts, is now a major part of the economics literature. The payout of cash to shareholders creates major conflicts that have received little attention.[1] Payouts to shareholders reduce the resources under managers' control, thereby reducing managers' power, and making it more likely they will incur the monitoring of the capital markets which occurs when the firm must obtain new capital (see M. Rozeff, 1982; F. H. Easterbrook, 1984). Financing projects internally avoids this monitoring and the possibility the funds will be unavailable or available only at high explicit prices.

Managers have incentives to cause their firms to grow beyond the optimal size. Growth increases managers' power by increasing the resources under their control. It is also associated with increases in managers' compensation, because changes in compensation are positively related to the growth

in sales (see Kevin Murphy, 1985). The tendency of firms to reward middle managers through promotion rather than year-to-year bonuses also creates a strong organizational bias toward growth to supply the new positions that such promotion-based reward systems require (see George Baker, 1986).

Competition in the product and factor markets tends to drive prices towards minimum average cost in an activity. Managers must therefore motivate their organizations to increase efficiency to enhance the probability of survival. However, product and factor market disciplinary forces are often weaker in new activities and activities that involve substantial economic rents or quasi rents.[2] In these cases, monitoring by the firm's internal control system and the market for corporate control are more important. Activities generating substantial economic rents or quasi rents are the types of activities that generate substantial amounts of free cash flow.

Free cash flow is cash flow in excess of that required to fund all projects that have positive net present values when discounted at the relevant cost of capital. Conflicts of interest between shareholders and managers over payout policies are especially severe when the organization generates substantial free cash flow. The problem is how to motivate managers to disgorge the cash rather than investing it at below the cost of capital or wasting it on organization inefficiencies.

The theory developed here explains 1) the benefits of debt in reducing agency costs of free cash flows, 2) how debt can substitute

*LaClare Professor of Finance and Business Administration and Director of the Managerial Economics Research Center, University of Rochester Graduate School of Management, Rochester, NY 14627, and Professor of Business Administration, Harvard Business School. This research is supported by the Division of Research, Harvard Business School, and the Managerial Economics Research Center, University of Rochester. I have benefited from discussions with George Baker, Gordon Donaldson, Allen Jacobs, Jay Light, Clifford Smith, Wolf Weinhold, and especially Armen Alchian and Richard Ruback.

[1] Gordon Donaldson (1984) in his study of 12 large *Fortune* 500 firms concludes that managers of these firms were not driven by maximization of the value of the firm, but rather by the maximization of "corporate wealth," defined as "*the aggregate purchasing power available to management for strategic purposes during any given planning period*" (p. 3). "In practical terms it is cash, credit, and other corporate purchasing power by which management commands goods and services" (p. 22).

[2] Rents are returns in excess of the opportunity cost of the resources to the activity. Quasi rents are returns in excess of the short-run opportunity cost of the resources to the activity.

for dividends, 3) why "diversification" programs are more likely to generate losses than takeovers or expansion in the same line of business or liquidation-motivated takeovers, 4) why the factors generating takeover activity in such diverse activities as broadcasting and tobacco are similar to those in oil, and 5) why bidders and some targets tend to perform abnormally well prior to takeover.

I. The Role of Debt in Motivating Organizational Efficiency

The agency costs of debt have been widely discussed, but the benefits of debt in motivating managers and their organizations to be efficient have been ignored. I call these effects the "control hypothesis" for debt creation.

Managers with substantial free cash flow can increase dividends or repurchase stock and thereby pay out current cash that would otherwise be invested in low-return projects or wasted. This leaves managers with control over the use of future free cash flows, but they can promise to pay out future cash flows by announcing a "permanent" increase in the dividend. Such promises are weak because dividends can be reduced in the future. The fact that capital markets punish dividend cuts with large stock price reductions is consistent with the agency costs of free cash flow.

Debt creation, without retention of the proceeds of the issue, enables managers to effectively bond their promise to pay out future cash flows. Thus, debt can be an effective substitute for dividends, something not generally recognized in the corporate finance literature. By issuing debt in exchange for stock, managers are bonding their promise to pay out future cash flows in a way that cannot be accomplished by simple dividend increases. In doing so, they give shareholder recipients of the debt the right to take the firm into bankruptcy court if they do not maintain their promise to make the interest and principle payments. Thus debt reduces the agency costs of free cash flow by reducing the cash flow available for spending at the discretion of managers. These control

effects of debt are a potential determinant of capital structure.

Issuing large amounts of debt to buy back stock also sets up the required organizational incentives to motivate managers and to help them overcome normal organizational resistance to retrenchment which the payout of free cash flow often requires. The threat caused by failure to make debt service payments serves as an effective motivating force to make such organizations more efficient. Stock repurchase for debt or cash also has tax advantages. (Interest payments are tax deductible to the corporation, and that part of the repurchase proceeds equal to the seller's tax basis in the stock is not taxed at all.)

Increased leverage also has costs. As leverage increases, the usual agency costs of debt rise, including bankruptcy costs. The optimal debt-equity ratio is the point at which firm value is maximized, the point where the marginal costs of debt just offset the marginal benefits.

The control hypothesis does not imply that debt issues will always have positive control effects. For example, these effects will not be as important for rapidly growing organizations with large and highly profitable investment projects but no free cash flow. Such organizations will have to go regularly to the financial markets to obtain capital. At these times the markets have an opportunity to evaluate the company, its management, and its proposed projects. Investment bankers and analysts play an important role in this monitoring, and the market's assessment is made evident by the price investors pay for the financial claims.

The control function of debt is more important in organizations that generate large cash flows but have low growth prospects, and even more important in organizations that must shrink. In these organizations the pressures to waste cash flows by investing them in uneconomic projects is most serious.

II. Evidence from Financial Restructuring

The free cash flow theory of capital structure helps explain previously puzzling results on the effects of financial restructuring. My paper with Clifford Smith (1985, Table 2) and Smith (1986, Tables 1 and 3) summarize more than a dozen studies of stock price changes at announcements of transactions which change capital structure. Most leverage-increasing transactions, including stock repurchases and exchange of debt or preferred for common, debt for preferred, and income bonds for preferred, result in significantly positive increases in common stock prices. The 2-day gains range from 21.9 percent (debt for common) to 2.2 percent (debt or income bonds for preferred). Most leverage-reducing transactions, including the sale of common, and exchange of common for debt or preferred, or preferred for debt, and the call of convertible bonds or convertible preferred forcing conversion into common, result in significant decreases in stock prices. The 2-day losses range from −9.9 percent (common for debt) to −.4 percent (for call of convertible preferred forcing conversion to common). Consistent with this, free cash flow theory predicts that, except for firms with profitable unfunded investment projects, prices will rise with unexpected increases in payouts to shareholders (or promises to do so), and prices will fall with reductions in payments or new requests for funds (or reductions in promises to make future payments).

The exceptions to the simple leverage change rule are targeted repurchases and the sale of debt (of all kinds) and preferred stock. These are associated with abnormal price declines (some of which are insignificant). The targeted repurchase price decline seems to be due to the reduced probability of takeover. The price decline on the sale of debt and preferred stock is consistent with the free cash flow theory because these sales bring new cash under the control of managers. Moreover, the magnitudes of the value changes are positively related to the change in the tightness of the commitment bonding the payment of future cash flows, for example, the effects of debt for preferred exchanges are smaller than the effects of debt for common exchanges. Tax effects can explain some of these results, but not all, for

example, the price increases on exchange of preferred for common, which has no tax effects.

III. Evidence from Leveraged Buyout and Going Private Transactions

Many of the benefits in going private and leveraged buyout (*LBO*) transactions seem to be due to the control function of debt. These transactions are creating a new organizational form that competes successfully with the open corporate form because of advantages in controlling the agency costs of free cash flow. In 1984, going private transactions totaled $10.8 billion and represented 27 percent of all public acquisitions (by number, see W. T. Grimm, 1985, Figs. 36 and 37). The evidence indicates premiums paid average over 50 percent.[3]

Desirable leveraged buyout candidates are frequently firms or divisions of larger firms that have stable business histories and substantial free cash flow (i.e., low growth prospects and high potential for generating cash flows)—situations where agency costs of free cash flow are likely to be high. The *LBO* transactions are frequently financed with high debt; 10 to 1 ratios of debt to equity are not uncommon. Moreover, the use of strip financing and the allocation of equity in the deals reveal a sensitivity to incentives, conflicts of interest, and bankruptcy costs.

Strip financing, the practice in which risky nonequity securities are held in approximately equal proportions, limits the conflict of interest among such securities' holders and therefore limits bankruptcy costs. A somewhat oversimplified example illustrates the point. Consider two firms identical in every respect except financing. Firm *A* is entirely financed with equity, and firm *B* is highly leveraged with senior subordinated debt, convertible debt and preferred as well

---

[3]See H. DeAngelo et al. (1984), and L. Lowenstein (1985). Lowenstein also mentions incentive effects of debt, but argues tax effects play a major role in explaining the value increase.

as equity. Suppose firm *B* securities are sold only in strips, that is, a buyer purchasing *X* percent of any security must purchase *X* percent of all securities, and the securities are "stapled" together so they cannot be separated later. Security holders of both firms have identical unlevered claims on the cash flow distribution, but organizationally the two firms are very different. If firm *B* managers withhold dividends to invest in value-reducing projects or if they are incompetent, strip holders have recourse to remedial powers not available to the equity holders of firm *A*. Each firm *B* security specifies the rights its holder has in the event of default on its dividend or coupon payment, for example, the right to take the firm into bankruptcy or to have board representation. As each security above the equity goes into default, the strip holder receives new rights to intercede in the organization. As a result, it is easier and quicker to replace managers in firm *B*.

Moreover, because every security holder in the highly levered firm *B* has the same claim on the firm, there are no conflicts among senior and junior claimants over reorganization of the claims in the event of default; to the strip holder it is a matter of moving funds from one pocket to another. Thus firm *B* need never go into bankruptcy, the reorganization can be accomplished voluntarily, quickly, and with less expense and disruption than through bankruptcy proceedings.

Strictly proportional holdings of all securities is not desirable, for example, because of IRS restrictions that deny tax deductibility of debt interest in such situations and limits on bank holdings of equity. However, riskless senior debt needn't be in the strip, and it is advantageous to have top-level managers and venture capitalists who promote the transactions hold a larger share of the equity. Securities commonly subject to strip practices are often called "mezzanine" financing and include securities with priority superior to common stock yet subordinate to senior debt.

Top-level managers frequently receive 15–20 percent of the equity. Venture capi-

talists and the funds they represent retain the major share of the equity. They control the board of directors and monitor managers. Managers and venture capitalists have a strong interest in making the venture successful because their equity interests are subordinate to other claims. Success requires (among other things) implementation of changes to avoid investment in low return projects to generate the cash for debt service and to increase the value of equity. Less than a handful of these ventures have ended in bankruptcy, although more have gone through private reorganizations. A thorough test of this organizational form requires the passage of time and another recession.

IV. Evidence from the Oil Industry

Radical changes in the energy market since 1973 simultaneously generated large increases in free cash flow in the petroleum industry and required a major shrinking of the industry. In this environment the agency costs of free cash flow were large, and the takeover market has played a critical role in reducing them. From 1973 to the late 1970's, crude oil prices increased tenfold. They were initially accompanied by increases in expected future oil prices and an expansion of the industry. As consumption of oil fell, expectations of future increases in oil prices fell. Real interest rates and exploration and development costs also increased. As a result the optimal level of refining and distribution capacity and crude reserves fell in the late 1970's and early 1980's, leaving the industry with excess capacity. At the same time profits were high. This occurred because the average productivity of resources in the industry increased while the marginal productivity decreased. Thus, contrary to popular beliefs, the industry had to shrink. In particular, crude oil reserves (the industry's major asset) were too high, and cutbacks in exploration and development (*E&D*) expenditures were required (see my 1986 paper).

Price increases generated large cash flows in the industry. For example, 1984 cash flows of the ten largest oil companies were \$48.5 billion, 28 percent of the total cash flows of the top 200 firms in Dun's *Business Month* survey. Consistent with the agency costs of free cash flow, management did not pay out the excess resources to shareholders. Instead, the industry continued to spend heavily on *E&D* activity even though average returns were below the cost of capital.

Oil industry managers also launched diversification programs to invest funds outside the industry. The programs involved purchases of companies in retailing (Marcor by Mobil), manufacturing (Reliance Electric by Exxon), office equipment (Vydec by Exxon), and mining (Kennecott by Sohio, Anaconda Minerals by Arco, Cyprus Mines by Amoco). These acquisitions turned out to be among the least successful of the last decade, partly because of bad luck (for example, the collapse of the minerals industry) and partly because of a lack of managerial expertise outside the oil industry. Although acquiring firm shareholders lost on these acquisitions, the purchases generated social benefits to the extent they diverted cash to shareholders (albeit to target shareholders) that otherwise would have been wasted on unprofitable real investment projects.

Two studies indicate that oil industry exploration and development expenditures have been too high since the late 1970's. John McConnell and Chris Muscarella (1986) find that announcements of increases in *E&D* expenditures by oil companies in the period 1975–81 were associated with systematic *decreases* in the announcing firm's stock price, and vice versa. These results are striking in comparison with their evidence that the opposite market reaction occurs to changes in investment expenditures by industrial firms, and similar SEC evidence on increases in *R&D* expenditures. (See Office of the Chief Economist, SEC, 1985.) B. Picchi's study of returns on *E&D* expenditures for 30 large oil firms indicates on average the industry did not earn "...even a 10% return on its pretax outlays" (1985, p. 5) in the period 1982–84. Estimates of the average ratio of the present value of future net cash flows of discoveries, extensions, and enhanced recovery to *E&D* expenditures for the industry ranged from less than 60 to 90

cents on every dollar invested in these activities.

V. Takeovers in the Oil Industry

Retrenchment requires cancellation or delay of many ongoing and planned projects. This threatens the careers of the people involved, and the resulting resistance means such changes frequently do not get made in the absence of a crisis. Takeover attempts can generate crises that bring about action where none would otherwise occur.

Partly as a result of Mesa Petroleum's efforts to extend the use of royalty trusts which reduce taxes and pass cash flows directly through to shareholders, firms in the oil industry were led to merge, and in the merging process they incurred large increases in debt, paid out large amounts of capital to shareholders, reduced excess expenditures on *E&D* and reduced excess capacity in refining and distribution. The result has been large gains in efficiency and in value. Total gains to shareholders in the Gulf/Chevron, Getty/Texaco, and Dupont/Conoco mergers, for example, were over $17 billion. More is possible. Allen Jacobs (1986) estimates total potential gains of about $200 billion from eliminating inefficiencies in 98 firms with significant oil reserves as of December 1984.

Actual takeover is not necessary to induce the required retrenchment and return of resources to shareholders. The restructuring of Phillips and Unocal (brought about by threat of takeover) and the voluntary Arco restructuring resulted in stockholder gains ranging from 20 to 35 percent of market value (totaling $6.6 billion). The restructuring involved repurchase of from 25 to 53 percent of equity (for over $4 billion in each case), substantially increased cash dividends, sales of assets, and major cutbacks in capital spending (including *E&D* expenditures). Diamond-Shamrock's reorganization is further support for the theory because its market value *fell* 2 percent on the announcement day. Its restructuring involved, among other things, *reducing* cash dividends by 43 percent, repurchasing 6 percent of its shares for $200 million, selling 12 percent of a newly created master limited partnership to the public, and *increasing* expenditures on oil and gas exploration by $100 million/year.

VI. Free Cash Flow Theory of Takeovers

Free cash flow is only one of approximately a dozen theories to explain takeovers, all of which I believe are of some relevance (see my 1986 paper). Here I sketch out some empirical predictions of the free cash flow theory, and what I believe are the facts that lend it credence.

The positive market response to debt creation in oil industry takeovers (as well as elsewhere, see Robert Bruner, 1985) is consistent with the notion that additional debt increases efficiency by forcing organizations with large cash flows but few high-return investment projects to disgorge cash to investors. The debt helps prevent such firms from wasting resources on low-return projects.

Free cash flow theory predicts which mergers and takeovers are more likely to destroy, rather than to create, value; it shows how takeovers are both evidence of the conflicts of interest between shareholders and managers, and a solution to the problem. Acquisitions are one way managers spend cash instead of paying it out to shareholders. Therefore, the theory implies managers of firms with unused borrowing power and large free cash flows are more likely to undertake low-benefit or even value-destroying mergers. Diversification programs generally fit this category, and the theory predicts they will generate lower total gains. The major benefit of such transactions may be that they involve less waste of resources than if the funds had been internally invested in unprofitable projects. Acquisitions not made with stock involve payout of resources to (target) shareholders and this can create net benefits even if the merger generates operating inefficiencies. Such low-return mergers are more likely in industries with large cash flows whose economics dictate that exit occur. In declining industries, mergers within the industry will create value, and mergers outside the industry are more likely to be low- or even negative-return projects. Oil fits this descrip-

tion and so does tobacco. Tobacco firms face declining demand due to changing smoking habits but generate large free cash flow and have been involved in major acquisitions recently. Forest products is another industry with excess capacity. Food industry mergers also appear to reflect the expenditure of free cash flow. The industry apparently generates large cash flows with few growth opportunities. It is therefore a good candidate for leveraged buyouts and these are now occurring. The $6.3 billion Beatrice *LBO* is the largest ever. The broadcasting industry generates rents in the form of large cash flows on its licenses and also fits the theory. Regulation limits the supply of licenses and the number owned by a single entity. Thus, profitable internal investments are limited and the industry's free cash flow has been spent on organizational inefficiencies and diversification programs—making these firms takeover targets. CBS's debt for stock restructuring fits the theory.

The theory predicts value increasing takeovers occur in response to breakdowns of internal control processes in firms with substantial free cash flow and organizational policies (including diversification programs) that are wasting resources. It predicts hostile takeovers, large increases in leverage, dismantlement of empires with few economies of scale or scope to give them economic purpose (for example, conglomerates), and much controversy as current managers object to loss of their jobs or the changes in organizational policies forced on them by threat of takeover.

The debt created in a hostile takeover (or takeover defense) of a firm suffering severe agency costs of free cash flow is often not permanent. In these situations, levering the firm so highly that it cannot continue to exist in its old form generates benefits. It creates the crisis to motivate cuts in expansion programs and the sale of those divisions which are more valuable outside the firm. The proceeds are used to reduce debt to a more normal or permanent level. This process results in a complete rethinking of the organization's strategy and its structure. When successful a much leaner and competitive organization results.

Consistent with the data, free cash flow theory predicts that many acquirers will tend to have exceptionally good performance prior to acquisition. (Again, the oil industry fits well.) That exceptional performance generates the free cash flow for the acquisition. Targets will be of two kinds: firms with poor management that have done poorly prior to the merger, and firms that have done exceptionally well and have large free cash flow which they refuse to pay out to shareholders. Both kinds of targets seem to exist, but more careful analysis is desirable (see D. Mueller, 1980).

The theory predicts that takeovers financed with cash and debt will generate larger benefits than those accomplished through exchange of stock. Stock acquisitions tend to be different from debt or cash acquisitions and more likely to be associated with growth opportunities and a shortage of free cash flow; but that is a topic for future consideration.

The agency cost of free cash flow is consistent with a wide range of data for which there has been no consistent explanation. I have found no data which is inconsistent with the theory, but it is rich in predictions which are yet to be tested.

REFERENCES

Baker, George, "Compensation and Hierarchies," Harvard Business School, January 1986.

Bruner, Robert F., "The Use of Excess Cash and Debt Capacity as a Motive for Merger," Colgate Darden Graduate School of Business, December 1985.

DeAngelo, H., DeAngelo, L. and Rice, E., "Going Private: Minority Freezeouts and Stockholder Wealth," Journal of Law and Economics, October 1984, 27, 367–401.

Donaldson, Gordon, Managing Corporate Wealth, New York: Praeger, 1984.

Easterbrook, F. H., "Two Agency-Cost Explanations of Dividends," American Economic Review, September 1984, 74, 650–59.

Grimm, W. T., Mergerstat Review, 1985.

Jacobs, E. Allen, "The Agency Cost of Corporate Control," MIT, February 6, 1986.

Jensen, Michael C., "The Takeover Controversy: Analysis and Evidence," Managerial Economics Research Center, Working Paper No. 86-01, University of Rochester, March 1986.

_____, "When Unocal Won Over Pickens, Shareholders and Society Lost," Financier, November 1985, 9, 50–52.

_____ and Smith, C. W., Jr., "Stockholder, Manager and Creditor Interests: Applications of Agency Theory," in E. Altman and M. Subrahmanyam, eds., Recent Advances in Corporate Finance, Homewood: Richard Irwin, 1985, 93–131.

Lowenstein, L., "Management Buyouts," Columbia Law Review, May 1985, 85, 730–84.

McConnell, John J. and Muscarella, Chris J., "Corporate Capital Expenditure Decisions and the Market Value of the Firm," Journal of Financial Economics, forthcoming 1986.

Mueller, D., The Determinants and Effects of Mergers, Cambridge: Oelgeschlager, 1980.

Murphy, Kevin J., "Corporate Performance and Managerial Remuneration: An Empirical Analysis," Journal of Accounting and Economics, April 1985, 7, 11–42.

Picchi, B., "Structure of the U.S. Oil Industry: Past and Future," Salomon Brothers, July 1985.

Rozeff, M., "Growth, Beta and Agency Costs as Determinants of Dividend Payout Ratios," Journal of Financial Research, Fall 1982, 5, 249–59.

Smith, Clifford W., "Investment Banking and the Capital Acquisition Process," Journal of Financial Economics, Nos. 1–2, 15, forthcoming, 1986.

Dun's Business Month, "Cash Flow: The Top 200," July 1985, 44–50.

Office of the Chief Economist, SEC, "Institutional Ownership, Tender Offers, and Long-Term Investments," April 1985.

MANAGERIAL CONTROL OF VOTING RIGHTS
Financing Policies and the Market for Corporate Control

René M. STULZ*

Ohio State University, Columbus, OH 43210-1309, USA

Received June 1986, final version received June 1987

This paper analyzes how managerial control of voting rights affects firm value and financing policies. It shows that an increase in the fraction of voting rights controlled by management decreases the probability of a successful tender offer and increases the premium offered if a tender offer is made. Depending on whether managerial control of voting rights is small or large, shareholders' wealth increases or falls when management strengthens its control of voting rights. Management can change the fraction of the votes it controls through capital structure changes, corporate charter amendments, and the acquisition of shareholder clienteles.

1. Introduction

Many papers analyze the role of managerial equity ownership in governing the conflict of interest between managers and outside shareholders. This literature takes the view that the value of the firm increases as the managers' stake in the firm's future cash flows increases. In Jensen and Meckling (1976), larger managerial equity ownership helps to align the incentives of managers with those of outside shareholders, as managers bear direct wealth consequences from their decisions. Further, Leland and Pyle (1977) show that managerial equity ownership conveys information to outside shareholders about managers' private valuation of the firm.

In this paper, we emphasize that the fraction α of the voting rights controlled by management is an important element of the ownership structure of publicly traded firms. We show that the value of the firm is positively related to α for low values of α and negatively related to α as α becomes large.

*Part of this research was done while I was visiting the Sloan School of Management at MIT and the Graduate School of Business at the University of Chicago. I thank Mark Bagnoli, Richard Cantor, Michael Dothan, George Constantinides, Ronen Israel, Kose John, Mike Long, John Long, Robert Merton, Merton Miller, Stew Myers, Ed Rice, Richard Ruback, Rob Vishny, Neil Wallace, Ralph Walkling, and participants at seminars at Harvard University, MIT, the University of Minnesota, the University of Chicago, the University of British Columbia, and the Ohio State University for useful comments. I am especially grateful to Harry DeAngelo, John Parsons, and Pat Reagan for useful discussions and comments. The paper benefited substantially from comments and suggestions from the referee, Andrei Shleifer, and from the editor, Michael Jensen.

Journal of Financial Economics 20 (1988) 25-54. © North-Holland Publishing Company.

Although managers can change α by buying or selling shares, we show that they can also do so through a variety of capital structure changes, through changes in the corporate charter, and through the acquisition of shareholder clienteles favorable to management. An important result from our analysis is that capital structure changes affect the value of the firm through their effect on α.

To demonstrate the importance of managers' control of voting rights, we consider a model in which the conflict of interest between management and outside shareholders arises solely from the fact that a successful tender offer affects the welfare of outside shareholders and managers differently. Although this assumption seems reasonable for corporations for which the threat of a hostile takeover attempt is significant, it is important to understand that the threat of a battle for corporate control is always present and hence always affects managers' actions. However, to keep our analysis tractable, we ignore the disciplining effects of the market for corporate control. In our model, managers control voting rights only because, by doing so, they affect the behavior of potential bidders and hence the probability of losing control. We show that the premium offered in a tender offer is an increasing function of the fraction of voting rights of the target controlled by management, while the probability of a hostile takeover falls with that fraction. Since α plays a crucial role in both the probability and the outcome of a hostile takeover attempt, one expects managers who value control to increase α when they learn that their firm has become a more attractive target. This is because the benefits managers derive from a large α increase with the probability of a takeover attempt, whereas the costs (for instance, the lack of diversification of their portfolio) remain the same.

In this paper, an increase in the fraction α of the voting rights controlled by managers has an ambiguous effect on the value of a potential target. On the one hand, a higher α adversely affects the value of the target as it decreases the probability of a hostile takeover attempt. On the other hand, the premium offered if such an attempt is made increases with α. If managers control a sufficiently large fraction of the votes and always oppose hostile takeover attempts, the value of the outside shares is lowest because no tender offers are ever made.[1] However, if managers control no votes a tender offer with a small premium can succeed even though, in general, the bidding firm would have been willing to offer a higher premium to acquire control. Hence, if $\alpha = 0$, an increase in α enables the target to get a larger fraction of the benefits from the takeover. This paper implies, therefore, that the value of the firm increases or falls when α increases depending on whether α is small or large, so that there is a unique value of α that maximizes the value of the firm. Morck, Shleifer and Vishny (1988) independently formulate and test this hypothesis, assuming

---

[1] Bradley and Kim (1985) show that tender offers for firms in which α exceeds 20% are rare.

that the fraction of the voting rights held by management is equal to the fraction of the firm's equity owned by management. They argue that when α is small, an increase in α makes the interests of management closer to those of shareholders, but that when α is large, an increase in α makes management more entrenched and less subjected to the discipline of the market for corporate control. Their empirical evidence shows that, after controlling for industry effects, Tobin's Q falls as α becomes large.

When managers control votes only through ownership of shares, it is likely that for a large all-equity firm managers control fewer votes than would be required to maximize the value of the firm. While a large investment in their company's shares makes it more likely that managers will keep control, it also forces them to bear a large amount of risk. We show that various contractual arrangements have the same benefits for managers as an increase in α brought about by a purchase of shares but different costs. Other types of contractual arrangements that increase management's bargaining power are available, such as those that decrease the value of control of the target for the bidder (poison pills, etc.), but they differ from those we focus on in this study.[2] Because takeover defenses that consolidate management's control of voting rights have effects similar to an outright purchase of shares by management, we are able to explain why outside shareholders sometimes vote for such defenses. It may also happen, however, that management controls too many voting rights, in the sense that the value of the outside shares would increase with a fall in α. In such cases, it becomes profitable for outside shareholders to make a takeover less costly for management, for instance through a golden parachute.

Whether management controls too few or too many votes, the firm's capital structure decision is relevant because of its effect on the distribution of voting rights. For instance, for fixed investment policy and fixed holdings of shares by management, an increase in leverage increases α and brings about an increase in the value of the outside shares if, previously, α was small. Hence, as in the Harris and Raviv (1988) model of proxy contests, managers may wish to change a firm's capital structure for the sole purpose of controlling a larger fraction of the voting rights with a given investment in their firm. In our model, an increase in leverage with fixed investment policy does not necessarily decrease the probability that management will be replaced by a competing management team. The reason is that an increase in debt increases α but also decreases the total value of equity, so that it becomes cheaper for a bidder who faces increasing marginal costs of borrowing (for instance, because existing debt has restrictive covenants) to acquire control. On the other hand, the covenants attached to new debt can substantially strengthen management's bargaining position and make a hostile takeover less likely.

---

[2] See Dann and DeAngelo (1988) for an analysis of various takeover defenses available to a corporation and of their effect on the value of the target.

The paper proceeds as follows. We derive the optimal behavior of the bidder in section 2. In section 3, we show how the value of the firm depends on α. Section 4 presents the determinants of the managers' choice of α. The next section derives the implications of our analysis for financing decisions and discusses some takeover defenses that have the same effect as an increase in α. We also compare the valuation effects of the announcement of financing decisions and takeover defenses in our analysis with the empirical evidence. We provide concluding remarks in section 6.

2. Managerial control of voting rights and tender offers

Consider an economy in which there are two relevant dates, dates 1 and 2, and in which all parties have the same information at date 1. At date 1, it is assumed that management controls the voting rights of a fraction α of the shares of an all-equity firm. We call those shareholders whose voting rights are not controlled by management outside shareholders. There is a continuum of atomistic outside shareholders who own shares at date 1. At date 1, some firm, called the bidder, decides whether to acquire information about the management's firm. If the bidder invests in information acquisition, it pays I at date 1 and receives information at date 2 describing the gain that would accrue to the bidder from control of the target. Given its information at date 2, the bidder decides whether to make a bid. To focus more readily on the key results of this paper, we assume that if the bidder's first attempt to acquire control of the target is not successful, its potential gain from control disappears. With this assumption, we do not have to analyze the gaming that often takes place once a bidder sets out to acquire control of a target. We will discuss where appropriate how relaxing this assumption would change our results. Furthermore, to focus the analysis, we assume until section 4 that the bidder's gain from control is too small to enable it to offer a premium large enough to induce management to tender the shares whose voting rights it controls. Although the objective function of management is discussed in section 4, for the moment it suffices to say that management values control and loses it if the takeover attempt succeeds.

We consider the case in which control of the target is guaranteed by possession of a simple majority of the shares. The bidder must therefore acquire half the shares for the takeover to be successful. To simplify the analysis, we consider only offers of the following kind: the bidder offers to buy exactly half the shares at a total price of $\frac{1}{2}y + P$, where (i) y is the date 2 value of the firm if no takeover attempt succeeds and is common knowledge when the bid is made, and (ii) P is the total premium offered by the bidder to acquire half the shares. If fewer than half the shares are tendered, the bidder buys no shares. We also assume that the total value of the shares not purchased by the bidder if the bid succeeds is equal to $\frac{1}{2}y$. This assumption implies that all the benefits from control accrue to the bidder who pays for these benefits the premium P. If the value of the shares not acquired with a successful bid is equal to $\frac{1}{2}y + \delta$ instead, where δ could be a function of the benefits that accrue to the bidder from control, the premium relevant for the shareholder' tendering decision is $P - \delta$, rather than P. It is necessary that $\delta < P$ for a takeover to have a positive probability of success.[3] We will discuss when appropriate how our results are affected when δ is positive but smaller than the premium.

Since the outside shareholders are atomistic, they cannot collude to force the bidder to offer a high premium, but instead compete among themselves for the premium.[4] While all shareholders would be better off if they did not tender for a low premium, i.e., one that is small compared with the bidder's potential gain from control, an individual shareholder has no private incentives not to tender when the fraction of the premium he expects to receive exceeds his opportunity cost from tendering. In the following, we assume that some shareholders have a positive opportunity cost of tendering and that not all of these shareholders face the same cost. An individual shareholder's opportunity cost of tendering is not common information and hence is not known by the bidder. Differing opportunity costs of tendering among shareholders imply that the supply curve of shares tendered increases with the premium offered by the bidder, as those shareholders with the lowest opportunity costs tender first. We assume that there is enough uncertainty about the distribution across shareholders of the opportunity costs of tendering that neither the bidder nor the target's managers know the true supply curve of shares tendered. The distribution of this curve is assumed to be such that, for most possible gains from control, it would not be profitable for the bidder to offer a premium which guarantees success of the tender offer. Further, we do not want the opportunity costs of tendering to eliminate competition among shareholders for the premium. To insure that competition among shareholders is economically significant, we assume that small bids have a nontrivial probability of success.

Assumptions implying that the expected fraction of the shares tendered is an increasing function of the premium offered by the bidder and that the bidder is uncertain about the fraction of the shares that will be tendered can be motivated by both empirical evidence and informal theoretical arguments. Empirically, there is evidence of bids that initially fail, but then succeed as the premium over the pre-offer price is increased, and there is evidence of bids

---

[3] See Bradley (1979) and Grossman and Hart (1980).

[4] This competition is discussed extensively in DeAngelo and Rice (1983). See also Bebchuk (1985), Bradley and Kim (1985), and the references in the previous footnote.

that are oversubscribed.[5] It has been shown that for share repurchases the number of shares purchased increases with the premium offered.[6] There is also direct evidence that the probability of success of a tender offer increases with the premium offered.[7]

Theoretical arguments that motivate an upward-sloping expected supply curve of shares can proceed along many routes. Although we do not want our analysis to be too intimately tied to a particular motivation for the upward-sloping expected supply curve, it is useful to derive one particular motivation that has implications consistent with our assumptions.[8] Suppose all outside shareholders have the same information but face different capital gains tax rates. A shareholder who tenders for cash must pay taxes on his capital gains, which represent his opportunity cost of tendering, whereas a shareholder who does not tender can keep postponing these taxes unless a successful tender offer is followed by a clean-up tender offer which involves an exchange of shares for cash. Consider the case in which a nontendering shareholder can postpone paying capital gains taxes indefinitely. This case does not preclude a clean-up tender offer, as the bidder can undertake a nontaxable exchange of shares. Let T_i be the fraction of his proceeds from tendering that shareholder i must pay in capital gains taxes. T_i depends both on the price the shareholder paid for his stake initially and on his personal tax rate. Shareholder i is better off if he tenders, and his share is accepted if $(1 - T_i)(y + 2P)$ exceeds y. Consequently, shareholder i tenders only if

$$T_i \le \frac{P}{\frac{1}{2}y + P} . \tag{1}$$

In this setting, a bidder who does not know how shareholders are distributed across tax rates is uncertain about the supply curve of shares tendered.

To facilitate our analysis, we make the following assumptions about the supply curve of shares tendered. If, once the bid is made, one samples among outside shareholders, each randomly chosen outside shareholder is assumed to tender with the same probability $s(P)$. We assume, for simplicity, that $s(P)$

---

[5]See, for instance, Bradley, Desai, and Kim (1983). Note, however, that the definition of the premium used here differs from the one commonly used in empirical analysis. The definition used in empirical work compares the price offered by the bidder with some pre-offer price. In this model, the pre-offer price depends on the expected premium and the probability of a tender offer. Nevertheless, if a tender offer takes place, the empirical measure of the premium is positively related to the measure used here.

[6]See Rosenfeld (1982) for direct evidence, and also Masulis (1980), Dann (1981), and Vermaelen (1981).

[7]See, for instance, Walkling (1985).

[8]Bebchuk (1985) provides a model in which an upward-sloping expected supply curve of shares arises from the fact that shareholders are heterogeneously informed about the value of the firm if it is not acquired.

does not depend on α. This implies that a firm does not attract different types of shareholders for different values of α. If the opportunity cost of tendering results from capital gains taxation, $s(P)$ is equal to the probability that a shareholder's tax rate is low enough to make it advantageous to tender. As there is uncertainty about the distribution of the opportunity costs of tendering, $s(P)$ is not known before a bid is made. We assume, however, that $s(P)$ is known to be distributed uniformly between $u(P)$ and $d(P)$ for $P \le \bar{P}$ and that the bidder never finds it profitable to offer a premium larger than $\bar{P}$. $u(P)$ and $d(P)$ are assumed to be increasing linear functions of P with equal slopes, so that the expected number of shares tendered at a premium P, $(1 - \alpha)\mathrm{E}(s(P))$, is a linear function of P, and $u(P) - d(P)$ is a constant. To insure that there is enough competition among shareholders, we assume that $u(P) > \frac{1}{2} + \gamma$ as $P \to 0$, where γ is a constant greater than zero. This assumption implies that a small bid has a nontrivial positive probability of success. While the assumption that a supply curve is linear is often made in economic analyses, the appendix shows that it could be substantially relaxed without affecting our results.

At date 2, target shareholders, the management, and the bidder first learn y, the value of the firm if no bid is made. y is drawn from a continuous distribution with density function $h(y)$. Once y is known, the bidder learns G if an investment in information is made at date 1, where G is the gain that accrues directly to the bidder from control of the target. We assume that G is drawn with probability p from a uniform distribution between 0 and $\bar{G}$ and is equal to some negative number $\underline{G}$ with probability $(1 - p)$. If $\underline{G}$ is low enough, the bidder never makes a bid without having acquired information. To simplify the discussion, we assume from now on that this is the case. G can take a negative value for many reasons. For instance, a bid may have a fixed cost which, in some states of the world, exceeds the benefits which accrue from control of the target.

The bidding firm chooses the premium given its perception of the probability of success of the bid as a function of the premium. Given a premium P, it follows from the central limit theorem that a fraction $(1 - \alpha)s(P)$ of the shareholders tender, i.e., with a continuum of outside shareholders, there is no uncertainty about the fraction of outside shareholders who tender if the probability that an individual shareholder tenders is known. Since the tender offer is successful if $(1 - \alpha)s(P)$ exceeds one half, it can succeed only if $s(P)$ is greater than $1/2(1 - \alpha)$. Let $z(\alpha)$ be equal to the fraction of the outside shareholders that must tender for the offer to be successful. Since the bidder does not know $s(P)$, the probability of success of the offer is the probability that $s(P)$ exceeds $z(\alpha)$. With our assumptions, this probability is given by

$$N(P, \alpha) = \frac{u(P) - z(\alpha)}{u(P) - d(P)}, \tag{2}$$

as long as the probability of success of the bid is less than one and greater than zero. The probability of success does not depend on the shareholders' perception of the value of the bidder's gain from control. This is because even if G is large compared to the payment offered by the bidder, shareholders cannot collude to make the bid fail to force the bidder to offer a higher payment. For an individual shareholder, the bidder's gain from control is irrelevant to his tendering decision because there is nothing he can do to appropriate a larger fraction of that gain.

Although the managers of the bidding firm maximize their own expected utility subject to constraints imposed by the shareholders, we assume for simplicity that they choose the optimal premium by maximizing the expected value of the bid. With this assumption, the bidding firm chooses P to maximize

$$[G-P]N\Omega, \tag{3}$$

where Ω is equal to zero if no bid is made and one otherwise. We will call the maximized value of (3) the expected value of the bid. Note that the bidder's actions when G is known do not depend on I, which is the sunk cost of acquiring information about the target. The expected value of the bid is shown in the appendix to be a concave function of the premium and it falls when P gets large. Hence, if a bid is made, there is a unique optimal premium. Further, the optimal premium increases with G, which is the bidder's gain from control.

In the absence of managerial holdings of shares, the bidder has to persuade half of the outside shareholders to tender to be successful. However, if α is positive, a larger fraction $z(\alpha) = 1/2(1-\alpha) > \frac{1}{2}$ of the outside shareholders must tender for the bidder to gain control. To keep the probability of success constant as α increases, the bidder must therefore increase the premium with α. As α increases, the probability of success falls for each premium because a larger fraction of the outside shareholders has to tender for the bid to succeed. It immediately follows that:

Result 1.   An increase in the fraction α of the voting rights controlled by management decreases the expected value of the bid to the bidder.

Proof.   See appendix.

For a given value of the gain from control G, the bidder increases the probability of success and decreases the expected value of the bid if it increases the premium offered. The bidder does not choose to offer a premium that insures success, but instead trades off the probability of success against the gain obtained if the bid is successful. For a given premium, an increase in

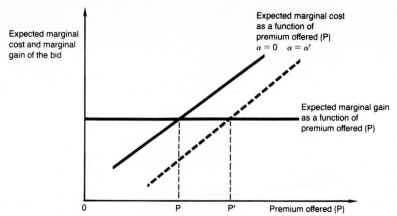

Fig. 1. Effect of an increase in α on the premium offered by the bidder. The bidder chooses a premium such that the expected marginal cost of increasing the premium equals the expected marginal gain. An increase in α leaves the expected marginal gain of increasing the premium unchanged but decreases the expected marginal cost, since it makes it less likely that the premium will have to be paid. This implies that an increase in α moves the expected marginal cost curve to the right, so that it intersects the expected marginal gain curve at a higher premium. Consequently, an increase in α increases the premium offered.

α does not affect the gain made by the bidder if the bid is successful, but it decreases the probability of success. Consequently, a higher α induces the bidder to offer a higher premium to make the tradeoff between the probability of success and the gain associated with a successful bid optimal. This explains the following result:

Result 2. From the bidder's perspective, the optimal premium is an increasing function of the fraction α of the voting rights of the target controlled by management as long as α is not so high that a bid is a negative net present value project.

Proof. See appendix.

Fig. 1 illustrates this result. The expected value of the bid for the bidder is equal to an expected gain, GN, minus an expected cost, C. The expected gain is the bidder's gain from control times the probability of success, and the expected cost is equal to the total premium offered times the probability of success, PN. The bidder chooses the premium offered to be such that the expected marginal gain from an increase in the premium equals the expected marginal cost. With our assumptions, the expected marginal gain is not affected by a change in α, since the effect of an increase in the premium offered on the probability of success does not depend on α.[9] However, an increase in α decreases the marginal expected cost by lowering the probability of success. With a higher α, an increase in the premium offered has a smaller cost because it is less likely that the premium will actually be paid. Fig. 1 shows how, with an increase in α, the marginal expected gain curve stays unchanged while the marginal expected cost curve moves to the right and intersects the marginal expected gain curve at a higher premium. Hence, the premium must increase with α as long as a bid is a positive net present value project. If outside shareholders can collude, they can make the bid a zero net present value project for the bidder irrespective of α. In that case, an increase in α cannot increase the premium.

3. The value of the firm and α

In this section, we address the question of how the date 1 value of the firm, $V(\alpha, 1)$, depends on the fraction of the firm's voting rights controlled by management. In the presence of capital gains taxes, shareholders have an opportunity cost of selling their shares and they may not all be made better off if managers take actions that maximize the market value of the firm. To avoid the unchartered territory where value maximization breaks down, we arbitrarily define $V(\alpha, 1)$ as the present value of the cash flows which accrue to shareholders and assume that they want $V(\alpha, 1)$ to be maximized. Taxes are ignored in the following analysis, so that $V(\alpha, 1)$ corresponds to the value of the firm from the perspective of an investor who pays no taxes. Furthermore, we assume that all cash flows are discounted at the rate of interest R. Using the analysis of section 2, it follows that

$$V(\alpha, 1) = \left(\frac{1}{1 + R} \right) \left[E(y) + ip \int_0^{\overline{G}} P(G, \alpha) N(P(G, \alpha), \alpha) \frac{\mathrm{d}G}{\overline{G}} \right], \quad (4)$$

where i is an indicator variable that takes value zero if the bidder makes no investment in information about the target and one otherwise. As all parties know α, I, and the distribution of the bidder's gain G (characterized by a

[9]Without our assumptions about the distribution of the fraction of shares held by outside investors that are tendered, the premium may fall with an increase in α. In particular Result 2 does not hold if the marginal contribution of an increase in the premium to the probability of success of the bid falls too much when α increases [formally, if $N_{P\alpha}$ is negative and $N_\alpha - (G - P)N_{P\alpha} > 0$]. The intuition for this condition is that, if $N_{P\alpha}$ is small, an increase in the premium has only a small impact on the probability of success of the bid, so that an increase in the premium increases the expected gain (GN) less than it increases the expected cost (PN) of the bid. In this case, the bidder is better off decreasing the premium offered if α increases. However, if $N_{P\alpha}$ is small enough to invalidate Result 2, there generally is no interior solution for the premium, as the second-order condition of the bidder's maximization problem [eq. (A.3) in the appendix] is unlikely to hold.

probability p that the gain is positive and distributed uniformly between zero and $\overline{G}$) before the shares are sold, they can infer i at date 1. Eq. (4) states that the value of the target is equal to the sum of two terms. The first term is the expected value of the firm in the absence of a takeover attempt, and the second is the expected value of the payment to target shareholders by a successful bidder times the probability that a successful bid will be made. For the bidder to invest in information, the net present value of doing so must be positive:

$$\left(\frac{1}{1+R}\right) p \int_0^{\overline{G}} (G - P(\alpha, G)) N(P(G, \alpha), \alpha)) \frac{dG}{\overline{G}} \geq I. \tag{5}$$

It immediately follows from this that:

Result 3.   If the target's value at date 1 is expressed as a function of the fraction of the voting rights controlled by managers, it reaches a maximum for some positive amount of that fraction and a minimum when management controls half or more of the shares.

Proof.   See appendix.

The intuition behind Result 3 can be explained as follows. The value of the target would be maximized if the target's shareholders could find a way to appropriate for themselves the benefits that otherwise would accrue to the bidder in the event of a successful bid. However, there is no action that an outside shareholder can take independently to insure that only bids having zero value for the bidder are successful. By increasing α, managers reduce the probability that a bid will succeed and make it more likely that a successful bid is a high bid. On the one hand, the probability of a successful bid falls as α increases and reaches zero when α equals one-half. On the other hand, the expected premium if a bid is successful is bounded by the gain from control for the bidder. This means that, as α becomes large, the product of the probability of a successful bid times the expected premium if such a bid takes place becomes small. Eventually, as α reaches one-half, no bid ever succeeds, so that the date 2 value of the firm is equal to its stand-alone date 2 value, y. However, Result 3 and this discussion rest on the assumption that management does not tender its shares at the highest premium that the bidder is willing to offer. This assumption is relaxed in the next section. It is interesting to note that, in this model, an increase in α is similar to establishing a minimum bid in an auction.[10] The benefit of establishing a minimum bid is

---

[10] Note that Shleifer and Vishny (1986b) provide an analysis in which the target implements a minimum bid once the bidder has already purchased shares by buying back those shares and entering a standstill agreement. See Riley and Samuelson (1981) for a discussion of the usefulness of establishing a minimum bid.

that it raises the expected value of the successful bid; the cost is that it decreases the probability of a successful bid.

If, contrary to our assumption, there is a second potential bidder, an increase in α will have less effect on the value of the target, because the first bidder takes into account that unless the premium offered is high enough, the second bidder will find it profitable to bid. Or, pursuing the auction analogy, the usefulness to the seller of establishing a minimum bid falls as the number of bidders becomes large. Hence, in this model, as the number of bidders increases, the benefit to shareholders of an increase in α when α is small falls while the cost is unchanged.[11] Note also that if nontendering shareholders receive more than $\frac{1}{2}y$ if the bid is successful, because the bidding firm faces constraints in its ability to appropriate the gains from the takeover, their opportunity cost of tendering is increased. This forces the bidder to offer a larger premium and hence has the same effect as an increase in the number of bidders.

Although our analysis shows that shareholders can benefit from an increase in α, such an increase has a cost for society as a whole. In our model any increase in the value of the target takes place at the expense of the bidder. However, an increase in α decreases the combined value of the target and the bidder because it makes unprofitable some bids that are profitable for $\alpha = 0$. Hence, a positive α leads to a waste of some opportunities for the bidder and the target to increase their combined value. Although a large α reduces the agency cost of equity financing, as discussed by Jensen and Meckling (1976) and others, and hence benefits society as a whole, this gain comes about because managers have a stake in future cash flows and not because they control voting rights. An analysis of the social costs and benefits of legislation that would restrict managerial control of voting rights is beyond the scope of this paper.

4. The choice of α by management

In this section, we study the determinants of α when management controls voting rights only by holding shares and the firm is an all-equity firm. Whereas our earlier analysis explicitly assumes that the premium offered is too small for managers to tender their shares, we now also consider the case in which the premium is high enough to persuade managers to tender and show that our previous results are not altered in this more general setting. For simplicity, we assume that managers act to maximize the following collective objective

---

[11]Previous papers focus on the benefits for the target of having multiple bidders. See Fishman (1985), Khanna (1985), P'ng (1985), and Shleifer and Vishny (1986b). In Riley and Samuelson (1980) the level of the minimum bid is not affected by the number of bidders, but the expected revenue from establishing a minimum bid is.

function:

$$\max \mathrm{E}[U(W(2)) + Q(1 - N)], \tag{6}$$

where $W(2)$ is the managers' wealth at the beginning of trading at date 2, i.e., when the outcome of the takeover attempt is known. Q is the managers' expected utility gain if a successful takeover does not occur and is independent of the change in the value of their holdings of their firm's shares. The probability that managers will get Q is one minus the probability of a successful takeover. It is assumed that U is a concave function of date 2 wealth and that it exhibits decreasing absolute risk aversion. In this simple approach, a positive Q means that the target's managers would be worse off if they lost their jobs. It may be that managers like to manage the target. However, in general, one would expect Q to be high whenever managers have skills that are unlikely to be highly valued by a potential bidder and are not very useful outside the target. An obvious example would be a situation in which the target is attractive because it owns stores in buildings that would be useful to the bidder. Presumably, the bidder, if successful, would close the stores and use the buildings for other purposes. Hence, managers who have become expert in managing the stores would lose a large part of their firm-specific human capital. One would also expect Q to be high whenever managers' compensation includes implicit promises of future payments. It is not always to the bidder's advantage to honor such commitments.[12] For instance, suppose that compensation contracts are structured so that effort increases the probability of being rewarded by a big prize – for instance, the job of chief executive, which has a salary chosen to make the prize attractive.[13] In such a situation, the management of the target may lose substantially if the top prize is taken away by the bidder, and Q is a measure of its loss in expected utility if a successful takeover changes the probability of obtaining this prize.

To determine managers' optimal holdings of shares in their firm, we first derive an expression for their wealth at date 2. We assume that at date 1 managers have wealth $W(1)$ and a stake in their firm worth $\alpha V(\alpha, 1)$. Managers' compensation from the firm is neglected in the following discussion. The compensation for the next period can be viewed as part of their wealth, while part of Q may reflect their compensation in subsequent periods. A useful extension of the present analysis would take into account the interaction between management's compensation and the probability of a change in control. It is assumed, for simplicity, that no asset can be used by managers to hedge their investment in their firm. In such a setting, there is no great loss of generality if one assumes that the investment opportunity set of managers

[12] Knoeber (1985) uses this argument to explain golden parachutes.
[13] See Lazear and Rosen (1981).

consists of only a risk-free bond with return R and the common stock of the firm. In this section, we also assume that there are no restrictions on short sales, so that managers can borrow at the rate R. Since capital gains taxes make it less likely that managers will tender, we assume that managers pay no taxes and discuss later how our results are changed when this assumption does not hold. At date 2, managers' wealth depends on the value of their shares. If no tender offer is made or if managers do not tender, the total value of their shares is αy. If managers tender, they also receive a fraction f of the premium. This fraction depends both on α and on the fraction of the shares tendered by outside shareholders. It follows from this that management's wealth at date 2 is

$$W(2) = [W(1) - \alpha V(\alpha, 1)](1 + R) + \alpha y + fP. \tag{7}$$

Managers' return from investing in their firm comes in two forms. First, managers get a pecuniary return from their investment that depends on their tendering policy. When managers tender less readily than other shareholders, their expected pecuniary rate of return is smaller than R as they may end up not tendering in the event of a successful bid. However, managers also benefit from the fact that their holdings of shares make it more likely that they will remain in control. At date 2, management tenders if its utility is maximized by doing so:

$$U([W(1) - \alpha V(\alpha, 1)](1 + R) + \alpha y + fP)N^* + Q(1 - N^*)$$
$$\geq U([W(1) - \alpha V(\alpha, 1)](1 + R) + \alpha y)N + Q(1 - N), \tag{8}$$

where N^* is the probability of success given that management tenders and N is the probability of success derived in section 2. To compute N^*, note that if management tenders, the offer is successful if a fraction $(\frac{1}{2} - \alpha)/(1 - \alpha)$ of the outside shareholders tenders. Hence, N^* can be computed by substituting this fraction in eq. (2). Inspection of eq. (8) reveals that, for a small enough premium, the left-hand side of the equation is smaller than the right-hand side, which means that it does not pay for management to tender when the premium is small. However, there is always a premium large enough that it pays for management to tender, as utility increases with date 2 wealth. Consequently, there is a premium P^* such that management tenders for all premia that exceed P^*. It immediately follows from eq. (8) that P^* is an increasing function of the benefit that management derives from control. However, for management not to tender, it must also be the case that the probability of success is higher when management tenders than when it does not, which means that management generally tenders in offers that are highly likely to succeed. If, contrary to our assumption in this section, management pays capital gains taxes, it may choose not to tender even when an offer is highly likely to succeed.

At this point, it is interesting to note that if the bidder can make repeated offers, it can learn about the true supply curve of shares. Hence, the bidder could, after having made repeated unsuccessful offers, offer a premium P' such that $s(P') = z(\alpha)$. If the bidder offers P', the offer succeeds with probability one, so that management tenders unless its opportunity cost of tendering exceeds the premium. However, as the offer is oversubscribed for that premium, management might be better off to tender at a lower premium P''. This is because the tender offer will succeed anyway, so that management wants to maximize its revenue from tendering. For a fixed supply curve of shares from outside shareholders, if management tenders at P'', a larger fraction of its shares will be accepted. In this case, it is not necessarily true that the premium for an offer that succeeds increases with α, since management might tender at a premium that induces less than half of the outside shareholders to tender. However, the probability that an offer will be made is still negatively related to α, since the bid cannot succeed unless it is profitable for the bidder even if it has to pay P', because otherwise management benefits from holding out. If it is costly to make a bid, a bidder does not generally find it profitable to make multiple offers that it expects to fail, so our assumption of no repeated bids leads to more plausible results. This discussion suggests, however, that this assumption could be relaxed, since our results obtain as long as there is substantial uncertainty about the supply curve of shares, so that management tenders only for a high premium.

We can now turn to the determinants of α. As it is risky for management to own shares, α is negatively related to managers' degree of relative risk aversion. Furthermore, because managers exhibit decreasing absolute risk aversion, α is an increasing function of managerial wealth. More important, however, α is positively related to the benefits that managers get from control and to the absolute value of the change in the probability of success of a bid brought about by an increase in α. It follows therefore that a decrease in the managers' benefits from control decreases α. Shareholders can engineer such a decrease by granting management a golden parachute, which suggests that the value of the firm should increase when a golden parachute is introduced in a firm with a large α. However, a golden parachute could also be introduced to reduce the value of the bid for a potential bidder, which would decrease the value of the firm irrespective of α. Although empirical researchers find that introducing a golden parachute can increase the value of a firm, such golden parachutes are likely to be introduced when the probability of a takeover attempt has increased, so that the positive abnormal returns associated with their introduction may just reflect the change in expectations about a successful takeover.[14]

---

[14] See Lambert and Larcker (1985).

We are now in a position to show that the results of sections 2 and 3 are not affected when management tenders for premia in excess of P^*. Note first that our results would no longer hold if it turns out that an increase in α decreases P^*. This is because, in this case, some bids would have a higher probability of success with higher values of α. It has been argued, for instance by Walkling and Long (1984), that an increase in α, by increasing the pecuniary loss to managers who refuse to tender, decreases P^*. However, in our present analysis, α is high when the benefits of control to management are high. Hence, a higher α is associated with a higher value of $Q(1 - N)$ and a smaller probability that management will tender for some, but not necessarily all, premia that the bidder might offer. This implies that our results of sections 2 and 3 still hold when management chooses to tender for some premia, at least for values of α smaller or equal to half the votes plus one. In the setting of this paper, there is no reason for managers to hold votes in excess of half the votes plus one. Hence, to explain such holdings of votes, one has to introduce considerations (for instance, incentive or asymmetric information effects) affecting managerial holdings of votes that are not captured in our model and may lead the value of the firm to increase with α when α exceeds one half.

It is important to understand that the results of sections 2 and 3 hold because managers' holdings of shares affect their probability of keeping the benefits from control. If there are no benefits from control, managers do not behave differently from other shareholders and they tender when doing so maximizes the value of their shares net of taxes. In this case, the relation between the value of the firm and α depends on the managers' tax status and on how their large shareholdings enable them to affect the outcome of the bid. It is interesting to note that our model implies that the value of the shares sold to the public in an initial public offering increases with α over some range of α if the potential shareholders believe that management is less likely to tender than outside shareholders. However, there is no apparent mechanism whereby managers can commit not to tender, so that if managers get no benefits from control, the value of the firm could be lower for a small positive α than for $\alpha = 0$. This is because managers might tender for a lower premium than the premium for which half the outside shareholders would tender when $\alpha = 0$.

5. Financing policies and management control of voting rights

Because of risk aversion and limited wealth, management is likely to own only a relatively small fraction of the shares of an all-equity corporation. Often, therefore, the value of an all-equity firm could be increased if management found ways to increase its control of voting rights. In this section, we show that all financing decisions affect management's control of voting rights for a given dollar investment by management in its corporation. Because the value of the firm was shown in earlier sections to depend on the distribution of voting rights, it follows that financing decisions affect the value of the firm. In particular, for low values of α, increases in leverage in general increase the value of the firm while decreases have the opposite effect. However, to highlight the valuation effects of changes in management's control of voting rights, we neglect the other determinants of the firm's capital structure that have traditionally been studied. Introducing these determinants would probably change the degree of leverage that maximizes the value of the firm, but not the result that the firm's value is not everywhere increasing in α. We conclude the section by discussing contractual arrangements that allow management to increase its control of voting rights while leaving other aspects of the firm's capital structure unchanged.

5.1. Leverage and management's control of voting rights

The analysis in section 4 assumes that managers can borrow to buy shares and face perfect capital markets. With such an assumption, it does not matter whether the firm or the managers borrow, so the value of the firm is independent of its capital structure but not of management's control of voting rights. However, this argument depends critically on the ability of managers to borrow on personal account at the same terms as the corporation.[15] In particular, managers must be able to enter into nonrecourse loans to purchase shares. If they cannot or if there is any other reason why managers cannot borrow at the same rate as the corporation, one would expect the firm to have debt outstanding. This is because with a debt issue managers can purchase a constant fraction of the shares at a lower cost and hence can achieve at more favorable terms what they would otherwise accomplish on personal account. While our model focuses on the possibility that managers will lose control through a hostile takeover, as more corporate debt is sold, the risk to managers of losing their position through bankruptcy increases and hence additional corporate debt becomes less advantageous.[16] Furthermore, as the firm issues more debt, the shares become more risky so that managers bear more risk for a given investment in the firm. As the debt–equity ratio increases, it is likely that at some point a further substitution of debt for equity leads managers to reduce their investment in the firm so that α falls. It follows that there are costs to increasing debt and that managers try to balance the marginal costs and benefits of debt when they choose the firm's debt–equity ratio. An

---

[15]Note that if outside shareholders cannot borrow and lend at the same terms as the corporation, they are not indifferent with respect to the capital structure of the firm. Although this result implies that there will be leverage-induced clienteles, it does not have useful implications for the capital structure of individual firms.

[16]Harris and Raviv (1988) have a model in which the advantage of debt is that it makes a change in control through a proxy contest less likely, while its cost is that it makes it more likely that managers will lose control to the creditors.

increase in the gain from control for a potential bidder increases the benefit to management of a high α, but does not change the costs associated with a high debt–equity ratio if no takeover attempt succeeds. This leads to the following result:

Result 4. If we hold constant the managers' investment in their own firm and if a change in the debt–equity ratio affects the potential bidder only because it changes management's control of voting rights, (a) there is a positive debt–equity ratio that maximizes the date 1 value of the firm, (b) the probability of a hostile takeover attempt is negatively related to the target's debt–equity ratio, and (c) an unexpected increase in the probability of a hostile takeover attempt increases the target's debt–equity ratio.

Palepu (1986) provides evidence to support this result. He studies a sample of 163 firms that were acquired during the period 1971–1979 and a random sample of 256 firms that had not been acquired as of 1979. He estimates a logistic multiple regression model in which the explanatory variables are firm characteristics hypothesized to affect a firm's probability of being taken over while the binary dependent variable takes the value one for acquired firms and zero otherwise. The estimate of the regression coefficient for leverage is negative and significant at the 0.05 level, so that a highly levered firm is less likely to be acquired than an unlevered firm.

One should note, however, that an increase in the debt–equity ratio can make a takeover less likely because it decreases the bidder's gain from control in addition to its effect on α. This may occur for at least three reasons. First, as suggested by Jensen (1986a, b), the issuance of new debt can be a way for management to bond itself to higher payout and reduced investment expenditures that raise the value of the firm and make acquisition of the target less valuable for a potential bidder. Second, the target's debt may include covenants which restrict the bidder's ability to use these assets in the way it wants to. For instance, the bidder may not be able to sell some of the target's assets without repurchasing the debt at a premium. Such covenants may be included in the bond indenture only because they make the target less attractive to a potential bidder. Hence, bond covenants themselves are a way for a target to decrease the probability of a successful bid, but such covenants decrease the value of the firm because they decrease the bidder's gain from control and hence decrease the premium offered. Third, an increase in the debt–equity ratio can make a takeover attempt less likely because the bidder may have included in its computation of the gain from the acquisition an increase in the debt of the target. Since an increase in the debt–equity ratio of the target reduces the target's ability to issue additional debt, the gain from the acquisition would fall as the debt–equity ratio increases.

Result 4 implies that an increase in leverage increases the value of the firm for low values of α. The empirical evidence on announcement effects of financing decisions shows that exchange offers that increase leverage increase the value of the firm, whereas exchange offers that decrease leverage decrease the value of the firm. Our analysis implies that, for a firm with a low α, the unexpected announcement of a leverage-increasing exchange offer has a positive effect on the value of the firm through its effect on α. This is because for low values of α an increase in leverage consolidates voting rights in the hands of management and hence enables it to force a bidder to pay a higher premium to acquire control. It should be emphasized, however, that the consolidation of voting rights is not the only possible positive effect on the value of the firm of an increase in α. Other favorable effects of an increase in leverage discussed in the literature include tax effects, information effects, and incentive effects.[17]

Interestingly, our model suggests a well-defined information effect of an unexpected change in leverage. Suppose that management has superior information about the probability that the firm will become a target given the existing value of α. Depending on whether it believes that probability has increased or decreased, management will choose to increase or decrease leverage. For low values of α, an increase in leverage would lead outside shareholders to believe the firm is moving toward the new, higher value of α that maximizes the value of the firm. However, if α becomes large as a result of the increase in leverage, the value of the firm would fall as a successful takeover becomes unlikely. Hence, whether the change in leverage conveys information about the probability of a takeover attempt or not, one would expect that the announcement effect of leverage-increasing exchange offers is related to α and can be negative when α is large, if the concentration of voting rights effect is economically significant. Dann and DeAngelo (1988) document negative average announcement effects for leverage-increasing transactions for a sample of firms involved in corporate control contests.

A final note of caution is required. Result 4 may not hold when the debt–equity ratio of the target affects the bidder's cost of borrowing. To see this, suppose the bidder faces increasing marginal costs of borrowing. For instance, issuing more debt could force the bidder to renegotiate with its bondholders to change some bond covenants. This would be costly and could induce the bidder to avoid making a bid that has to be financed with debt unless the gain from control for the bid is high. As the target increases its debt, the total value of its equity and the bidder's borrowing costs to acquire control fall. In this case, a bid may become more likely as the debt–equity ratio

---

[17]Smith (1986) reviews the empirical evidence and the hypotheses offered to explain it. Jensen (1986a, b) offers a new explanation of the empirical evidence which relies on the fact that, for firms with free cash flow, a leverage increase bonds management to new payout and investment policies more favorable to shareholders' interests.

increases.[18] Because the total premium paid by the bidder increases with α, the value of the target is still increased by the change in the debt–equity ratio when α is small. However, in this case, an increase in the debt–equity ratio could mean that managers are more likely to lose control. One would not expect such cases to be frequent, because bidders are usually firms for which bond covenants are unlikely to become binding in the short run. Further, newly issued bonds could incorporate covenants that decrease a bidder's possible gain from control (for instance, by restricting the sale of the target's assets) and hence make a bid less likely even though a bidder would have to issue less debt to acquire the target. Nevertheless, this case is important because it shows that, sometimes, it will pay for a firm to decrease its debt–equity ratio to obtain a better bargaining position with a bidder.

5.2. Stock repurchases

Although many papers have been devoted to the study of stock repurchases, most do not address why takeover targets find such repurchases desirable.[19] In the standard corporate finance literature, stock repurchases are generally viewed as a way for managers to signal greater earning opportunities. This literature does not explain, however, why greater earning opportunities should come up just when a bidder makes a bid or why, if management already knew these opportunities, it waited to act until a bidder made himself known. Jensen (1986a, b) argues that such stock repurchases decrease the resources available to management and hence prevent the management of firms with limited growth opportunities from investing these resources in negative net present value projects. His analysis implies that stock repurchases are more likely when the increased likelihood of a takeover contest puts management under pressure to make the target less attractive to a hostile bidder.

Although a share repurchase can decrease the bidder's gain from acquiring control of the target, it also follows from our analysis that a share repurchase can make it harder for a bidder to acquire control because it increases managers' control of voting rights. For low values of α, a share repurchase increases the value of the target even in the absence of its effects on the management's actions discussed in Jensen (1986a, b). However, for large values of α, our analysis implies that share repurchases can decrease the value of the firm. Dann and DeAngelo (1988) provide empirical evidence on share repurchases during takeover contests. Interestingly, they find that the average announcement effect of the repurchases in their sample is negative. Some of the repurchases they discuss seem to be strongly motivated by managers'

---

[18] Stiglitz (1972) argues that because of this phenomenon the probability of a takeover increases with the debt–equity ratio.

[19] See, for instance, Dann (1981), Vermaelen (1981), Masulis (1980), and Rosenfeld (1982).

intention to consolidate their voting power as they are associated with private placements of shares to management, investors allied with management, or pension funds under the control of management. The other repurchases they discuss as well as those discussed in Jensen (1986a, b) are better explained as ways for management to bond itself to new investment and payout policies. The motivation for repurchases discussed in Jensen and the motivation emphasized here are not mutually exclusive and each can contribute, in varying degrees, to explaining particular stock repurchases.

The concentration of the vote effect of an increase in α increases the value of the firm for low values of α and decreases it for high values of α. Vermaelen (1981) regresses the announcement effect on the fraction of insider holdings. For one subperiod in his sample, he finds that in a multivariate regression the coefficient of the announcement effect on the fraction of insider holdings is significantly different from zero at the 0.05 level. This evidence could mean that the positive signalling, tax, or leverage-increasing incentive effects of stock repurchases dominate the concentration of the vote effect for high values of α. However, Vermaelen's result does not hold for other subperiods in his sample. As more recent repurchases seem to be taking place around takeover contests it would be interesting to study the relation between announcement effects of stock repurchases and α in a sample that includes the more recent experience.

5.3. Convertible debt and delayed conversion

Ingersoll (1977a) and Brennan and Schwartz (1977) show that in perfect markets a convertible security should be called as soon as the value of the asset to be exchanged for the security equals the call value plus the accrued interest. Yet Ingersoll (1977b) documents that most firms do not follow this policy. In his sample, corporations waited, on average, until the value of the common stock to be exchanged for the debt was 83.5% in excess of the call value plus the accrued interest of bonds convertible into stock, while the value of the preferred stock was 69.9% in excess. In the context of the present paper, forcing conversion of debt into common stock decreases α.[20] If the holders of convertible debt are less likely to convert and tender than holders of common stock, forced conversion has a cost created by the redistribution of voting rights that has been neglected in the literature. As holders of a convertible security who tender lose either a put option in the case of convertible debt or, possibly, the right to higher dividends with convertible preferred stock, it seems likely that holders of convertible securities face a higher opportunity cost of tendering than holders of common stock. Further, holders of convertible securities may not be able to convert in time to participate in the tender

---

[20] See Ingersoll (1977b), Harris and Raviv (1985), and Constantinides and Grundy (1986) for analyses which offer hypotheses as to why convertibles are called late.

offer. Mikkelson (1981) documents that the announcement of forced conversion of debt convertible into common stock significantly decreases the value of the firm, while the decrease in the value of the firm resulting from the announcement of forced conversion of preferred stock into common stock is not statistically different from zero. Since, on average, preferred stock seems to have less valuable voting rights than common stock, forced conversion of debt into common stock would be more likely to signal a decreased probability of a tender offer than forced conversion of preferred stock into common stock. This could help explain the stronger adverse impact on the value of the firm of the forced conversion of debt convertible into common stock. Note, however, that in the case in which the bidder faces increasing marginal costs of borrowing, forced conversion of a convertible would make it more difficult for the bidder to acquire control as more borrowing would be required.

5.4. Supermajority rules and differential voting rights

Instead of increasing their control of voting rights directly, managers can decrease the importance of voting rights held by other shareholders. One way to do this is through a supermajority rule. A supermajority rule is viewed here, for simplicity, as one according to which the bidder gains effective control of the target only if some fraction $\gamma > \frac{1}{2}$ of the shares has been acquired. The introduction of a supermajority rule is equivalent to an increase in α as it implies that, even if $\alpha = 0$, the marginal shareholder who tenders requires a higher premium than if $\gamma = \frac{1}{2}$. In our model, therefore, an increase in γ from $\gamma = \frac{1}{2}$ increases the value of the firm if α is smaller than the value of α that would maximize the value of the firm and decreases it otherwise. DeAngelo and Rice (1983), Linn and McConnell (1983), and Jarrell and Poulsen (1987) study the change in the value of the firm associated with the announcement of the introduction of antitakeover amendments. On average, the introduction of supermajority amendments does appear to reduce the value of a firm, but the announcement effect seems to vary considerably in both sign and magnitude among firms. It would therefore be useful to re-examine these announcement effects to see whether α can provide some explanation for their cross-sectional distribution. Our model implies that negative announcement effects are more likely to be associated with firms in which α is large than with other firms. Alexander (1986), regressing the announcement effects of antitakeover amendments on a constant and the fraction of the shares held by members of the board of directors, finds that the announcement effect is negatively related to the fraction of the shares held by members of the board. Jarrell and Poulsen (1987) obtain a similar result.

In some cases, supermajority rules can achieve an increase in the value of the firm that cannot be accomplished through an increase in α. To see this, consider the case in which management is not made worse off by a takeover attempt. In this case, the value of the firm would increase with an increase in α provided that managers could commit not to tender, because a bid would succeed only with the support of shareholders with higher opportunity costs of tendering. As argued in the previous section, however, there is no mechanism whereby managers can commit not to tender. Hence, in this case, the value of the firm may not depend on α. However, management can achieve the same effect as an increase in α associated with a credible commitment not to tender by introducing a supermajority rule. The disadvantage of a supermajority rule is that it is not easy to remove when shareholders might be better off without it.

By introducing differential voting rights, management can also decrease the importance of voting rights held by other shareholders. Consider a firm with two classes of common stock that differ only in their voting rights. For instance, both types of shares receive identical payouts, but shares of one type have two votes, whereas shares of the other type have only one vote each. If management holds the shares with the higher voting rights, it holds a larger fraction of the voting rights for a given investment than it would without the existence of two classes of common stock. Hence, the existence of differential voting rights brings about an increase in α when managers hold a disproportionate fraction of the shares with superior voting rights. The analysis in this paper implies that one would expect shares with higher voting rights to be held mainly by managers. DeAngelo and DeAngelo (1985) and Partch (1987) document that this is indeed the case. Our analysis also indicates that the value of the firm falls when managers introduce shares with higher voting rights to acquire a veto right on future proposed control changes.

If some shares with higher voting rights are traded, one would expect those shares to trade at a premium as long as the probability of a takeover is not zero and to receive a higher premium if a successful tender offer is made. Several papers document that, usually, shares with higher voting rights trade at a premium over other shares issued by the same firm.[21] Further, DeAngelo and DeAngelo (1985) study cases in which firms with more than one type of shares were acquired by other firms and show that shares with higher voting rights received a higher premium. Partch (1987) studies a sample of firms that issued shares with limited voting rights and finds that, on average, the creation of such shares increased shareholder wealth. However, as two-thirds of the shares with limited voting rights in her sample also receive a preferential dividend, she is unable to distinguish between the effect of a change in payout policy and the effect of a change in the distribution of voting rights at conventional significance levels. Pinegar and Lease (1986) study the announcement effect on a firm's common stock of an offer to exchange common stock

---

[21] See, for instance, DeAngelo and DeAngelo (1985) and Lease, McConnell, and Mikkelson (1983, 1984).

for preferred stock. They find that the announcement effect of such an offer is negatively related to the voting rights of the preferred stock. In other words, shareholders benefit more from an offer to exchange common stock for preferred stock when the preferred stock has no voting rights than otherwise, which would be consistent with our analysis if these firms have low α's. This suggests that announcement effects of a capital structure change are related to the changes in the distribution of voting rights they bring about.

5.5. Shareholder clienteles

Management can increase α through contractual arrangements that give it the right to vote shares it does not own or enable it to influence how such shares are voted. These contractual arrangements are likely to be costly for management, as they can force it to relinquish some decision rights. Our analysis suggests that, for low values of α, the announcement effect of new contractual arrangements that increase α should be positive as they move α closer to the value that maximizes the value of the firm. A discussion of the main empirical implications of our analysis for such contractual arrangements follows.

5.5.1. ESOP's and pension funds

Management generally acts as a trustee of the firm's pension fund and of the firm's stock ownership plan, and hence it can significantly influence how the firm's shares held by the pension fund or the stock ownership plan are voted. One would therefore expect that the introduction of an ESOP and purchases of the firm's shares by its pension fund or the ESOP would have a positive concentration of the voting rights effect on the value of the firm when α is small. One should not forget, however, that purchases of shares by the firm's ESOP or pension fund can also affect the value of the firm for other reasons (for instance, they can have tax effects).

5.5.2. Voting trusts

DeAngelo and DeAngelo (1985) document instances in which management has the right to vote shares that it does not own that are held in trust. The establishment of such a trust could have a positive effect on the value of the firm as it increases α. However, when the establishment of such a trust leads to a large value of α, i.e., one that is close to or exceeds one half, one would expect the value of the firm to fall. The value of the firm's equity can also increase or fall when shares are acquired by investors friendly to management depending on whether α is small or large.[22] Dann and DeAngelo (1988) document instances during takeover contests in which management places shares with friendly investors and show that, on average, such placements decrease the value of equity even when they do not decrease the firm's leverage.

5.5.3. Standstill agreements

Typically, a standstill agreement that limits ownership of target shares by an investor also stipulates that the investor will vote with management in a corporate control contest. This suggests that, in some cases, a standstill agreement could increase the value of the firm's equity because it concentrates control of the votes in management's hands. Dann and DeAngelo (1983) find that standstill agreements typically decrease the value of the target's equity. This could mean that standstill agreements are used more often by firms with large α's. A more plausible explanation however, is that besides concentrating voting rights in the hands of management, a standstill agreement effectively eliminates a bidder. This would decrease the value of the firm in our analysis.

5.5.4. Financial restructurings

So far, we have assumed that financial transactions leave an individual shareholder's probability of tendering unchanged for a given premium. However, a financial restructuring can change this probability. For instance, a share repurchase buys back shares from those shareholders who have the lowest opportunity costs of tendering, so that a subsequent bidder has to buy shares from shareholders who have higher opportunity costs of tendering. In our model, such a share repurchase decreases the probability of success of a bid for a low premium and leads the bidder to offer a higher premium. This effect of a share repurchase can take place even if $\alpha = 0$ and hence is not directly related to the main theme of this paper. However, it follows from this discussion that the effect of a given α on the premium offered can be affected

---

[22] In this model a large shareholder plays a different role than in the model of Shleifer and Vishny (1986a). In their model, some takeovers cannot take place in the absence of a large shareholder, even though they would make the target's shareholders better off, because the bidder cannot exclude the target's nontendering shareholders from the gains created by its improvements in the target's management. The large shareholder can facilitate a takeover by giving up some of the gains and hence make the takeover a positive net present value project for the bidder. In the Shleifer and Vishny (1986a) model, the premium offered in a takeover attempt falls with the proportion of shares held by the large shareholder, while the value of the target increases. Following an increase in the large shareholder's holdings, a takeover becomes more likely because takeovers which generate lower gains can take place.

by changes in the distribution of shareholders' opportunity costs of tendering through financial restructurings.

6. Conclusion

This paper shows how the value of a firm that is a potential takeover target depends on the fraction of the voting stock held by management. The result that the value of the firm depends critically on the distribution of the votes between management and outside shareholders is shown to have implications for how one views various takeover defenses and for the firm's financial policies.

Some interesting extensions of the previous analysis are the following. First, we assume that the conflict of interest between shareholders and managers arises only from the fact that a successful takeover always benefits shareholders but may hurt managers. Thus our analysis ignores the positive incentive effects of a large α, stressed by Jensen and Meckling (1976), and of the market for corporate control discussed in Jensen and Ruback (1983).[23] It is possible that an analysis that includes the incentive effects of α would show that, in some cases, the value of the firm increases monotonically with α because these effects dominate the distribution of the vote effect studied in this paper.

Second, we assume the target's management cannot increase its bargaining power other than through an increase in α. It would be interesting to see how our analysis extends to the case in which management can increase its bargaining power in other ways, for instance by introducing a poison pill, and how the distribution of voting rights affects management's ability to bargain with a bidder.[24]

Finally, we ignore informational asymmetries. In general, one would expect management to know more about the target than either outside shareholders or the bidder. This introduces a new reason for management to resist, in that it may have information that leads it to believe the firm is undervalued.[25] In such a situation, the managers' ability to block a low bid would increase the value of the firm. Hence, this type of informational asymmetry could bring about a higher optimal value for α. Although constructing a model that incorporates distribution-of-votes effects, incentive effects, and informational asymmetries is a challenging task well beyond the scope of this paper, the results presented here indicate that research along these lines would be helpful

---

[23] See Scharfstein (1985) for a model that deals with the incentive effects of the market for corporate control.

[24] See Parsons (1985) for a bargaining model of tender offers.

[25] See Baron (1983) for a model that deals with these informational asymmetries.

to understand better how the market for corporate control works and how corporate capital structures are selected.

Appendix

Let N_α and N_P be, respectively, the partial derivatives of N with respect to α and P. It is easy to verify that $N_\alpha < 0$ and $N_P > 0$.

Result 1. If a bid is made, let $Y = [G - P]N$. Using the envelope theorem, it immediately follows that

$$\frac{dY}{d\alpha} = [G - P]N_\alpha < 0. \tag{A.1}$$

Result 2. The optimal premium satisfies:

$$[G - P]N_P = N, \tag{A.2}$$

$$[G - P]N_{PP} - 2N_P < 0, \tag{A.3}$$

$$[G - P]N \ge 0. \tag{A.4}$$

(A.2) is the first-order condition, (A.3) the second-order condition, and (A.4) represents the constraint that a bid has to be a positive NPV project. With our assumptions, N_P is a constant, so that $N_{PP} = 0$ and the second-order condition (A.3) is always satisfied.

Differentiating (A.2) using the envelope theorem yields

$$\frac{dP}{d\alpha} = \frac{-[G - P]N_{P\alpha} + N_\alpha}{[G - P]N_{PP} - 2N_P} = \frac{-N_\alpha}{2N_P} > 0, \tag{A.5}$$

where the second equality follows from the fact that N_P is a constant.

$dV/d\alpha$. Differentiating $V(\alpha, 1)$ with respect to α yields

$$\frac{dV}{d\alpha} = P \int_0^{\bar{G}} \left(\frac{1}{1 + R} \right) [P_\alpha N + PN_P P_\alpha + PN_\alpha] \frac{dG}{\bar{G}}. \tag{A.6}$$

To evaluate the term in square brackets, we can use eq. (A.5) to rewrite this term as follows:

$$P_\alpha N + PN_P P_\alpha + PN_\alpha = \tfrac{1}{2}[PN_P - N](N_\alpha/N_P). \tag{A.7}$$

Note now that eq. (A.2) implies that $N = [G - P]N_P$. Using (A.2) to eliminate N in (A.7) yields

$$\tfrac{1}{2}[PN_P - N](N_\alpha/N_P) = \tfrac{1}{2}[2P - G]N_\alpha. \tag{A.8}$$

Consequently, the term in square brackets in eq. (A.6) is positive whenever G is large in comparison with P. As $u(P)$ and $d(P)$ are assumed to be linear functions of P with identical slopes, we can rewrite them as $u(P) = a + \beta P$ and $d(P) = A + \beta P$. Using eq. (A.2), we get the following solution for the premium:

$$P = \frac{1}{2\beta}[G\beta - a + z(\alpha)]. \tag{A.9}$$

Eq. (A.9) implies that if the premium is optimally chosen, G exceeds $2P$ for $\alpha = 0$, as $-a + z(0)$ is negative by assumption. Hence, $dV/d\alpha$ is positive when $\alpha = 0$.

Different supply functions. Our results still hold if N_{PP} and $N_{P\alpha}$ differ from zero provided that (a) there is a unique interior solution for the premium, (b) $N_\alpha + (P - G)N_{P\alpha} < 0$, and (c) $G > 2P$ over a sufficient range of values for G for $\alpha = 0$. Condition (b) is likely to hold whenever there is a unique interior solution for the premium. This follows from the fact that an increase in α has the opposite effect on N of a fall in the premium. By this argument, one would expect $N_{P\alpha}$ to have the opposite sign from N_{PP}. However, if N_{PP} is positive and $G - P$ is large, the second-order condition (A.3) does not hold. Hence, one would expect $N_{P\alpha}$ to be positive, which implies that condition (b) holds. Condition (c) holds whenever competition among shareholders for the premium is strong, so that the premium offered when $\alpha = 0$ is small compared with the gain to the bidder.

References

Alexander, C., 1986, Ownership structure, efficiency and entrenchment and antitakeover charter amendments, Unpublished paper (University of California, Los Angeles, CA).

Baron, 1983, Tender offers and management resistance, Journal of Finance 38, 331–342.

Bradley, M. and E.H. Kim, 1985, The tender offer as a takeover device: Its evolution, the free rider problem and the prisoner's dilemma, Unpublished manuscript.

Bradley, M., A. Desai, and E.H. Kim, 1983, The rationale behind interfirm tender offers: Information or synergy?, Journal of Financial Economics 11, 183–207.

Brennan, M. and E. Schwartz, 1977, Convertible bonds: Valuation and optimal strategies for call and conversion, Journal of Finance 32, 1699–1715.

Constantinides, G.M. and P.D. Grundy, 1986, Call and conversion of convertible corporate bonds: Theory and evidence, Unpublished paper (University of Chicago, Chicago, IL).

Dann, L., 1981, Common stock repurchases: An analysis of returns to bondholders and stockholders, Journal of Financial Economics 9, 113–138.

Dann, L. and H. DeAngelo, 1983, Standstill agreements, privately negotiated stock repurchases and the market for corporate control, Journal of Financial Economics 11, 275–300.

Dann, L. and H. DeAngelo, 1988, Corporate financial policy and corporate control: A study of defensive adjustments in asset and ownership structure, Journal of Financial Economics, this issue.

DeAngelo, H. and L. DeAngelo, 1985, Managerial ownership of voting rights: A study of public corporations with dual classes of common stock, Journal of Financial Economics 14, 33–70.

DeAngelo, H. and E. Rice, 1983, 'Antitakeover' charter amendments and stockholder wealth, Journal of Financial Economics 11, 329–360.

Fishman, M., 1985, A theory of takeover bidding, Unpublished manuscript.

Grossman, S. and Oliver Hart, 1980, Takeover bids, the free-rider problems, and the theory of the corporation, Bell Journal of Economics, 42–64.

Harris, M. and A. Raviv, 1985, A sequential signalling model of convertible debt call policy, Journal of Finance 40, 1263–1981.

Harris, M. and A. Raviv, 1988, Corporate control contests and capital structure, Journal of Financial Economics, this issue.

Ingersoll, J., 1977, An examination of corporate call policies on convertible securities, Journal of Finance 32, 463–478.

Jarrell, G. and A. Poulsen, 1987, Shark repellents and stock prices: The effects of antitakeover amendments since 1980, Journal of Financial Economics 19, 127–168.

Jensen, M.C., 1986a, Agency costs of free cash flows, corporate finance, and takeovers, American Economic Review 76, 323–329.

Jensen, M.C., 1986b, The takeover controversy: Analysis and evidence, Midland Corporate Journal 4, 6–32.

Jensen, M.C. and W.H. Meckling, 1976, Theory of the firm: Managerial behavior, agency costs, and ownership structure, Journal of Financial Economics 3, 305–360.

Jensen, M.C. and R.S. Ruback, 1983, The market for corporate control: The scientific evidence, Journal of Financial Economics 11, 5–51.

Khanna, N., 1985, Optimal bidding for tender offers, Unpublished manuscript.

Knoeber, C.R., 1986, Golden parachutes, shark repellents and hostile tender offers, American Economic Review 76, 155–168.

Lambert, R.A. and D.F. Larcker, 1985, Golden parachutes, executive decision-making, and shareholder wealth, Journal of Accounting and Economics 7, 179–204.

Lease, R.D., J.J. McConnell, and W.H. Mikkelson, 1983, The market value of control in publicly traded corporations, Journal of Financial Economics 11, 439–472.

Lease, R.D., J.J. McConnell, and W.H. Mikkelson, 1984, The market value of differential voting rights in closely held corporations, Journal of Business 57, 443–467.

Leland, H. and D. Pyle, 1977, Information asymmetries, financial structure and financial intermediation, Journal of Finance 32, 737–48.

Levy, H., 1983, Economic evaluation of voting power of common stock, Journal of Finance 38, 79–93.

Linn, S.C. and J.J. McConnell, 1983, An empirical investigation of the impact of 'antitakeover' amendments on common stock prices, Journal of Financial Economics 11, 361–400.

Masulis, R.M., 1980, Stock repurchase by tender offer: An analysis of the causes of common stock price changes, Journal of Finance 35, 305–319.

Mikkelson, W.H., 1981, Convertible calls and security returns, Journal of Financial Economics 9, 237–264.

Morck, R., A. Shleifer, and R.W. Vishny, 1988, Management ownership and market valuation: An empirical analysis, Journal of Financial Economics, this issue.

Palepu, K.G., 1986, Predicting takeover targets: A methodological and empirical analysis, Journal of Accounting and Economics, 3–37.

Parsons, J., 1985, A bargaining model of two-tiered tender offers, Unpublished paper.

Partch, M.M., 1987, The creation of a class of limited voting common stock and shareholder wealth, Journal of Financial Economics 18, 313–339.

Pinegar, J.M. and R.C. Lease, 1986, The impact of preferred-for-common exchange offers on firm value, Journal of Finance 41, 795–815.

P'ng, I.P.L., 1985, The information conveyed by a tender offer and the takeover price of a target firm, Working paper (University of California, Los Angeles, CA).

Riley, J.G. and W.F. Samuelson, 1981, Optimal auctions, American Economic Review 71, 381–392.

Rosenfeld, A., 1982, Repurchase offers: Information adjusted premiums and shareholders' response, MERC monograph series MT-82-01 (University of Rochester, Rochester, NY).

Scharfstein, J., 1985, The disciplinary role of takeovers, Unpublished manuscript.

Shleifer, A. and R.W. Vishny, 1986a, Large shareholders and corporate control, Journal of Political Economy 94, 461–488.

Shleifer, A. and R.W. Vishny, 1986b, Greenmail, white knights, and shareholder's interest, Rand Journal of Economics 3, 293–309.

Smith, C.W., 1986, Investment banking and the capital acquisition process, Journal of Financial Economics 15, 3–29.

Stiglitz, J., 1972, Some aspects of the pure theory of corporate finance: Bankruptcies and takeovers, Bell Journal of Economics and Management Science 3, 458–483.

Vermaelen, T., 1981, Common stock repurchases and market signalling, Journal of Financial Economics 9, 139–183.

Walkling, R.A., 1985, Predicting tender offer success: A logistic analysis, Journal of Financial and Quantitative Analysis 20, 461–478.

Walkling, R.A. and M.S. Long, 1984, Agency theory, managerial welfare and takeover bid resistance, Rand Journal of Economics 1, 54–68.